SAGE
Premium
Video

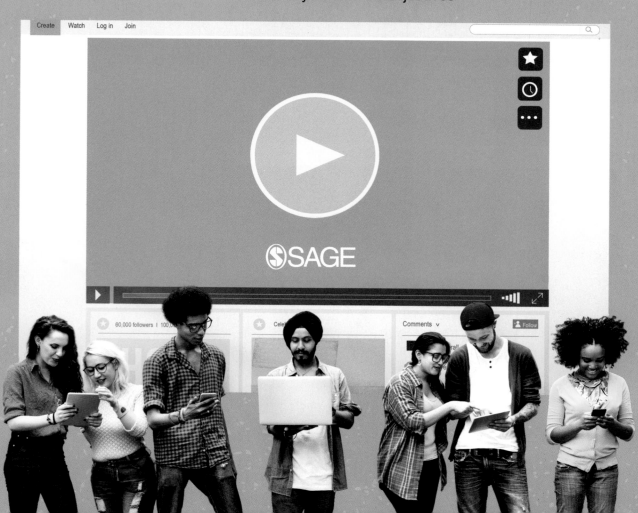

The
Hallmark
Features

A COMPLETE LEARNING PACKAGE

Fundamentals of Human Resource Management: Functions, Applications, and Skill Development helps students of all majors build the skills they need to recruit, select, train, and develop people.

- **CASE STUDIES** illustrate how specific organizations use the HRM function and include critical thinking questions that challenge students to identify chapter concepts.

- **TRENDS AND ISSUES IN HRM** at the end of every chapter introduce students to important developments in the HR field, including technology, diversity, automation, the agile workplace, generational differences, and gamification.

- **SKILL-BUILDING EXERCISES** provide students with hands-on opportunities to experience human resources and develop essential skills.

Case 8.1 Not Spilling the Beans at Jelly Belly: Developing a More Accurate Performance Appraisal System

Candy making is a fun business, and so it is no surprise that it is fun to work at the Jelly Belly Candy Company of Fairfield, California. Although this company has cheesecake, buttered popcorn, orange sherbet, and jalapeño on the menu, they are most known for making Jelly beans—fifty "official" flavors, with new and sometimes startlingly flavored (and named) versions introduced periodically, such as Chili Mango. The company's other products include gumballs, gummies, and sour candies in Jelly Belly flavors. Its more than 100 confections also include candy corn, sour candies, jellies, novelty candy, chocolates, chocolate-covered nuts, cinnamon confections, and licorice, along with seasonal offerings. Jelly Belly's candy is sold in more than 70 countries worldwide. In addition to making candy, the company dabbles in retail. It operates half a dozen retail Jelly Belly candy stores in California, as well as a visitor center/warehouse (with tours) in Pleasant Prairie, Wisconsin.

Jelly Belly Candy Company is dedicated the highest-quality c... customer serv... able r

other was doing its employee performance appraisals manually, using paper forms. The task of creating and consolidating the performance management process fell to Margie Poulos, HR manager of Jelly Belly's Midwest operations. She and a small team of Jelly Belly HR staff were charged with finding a single automated system that could be used for all of Jelly Belly's 600 employees in three locations.

The driving factor behind Jelly Belly's performance management was the belief that thorough, accurate reviews help employees to better understand what is expected of them, so they can set clear, measurable objectives. That translates into higher employee satisfaction, said Jeff Brown, Jelly Belly's director of human resources. "When ... gotten a thoro... most ...

do other things that may cause our workforce to become more satisfied. We can adjust work hours (minimally), make benefits packages better, and maybe make work schedules a little better. As discussed, we can also use job design flexibility. Any of these might cause turnover to go down. But this won't happen overnight because it takes some time to change people's opinions of the organization. In addition, this option takes a while, doesn't it? We have to go

New Hires

Our next option is to *hire new employees.* But this option takes a while, doesn't it? We have to go through a long process of analyzing the job, recruiting people, selecting employees, training, and working through a learning curve to get them capable of doing the work. We can see that this is a slow method of resolving a worker shortage. It is also not easy to take back.

Trends and Issues in HRM

In this chapter's trends and issues section, we will review Gig Work and the Agile Workforce. Secondly, we will brief you on Automation at Work in modern companies.

Gig Work and the Agile Workforce

Let's take a closer look at the changing shape of the workforce. The last edition of this text, published 3 years ago, noted that gig work was accounting for a little over 7% of the workforce in the United States. The most recent estimates for the various types of gig work—mostly forms of contract or temporary labor—are between 20% and 30%, and that is expected to grow to nearly 50% of the labor force by 2025.

Certainly, gig work is not going to overtake regular employment as the primary means of labor engagement any time soon, but as an optional form of work it is increasing at a massive rate. McKinsey Global Institute recently identified four types of independent workers: "free agents," who choose gig work and make a living doing it; "casual earners," who supplement their regular work with gigs; "reluctants," who work primarily through gigs but would rather have a regular job; and the "financially strapped," who do supplemental work because they need the money. M...nsey says that that as many as 162 million people do gig work in the United States and the ... of the European Union.

...ment has taken notice of gig work also. The Bureau of Labor Statistics ... to count how many gig workers there really are in the ... (DOL) and the Equal Employment Opportunity ...h gig workers may be misclassified as ... of the EEOC and the DOL is ... when they are really ... purposes

interview questions while not going into any details of the job responsibilities or even some background about the firm. Most answers to the manager's questions required a yes/no response. She did not receive a tour of the store nor did she meet any of the store employees, including those she dealt with earlier. Krissy tried to ask several of her prepared questions in order to develop a relationship with the manager, yet each was answered in a very curt, perfunctory manner. Krissy walked out of the store feeling that she had the worst interview in the history of job interviews.

Two days later Krissy was astonished when she was asked to have a Skype interview with the regional district manager at Links. This manager was quite positive, emphasizing the importance of the New York store as the "showcase" for Links of London products and services; service had to be "of the highest quality" with the customer always coming first. The regional district manager was supportive of her efforts to obtain a graduate degree and indicated the financial support she would receive from the firm for her continued education. When the job offer came "out of the blue" 3 weeks later to start immediately, Krissy didn't know what to do or what to think. No one had contacted her references throughout the process to verify her abilities. There seemed to be several loose links in the chain of command at Links of London that tarnished their golden image.

Questions

1. What types of "fit" was Links of London looking for in their employees, according to their career services website?

2. What are the steps in the selection process, and where did this process seem to falter with Krissy?

3. What determines if a question is acceptable in a pre-employment inquiry, and what questions might have been deemed unacceptable on Links's job application?

4. Krissy took a personality test as well as a test of her integrity yet not a job-specific cognitive test. What might be the firm's rationale for using the tests they did?

5. What type of interview did the store manager seem to conduct using what type of questions?

6. What steps should have been taken when conducting the interview? Did the store manager miss any of them?

7. If you were Krissy, would you accept the job offer?

Case is derived from a previously published case (see reference 2) and includes fictitious material added to enhance the case solely for instructional purposes.

Skill Builder 6.1 Interviewing

Objective

To develop your ability to develop interview questions

To develop your ability to interview and to be interviewed

Skills

The primary skills developed through this exercise are as follows:

1. *HR management skills*—Technical, interpersonal, business, and conceptual and design skills

2. *SHRM 2018 Curriculum Guidebook*—N: Staffing (Recruitment and Selection)

Preparation

Assume you are the HR director and you need to hire a new college grad for an entry-level HR position.

Because you are not a large company, you have a small staff and the new hire will help out in a wide variety of HR functions. Develop a list of at least 10 questions you would ask the candidates during a job interview for the position.

Apply It

What did I learn from this experience? How will I use this knowledge in the future?

_____

_____

Your instructor may ask you to do this Skill Builder in class by breaking into groups of two or three and actually conducting interviews using your questions. If so, the instructor will provide ...sary inform...

SAGE
Publishing:
Our Story

At SAGE, we mean business. We believe in creating evidence-based, cutting-edge content that helps you prepare your students to succeed in today's ever-changing business world. We strive to provide you with the tools you need to develop the next generation of leaders, managers, and entrepreneurs.

- We invest in the right **AUTHORS** who distill research findings and industry ideas into practical applications.

- We keep our prices **AFFORDABLE** and provide multiple **FORMAT OPTIONS** for students.

- We remain permanently independent and fiercely committed to **QUALITY CONTENT** and **INNOVATIVE RESOURCES**.

FUNDAMENTALS OF HUMAN RESOURCE MANAGEMENT

FUNCTIONS, APPLICATIONS, SKILL DEVELOPMENT

SECOND EDITION

ROBERT N. LUSSIER

Springfield College

JOHN R. HENDON

University of Arkansas at Little Rock

Los Angeles | London | New Delhi
Singapore | Washington DC | Melbourne

FOR INFORMATION:

SAGE Publications, Inc.
2455 Teller Road
Thousand Oaks, California 91320
E-mail: order@sagepub.com

SAGE Publications Ltd.
1 Oliver's Yard
55 City Road
London EC1Y 1SP
United Kingdom

SAGE Publications India Pvt. Ltd.
B 1/I 1 Mohan Cooperative Industrial Area
Mathura Road, New Delhi 110 044
India

SAGE Publications Asia-Pacific Pte. Ltd.
18 Cross Street #10-10/11/12
China Square Central
Singapore 048423

Acquisitions Editor: Maggie Stanley
Senior Content Development Editor: Darcy Scelsi
Editorial Assistant: Janeane Calderon
Marketing Manager: Sarah Panella
Production Editor: Veronica Stapleton Hooper
Copy Editor: Colleen Brennan
Typesetter: C&M Digitals (P) Ltd.
Proofreader: Sally Jaskold
Indexer: Sheila Bodell
Cover Designer: Gail Buschman

Printed in Canada

ISBN (pbk): 978-1-5443-2448-7

This book is printed on acid-free paper.

19 20 21 22 23 10 9 8 7 6 5 4 3 2 1

• Brief Contents •

Preface		**xxiii**
Acknowledgments		**xxxi**
About the Authors		**xxxii**
PART I •	**THE HUMAN RESOURCE MANAGEMENT ENVIRONMENT**	**1**
Chapter 1 •	Today's Human Resource Management Process	2
Chapter 2 •	Strategy-Driven Human Resource Management	28
Chapter 3 •	The Legal Environment	54
PART II •	**STAFFING**	**81**
Chapter 4 •	Workforce Planning: Job Analysis, Design, and Employment Forecasting	82
Chapter 5 •	Recruiting Job Candidates	112
Chapter 6 •	Selecting New Employees	136
PART III •	**DEVELOPING AND MANAGING**	**165**
Chapter 7 •	Training, Learning, Talent Management, and Development	166
Chapter 8 •	Performance Management and Appraisal	192
Chapter 9 •	Employee Rights and Labor Relations	222
PART IV •	**COMPENSATING**	**251**
Chapter 10 •	Compensation Management	252
Chapter 11 •	Employee Incentives and Benefits	280
PART V •	**PROTECTING AND EXPANDING ORGANIZATIONAL OUTREACH**	**309**
Chapter 12 •	Workplace Safety, Health, and Security	310
Chapter 13 •	Ethics, Sustainability, Diversity, and Inclusion	334
Chapter 14 •	Global Issues for Human Resource Managers	362
Glossary		**385**
Notes		**390**
Index		**419**

• Detailed Contents •

Preface   xxiii

Acknowledgments   xxxi

About the Authors   xxxii

PART I • THE HUMAN RESOURCE MANAGEMENT ENVIRONMENT   1

Chapter 1 • Today's Human Resource Management Process   2

Why Study Human Resource Management (HRM)?   4

  Employee Engagement   4

  Student Engagement and Skill Development   5

HRM Past and Present   5

  Today's HRM Challenges   6

  Labor Demographics   7

  Technology and Knowledge   7

    Knowledge Workers and the Knowledge-Based Firm   8

    The Pace of Technological Change   8

    Knowledge Workers Are in Short Supply   8

  Technology's Effect on Efficiency   8

  The Purpose for Managing Human Resources   9

Disciplines Within HRM   9

  The Legal Environment: EEO and Diversity Management   9

  Staffing   10

  Training and Development   10

  Employee Relations   10

  Labor and Industrial Relations   10

  Compensation and Benefits   10

  Safety and Security   10

  Ethics and Sustainability   11

HRM Responsibilities   14

  Line Versus Staff Management   14

  Major HR Responsibilities of HR Staff and Line Management   14

HRM Skills   15

  Technical Skills   15

  Interpersonal Skills   15

  Conceptual and Design Skills   16

  Business Skills   16

Resources for HRM Careers   17

  Society for Human Resource Management (SHRM)   17

  Other HR Organizations   17

  Professional Responsibility and Liability   18

Practitioner's Model for HRM   18

  The Model   18

    Section I: Current HRM Practices, Strategic Planning, and HR Laws   18

    Section II: Staffing   18

    Section III: Developing and Managing   19

    Section IV: Compensating   19

    Section V: Protecting and Expanding Stakeholder Reach   20

Trends and Issues in HRM   20
    Employee Engagement Improves Productivity   **20**
    HRM and Organizational Agility   **20**
Chapter Summary   21
Key Terms   23
Key Terms Review   23
Communication Skills   24
Case 1.1 Fracturing the Labor Market: Employment in the Oil Services Industry   25
Skill Builders   26

Chapter 2 • Strategy-Driven Human Resource Management   **28**

An Introduction to Strategic Planning and the Environment   30
    HR Management's Role in Strategic Planning   **31**
    The External Environment   **31**
Strategy   33
    What Is Strategy?   **34**
    Vision, Mission, and Objectives   **34**
        The Vision   34
        The Mission   34
        Putting the Vision and Mission Together   35
        Setting Objectives   35
    Generic Strategies   **37**
        Cost Leadership   37
        Differentiation   37
        Focus or Niche   37
    How Strategy Affects HRM   **37**
        HRM and Cost Leadership   38
        HRM and Differentiation   38
        HRM and Focus Strategy   38
    HRM Promotes Strategy Through High Performance Work Practices   **38**
Structure   39
    Basics of Organizational Structure   **39**
    How Does Structure Affect Employee Behavior?   **40**
    How Does Structure Affect HRM?   **40**
Organizational Culture   40
    What Is Organizational Culture?   **40**
        Artifacts of Organizational Culture   40
    How Culture Controls Employee Behavior in Organizations   **41**
    Social Media and Culture Management   **41**
An Introduction to Data Analytics and HR Technology   42
    Big Data   **42**
    A Brief on Data Analytics   **42**
    HR Technology   **43**
    Desired Outcomes   **43**
Human Resource Management Systems (HRMS)   43
    What Are HRMS?   **44**
    How Do HRMS Assist in Making Decisions?   **44**
Measurement Tools for Strategic HRM   44
    Economic Value Added (EVA)   **44**
    Return on Investment (ROI)   **45**
Trends and Issues in HRM   46
    Structure, Culture, and Technology Are Misaligned   **46**
    Continuing Globalization Increases the Need for Strategic and HRM Planning   **46**
Chapter Summary   47
Key Terms   49

Key Terms Review   49

Communication Skills   49

Case 2.1 Catalya Hats: Pulling a Rabbit Out of the Hat or Coming Up
Empty Handed?   50

Skill Builders   52

Chapter 3 • The Legal Environment   54

The Legal Environment for HRM and a User's Guide to Managing People   56

The OUCH Test Guide   **56**

Objective   56

Uniform in Application   56

Consistent in Effect   57

Has Job Relatedness   58

Major Employment Laws   58

Equal Pay Act of 1963   **59**

Title VII of the Civil Rights Act of 1964 (CRA)   **59**

Types of Discrimination   59

Organizational Defenses Against Discrimination Charges   61

Age Discrimination in Employment Act of 1967 (ADEA)   **62**

Vietnam Era Veterans Readjustment Assistance Act of 1974 (VEVRAA)   **62**

Pregnancy Discrimination Act of 1978 (PDA)   **62**

Americans with Disabilities Act of 1990 (ADA), as Amended in 2008   **62**

Civil Rights Act of 1991   **63**

**Uniformed Services Employment and Reemployment Rights
Act of 1994 (USERRA)**   **64**

Veterans Benefits Improvement Act of 2004 (VBIA)   **65**

Title II of the Genetic Information Nondiscrimination Act of 2008 (GINA)   **65**

Lilly Ledbetter Fair Pay Act of 2009 (LLFPA)   **65**

Equal Employment Opportunity Commission (EEOC)   66

What Does the EEOC Do?   **66**

Other EEOC Enforcement Actions   **66**

Employee Rights Under the EEOC   **67**

Employer Rights and Prohibitions   **67**

Retaliation   67

Constructive Damage   67

HR Leadership   **67**

Sexual Harassment   68

Types of Sexual Harassment   **68**

Quid Pro Quo Harassment   68

Hostile Work Environment   68

What Constitutes Sexual Harassment?   **69**

Filing Complaints and HR's Response   **69**

Is It Really Sexual Harassment?   69

HR Disciplinary Action and Cover-Ups   69

Reducing Organizational Risk From Sexual Harassment Lawsuits   **70**

Religious Discrimination   71

Trends and Issues in HRM   71

Sexual Orientation and Gender Identity Discrimination   **72**

Technology May Create Dangers in Equal Opportunity and Diversity Management   **72**

Chapter Summary   73

Key Terms   74

Key Terms Review   74

Communication Skills   76

Case 3.1 When Religion Is on the Agenda   76

Skill Builders   78

PART II • STAFFING   81

Chapter 4 • Workforce Planning: Job Analysis, Design, and Employment Forecasting   82

Workforce Planning and Workflow Analysis   84

Workflow Analysis   **84**

Organizational Output   84

Tasks and Inputs   84

Job Analysis   85

Why Do We Need to Analyze Jobs?   **86**

Job Analysis Databases   **86**

Job Analysis Methods   **87**

Questionnaires   87

Interviews   87

Diaries   88

Observation   88

Outcomes: Job Description and Job Specification   **89**

Job Design/Redesign   90

Organizational Structure and Job Design   **90**

Approaches to Job Design and Redesign   **90**

The Job Characteristics Model (JCM)   91

Designing Motivational Jobs   93

Job Simplification   **93**

Job Expansion   **94**

Job Rotation   94

Job Enlargement   94

Job Enrichment   94

Flexible Job Design   **94**

HR Forecasting   96

Reliability   **96**

Validity   **96**

Forecasting Methods   97

Quantitative Forecasting   **97**

Qualitative Forecasting   **97**

Methods for Reconciling a Labor Surplus   99

Downsizing and Layoffs   **99**

Pay Reduction   **100**

Work Sharing   **100**

Natural Attrition   **100**

Hiring Freezes   **100**

Retraining and Transfers   **100**

Early Retirement   **100**

Methods for Reconciling a Labor Shortage   101

Overtime   **101**

Temporary or Contract Workers   **101**

Technological Innovation   **102**

Retraining Workers   **102**

Outsourcing   **102**

Turnover Reduction   **102**

New Hires   **103**

Trends and Issues in HRM   103

Gig Work and the Agile Workforce   **103**

Automation at Work   **103**

Chapter Summary   104

Key Terms   106

Key Terms Review   106

Communication Skills 107

Case 4.1 Walmart's Everyday Hiring Strategy: Fueling Future Consumer
   Demand With Passion and Talent 107

Skill Builders 109

Chapter 5 • Recruiting Job Candidates 112

The Recruiting Process 114

External Forces Acting on Recruiting Efforts 114

The Labor Market 114

Social and Legal Environment 115

Organizational Recruiting Considerations 115

What Policies to Set 115

When to Recruit 115

Alternatives to Recruitment 115

Reach of the Recruiting Effort 116

The Technology Recruiting Revolution 116

Issues With Technology Recruiting 117

Internal or External Recruiting? 117

Internal Recruiting 117

Advantages and Disadvantages of Internal Recruiting 117

External Recruiting 118

Walk-Ins 118

Educational Institutions 118

Employment Agencies 118

Advertising 120

Advantages and Disadvantages of External Recruiting 120

Challenges and Constraints in Recruiting 121

Budgetary Constraints 121

Policy Constraints and Organizational Image 121

Job Characteristics 122

The Recruiter–Candidate Interaction and the Realistic Job Preview (RJP) 122

Evaluation of Recruiting Programs 124

Yield Ratio 124

Cost per Hire 125

Number of Hires 125

Time Required to Hire 125

New Hire Turnover 126

New Hire Performance 126

Trends and Issues in HRM 126

Millennial Versus Generation Z: Aren't They All the Same? 127

Look for Grit, Not Just Talent 128

Chapter Summary 128

Key Terms 129

Key Terms Review 130

Communication Skills 130

Case 5.1 Trying to Build When Nobody Wants to Work 131

Skill Builders 133

Chapter 6 • Selecting New Employees 136

The Selection Process 138

The Importance of the Selection Process 138

Bad Hires Cost Time and Money 138

Bad Hires Result in Lower Productivity 138

Bad Hires Can Be Negligent Hires 138

Steps in the Selection Process 139

Looking for "Fit" 140

Personality-Job Fit	**140**
Ability-Job Fit	**140**
Person-Organization Fit	**140**
Uniform Guidelines on Employee Selection Procedures	141
What Qualifies as an Employment Test?	**141**
Valid and Reliable Measures	**142**
Criterion-Related Validity	142
Content Validity	142
Construct Validity	142
Reliability	143
The Relationship Between Reliability and Validity	143
Applications and Preliminary Screening	144
Applications and Résumés	**144**
Pre-Employment Inquiries	**144**
Testing and Legal Issues	144
The EEOC and Employment Testing	**146**
Polygraphs and Genetic Testing	**146**
Genetic Testing	146
Written Testing	**146**
Skills Tests	147
Personality and Interest Tests	147
Cognitive Ability Tests	147
Honesty or Integrity Tests	148
Physical Testing	**148**
Physical Skills Tests	148
Physical Exams	148
Drug Testing	149
Fitness-for-Duty Testing	149
To Test or Not to Test	149
Selection Interviews	150
Interviewing	**150**
Types of Interviews and Questions	**151**
Types of Interviews	151
Types of Questions	151
Preparing for and Conducting the Interview	**153**
Background Checks	153
Credit Checks	**154**
Criminal Background Checks	**155**
Reference Checks	**155**
Social Media and Web Searches	**155**
Selecting the Candidate and Offering the Job	156
Hiring	**157**
Trends and Issues in HRM	157
Federal Regulation Limits Selection Testing	**157**
The Global Workforce and Immigration	**158**
Chapter Summary	159
Key Terms	160
Key Terms Review	160
Communication Skills	161
Case 6.1 A Kink in Links of London's Selection Process	161
Skill Builders	163
PART III • DEVELOPING AND MANAGING	**165**
Chapter 7 • Training, Learning, Talent Management, and Development	**166**
The Need for Training and Development	168
Training and Development	**168**

When Is Training Needed?	**168**
New Employee Onboarding	169
New Job Requirements or Processes	169
Remediation	170
Employee Development for Advancement	170
The Training Process and Needs Assessment	170
Steps in the Training Process	**170**
Interrelationship of the Training Process Steps	170
Needs Assessment	**171**
Employee Readiness	**171**
Ability	171
Willingness	172
Learning and Shaping Behavior	172
Learning	**172**
Learning Theories	**173**
Shaping Behavior	**173**
Positive Reinforcement	174
Negative Reinforcement	174
Punishment	174
Extinction	174
Shaping (Changing) Behavior	175
Increasing Targeted Behavior	175
Decreasing Targeted Behavior	175
Design and Delivery of Training	175
On-the-Job Training (OJT)	**178**
Classroom Training	**178**
Distance or E-Learning	**178**
Microlearning	178
Simulations	**179**
Assessing Training	180
Assessment Methods	**180**
Talent Management and Development	181
Careers	**181**
Common Methods of Employee Development	**181**
Outsourcing	182
Formal Education	182
Experience	182
Employment Assessment	182
A Model of Career Development Consequences	**182**
Exploration	183
Establishment	183
Maintenance	183
Disengagement	183
Trends and Issues in HRM	185
Gamification—A Phoenix Rising?	**185**
The Corporate Learning Imperative	**185**
Chapter Summary	186
Key Terms	187
Key Terms Review	187
Communication Skills	188
Case 7.1 Doing Crunches at Nestlé: Continuous Improvement of Human Assets	188
Skill Builders	190
Chapter 8 • Performance Management and Appraisal	**192**
Performance Management Systems	194
Is It Time to Delete the Annual Appraisal Process?	**194**
Performance Management Versus Performance Appraisal	**195**

The Performance Appraisal Process — **195**
Accurate Performance Measures — **196**
You Get What You Reinforce — 197
Valid and Reliable — 197
Acceptable and Feasible — 197
Specific — 197
Based on the Mission and Objectives — 197

Why Do We Conduct Performance Appraisals? — 198
Communication (Informing) — **198**
Decision Making (Evaluating) — **198**
Motivation (Engaging) — **198**

What Do We Assess? — 198
Trait Appraisals — **199**
Give Traits the OUCH Test — 199
Should We Measure Traits? — 199
Behavioral Appraisals — **199**
Give Behavior the OUCH Test — 199
Should We Measure Behavior? — 199
Results Appraisals — **200**
Give Results the OUCH Test — 200
Should We Measure Results? — 200

How Do We Use Appraisal Methods and Forms? — 201
Critical Incidents Method — **201**
Management by Objectives (MBO) Method — **201**
Step 1: Set Individual Objectives and Plans — 202
Step 2: Give Feedback and Continually Evaluate Performance — 202
Step 3: Reward According to Performance — 202
Narrative Method or Form — **202**
Graphic Rating Scale Form — **202**
Behaviorally Anchored Rating Scale (BARS) Form — **203**
Ranking Method — **204**
Which Option Is Best? — **204**

Who Should Assess Performance? — 205
Supervisor — **205**
Problems With Supervisor Evaluations — 205
Avoiding Supervisor Review Problems — 205
Peers — **205**
Problems With Peer Reviews — 206
Avoiding Peer Review Problems — 206
Subordinates — **206**
Problems With Subordinate Reviews — 206
Avoiding Subordinate Review Problems — 206
Self — **206**
Problems With Self-Assessments — 207
Avoiding Self-Assessment Problems — 207
Customers — **207**
Problems With Customer Assessments — 207
Avoiding Customer Assessment Problems — 207
360-Degree Evaluations — **207**
Problems With 360-Degree Evaluations — 208
Avoiding 360-Degree Evaluation Problems — 208

Performance Appraisal Problems — 208
Common Problems Within the Performance Appraisal Process — **208**
Bias — 209
Stereotyping — 209
Halo Error — 209

Distributional Errors	209
Similarity Error	209
Proximity Error	209
Recency Error	209
Contrast Error	210
Avoiding Performance Appraisal Process Problems	**210**
Develop Accurate Performance Measures	210
Use Multiple Criteria	210
Minimize the Use of Trait-Based Evaluations	210
Give the Measures the OUCH Test	210
Train Evaluators	210
Use Multiple Raters	211
Effective Ongoing Coaching	211
Debriefing the Appraisal	212
The Evaluative Performance Appraisal Interview	**212**
Conducting an Evaluative Interview	212
The Developmental Performance Appraisal Interview	**213**
Conducting a Developmental Interview	213
Being Evaluated	213
Trends and Issues in HRM	214
Building Engagement Through Performance Management	**214**
Electronic Performance Monitoring	**214**
Chapter Summary	215
Key Terms	216
Key Terms Review	216
Communication Skills	217
Case 8.1 Not Spilling the Beans at Jelly Belly: Developing a More Accurate Performance Appraisal System	218
Skill Builders	219
Chapter 9 • Employee Rights and Labor Relations	**222**
Managing and Leading Your Workforce	224
Trust and Communication	**224**
Listening Skills	225
Job Satisfaction	227
Measuring Job Satisfaction	**227**
The Faces Scale of Job Satisfaction Measurement	227
The Questionnaire Job Satisfaction Measurement	227
Pulse Surveys	227
Determinants of Job Satisfaction	**228**
Commonly Accepted Employee Rights	230
Right of Free Consent	**230**
Right to Due Process	**230**
Right to Life and Safety	**230**
Right of Freedom of Conscience (Limited)	**231**
Right to Privacy (Limited)	**231**
Right to Free Speech (Limited)	**231**
Management Rights	232
Codes of Conduct	**232**
Employment-at-Will	**232**
Coaching, Counseling, and Discipline	233
Coaching	**233**
The Coaching Model	233
Management Counseling	**233**
Problem Employees	234

Disciplining **234**
 Just Cause 234
 Guidelines for Effective Discipline 235
 Progressive Discipline 236
 The Discipline Model 237
 Causes of Immediate Termination 238
Legal Issues in Labor Relations 239
 The Railway Labor Act (RLA) of 1926 **239**
 The National Labor Relations Act (NLRA) of 1935 (Wagner Act) **239**
 The Labor Management Relations Act (LMRA) of 1947 (Taft-Hartley Act) **240**
 The Worker Adjustment and Retraining Notification Act of 1988 (WARN Act) **241**
Unions and Labor Rights 241
 Union Organizing **241**
  The No TIPS Rules 242
 Labor Relations and Collective Bargaining **242**
 Grievances **243**
 Decertification Elections **243**
Trends and Issues in HRM 243
 Good Feedback Makes a Good Manager **243**
 Social Media and the Web Continue to Create Managerial Nightmares **244**
Chapter Summary 245
Key Terms 246
Key Terms Review 246
Communication Skills 247
Case 9.1 Willful Violation, or a Problem That Can Be Corrected? 247
Skill Builders 248

PART IV • COMPENSATING **251**

Chapter 10 • Compensation Management **252**

Compensation Management 254
 The Compensation System **254**
  Types of Compensation 254
Motivation and Compensation Planning 255
 Expectancy Theory **255**
 Equity Theory **256**
Compensation Strategy 257
 Ability to Pay **257**
 At, Above, or Below the Market? **257**
 What Types of Compensation? **257**
 Pay for Performance or Pay for Longevity? **258**
 Skill-Based or Competency-Based Pay? **258**
 Wage Compression **258**
 Pay Secrecy **259**
Legal and Fairness Issues in Compensation 259
 Fair Labor Standards Act of 1938 (Amended) **259**
  Minimum Wage 260
  Exempt or Nonexempt 260
  Overtime 260
  Child Labor 262
  Employee Misclassification Under the FLSA 262
 Pay Equity and Comparable Worth **263**
 Other Legal Issues **263**
Job Evaluation 264
 External Versus Internal Methods **264**

        Job Ranking Method   **264**

        Point-Factor Method   **264**

        Factor Comparison Method   **265**

    Developing a Pay System   266

        Job Structure and Pay Levels   **266**

        Creation of Pay Levels   267

        Product Market Competition and Labor Market Competition   267

        Benchmarking Pay Survey Data   268

        Pay Structure   **269**

        Delayering and Broadbanding   270

    Trends and Issues in HRM   272

        Designation of Independent Contractors Continues to Be an Issue   **272**

        The Stubborn Gender Wage Gap—Can It Be Fixed?   **272**

    Chapter Summary   273

    Key Terms   275

    Key Terms Review   275

    Communication Skills   276

    Case 10.1 Discounting Everything but Compensation at Costco   276

    Skill Builders   278

Chapter 11 • Employee Incentives and Benefits   **280**

    The Strategic Value of Incentives and Benefits   282

    Individual Incentives, or Variable Pay   282

        Advantages and Disadvantages of Individual Incentives   **283**

        Individual Incentive Options   **283**

        Bonus   283

        Commissions   283

        Merit Pay   284

        Piecework Plans   284

        Standard Hour Plans   284

    Group Incentives   284

        Advantages and Disadvantages of Group Incentives   **284**

        Group Incentive Options   **285**

        Profit Sharing Plans   286

        Gainsharing Plans   286

        Employee Stock Plans   286

    Executive Compensation   287

        The Dodd-Frank Wall Street Reform and Consumer Protection Act of 2010   **288**

        Shareholder "Say on Pay" and "Golden Parachute" Votes   288

        Executive Compensation Ratios   289

        Executive Incentives   **289**

    Statutory Benefits   289

        Social Security and Medicare   **289**

        Retirement   290

        Disability and Survivor Benefits   290

        Medicare   290

        Workers' Compensation   **290**

        Unemployment Insurance   **290**

        Family and Medical Leave Act of 1993 (FMLA)   **291**

        The Affordable Care Act of 2010 (ACA)   **292**

    Statutory Requirements When Providing Certain Voluntary Benefits   292

        Consolidated Omnibus Budget and Reconciliation Act of 1985 (COBRA)   **292**

        Health Insurance Portability and Accountability Act of 1996 (HIPAA)   **292**

        Employee Retirement Income Security Act of 1974 (ERISA)   **292**

Eligibility	293
Vesting	293
Portability	293
Fiduciary Responsibility	293
PBGC	293
Voluntary Benefits	294
Group Health Insurance	**294**
Traditional Plans (Also Called Fee-for-Service)	294
Health Maintenance Organizations (HMOs)	294
Preferred Provider Organizations (PPOs)	294
Health or Medical Savings Accounts (HSAs/MSAs) and Health Reimbursement Accounts (HRAs)	295
High-Deductible Health Plan (HDHP)	295
Retirement Benefits	**296**
Defined Benefit Versus Defined Contribution Plans	296
Shift From Defined Benefit to Defined Contribution Plans	296
401(k) Plans	296
IRAs and Roth IRAs	296
Paid Time Off	**297**
Vacation or Annual Leave	297
Sick Leave	297
Holiday Pay	297
Paid Personal Leave	297
Other Employee Benefits	**297**
Employee Insurance Options	297
Employee Services	298
Flexible Benefit (Cafeteria) Plans	299
Modular Plans	**299**
Core-Plus Plans	**299**
Full-Choice Plans	**300**
Trends and Issues in HRM	300
Does Incentive Pay Actually Improve Performance?	**300**
Benefits for Domestic Partners	**301**
Chapter Summary	302
Key Terms	303
Key Terms Review	303
Communication Skills	304
Case 11.1 Best Buy or Best Scam? Trying to Get Commission Results on So-Called Non-Commission Pay	305
Skill Builders	306

PART V • PROTECTING AND EXPANDING ORGANIZATIONAL OUTREACH — 309

Chapter 12 • Workplace Safety, Health, and Security — 310

Workplace Safety and OSHA	312
The Occupational Safety and Health Act (OSH Act)	**312**
The Occupational Safety and Health Administration (OSHA)	313
What Does OSHA Do?	**313**
Employer and Employee Rights and Responsibilities Under OSHA	**313**
Employer Rights	313
Employee Rights	315
Hazard Communication Standards	316
Violations, Citations, and Penalties	317
National Institute of Occupational Safety and Health (NIOSH)	**317**
Employee Health	318

Employee Assistance Programs (EAPs) and Employee Wellness
    Programs (EWPs)   **318**
    EAPs   318
    EWPs   318
Ergonomics and Musculoskeletal Disorders (MSDs)   **318**
Safety and Health Management and Training   **319**

Stress   319
Functional and Dysfunctional Stress   **319**
    Functional Stress   319
    Dysfunctional Stress   320
    Causes of Stress   320
    Negative Consequences of Dysfunctional Stress   321
Stress Management   **321**
    Time Management   321
    Relaxation   321
    Nutrition   322
    Exercise   323
    Positive Thinking   323
    Support Network   323
    Cut Back Smart Phone Checking   323
The Stress Tug-of-War   **323**

Workplace Security   324
Cyber Security   **324**
Workplace Violence   **325**
    Signs of Potential Violence   325
    Organizational Prevention of Violence   326
Social Media for Workplace Safety and Security   **326**
Employee Selection and Screening   **326**
General Security Policies, Including Business Continuity and Recovery   **327**

Trends and Issues in HRM   328
OSHA Changes Rules on Post-Incident Drug Testing   **328**
eDocAmerica—Health and Wellness Online   **328**

Chapter Summary   329
Key Terms   330
Key Terms Review   330
Communication Skills   331
Case 12.1 You Are Not Hurt? Good—You're Fired!   331
Skill Builders   333

Chapter 13 • Ethics, Sustainability, Diversity, and Inclusion   **334**

Ethical Organizations   336
Corporate Philanthropy—Ethics Defined   **336**
Contributing Factors to Unethical Behavior   **338**
    Personality Traits and Attitudes   338
    Moral Development   338
    The Situation   338
    Justification of Unethical Behavior   339
Ethical Approaches   **339**
    Golden Rule   339
    Four-Way Test   340
    Stakeholders' Approach to Ethics   340
    Discernment and Advice   340

Codes of Ethics   341
Creating and Maintaining Ethical Organizations   **341**
    Authority   342
    Responsibility   342

Accountability 342
Managers Face Ethical Questions on a Daily Basis 343
Bribery 343
Corrupt Payments to Government Officials 343
Employment and Personnel Issues 343
Marketing Practices 344
Impact on the Economy and Environment 344
Employee and Customer Privacy 344
Diversity and Inclusion 345
Equal Employment Opportunity and Affirmative Action 345
Executive Order 11246 Defined Federal Contractor 346
Federal Court Orders for Affirmative Action Programs 346
Reverse Discrimination 346
Diversity and Inclusion in the Workforce 346
Demographic Diversity 347
Benefits of a Diverse and Inclusive Workforce 347
Creativity and Innovation 347
Challenges to Diversity and Inclusion 348
Managing Diversity 348
Inclusive Equal Opportunity for All 348
Diversity Recruiting and Promoting 348
Diversity Training 349
Mentor Programs 349
Network Diversity Groups 349
Corporate Social Responsibility (CSR) 349
CSR Defined 349
The Business Case for CSR 350
Stakeholders, Laws, and CSR 350
Levels of Corporate Social Responsibility 350
Sustainability 351
HR and Organizational Sustainability 351
Sustainability Practices and Green Companies 351
The Need for Management Commitment 352
Sustainability Training 352
The Sustainable Organization 353
Trends and Issues in HRM 354
Sustainability-Based Benefits 354
Does Diversity Training Work? 354
Chapter Summary 355
Key Terms 356
Key Terms Review 356
Communication Skills 357
Case 13.1 CEO Compensation: Do They Deserve Rock Star Pay? 357
Skill Builders 359

Chapter 14 • **Global Issues for Human Resource Managers** 362
Globalization of Business and Human Resource Management 364
Reasons for Business Globalization 364
Find New Customers 364
Declining Barriers of Distance and Culture 364
The Global Village 365
Declining Trade Barriers and the WTO 365
The Rise of Trade Blocs 365
To Remain Competitive! 365
Is HRM Different in Global Firms? 366
Legal, Ethical, and Cultural Issues 367

International Labor Laws   **367**

U.S. Law   **368**

National Culture   **368**

Cultural Differences and Management   368

Hofstede's Model of National Culture   369

Global Staffing   371

Skills and Traits for Global Managers   **371**

Staffing Choice: Home-, Host-, or Third-Country Employees   **372**

Outsourcing as an Alternative to International Expansion   **372**

Developing and Managing Global Human Resources   373

Recruiting and Selection   **374**

Expatriate Training and Preparation   **374**

Cultural Training   374

Communication Training   375

Repatriation After Foreign Assignments   **376**

Compensating Your Global Workforce   376

Pay   **376**

Balance Sheet Approach   377

Split-Pay Approach   377

Other Approaches   377

Incentives in Global Firms   **377**

Benefit Programs Around the World   **378**

Trends and Issues in HRM   378

Globalization of Business Continues as a Trend!   **379**

The Worldwide Labor Environment   **379**

Brazil   379

South Korea   379

Chapter Summary   380

Key Terms   381

Key Terms Review   381

Communication Skills   381

Case 14.1 The Great Singapore Sale at Jurong Point:
Finding and Retaining Bargain Employees   382

Skill Builders   383

Glossary   **385**

Notes   **390**

Index   **419**

• Preface •

In his book *Power Tools,* John Nirenberg asks, "Why are so many well-intended students learning so much and yet able to apply so little in their personal and professional lives?" The world of business and human resource management (HRM) has changed, and so should how it is taught. Increasing numbers of students want more than lectures to gain an understanding of the concepts of HRM. They want their courses to be relevant and to apply what they learn, and they want to develop skills they can use in their everyday life and at work. It's not enough to learn about HRM; they want to learn how to be HR managers. This is why we wrote the book. After reviewing and using a variety of HRM books for more than a decade, we didn't find any that (1) could be easily read and understood by students and (2) effectively taught students how to be HR managers. We wrote this text out of our desire to prepare students to be successful HR managers and/or to use HRM skills as line managers or employees. As the subtitle states, this book not only presents the important HRM concepts and functions but also takes students to the next level by actually engaging them by teaching them to apply the concepts through critical thinking and to develop HRM skills they can use in their personal and professional lives.

Market and Course

This book is for undergraduate- and graduate-level courses in human resource management (HRM), including personnel management. It is appropriate for a first course in an HRM major, as well as required and elective courses found in business schools. This textbook is also appropriate for HRM courses taught in other disciplines, such as education and psychology, particularly industrial psychology and organizational psychology, and can be utilized for training courses in supervision. The level of the text assumes no prior background in business or HRM. This book is an excellent choice for online and hybrid courses in HRM.

Learning by Doing: A Practical Approach

I (Lussier) started writing management textbooks in 1988—prior to the calls by the Association to Advance Collegiate Schools of Business (AACSB) for skill development—to help professors teach their students how to apply concepts and develop management skills. Pfeffer and Sutton (*The Knowing-Doing Gap,* 2000) concluded that the most important insight from their research is that knowledge that is actually implemented is much more likely to be acquired from learning by doing than from learning by reading, listening, or thinking. We designed this book to give students the opportunity to "learn by doing" with the following approaches:

- A practical **"how-to-manage"** approach that is strategy driven.

- The only HR text where primary content areas identified in the Society of Human Resource Management **2018 Curriculum Guidebook** as *required* for undergraduate students is specifically identified in the text where the material is covered (over 270 items). In addition, many of the *secondary* and *graduate students only* items are also identified as they occur in the text.

- Six types of high-quality **application materials** use the concepts to develop critical-thinking skills.

- Four types of high-quality **skill-builder exercises** help to develop HR management skills that can be utilized in students' professional and personal lives.

- A selection of **videos** that reinforce HRM-related abilities and skills.

- A flexible approach that meets the preferred teaching style of professors and learning styles of today's students who want to be engaged with active learning.

A New Generation of Learners

Today's students, including millennials and Generation Z (also referred to as the post-millennials), succeed when they are fully engaged in learning on multiple levels; traditional methods of teaching do not always meet their needs. Our text is flexible enough to accompany lecture-based teaching, and also offers a wide range of engaging activities that accommodate a variety of contemporary learning styles. Many of the specific learning preferences of today's students have been addressed in the book's overall approach, organization, and distinctive features.

Active Learning

A desire for **active learning** is addressed with a large variety of activities and skill-building tools.

Practical Approaches

A desire for **application and skills** in personal and professional realms is addressed by a variety of features throughout the text. **Immediate application and ongoing self-assessment** are found in the Work Application prompts (found online and in the Instructor Manual) and Self-Assessment tools. Organization tools such as **checklists, summaries, and "how to"** instructions are integrated throughout the book, for example, the marginal references to SHRM curriculum guidelines.

Accessible Content

Chunking of content into easily digested segments helps students to organize study time. **Visual learning** preferences are accommodated in colorful exhibits, models, and figures throughout the text, along with an ancillary package that includes visual learning options. **Internet learning** preferences are recognized in a robust Web-based package, which includes video and interactive features for students.

A Three-Pronged Approach

We have created a concise textbook intended to develop the full range of HRM competencies. As the subtitle of this book implies, we provide a balanced, three-pronged approach to the curriculum.

Concepts/Functions

The following features are provided to support the first step in the three-pronged approach.

HRM functions. Chapter 1 presents eight major HRM functions identified by SHRM with questions that need to be answered. The book is structured around the eight functions in five parts (see the table of contents for details). These functions are emphasized in order to show students the depth of knowledge that is required of the contemporary HR manager.

Pedagogical aids. Each chapter includes Learning Outcomes, Chapter Summary, Key Terms and Key Terms Review, Communication Skills questions, Case study followed by questions, and Skill Builders.

SHRM's Required Content, as well as many Secondary and Graduate-only HR Content Areas from the *SHRM Human Resource Curriculum: Guidebook and Templates for Undergraduate and Graduate Programs* (SHRM, 2018), are annotated for easy reference where they appear in each chapter of the text. An in-text reference (e.g., **SHRM C:17**) identifies the *SHRM Curriculum Guidebook* topic being covered, and a reference number links to an appendix covering the entire *SHRM Curriculum Guidebook*. Nearly all of the Primary Content Areas and Subtopics identified in the *SHRM Curriculum Guidebook* are introduced within the text.

Applications

The following features are provided to support the second step in the three-pronged approach.

Practitioner's Perspective illustrates how a real-life human resource manager currently employed by the state of Arkansas works within the various HRM functions in her daily activities.

Organizational examples of HRM concepts and functions appear throughout the book.

Work Applications incorporate open-ended questions that require students to explain how the HRM concepts apply to their own work experience. Student experience can be present, past, summer, full-time, part-time employment, or volunteer work. The Work Applications associated with the prompts in the text can be found online and in the Instructor Manual.

Applying the Concept features ask students to determine the most appropriate HRM concept to be used in a specific short example.

Ethical Dilemma features give students examples of real-world situations in which they need to make a choice using the concepts and skills presented in the chapter.

Cases at the end of each chapter illustrate how specific organizations use the HRM functions. Critical-thinking questions challenge students to identify and apply the chapter concepts that are illustrated in each case.

Skill Development

The following features are provided to support the third step in the three-pronged approach.

Self-Assessments help students to gain personal knowledge of how they will complete the HRM functions in the real world. All information for completing and scoring is contained within the text.

Communication Skills at the end of each chapter include questions for class discussion, presentations, and/or written assignments to develop critical-thinking communication skills; they are based on HR content areas.

Skill Builders develop skills that can be used in students' personal and professional lives. Many of the exercises in similar textbooks tend to be discussion-oriented exercises that don't actually develop a skill that can be used immediately on the job.

New to This Edition

All SHRM Guidelines are updated to the 2018 release. A full correlation to the SHRM Guidelines can be found online. All Work Application prompts have been moved online and are in the Instructor Manual.

Chapter 1

- Reorganized content for better flow and clarity

- Updated statistics

- Added subheadings to improve readability

- Provided updates to industry changes, such as title changes, role changes, and technological innovations

- Trends and Issues in HRM (new discussions): "Employee Engagement Improves Productivity" and "HRM and Organizational Agility"

- New Case: Fracturing the Labor Market: Employment in the Oil Services Industry

Chapter 2

- Reorganized some chapter content to improve flow and clarity

- Added discussion of the role of HR management in strategic planning

- Updated statistics and examples from current events and trends in industry

- Updated discussion of the role of data analytics in HRM

- Updated terminology from HRIS to HRMS

- Trends and Issues in HRM (new discussion): "Structure, Culture, and Technology Are Misaligned"

- New Case: Catalya Hats: Pulling a Rabbit Out of the Hat or Coming Up Empty Handed?

Chapter 3

- New chapter title: The Legal Environment

- Moved content on equal employment opportunity (EEO), affirmative action, and diversity to Chapter 13

- Added discussion on the role and responsibilities of HR to ensure compliance with the law and avoidance of sexual harassment issues

- Expanded discussion of religious discrimination

- New Skill Builder 3.2 (first edition's Skill Builder 3.2 is now Skill Builder 13.3)

- Trends and Issues in HRM (new discussions): "Sexual Orientation and Gender Identity Discrimination" and "Technology May Create New Dangers in Equal Opportunity and Diversity Management"

- New Case: When Religion Is on the Agenda

Chapter 4

- New chapter title: Workforce Planning: Job Analysis, Design, and Employment Forecasting

- Revised Learning Outcomes

- Updated content throughout the chapter

- Added new Self-Assessment

- Trends and Issues in HRM (new discussions): "Gig Work and the Agile Workforce" and "Automation at Work"

- New Case: Walmart's Everyday Hiring Strategy: Fueling Future Consumer Demand With Passion and Talent

Chapter 5

- Thoroughly revised and updated to reflect more current examples and technologies in this area of the field of HR

- Expanded discussion on technology and online recruiting

- Trends and Issues in HRM (new discussions): "Millennial vs. Generation Z: Aren't They All the Same?" and "Look for Grit, Not Just Talent"

- New Case: Trying to Build When Nobody Wants to Work

Chapter 6

- Expanded discussion of the fit of the candidate and the organization, focusing more on cultural fit and providing real-world examples

- Added new Self-Assessment: O*Net Interest Profiler Revisited

- Updated information on applications and résumés

- Updated statistics on written testing

- Revised and updated discussion of drug testing

- Expanded discussion on types of interviews and interview questions

- Revised content addressing criminal background checks

- Trends and Issues in HRM (new discussions): "Federal Regulation Limits Selection Testing" and "The Global Workforce and Immigration"

- New Case: A Kink in Links of London's Selection Process

Chapter 7

- Updated section "When Is Training Needed?" with current terminology and examples

- Added discussion of using simulations as a training method

- Added discussion of outsourcing as a method of employee development

- Trends and Issues in HRM (new discussions): "Gamification—A Phoenix Rising" and "The Corporate Learning Imperative"

- New Case: Doing Crunches at Nestlé: Continuous Improvement of Human Assets

Chapter 8

- Revised section "Performance Management Systems," introducing current debate in the field to modify or discontinue annual performance ratings

- Updated and revised section "Who Should Assess Performance?" specific to supervisors and peers

- Added discussion of effective coaching in relation to avoiding common errors

- Thoroughly revised section "Debriefing the Appraisal," with emphasis on and discussion of the importance of coaching

- Expanded discussion of the developmental performance appraisal interview

- Trends and Issues in HRM (new discussions): "Building Engagement Through Performance Management" and "Electronic Performance Monitoring"

- New Case: Not Spilling the Beans at Jelly Belly: Developing a More Accurate Performance Appraisal System

Chapter 9

- Fully revised and expanded discussion of "Managing and Leading Your Workforce"

- Added discussion of pulse surveys

- Made significant revisions to content on coaching

- Updated and revised content on union organizing and membership

- Trends and Issues in HRM (new discussions): "Good Feedback Makes a Good Manager" and "Social Media and the Web Continue to Create Managerial Nightmares"

- New Case: Willful Violation, or a Problem That Can Be Corrected?

Chapter 10

- Significantly revised and updated to reflect current trends, laws, and statistics in the area of compensation

- Revamped discussion of "Compensation Management," placing greater emphasis on its growing importance to the firm

- Completely revamped discussion on "Compensation Strategy" to replace "Organizational Philosophy"

- Updated minimum wage discussion

- Trends and Issues in HRM (new discussions): "Designation of Independent Contractors Continues to Be an Issue" and "The Stubborn Gender Wage Gap—Can It Be Fixed?"

- New Case: Discounting Everything but Compensation at Costco

Chapter 11

- Significantly revised and updated to reflect current trends, laws, and statistics in the area of incentives and benefits, shifting focus to strategic use of both

- Trends and Issues in HRM (new discussions): "Does Incentive Pay Actually Improve Performance" and "Benefits for Domestic Partners"

- New Case: Best Buy or Best Scam? Trying to Get Commission Results on So-Called Non-Commission Pay

Chapter 12

- Updated statistics throughout the chapter

- Expanded discussion of cyber security

- Trends and Issues in HRM (new discussions): "OSHA Changes Rules on Post-Incident Drug Testing" and "eDocAmerica—Health and Wellness Online"

- New Case: You Are Not Hurt? Good—You're Fired!

Chapter 13

- New chapter title: Ethics, Sustainability, Diversity, and Inclusion

- Moved section "EEO, Affirmative Action, and Diversity" (formerly in Chapter 3) to this chapter, retitling it "Diversity and Inclusion" and expanding coverage to include differences between diversity and inclusion

- Expanded section titled "Demographic Diversity"

- Added new discussion, "Managing Diversity," covering the five HR initiatives used to increase equal opportunity

- Added new Self-Assessment covering diversity

- New Case: CEO Compensation: Do They Deserve Rock Star Pay?

Chapter 14

- Updated statistics and political trends impacting global economies and businesses

- Trends and Issues in HRM (new discussion): Globalization of Business Continues as a Trend!

- New Case: Germany "Italian Style": An Interview With Bari Italy HR Director Francesco Basile of Bosch

Ancillaries

http://edge.sagepub.com/fundamentalsofhrm2e

SAGE edge offers a robust online environment featuring an impressive array of tools and resources for review, study, and further exploration, keeping both instructors and students on the cutting edge of teaching and learning.

   SAGE edge for Instructors supports teaching by making it easy to integrate quality content, creating a rich learning environment for students.

- **Test banks** built on Bloom's taxonomy and tied to the book's learning objectives provide a diverse range of pre-written options as well as the opportunity to edit any question and/or insert personalized questions to effectively assess students' progress and understanding.

- **Sample course syllabi** for semester and quarter courses provide suggested models for structuring one's course.

- Editable, chapter-specific **PowerPoint® slides** offer complete flexibility for creating a multimedia presentation for the course.

- **Multimedia content** includes videos that appeal to students with different learning styles.

- The **Instructor's Manual** provides answers to Applying the Concept and Skill Builder activities and case notes, as well as chapter work applications.

- **SHRM Correlation Guide** for ease in finding content in the book for each SHRM Guideline covered.

SAGE edge for Students provides a personalized approach to help students accomplish their coursework goals in an easy-to-use learning environment.

- Mobile-friendly **eFlashcards** strengthen understanding of key terms and concepts.

- Mobile-friendly practice **quizzes** allow for independent assessment by students of their mastery of course material.

- **Chapter learning objectives and summaries** help students reinforce the most important material.

- **Multimedia content** includes video and web resources that appeal to students with different learning styles.

- **SHRM Correlation Guide** for ease in finding content in the book for each SHRM Guideline covered.

SAGE coursepacks

SAGE coursepacks for Instructors make it easy to import our quality content into your school's LMS. Intuitive and simple to use, it allows you to

Say NO to . . .

- required access codes
- learning a new system

Say YES to . . .

- using only the content you want and need
- high-quality assessment and multimedia exercises

For use in: Blackboard, Canvas, Brightspace by Desire2Learn (D2L), and Moodle

Don't use an LMS platform? No problem, you can still access many of the online resources for your text via SAGE edge.

SAGE coursepacks include:

- Our content delivered **directly into your LMS**

- Intuitive, simple format that makes it easy to integrate the material into your course with minimal effort

- Pedagogically **robust assessment tools** that foster review, practice, and critical thinking, and offer a more complete way to measure student engagement, including:
  - Diagnostic chapter **pre tests and post tests** that identify opportunities for improvement, track student progress, and ensure mastery of key learning objectives
  - **Test banks** built on Bloom's Taxonomy that provide a diverse range of test items with ExamView test generation. Questions are also correlated to the current AACSB Standards.

- ○ **Activity and quiz options** that allow you to choose only the assignments and tests you want
- ○ **Instructions** on how to use and integrate the comprehensive assessments and resources provided

- **Assignable SAGE Premium Video** (available via the interactive eBook version, linked through SAGE coursepacks) that is tied to learning objectives, curated, and produced exclusively for this text to bring concepts to life and appeal to different learning styles, featuring:
  - ○ **Corresponding multimedia assessment options** that automatically feed to your gradebook
  - ○ *HRM in Action* animated videos that highlight key concepts in human resource management

- Comprehensive, downloadable, easy-to-use *Media Guide in the Coursepack* **for every video resource**, listing the chapter to which the video content is tied, matching learning objective(s), a helpful description of the video content, and assessment questions

- **Multimedia content** includes links to video, audio, web, and data that are tied to learning objectives and enhance exploration of key topics to make learning easier

- Editable, chapter-specific **PowerPoint® slides** that offer flexibility when creating multimedia lectures so you don't have to start from scratch but you can customize to your exact needs

- **Sample course syllabi** with suggested models for structuring your course that give you options to customize your course in a way that is perfect for you

- **Integrated links to the interactive eBook** that make it easy for your students to maximize their study time with this "anywhere, anytime" mobile-friendly version of the text. It also offers access to more digital tools and resources, including SAGE Premium Video

- Selected tables and figures from the textbook

• Acknowledgments •

We would like to thank our team at SAGE Publications, which helped bring this book to fruition. Our first executive editor, Patricia Quinlin, who brought us to SAGE, and editor Lisa Cuevas Shaw shepherded the development of the first edition of *Human Resource Management* from its inception. Our current editor, Maggie Stanley, as well as Darcy Scelsi and Janeane Calderon, provided additional assistance and support. We are grateful to Gail Buschman for a cover and interior design that sets this book apart. During the production process, Veronica Stapleton Hooper provided professionalism and valuable support. Sarah Panella lent her marketing experience and skills to promoting the book.

We would like to acknowledge our colleagues at SHRM who provided organizational resources—in particular the 2018 *SHRM HR Curriculum Guidebook and Template*—to ensure that *Fundamentals of Human Resource Management* is *the* textbook of choice for future HR practitioners. We would also like to recognize Cindy Wright of the Department of Human Services for Arkansas for her vital contribution of chapter-opening vignettes ("Practitioner's Perspective"), which feature her personal insight and experience as an HR professional. Excellent case material has been provided by Can Guler, Komal Thakker, and Herbert Sherman of the Department of Management Sciences, School of Business Brooklyn Campus, Long Island University, and by Robert Wayland, University of Arkansas at Little Rock.

Thanks to the following reviewers who participated throughout all stages of the book's development:

First Edition Reviewers

Richard Bahner, *Kean University*

Tony Bledsoe, *Meredith College*

Tony Daniel, *Shorter University*

Kelly Hall, *Stetson University*

Reggie Hall, *Tarleton State University*

Joni Koegel, *Cazenovia College*

Cindy Lanphear, *University of the Ozarks*

Wai Kwan (Elaine) Lau, *Marshall University*

Brian Martinson, *Tarleton State University*

Kelly Mollica, *University of Memphis*

Hudson Nwakanma, *Florida A&M University*

Julie Palmer, *Webster University*

Samuel L. Rohr, *Purdue University North Central*

Katina Sawyer, *Villanova University*

Andrea Smith-Hunter, *Siena College*

Marie A. Valentin, *Texas A&M University*

Second Edition Reviewers

Callie Burnley, *California State University Polytechnic, Pomona and Chaffey College*

Yi-Yu Chen, *New Jersey City University*

Issam Ghazzawi, *University of La Verne*

Joni A. Koegel, *Cazenovia College*

Loren Kuzuhara, *University of Wisconsin–Madison*

Julia Levashina, *Kent State University*

Kelly Mollica, *University of Memphis Lambuth Campus*

Thomas J. Norman, *California State University, Dominguez Hills*

Katina Sawyer, *Villanova University*

Steven Austin Stovall, *Wilmington College*

• About the Authors •

Robert N. Lussier is a professor of management at Springfield College. Through teaching management courses for more than 25 years, he has developed innovative methods for applying concepts and developing skills that can be used both personally and professionally. A prolific writer, Dr. Lussier has more than 425 publications to his credit, including *Management* 7e (SAGE), *Human Relations* 10e (McGraw-Hill), and *Leadership* 6e (South Western/Cengage) and has published in top tier academic journals. He holds a bachelor of science degree in business administration from Salem State College, master's degrees in business and education from Suffolk University, and a doctorate in management from the University of New Haven. He served as founding director of Israel Programs and has taught courses in Israel.

John R. Hendon is a seven-time entrepreneur and former director of operations for a $60 million company. He brought his experience and interests to the classroom full time in 1994 and has been a faculty member in the Department of Management at the University of Arkansas at Little Rock for over 20 years. An active member of the Society for Human Resource Management, he teaches in the areas of human resource management, strategy, and organizational management, and researches in a number of areas in the management field, specializing in entrepreneurial research. John is also currently the president of The VMP Group, an Arkansas-based business consulting firm. John's company consults with a variety of businesses on human resources, family business, strategic planning, organizational design, and leadership. He has provided professional assistance in the start-up and operation of dozens of Arkansas- and California-based businesses and nonprofits, government agencies, and utilities. John holds an MBA degree from San Diego State University and a BS in education from the University of Central Arkansas.

To my wife, Marie, and our six children,
Jesse, Justin, Danielle, Nicole, Brian, and Renee
R.N.L.

For my father, Charles "Chuck" Hendon, who taught me perseverance
J.R.H.

The Human Resource Management Environment

PART I

1 **Today's Human Resource Management Process**

2 **Strategy-Driven Human Resource Management**

3 **The Legal Environment**

PRACTITIONER'S MODEL

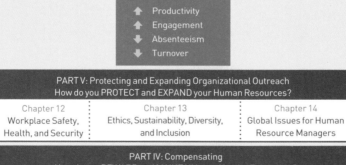

↑ Productivity
↑ Engagement
↓ Absenteeism
↓ Turnover

PART V: Protecting and Expanding Organizational Outreach
How do you PROTECT and EXPAND your Human Resources?

| Chapter 12 Workplace Safety, Health, and Security | Chapter 13 Ethics, Sustainability, Diversity, and Inclusion | Chapter 14 Global Issues for Human Resource Managers |

PART IV: Compensating
How do you REWARD and MAINTAIN your Human Resources?

| Chapter 10 Compensation Management | Chapter 11 Employee Incentives and Benefits |

PART III: Developing and Managing
How do you MANAGE your Human Resources?

| Chapter 7 Training, Learning, Talent Management, and Development | Chapter 8 Performance Management and Appraisal | Chapter 9 Employee Rights and Labor Relations |

PART II: Staffing
What HRM Functions do you NEED for sustainability?

| Chapter 4 Workforce Planning: Job Analysis, Design, and Employment Forecasting | Chapter 5 Recruiting Job Candidates | Chapter 6 Selecting New Employees |

PART I: The Human Resource Management Environment
What HRM issues are CRITICAL to your organization's long-term sustainability?

| Chapter 1 Today's Human Resource Management Process | Chapter 2 Strategy-Driven Human Resource Management | Chapter 3 The Legal Environment |

1

©iStockphoto.com/LumineImages

Today's Human Resource Management Process

Learning Outcomes

After studying this chapter, you should be able to do the following:

1.1 Explain why all managers need to understand the basics of HRM. **PAGE 4**

1.2 Discuss how HRM helps meet management challenges to improve organizational revenues. **PAGE 5**

1.3 Describe the major HRM discipline areas. **PAGE 9**

1.4 Recall the primary difference between line and staff managers by their major HR responsibilities. **PAGE 14**

1.5 Summarize the major HRM skill sets. **PAGE 15**

1.6 Identify the most common HRM certification programs and their parent organizations. **PAGE 17**

1.7 Explain the practitioner's model for HRM and how it applies to this book. **PAGE 18**

SHRM HR Content

See Online: *SHRM 2018 Curriculum Guidebook* for the complete list

C. Employee and Labor Relations
- 4. Attendance
- 16. Employee engagement
- 17. Employee involvement
- 19. Employee retention

D. Employment Law
- 36. Professional liability

E. Globalization
- 6-c. Global benefits—Global labor markets
- 6-d. Global benefits—Global talent shortages

G. HR's Role in Organizations
- 1. It is expected that faculty will discuss HR's role regarding each of the individual HR disciplines . . .

L. Organizational Development
- 5. Improving organizational effectiveness
- 6. Knowledge management
- 10. Organizational effectiveness
- 13. Ongoing performance and productivity initiatives

O. Strategic HR
- 1-g. Strategic management—Organizational effectiveness
- 1-j. Strategic management—Sustainability/corporate social responsibility
- 2-a. HR strategies—Ethics
- 2-c. HR strategies—Internal consulting
- 2-g. HR strategies—The role of the chief human resource officer (CHRO)

Practitioner's Perspective

Cindy reflected on the current state of the HR field: Choice and change—two things you can rely on today! No longer merely concerned with hiring, firing, and record keeping, the average human resource (HR) department increasingly partners with the strategic planners in the executive suite, thanks to HR-based education and certifications. HR certification is available through the HR Certification Institute (HRCI) with PHR, SPHR, and GPHR designations, and the Society for Human Resource Management (SHRM) also offers its own program of certification with SHRM-CP and SHRM-SCP.

My professional progress began with membership in HR organizations. First, I became a SHRM student member, which provided access to SHRM's website—which was in turn valuable for research while I was a student. I still use it frequently. Next, my involvement spread to the local HR association. The chapter meetings provided excellent opportunities for education through the monthly programs, as well as for networking and swapping "best practices" with my colleagues. My involvement inspired me to become certified as a professional. But beyond that, I have found that those who invest in certification tend to become more involved in their profession and, by extension, more successful.

(Continued)

(Continued)

I invite you to join me as we explore the field of human resource management (HRM). Chapter 1 gives an overview of HRM as a profession.

Cindy Wright, PHR, came late to the human resources profession, and perhaps that explains some of her passion for the field. Wright graduated summa cum laude with a business administration degree, with an emphasis in human resources. She was recognized as "Outstanding Graduate" by the Human Resources Management department. After employment as a benefits administrator for 7,000 telecommunications retirees, then as an HR generalist for a gas well drilling company of 500 employees, Wright is now working in personnel management for the Department of

Human Services in the Division of Behavioral Health Services. Besides membership in the profession's national organization, the Society for Human Resource Management (SHRM), Wright has been active in the local affiliated chapter, the Central Arkansas Human Resources Association (CAHRA). Wright served as vice president of administration for the chapter's board as well as chair of the College Relation Committee. She was recognized by her peers with the "Rising Star" award for her work in creating a student chapter membership and was involved in the initial efforts to create satellite CAHRA chapters. Wright's mission is to provide assistance to others interested in entering into and advancing within the human resources profession.

Why Study Human Resource Management (HRM)?

>> **LO 1.1 Explain why all managers need to understand the basics of HRM.**

It's natural to think, "What can I get from this book?" or "What's in it for me?" Success in our professional and personal lives is about creating relationships,[1] and students generally understand the importance of relationships.[2] The better you can work with people, the more successful you will be in your personal and professional lives—whether as an employee, a line manager, or a human resource manager. And that's what this book is all about.

In a modern organization, **human resources (HR)**—*the people within an organization*—are one of the primary means of creating a competitive advantage, because the way we manage people directly affects their work performance.[3] Most organizations of comparable size and scope within an industry generally have access to the same material- and facilities-based resources that any other organization within the industry may have, making it very difficult to create a competitive advantage based on material, facility, or other tangible resources. What this frequently leaves is people as the organization's most valuable asset.[4] If the organization can manage its people more successfully than its competitors do, if it can get its employees *engaged* in the day-to-day success of the organization, and if it can get them to stay with the organization, then it has a much greater chance of being successful—with the term *successful* defined in this case as being more productive and more profitable than the competition.[5] Managers are responsible for getting the job done through employees,[6] so the organization's human resources are nearly always its most valuable resource. (SHRM guides are available at the beginning of each chapter as well as on the companion website. We will explain them in the section of this chapter titled "Resources for HRM Careers.")

Human resources (HR) The people within an organization

Employee Engagement

While job satisfaction can be an important aspect of employee engagement, the overall concept of **employee engagement** is much larger: It is *a combination of job satisfaction, ability, and a willingness to perform for the organization at a high level and over an extended period of time.* **Google** is an example of an organization that takes the concept of employee engagement very seriously. **Google**'s "Project Oxygen" is one attempt to analyze what makes a better boss and use that information to train managers to be more consistent and interactive.[7] This training is designed to create greater employee satisfaction and engagement, for very practical reasons. An article by the Queen's Centre for Business Venturing in Canada notes that companies with the highest employee engagement over a 10-year period achieved 65% greater share-price increase; 15% greater employee productivity; 30% greater customer satisfaction; plus other significant advantages over their less engaged competitors.[8] Companies with high levels of satisfaction and engagement also outperform those with less engaged employees in return on investment (ROI), operating income, growth rate, and long-term company valuation.[9] So **Google** has good reason for training managers to be more engaging. The role of modern managers also continues to change, requiring today's organizational leaders to deal with increasingly dynamic and complex environments.[10] **(SHRM C:17 and C:16)**

Employee engagement A combination of job satisfaction, ability, and a willingness to perform for the organization at a high level and over an extended period of time

Student Engagement and Skill Development

Today's students want to be actively engaged in their education. They don't simply want to learn HRM concepts, they want to be able to apply the concepts with critical thinking, and develop skills they can use in their personal and professional lives.[11] Organizations also want managers to have the ability to apply concepts and skills at work.[12] This is the reason our book uses a three-pronged approach, with these objectives:

- To teach you the important functions and concepts of HRM

- To develop your ability to apply HRM functions and concepts through critical thinking

- To develop your HRM skills in your personal and professional lives

We offer some unique features to further each of the three objectives, as summarized in Exhibit 1.1.

EXHIBIT 1.1 ● Features of This Book's Three-Pronged Approach		
Features That Present HRM Functions and Important Concepts	**Features to Apply the HRM Functions and Concepts That You Learn**	**Features That Foster Skill Development**
• Learning Outcomes	• Practitioner's Perspective	• Self-Assessments
• Key Terms	• Organizational Examples	• Communication Skills Questions
• Step-by-Step Behavior Models	• Work Applications	• Ethical Dilemmas
• Chapter Summaries With Glossaries	• Applying the Concepts	• Skill Builder Exercises
• Review Questions	• Cases	
	• Videos	

This book will teach you how to get people engaged and get the results necessary to succeed against tough competitors in today's business environment.[13] We will focus on HR management, but the principles apply to any form of management. The bottom line is that if you learn these skills and apply them successfully in *any* manager role, you will get your employees engaged and improve productivity. That is what will get you noticed by senior management and allow you to move up the organizational ladder. So, let's get started!

HRM Past and Present

>> LO 1.2 Discuss how HRM helps meet management challenges to improve organizational revenues.

Back in the mid-1970s—when there weren't even any computers available to most managers!—being the human resource manager (we usually called them personnel managers then) was considered to be a bit easier than other management jobs. HR managers were only expected to be paper pushers who could keep all of the personnel files straight. They had very little to do with the management of the organization's business processes.

In these types of organizations, the HR department was considered a cost center.[14] A **cost center** is *a division or department that brings in no revenue or profit for the organization—running this function only costs the organization money.* As you can easily see, we don't want many (or any) cost centers if we can help it. We need revenue centers instead.

Revenue centers, however, are *divisions or departments that generate monetary returns for the organization.* Where cost centers eat up available funds, revenue centers provide funds for the organization to operate. So, what's a good HR manager to do? HR departments are not able to

Cost center A division or department that brings in no revenue or profit for the organization—running this function only costs the organization money

Revenue centers Divisions or departments that generate monetary returns for the organization

Productivity center A revenue center that enhances the profitability of the organization through enhancing the productivity of the people within the organization

Productivity The amount of output that an organization gets per unit of input, with human input usually expressed in terms of units of time

Effectiveness A function of getting the job done whenever and however it must be done

Efficiency A function of how many organizational resources we used in getting the job done

generate revenue *directly* because of their tasking within the organization, but they can generate significant revenue and profit in an indirect fashion as *productivity centers.*

A **productivity center** is *a revenue center that enhances the profitability of the organization through enhancing the productivity of the people within the organization.* Today's HR managers are no longer running an organizational cost center. HRM enhances the revenues of the organization—by being a productivity center. **Productivity** is *the amount of output that an organization gets per unit of input, with human input usually expressed in terms of units of time.* **(SHRM L:13)**

But how can we become more productive? Productivity is the end result of two components that managers work to create and improve within the organization:

- **Effectiveness**—*a function of getting the job done whenever and however it must be done.* It answers the question, "Did we do the right things?"

- **Efficiency**—*a function of how many organizational resources we used in getting the job done.* It answers the question, "Did we do things right?"

Both of these are important, but most of the time, we are focused on efficiency.[15] Our people allow us to be more efficient as an organization *if* they are used in the correct manner. This course is about how to make our people more efficient. **(SHRM L:5, L:10, O:1-g)**

Companies around the world are taking this need for efficiency very seriously, and new technologies and new ways of working are helping companies improve their efficiency. Chief human resource officers (CHROs) are concerned about employee engagement and productivity, and especially about improving efficiency,[16] so companies put some of their best managers in the HRM job. In addition to improving efficiency, Fortune 500 firms that have a senior HR manager in the "C-suite"—meaning having a CHRO in addition to having a chief operations officer (COO), a chief finance officer (CFO), etc.—increased profitability by 105% over peer companies that did not have a CHRO![17] **(SHRM O:2-g)**

As the HR management responsibilities have changed over the years, so have their titles. The prior title Personnel Manager is not commonly used today. HRM is still popular, but some companies are using different titles, such as VP of People and Culture at **Birchbox**,[18] People Operations at **Google** and **Southwest**, Employee Experience at **Airbnb**, and Employee Success at **Salesforce**.[19]

If you are interested in a HR career in a large company, the number of jobs has been increasing over the years. In 2007, the ratio of HR staff to workers was 1 HR staff member for every 100 workers. By 2017, the ratio had increased to 1.4:100.[20]

HR management deals primarily with improving the efficiency of the people within our organization—getting more per unit of time. If our people are inefficient over long periods of time, our organization will fail. If we don't use our people efficiently, we're ultimately going to be forced out of business by somebody who is better at using those resources than we are.

Today's HRM Challenges

As the HR responsibilities and complexity of the function increases, so have the challenges they face.[21] A recent SHRM survey of HR and non-HR executives asked what challenges they think will be most significant over the next 10 years. Here is a brief review of what they said.[22]

The three biggest challenges according to HR executives:

1. Maintaining high levels of employee engagement

2. Developing next generation organization leaders

3. Maintaining competitive compensation and benefits offerings

The biggest challenges according to non-HR executives were very similar:

1. Developing next generation organizational leaders

2. Managing the loss of key workers and their skill sets

3. Maintaining competitive benefits and compensation offerings

The HR competencies that will be the most critical:[23]

1. Business acumen: ability to understand and apply information to contribute to the organization's strategic plan

2. Organizational leadership and navigation: ability to direct and contribute to initiatives and processes within the organization

3. Critical evaluation: ability to interpret information to make business decisions and recommendations

4. HR expertise: ability to apply the principles and practices of HRM to contribute to the success of the business (the focus of this book)

Can you see how these challenges and the competencies could have an effect on productivity? We have pursued better selection and retention strategies for a number of years, and we have become much better at identifying future leaders and managing organizational relationships, culture, and structure.

Where we have not done as well—at least in most organizations to this point—is in business acumen, especially in quantitative areas dealing with metrics and data analytics. This is an area that is exploding in HR departments all over the world. The ability to analyze large data sets allows HRMs to work toward overcoming another of their challenges—creating strategic agility *and* greater productivity.[24] We will introduce you to some of the basic HR metrics as we go through this text, but first let's look at the demographics issue.

▲
Part of the diversity in today's workforce is people retiring later in life and working part-time.

Labor Demographics

We face significant demographic changes in the labor force that will be available to our companies over the next 20 to 30 years, and these changing demographics will affect our ability to maintain and improve productivity over the long term.

While there continue to be arguments concerning whether or not there is a skilled worker shortage worldwide, anecdotally at least companies are seeing a reduction in the number and quality of potential employees, plus greater gender, ethnic, and age diversity than at any time in the past. Partly as a result of the perceived shortage of skilled labor, we are seeing a greater number of older employees with high-level skill sets remain in the workforce. According to the U.S. Bureau of Labor Statistics, "Over the entire 2014–24 decade, the labor force growth rate of the 65- to 74-year-old age group is expected to be about 55 [percent], and the labor force growth rate of the 75-and-older age group is expected to be about 86 percent, compared with a 5-percent increase for the labor force as a whole."[25] So as a manager in a modern organization, your workforce will look much older than it has historically.

Your organization will also look more culturally diverse—even compared to today. The growth in immigrant workers will be substantial. Hispanic workers (of all nationalities) alone are predicted to be approximately 24% of the workforce in 2050, but today, they only make up about 14% of the workforce. Asian workers are expected to move up from about 4% now to about 8% of the workforce in 2050. But the gender mix will stay fairly close to what it is today. The percentage of women in the workforce has stabilized at about 47% or 48%.[26]

All of this means that managers will need to be more culturally aware and able to deal with individuals with significantly different work ethics, cultural norms, and even languages. **(SHRM E:6-c)**

Technology and Knowledge

The 20th century saw the growth and decline of the Industrial Age in the United States and most other developed countries around the world. However, as we neared the end of the

▲
Today's technology improves the effectiveness and efficiency of HR managers, leading to higher levels of productivity throughout the organization.

Information Age An era that began around 1980, in which information became one of the main products used in organizations; it is characterized by exponential increases in available information in all industries

Knowledge workers Workers who "use their head more than their hands" and who gather and interpret information to improve a product or process for their organizations

20th century, we started to enter the **Information Age**— *an era that began around 1980, in which information became one of the main products used in organizations; it is characterized by exponential increases in available information in all industries.* This was when assembly line work began to be taken over more and more by computers, robots, and other machines, and it was when the humans in our organizations were beginning to provide more than just labor; they started to provide intelligence—or knowledge. In the Information Age, we began to see a new kind of worker—knowledge workers.

Knowledge Workers and the Knowledge-Based Firm

Knowledge workers are *workers who "use their head more than their hands" and who gather and interpret information to improve a product or process for their organizations.* There has been a lot written in the past 20 years on knowledge workers, but we can boil it down to the fact that most workers in modern organizations are not working primarily with their hands; they work with their minds. In essence, knowledge workers manage knowledge for the firm. **(SHRM L:6)**

The Pace of Technological Change

Technology is currently outstripping our ability to use it. Computers get faster and faster, but the human beings that have to use them don't. What does this mean to a business? It means that if we can figure out ways to take advantage of technology better and quicker than our competitors can, then we can create a sustainable competitive advantage. We must continually figure out ways to use technology more successfully through hiring and training better and more capable employees—our *human* resources. If we do this, then our people will continually figure out ways to take advantage of it before our competitors.

Knowledge Workers Are in Short Supply

However, there is a continuous shortage of knowledge workers available. In fact, "The majority of jobs being created in the United States require skills possessed by only 20% of the current workforce."[27] And the news is the same globally. This means that for the foreseeable future, we will have a shortage of knowledge workers. So each HR manager is going to be competing with every other HR manager in the world for that 20% of the workforce that comprises the pool of knowledge workers. Only if the organization manages its people successfully and maintains a reasonable working environment will it have any chance of filling most of the jobs that it has available. **(SHRM E: 6-d)**

Technology's Effect on Efficiency

Senior HR managers, knowing the limits placed on them by the shortage of knowledge workers, have learned that one way to improve efficiency of their workers is through use of technology— especially analytics. Old ways of doing work have become too slow in almost all cases—with competitors constantly innovating processes, and customers and employees demanding that we use technology tools to speed up both work and feedback on the work that is done.[28] Using technology allows us to gather, analyze, and manage large amounts of data much more quickly than we have ever been able to do before. This in turn allows managers—including HR managers—to find commonalities in the data that can help them create new and more efficient processes. One example will help show what we are talking about:

Sysco, a food service company with more than 50,000 employees, was able to identify "what actions by management will have the greatest impact on the business" through the use of survey data. Using some of this information, they were able to improve retention for their delivery associates from 65% to 85%, which in turn saved the company about "$50 million in hiring and training costs for new associates."[29]

The Purpose for Managing Human Resources

Before we go further, let's look at some of the things that managers tell us they *must* control in order to manage people through today's business challenges, but they can't *directly* manipulate. Every time we survey managers in any industry or any department about managing, they bring up the following issues as being among the most important and most difficult things they deal with:[30]

1. *Productivity*—previously defined

2. *Employee engagement*—previously defined

3. *Turnover*—permanent loss of workers from the organization. When people quit, it is considered voluntary turnover, while when people are fired, it is involuntary turnover.

4. *Absenteeism*—temporary absence of employees from the workplace

Note that each of these issues deals with people: not computers, not buildings, not finances—people! We have already introduced you to productivity and employee engagement, but what about the other two items? Let's take a moment for a more detailed look at each of them.

Turnover is *the permanent loss of workers from the organization.* There is strong and "growing recognition that collective turnover can have important consequences for organizational productivity, performance, and—potentially—competitive advantage."[31] As we will discuss throughout the book, turnover is very costly, so we want to minimize turnover. **(SHRM C:19)**

How about absenteeism? **Absenteeism** is *the failure of an employee to report to the workplace as scheduled.* On an annual basis, absenteeism costs in the United States went from an estimated $30 billion in 1984[32] to anywhere from $100 to $150 billion per year in 2011.[33,34] We likely lose productivity, and if some of our workers are frequently absent, it causes lower job satisfaction in others who have to continually "take up the slack" for their absent coworker. **(SHRM C:4)**

Note that these four issues are interrelated. Absenteeism is costly, is often due to a lack of employee engagement, and leads to lower productivity.[35] People tend to leave their jobs (turnover) when they aren't engaged in their work, and while they are being replaced and sometimes after, organizational productivity goes down.[36]

So the bottom line is this: As managers, we always need to be doing things that will improve productivity and employee engagement and that will reduce absenteeism and turnover. These items are critical. Everything in HRM revolves around these four things.

Turnover The permanent loss of workers from the organization

Absenteeism The failure of an employee to report to the workplace as scheduled

Disciplines Within HRM

>> **LO 1.3 Describe the major HRM discipline areas.**

HRM is an exciting field with many different paths that you can take over the course of your career.[37] The field is so broad you could do something different each year for a 40-year career and never exactly duplicate an earlier job. Although there are many different jobs in the field, most of them fall into a few categories. Let's briefly take a look at each of these disciplines or specialties. But first, complete the self-assessment (at the end of this section, p. 11) to help you better understand your overall interest in HR and which specialties interest you more. This section presents the disciplines discussed in detail throughout the book, so we will keep it short here.

The Legal Environment: EEO and Diversity Management

Equal employment opportunity (EEO) and diversity management specialists ensure compliance with equal opportunity laws and regulations as well as organizational affirmative action plans (when such plans are required or desired). They also have responsibilities related to the management of diverse employee groups within the company.

The HR legal and regulatory environment is critical to every organization today. This is also quite likely the area that changes more than any other in HRM. Every court case dealing with the HR environment inside any organization has the potential to affect every organization. Even if the court ruling doesn't change the way a company has to do business, if a federal or state legislature sees the ruling as unfair, then it may change the law and thus affect each organization under its jurisdiction. We discuss this discipline in Chapter 3.

Staffing

Staffing includes all of the things we need to do to get people interested in working for our company—going through the recruiting process, selecting the best candidates who apply, and getting them settled into their new jobs. However, this area can literally make or break the organization in its ability to be productive.[38] If we attract and hire the right types of people with the right attitudes and skills, then the organization will have a good start at being successful. We discuss staffing in Chapters 4, 5, and 6.

Training and Development

Next, we have the training and development discipline. We train people for a variety of reasons, from teaching them their basic job to teaching them the things they will need in order to move up in the organization as people above them resign or retire.

As a training and development specialist, you would have responsibility for the training processes within the organization as well as for the development of curricula and lesson plans and the delivery of training courses. You would also be involved with the development of talent within the company so employees are trained and ready to move into more senior positions as those positions become vacant. We discuss training and development in Chapter 7.

Employee Relations

This specialty covers a wide array of items such as coaching, counselling, and disciplining the workforce as needed. It also involves leadership and team-building efforts within the organization. We also measure and evaluate job satisfaction and employee engagement as part of employee relations. HR managers in this function have to keep up with the many and varied laws relating to employee relations, and this specialty also involves the management of employee communication. We discuss employee relations in Chapter 9.

Labor and Industrial Relations

The labor and industrial relations specialist works with the laws and regulations that control the organization's labor-related relationships with their workforce. HR managers who work in this area might be involved in union votes, negotiations for union agreements, collective bargaining, grievances, and other items that affect the union-management relationship within the organization. This area also includes all labor relations activities, even in nonunion businesses. We also discuss labor and industrial relations in Chapter 9.

Compensation and Benefits

The compensation and benefits specialist helps decide the total compensation package the organization will use to attract and retain the best mix of people with skills that are specifically suited to the organization. A manager will have to understand the federal and state laws dealing with compensation. You would also deal directly with all of the federal and state compensation laws to ensure compliance in organizational pay and benefits procedures. We discuss compensation in Chapter 10 and benefits in Chapter 11.

Safety and Security

In the safety and security discipline, you might work in the area of occupational safety and/or health to make sure we don't injure our people or cause them to become sick because of exposure to some substance they work with. This discipline also includes fields such as stress management and employee assistance programs, which help employees cope with the demands of their jobs on a daily basis. And finally, this function works to ensure that employees are secure from physical harm inflicted by other workers, outsiders, or even acts of nature. We discuss safety and security in Chapter 12.

Ethics and Sustainability

In this specialty, you would bear responsibility for seeing to it that the organization acts in an ethical and socially responsible manner. You might work on codes of ethics and also make sure employees live by those codes, such as by maintaining ways in which employees can report violations of ethics (also known as *whistle-blowing*). We discuss ethics and sustainability in Chapter 13. **(SHRM O:1-j and O:2-a)**

Sustainability is meeting the needs of today without sacrificing future generations' ability to meet their needs.[39] Some companies have historically done a relatively poor job of maintaining the environment in some countries in which they operated.

If you take a look at the table of contents as well as the practitioner's model later in this chapter, you will realize this book is organized to discuss the eight areas of HRM discussed here.

1.1 SELF-ASSESSMENT
HR DISCIPLINES

Following are 24 HR activities that you could be involved in. Rate your interest in each specialty with a number (1–7) that represents your interest in the activity.

I'm not really interested in doing this						I'm really interested in doing this
1	2	3	4	5	6	7

1. _____ Working to make sure everyone in the firm is treated fairly

2. _____ Working against discrimination and helping minorities to get hired and promoted

3. _____ Knowing the laws, helping the firm implement laws, and reporting how the firm complies with the HR laws

4. _____ Working to get people to apply for jobs, such as writing advertisements and attending job fairs

5. _____ Interviewing job candidates

6. _____ Orienting new employees to the firm and their jobs

7. _____ Teaching employees how to do their current jobs

8. _____ Developing employees' general skills so they can progress in the firm

9. _____ Designing curricula and lesson plans for others to teach employees

10. _____ Coaching, counseling, and disciplining employees whose work quality is not up to standards

11. _____ Working with teams and helping resolve conflicts

12. _____ Working to understand and improve the level of job satisfaction throughout the firm

13. _____ Working with union employees

14. _____ Collective bargaining with unions

15. _____ Solving employee complaints

16. _____ Working to determine fair pay for different jobs, including investigating competitors' pay scales

17. _____ Creating incentives to motivate and reward productive employees

18. _____ Finding good benefits providers, such as lower-cost and higher-quality health insurance providers

19. _____ Making sure that employees don't get hurt on the job

20. _____ Working to keep employees healthy, such as developing diet and exercise programs

(Continued)

(Continued)

21. _____ Ensuring the security of the facilities and employees, issuing IDs, and keeping employee records confidential

22. _____ Ensuring that employees are ethical, such as developing and enforcing codes of ethics

23. _____ Enforcing ethical standards, such as maintaining methods for employees to confidentially report ethics violations

24. _____ Working to help the organization develop methods to improve efficiency while protecting our environment

Scoring and Interpreting Individual Discipline Results

Place your rating numbers (1–7) below and total the three scores for each discipline. Then rank your totals from 1 to 8 to determine which disciplines interest you most.

Legal Environment: EEO and Diversity Management

1 _____

2 _____

3 _____

_____ Total (Rank this total: _____ [1–8])

Staffing

4 _____

5 _____

6 _____

_____ Total (Rank this total: _____ [1–8])

Training and Development

7 _____

8 _____

9 _____

_____ Total (Rank this total: _____ [1–8])

Employee Relations

10 _____

11 _____

12 _____

_____ Total (Rank this total: _____ [1–8])

Labor and Industrial Relations

13 _____

14 _____

15 _____

_____ Total (Rank this total: _____ [1–8])

Compensation and Benefits

16 _____

17 _____

18 _____

_____ Total (Rank this total: _____ [1–8])

Safety and Security

19 _____

20 _____

21 _____

_____ Total (Rank this total: _____ [1–8])

Ethics and Sustainability

22 _____

23 _____

24 _____

_____ Total (Rank this total: _____ [1–8])

The higher your total in each discipline, the greater your interest in that area of HR at this point in time. Of course, your interest levels can change as you learn more about each discipline. You will also be doing self-assessments in all the other chapters that relate to these eight disciplines.

Scoring and Interpreting Total Discipline Results

Now add up your grand total interest score from all 24 activities and write it here: _____. Then compare it to the continuum below to gauge your overall level of interest in working in human resources:

Low interest in HR						High interest in HR
24	50	75	100	125	150	168

The higher your score, the greater is your overall interest in HR, again at this time only.

You should realize this self-assessment is only designed to show your current level of interest. It may not predict how much you will enjoy working in any HR discipline in the future. For example, if you get a real job in an area where you gave yourself a low score today, you could end up finding it very interesting. The self-assessments throughout this book are designed to give you a better understanding of your interest and aptitudes at the present time, and they are open to your interpretations. For example, some people tend to rate themselves much lower or higher than others even though they have the same level of interest—so don't be too

concerned about your score. There are *no* correct answers or scores. Some people with lower scores may actually enjoy the course more than those with higher scores. The purpose of these self-assessments is to help you gain self-knowledge and get you thinking about how the topic of HRM relates to you.

So at this point, you should have a better idea of what the eight HR disciplines are and which areas are of more and less interest to you. But as you read the rest of this chapter and the others and learn more about each discipline, you may change your mind.

1.1 APPLYING THE CONCEPT
HRM DISCIPLINES

Identify each HRM discipline and write the letter corresponding to it before the activity involving it.

a. Legal Environment: EEO and Diversity Management

b. Staffing

c. Training and Development

d. Employee Relations

e. Labor and Industrial Relations

f. Compensation and Benefits

g. Safety and Security

h. Ethics and Sustainability

_____ 1. The HR manager is writing an ad to recruit a job candidate.

_____ 2. The HR manager is investigating an employee complaint of racial discrimination.

_____ 3. The HR manager is taking a class in preparation for the exam to become certified as a Professional in Human Resources (PHR).

_____ 4. The HR manager is working with an insurance company to try to keep the high cost of health insurance down.

_____ 5. The HR manager is replacing the office copier with a more energy-efficient model.

_____ 6. The HR manager is having a new software program installed to protect employee records from theft.

_____ 7. The HR manager is working on the new collective bargaining contract with the Teamsters Union.

_____ 8. The HR manager is looking for potential new employees at the LinkedIn website.

_____ 9. The HR manager is filling out an accident report with a production worker who got hurt on the job.

_____ 10. The HR manager is reviewing a report that compares its wages and salaries to other businesses in the area.

_____ 11. The HR manager is giving priority to promoting a member of a minority group to a management position.

_____ 12. The HR manager is teaching the new employee how to use the HR software program.

_____ 13. The HR manager is referring an employee to a marriage counselor.

HRM Responsibilities

>> **LO 1.4 Recall the primary difference between line and staff managers by their major HR responsibilities.**

Now that we know the HR disciplines, it's time to learn the difference between line and staff managers and how their HR responsibilities within the disciplines are different while being related.

Line Versus Staff Management

Line managers are *the individuals who create, manage, and maintain the people and organizational processes that create whatever it is that the business sells.* Put simply, they are the people who control the actual operations of the organization. A line manager may have direct control over staff employees, but a staff manager would not generally have any direct control of line employees. HR managers, on the other hand, would generally be **staff managers**, *individuals who advise line managers in some field of expertise.* These managers, including accountants, lawyers, and HR staff, act basically as internal consultants for the company. So HR managers have staff authority to advise the operational managers concerning the HR disciplines.

Major HR Responsibilities of HR Staff and Line Management

All managers are responsible for meeting the organization's goals through effective management of its human resources. However, their major HR responsibilities are different. The HR staff have the primary responsibility of developing the HR policies and programs for everyone in the organization to implement on a daily basis. The line managers, therefore, are responsible for implementing the HR policies within their departments. Let's review the HR disciplines and discuss some differences. **(SHRM O:2-c and G:1)**

- **The Legal Environment: EEO and Diversity Management**. The HR staff need to know the laws and train the line managers how to operate within the law, such as what line managers can and can't ask during the interview process to follow EEO laws. HR staff may develop diversity programs and teach line managers how to work with a diversity of employees.

- **Staffing**. The HR staff generally recruit candidates, but line managers usually select who is hired.

- **Training and Development**. HR staff develop training programs, including training line managers how to be effective managers. HR may teach many employees how to do their jobs, but line managers tend to provide ongoing on-the-job training.

- **Employee Relations**. HR staff develop policies, but line managers are constantly dealing with employee relations. HR may train line managers on how to coach and discipline employees.

- **Labor and Industrial Relations**. HR is responsible for policies and training to make sure the labor laws are followed and line managers implement them. If the organization has a union, HR often helps in the contract negotiations.

- **Compensation and Benefits**. HR is responsible for developing the pay system including salary and benefits, but line managers can often have some input into how much an individual is paid, including raises.

- **Safety and Security**. HR is responsible for knowing the safety laws (OSHA) and ensuring that line managers train and manage their employees to follow the safety rules.

- **Ethics and Sustainability**. HR may develop ethics codes for everyone in the organization to follow, and line managers are responsible for making ethical decisions and helping their employees do likewise.

Line managers The individuals who create, manage, and maintain the people and organizational processes that create whatever it is that the business sells

Staff managers Individuals who advise line managers in some field of expertise

1.1 ETHICAL DILEMMA: WHAT WOULD YOU DO?

Our first HR discipline is to know and obey the laws, and the last discipline is ethics and sustainability. A long debated issue is (a) should a company focus on making a profit and doing so within the law, or (b) should a company go beyond the law to be ethical and socially responsible? Some experts state that (c) by being ethical and socially responsible the firm will be more profitable, whereas (d) others say that one shouldn't consider profits—a company should be ethical and socially responsible simply because it is the right thing to do. **Apple**'s cofounder **Steve Jobs** primarily believed in focusing on profits, whereas current CEO **Tim Cook** has changed policies to be more socially responsible by giving more resources to nonprofit organizations.

1. Do you agree with (a) focusing on profits, or (b) going beyond to be ethical and socially responsible?

2. Do you agree with (c) being ethical and socially responsible if it is profitable, or (d) that a company should be ethical simply because it is the right thing to do?

3. Review the HR disciplines and describe how a company can be ethical and socially responsible in performing these functions.

HRM Skills

>> **LO 1.5 Summarize the major HRM skill sets.**

All managers require a mix of technical, interpersonal, conceptual and design, and business skills in order to successfully carry out their jobs (see Exhibit 1.2).[40] The set of necessary HR skills is similar to the skills needed by other managers, but of course it emphasizes people skills more than some other management positions do. The recent SHRM competency model discusses four basic "competency clusters" that match up well with the following four skill sets.[41]

Technical Skills

The first skill set an HR manager must develop to be successful, and the easiest one to develop, is technical skills.[42] **Technical skills** are *the ability to use methods and techniques to perform a task.* HR managers require many skills, including comprehensive knowledge of laws, rules, and regulations relating to HR; computer skills; interviewing and training skills; understanding of performance appraisal processes; and many others. This skill set is part of the SHRM *technical expertise* competency. We will cover many of these skills in the remaining chapters of this book.

Technical skills The ability to use methods and techniques to perform a task

Interpersonal Skills

The second major skill set is **interpersonal skills**, which comprise *the ability to understand, communicate, and work well with individuals and groups through developing effective relationships.*

Interpersonal skills The ability to understand, communicate, and work well with individuals and groups through developing effective relationships

EXHIBIT 1.2 ● HRM Skills

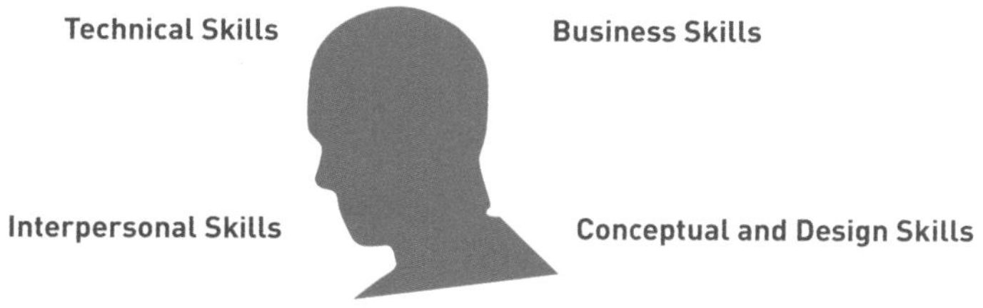

Technical Skills

Business Skills

Interpersonal Skills

Conceptual and Design Skills

The resources you need to get the job done are made available through relationships with people both inside the organization (i.e., coworkers and supervisors) and outside the organization (i.e., customers, suppliers, and others).[43] This skill set is identified as *interpersonal proficiency* in the SHRM competency model.

We will focus on interpersonal skills throughout this book, and you will have the opportunity to develop *your* interpersonal skills through this course.

HR managers must have strong people skills, including being empathetic. **Empathy** is simply *being able to put yourself in another person's place—to understand not only what that person is saying but why the individual is communicating that information to you*. Empathy involves the ability to consider what the individual is feeling while remaining emotionally detached from the situation.

Empathy Being able to put yourself in another person's place—to understand not only what that person is saying but why the individual is communicating that information to you

Conceptual and Design Skills

Conceptual and design skills help in decision making. Leaders' decisions determine the success or failure of the organization.[44] So organizations train their people to improve their decision-making skills.[45] **Conceptual and design skills** include *the ability to evaluate a situation, identify alternatives, select a reasonable alternative, and make a decision to implement a solution to a problem*. Learning this skill set is necessary if you are going to become capable in the SHRM *leadership proficiency* competency.

Conceptual and design skills The ability to evaluate a situation, identify alternatives, select a reasonable alternative, and make a decision to implement a solution to a problem

Business Skills

Finally, SHRM's *business-oriented proficiency* competency is a mandatory HRM skill. **Business skills** are *the analytical and quantitative skills—including in-depth knowledge of how the business works and its budgeting and strategic planning processes—that are necessary for a manager to understand and contribute to the profitability of the organization*. HR professionals must have knowledge of the organization and its strategies if they are to contribute strategically. This also means they must have understanding of the financial, technological, and other facets of the industry and the organization. Today, HR managers must gain the capability to manipulate large amounts of data using data analytics programs and HR metrics.

Business skills The analytical and quantitative skills—including in-depth knowledge of how the business works and its budgeting and strategic planning processes—that are necessary for a manager to understand and contribute to the profitability of the organization

1.2 APPLYING THE CONCEPT
HRM SKILLS

Identify each activity as being one of the following types of HRM skills and write the letter corresponding to each skill before the activity or activities describing it.

a. Technical

b. Interpersonal

c. Conceptual and design

d. Business

_____ 14. The HR manager is working on the strategic planning process.

_____ 15. The HR manager is working on determining why more employees have been coming to work late recently.

_____ 16. The HR manager is filling out a complex government form.

_____ 17. The HR manager is talking socially with a few of her staff members.

_____ 18. The HR manager is praising a staff member for finishing a job analysis ahead of schedule.

_____ 19. The HR manager is assigning projects to various staff members.

_____ 20. The HR manager is communicating with employees throughout the company via email.

Resources for HRM Careers

>> **LO 1.6 Identify the most common HRM certification programs and their parent organizations.**

If you are interested in HRM as a career, there are several professional associations and certification programs associated with HR management that will help you get into these jobs and help you advance more quickly in the future. We've listed some of them in this section, and there are several others within specific HR disciplines that are not discussed here.

Society for Human Resource Management (SHRM)

The **Society for Human Resource Management (SHRM)** is *the largest and most recognized of the HRM advocacy organizations in the United States.* According to its website, SHRM is "the world's largest HR professional society . . . representing more than 285,000 members in over 165 countries."[46]

What does SHRM do? Probably the biggest part of its work is dedicated to (1) advocacy for national HR laws and policies for organizations and (2) training and certification of HR professionals in a number of specialty areas. SHRM's new "competency-based" certification programs include the SHRM Certified Professional and Senior Certified Professional (SHRM-CP and SHRM-SCP).

SHRM is an outstanding organization that anyone thinking about a career in human resources should consider joining. Student memberships have always been and continue to be very inexpensive, especially considering all that is available to members of the organization.

SHRM also provides a curriculum guide for colleges and universities that offer HRM degree programs. The guide identifies specific areas in which SHRM believes students should gain competence as HRM majors. Because SHRM is such a significant force in each of the HRM fields, we have decided to show you where each of the required curriculum areas is covered within this text. In each chapter, you will see notes within the content when a *SHRM required* topic is discussed. These notes are alphanumerically keyed to the information in the Appendix *SHRM 2018 Curriculum Guidebook.* You might want to pay special attention to these notes if you have plans to become an HR manager.

If you do decide to work toward a goal of becoming an HR manager, you will need to think about taking the SHRM-CP Exam. To get more information about the SHRM-CP Exam and when you are eligible to take it, go to the SHRM website at http://www.shrm.org.

▲
Taking and passing the SHRM Assurance of Learning Exam is an important step on the path to becoming an HR manager.

Other HR Organizations

In addition to SHRM, there are three organizations that have certification programs that are recognized in many countries around the world. The first one is the **Association for Talent Development (ATD)**. As its name implies, ATD primarily focuses on supporting those who develop the knowledge and skills of employees in organizations around the world.[47] Its major certification is the Certified Professional in Learning and Performance (CPLP). According to the ATD websites, CPLP certification is designed to "Validate your knowledge and skills in the talent development profession."[48]

The **Human Resource Certification Institute (HRCI)** is the second organization that provides some of the most respected certifications for HR personnel anywhere in the world.[49] The three biggest HRCI certification programs are the PHR, SPHR, and GPHR certifications. PHR stands for Professional in Human Resources, SPHR stands for Senior Professional in Human Resources, and GPHR stands for Global Professional in Human Resources. These certifications are recognized by organizations worldwide as verification of a high level of training.

The third major organization is **WorldatWork**.[50] Certifications from this organization include Certified Compensation Professional (CCP), Advanced Certified Compensation Professional (ACCP), Certified Benefits Professional (CBP), Global Remuneration Professional (GRP), Work-Life Certified Professional (WLCP), Certified Sales Compensation Professional (CSCP), and Certified Executive Compensation Professional (CECP).

Professional Responsibility and Liability

Like all managers, HR managers should try to do what is best for the organization and employees—creating a win-win situation for both. Unfortunately, you can't always do so. And your first responsibility is to the organization. Managers have a type of fiduciary responsibility to act for and on behalf of the owners' interest—not employees. HRM departments exist primarily to serve top management.[51] For example, employees don't always agree with the HR policies and rules, such as when **Amazon** does not pay employees for time waiting to get through security. You may have to lay off employees, such as happened at **Sears**, which needed to cut company costs, but this obviously results in lost jobs—more of a win-lose situation.

Do you realize that you can be held personally liable for your actions on the job? If you break the law, you can be sued and possibly face criminal charges. This is one of the many reasons why you really want to understand all of the HRM concepts. You need to be aware of the potential for personal liability, and in some cases, you may even need to consider professional liability insurance—for instance, if you are an HRM consultant to outside organizations. **(SHRM D:36)**

Practitioner's Model for HRM

>> **LO 1.7 Explain the practitioner's model for HRM and how it applies to this book.**

We have given you a (very) brief history of the HRM world and what HR management does for the organization. Now we need to start talking about some of the detailed information you will need to know in order to be a successful manager for your organization. How will we do that? We are going to work through what you need to know using a practitioner's model for HRM, shown in Exhibit 1.3, which is the foundation for this book.

The Model

The practitioner's model is designed to show you how each of the areas within HRM interacts and which items you must deal with before you can go on to successfully work on the next section—kind of like building a foundation before you build a house. Let's discuss the details of each section of the model separately. As we discuss each section, refer back to Exhibit 1.3 for a visual of the section.

Section I: Current HRM Practices, Strategic Planning, and HR Laws

You have already begun Section I, where we discuss modern HRM, including the necessity of having strategy-driven HRM and a strong understanding of the basic HR legal environment. This is the basis for everything else that an HR manager will do, so it is the foundation of our diagram. These are the things that are *most critical* to the organization's basic stability and success, because if we don't get them right, we will probably not be around long enough as an organization to be successful in the sections resting on this one.

Section II: Staffing

Now that we have a stable organization with some form of direction, we start to look at getting the right people into the right jobs. We first look at identifying the jobs that will need to be filled and then work through how to recruit the right numbers and types of people to fill those jobs. Finally, we find out what our options are concerning methods to select the best of those job candidates whom we have recruited.

EXHIBIT 1.3 ● **The Practitioner's Model for HRM**

↑ Productivity
↑ Engagement
↓ Absenteeism
↓ Turnover

PART V: Protecting and Expanding Organizational Outreach How do you PROTECT and EXPAND your Human Resources?		
Chapter 12 Workplace Safety, Health, and Security	Chapter 13 Ethics, Sustainability, Diversity, and Inclusion	Chapter 14 Global Issues for Human Resource Managers

PART IV: Compensating How do you REWARD and MAINTAIN your Human Resources?	
Chapter 10 Compensation Management	Chapter 11 Employee Incentives and Benefits

PART III: Developing and Managing How do you MANAGE your Human Resources?		
Chapter 7 Training, Learning, Talent Management, and Development	Chapter 8 Performance Management and Appraisal	Chapter 9 Employee Rights and Labor Relations

PART II: Staffing What HRM Functions do you NEED for sustainability?		
Chapter 4 Workforce Planning: Job Analysis, Design, and Employment Forecasting	Chapter 5 Recruiting Job Candidates	Chapter 6 Selecting New Employees

PART I: The Human Resource Management Environment What HRM issues are CRITICAL to your organization's long-term sustainability?		
Chapter 1 Today's Human Resource Management Process	Chapter 2 Strategy-Driven Human Resource Management	Chapter 3 The Legal Environment

Section III: Developing and Managing

In the third section, we learn how to manage our people once they have been hired. We have to train people to do jobs; we have to evaluate them in some formal manner so they know how well they are doing; and we have to develop them so they can fill higher-level positions as we need people to step up into those positions. We sometimes have to coach, counsel, and/or discipline our employees as well, so we need to learn how to do those things. Finally, Section III addresses the role of employee and labor relations.

Section IV: Compensating

The fourth section will cover the compensation and benefits packages to keep our people satisfied (or at least not dissatisfied). Both direct compensation, in the form of base pay and incentives, and indirect pay, in the form of worker benefits, provide us with some level of control over what our employees decide to do for the organization. Section IV shows us how to *reward and maintain* our workforce, since they are so critical to our ongoing success.

Section V: Protecting and Expanding Stakeholder Reach

The last section's topics include managing safety and health, providing ethical and social responsibility guidelines to members of the organization, and the globalization issues involved in working in multiple countries and cultures. In addition to safety and health, two areas have become far more important since the beginning of the Information Age in the early 1980s: (1) ethical, sustainable, and socially responsible organizations; and (2) the ability to operate in a global business environment.

Trends and Issues in HRM

In each chapter of this text, we will briefly discuss some of the most important trends and issues in HRM today. These trends and issues will cover areas such as the use of technology in HRM, global HRM, ethical issues in HR, and diversity and equal opportunity. For this chapter, we have chosen the issues of (a) how employee engagement improves productivity and (b) HRM and organizational agility.

Employee Engagement Improves Productivity

Remember that employee engagement is a combination of job satisfaction, ability, and a willingness to perform for the organization at a high level and over an extended period of time. This combination of satisfaction, ability, and willingness is more critical today than ever before.[52] However, one Gallup survey recently noted that only about 32% of U.S. workers are engaged with their work, and worldwide it is even worse at a dismal 13% engagement.[53] In another survey, Gallup reported that companies with the most engaged workforce had 147% higher earnings per share, better productivity and profitability, and lower absenteeism and turnover than their competitors, so there is certainly strong reason to work toward a more engaged workforce.[54]

Many managers and employees think that compensation is the most important item in employee engagement, but that is simply not the case—at least in most organizations.[55] Overall compensation and benefits matter, but they are not enough. So how do we improve engagement? Take a look at the following tips.

1. Give them the right tools—mobile, social, digital tools that provide immediate information and feedback.[56]

2. Create trust—"walk the talk," as Jack Welch says.[57]

3. Listen—and then act on the information received. "Not only does a comprehensive approach to listening help an organization pinpoint and quickly address problems, it makes people feel valued."[58]

4. Employees are more important than clients/customers. Manage and lead the individual employee—they are *individuals!*[59]

5. Treat *all* employees with respect. This was the number one factor in job satisfaction, and therefore in employee engagement, in a 2016 SHRM survey.[60]

Obviously, this is a cursory look at engagement, but we will discuss every one of these issues in more depth as we go through the remainder of the text. For now, just understand the importance of improved employee engagement.

HRM and Organizational Agility

One of the words being used to describe successful organizations in today's environment is *agile*. The agile organization not only accepts change and disruption, it thrives in such environments.

Because nearly every industry is being disrupted by technology, agility is becoming a requirement in order to become, or remain, an industry leader.[61] How can HRM help the organization become agile?

- Create a digital culture.[62] To do this, HR and line managers must become comfortable with mobile and on-demand technology that allows the organization to be more agile and respond more quickly to outside forces. Digital technology can be used in nearly every area of HRM,[63] including recruiting, selection, organizational safety, training and development, performance management and appraisal, and tracking individual compensation.

- Develop the ability to not only survive but also thrive on change.[64,65] Along with creating a culture that is comfortable with digital technology and tools, the business needs to pay close attention to making people at all levels comfortable with immediate and continuing change.

- Explore the value of "on-demand" workers. Full-time employees need to work seamlessly with consultants, temporary workers, part-timers, and partner organization employees. They will need to be able to create and maintain these relationships as long as necessary, modify them when needed, and cut off their interaction when the relationship no longer adds value.

- Review legacy processes and structures for adaptability to the agile workplace. Many companies have internal structures and processes that were designed to improve efficiency, but at the expense of adaptability.[66] If the organization is going to be able to become agile, we have to review the company structure and processes to see what can be kept without significant effect on the ability to adapt to new environments and what has to be modified.

Chapter Summary

1.1 Explain why all managers need to understand the basics of HRM.

In a modern organization, human resources are one of the primary means of creating a competitive advantage for the organization, because the ways we manage people directly affects their performance. Companies with the highest employee engagement over a 10-year period achieved 65% greater share-price increase; 15% greater employee productivity; 30% greater customer satisfaction; plus other significant advantages over their less engaged competitors. HRM provides all managers with tools to engage their employees and as a result increase employee productivity and company profitability.

1.2 Discuss how HRM helps meet management challenges to improve organizational revenues.

Today's HR department acts as a productivity center rather than a cost center, enhancing the profitability of the company by improving employee productivity. HRM practices primarily help to improve organizational efficiency. Employees become more efficient if they are used correctly, which means that managers don't use up their time (the valuable resource that we get from employees) in an inefficient manner. HR also assists in managing technology for efficiency, and managing the four dependent variables that concern line managers.

1.3   Describe the major HRM discipline areas.

- *The legal environment: EEO and diversity management.* This discipline deals with equal opportunity laws and regulations as well as management of a diverse workforce.

- *Staffing.* This discipline manages the processes involved in job analysis, recruiting, and selection into the organization.

- *Training and development.* This discipline has responsibility for the training processes within the organization, for developing curricula and lesson plans, and for delivery of training courses. It is also involved with development of talent within the company to provide a group of employees who will be able to move into more senior positions that become vacant.

- *Employee relations.* This area involves the coaching, counseling, and discipline processes, along with employee communication and stress management. It is also typically responsible for the management of job satisfaction and employee engagement.

- *Labor and industrial relations.* This discipline works with the laws and regulations that control the organization's relationships with its workforce. It also works with any union-management contracts, including but not limited to union votes, grievances, contract negotiations, and bargaining with union representatives.

- *Compensation and benefits.* This discipline works with pay of various types and with benefits packages, all of which are designed to attract and keep the right mix of employees in the organization. It also deals directly with all of the federal and state compensation laws to ensure compliance.

- *Safety and security.* This discipline works to ensure that the environment on the job is safe for all workers so that on-the-job injuries and illnesses are minimized to the greatest extent possible. It also involves managing the organization's planning for securing the workforce, both from being harmed by other people and from natural disasters such as earthquakes or tornados.

- *Ethics and sustainability.* This discipline bears responsibility for seeing to it that the organization acts in an ethical and socially responsible manner, to minimize harm to the environment and its various stakeholders. It involves managing the sustainability efforts in the organization to minimize the depletion of worldwide resources caused by the organization carrying out its processes.

1.4   Recall the primary difference between line and staff managers by their major HR responsibilities.

The HR staff have the primary responsibility of developing the policies and programs with its HR disciplines for everyone in the organization to implement on a daily basis. The line managers are responsible for implementing the HR policies and all other processes within their departments.

1.5   Summarize the major HRM skill sets.

The HRM skill sets include technical skills, interpersonal skills, conceptual and design skills, and business skills. *Technical skills* include the ability to use specialized knowledge, methods, and techniques to perform a task. *Interpersonal skills* provide the ability to understand, communicate, and work well with individuals and groups through developing effective relationships. *Conceptual and design skills* provide the ability to evaluate a situation, identify alternatives, select an alternative, and implement a solution to the problem. Finally, *business skills* provide analytical and quantitative skills, including the in-depth knowledge of how the business works and of its budgeting and strategic planning processes.

1.6   Identify the most common HRM certification programs and their parent organizations.

The primary certifications are carried out by SHRM, ATD, HRCI, and WorldatWork. SHRM's "competency-based" certification programs include the SHRM Certified Professional and Senior Certified Professional (SHRM-CP and SHRM-SCP). ATD training and development certifications include the Certified Professional in Learning and Performance (CPLP) and the Human Performance Improvement (HPI) certification. HRCI maintains certification programs for Professional in Human Resources (PHR), a senior version (SPHR), and a global version (GPHR). Finally, certifications from WorldatWork include Certified Compensation Professional (CCP), Certified Benefits Professional (CBP), Global Remuneration Professional (GRP), and others.

1.7   Explain the practitioner's model for HRM and how it applies to this book.

The practitioner's model shows the relationships between each of the functions and disciplines within

HRM. On the first level are the items that are absolutely critical to the organization if it is going to continue to operate (and stay within federal and state laws while doing so) and be stable and successful for a significant period of time. The second level encompasses those things that are required to identify the kinds of jobs that must be filled and then recruit and select the right types of people into those jobs so the company can maximize productivity over the long term. These items will allow the organization to get its work done successfully over long periods of time. In the third tier, we concern ourselves with management of the human resources that we selected in the second level. We have to get them training to do their jobs and allow them to perform those jobs for a period of time. We then have to appraise their performance and, if necessary, correct behaviors that are not allowing them to reach their maximum potential. As this is occurring, we need to ensure that we maintain positive relationships with our employees so they remain engaged and productive. In the fourth tier, we want to make sure we reward our workforce reasonably through fair and reasonable compensation planning to minimize unnecessary turnover and dissatisfaction. In the last tier, we provide for employee safety and health, and also turn our attention to organizational ethics and the issues surrounding global business operations because these issues will allow us to sustain our workforce and continue to thrive.

Key Terms

absenteeism, 9	employee engagement, 4	productivity center, 6
business skills, 16	human resources (HR), 4	revenue centers, 5
conceptual and design skills, 16	Information Age, 8	Society for Human Resource
cost center, 5	interpersonal skills, 15	Management (SHRM),17
effectiveness, 6	knowledge workers, 8	staff managers, 14
efficiency, 6	line managers, 14	technical skills, 15
empathy, 16	productivity, 6	turnover, 9

Key Terms Review

Complete each of the following statements using one of this chapter's key terms.

1. _____ are the people within an organization.

2. _____ is a combination of job satisfaction, ability, and a "willingness to perform" for the organization at a high level, and over an extended period of time.

3. _____ is a division or department within an organization that brings in no revenue or profit—in other words it costs money for the organization to run this function.

4. _____ are divisions or departments that generate monetary returns for the organization.

5. _____ is a revenue center that enhances profitability of the organization through enhancing the productivity of the people within the organization.

6. _____ is the amount of output that an organization gets per unit of input, with human input usually expressed in terms of units of time.

7. _____ answers the question "Did we do the right things?" It is a function of getting the job done whenever and however it must be done.

8. _____ is a function of how many organizational resources we used in getting the job done; it answers the question "Did we do things right?"

9. _____ is the permanent loss of workers from the organization.

10. _____ is the failure of an employee to report to the workplace as scheduled.

11. _____ is an era that began around 1980 in which information became one of the main products used in organizations; it is characterized by exponential increases in available information in all industries.

12. _____ are workers who "use their head more than their hands" to gather and interpret information in order to improve a product or process for their organizations.

13. _____ include the ability to use methods and techniques to perform a task.

14. _____ are the ability to understand, communicate, and work well with individuals and groups through developing effective relationships.

15. _____ is being able to put yourself in another person's place—to understand not only what they are saying but why they are communicating that information to you.

16. _____ are made up of the ability to evaluate a situation, identify alternatives, select an alternative, and make a decision to implement a solution to a problem.

17. _____ are the analytical and quantitative skills, including in-depth knowledge of how the business works and its budgeting and strategic planning processes that are necessary for a manager to understand and contribute to the profitability of their organization.

18. _____ are the individuals who create, manage, and maintain the people and organizational processes that create whatever it is that a business sells.

19. _____ are the individuals that advise line management of the firm in their area of expertise.

20. _____ is the largest and most recognized of the HRM advocacy organizations in the United States.

Communication Skills

The following critical-thinking questions can be used for class discussion and/or for written assignments to develop communication skills. Be sure to give complete explanations for all answers.

1. Why is it important for all business majors to take this course in HRM?

2. Are you interested in becoming an HR manager? Why or why not?

3. Do you agree with the statement "Effectively utilizing the human resources within the organization is one of the few ways to create a competitive advantage in a modern business"? Why or why not?

4. Is employee engagement possible in an age when people tend to have very little loyalty to their employers and vice versa? How would you work to increase employee engagement as a manager?

5. Can HRM really create revenue for the organization? If so, how?

6. Identify some things (other than increasing pay) that could be done by a manager to increase productivity and employee engagement and decrease absenteeism and turnover. Make a list for each item.

7. If you were the HR manager for your organization, what would you do to increase the number of applicants who apply for "knowledge worker" positions in your organization? Assume you can't pay them more.

8. Is there anything that an individual within an organization can do to help improve relations among diverse workers? If so, what?

9. Some say that for managers, hard skills (technical and business skills) are more important than soft skills (interpersonal skills and conceptual and design skills). What do you think, and why?

10. Are external certification programs (in all jobs) becoming more important? Why?

Case 1.1 Fracturing the Labor Market: Employment in the Oil Services Industry

When oil hit $26.21 a barrel in 2016, down from nearly $100 a barrel from 5 years earlier, jobs in the oil service industry were rare and people out of work. "Everyone [was] so hungry, it [was] like we were hanging a steak in front of a bunch of starving people," said Joseph Triepke, founder of the industry research company Infill Thinking in Dallas. A year later with oil at $55 a barrel, an employer like Piotr Galitzine is having a hard time keeping up with his orders and running 24/7 one of his Houston-based steel-pipe shops.[67]

The rising oil prices are fueling orders with the oilfield-equipment giant National Oilwell Varco Inc. as well, with a 10-year shift in their business from offshore gear to land-based. "It's tough," said the chief executive officer of Agility Energy Inc. "We've got commitments that are very difficult to keep right now because we can't get the drivers."[68] Surprising since truckers who haul fracking sand have a starting pay of around $80,000/year.

Yet this shift of employment in this market segment is not evident when looking at the larger labor picture since unemployment for the most part has been unchanged. The Bureau of Labor Statistics (the government agency charged with tracking U.S. employment) reported that long-term unemployment, defined as those being out of work for more than 26 weeks, remained stable at 1.8 million in February 2017. This constituted 23.8% of total unemployment. The annual rate of total unemployment dropped from 4.9% to 4.7% with the total number of unemployed remaining constant at 7.5 million.

Construction employment accounted for the largest growth in February 2017. Construction in general over the last 6 months accounted for job growth of 177,000 with a 1-month gain of 58,000 jobs. Heavy and civil engineering construction added 15,000 jobs while specialty trade contractors accounted for 36,000 jobs.[69]

With the price of crude oil doubling over the past 3 years, oil companies are quite busy. This growth has been supported by new technology that allows for faster drilling, more intelligent fracking, and locating a greater quantity of rich oil deposits. This boom could be very short-lived given the fact that finding good shale formations are hit-or-miss. Once found, the fracking process begins—the adjacent rock is bombarded with chemicals, water, and sand. The most stress-free drilling is in pancaked layered formations (predominately found in the Permian Basin of New Mexico and west Texas).

When business booms, so does employment. Canada and the United States are outpacing worldwide expenditures on production and exploration by 4:1, with the U.S. outpacing the last oil surge with an additional 125,000 barrels a day since September 2016.

"Every time I push that computer button that says 'approved' on the rehire, I feel better."[70] CEO Galitzine of pipe-supplier TMK Ispco, the U.S. unit of Russia's TMK PJSC, said that just over the past 4 months he has hired nearly 300 employees, increasing the number of his workers to the highest level since January 2016; yet he feels this boom of oils prices may not last.

"When we were at $100, to look at $50 would have been very scary . . . Now, the confidence $100 used to instill can probably be had at $65 . . . That's how much cost has been squeezed out of the supply chain. So $65 is the new $100."[71]

Is Galitzine right? Supply and demand drives the industry and Galitzine is tracking how growth in shale drilling is offsetting the November reduction of 1.2 million barrels a day of crude from the 13-member Organization of Petroleum Exporting Countries and Russia.

Bryan Sheffield, chief executive officer of Parsley Energy Inc., is worried that the boom/bust cycle will repeat itself, he just doesn't know when. "For every barrel that OPEC cuts, the American shale drillers are putting on half a barrel. If that remains, then I think we're okay." If shale fields start churning out much more, "then who knows what's going to happen to the price of oil," he said. "Probably nothing good."[72]

Questions

1. One of the two main goals of strategic HRM is to ensure the correct number of employees with the types of skills the organization requires. Given the boom/bust nature of the oil services industry, what external factors in this case should an HRM manager monitor to ensure that employment needs are met?

2. What types of jobs and related skill sets seem to be in short supply currently in the oil supply industry given the increase in construction employment in the past year? Which of the three new HRM challenges and four reasons

for managing human resources does this issue mostly closely address?

3. HR managers have several disciplines of responsibilities. Which disciplines does this case directly and indirectly address?

4. Given the feast/famine cycle in the oil supplier industry, what trends and issues in HR address

the necessity of retaining these firms' best employees?

5. The people quoted in the case are all CEOs of their firms and not HRM managers. Why would CEOs concern themselves with HR issues if these issues are the responsibility of HR managers?

Skill Builder 1.1 Getting to Know You

Objectives

1. To get acquainted with some of your classmates

2. To gain a better understanding of what the course covers

3. To get to know more about your instructor

Skills

The primary skills developed through this exercise are as follows:

1. *HR management skills*—**Interpersonal skills**

2. *SHRM 2018 Curriculum Guidebook*—C: **Employee and Labor Relations**

Procedure 1 (5–8 minutes)

Break into groups of five or six, preferably with people you do not know. Have each member tell the group their name and two or three significant things about themselves. Then have all group members ask each other questions to get to know each other better.

Procedure 2 (4–8 minutes)

Can everyone in the group address every other person by name? If not, have each member repeat their name. Then each person in the group should repeat the names of all the group members until each person knows everyone's first name.

Application

What can you do to improve your ability to remember people's names?

_____

_____

_____

_____

Procedure 3 (5–10 minutes)

Elect a spokesperson for your group. Look over the following categories and decide on some specific questions you would like your spokesperson to ask the instructor from one or more of the categories. The spokesperson will not identify who asked the questions. You do not have to have questions for each area.

- *Course expectations.* What do you expect to cover or hope to learn from this course?

- *Doubts or concerns.* Is there anything about the course that you don't understand?

- *Questions about the instructor.* List questions you'd like to ask the instructor to get to know him or her better.

Procedure 4 (10–20 minutes)

Each spokesperson asks the instructor one question at a time until all questions have been answered. Spokespeople should skip questions already asked by other groups.

Apply It

What did I learn from this experience? How will I use this knowledge in the future?

_____

_____

_____

Skill Builder 1.2 Comparing HR Management Skills and HR Responsibilities

Objective

To better understand the importance of good HR management skills and implementing HR responsibilities effectively

Skills

The primary skills developed through this exercise are as follows:

1. *HR management skills*—**Conceptual and design**

2. *SHRM 2018 Curriculum Guidebook*—**C: Employee and Labor Relations**

Compare Your Supervisors' HR Management Skills and HR Responsibilities Effectiveness

Recall the best supervisor or boss you ever worked for and the worst one you ever worked for (preferably line managers, not HR managers). Compare these two people by writing brief notes in the following chart about each person's HR management skills and HR responsibilities.

HR Management Skills and HR Responsibilities

Skills and Responsibilities	Supervisor or Boss	
	Best	Worst
Technical		
Interpersonal		

Skills and Responsibilities	Supervisor or Boss	
	Best	Worst
Conceptual and Design		
Business Skills		
Legal Considerations		
Staffing		
Training and Development		
Employee and Labor Relations		
Safety and Security		
Ethics		

Based on your own experiences with a good boss and a poor one, what do you believe are the key differences between good and poor managers?

Apply It

What did I learn from this exercise? How will I use this knowledge in the future?

_____

_____

_____

©iStockphoto.com/FlamingoImages

Strategy-Driven Human Resource Management

Learning Outcomes

After studying this chapter, you should be able to do the following:

2.1 Discuss the strategic planning process by classifying the major components of the external environment. **PAGE 30**

2.2 Discuss how visions, missions, and objectives help to define the organization's strategy. **PAGE 33**

2.3 Explain the three major generic strategies. **PAGE 33**

2.4 Summarize the importance of the major components of organizational structure. **PAGE 39**

2.5 Discuss how organizational culture affects the members of the organization. **PAGE 40**

2.6 Define data analytics by how it helps organizations make important decisions. **PAGE 42**

2.7 Identify how human resource management systems (HRMS) can help HR make decisions. **PAGE 43**

2.8 Recall the common measurement tools for strategic human resource management (HRM). **PAGE 44**

SHRM HR Content

See Online: *SHRM 2018 Curriculum Guidebook* for the complete list

C. Employee and Labor Relations
   29. Managing/creating a positive organizational culture

H. Human Resource Information Systems (HRIS)
   5. Using HR data for enterprise management

I. Job Analysis and Job Design
   6. Organization design (missions, functions, and other aspects of work units for horizontal and vertical differentiation)

K. Metrics and Measurement of HR
   5. Economic value added
   8. Return on investment (ROI)

L. Organizational Development
   12. Organizational structure and job design

O. Strategic HR
   1. Strategic management
   1-a. Strategic management—Competitive advantage
   1-b. Strategic management—Competitive strategy
   1-c. Strategic management—Enhancing firm competitiveness
   1-f. Strategic management—Mission and vision
   1-h. Strategic management—Strategy implementation
   1-i. Strategic management—Strategy formulation
   2-d. HR strategies—Linking HR strategy to organizational strategy
   2-e. HR strategies—Measuring HR effectiveness

Practitioner's Perspective

Cindy notes that one thing many family get-togethers have in common is storytelling—reminiscing about common experiences and outstanding members. These stories are part of the ties that bind and define the group, and the same is true for your work "family."

For example, take this story about Bill, an executive who started work as an emergency medical technician (EMT). One time while Bill was moving a nursing home resident, the resident's bedridden roommate feebly attempted to say good-bye. Young and impatient, Bill didn't stop to let the two talk but hurried off to the hospital with his passenger.

The next time he was at that location, Bill was pulled aside by a nurse who said, "What I am about to say will break your heart, but it will make you a better man. The woman you transported died in the hospital that night. The roommate was her husband of 70 years, and you didn't give him time to say good-bye." Ever afterward in his career, Bill's motto was "Patients First," and that goal permeates his institution even today in everything it does.

What else defines company culture? Chapter 2 examines strategies, mission statements, vision, and values—all important pieces of a company's identity.

An Introduction to Strategic Planning and the Environment

>> **LO 2.1 Discuss the strategic planning process by classifying the major components of the external environment.**

Strategy and strategic planning provide us with a process of looking at our organization and its environment—both today and in the expected future—and determining what our organization decides to do to meet the requirements of that expected future (see Exhibit 2.1). This process of analyzing the environment and building a coherent strategy is more critical today than it has ever been before. This is because in most worldwide industries today, we have far more competition and capacity than ever before, making it more difficult to create the sustainable competitive advantage that we need in order to survive over the long term. Successful companies move forward via careful planning.[1]

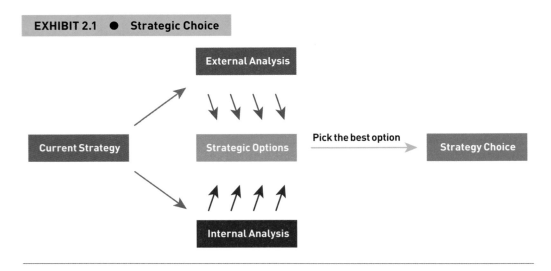

EXHIBIT 2.1 ● Strategic Choice

There is an old saying: "When you fail to plan, you plan to fail." Research supports this saying and confirms the importance of planning,[2] as there is a link between planning and performance.[3] Some managers complain they don't have time to plan, yet research shows that managers who plan are more effective and efficient than nonplanners. Before we get into the details of strategic planning, complete Self-Assessment 2.1 to determine your level of planning.

2.1 SELF-ASSESSMENT

LEVEL OF PLANNING

Write a number from 1 to 5 before each statement to indicate how well each statement describes your behavior.

Describes me			Does not describe me	
5	4	3	2	1

_____ 1. Whenever I start a project of any kind, I have a specific end result in mind.

_____ 2. When setting objectives, I state only the end result to be accomplished; I don't specify how the result will be accomplished.

_____ 3. I have specific and measurable objectives; for example, I know the specific grade I want to earn in this course.

_____ 4. I set objectives that are difficult but achievable.

_____ 5. I set deadlines when I have something I need to accomplish, and I meet those deadlines.

_____ 6. I have a long-term goal (what I will be doing in 3–5 years) and short-term objectives that will get me there.

_____ 7. I have written objectives stating what I want to accomplish.

_____ 8. I know my strengths and weaknesses, am aware of threats, and seek opportunities.

_____ 9. I analyze a problem and consider alternative actions, rather than immediately jumping in with a solution.

_____10. I spend most of my day doing what I plan to do, rather than dealing with emergencies and trying to get organized.

_____11. I use a calendar, appointment book, or some form of to-do list.

_____12. I ask others for advice.

_____13. I follow appropriate policies, procedures, and rules.

_____14. I develop contingency plans in case my plans do not work out as I expect them to.

_____15. I implement my plans and determine if I have met my objectives.

Add up the numbers you assigned to the statements to see where you fall on the continuum below.

Planner						Nonplanner
75	65	55	45	35	25	15

Don't be too disappointed if your score isn't as high as you would like. All of these items are characteristics of effective planning. Review the items that did not describe you and consider making an effort to implement those characteristics of planning.

HR Management's Role in Strategic Planning

As discussed in Chapter 1, the role of HRM has expanded over the years. Organizations today realize the importance of HRM. That is why more than half of HRM top executives at major corporations now report directly to the CEO.[4] HRM also develops its own strategic plans to help align HR practices with the business strategy,[5] because organizations that hire and retain motivated and productive people gain a long-lasting competitive advantage.[6] But CEOs have little faith that HR is capable of strategic planning for talent acquisition and development, or linking HR planning to organizational strategies.[7] CEOs also lack trust in HR efforts to utilize analytics for decision making.[8] Only about 1 in 10 CEOs say their HR leaders are capable in these areas. Therefore, we need to increase our efforts in HRM education to create strategic HR leaders.

In this chapter, we focus on the organization's environment. The environment has two parts: internal and external. First, let's briefly discuss the external environment. Then, in the next section, we will describe in detail three key aspects of the internal environment: strategy, structure, and culture.

The External Environment

The external environment consists of a series of influences originating outside the organization that the company cannot control. Each of these forces acts on the firm and requires it to change and adapt, usually in the form of strategic responses to these environmental changes.[9] The successful companies are the ones that keep changing.[10] It is also important to have good relationships with external stakeholders because they provide access to resources.[11] The nine major forces originating in the external environment are shown in Exhibit 2.2, along with an explanation of each.

- _Customers._ Without customers, there's no need for an organization. Therefore, companies must continually improve products and services to create value for their customers.[12] This process of improvement requires skilled employees who are willing to use their creativity to add to the organization's knowledge and thereby help manage products and services for customers.

- _Competition._ Businesses must compete for customers, and their performance is not simply a function of their own actions. Each firm's performance must be understood relative

EXHIBIT 2.2 ● The External Environment

to the actions of its *competitors*.[13] Organizations also frequently compete for the same employees and sometimes for suppliers.[14] Also, changes in competitors' strategies often affect the performance of the organization.

- *Suppliers.* Organizations buy resources from suppliers. Therefore, partnerships with *suppliers* also affect firm performance.[15] The Japanese earthquake and tsunami in Fukushima affected virtually every company in the auto industry because electronic components made in northern Japan were unavailable for an extended period of time.[16] It is important to develop close working relationships with your suppliers.[17]

- *Labor Force.* The talent pool available to an organization from which to hire new employees has a direct effect on the organization's performance. **Facebook** planned to hire more than 3,000 people in 2017 just to improve their ability to review questionable posts, along with thousands of others for various jobs within the company.[18]

- *Shareholders.* The owners of a corporation, known as shareholders, influence management.[19] Most shareholders of large corporations are not involved in the day-to-day operation of the firm, but they do vote for the directors of the corporation. The board of directors is also generally not involved in the day-to-day management of the firm, but may hire or fire top management. The top manager (usually the CEO) reports to the board of directors, and if the organization does not perform well, the board can fire that manager and others.[20]

- *Society.* Our society, to a great extent, determines what acceptable business practices are.[21] Individuals and various groups of stakeholders work in a number of ways to pressure businesses to make changes. For example, protesters held up completion of the **Dakota Access** oil pipeline for almost a year when they were concerned for the safety of a Native American source for drinking water.[22]

Technology is one of the nine major forces originating in the external environment. Companies that continue to innovate their technology, like Apple, will have an advantage over the competition.

- *Technology.* Few organizations operate today as they did even a decade ago. Products not envisioned a few years ago are now being mass-produced, which creates new business opportunities. Businesses that don't keep up with technology, like **BlackBerry** (the prior cell phone dominator), lose business to those creating the latest business innovations, like **Apple** and **Samsung**.

- *The Economy.* No corporation has control over economic growth, inflation, interest rates, foreign exchange rates, or other such factors; thus, the economy has a direct impact on the firm's performance and profits. We always have to take the economy into account when performing strategic planning activities.

- *Governments*. As a business owner or manager, you can't just run your business any way you want to because federal, state, and local governments develop the laws and regulations that determine what your business can and can't do.[23] So although you can try to influence the government, it clearly affects your business.[24] To learn more about the U.S. federal government, visit its official web portal at http://www.usa.gov/.

According to **Russell Ackoff**, interactive managers design a desirable future and invent ways of bringing it about.[25] They believe they are capable of creating a significant part of the future and controlling its effects on them. They try to prevent threats, not merely prepare for them, and to create opportunities, not merely exploit them. Rather than reacting or responding, interactive managers make things happen for their benefit and for that of their stakeholders. **Apple** was interactive when it created the first PC, changed how we listen to and buy music, and introduced us to new ways of using our phones.

2.1 APPLYING THE CONCEPT
THE EXTERNAL ENVIRONMENT

Read each statement and write in the letter corresponding to the external environmental factor it refers to.

a. Customers

b. Competition

c. Suppliers

d. Labor force

e. Shareholders

f. Society

g. Technology

h. The economy

i. Governments

_____ 1. The CEO was fired by the owners because our company is not profitable.

_____ 2. **GE** wanted to acquire our company, but the Securities and Exchange Commission (SEC) said that would be in violation of antitrust laws, thereby preventing the deal.

_____ 3. Karen bought a new oven that will cook our pizza in half the time and make it taste even better.

_____ 4. **eHarmony**, an online dating service, is losing some customers to other services focusing on Christian, African-American, and older people seeking matches.

_____ 5. Our purchasing agent just closed a deal that will let us buy sugar for a few cents less per pound, saving us thousands of dollars per year.

In addition to our analysis of the major external environmental factors that we can't control, we need to review some critical internal organizational factors that we can control to decide what we want to do as an organization as we move into the future. The major factors in our analysis of the internal environment are shown in Exhibit 2.3 and are discussed in this and the next three sections.

Strategy

>> **LO 2.2 Discuss how visions, missions, and objectives help to define the organization's strategy.**

>> **LO 2.3 Explain the three major generic strategies.**

Strategy and the strategic planning process have a long history, and businesses have adapted the principles to their own use. "Many military historians and contemporary

EXHIBIT 2.3 ● The Internal Environment

business students view the Chinese military strategist **Sun Tzu** (ca. 500 BC) as the developer of 'the Bible' of strategy . . . Sun Tzu's principles are divided into two components: 1) knowing oneself and 2) knowing the enemy."[26] To put Sun Tzu's words in a contemporary business context, we need to know our internal and external environments. But how does a modern business go about creating and implementing a strategic plan? Well, strategic planning follows a process,[27] so let's discuss that process now.

What Is Strategy?

Research has shown that HRM is an important strategic business function that influences the performance of both large and small firms.[28] But what is strategy? At its most basic level, a **strategy** is *a plan of action designed to achieve a particular set of objectives*. It looks at the external (industry and macro-) environment and the internal (organizational) environment in order to create strategic advantage. Strategic advantage occurs when you analyze the environment better and react to it quicker than your competitors do while using all of your internal resources efficiently, thus creating the sustainable competitive advantage that we introduced in Chapter 1. **(SHRM O-1 and O:1-b)**

In this section, we look at the following three major strategic questions to analyze what kind of strategic plan we need:[29] (1) What is our present situation (where are we now)? (2) Where do we want to go? (3) How do we plan to get there?

You would think that answering question 1 would be easy—but you must answer many other questions before you can confidently answer "Where are we now?" These other questions include "Are we making a profit?" "Do our products satisfy our customers' current needs?" "Do we have the right kind of workforce in place at this time?" "Is our technology working like it should?" "Do we have sufficient physical resources like plant, machinery and equipment, and retail locations?" "Are our advertising and marketing programs successful?" and many more. Answering these questions creates a picture of your organization—a snapshot at a particular point in time—and that picture has to be comprehensive so you know what is happening, good and bad, within the organization in significant detail. If you think about each of these other questions for just a second, you will see how complex answering question 1 really becomes.

Question 2 is basically asking us what we plan to "look like" as an organization at a particular point in the future, meaning it's asking us what are our *vision, mission, and objectives* for the organization.

Answering question 3 then gives us the necessary information to create the plan that will allow us to reach the goals that we identify in our answer to question 2 so that we can become the organization that we envision and at the same time create a sustainable competitive advantage. **(SHRM O:1-a)**

Vision, Mission, and Objectives

A vision and a mission are two of the most critical components of any successful corporate strategy. Together, they provide the information necessary to focus every employee on the company's goals and objectives. **(SHRM O:1-f)**

The Vision

A **vision** is *what we expect to become as an organization at a particular point in time in the future*. The vision by necessity is a fuzzy thing; it is not specific in that it doesn't say *how* we're going to achieve it. It is who we are, what we stand for, what we believe in, and what we want to become. Despite their fuzziness, visions are very powerful when used correctly. A vision provides a focus point for the future; it tells the company where it is headed.[30] If everyone is focused on the same future end state, they will work toward that same end state.

So the vision answers the question "What do we want to become as an organization?" But the firm is only successful when the followers share the leader's vision,[31] and HR is where many organizations perform the culture training that promotes a shared vision within the organization.

The Mission

In contrast, the mission is where we start to become specific. The **mission statement** *lays out our expectations of what we're going to do in order to become the organization that we have envisioned*. The mission is more specific than the vision, which means that it generally must be a bit longer-winded. The mission statement takes into account things like whom we serve (in terms of customer groups, types of products and services, technologies we use, etc.) and how we serve them. Fundamentally, it answers the question "What do we need to do in order to become what we have envisioned?"

Putting the Vision and Mission Together

Let's use as an example the vision and mission statements of the **College of Business of the University of Arkansas at Little Rock**. Its vision statement is as follows: "The College of Business serves as a catalyst to advance education and economic development in the State of Arkansas."[32] Notice that this vision statement does not tell you how the college will be a catalyst or what it is going to do. But what is a catalyst? It's "a substance that modifies and increases the rate of a reaction without being consumed in the process."[33] So, that means the college is going to be an organization that increases the rate of change in education and economic development in its home state.

▲
Trader Joe's is known for its strong company vision and mission.

We then look at the mission of the organization, which tells us how the organization expects to do what the vision puts forth. The mission statement of this college of business says, "The mission of the College of Business is to prepare students to succeed as business professionals in a global economy and to contribute to the growth and viability of the region we serve."[34] So the college of business will achieve its vision by providing education that gives its students the tools they need to succeed in business and create change in the state. This, in turn, will act to improve the state's economic fortunes.

When you put the vision and mission together, all the people in the organization get a more complete picture of the direction in which they are expected to go. This allows them all to focus on going in that direction, and that in turn makes it much easier for them to help the organization achieve its goals. *The fact that they create a focus is the thing that makes a vision and mission so powerful.* If everyone in the organization is focused on the same end result, it is much more likely that the organization will achieve that end result.

A strong vision and a good mission statement are critical parts of the strategic planning process. *Everything* else in strategic planning comes from the vision and mission.

Vision + Mission = FOCUS!

Top management needs to articulate a compelling vision so clearly that it can be seen almost as a movie in one's head, but it's not easy.[35] Companies including **Twitter** struggle to define a clear vision, and **Airbnb** has had difficulty defining its mission and brand.[36]

Finally, organizations go through a series of analyses of both external and internal factors to come up with the plan of action that answers question 3. Strategic planners look at each of the environmental factors we noted earlier, and they analyze the company's capabilities and limitations to come up with objectives and a workable plan. We will discuss some of these factors in the following sections.

Setting Objectives

After developing our vision and mission, the next step is to set objectives that flow from the mission to address strategic issues. Successful managers have a goal orientation,[37] and many have daily goals,[38] which means they set and achieve objectives. In a survey of CEOs, the second biggest challenge facing leaders today is staying focused, and setting objectives helps.[39]

Before you develop any plan, you begin with the end result you want to accomplish; objectives do not state how they will be accomplished, the plan does. Goal orientation can also be learned,[40] and using the objective-setting model and completing Skill Builder 2.1 can help. **Objectives** *state what is to be accomplished in singular, specific, and measurable terms, with a target date.*

Objectives Statements of what is to be accomplished in singular, specific, and measurable terms, with a target date

Here is a model adapted from **Max Weber** to help you write effective objectives, followed by a few company examples.

(1) To + (2) action verb + (3) singular, specific, measurable result + (4) target date

McDonald's: (1) To (2) increase (3) the percentage of franchised units to 90% (4) by 2018.[41]

Apple: To build a car by year-end 2019.[42]

Starbucks: To open 1,400 stores in China by 2019.[43]

Anheuser-Busch InBev: To increase revenues to $100 billion by 2020.[44]

Tesla: To increase annual sales to 500,000 vehicles by 2020.[45]

Ford: To sell driverless cars without steering wheels or pedals by 2021.[46]

GM: To sell 2 million cars a year through 2030.[47]

2.2 APPLYING THE CONCEPT
WRITING OBJECTIVES

For each objective, write in the letter corresponding to which "must" criterion is not met.

a. Single result

b. Specific

c. Measurable

d. Target date

_____   6. To start working out aerobically within a few weeks

_____   7. To double ticket sales

_____   8. To sell 7% more sandwiches and 15% more chips in 2020

_____   9. To decrease the number of sales returns by year end of 2020

_____   10. To be perceived as the best restaurant in the Boston area by 2020

2.1 ETHICAL DILEMMA: WHAT WOULD YOU DO?

A major objective of all businesses is to make a profit and to develop strategies to increase profits, and most businesses try to legally minimize the taxes they pay. Some U.S. corporations have used the strategy of inversion—to acquire a foreign company and move headquarters overseas—to reduce the corporate taxes they pay. **Burger King Worldwide's** acquisition of Canada's **Tim Hortons** was an inversion.[48] **Apple** and other corporations kept cash overseas to keep it from being taxed in the United States.

Some members of Congress say that individuals also use legal tax deductions, sometimes called loopholes, to lower their personal income taxes and that this is unethical. But most businesses and people take all the deductions and other methods they can to pay less taxes.

1. Are inversions and keeping money in other countries to avoid paying taxes ethical or unethical?

2. If you became the new CEO of Burger King, would you have the company pay a higher U.S. corporate tax even though it is not required to do so by law?

3. As an individual taxpayer, will (or do) you take deductions to lower the amount you pay in taxes?

4. Are your answers to questions 2 and 3 consistent, or do you believe businesses should pay the extra taxes but individuals shouldn't?

5. Review the HR disciplines and describe how a company can be ethical and socially responsible in performing these functions.

Generic Strategies

There are several generic strategy types that we are able to categorize. However, we will keep this simple and break the types of strategies down into three common categories developed by **Michael Porter**: cost leadership, differentiation, and focus or niche strategies.[49]

Cost Leadership

Cost leaders do everything they can to lower the internal organizational costs required to produce their products or services. **Walmart** has had great success with this strategy. During the 2007–2009 recession and even afterward, Walmart reduced its prices even more aggressively to combat loss of business to "dollar" stores.[50] **Southwest** hung up its low-cost jersey, increasing costs as it grew to be the airline with the most passengers in the United States.[51] **Allegiant**, **Spirit**, and **JetBlue** have become today's low-cost carriers.[52]

Differentiation

This strategy attempts to create an impression of difference for the company's product or service in the mind of the customer,[53] focusing on being sufficiently distinctive.[54] The differentiator company stresses its advantage over its competitors.[55] If a company like **Apple** is successful in creating this impression, it can charge a higher price for its product or service than can its competitors.[56] **Nike, Harley Davidson, Margaritaville**, and others place their corporate name prominently on their products to differentiate those products from those of the competition. **Coca-Cola** uses its scripted name logo and contour bottle.

Focus or Niche

With this strategy, the company focuses on a specific portion of a larger market. For instance, the company may focus on a regional market, a particular product line, or a buyer group. Within a particular target segment or market niche, the firm may use either a differentiation or a cost leadership strategy. It is hard to compete head-on with the big companies like **Coca-Cola** and **Pepsi**, but the much smaller **Dr Pepper Snapple Group's** two non-colas have a differentiated taste for a much smaller target market, and the company is very profitable.[57] **Ebony** and **Jet** magazines target African-Americans, and **Rolex** watches have a market niche of upper-income people. **Right Guard** deodorant is aimed at men, and **Secret** at women.

2.3 APPLYING THE CONCEPT
GENERIC STRATEGIES

Identify which strategy is used by each brand or company listed, and write the letter corresponding to the company's strategy by the company's name.

a. Cost leadership

b. Differentiation

c. Focus or niche

_____ 11. **Gucci** handbags

_____ 12. **Ironman** magazine

_____ 13. **Rolex** watches

_____ 14. **TOMS** shoes

_____ 15. **Target** stores

How Strategy Affects HRM

There are several areas where the generic corporate strategy affects how we do our jobs within HR. Let's take a look at a few of the significant differences between generic strategies. We will continue to discuss these areas in greater detail as we progress through the book.

HRM and Cost Leadership

If our organization is following a generic cost leadership strategy, we are going to be most interested in minimizing all internal costs, including employee costs, to maximize efficiency and effectiveness.[58] We will probably create specific job descriptions that are highly specialized within the organization so we have people doing the same thing repeatedly, as is the case with McDonald's, for example. We will also have a specific job description for each position and job-specific training with very little, if any, cross-training. We may provide incentives that emphasize cost controls and efficiency.

HRM and Differentiation

On the other hand, if our organization is following a differentiator strategy, we're going to be more concerned with employees who have the ability to innovate and create new processes and who can work in uncertain environments within cross-functional teams.[59] In a differentiator organization, we will most likely have much broader job classifications, as well as broader work-planning processes. Individuals will be hired and paid based on individual knowledge and capabilities rather than skills related to the job they fill when they enter the organization. Incentive programs will more often reward tenacity, innovation, and creativity.

HRM and Focus Strategy

Companies that have a specific focus or niche can garner a target audience looking for something specific, allowing the company to profit alongside larger, more dominant competitors.

HRM Promotes Strategy Through High Performance Work Practices

HR managers need to recruit, select, train, evaluate, and interact with employees differently based on different organizational strategies. The same holds true when looking at different sets of company objectives, different competitors, and many other industry and company characteristics.

In most large organizations today, we do not manage our people based on low-cost leader strategies. We manage the company's human resources through a set of high performance work practices. According to the **U.S. Department of Health and Human Services**, **high performance work practices (HPWPs)** are *practices that have been shown to improve an organization's capacity to effectively attract, select, hire, develop, and retain high-performing personnel.*[60] These practices are designed to improve employee commitment and increase involvement in the organization. There are also research claims that increased implementation of HPWPs results in better financial performance and employee outcomes.[61] **(SHRM O:1-h)**

Among the common HPWPs are:

High performance work practices (HPWPs) Practices that have been shown to improve an organization's capacity to effectively attract, select, hire, develop, and retain high-performing personnel

- Actions to maximize employee engagement

- Talent acquisition and development programs

- Employee empowerment

- Aligning leadership with the strategy through managerial training, career development, and succession planning

There are many other pieces to a potential high performance work system (the set of practices that we choose). Regardless of the specific practices that you select, the intended outcomes are increases in productivity and engagement, while lowering absenteeism and voluntary turnover.

HR managers have primary responsibility to evaluate all of the organizational characteristics to determine what kinds of people to bring into the organization and then how to continuously engage and develop those people once they have become a part of the company. This is the reason it's so critical for HR managers to understand organizational strategy.[62]

In fact, as you go through the remainder of this book, you will see continuing references to how HRM will affect the company's ability to do its work over the long term. Everything that HR does must mesh with the chosen strategy to provide the right kinds of employees, who will learn and do the right types of jobs so the company can achieve its goals. So, essentially, this book focuses on developing high performance work practices.

Structure

>> **LO 2.4 Summarize the importance of the major components of organizational structure.**

The selection of a proper organizational structure is critical to successfully implement strategy.[63] **Organizational structure** refers to *the way in which an organization groups its resources to accomplish its mission.*

In HRM, managers need to have an understanding of organizational structure to do their jobs correctly. An organization is a system that is typically, but not always, structured into departments such as finance, marketing, production, human resources, and so on. Each of these departments affects the organization as a whole, and each department is affected by the other departments. All of an organization's resources must be structured effectively if it is to achieve its mission.[64] **(SHRM O:2-d, O:1-c, O:1-i)**

> **Organizational structure** The way in which an organization groups its resources to accomplish its mission

Basics of Organizational Structure

Managers design formal structures to organize a company's resources,[65] and the structure of the firm must align with the environment in which it operates[66] to achieve the strategic objectives.[67] One way to look at organizational structure is to identify a series of fundamental components. Each of these components identifies a way in which we divide the organization up and group its resources to make them more efficient and effective. Let's discuss complexity, formalization, and centralization as structural components. **(SHRM I:6)**

Complexity is *the degree to which different parts of the organization are segregated from one another.* Organizations can be broken up vertically, using management layers; horizontally, with departments or divisions; or separated physically, for instance, with marketing functions in New York and manufacturing in Guadalajara. Each of these demonstrates a way in which we break the organization up into smaller and more differentiated pieces.

> **Complexity** Degree to which different parts of the organization are segregated from one another

We want to minimize complexity as much as possible in order to minimize organizational costs. For example, **Microsoft** is currently working through changes to its organizational complexity under CEO **Satya Nadella** because its historical structure has become too slow and expensive.[68]

Formalization is *the degree to which jobs are standardized within an organization, meaning the degree to which we have created policies, procedures, and rules that "program" the jobs of the employees.* If we make things routine by creating standard operating procedures and other standard processes, we can usually increase the efficiency and effectiveness of the people within the organization.[69]

> **Formalization** Degree to which jobs are standardized within an organization, meaning the degree to which we have created policies, procedures, and rules that "program" the jobs of the employees

How much we're able to formalize jobs within the organization, though, depends on what the organization is designed to do. If the organization is designed to do the same thing over and over, such as produce a low-cost commodity, then we can usually formalize many of its procedures, like at **McDonald's**. On the other hand, if the organization is designed to do unique and nonroutine things, then we will probably not be able to formalize very much of what the organization does.[70]

Centralization, the third major component of organizational structure, is *the degree to which decision making is concentrated within the organization.* The degree of centralization in an organization has to do with dispersion of authority for decision making and delegation of authority. If we can concentrate authority in decision making with one or a few individuals, we can concentrate on hiring people who are very good at making business decisions in those few positions and not worry about the decision-making skills of the rest of our employees.[71]

> **Centralization** Degree to which decision making is concentrated within the organization

However, there's a trade-off to centralized decision making. As the organization gets larger, we may have to go through many layers of the organization in order to get a decision made. This can slow down the processes within the firm. For example, **TEPCO** was criticized for having a complex bureaucratic decision-making process that led to the meltdown of three reactors at one of its nuclear plants in Japan.[72]

Is there one "best" structure? No. The best structure is one that fits the firm's current competitive situation as well as its internal capabilities and that enables it to implement its strategies successfully. **Warren Buffett** advises businesses to keep things simple,[73] and **Peter Drucker** may have said it as well as anyone when he noted, "The simplest organization structure that will do the job is the best one."[74]

How Does Structure Affect Employee Behavior?

Here is a general answer to how structure affects our employees' behavior. With high complexity, formalization, and centralization, employees focus on following the policies and rules within the limited scope of their highly specialized jobs without making decisions—like **McDonald's**. With low complexity, formalization, and centralization, employees can be more creative to get the job done the way they want to—like **Zappos,** where there are no departments or standard procedures and employees are expected to "think on your feet" and make decisions.[75] **(SHRM L:12)**

How Does Structure Affect HRM?

As the HR manager, would your job change if your organization adopted the structure of one of the two companies mentioned in the previous paragraph? Would you need to recruit and hire different types of people in a bureaucratic organization like **McDonald's** than you would in an entrepreneurial organization like **Zappos**? Indeed, you would—even at managerial levels. In the more bureaucratic organization, you would most likely hire people who had significant depth of expertise in a narrow area within their field of knowledge so that they could apply that expertise in a highly efficient manner. Your training programs would also probably be more specific and geared toward particular jobs. In fact, the organizational structure will affect virtually every function of the HR manager. So, in order to be a successful HR manager, you have to understand and adapt to the particular organizational structure of your firm.

Organizational Culture

>> **LO 2.5 Discuss how organizational culture affects the members of the organization.**

Organizational culture should be how the firm achieves its vision and mission by living its values and beliefs on a daily basis.[76] Fostering the right organizational culture is one of the most important responsibilities of the CEO, HR managers, and other corporate executives.[77] Any group of people that gather together anywhere at any point in time create a unique group culture. They have their own group standards, called norms, which create pressure for the group's members to conform. Social groups have societal cultures, nations have national cultures, and organizations have their own distinct organizational cultures. **(SHRM C:29)**

What Is Organizational Culture?

Organizational culture The values, beliefs, and assumptions about appropriate behavior that members of an organization share

Organizational culture consists of *the values, beliefs, and assumptions about appropriate behavior that members of an organization share.* Culture describes how employees do what they do (standards of behavior) and why they do what they do (values, profits, customers, employees, society). Every organization has a culture, and success depends on the health and strength of its culture.[78]

A critical role of HRM today is to help create a workplace culture with its own standards of behavior and hold everyone to these standards.[79] HRM also needs to recruit and hire people that fit the organizational culture to achieve its strategic objectives.[80] Organizational culture is primarily learned through HR orientation and training, observing people, and artifacts in the organization.

Artifacts of Organizational Culture

Five artifacts of organizational culture help employees learn the culture:

1. *Heroes,* such as founders Steve Jobs of **Apple**, Mark Zuckerberg of **Facebook**, Elon Musk of **Tesla**, and others who have made outstanding contributions to their organizations.

2. *Stories,* often about founders and others who have made extraordinary efforts. These include stories about Sam Walton visiting every **Walmart** store yearly, or someone driving through a blizzard to deliver a product or service. Public statements and speeches can also be considered stories.

3. *Slogans,* such as at **McDonald's** Q, S, C, V (quality, service, cleanliness, and value).

4. *Symbols,* such as logos, plaques, pens, jackets, or a pink Cadillac at the cosmetics firm **Mary Kay**.

5. *Ceremonies,* such as awards luncheons and dinners for top achievers at **Macy's**.

How Culture Controls Employee Behavior in Organizations

Organizational culture is a very powerful force in controlling how people act within its boundaries. For instance, if the culture says that we value hard work and productivity but an individual on one of the teams fails to do his or her part, then the other members of the team are quite likely to peer-pressure that individual to conform to the culture or to leave the organization. Since assumptions, values, and beliefs are so strong, all individuals will most likely conform to those behaviors that the culture values.

You may not believe that culture has the ability to cause you to change the way you act, but it does. Have you ever done something to fit in, or have you ever done something you really didn't want to do because of peer pressure? Doesn't peer pressure control most people—at least sometimes? Think about the way you act as part of your family, and then compare that to the way you act as a student at school, with a group of your friends, or as an employee at work. Chances are quite high that you act differently within these different "cultures." We all act to conform, for the most part, to the culture that we happen to be in at a point in time, because the culture's values push us to act that way.

In a strong organizational culture, employees tend to dress and behave in similar ways.

Social Media and Culture Management

Social media is one of the mechanisms we now use to both monitor and—at least partially—control organizational environments.[81] Companies can monitor the internal environment using social media venues, which gives management a feel for the culture within the organization. They can also actively seek out information internally using various forms of social media[82] and can even ask company members to interact on social media platforms such as **LinkedIn** and **Facebook**. Have you ever known someone whose organization asked employees to "like" them on **Facebook**? This mechanism is becoming more important every day and will continue to do so for the immediate future.

The same is true for the external environment, from following competitors on social media sites to utilizing government webpages and media links. Governments and other entities are even using social media to extend their reach into communities that are generally hard to reach because they don't pay much attention to standard methods of communication like State of the Union addresses and regulatory bulletins. In the United States, **President Obama**'s administration turned to social media to attract younger individuals (who don't tend to get as involved with government issues) to the federal health care exchanges. The administration did this because the Affordable Care Act required younger people to sign up to offset the higher cost of insuring older individuals.[83]

EXHIBIT 2.4 ● The Internal and External Environment

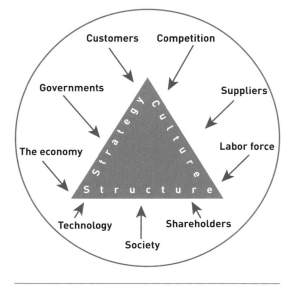

Social media continues to become more important to business and government. You can bet that governments will pay more attention to social media in the future, since many of the "Arab Spring" uprisings were coordinated via social media.[84] This is just one example of the power of social media sites.

Recall that each organization has an internal and an external environment. Exhibit 2.4 puts together the internal and external components making up that environment.

2.4 APPLYING THE CONCEPT
THE INTERNAL ENVIRONMENT

Identify which internal environmental factor is referred to in each statement, and then write the letter corresponding to that factor before the statement.

a. Strategy

b. Structure

c. Culture

_____ 16. "At **Victoria's Secret**, we focus on selling clothes and other products to women."

_____ 17. "At the **SEC**, we have several layers of management."

_____ 18. "At **Ford**, quality is job one."

_____ 19. "Walking around the office at **Bank of America**, I realized that I would have to wear a jacket and tie every day."

_____ 20. "I work in the production department at **Ford**, and she works in the marketing department."

An Introduction to Data Analytics and HR Technology

>> **LO 2.6 Define data analytics by how it helps organizations make important decisions.**

According to a recent SHRM symposium, "HR is ripe for disruption and transformation."[85] As HR practices are more automated and data-driven, HR managers will have to become even more knowledgeable of data management and manipulation in order to continue to do their jobs.[86] Data scientists are in demand.[87] One area of required knowledge is data analytics. **Data analytics** is *the process of accessing large amounts of data in order to analyze those data and gain insight into significant trends or patterns within organizations or industries.* This ability to create huge amounts of data has led to the concept of "big data."

Data analytics Process of accessing large amounts of data in order to analyze those data and gain insight into significant trends or patterns within organizations or industries

Big Data

Big data involves the collection of extremely large data sets. It can reveal patterns and opportunities that 99% of businesspeople would miss.[88] Have you ever been online or in a store and received customized ads for products you bought in the past or are likely to buy, or ads telling you it's time to reorder? That's big data. ***Fortune* 500** executives are all talking about big data[89] because it allows us to make important organizational decisions—especially strategic decisions—faster.[90]

Jack Ma, chairman of Alibaba, says, "Data will become the biggest production material in the future."[91] Executives must transform into math machines,[92] because whoever has the most exact data—and knows how to use it—wins today.[93] **United Airlines** uses big data to decide where to fly, how often, how many people to carry, and how big or small a plane to use.[94]

A Brief on Data Analytics

Companies like **Google** grew up on data analytics. Director of research **Peter Norvig** once said, "We don't have better algorithms than anyone else; we just have more data."[95] And **Google** analyzes *all* of that data looking for patterns that it can use. Many other companies have joined this movement, including some powerful outsourcers like **Facebook**, **IBM**, and **Oracle**, who are selling big data services.[96] Other companies are doing their own big data analysis, using big data as a competitive weapon, according to a McKinsey & Company report.[97]

Analysis of big data is providing information that HR managers can immediately act on as well. A recent analytical study showed "the communication skills and personal warmth of an employee's supervisor are often crucial in determining the employee's tenure and performance."[98] A lot of HR managers have anecdotally passed this information on to their line managers for many years.

Because of big data, we can now analyze thousands or even millions of interactions between people in and between organizations and look for patterns to those interactions. According to a report in the *Harvard Business Review,* "We can measure, and therefore manage, more precisely than ever."[99] If we find a pattern, it may tell us what we should do based on data rather than instinct. We can "directly translate that [pattern] knowledge into improved decision making and performance."[100]

HR Technology

HR managers must become comfortable with collecting and analyzing big data to drive results.[101] Analytics tools and other HR technology can be used for many HR functions, such as talent acquisition, training and development, productivity analysis, motivation, retention, and engagement.[102] However, organizational silos, skills shortages, and suspicion about reducing human beings to data points are "preventing HR departments from effectively using talent analytics."[103]

The convergence of HRM and big data is sometimes called *workforce science,* as "This is absolutely the way forward."[104] The ability to measure actions and reactions in large numbers and find patterns in them is going to change the management of people in organizations, not just in the long term but in the immediate future. In fact, it is already happening. Again, **Google** uses data analysis in HR just as much as it does in the marketing of products and services. **Google** knows, for instance, that its most innovative workers "are those who have a strong sense of mission about their work and . . . have autonomy."[105]

In addition to analytics, HR has begun using other technologies to reach and inform workers to a much greater extent than ever before. Part of this shift is because most employees are now comfortable with using technology. Virtually all HR record keeping in business today is done through databases where information only has to be entered one time. According to **Insperity**, an HR technology company, just about every aspect of employment, from selection and onboarding to training, compensation and benefits, performance reviews, and mobile workforce management is being managed through a variety of computers and personal technology devices such as smart phones and tablets.[106]

Desired Outcomes

Businesses are increasingly looking at internal people processes in order to predict the impact of those processes on their business results.[107] Thus, the desired outcomes are increased performance, and "companies that are highly skilled in core HR practices experience up to 3.5 times the revenue growth and as much as 2.1 times the profit margins of less capable companies."[108] That is a shocking differential between skilled and less skilled organizations. HR managers who understand and use such metrics can gain their "seat at the table" when strategy is being discussed in their firms. There is no doubt that data analytics is becoming a critical area of expertise for HR managers—especially at higher management levels.

Human Resource Management Systems (HRMS)

>> **LO 2.7 Identify how human resource management systems (HRMS) can help HR make decisions.**

Most organizations today use complex computer systems to manage and manipulate data. Human resource management systems (HRMS) are one type of system used to manage and analyze data in organizations, as HR uses data to influence business performance.[109]

What Are HRMS?

Human resource management systems (HRMS) are *interacting database systems that aim at generating and delivering HR information and allow us to automate some human resource management functions.*[110] A slightly older term for such systems that you may hear is human resource information systems (HRIS). Some of the most common features in HRMS include modules for tracking attendance and leave, job, and pay history and logging appraisal scores and review dates. Others include modules for benefits enrollment and tracking, succession management, training management, and time logging. There are additional modules available depending on the size and type of the organization.[111] **(SHRM H:5)**

How Do HRMS Assist in Making Decisions?

Today's HRMS platforms include such key features as workforce management, performance monitoring of the recruiting process, e-mail alert systems, and predictive analytics.[112] These new systems are very user-friendly. We can use the information stored in the database to make daily decisions within the HR department. For example, since training records are available in the HRMS, if we need to determine who has completed conflict management coursework for a new team being created in the company, we can quickly identify individuals with that skill set. We can also use the same databases when considering promotions, transfers, and many other daily activities that are required inside the organization.

Measurement Tools for Strategic HRM

>> **LO 2.8 Recall the common measurement tools for strategic human resource management (HRM).**

Housed within many HRMS are statistical packages for HRM. Just as we have to quantify and measure other parts of the organization, we also have measurement tools specific to HRM. Two of the most common tools are economic value added (EVA) and return on investment (ROI). Let's take a brief look at each of these tools.

Economic Value Added (EVA)

Economic value added (EVA) is designed as a method for calculating the creation of value for the organization's shareholders. **Economic value added (EVA)** is a *measure of profits that remain after the cost of capital has been deducted from operating profits.* It provides shareholders and managers with a better understanding of how the business is performing overall. As an equation, EVA would look like this:

$$\text{EVA} = \text{Net operating profit after tax} - (\text{Capital used} \times \text{Cost of capital})^{[113]}$$

EVA is a measure of how much money we made through our operations minus the amount of money we had to spend or borrow (at a particular interest rate) in order to perform those operations. For a company to grow, it must generate average returns higher than its capital costs. **(SHRM K:5 and O:2-e)**

As an example, let's look at a fictitious company's incentive program to see if we gained value. Acme Mega Corp decided to create a bonus program to increase productivity. They set aside $1 million for the program, and their cost to acquire the million dollars was 6%. For now, don't worry too much about why it was 6%. You will learn about weighted average cost of capital (WACC) and other financial measures later. Ultimately Acme was able to measure *productivity improvements* at the end of one year of the incentive program, and they increased productivity by $1.2 million (after taxes were calculated on the increased productivity). The EVA calculation would be as follows:

$$\text{EVA} = \text{Net operating profit after tax} - (\text{Capital used} \times \text{Cost of capital})$$

$$\text{EVA} = \$1,200,000 - (\$1,000,000 \times 1.06) = \$1,200,000 - \$1,060,000 = \$140,000$$

So we made $140,000 on our $1 million investment—a 14% return.

Return on Investment (ROI)

Return on investment (ROI) is a *measure of the financial return we receive because of something that we do to invest in our organization or its people.* ROI is most commonly used in financial analyses, but many areas of HR lend themselves to ROI calculations. These areas include training, outsourcing, benefits, diversity, and many others. In each of these areas, we can calculate the cost of the process—whether that process is training, diversity management, or anything else—and compare that to the returns we get from the process. **(SHRM K:8)**

To calculate ROI, you need two figures: the cost of the investment and the gain that you receive from making the investment. From there, the calculation is pretty simple:

$$\text{ROI} = \frac{\text{Gain from investment} - \text{Cost of investment}}{\text{Cost of investment}}$$

Return on investment (ROI) Measure of the financial return we receive because of something that we do to invest in our organization or its people

So, as an example, if we create a training course to improve the skills of our assembly workers and send all of the workers through the training, that training will cost us $1 million. We know that historically, during a normal year of production, the assembly workers have been able to assemble $5 million worth of our product. However, after the training is complete, we measure our assembly process over the ensuing year and find that our amount of product created that year has increased to $8 million. This gives us a $3 million gain from the investment. We can plug these numbers into our calculation and find out the following:

$$\text{ROI} = \frac{\$3,000,000 - \$1,000,000}{\$1,000,000} = \frac{\$2,000,000}{\$1,000,000} = 2 \text{ or } 200\%$$

It is always important to calculate at least a rough ROI for any investment in organizational resources. There's a definite need to understand how much we get in return for an investment. Don't just assume the return on investment is always positive—because it's not.

2.5 APPLYING THE CONCEPT
RETURN ON INVESTMENT (ROI)

For all your HR investment programs, the objective is to get at least 0.25 or 25% ROI. In each of the four HR programs:

1. Calculate the ROI and place the number and percentage (%) on the line before the number.

2. State if it (a) does or (b) doesn't meet the objective on the line after the number and explain the results of the ROI calculations.

_____ 21. _____. HR developed a new program to reduce absenteeism. The program cost $1,000. Absenteeism decreased, resulting in a cost savings of $2,000.

_____ 22. _____. HR developed a new program to improve employee morale. Morale increased at an estimated cost savings of $6,000, and the program cost $5,000.

_____ 23. _____. HR developed a new program to increase the percentage of minorities employed during the next 6 months. Although you hired more minorities, some current employees left the company and you hired more whites, resulting in a 1% gain, at an estimated value of $5,000. The extra recruiting cost targeted at minorities was $50,000.

_____ 24. _____. HR developed a new safety training program to decrease the number of accidents, resulting in paying employees while out of work due to injuries. The training cost $40,000, and the savings was $100,500.

Trends and Issues in HRM

Here we continue our discussion of some of the most important trends and issues in HRM today. In this chapter, we chose the following issues: (a) the misalignment of structure, culture, and technology; and (b) how continuing globalization is increasing the need for strategic and HRM planning.

▲
Taking a company global requires effective strategic and HRM planning.

©iStockphoto.com/simonkr

Structure, Culture, and Technology Are Misaligned

A 2017 Deloitte Global Human Capital Trends report noted, "Technology is advancing at an unprecedented rate. Individuals are relatively quick to adapt, *but organizations move at a slower pace.* Many still retain industrial age structure and practices that are long outdated."[114] We briefed you on the general issue of organizational agility in Chapter 1, but here we want to quickly review the inertia that is caused by organizational structure and culture and show why companies have to make a concerted effort to modify those elements to become more agile.

Recall from earlier in the chapter that strong (centralized, formalized, and moderately complex) organizational structures can provide positive control over what happens within a company. This control is a desired state for the leaders because it helps stabilize the firm. But, in order to adapt to technologies that are "advancing at an unprecedented rate," companies will need to let go of some of that control. Managers and executives will have to *decentralize,* lower *formalization,* and allow even more *complexity* so that line employees can react quickly when necessary.

Similarly, a strong culture can be a serious impediment to agility. Remember that culture is based on a collective set of values that members of the organization share and that are extremely hard to change—at least quickly. So strong company cultures will resist quick changes. If a company is going to need to adapt fast to changes in lots of areas, inflexible cultures will have to be modified. In a battle between culture and market forces, culture will win almost every time. So we have to modify the culture to be more agile or we will never be able to create or maintain a sustainable competitive advantage over competitors.

Continuing Globalization Increases the Need for Strategic and HRM Planning

You may think that with the current state of affairs, where federal governments from North America to the European Union are retrenching and breaking off trade and business partnerships with former partners in other countries, that globalization is becoming a less significant issue. However, you would be wrong. As business in most industries continues to globalize out of necessity, competition will inevitably increase. Competitors need to gain access to more markets, and as more competitors gain access to more and more markets, competition will steadily increase. This increasing competition puts pressure on businesses to create a plan to overcome their competitors' advantages.

Remember that strategic planning is designed to analyze the competitive landscape our organization faces and create a workable plan that will allow us to compete within that landscape. So as competition increases, developing a good, solid "global" strategy and implementing continuous reviews of our strategic plans become more and more significant.

For HRM, this means that HR managers will need to become better at managing expatriate employees, paying wages across national borders, managing disparate country laws and regulations, and much more. We will discuss the globalization issues for HRM in more detail in Chapter 14.

Chapter Summary

2.1 Discuss the strategic planning process by classifying the major components of the external environment.

Strategic planning provides a process to evaluate our organization and its environment—both today and in the expected future—and determine what our organization wants to do to meet the requirements of that expected future. There are nine major external environmental forces that must be taken into account:

- *Customers*. Companies must continually improve products to create value for their customers.

- *Competition*. Organizations must compete against each other for customers, for the same employees, and sometimes for suppliers. Competitors' changing strategic moves affect the performance of the organization.

- *Suppliers*. The firm's performance is affected by its suppliers. Therefore, it is important to develop close working relationships with your suppliers.

- *Labor Force*. The recruits available to, and the employees of, an organization have a direct effect on its performance. Management must recruit human resources from the available labor force outside the company's boundaries.

- *Shareholders*. The owners of a corporation, known as shareholders, influence management. Most shareholders of large corporations are not involved in the day-to-day operation of the firm, but they do vote for the board of directors, and the top manager reports to the board of directors.

- *Society*. Individuals and groups within society have formed to pressure business for changes. People who live in the same area with the business do not want it to pollute the air or water or otherwise abuse natural resources.

- *Technology*. Computers and the Internet have changed the speed and the manner in which organizations conduct and transact business. Changing technologies require technologically savvy employees who have the ability to adapt to new processes.

- *The Economy*. No organization has control over economic growth, inflation, interest rates, foreign exchange rates, and so on. In general, as measured by gross domestic product (GDP), businesses do better when the economy is growing than they do during recessions.

- *Governments*. National, state, and local governments all set laws and regulations that businesses must obey. To a large extent, a business may not do whatever it wants to do; the government tells business what it can and cannot do.

2.2 Discuss how visions, missions, and objectives help to define the organization's strategy.

A strategy is a plan of action designed to achieve a particular set of objectives. Visions and mission statements help focus organizational activities on achieving the strategic goals of the organization. The vision is what we expect to become as an organization at a particular point in time in the future. The vision is who we are, what we stand for, what we believe in, and what we want to become. The mission is where we start to become specific. It lays out our expectations of what we're going to do in order to become the organization that we have envisioned. When you put the vision and mission together, all the people in the organization get a more complete picture of the direction in which they are expected to go. Setting objectives creates targets that enable management to measure its progress at achieving its vision and mission and other goals.

2.3 Explain the three major generic strategies.

- Cost Leadership—Cost leaders do everything they can to lower the internal organizational costs required to produce their products or services. This can give them a powerful edge in commodity product/service environments.

- Differentiation—This strategy attempts to create an impression of difference for the company's product or service in the mind of the customer. The differentiator company stresses its advantages to the customer over its competitors.

- Focus/Niche—With this strategy, the company focuses on a specific portion, or segment, of a larger market. Within a particular target segment or market niche, the firm may use either a differentiation or a cost leadership strategy.

2.4 Summarize the importance of the major components of organizational structure.

Organizational structure refers to the way in which an organization groups its resources to accomplish its mission. Organizations structure their resources to transform inputs and outputs. All of an organization's resources must be structured effectively to achieve its mission. As a manager in any department, you will be responsible for part of the organization's structure.

All of an organization's resources must be structured effectively if it is to achieve its mission. Structure is made up of three major components:

- *Complexity* is the degree to which three types of differentiation exist within the organization. These three types are vertical differentiation, horizontal differentiation, and spatial differentiation. The more the organization is divided—whether vertically, horizontally, or spatially—the more difficult it is to manage.

- *Formalization* is the degree to which jobs are standardized within an organization. The more we can standardize the organization and its processes, the easier it is to control those processes.

- *Centralization* is the degree to which decision making is concentrated within the organization at a single point—usually at the top. A highly centralized organization would have all authority concentrated at the top, while a decentralized organization would have authority spread throughout. If authority can be centralized, we can take advantage of learning curve effects that help to improve our decision making over time.

2.5 Discuss how organizational culture affects the members of the organization.

Organizational culture consists of the values, beliefs, and assumptions about appropriate behavior that members of an organization share. Organizational culture is primarily learned through observing people and events in the organization. Because organizational culture is based at least partly on assumptions, values, and beliefs, the culture can control how people act within its boundaries. Because assumptions, values, and beliefs are such strong influences, individuals will generally act to conform to the culture. For the most part, we all act to conform to the culture that we happen to be in at any given point in time, and that's because cultural values push us to act that way.

2.6 Define data analytics by how it helps organizations make important decisions.

Data analytics is the process of accessing large amounts of data in order to analyze those data and gain insight into significant trends or patterns within organizations or industries. Analytics tools and processes can be used to guide decision making for many HR functions, such as talent acquisition and management, training and development, work and job analysis, productivity analysis, motivation, retention, and engagement. Data analytics on a large scale, or *big data,* will change how people are managed within organizations and ideally lead to increased performance of the organization.

2.7 Identify how human resource management systems (HRMS) can help HR make decisions.

Human resource management systems (HRMS) are interacting database systems that aim to generate and deliver HR information and allow us to automate some HRM functions. They are primarily database management systems, designed especially for use in HR functions.

HRMS allow us to maintain control of our HR information and make it available for use during the strategic planning process. Having this information immediately available makes the strategic planning process both quicker and smoother. We can also use the information stored in the database to make daily decisions within the HR department, such as a decision on whom to send to a particular training class. We can also use these databases when considering promotions, transfers, team assignments, and many other daily activities that are required inside the organization.

2.8 Recall the common measurement tools for strategic human resource management (HRM).

We discussed two common tools in this chapter: economic value added (EVA) and return on investment (ROI).

EVA is a measure of profits that remain after the cost of capital has been deducted from operating profits. ROI is a measure of the financial return we receive because of something that we do to invest in our organization or its people.

Key Terms

centralization, 39
complexity, 39
data analytics, 42
economic value added
  (EVA), 44
formalization, 39

high performance work practices
  (HPWPs), 38
human resource management
  systems (HRMS), 44
mission statement, 34
objectives, 35

organizational culture, 40
organizational structure, 39
return on investment (ROI), 45
strategy, 34
vision, 34

Key Terms Review

Complete each of the following statements using one of this chapter's key terms.

1. _____ is a plan of action to achieve a particular set of objectives.

2. _____ is what we expect to become as an organization at a particular future point in time.

3. _____ is our expectations of what we're going to do in order to become the organization that we envisioned.

4. _____ are practices that have been shown to improve an organization's capacity to effectively attract, select, hire, develop, and retain high-performing personnel.

5. _____ refers to the way in which an organization groups its resources to accomplish its mission.

6. _____ is the degree of three types of differentiation within the organization.

7. _____ is the degree to which jobs are standardized within an organization.

8. _____ is the degree to which decision making is concentrated within the organization at a single point—usually at the top of the organization.

9. _____ consists of the values, beliefs, and assumptions about appropriate behavior that members of an organization share.

10. _____ is the process of accessing large amounts of data in order to analyze those data and gain insights into significant trends or patterns within organizations or industries.

11. _____ are interacting database systems that aim at generating and delivering HR information and allow us to automate some human resource management functions.

12. _____ is a measure of profits that remain after the cost of capital has been deducted from operating profits.

13. _____ is a measure of the financial return we receive because of something that we do to invest in our organization or its people.

Communication Skills

The following critical-thinking questions can be used for class discussion and/or for written assignments to develop communication skills. Be sure to give complete explanations for all answers.

1. Can you name a business that you know of in which competition has increased significantly in the past few years? Why do you think competition has increased in this case?

2. What are some of the ways in which the environmental factors that we discussed in this chapter directly affect the organization?

3. Do you agree that every organization needs a strategic plan? Why or why not?

4. Think about the technological changes that have occurred since you were born. Do you think those changes have affected the strategic planning process? How?

5. What should a mission statement focus on—customers, competitors, products/services, the employee environment, or something else? Identify why you chose a particular answer.

6. We discussed the three major generic strategies in this chapter. Can you think of examples of each of the three strategies in specific businesses

you know of? In your opinion, how successful have these companies been with their strategy?

7. If you were going to design the structure for a new, innovative start-up company, what kind of structure would you try to create in regard to level of complexity, formalization, and centralization? Why would you set up this type of structure?

8. Which of the five artifacts, or important ways in which employees learn about culture, do you think is most important? Why?

9. Name some situations in HRM when you would want to use either economic value added (EVA) or return on investment (ROI) as an analytical tool.

Case 2.1 Catalya Hats: Pulling a Rabbit Out of the Hat or Coming Up Empty Handed?[115]

Catalya Hats, a millinery company, began from a simple design of a Panama hat in Ricardo Catalya's home in Ecuador. Mr. Catalya had no idea that when he created his first Panama hat in 1906 to protect himself from the sun, it would become an iconic fashion classic. His hats were crafted from the finest natural toquilla straw fiber; no two fibers were the same. In fact, each hat had its own character because the materials were different in shape and color. Toquilla comes from a straw plant and cannot be woven by a machine; it can only be woven by hand. Depending on the weave count, one hat could take anywhere between 1 week to 3 months to manufacture.

It did not take long for many powerful businesspersons and celebrities from the United States to take recognition of these handcrafted pieces. The company's strategy was to become a globally integrated quality hat company. For over 100 years, the industry has praised the company, and helped the company raise its annual revenue to $25.5 million by 2006.

Nearly all of the top managers started their careers with the firm and had worked their way up to their

current positions. The firm's practice, started by its founder, was for all employees to learn the business from the ground up, starting with working on the production line assisting the hat makers (regardless of their actual field of expertise) and then rotating through every job dealing with hat production and distribution including actual hat making. This approach to employee training ensured that everyone in the firm, regardless of their specific tasks and responsibilities, had a personal connection to not only every job performed but also to most of the people who performed the jobs.

The company's accomplishments were due in no small part to its cross-functional corporate structure, a structure that reinforced egalitarian decision making. By definition, the company's team or project members came from more than one functional area of the company, working together toward a common goal and a common bond: a love of hats. This structure ensured that the work groups were able to carry out the company's mission of making every hat a unique experience. Catalya's organizational culture was family-based and family-driven and embodied through the managers' and employees' work attitudes and behaviors. The top-level managers were the leaders who set and implemented these values and beliefs as well as how an employee should be treated; they role-modeled how an employee should perform when representing the firm both within and without.

The firm finally maxed out its production capacity at the turn of the 21st century, stalling the family's plans for international growth and expansion. Although profitable, the family did not have the financial wherewithal to support a sizable plant investment and so continued focusing just on process and production improvements through technological innovation. In 2016, the firm was reluctantly sold to a private investor, Ralph Dweck, who had the capital needed to expand the name and brand. An essential part of the purchasing agreement was that Dweck agreed to retain the current employees and staff for a minimum of 2 years and that he would remain true to the quality and traditions of the firm. Dweck understood that his new staff may not see or agree with his "big picture," his vision for international growth and expansion, and hoped that he could move them out of their "familial" surroundings and transition them into a more corporate, professional milieu and mindset.

At the first major executive meeting, Dweck rolled out his plans to enter into new international markets and distribution channels. Everyone seemed onboard with these growth plans until Dweck discussed the need to find international business partners in order to expand the firm's operation. These partners, specifically firms with innovative technology and excess production capability, would dramatically increase the firm's production capacity while leveraging Catalya's good name. Some form of outsourcing of production seemed to make the most sense to Dweck, given the limited financial investment required. Nonetheless, his proposal received opposition from many of the top managers within the firm.

Brian Bianco, the vice president of operations argued that no one could make Catalya hats like Catalya employees and that unless these "partners" were going to be trained by Catalya hat makers, the products would be of inferior quality. He proposed instead to increase the current plant size and capacity, take on a larger work force, and continue the tradition of producing high-quality hats made in Ecuador. He felt

that local monitoring and quality control techniques would ensure that the firm would maintain high production standards, standards that would allow the firm to continue to excel as a top-flight connoisseur hat maker.

Evelyn Choi, manager of production, echoed his concerns about outsourcing production, reminding everyone of Ricardo Catalya's legacy and the pride employees had in working for such a prestigious firm. Janice Warling in public relations thought that they would garner far more public support by "making local, being global" and that they could leverage the "fair trade" movement by touting how well their workers were paid as well as their pristine working conditions. She thought that they could even seek government funding and support to help them grow the business (low or no interest loans, tax abatements or rebates, etc.). Tori Baugmart, the vice president of human resources, reinforced these sentiments and indicated that labor was plentiful, fairly well skilled, and not overly costly compared with other workforces.

In response to these negative comments, Dweck tried to explain to his team the need to ride the wave of consumer demand for these hats without committing a huge amount of resources for gearing up production. He was afraid that this increased demand might be short-lived, having quadrupled in the past 5 years, and that the firm might get caught in a fad downturn rather than climbing up the surging wave of a fashion trend. Outsourcing seemed to be the best short-term solution to solving the supply gap, a gap that could not be shrunk through price increases.

Questions

1. What is Catalya Hats' vision/mission, and how might it explain why the Catalya family sold their firm to a private investor, Ralph Dweck?

2. What external environmental factors underlie the discussion of whether production of Catalya hats should or should not be outsourced?

3. What is the strategy of Catalya Hats, and how does it affect its HR policies?

4. What was the firm's basic structure, and how did it reinforce their strategy?

5. How did the firm's culture support their strategy?

Skill Builder 2.1 Writing Objectives

For this exercise, you will first work at improving ineffective objectives. Then you will write nine objectives for yourself.

Objective

To develop your skill at writing objectives

Skills

The primary skills developed through this exercise are as follows:

1. *HR management skills*—Conceptual and design

2. *SHRM 2018 Curriculum Guidebook*—O: Strategic HR

Part 1

Indicate which of the criteria each of the following objectives fails to meet in the model and rewrite the objective so that it meets all those criteria. When writing objectives, use the following model:

To + action verb + single, specific, and measurable result + target date

1. To improve our company image by the end of 2020

   Criteria not met: _____

   Improved objective: _____

2. To increase the number of customers by 10%

   Criteria not met: _____

   Improved objective: _____

3. To increase profits during 2020

   Criteria not met: _____

   Improved objective: _____

4. To sell 5% more hot dogs and 13% more soda at the baseball game on Sunday, June 14, 2019

   Criteria not met: _____

   Improved objective: _____

Part 2

Write three educational, three personal, and three career objectives you want to accomplish. These may be short-term (something you want to accomplish today), long-term (something you want to have accomplished 20 years from now), or medium-term objectives. Be sure to structure your objectives using the model and meeting the criteria for effective objectives.

- Educational Objectives

- Personal Objectives

- Career Objectives

Apply It

What did I learn from this experience? How will I use this knowledge in the future?

_____

_____

_____

_____

Your instructor may ask you to do this Skill Builder in class in a group. If so, the instructor will provide you with any necessary information or additional instructions.

Case created by Herbert Sherman, PhD, and Theodore Vallas, Department of Management Sciences, Long Island University School of Business, Brooklyn Campus

Skill Builder 2.2 Strategic Planning at Your College

This exercise enables you to apply the strategic planning process to your college or university as an individual and/or a group. Complete each step by typing or writing out your answers. You can also conduct this exercise for another organization.

Objective

To develop your strategic planning skills by analyzing the internal environment of strategy, structure, and culture

Skills

The primary skills developed through this exercise are as follows:

1. *HR management skills*—Business and conceptual and design

2. *SHRM 2018 Curriculum Guidebook*—O: Strategic HR

Part A: Strategy

Step 1: Develop a Mission

1. What is the vision and mission statement of your university/college or school/department?

2. Is the mission statement easy to understand and remember?

3. How would you improve the mission statement?

Step 2: Identify a Strategy

Which of the three generic strategies does your school or department use?

Step 3: Conduct Strategic Analysis

1. Complete a SWOT analysis by identifying the strengths, weaknesses, opportunities, and threats facing your school.

2. Determine the competitive advantage (if any) of your university/college or school/department.

Step 4: Set Objectives

What are some objectives of your university/college or school/department?

Step 5: Implement, Monitor, and Evaluate Strategies

How would you rate your university/college's or school/department's strategic planning? How could it be improved?

Part B: Structure

Describe your school or department's organizational structure in terms of its complexity, formalization, and centralization.

Part C: Culture

Identify artifacts in each of the categories of heroes, stories, slogans, symbols, and ceremonies.

Identify the cultural levels of the organization's behaviors, values and beliefs, and assumptions.

Apply It

What did I learn from this experience? How will I use this knowledge in the future?

_____

_____

_____

_____

Your instructor may ask you to do this Skill Builder in class in a group. If so, the instructor will provide you with any necessary information or additional instructions.

©iStockphoto.com/sturti

3

The Legal Environment

Learning Outcomes

After studying this chapter, you should be able to do the following:

3.1 Identify the four components of the OUCH test by describing when it is useful in an organizational setting. **PAGE 56**

3.2 Discuss the major equal employment opportunity (EEO) laws specifying the groups of people each law protects. **PAGE 58**

3.3 Briefly discuss the major functions of the Equal Employment Opportunity Commission (EEOC). **PAGE 66**

3.4 Compare the two primary types of sexual harassment. **PAGE 68**

3.5 Briefly discuss the employer's requirements concerning avoidance of religious discrimination in the workplace. **PAGE 71**

SHRM HR Content

See Online: *SHRM 2018 Curriculum Guidebook* for the complete list

D. Employment Law

2. Age Discrimination in Employment Act of 1967
3. Americans with Disabilities Act of 1990 and as amended in 2008
6. Equal Pay Act of 1963
11. Genetic Information Nondiscrimination Act (GINA)
16. Lilly Ledbetter Fair Pay Act
19. Pregnancy Discrimination Act of 1978
22. Title VII of the Civil Rights Act of 1964 and 1991
23. Uniformed Services Employment and Reemployment Rights Act of 1994 (USERRA)
28. Disparate impact
29. Disparate treatment
34. Enforcement agencies (EEOC, OFCCP)
37. Types of discrimination
38-a. Unlawful harassment—Sexual
38-b. Unlawful harassment—Religious

38-c. Unlawful harassment—Disability
40. ADA (Reasonable accommodation)

I. Job Analysis and Job Design

1-a. Compliance with legal requirements—Equal employment (job-relatedness, bona fide occupational qualifications, and the reasonable accommodation process)

J. Managing a Diverse Workforce

5. Equal employment opportunity (EEO)
6. Gay, lesbian, bisexual, transgender (GLBT)/sexual orientation issues
9. Individuals with disabilities
12. Religion

N. Staffing (Recruitment and Selection)

2. Bona fide occupational qualifications (BFOQs)

Practitioner's Perspective

Cindy says: One of the reasons some agree with the Dilbert comic strip depiction of the HR manager as devoid of feeling is due to the necessity of fair and uniform enforcement of government rules and regulations, as well as the company's own policies and procedures. Aaron—a favorite with the patients and a willing overtime worker—misread the schedule and missed a day of work at the hospital. A no-call/no-show (NC/NS) merits a written warning, but Aaron's supervisor didn't want to administer the discipline.

"Well," I asked, "what if we were talking about another less exemplary employee? What about, oh, let's say—Sandy? What would you do if she was NC/NS?"

"Hey, no problem there—I'd write up Sandy in an instant!" replied the supervisor.

"Wait—wouldn't that be discrimination?" Different treatment of individuals who are in similar circumstances opens the door to legal liability. In Chapter 3, we'll explore why HR is required to advise and assist with compliance issues—no matter how "heartless" it may appear.

The Legal Environment for HRM and a User's Guide to Managing People

>> **LO 3.1 Identify the four components of the OUCH test by describing when it is useful in an organizational setting.**

We all have to obey the law in our personal and professional lives. The external environment (Chapter 2) and the HRM discipline area of *EEO and Diversity Management* (Chapter 1) has a major impact on HRM practices. Organizations are not completely free to hire, promote, or fire whomever they want. The HR department usually has the responsibility of seeing that the organization complies with the law.[1] In this chapter, we will explore some of the laws that HR managers have to work with on a daily basis in order to maintain fairness in the workplace.

We have grown to believe in the value of a diverse workforce,[2] and one of the primary jobs of an HR manager is to assist in avoiding any discriminatory employment situations that can create legal, ethical, or social problems with organizational stakeholders. As a result, one of the first things we need to do in this chapter is define **discrimination**, which is *the act of making distinctions or choosing one thing over another; in HR, it is making distinctions among people.*

From this definition you can see that if managers don't discriminate, then they're not doing their job. However, we absolutely want to avoid *illegal* discrimination based on a person's membership in a protected class, and we want to avoid unfair treatment of any of our employees at all times. **Illegal discrimination** is *the act of making distinctions that harm people and that are based on those people's membership in a protected class.* This chapter will teach you some of the tools that we can use to avoid illegal discrimination.

The OUCH Test Guide

Before we start talking about equal employment opportunity and all of the forms of illegal discrimination in the workplace, let's introduce you to the OUCH test.[3] The **OUCH test** is *a rule of thumb used whenever you are contemplating any employment action, to maintain fairness and equity for all of your employees or applicants.* Every manager should use this test whenever contemplating any action that involves their employees.

OUCH is an acronym that stands for (see Exhibit 3.1):

- **O**bjective
- **U**niform in application
- **C**onsistent in effect
- **H**as job relatedness

Discrimination The act of making distinctions or choosing one thing over another; in HR, it is making distinctions among people

Illegal discrimination The act of making distinctions that harm people and that are based on those people's membership in a protected class

OUCH test A rule of thumb used whenever you are contemplating any employment action, to maintain fairness and equity for all of your employees or applicants

Objective

Is the action objective, or is it subjective? Something that is objective is based on fact, or quantifiable evidence, not on personal feelings or prejudices. Something that is subjective is based on your emotional state/feelings or opinion. You should make your employment actions as objective as possible, in all cases.

Uniform in Application

If you apply an action in an employment situation, are you applying that same action in all cases of the same type? If you ask someone to perform a test, you need to create the exact same testing circumstances, as much as you can control them. For instance, if one person took an exam in a quiet room and the other in a noisy hallway, your actions would not be uniform in application.

EXHIBIT 3.1 ● The OUCH Test

Objective	Fact-based and quantifiable, not subjective or emotional
Uniform in Application	Apply the same "tests" in the same ways
Consistent in Effect	Ensure the result is not significantly different for different groups
Has Job Relatedness	Action must relate to the essential job functions

Consistent in Effect

Does the action have a significantly different effect on one or more protected groups than it has on the majority group? We have to try to make sure that we don't affect one of the many legally protected groups disproportionately with an employment action. But how can we know?

We have the **Four-Fifths Rule**,[4] *a test used by various federal courts, the Department of Labor, and the EEOC to determine whether disparate impact exists in an employment test.* This rule has been cited in numerous federal court cases, and it says that if the selection ratio for any group (e.g., Asian males) is less than four-fifths of the selection rate for the majority group (e.g., white males) in any employment action, then it constitutes evidence of potential disparate impact (we will explain disparate impact in more detail shortly).

For an example, take a look at Exhibit 3.2. Let's suppose we live in an area that is basically evenly split between African-American and white, non-Hispanic populations. You are planning on hiring about 40 new employees for a general position in your company. You decide to give each of the potential employees a written test. If the results of the test disproportionately rule out the African-American applicants, then your written test is not consistent in effect. So let's look at the numbers in Exhibit 3.2.

In the first example, the selection rate of African-American males (the protected group in this case) was 17%, which is above the Four-Fifths Rule threshold of 16%. Therefore, we are "consistent in effect," based on the Four-Fifths Rule.

However, in the second example, the selection rate of African-American males was 22.5%, and the minimum value by the Four-Fifths Rule was 23.2%. As a result, we would be outside the boundaries of being consistent in effect in this case.

If we are out of compliance with the Four-Fifths Rule, have we automatically broken the law? No.[5] We do have to investigate why we are outside the four-fifths parameter, though. If there is a legitimate reason for the discrepancy that we can prove in a court case, then we are probably

Four-Fifths Rule A test used by various federal courts, the Department of Labor, and the EEOC to determine whether disparate impact exists in an employment test

EXHIBIT 3.2 ● The Four-Fifths Rule

Example 1: You are planning to hire about 40 new employees. The statistical information on applicants is below:		
	White Males	**African-American Males**
Applicants	100	100
Selected	20	17
Selection rate	20% (20/100)	17% (17/100)

4/5ths = 80%, so 80% of 20% (0.80 × 0.20) = 16%.

The selection rate of 17% is greater than 16%, so the Four-Fifths Rule is met.

Example 2: What if you didn't have equal numbers of applicants in each group?		
	White Males	**African-American Males**
Applicants	100	40
Selected	29	9
Selection rate	29%	22.5% of 40

4/5ths = 80%, so 0.80 × 0.29 = 0.232 or 23.2%

The selection rate of 22.5% is *less* than the 23.2% required, so the Four-Fifths Rule is *not* met.

You would have to hire 9.28 or more people (23.2% of 40 = 9.28) in this case to be in compliance with the Four-Fifths Rule. You can't have 28% of a person, so you need to round up to 10 to be within the requirement. Therefore, you need one more African-American male to meet the 4/5 ratio requirement.

OK with a selection rate that is outside the parameters. We *can* also look at six-fifths to determine the possibility of reverse discrimination, which is discrimination against the majority group. So we would want to have between 16 and 24 African-American males selected in the first example, since 6/5 of 20 is 24.

Consistency in effect is by far the most complex of the four OUCH test factors. However, it is also very important in allowing us to show consistency in our actions as managers in an organization.

Has Job Relatedness

Is the action directly related to the primary aspects, or essential functions of the job in question?[6] In other words, if your job has nothing to do with making coffee for the office in the morning, I cannot base any employment action such as a hiring or firing on whether or not you do a good job making the coffee.

Remember that the OUCH test is a rule of thumb and does not work perfectly. It is not a legal test by itself. It is a good guide to nondiscriminatory practices, but it is only a guide. Now let's take a look at some of the specific legal requirements in the workplace.

Major Employment Laws

>> **LO 3.2 Discuss the major equal employment opportunity (EEO) laws specifying the groups of people each law protects.**

In any job within any organization today, you will need a basic understanding of the major employment laws that are currently in effect. If you don't understand what is legal and what isn't, you can inadvertently make mistakes that may cost your employer large amounts of money and time. Let's take a chronological look at some of the laws, listed in Exhibit 3.3.

EXHIBIT 3.3 ● Major EEO Laws in Chronological Order

Law	Description
Equal Pay Act of 1963	Requires that all employees be paid equally if they are doing equal work under similar working conditions
Title VII of the Civil Rights Act of 1964	Prohibits discrimination on the basis of race, color, religion, sex, or national origin in all areas of the employment relationship
Age Discrimination in Employment Act of 1967	Prohibits age discrimination against people 40 years of age or older and restricts mandatory retirement
Vietnam Era Veterans Readjustment Assistance Act of 1974	Prohibits discrimination against Vietnam veterans by all employers with federal contracts or subcontracts of $100,000 or more; also requires that affirmative action be taken
Pregnancy Discrimination Act of 1978	Prohibits discrimination against women affected by pregnancy, childbirth, or related medical conditions
Americans with Disabilities Act of 1990	Strengthened the Rehabilitation Act of 1973 to require employers to provide "reasonable accommodations" to allow disabled employees to work
Civil Rights Act of 1991	Strengthened civil rights by providing for possible compensatory and punitive damages for discrimination
Uniformed Services Employment and Reemployment Rights Act (USERRA) of 1994	Ensures the civilian reemployment rights of military members who were called away from their regular (nonmilitary) jobs by U.S. government orders

Law	Description
Veterans Benefits Improvement Act of 2004	Amends USERRA to extend health care coverage while away on duty, and requires employers to post a notice of benefits, duties, and rights of reemployment
Genetic Information Nondiscrimination Act of 2008	Prohibits the use of genetic information in employment, prohibits intentional acquisition of same, and imposes confidentiality requirements
Lilly Ledbetter Fair Pay Act of 2009	Amends the 1964 CRA to extend the period of time in which an employee is allowed to file a lawsuit over pay discrimination

Equal Pay Act of 1963

The Equal Pay Act requires that all employees who do the same job, in the same organization, must receive the same pay. It defines *equal* in terms of "equal skill, effort, and responsibility, and . . . performed under similar working conditions."[7] However, if pay differences are the result of differences in *seniority, merit, quantity or quality of production, or any factor other than sex* (e.g., shift differentials and training programs), then pay differences are legally allowable.[8] While originally designed to equalize pay between men and women, the act hasn't been fully successful. But our next law added serious consequences to such unequal treatment. However, before reading the reality of equal opportunity, complete Self-Assessment 3.1. **(SHRM D:6)**

Reality. Today, women make up about half of the U.S. workforce,[9] but they are only paid 77 cents on the dollar compared to their white male counterparts, and women of color only earn 65 cents.[10] And the best-paid jobs have the biggest gaps, as women have fewer opportunities for advancement. Women are underrepresented at every management level. Men are 30% more likely than women to be promoted into a managerial role.[11]

These two gaps are much wider in many other countries. In fact, the **World Economic Forum** estimated that at the current rate of global pay and employment opportunity, the gender gap will take 217 years to close.[12] If women globally were offered the same economic opportunities as men, an estimated $28 trillion would be added to global gross domestic product by 2025.[13] A major challenge for HR managers is to close the gaps at their organizations. Following the guidelines in this book can help you close those gaps.

Title VII of the Civil Rights Act of 1964 (CRA)

This act changed the way that virtually every organization in the country did business, and it also helped change employers' attitudes about discrimination. The 1964 CRA states that it is illegal for an employer "(1) to fail or refuse to hire or to discharge any individual, or otherwise to discriminate against any individual with respect to his compensation, terms, conditions, or privileges of employment, because of such individual's race, color, religion, sex, or national origin; or (2) to limit, segregate, or classify his employees or applicants for employment in any way which would deprive or tend to deprive any individual of employment opportunities or otherwise adversely affect his status as an employee, because of such individual's race, color, religion, sex, or national origin."[14]

The act applies to organizations with 15 or more employees who are working 20 or more weeks a year and who are involved in interstate commerce. The law also generally applies to state and local governments; educational institutions, public or private; all employment agencies; and all labor associations of any type. **(SHRM D:22 and D:37)**

Let's discuss some of the important concepts introduced by the CRA of 1964.

Types of Discrimination

The 1964 CRA identified three types of discrimination: disparate treatment, disparate impact, and pattern or practice. Subsequent court rulings helped to further define the three types.

3.1 SELF-ASSESSMENT
ATTITUDES ABOUT WOMEN AND MINORITIES ADVANCING

Be honest in this self-assessment, as your assessment will not be accurate if you aren't. Also, you should not be asked to share your score with others.

Each question below is actually two questions. It asks you about your attitude toward women, and it also asks you about your attitude toward minorities. Therefore, you should give two answers to each question: one regarding women and the other regarding minorities. Write the number corresponding to your answer (5 = agree, 3 = don't know, 1 = disagree) about women in the Women column, and write the number corresponding to your answer about minorities in the Minorities column.

Agree				Disagree
5	4	3	2	1

Women	Minorities
_____ 1. Women/Minorities lack motivation to get ahead.	1. _____
_____ 2. Women/Minorities lack the education necessary to get ahead.	2. _____
_____ 3. Women/Minorities working has caused rising unemployment among white men.	3. _____
_____ 4. Women/Minorities are not strong enough or emotionally stable enough to succeed in high-pressure jobs.	4. _____
_____ 5. Women/Minorities have a lower commitment to work than do white men.	5. _____
_____ 6. Women/Minorities are too emotional to be effective managers.	6. _____
_____ 7. Women/Minority managers have difficulty in situations calling for quick and precise decisions.	7. _____
_____ 8. Women/Minorities have a higher turnover rate than do white men.	8. _____
_____ 9. Women/Minorities are out of work more often than are white men.	9. _____
_____ 10. Women/Minorities have less interest in advancing than do white men.	10. _____
_____ Total	Total _____

Women: To determine your attitude score toward women, add up the total of your 10 answers in the Women column and place the total on the Total line and on the following continuum. The higher your total score, the more negative your attitude.

10	20	30	40	50

Positive attitude   Negative attitude

Minorities: To determine your attitude score toward minorities, add up the total of your 10 answers from the Minorities column and place the total on the Total line and on the following continuum. The higher your total score, the more negative your attitude.

10	20	30	40	50

Positive attitude   Negative attitude

Each statement is a negative attitude about women and minorities at work. However, research has shown all of these statements to be false; they are considered myths. Such statements stereotype women and minorities unfairly and prevent them from advancing in organizations through gaining salary increases and promotions. Thus, part of managing diversity and diversity training is to help overcome these negative attitudes to provide equal opportunities for ALL.

Disparate treatment exists *when individuals in similar situations are intentionally treated differently and the different treatment is based on an individual's membership in a protected class.* In a court case, the plaintiff must prove that the employer intended to discriminate in order to prove disparate treatment.[15] Disparate treatment is generally illegal unless the employer can show that there was a "bona fide occupational qualification" (or BFOQ) that caused the need to intentionally disallow members of a protected group from applying for or getting the job. **(SHRM D:29)**

Disparate impact occurs *when an officially neutral employment practice disproportionately excludes the member of a protected group; it is generally considered to be unintentional, but intent is irrelevant.*[16] **(SHRM D:28)**

Disparate impact is generally judged by use of the Four-Fifths Rule that we introduced in the OUCH test. If our investigation shows an employment test or measure was biased toward or against a certain group, then we have to correct the test or measure unless there was a legitimate reason to measure that particular characteristic. However, if our investigation shows the test was valid and reliable and that there was some other legitimate reason why we did not meet the four-fifths standard, then illegal discrimination *may* not exist.

Pattern or practice discrimination occurs *when a person or group engages in a sequence of actions over a significant period of time that is intended to deny the rights provided by Title VII of the 1964 CRA to a member of a protected class.* If there is reasonable cause to believe that any organization is engaging in pattern or practice discrimination, the U.S. Attorney General may bring a federal lawsuit against it.[17] In general, no individual can directly bring a pattern-or-practice lawsuit against an organization. As with disparate treatment, it must be proven that the employer intended to discriminate against a particular class of individuals and did so over a protracted period of time.

See Exhibit 3.4 for types of discrimination and types of organizational defenses against illegal discrimination charges.

Disparate treatment When individuals in similar situations are intentionally treated differently and the different treatment is based on an individual's membership in a protected class

Disparate impact When an officially neutral employment practice disproportionately excludes the members of a protected group; it is generally considered to be unintentional, but intent is irrelevant

Pattern or practice discrimination When a person or group engages in a sequence of actions over a significant period of time that is intended to deny the rights provided by Title VII of the 1964 CRA to a member of a protected class

EXHIBIT 3.4 ● Organizational Defenses to Discrimination Charges

Discrimination Type	Intent	Organizational Defense
Disparate Treatment	Intentional	BFOQ
Disparate Impact	Unintentional	BFOQ or business necessity *and* job relatedness
Pattern or Practice	Intentional	BFOQ (unlikely defense)

Organizational Defenses Against Discrimination Charges

The organization can defend itself against discrimination charges by showing either that there was a need for a particular characteristic or qualification for a specific job or that there was a *requirement* that the business do certain things in order to remain viable and profitable so that we didn't harm *all* of our employees by failing and shutting down. Let's review these defenses.

The first defense is a **bona fide occupational qualification (BFOQ)**, *a qualification that is absolutely required in order for an individual to be able to successfully do a particular job.* The qualification cannot just be a desirable quality within the job applicant—it must be mandatory.[18] A BFOQ defense can be used against both disparate impact and disparate treatment allegations. **(SHRM I:1-a and N:2)**

Business necessity exists *when a particular practice is necessary for the safe and efficient operation of the business and when there is a specific business purpose for applying a particular standard that may, in fact, be discriminatory.* A business necessity defense is applied by an employer in order to show that a particular practice was necessary for the safe and efficient operation of the business. Business necessity defenses must be combined with a test for job relatedness. However, business necessity is specifically prohibited as a defense against disparate treatment.[19]

Bona fide occupational qualification (BFOQ) A qualification that is absolutely required in order for an individual to be able to successfully do a particular job

Business necessity When a particular practice is necessary for the safe and efficient operation of the business and when there is a specific business purpose for applying a particular standard that may, in fact, be discriminatory

Job relatedness When a test for employment is a legitimate measure of an individual's ability to do the essential functions of a job

Job relatedness is shown *when a test for employment is a legitimate measure of an individual's ability to do the essential functions of a job.* For job relatedness to act as a defense against a charge of discrimination, it first has to be a business necessity, and then the employer must be able to show that the test for the employment action was a legitimate (valid) measure of an individual's ability to do the job.[20]

3.1 APPLYING THE CONCEPT

BFOQ

State if each of the following would or wouldn't meet the test of a BFOQ:

a. It is a legal BFOQ

b. It is NOT a legal BFOQ

_____ 1. For the job of modeling women's clothing, applicants must be female.

_____ 2. For a job of loading packages onto trucks to be delivered, applicants must be able to lift 35 pounds.

_____ 3. For the job of teaching business at a Catholic college, applicants must be practicing Catholics.

_____ 4. For the job of attendant in a men's locker facility at a gym, applicants must be male.

_____ 5. For the job of a guard in a prison with male inmates, applicants must be men.

Age Discrimination in Employment Act of 1967 (ADEA)

The ADEA prohibits discrimination against employees age 40 or older, so it added the "protected class" of *age*. In this case, it applies if the organization has 20 or more workers instead of 15. The wording of this act almost exactly mirrors Title VII with the exception of the 20-worker minimum. This mirroring of the 1964 CRA is true of nearly all of the protected class discrimination laws that came about after 1964. **(SHRM D:2)**

Vietnam Era Veterans Readjustment Assistance Act of 1974 (VEVRAA)

This act again provides basically the same protection as the CRA does, but for Vietnam veterans. However, it only applies to federal contractors. It requires that "employers with federal contracts or subcontracts of $100,000 or more provide equal opportunity *and* affirmative action for Vietnam era veterans, special disabled veterans, and veterans who served on active duty during a war or in a campaign or expedition for which a campaign badge has been authorized."[21]

Pregnancy Discrimination Act of 1978 (PDA)

The PDA prohibits discrimination against women affected by pregnancy, childbirth, or related medical conditions as unlawful sex discrimination under Title VII and requires that they be treated as all other employees for employment-related purposes, including benefits.[22] Again, this law is mandatory for companies with 15 or more employees, including employment agencies, labor organizations, and state and local governments. **(SHRM D:19)**

Americans with Disabilities Act of 1990 (ADA), as Amended in 2008

Disability A physical or mental impairment that substantially limits one or more major life activities, a record of having such an impairment, or being regarded as having such an impairment

The ADA is one of the most significant employment laws ever passed in the United States. It prohibits discrimination based on disability in all employment practices, and applies to virtually *all* employers with 15 or more employees in the same basic ways as the CRA of 1964 does. The ADA defines a **disability** as *a physical or mental impairment that substantially limits one or more major life activities, a record of having such an impairment, or being regarded as having such an impairment.*[23] **(SHRM D:3, D:38-c, J:9, and D:40)**

What does the ADA require of employers? An organization must make "reasonable accommodations" to the physical or mental limitations of an individual with a disability who was otherwise qualified to perform the "essential functions" of the job, unless it would impose an "undue hardship" on the organization's operation.[24]

A **reasonable accommodation** is *an accommodation made by an employer to allow someone who is disabled but otherwise qualified to do the essential functions of a job to be able to perform that job.* Reasonable accommodations are usually inexpensive and easy to implement. For example, if a job requires that the employee use a computer keyboard and a blind individual applies for that job, the organization can make a reasonable accommodation by purchasing a Braille keyboard. In this case, Braille keyboards are inexpensive and provide the blind individual with the ability to do the job based on the reasonable accommodation provided.

In defining reasonable accommodations, we have to distinguish between "essential" and "marginal" job functions. **Essential functions** are *the fundamental duties of the position.* Based on many court decisions, a function can generally be considered essential if it meets one of the following criteria:

1. The function is something that is done routinely and frequently in the job.

2. The function is done only on occasion, but it is an important part of the job.

3. The function may never be performed by the employee, but if it were necessary, it would be critical that it be done right.

Marginal job functions, on the other hand, are *those functions that may be performed on the job but need not be performed by all holders of the job.* Individuals with disabilities *cannot* be denied employment if they cannot perform marginal job functions.[25]

Under the ADA, employers are:[26]

- Not required to make reasonable accommodations if the applicant or employee does not request it;

- Not required to make reasonable accommodations if applicants don't meet required qualifications for a job;

- Not required to lower quality standards or provide personal use items such as glasses or hearing aids to make reasonable accommodations; and

- Not required to make reasonable accommodations if to do so would be an undue hardship.

An **undue hardship** exists *when the level of difficulty for an organization to provide accommodations, determined by looking at the nature and cost of the accommodation and the overall financial resources of the facility, becomes a significant burden on the organization.* However, an undue hardship may be different for different companies. For instance, a small company may have an undue burden based on a relatively low-cost accommodation to a disabled individual, while a larger company could not claim undue hardship for the same accommodation.

The biggest problem that employers have with the ADA is the fact that it contains a number of words and phrases that can be interpreted in different ways. A 2008 amendment to the original law—the ADAAA—clarified some of the terms in the act,[27] but the law is still difficult to interpret and follow. Because of these poorly defined terms, companies have had a difficult time in applying the ADA in a consistent manner, and as a result, they have quite likely been involved in more lawsuits per disabled employee than with any other protected group.[28]

Civil Rights Act of 1991

The CRA of 1991 was enacted as an amendment designed to correct a few major omissions of the 1964 CRA as well as to overturn several U.S. court decisions.[29] One of the major changes in the amendment was the addition of compensatory and punitive damages in cases of intentional discrimination under Title VII and the ADA, when intentional or reckless discrimination is proven. **Compensatory damages** are *monetary damages awarded by the court that compensate the injured person for losses.* Such losses can include future pecuniary loss (potential future

Reasonable accommodation An accommodation made by an employer to allow someone who is disabled but otherwise qualified to do the essential functions of a job to be able to perform that job

Essential functions The fundamental duties of the position

Marginal job functions Those functions that may be performed on the job but need not be performed by all holders of the job

Undue hardship When the level of difficulty for an organization to provide accommodations, determined by looking at the nature and cost of the accommodation and the overall financial resources of the facility, becomes a significant burden on the organization

Compensatory damages Monetary damages awarded by the court that compensate the injured person for losses

monetary losses like loss of earnings capacity), emotional pain, suffering, and loss of enjoyment of life. **Punitive damages** are *monetary damages awarded by the court that are designed to punish an injuring party that has intentionally inflicted harm on others*. They are meant to discourage employers from intentionally discriminating, and they do this by providing for payments to the plaintiff beyond the actual damages suffered.

However, the act also provides for a sliding scale of upper limits or "caps" on the combined amount of compensatory and punitive damages based on the number of employees employed by the employer. The limitations are shown in Exhibit 3.5.[30]

Another major area in which the 1991 act changed the original CRA is in the application of quotas for protected group members. Quotas were made explicitly illegal by the 1991 act. The act also prohibits "discriminatory use" of test scores, which is commonly called race norming. **Race norming** exists *when different groups of people have different scores designated as "passing" grades on a test for employment*. The 1991 act basically equated this with quotas and, as such, made it illegal.[31]

EXHIBIT 3.5 ● Caps on Compensatory and Punitive Damages by Employer Size

Employer Size	Caps on Damages
15 to 100 employees	$ 50,000
101 to 200 employees	$100,000
201 to 500 employees	$200,000
501 employees or more	$300,000

3.1 ETHICAL DILEMMA: WHAT WOULD YOU DO?

The United States was once known as the "melting pot," as people from all over the world came to the country and adjusted to its culture. In the past, generally, immigrants had to learn English to get a job. Today, however, many organizations hire people who can't speak English, and they use translators and have policies written in multiple languages for these employees. Government agencies at the federal, state, and local levels are also providing translators and written materials in other languages.

1. Why are some organizations no longer requiring workers to speak English?

2. Should a worker be required to be able to speak English to get a job in the United States?

3. Is it ethical to (or not to) hire people who can't speak English and to provide translators and policies written in multiple languages?

Uniformed Services Employment and Reemployment Rights Act of 1994 (USERRA)

USERRA was passed to ensure the civilian reemployment rights of military members who were called away from their regular (nonmilitary) jobs by U.S. government orders. Unlike other EEO laws, there is no minimum number of employees required for coverage by USERRA.[32] Per the U.S. Department of Labor, "USERRA is intended to minimize the disadvantages to an individual that occur when that person needs to be absent from his or her civilian employment to serve in this country's uniformed services. USERRA makes major improvements in protecting service member rights and benefits by clarifying the law and improving enforcement mechanisms."[33] **(SHRM D:23)**

USERRA covers virtually every individual in the country who serves or has served in the uniformed services, and it applies to all employers in the public and private sectors, including federal employers. It also provides protection for disabled veterans, requiring employers to make reasonable efforts to accommodate their disabilities.[34] Under USERRA, the employee returning from military service is not only entitled to the job that they had when they left, but they are entitled to any "escalation," or any job or pay/benefits increase they would have attained, if they had not been called away.[35]

Veterans Benefits Improvement Act of 2004 (VBIA)

The VBIA is an amendment to USERRA. It extended the requirement for employers to maintain health care coverage for employees who were serving on active duty in the military (originally, this period was 18 months, but the VBIA changed it to 2 years), and it also required employers to post a notice of benefits, duties, and rights under USERRA/VBIA.[36]

▲ The Uniformed Services Employment and Reemployment Rights Act (USERRA) was passed in 1994. This measure protects military members from losing their civilian jobs should they be called away by U.S. government orders.

Title II of the Genetic Information Nondiscrimination Act of 2008 (GINA)

Title II of the Genetic Information Nondiscrimination Act of 2008 (GINA) "prohibits the use of genetic information in employment, prohibits the intentional acquisition of genetic information about applicants and employees, and imposes strict confidentiality requirements."[37] **(SHRM D:11)**

Because companies were starting to use genetic tests to make employment and health care decisions, Congress decided to address their use so that the general public would not fear adverse employment-related or health coverage–related consequences for having a genetic test or participating in research studies that examine genetic information.[38] The result was GINA.

Lilly Ledbetter Fair Pay Act of 2009 (LLFPA)

This law amended Title VII of the 1964 CRA. In practical terms, the LLFPA extends the period of time in which an employee is allowed to file a lawsuit for compensation (pay) discrimination. The 1964 CRA only allowed 180 days from the time of the discriminatory action for an individual employee to file a lawsuit. The LLFPA allows an individual to file a lawsuit within 180 days after "any application" of that discriminatory compensation decision, including every time the individual gets paid, as long as the discrimination is continuing, which would usually be for the entire period of their employment. **(SHRM D:16)**

3.2 APPLYING THE CONCEPT
EMPLOYMENT LAWS

Review the laws listed below and then write the letter corresponding to each law before the statement(s) describing a situation where that law would apply.

a. Equal Pay

b. Title VII CRA 1964

c. ADEA

d. VEVRAA

e. PDA

f. ADA

(Continued)

(Continued)

g. CRA 1991

h. USERRA

i. VBIA

j. GINA

k. LLFPA

_____ 6. I had to take a medical test, and the company found out that I am at high risk to get cancer. So it decided not to hire me, so it could save money on medical insurance.

_____ 7. Although I was the best qualified, I was intentionally not promoted because I am a woman.

_____ 8. I can't understand why this firm doesn't want to hire me just because I served my country. I didn't want to go and fight overseas, but I was drafted into the army in 1969 and had no choice; I didn't want to go to jail for draft evasion.

_____ 9. My boss is laying me off because I serve in the National Guard and will be deployed overseas for 6 months. As a result, I will have to find a new job when I get back.

_____ 10. The firm is laying me off to hire some younger person to save money. Is this what I deserve for my 20 years of dedication?

_____ 11. I'm being paid less than the men who do the same jobs, just because I'm a woman.

_____ 12. The firm hired this new guy and bought a special low desk because he is so short.

_____ 13. I'm suing the firm for lost wages because they intentionally discriminated against me and fired me when I complained about it.

Equal Employment Opportunity Commission (EEOC)

>> **LO 3.3 Briefly discuss the major functions of the Equal Employment Opportunity Commission (EEOC).**

The various federal equal employment opportunity (EEO) laws are enforced by the Equal Employment Opportunity Commission (EEOC). The EEOC is a federal agency that has significant power over employers in the process of investigating complaints of illegal discrimination.[39]

What Does the EEOC Do?

The EEOC has three significant responsibilities: (1) investigating and resolving discrimination complaints through either conciliation or litigation, (2) gathering and compiling statistical information on such complaints, and (3) running education and outreach programs on what constitutes illegal discrimination.[40] Additionally, every company with more than 100 employees or with more than 50 employees *and* with federal contracts totalling $50,000 or more must file an EEO-1 Report with the EEOC each year.[41] The EEO-1 identifies the company's EEO compliance data based on protected classifications within federal law. **(SHRM D:34)**

Deadlines for filing complaints vary widely, but generally, a discrimination complaint must be filed with the EEOC within 180 days of the date of discrimination. If the EEOC determines that discrimination has taken place, it will attempt to provide reconciliation between the parties. If the EEOC cannot come to an agreement with the organization, there are two options:

1. The agency may aid the alleged victim in bringing suit in federal court.

2. It can issue a "right-to-sue" letter to the alleged victim. A **right-to-sue** is *a notice from the EEOC, issued if it elects not to prosecute an individual discrimination complaint within the agency, that gives the recipient the right to go directly to the courts with the complaint.*

Right-to-sue A notice from the EEOC, issued if it elects not to prosecute an individual discrimination complaint within the agency, that gives the recipient the right to go directly to the courts with the complaint.

Other EEOC Enforcement Actions

The EEOC and other federal agencies have begun to act directly against companies in many cases without a complaint being filed when they suspect systemic discrimination.[42] *Systemic discrimination* (23% of EEOC's active cases in 2013)[43] is defined by the EEOC as "a pattern or practice, policy, or class case where the alleged discrimination has a broad impact on an industry, profession, company, or geographic area."[44] In one year alone, more than 300 systemic investigations resulted in 63 settlements or conciliation agreements worth more than $40 million.[45]

Employee Rights Under the EEOC

Employees have the right to bring discrimination complaints against their employer by filing a complaint with the EEOC. They also have the right to participate in an EEOC investigation, hearing, or other proceeding without threat of retaliation; rights related to the arbitration and settlement of the complaint; and the right to sue the employer directly in court over claims of illegal discrimination, even if the EEOC does not support their claim. For information on how to submit a written complaint, go to the EEOC website (http://www.eeoc.gov). **(SHRM J:5)**

Reality. The majority of workplace harassment cases are never reported because employees fear retaliation. A **LegalZoom** survey found that just 25% of workers believe their employers quickly and effectively resolve workplace issues.[46]

Employer Rights and Prohibitions

The employer has a right to defend the organization using the defenses noted earlier: BFOQ, business necessity, and job relatedness. However, the employer does not have a right to *retaliate* against individuals who participate in an EEOC action. The employer also is prohibited from creating a work environment that would lead to charges of *constructive discharge*.

Retaliation

In addition to providing defenses against discrimination claims, the 1964 Civil Rights Act identifies a situation in which organizations can be held liable for harming the employee because of retaliation.[47] **Retaliation** is *a situation where the organization takes an "adverse employment action" against an employee because the employee brought discrimination charges against the organization or supported someone who brought discrimination charges against the company.* An **adverse employment action** is *any action such as firings, demotions, schedule reductions, or changes that would harm the individual employee.* Each of the EEO laws identifies retaliation as illegal harassment based on the protected class identified within that law.

Managers need to be aware that there are severe penalties for engaging in retaliation against an employee or applicant for participating in protected activity. In 2017, almost 50% of all EEOC complaints had a retaliation claim as at least a component of the complaint.[48]

> **Retaliation** A situation where the organization takes an "adverse employment action" against an employee because the employee brought discrimination charges against the organization or supported someone who brought discrimination charges against the company

> **Adverse employment action** Any action such as firings, demotions, schedule reductions, or changes that would harm the individual employee

Constructive Discharge

The organization can also be accused of "constructive discharge" due to discriminatory actions on the job. **Constructive discharge** exists *when an employee is put under such extreme pressure by management that continued employment becomes intolerable and, as a result, the employee quits, or resigns from, the organization.* In a 2004 decision,[49] the Supreme Court noted that the U.S. Court of Appeals had identified constructive discharge as "(1) he or she suffered harassment or discrimination so intolerable that a reasonable person in the same position would have felt compelled to resign . . . ; and (2) the employee's reaction to the workplace situation—that is, his or her decision to resign—was reasonable given the totality of circumstances."

If an individual can show that constructive discharge caused them to resign from the organization, then the individual would be eligible for all employee rights associated with being involuntarily terminated from the company.

> **Constructive discharge** When an employee is put under such extreme pressure by management that continued employment becomes intolerable and, as a result, the employee quits, or resigns from, the organization

HR Leadership

Some 75% of employees don't believe their employers are quick and effective at dealing with workplace issues and they fear retaliation for complaining.[50] Ignoring complaints, not taking corrective action to correct problems, cover-ups, and retaliation often lead to lower productivity. So, a major challenge for HR staff with limited resources is to help create a culture without fear of retaliation that resolves worker issues in a timely manner. We'll tell you how to deal with complaints in Chapter 9.

Discrimination is a significant factor in holding both women and minorities back from the top jobs.[51] The United States has the EEOC to handle legal charges of sex-based discrimination. However, despite legislative remedies, they haven't made much progress in the United States.[52]

We can't expect the EEOC to create equal opportunity for all. To bring about equality, HR must lead the way following the laws and guidelines throughout this book and assist all managers in truly creating equal opportunities for all. Creating equal opportunity for all and selecting the best qualified person for the position isn't only the right ethical thing to do, it increases individual productivity and the organization's productivity. We will discuss how to manage diversity and inclusion in Chapter 13 to create equal opportunity for all.

Sexual Harassment

>> **LO 3.4 Compare the two primary types of sexual harassment.**

Sexual harassment is included as part of the 1964 CRA (the prohibition of discrimination based on sex), but it is one of the two items we mentioned earlier in the chapter that was not specifically recognized as a separate type of discrimination until federal courts started hearing cases on the act. Sexual harassment is a pervasive issue in organizations, as illustrated by the sheer number of cases identified in the "#MeToo" movement,[53] so we need to understand what it is and how to avoid creating a situation where it can occur at work. **(SHRM D:38a)**

Types of Sexual Harassment

Defined by the EEOC, **sexual harassment** is *unwelcome sexual advances, requests for sexual favors, and other verbal or physical conduct of a sexual nature when submission to or rejection of this conduct explicitly or implicitly affects an individual's employment, unreasonably interferes with an individual's work performance, or creates an intimidating, hostile, or offensive work environment.*[54] There are two types of sexual harassment specifically delineated in law: quid pro quo harassment and hostile work environment. Both are discussed below.

Quid Pro Quo Harassment

Literally, quid pro quo means "this for that." **Quid pro quo harassment** is *harassment that occurs when some type of benefit or punishment is made contingent upon the employee submitting to sexual advances.* "If you do something sexual for me, I will do something for you." Quid pro quo is a direct form of harassment aimed at an individual and is most commonly seen in supervisor–subordinate relationships, although this is not always the case. It is, however, based on the power of one individual over another. Hollywood producer **Harvey Weinstein** has been accused of being one of the more notorious quid pro quo harassers of young actresses trying to get parts in big-budget films, and he will most likely go to prison because of such harassment.

Hostile Work Environment

Hostile work environment is *harassment that occurs when someone's behavior at work creates an environment that is sexual in nature and that makes it difficult for someone of a particular sex to work in that environment.* Hostile work environment sexual harassment happens when a "reasonable person" determines that the behavior in question goes beyond normal human interaction and the jokes and kidding that accompany such interaction, instead rising to a level that such a reasonable person would consider the act or acts to be both harassing and sexual in nature.[55] For the purposes of the law, a **reasonable person** is *the "average" person who would look at the situation and its intensity to determine whether the accused person was wrong in their actions.*

Sexual harassment Unwelcome sexual advances, requests for sexual favors, and other verbal or physical conduct of a sexual nature when submission to or rejection of this conduct explicitly or implicitly affects an individual's employment, unreasonably interferes with an individual's work performance, or creates an intimidating, hostile, or offensive work environment

Quid pro quo harassment Harassment that occurs when some type of benefit or punishment is made contingent upon the employee submitting to sexual advances

Hostile work environment Harassment that occurs when someone's behavior at work creates an environment that is sexual in nature and that makes it difficult for someone of a particular sex to work in that environment

Reasonable person The "average" person who would look at the situation and its intensity to determine whether the accused person was wrong in their actions

What Constitutes Sexual Harassment?

Sexual harassment does not have to occur between a male and female or between a supervisor and subordinates. Same-sex harassment and female-to-male harassment also occur at work.[56]

As in other forms of illegal discrimination, the plaintiff only has to show a prima facie (literally "on the face of it," meaning it looks like harassment to a reasonable person) case that harassment has occurred. To qualify as a prima facie case of sexual harassment, the work situation must include the following characteristics:[57]

1. The plaintiff is a member of a protected class;

2. The harassment was based on sex;

3. The person was subject to unwelcome sexual advances; *or*

4. The harassment was sufficiently severe enough to alter the terms, conditions, or privileges of employment.

In order for the organization to be considered for liability, two critical conditions must exist:[58]

1. The plaintiff did not solicit or incite the advances.

2. The harassment was undesirable, and was severe enough to alter the terms, conditions, and privileges of employment.

Filing Complaints and HR's Response

One thing many employees don't know, and need to, is that the Supreme Court determined that in order to get legal recourse, employees have to first file harassment complaints with the HR department.[59] HR needs to develop and make the policies and process of filing a complaint clear to all employees. If the employee is not satisfied with any investigation and action taken by the organization, then they can take the complaint to the EEOC and courts.

Is It Really Sexual Harassment?

In some situations, sexual harassment is clear and one offense is too many (such as quid pro quo harassment) and should be reported to the HR department. However, there is a lot of gray area, such as asking to go out on a date, sexual talk and pictures, and telling dirty jokes. To some employees, these behaviors are welcome; but to others, these behaviors can be considered a hostile work environment.

In these situations, where you feel as if you are being sexually harassed, you should clearly tell the person not to repeat the behavior because it is sexual harassment and that you will report them if they do it again. If the behavior is repeated, file the complaint with HR. Applying the Concept 3.3 can help you better understand what is and isn't sexual harassment.

HR Disciplinary Action and Cover-Ups

To avoid EEOC complaints and lawsuits, HR needs to do a good job of investigating the complaint and disciplining in a timely manner. However, this does not always happen. The University of Michigan took no action for years to stop its Olympic physician, **Dr. Larry Nassar**, from sexually abusing hundreds of young gymnasts. Fox's **Roger Ailes** and **Bill O'Reilly** had their alleged sexual harassment complaints repeatedly covered up by confidentiality provisions in settlement agreements and alleged multimillion-dollar payoffs.

You shouldn't give high performers a pass to keep them. Could you live with yourself knowing you allowed sexual assault and harassment to happen and continue to negatively affect the lives of others? No one should have to be uncomfortable at work because of sexual harassment.

3.3 APPLYING THE CONCEPT

SEXUAL HARASSMENT

Write the letter and number codes listed below before each statement to indicate the kind of behavior it describes.

a. Sexual harassment: After the harassment letter, write in if it is (1) quid pro quo or (2) hostile work environment harassment (i.e., write a/1 or a/2).

b. Not sexual harassment

_____ 14. Karen tells her coworker Jim an explicitly sexual joke, even though twice before, Jim told her not to tell him any dirty jokes.

_____ 15. Ricky-Joe typically puts his hand on his secretary's shoulder as he talks to her, and she is comfortable with this behavior.

_____ 16. José, the supervisor, tells his secretary, Latoya, that he'd like to take her out for the first time today.

_____ 17. Cindy tells her assistant, Juan, that he will have to go to a motel with her if he wants to be recommended for a promotion.

_____ 18. Jack and Jill have each hung up pictures of nude men and women on the walls near their desks, in view of other employees who walk by.

_____ 19. As coworker Rachel talks to Carlos, he is surprised and uncomfortable because she gently rubbed his buttock.

_____ 20. Hank and some of the other guys regularly come over to Jean's desk and look down at her breast as they make small talk.

Reducing Organizational Risk From Sexual Harassment Lawsuits

The HR department has the responsibility of educating employees about how to avoid, and how to report, sexual harassment. They also need to investigate the offense and take action to stop the behavior, punish offenders, and prevent future harassment. Many HR departments require all employees to complete a sexual harassment training course and pass a test, often online. Exhibit 3.6 shows five important steps to follow to avoid sexual harassment liability.[60]

Unfortunately, we sometimes end up in court over harassment allegations. Once the plaintiff has shown a prima facie case supporting the accusation, the courts will determine whether the organization is liable for the actions of its employee based on the answers to two primary questions:

1. Did the employer know about, or should the employer have known about, the harassment?

2. Did the employer act to stop the behavior?

EXHIBIT 3.6 ● Limiting Organizational Liability for Sexual Harassment

1. Develop a policy statement making it clear that sexual harassment will not be tolerated. You have to delineate what is acceptable and what is not. The policy should also state that anyone participating in a sexual harassment complaint or investigation should not be retaliated against.

2. Communicate the policy by training all employees to identify inappropriate workplace behavior. Make sure that everyone is aware of the policy.

3. Develop a mechanism for reporting sexual harassment that encourages people to speak out. It is critical in this case to create a mechanism outside of the normal chain of command. The typical case of harassment is between an individual and the immediate supervisor. Because of this, if the organization does not have a way to report the behavior outside the normal supervisory chain of command, the courts will consider that the company does not have a mechanism for reporting.

4. Ensure that just cause procedures (we will talk about these in Chapter 9) are followed when investigating the complaint.

5. Prepare to carry out prompt disciplinary action against those who commit sexual harassment.

In general, if the employer knew or should have known about the harassment and did nothing to stop the behavior, then the employer can be held liable. Sexual harassment should be treated very seriously, because the consequences can be grave for the organization if managers don't do what they should to prevent the harassment. **Weinstein**'s company declared bankruptcy just a few months after his first accusers came forward.[61]

Religious Discrimination

>> **LO 3.5 Briefly discuss the employer's requirements concerning avoidance of religious discrimination in the workplace.**

This chapter's topics include employment laws related to discrimination. The major groups that are protected against discrimination by (law) include *age* (ADEA law), *gender* (equal pay, CRA, sexual harassment), *race and ethnicity* (CRA), *disability* (ADA), and *religion* (CRA). The last one we haven't given basic coverage is religion, which we do in this section. A newer, still evolving group of *sexual orientation and gender identity* protection and discrimination will be discussed in the Trends and Issues section.

Religion-based discrimination and the ability of employers to create work rules that may affect religious freedom continues to be an issue in the workplace.[62] The issue of standards of dress in a number of religions, most notably Islam's standards for women's attire in public (including the hijab, niqab, and burqa), has become a point of contention in some workplaces. If an employer sees the niqab as a symbol of repression, can the employer deny the right to wear such head coverings and use the antidiscrimination statutes concerning gender as justification? Can an employer require drivers that work for them to deliver alcohol to customer warehouses when the drivers may have a religious opposition to drinking alcohol?[63]

Religion is generally a less obvious characteristic than gender or race, though, and it is usually not a characteristic on which we base decisions. However, if a person's religion requires a certain type of dress, or observation of religious holidays or days of worship that are not in keeping with the normal workday practices of the organization, and if the individual requests accommodation for these religious beliefs, then we generally would need to make every reasonable effort to accommodate such requests. Employers are required to provide such a "reasonable accommodation" for requests that are based on "employees' sincerely held religious beliefs or practices, unless doing so would impose an 'undue hardship' on their business operations."[64]

There are many religious freedom questions that we are dealing with in companies today, and there are certainly no easy answers. However, HR and line managers should clearly describe the job and working days and hours required. If the employee agrees to accept the job described, they are required to do the job. So, if the employee refuses to deliver alcohol or work specific, agreed-upon hours to attend religious services, they are not performing their job, which is grounds for dismissal. But, to promote diversity and inclusion, and to fill jobs with qualified employees, many companies accommodate religious requests as much as possible. **(SHRM D:38-b and J:12)**

▲
Religion is identified as a protected class in the 1964 Civil Rights Act, meaning that an employer cannot consider an individual's religion when making employment decisions.

©iStockphoto.com/JohnnyGreig

Trends and Issues in HRM

We again end this chapter with two significant issues affecting HRM. These issues include information on sexual orientation discrimination and a brief discussion on using technology blindly when taking employment actions.

Sexual Orientation and Gender Identity Discrimination

Is sexual orientation discrimination illegal? That depends on who you ask. As of early 2017, two federal appeals courts had provided rulings which said that sexual orientation was not explicitly prohibited under Title VII of the 1964 Civil Rights Act. In fact, "Federal courts have by an overwhelming margin refused to apply Title VII to claims of sexual orientation discrimination."[65] **(SHRM J:6)**

However, at the same time, the EEOC—the federal agency charged with investigating claims of discrimination—has stated that sexual orientation or gender identity discrimination is a form of sex discrimination, and many experts in HR law are recommending to companies that they not participate in any discrimination based on sexual orientation or gender identity for solid business reasons. It also appears as if business has listened and is willing to provide equity and fairness to all of their employees to the best of their collective abilities. According to the Corporate Equality Index from the Human Rights Campaign Foundation, as of 2017, 92% of the Fortune 500 firms include sexual orientation in their nondiscrimination policies and 82% include gender identity.[66] There are also other outside pressures on business that have increased the willingness of organizations to provide equity to all employees.

Remember that states and even cities have the ability to make laws concerning equal opportunity and fairness in the workplace. According to the Society for Human Resource Management (SHRM):[67]

- 22 states and the District of Columbia prohibit discrimination relating to sexual orientation.

- 19 states and the District of Columbia prohibit discrimination in private and public employment related to gender identity.

- More than 255 local municipalities provide protections in private and public employment against discrimination based on sexual orientation and/or gender identity.

In this situation, as in so many other issues of potential bias in hiring, it just does not make sense to discriminate. Logic says that if we artificially remove the people of any group from consideration for employment (including promotion and all other employment actions), we are almost certain to be removing some of the best qualified individuals from the candidate pool. With significant shortages of skilled employees in almost every area of work, this is simply foolish and will harm the organization in its ability to field the best talent on a daily basis. So even though the issue has not been determined in court or in Congress, it just makes sense to treat all individuals the same—and it's the right thing to do.

Technology May Create New Dangers in Equal Opportunity and Diversity Management

Many people in today's workforce have grown up with the idea that technology will solve all of their problems. However, if this is the case, then why are virtually *all* major technology companies being criticized over their lack of diversity? A quick Internet search shows that **Qualcomm** settled a gender-bias lawsuit for $19.5 million in 2016[68] while **HP** was accused of age-bias the same year.[69] "**Airbnb**, **Uber**, and **Lyft** were all accused of discrimination against black customers trying to book lodging and hail rides."[70] **Yahoo** was accused of gender bias against men, and **Palantir** of bias against Asian engineers. And this is all just in 2016. In 2017, **Google** was accused of systematically underpaying female employees, as was **Oracle**. And **Susan Fowler**, an engineer for **Uber**, filed a rather lurid sexual harassment claim against the company.[71]

What is going on? **Google**, for example, is known for trying to take the bias out of hiring by creating algorithms to identify candidates for employment. But how do the algorithms get created? By looking at successful past hires that are overwhelmingly white males and trying to identify commonalities among those hiring successes. This method would almost have to create a bias, unless the researchers made a concerted effort to take any factors that correlated with gender, age, ethnicity, race, and multiple other bias categories out of the equations. A reasonably new concept of "candidate personas" is being used in creating many of these algorithms. Notes one HR technology provider, "the easiest way to begin a candidate persona is to research the people who have been hired before in the role,"[72] but such a beginning may knock out people who haven't had the opportunity to walk a particular path at work and therefore can never meet the ideal candidate requirements. Technology has a tendency to make these problems even more significant than having a manager hire new employees based on their opinion, because biases are now built in to the system that then throws out all of the candidates who are not ideal. In *Weapons of Math Destruction: How Big Data Increases Inequality and Threatens Democracy,* author Cathy O'Neil says that these algorithms are "ticking time-bombs that are well-intended but ultimately reinforce harmful stereotypes."[73]

What does a great HR manager need to do? First, you need to understand that just because a candidate pool was generated by a computer does not mean that it is unbiased. Remember the "garbage-in, garbage-out" rule of computing. Second, analyze the inputs to the algorithm (assuming it was designed by your company or you can get the input information from the firm that did design it). Look for implicit biases in the input data. Finally, test the candidate pools that result from such algorithms against the OUCH test, and specifically against the four-fifths rule, to look for disparate impact.[74]

Chapter Summary

3.1 Identify the four components of the OUCH test by describing when it is useful in an organizational setting.

The OUCH test is a rule of thumb you should use whenever you are contemplating any employment action. You use it to maintain equity for all of your employees or applicants. **OUCH** is an acronym that stands for **O**bjective, **U**niform in application, **C**onsistent in effect, and **H**as job relatedness. An employment action should generally be objective instead of subjective; we should apply all employment tests the same way, every time, with everyone, to the best of our ability; the employment action should not have an inconsistent effect on any protected groups; and the test must be directly related to the job to which we are applying it.

3.2 Discuss the major equal employment opportunity (EEO) laws specifying the groups of people each law protects.

The Equal Pay Act of 1963 requires that women be paid equal to men if they are doing the same work.

The Civil Rights Act of 1964 prohibits discrimination on the basis of race, color, religion, sex, or national origin, in all areas of the employment relationship.

The Age Discrimination in Employment Act of 1967 prohibits age discrimination against people 40 years of age or older, and it restricts mandatory retirement.

The Vietnam Era Veterans Readjustment Assistance Act of 1974 prohibits discrimination against Vietnam veterans by all employers with federal contracts or subcontracts of $100,000 or more. It also requires that affirmative action be taken.

The Pregnancy Discrimination Act of 1978 prohibits discrimination against women affected by pregnancy, childbirth, or related medical conditions, and it treats such discrimination as unlawful sex discrimination.

The Americans with Disabilities Act of 1990 requires employers to provide "reasonable accommodations" to allow disabled employees to work.

The Civil Rights Act of 1991 strengthened civil rights by providing for possible compensatory and punitive damages for discrimination.

The Uniformed Services Employment and Reemployment Rights Act (USERRA) ensures the civilian reemployment rights of military members who were called away from their regular (nonmilitary) jobs by U.S. government orders.

The Veterans Benefits Improvement Act of 2004 amends USERRA to extend health care coverage while away on duty, and it requires employers to post a notice of benefits, duties, and rights of reemployment.

The Genetic Information Nondiscrimination Act of 2008 prohibits the use of genetic information in employment, prohibits intentional acquisition of the same, and imposes confidentiality requirements.

The Lilly Ledbetter Fair Pay Act of 2009 amends the 1964 CRA to extend the period of time in which an employee is allowed to file a lawsuit over pay discrimination.

3.3 Briefly discuss the major functions of the Equal Employment Opportunity Commission (EEOC).

The EEOC is a federal agency that investigates complaints of illegal discrimination based on race, color, religion, sex (including pregnancy), national origin, age (40 or older), disability, or genetic information.

The EEOC has three significant functions: investigating and resolving discrimination complaints through either conciliation or litigation, gathering and compiling statistical information on such complaints, and running education and outreach programs on what constitutes illegal discrimination.

3.4 Compare the two primary types of sexual harassment.

Quid pro quo harassment occurs when some type of benefit or punishment is made contingent upon the employee submitting to sexual advances. In other words, if you do something for me, I will do something for you, or conversely, if you refuse to do something for me, I will harm you.

Hostile work environment harassment occurs when someone's behavior at work creates an environment that is sexual in nature and makes it difficult for someone of a particular sex to work in that environment. Hostile environment sexual harassment happens when a "reasonable person" would determine that the environment went beyond normal human interactions and the jokes and kidding that go with those interactions and rose to the level that such a reasonable person would consider the act or acts to be both harassing and sexual in nature.

3.5 Briefly discuss the employer's requirements concerning avoidance of religious discrimination in the workplace.

Religion is one of the identified protected classes in the 1964 Civil Rights Act. As such, we can't use it as a factor in making "any employment decision" with our employees. Issues such as standards of dress, time off for religious holidays, adherence to strongly held religious beliefs, and other questions of religious freedom should be accommodated to the best of our ability to avoid inadvertent violation of the law.

Key Terms

adverse employment action, 67
bona fide occupational
    qualification (BFOQ), 61
business necessity, 61
compensatory damages, 63
constructive discharge, 67
disability, 62
discrimination, 56
disparate impact, 61
disparate treatment, 61

essential functions, 63
Four-Fifths Rule, 57
hostile work environment, 68
illegal discrimination, 56
job relatedness, 62
marginal job functions, 63
OUCH test, 56
pattern or practice
    discrimination, 61
punitive damages, 64

quid pro quo harassment, 68
race norming, 64
reasonable accommodation, 63
reasonable person, 68
retaliation, 67
right-to-sue, 66
sexual harassment, 68
undue hardship, 63

Key Terms Review

Complete each of the following statements using one of this chapter's key terms.

1. _____ is the act of making distinctions or choosing one thing over another; in HR, it is distinctions among people.

2. _____ is making distinctions that harm people by using a person's membership in a protected class.

3. _____ is a rule of thumb used whenever you are contemplating any employment action,

to maintain fairness and equity for all of your employees or applicants.

4. _____ is a test used by various federal courts, the Department of Labor, and the EEOC to determine whether disparate impact exists in an employment test.

5. _____ exists when individuals in similar situations are intentionally treated differently and the different treatment is based on an individual's membership in a protected class.

6. _____ occurs when an officially neutral employment practice disproportionately excludes the members of a protected group; it is generally considered to be unintentional, but intent is irrelevant.

7. _____ occurs when, over a significant period of time, a person or group engages in a sequence of actions that is intended to deny the rights provided by Title VII (the 1964 CRA) to a member of a protected class.

8. _____ is a qualification that is absolutely required for an individual to successfully do a particular job.

9. _____ exists when a particular practice is necessary for the safe and efficient operation of the business, and when there is a specific business purpose for applying a particular standard that may, in fact, be discriminatory.

10. _____ exists when a test for employment is a legitimate measure of an individual's ability to do the essential functions of a job.

11. _____ is a physical or mental impairment that substantially limits one or more major life activities, a record of having such an impairment, or a condition of being regarded as having such an impairment.

12. _____ is an accommodation made by an employer to allow someone who is disabled but otherwise qualified to do the essential functions of a job to be able to perform that job.

13. _____ consist of the fundamental duties of the position.

14. _____ are those functions that may be performed on the job but need not be performed by all holders of the job.

15. _____ occurs when the level of difficulty for an organization to provide accommodations, determined by looking at the nature and cost of the accommodation and the overall financial resources of the facility, becomes a significant burden on the organization.

16. _____ consist of monetary damages awarded by the court that compensate the person who was injured for their losses.

17. _____ consist of monetary damages awarded by the court that are designed to punish an injuring party that intentionally inflicted harm on others.

18. _____ occurs when different groups of people have different scores designated as "passing" grades on a test for employment.

19. _____ is a notice from the EEOC, if they elect not to prosecute an individual discrimination complaint within the agency, that gives the recipient the right to go directly to the courts with a complaint.

20. _____ is a situation in which the organization takes an "adverse employment action" against an employee because the employee brought discrimination charges against the organization or supported someone who brought discrimination charges against the company.

21. _____ consists of any action such as firings, demotions, schedule reductions, or changes that would harm the individual employee.

22. _____ exists when an employee is put under such extreme pressure by management that continued employment becomes intolerable for the employee and, as a result of the intolerable conditions, the employee resigns from the organization.

23. _____ consists of unwelcome sexual advances, requests for sexual favors, and other verbal or physical conduct of a sexual nature; when submission to or rejection of this conduct explicitly or implicitly affects an individual's employment; unreasonably interferes with an individual's work performance; or creates an intimidating, hostile, or offensive work environment.

24. _____ is harassment that occurs when some type of benefit or punishment is made contingent upon the employee submitting to sexual advances.

25. _____ is harassment that occurs when someone's behavior at work creates an environment that is sexual in nature and makes it difficult for someone of a particular sex to work in that environment.

26. _____ is the "average" person who would look at the situation and its intensity to determine whether the accused person was wrong in their actions.

Communication Skills

The following critical-thinking questions can be used for class discussion and/or for written assignments to develop communication skills. Be sure to give complete explanations for all answers.

1. Do you agree that applying the OUCH test to an employment situation will minimize illegal discrimination? Why or why not?

2. Are there any groups of people in the United States that you think should be covered by federal laws as a protected group but are not currently covered? Why or why not?

3. In your opinion, is most discrimination in the United States unintentional (disparate impact), or is most discrimination intentional (disparate treatment)? Why do you think so?

4. What is your opinion of organizations using bona fide occupational qualifications (BFOQs) to limit who they will consider for a job?

5. Do you agree that most employers probably want to obey the Americans with Disabilities Act but don't know exactly what they are required to do under the law? Do you think that most employers would rather not hire disabled people? Justify your answer.

6. How would you define the terms "reasonable accommodation" and "undue hardship" if you were asked by one of your company managers?

7. Do you think that sexual harassment in the workplace is overreported or underreported? Justify your answer.

Case 3.1 When Religion Is on the Agenda

The Loxedose Company near Chicago transfers computer models into hard physical copies. Computer programmers design the representation, and machines sculpt the product line by line from the bottom to the top by adding levels of materials that adhere and are durable.

Two managers who founded the company celebrate individual and company successes. For example, Founders Day, August 25, features all 30 members of the company (or whoever is available) helping blow out the company birthday cake. Labor Day features a camping trip for those interested, at a manager's cabin at the largest lake in the area. Halloween features most employees wearing a costume, unless they are out on a sales or delivery run. Thanksgiving features a turkey lunch, whether vegetarians like it or not.

The managers believe that everyone should be working together and celebrating together. Accordingly, Christmas is not only a great year-end celebration but also a super holiday party. Traditionally, gifts are exchanged, Christmas carols are sung, and computer-designed trophies are given to the employees with bonus checks attached. Employees have to be present to receive the prizes made from Loxedose computer designs and materials.

This year, Loxedose hired a married couple, Omar and Judy, to be a part of the sales staff. Omar is from Saudi Arabia and is studying at a university in Chicago. His wife is an American who attends the same university.

Judy joined the Islamic faith when she married Omar. She was a Christian early in her life and then was unchurched through many years before she met Omar.

The Christmas party is a mandatory meeting and celebration. Employees have to be there to pick up their trophy along with their $200 bonus check. Whereas Judy was OK with going to the celebration this year, Omar was not because Christmas is a Christian celebration. Judy decided to go to the Christmas party without Omar to pick up Omar's statue along with hers.

The party started just fine with an exchange of presents, a birthday cake for Jesus, and a bunch of thank-yous from top management. When it came to giving out the celebratory statues and money, the managers stated you had to be there to receive these gifts. Omar and Judy were mentioned together so Judy started picking up both statues when the company managers insisted Omar had to be there to receive his statue. Judy protested, saying this gathering was part of a Christmas celebration that was not part of Omar's religion. Omar's statue and money remained at the celebration.

Judy and Omar protested to management that they were discriminating based on religion because the bonus based on performance was distributed through the Christmas party and not offered if the employee didn't attend. All employees should have an equal right to get the bonus. Furthermore, not everyone will always be able to attend the parties because of illnesses, family matters, and other issues.

The managers proposed creating a new employee handbook policy associated with celebrations, awards, and religion. The following choices were suggested in a company meeting:

1. Celebrations within the company are important because they bring the employees together beyond the basic job. Employees will be required to attend Christian celebrations during work hours because that is the dominant religion.

2. Celebrations within the company are important because they bring the employees together beyond the basic job. Employees will be required to attend celebrations unless there are religious reasons or other reasons approved by management.

3. Celebrations within the company are important because they bring the employees together

beyond the basic job. However, no celebrations shall be related to any, or for any, religious holiday, in order to respect the beliefs of those who do not celebrate as such. Anyone missing any party needs prior approval from management.

4. Celebrations within the company are optional. However, rewards will be provided for performance at a December party. If no reward is received at the party, it will be delivered to the employee the next day.

5. No statues or awards will be given at company celebrations. They will be mailed to employees or added to payroll automatically.

Top management strongly opposes the last two proposals because they would actually destroy the effect of providing awards in front of everyone. They prefer the second proposal because everyone would need to contact management and management would have control of who would be at the celebration. Omar and Judy do not like the fact that they would be forced (in Proposal 2) to reject the Christmas party because it is Christian. They much prefer Proposal 3, which eliminates religion-related celebrations. Top management does not like Proposal 3 because it thinks religion-based celebrations are an important part of life.

Questions

1. Does the current policy pass the OUCH test?

2. Does management have a legal defense to discriminate by requiring attendance at religious-based events? Which defense is management using for keeping the policy?

3. Which employment law or laws does this case involve? How would the law(s) that you identified apply in this case?

4. Which employee handbook proposal should the company incorporate (if any) and why?

5. How effective in the company's culture is giving out awards in front of everyone else?

6. Should religious parties be optional? Mandatory? Offered? Not offered?

Case created by Gundars Kaupins of Boise State University

Skill Builder 3.1 The Four-Fifths Rule

For this exercise, you will do some math.

Objective

To develop your skill at understanding and calculating the Four-Fifths Rule

Skills

The primary skills developed through this exercise are as follows:

1. *HR management skills*—Analytical and quantitative business skills

2. *SHRM 2018 Curriculum Guidebook*—K: Metrics and Measurement of HR

Complete the following Four-Fifths Problems

1.

	Males	Females
Applicants	100	100
Selected	50	40
Selection rate	50% (50/100)	40% (40/100)

4/5 = _____ %.

The selection rate of _____% is equal to, less than, or greater than _____% or 4/5.

Therefore, the Four-Fifths Rule is or is not met. How many total females and how many more females should be hired? _____

2.

	White	Nonwhite
Applicants	120	75
Selected	80	25
Selection rate	_____	_____

4/5 = _____ %.

The selection rate of _____% is equal to, less than, or greater than _____% or 4/5.

Therefore, the Four-Fifths Rule is or is not met. How many total and how many more nonwhites should be hired? _____

3.

	White Females	Nonwhite Females
Applicants	63	109
Selected	17	22
Selection rate	_____	_____

4/5 = _____ %.

The selection rate of _____% is equal to, less than, or greater than _____% or 4/5.

Therefore, the Four-Fifths Rule is or is not met. How many total and how many more nonwhite females should be hired? _____

Skill Builder 3.2 Diversity and Discrimination

Objective

To become more aware of and sensitive to diversity and discrimination

Skills

The primary skills developed through this exercise are as follows:

1. *HR management skills*—Interpersonal skills

2. *SHRM 2018 Curriculum Guidebook*—P: Training and Development

Answer the questions in the following paragraph:

Prejudice or Stereotype

We have all faced prejudice or stereotyping sometime in our lives by family, friends, classmates, team members, coworkers—parents, teachers, coaches, or bosses. Describe a situation in which you encountered prejudice and/or were stereotyped. Were you ever disrespected (called names, or put down in some way), mistreated, unfairly treated, not accepted by others because of your age, sex, race, color, ability (disability, intelligence, athleticism, relevant skills to the group), religion, appearance (looks/clothes), or in some other way that made you different from others? Or have you ever been in a group of so-called friends, at school, sports, job, etc., where you didn't feel valued and included (or were not included in an activity) because you were different?

Illegal Discrimination at Work

Write a short overview of an illegal discrimination at work, such as not being hired or promoted. The person can be you, someone you know, or someone you heard or read about.

Apply It

What did I learn from this experience? How will I use this knowledge in the future?

_____

_____

_____

Your instructor may ask you to do this Skill Builder in class in a group. If so, the instructor will provide you with any necessary information or additional instructions.

Staffing

4   **Workforce Planning: Job Analysis, Design, and Employment Forecasting**

5   **Recruiting Job Candidates**

6   **Selecting New Employees**

PART II

PRACTITIONER'S MODEL

- ⬆ Productivity
- ⬆ Engagement
- ⬇ Absenteeism
- ⬇ Turnover

PART V: Protecting and Expanding Organizational Outreach
How do you PROTECT and EXPAND your Human Resources?

Chapter 12 Workplace Safety, Health, and Security	Chapter 13 Ethics, Sustainability, Diversity, and Inclusion	Chapter 14 Global Issues for Human Resource Managers

PART IV: Compensating
How do you REWARD and MAINTAIN your Human Resources?

Chapter 10 Compensation Management	Chapter 11 Employee Incentives and Benefits

PART III: Developing and Managing
How do you MANAGE your Human Resources?

Chapter 7 Training, Learning, Talent Management, and Development	Chapter 8 Performance Management and Appraisal	Chapter 9 Employee Rights and Labor Relations

PART II: Staffing
What HRM Functions do you NEED for sustainability?

Chapter 4 Workforce Planning: Job Analysis, Design, and Employment Forecasting	Chapter 5 Recruiting Job Candidates	Chapter 6 Selecting New Employees

PART I: The Human Resource Management Environment
What HRM issues are CRITICAL to your organization's long-term sustainability?

Chapter 1 Today's Human Resource Management Process	Chapter 2 Strategy-Driven Human Resource Management	Chapter 3 The Legal Environment

©iStockphoto/monkeybusinessimages

Workforce Planning

Job Analysis, Design, and Employment Forecasting

Learning Outcomes

After studying this chapter, you should be able to do the following:

4.1   Describe the process of workflow analysis, identifying why it is important to HRM. **PAGE 84**

4.2   Discuss the reason for job analysis, stating the expected outcomes of the process. **PAGE 85**

4.3   Identify the four major methods used for job analysis. **PAGE 85**

4.4   Discuss the four major approaches to job design. **PAGE 90**

4.5   Identify the components of the job characteristics model (JCM). **PAGE 91**

4.6   Explain the three major tools for motivational job design. **PAGE 93**

4.7   Discuss two types of HR forecasting. **PAGE 96**

4.8   Explain the three most common quantitative HR forecasting methods. **PAGE 96**

4.9   Identify the seven major options for managing a labor surplus. **PAGE 99**

4.10 Identify the seven major options for overcoming a labor shortage. **PAGE 101**

SHRM HR Content

See Online: *SHRM 2018 Curriculum Guidebook* for the complete list

B. Compensation and Benefits

Employee Benefits

27.   Early retirement programs and buy-out

I. Job Analysis and Job Design

4.   Job/role design (roles, duties, and responsibilities)

5.   HR planning (skill inventories and supply/demand forecasting)

9-a. Work flow analysis—Analyzing work inputs and outputs

10.   Work management (work processes and outsourcing)

K. Metrics and Measurement of HR

1.   Analyzing and interpreting metrics

6.   Forecasting

7.   Quantitative analysis

9.   Trend and ratio analysis projections

N. Staffing (Recruitment and Selection)

3-b. Determining labor demand and supply—Forecasting

5.   Employment relationship: Employees, contractors, temporary workers

O. Strategic HR

2-h. HR strategies—Trends and forecasting in HR

P. Training and Development

6-g. Selecting training methods—Job rotation

Q. Workforce Planning and Talent Management

1.   Downsizing/rightsizing

2.   Labor supply and demand

3.   Planning: Forecasting requirements and availabilities, gap analysis, action planning, core/flexible workforce

S. Downsizing/Rightsizing

1.   Alternatives to employment downsizing

2.   Approaches to reducing staff size

3.   Consequences of employment downsizing

5.   Employment downsizing

8.   Importance of focusing on individual jobs vs. individual staff members

9.   Layoffs

11.   Reductions in force

13.   Why downsizing happens

14.   When downsizing is the answer

Practitioner's Perspective

Cindy's day started when an executive burst into the HR office. "Hold everything!" he shouted. "Doug just announced he's retiring unexpectedly, and we've got to start advertising for someone to replace him immediately. I don't know how we can manage without him!"

"Calm down—we can do this," she replied. "Just send us your succession planning matrix and his functional job description, and we'll start the process to replace him."

"I hate to admit it, but I never completed that matrix, and I don't have an updated job description for Doug," the manager replied sheepishly. "There have been so many changes with the department reorganizations this year that we need to reconfigure everything."

While hiring someone new is the perfect time to update the job description for a position, it is not the best time to create one. Why is it important to have a current job description, and how does one go about writing one? Chapter 4 shows how to successfully identify and document motivational positions.

Workforce Planning and Workflow Analysis

>> **LO 4.1 Describe the process of workflow analysis, identifying why it is important to HRM.**

Now that we have learned some of the basics concerning how to treat our human resources fairly and equitably, we need to start putting people to work in the organization. People are the most important resource,[1] so how we manage people is critical,[2] as it gives the firm a competitive advantage.[3] Let's start with the realization that in order for the organization to maximize productivity, we must match the right people with the right jobs.[4] Why? Because mismatched workers tend to be subpar performers[5] that have low engagement, leading to absenteeism, higher turnover, and lower levels of productivity than those who are matched effectively.[6] The first step to matching people to the right jobs is to determine what jobs we need to have performed and the qualifications needed to do the jobs. Then we can match employees to those jobs. Let's start by taking a brief look at workflow analysis.

Workflow Analysis

Workflow analysis The tool used to identify what has to be done within the organization to produce a product or service

Imagine that we are starting up a brand new company. The first thing we have to know is what we expect the organization to do. Do we plan to make products (e.g., **Samsung**), or do we plan to provide services (e.g., **Netflix**)? Per our discussion of organizational structure in Chapter 2, the way in which we put the organization together will depend on what we expect it to do, and that in turn will help determine the workflow. **Workflow analysis** is *the tool used to identify what has to be done within the organization to produce a product or service.* For each product or service that we provide in the organization, we have to identify the "series of tasks . . . that need to be completed in order to take the work from initiation to completion."[7] **(SHRM I:9-a)**

Organizational Output

The first thing we analyze is the end result of our processes: our expected organizational outputs, or what the customer wants from us.[8,9] So we are actually working backward. If we decide that we are going to make desks but we don't identify what kind of desks we're going to make, then do we need skilled craftsman, metalworkers, or just unskilled assemblers? The answer is, of course, that it depends on what kind of desk we plan to make. So identifying the end result is a critical first step in identifying the workflows needed to create that result. **(SHRM I:10)**

Tasks and Inputs

Once we identify the result we expect, we can then determine the steps or activities required to create the end result we've identified. Finally, based on the steps that we identify and the tasks that will have to be performed, we can identify the inputs that are going to be necessary to carry out the steps and perform the same tasks.[10]

There is a simple mnemonic (a memory tool) available to remember what resource inputs we have available. It is called the 4 Ms:[11]

1. *Machines*—resources such as tools, equipment, manufacturing machinery, and other machines that are used in completing work

2. *Material*—any physical resource (e.g., wood, metal, buildings, real estate, etc.) used in production

3. *Manpower*—the people that are needed in a particular production process—both quantity and types

4. *Money*—the capital that must be spent to perform our processes

These four large categories of resources are what we use up in doing what we intend to do.[12] Whenever we look at workflow analysis, we have to identify which of the 4 Ms and how much of each we are using up in a particular process. The final result of our workflow analysis is shown in Exhibit 4.1.

EXHIBIT 4.1 ● Workflow Analysis

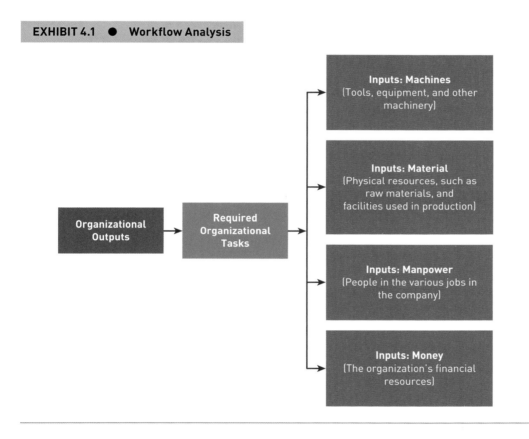

Job Analysis

>> **LO 4.2 Discuss the reason for job analysis, stating the expected outcomes of the process.**

>> **LO 4.3 Identify the four major methods used for job analysis.**

Once we understand the workflows in the organization, the next thing we need to do is figure out which parts of the workflows are done by each person. This is the concept of job analysis. Before you begin to search for a new employee, you need to conduct a job analysis.[13] **Job analysis** is *the process used to identify the work performed and the working conditions for each of the jobs within our organizations.* Job analysis analyzes one small part of the workflow, and the results of the analysis will include duties, responsibilities, skills, knowledge required, outcomes, conditions under which the worker must operate, and possibly other factors.[14]

Job analysis The process used to identify the work performed and the working conditions for each of the jobs within our organizations

Why Do We Need to Analyze Jobs?

Job analysis is the basis of just about everything HR does.[15] If you think about it, you will quickly realize that we need to identify and correctly analyze the jobs in the organization in order to perform *any* of the following functions:

1. *Human resource planning.* Job analysis helps us design jobs better to get the results we need. (We will talk about job design shortly.)

2. *Job evaluation for compensation.* If we don't know what the job consists of, how can we determine how much the job is worth to the organization so we know how much to pay the person?

3. *Staffing (recruiting and selection).* If we don't know what an employee is going to do and how much we will pay that employee, then how do we know whom to recruit and hire?

4. *Training.* If we don't know what the job consists of, how can we teach people to do the job?

5. *Performance management.* How can we evaluate performance if we don't know what the worker's job consists of?

6. *Maintain a safe work environment.* Job analysis will help us identify hazards the job incumbent will need to understand, as well as any required personal protective equipment and training the person will need to safely carry out the job.

So job analysis is important to the HR department, but how does it affect other managers? Think about the following issues that *any* organizational manager may face on a routine basis:

1. Managers must have detailed information about all the jobs in their work groups so they can manage the workflow processes.

2. Managers need to understand job requirements in their work groups so they can make intelligent hiring, training, and promotion decisions.

3. Every manager is responsible for conducting performance evaluations in some form, whether on an annual or a rolling basis, to ensure that all employees are performing their jobs satisfactorily.

So we can see that job analysis is very important to both HR and line managers. But how do you analyze a job?

Job Analysis Databases

There are various commercial databases that can be of some help to those performing job analysis. The free **U.S. Department of Labor's O*NET** contains hundreds of standardized and occupation-specific descriptors on almost 1,000 occupations covering the entire U.S. economy.[16] You can also use it to better understand jobs and the qualifications you need in career exploration options. To learn more about O*NET OnLine visit www.onetonline.org, which is the website for Self-Assessment 4.1.

Using a database can be a good starting point for job analysis. However, each job analysis will most likely need to be customized. The O*NET Toolkit for Business (visit https://www.onetcen ter.org/action.html#toolkit-for-business) provides a wealth of background information on the features of O*NET. It details O*NET's many uses for human resource professionals and employers that includes a link to "Job Description Writer" that lets you find a current job description and edit it. You can check it out at https://www.careeronestop.org/BusinessCenter/Toolkit/GettingStarted.aspx. Whether or not you can find a job description on a database, you need to conduct your own job analysis to verify that the job in your company matches well with the job in the database. How to do so is our next topic.

4.1 SELF-ASSESSMENT

O*NET INTEREST PROFILER

The O*NET Interest Profiler (https://www.onetcenter.org/ IP.html) can help you find out what your interests are and how they relate to the world of work. You can find out what you like to do, and it helps you decide what kinds of careers you might want to explore. In textbook terms, it will help you match your interest to jobs. Input the URL for the Interest Profiler above into your browser, then click the "O*NET IP Short Form for the Web-based version." Click "Take the Web-based Interest Profiler Now" and complete the 60 question self-assessment as instructed and get your results.

Job Analysis Methods

Four commonly used methods of job analysis include the use of questionnaires, interviews, diaries, and observation.[17] The necessary result that we are looking for with all four methods is a job description and specification for a person to be successful in the position. Let's discuss the four methods.[18]

Questionnaires

A number of highly valid and reliable questionnaires can be given to different people in order to analyze the job in question. A questionnaire may be given to the current jobholder (the incumbent), the supervisor, or others who are affected by the way the job is done in the organization. Most of the questionnaires follow similar processes. Each asks questions that help to identify the functions that are a part of a particular job, and then, in most cases, assigns a point value to that function.[19] The *Position Analysis Questionnaire* and the *Management Position Description Questionnaire* are two examples of this type of job analysis.[20]

Questionnaire Advantages

- Quick way to get information from large number of sources

- Usually easy to quantify

- Relatively low cost

- Generally valid and reliable instruments

- No need for a trained interviewer or observer

Questionnaire Disadvantages

- Incomplete responses (nobody is interviewing or observing actions, so there is no follow-up)

- Responses may be hard to interpret

- Low response rates are possible if there is no supervisory follow-up

Interviews

In job analysis interviews, trained interviewers usually ask questions of the incumbent, and the answers are compiled into a profile of the job. Untrained interviewers are much more likely to violate the OUCH test during the interview process and invalidate the job analysis outcome because of it.[21] The interviewer asks job-related questions, and the incumbent describes the job based on the questions asked.

Interview Advantages

- The incumbent is most familiar with the job
- Can include qualitative data
- Allows the interviewer to follow up confusing or incomplete answers
- Simple, quick, and more comprehensive than some other forms
- Provides an opportunity to explain the need for the analysis and answer questions

Interview Disadvantages

- Dependent on trained interviewer and well-designed questions
- Workers may exaggerate their job duties
- Time-consuming and may not be cost efficient

An employee's diary or log outlining their daily tasks and activities can be used as the basis for a job description.

Diaries

Here the worker maintains a work log, or *diary*, in which the employee writes down the tasks accomplished while going about the job.[22] This log becomes the document from which we build the description of the job. Diaries will be more valuable than some of the other methods when it is difficult to directly observe what is done in a job.

Diary Advantages

- Participatory form of analysis
- May collect data as they happen
- The worker knows the job and what is important
- Useful for jobs that are difficult to observe

Diary Disadvantages

- Relies on worker writing all work down
- Worker may rely on memory of things done earlier in the day
- Information distortion
- Data are not in a standard format—makes quantifying difficult

Observation

We can also use observation of the person at work, in which an observer shadows the worker and logs tasks the worker performs over a period of time.[23] A trained observer will usually identify tasks that workers don't even think about doing and therefore wouldn't have noted in a log or diary.

Observation Advantages

- First-hand knowledge
- Allows the analyst to see the work environment, view the tools and equipment the worker uses, observe the worker's interrelationships with other workers, and gauge the complexity of the job

- Reduces information distortion common in some other methods
- Relatively simple to use

Observation Disadvantages

- Observer may affect the job incumbent's performance
- Inappropriate for jobs that involve significant mental effort
- May lack validity and reliability
- Time-consuming
- Requires a trained observer

The four methods listed above are certainly not the only methods of job analysis, and they may not even be the best options for a particular situation. There are other options, including the use of subject matter experts, work sampling, videotaping of jobs, and others. However, these four types of analysis demonstrate the basic process of job analysis. We can also use multiple methods if one method alone will not provide a good analysis.

Outcomes: Job Description and Job Specification

The two primary outcomes for most job analysis projects are the job description and the job specification. The **job description** *identifies the major tasks, duties, and responsibilities that are components of a job,* while the **job specification** *identifies the qualifications of a person who should be capable of doing the job tasks noted in the job description.* These two outcomes are routinely written into one document. With a quick search of job search sites on the Web (**Indeed**, **Monster .com**, etc.), you can find thousands of examples of a job description and specification, and you can also find hundreds of samples at **O*NET**.

The job *description* describes the job itself, not the person who will do the job. It should identify skills needed[24] and give you and the applicant a clear understanding of the expectations in performing the job,[25] so that everyone "really" knows what the position entails. The job *specification* identifies the qualifications needed by the person who is to fill a position. It identifies the right person that matches the job you want done.[26]

We will use the job specification to go out and recruit (Chapter 5) when we have an opening for the job. The job analysis should be periodically updated as the job and qualifications to do the job change in a dynamic business environment.

Job description Identification of the major tasks, duties, and responsibilities that are components of a job

Job specification Identification of the qualifications of a person who should be capable of doing the job tasks noted in the job description

4.1 APPLYING THE CONCEPT
JOB ANALYSIS METHODS

Review the following job analysis methods and then write the letter corresponding to each method before the situation in which it would be the most appropriate.

a. Questionnaire
b. Interview
c. Diary
d. Observation

_____ 1. On your staff, you have an industrial engineer who is an efficiency expert. You want her to improve the productivity of your machinists.

_____ 2. You have professionals who work independently using different methods of developing computer games.

_____ 3. In your call center, where hundreds of employees make cold calls to sell your products, there is a high turnover rate that you want to improve.

_____ 4. You have several service call employees who repair a variety of computers. You would like to have a better idea of what types of computers they are fixing.

Job Design/Redesign

>> **LO 4.4 Discuss the four major approaches to job design.**

Job or work design is about creating jobs.[27] Tasks to be performed in organizations are grouped, usually into functional departments, and the tasks are further grouped into jobs for each employee, providing structures and processes. **Job design** is *the process of identifying tasks that each employee is responsible for completing, as well as identifying how those tasks will be accomplished.* Job design is crucial because it affects job satisfaction, engagement, and productivity,[28] along with a large number of other functions in HRM.[29]

Job redesign refers to changing the tasks or the way work is performed in an existing job. Job design, which includes redesign, is about working smarter, not harder, to find new ways of doing things that boost productivity.[30]

Organizational Structure and Job Design

The way we combine the components of an organizational structure causes employees to act in different ways (Chapter 2). Jobs in the organization have to be designed to fit within the confines of the structure we have designed.[31]

If we have a more relaxed, flatter structure with lots of autonomy for our workers, as we would see in companies with high performance work practices,[32] we need to design our jobs to take advantage of that autonomy or self-direction on the part of our employees. If, on the other hand, we have a rigid, bureaucratic organizational structure with strong centralized decision making and control, then our jobs have to be designed so that they can be readily controlled by a central authority. **(SHRM I:4)**

Approaches to Job Design and Redesign

Job design/redesign can take several forms, depending on what we are trying to accomplish in the organization. There are four primary approaches to job design: mechanistic, biological, perceptual-motor, and motivational.[33]

1. **Mechanistic job design** *focuses on designing jobs around the concepts of task specialization, skill simplification, and repetition.* When we design a mechanistic job, we will try to make the job simple and repetitive so that the worker can get very good and very fast at doing it. An example of mechanistic job design in manufacturing would be attaching the desktop to its base using six fasteners and then going to the next desk to do the same thing again. The biggest problem in mechanistic job design is that we might overspecialize the work to the point that it becomes too repetitive and thus very boring.[34]

2. **Biological job design** *focuses on minimizing the physical strain on the worker by structuring the physical work environment around the way the body works.* Here we make the job physically easier so that workers can be more efficient and so that it is less likely they will be injured and have to miss work. An example of biological job design would involve installing a conveyor belt that lifts and adjusts to the correct level so each person can assemble their parts of the final product within a comfortable range of motion. This allows the workers to do their jobs with minimal physical strain. Again, though, this approach does little to make workers more motivated or satisfied with their work.

3. **Perceptual-motor job design** *focuses on designing jobs with tasks that remain within the worker's normal mental capabilities and limitations.* Instead of trying to minimize the physical strain on the workforce, the goal is to design jobs in a way that ensures they moderate the mental strain on a worker.[35] For example, we might use it to break down an executive assistant's job into a report writer and a scheduler job, because the sets of skills needed in these two areas are significantly different. One more time, we may create jobs that are not very motivating.

4. **Motivational job design** *focuses on the job characteristics that affect the psychological meaning and motivational potential of the job; this approach views attitudinal variables as the most important outcomes of job design.* The theory is that if workers are more motivated, they will produce more work. It is to this last approach to job design that we can apply the job characteristics model, which we will discuss next.

Job design The process of identifying tasks that each employee is responsible for completing, as well as identifying how those tasks will be accomplished

Mechanistic job design Designing jobs around the concepts of task specialization, skill simplification, and repetition

Biological job design Designing jobs by focusing on minimizing the physical strain on the worker by structuring the physical work environment around the way the body works

Perceptual-motor job design Designing jobs with tasks that remain within the worker's normal mental capabilities and limitations

Motivational job design Designing jobs by focusing on the job characteristics that affect the psychological meaning and motivational potential of the job; this approach views attitudinal variables as the most important outcomes of job design

4.2 SELF-ASSESSMENT

ORGANIZATIONAL STRUCTURE AND JOB DESIGN PREFERENCE

Individuals differ in the type of organizations and job designs in which they prefer to work. To determine your preference, evaluate each of the following 10 statements, using the scale below. Assign each statement a number from 1 to 5, representing your level of agreement with the statement (5 = strong agreement, 3 = not sure, 1 = strong disagreement).

I agree				I disagree
5	4	3	2	1

_____ 1. I prefer having just one boss telling me what to do, rather than multiple people.

_____ 2. I prefer to just perform my job, rather than being concerned about organizational objectives and being involved in setting them.

_____ 3. I prefer knowing the reporting relationship, knowing who is whose boss, and working through proper channels—rather than just working directly with a variety of people based on the situation.

_____ 4. I prefer having a clear job description so I know just what I need to do at work, rather than having the ambiguity of not being sure and doing whatever needs to be done.

_____ 5. I prefer being a specialist doing one job really well, rather than being a generalist doing several things not as well.

_____ 6. I prefer doing my own thing that contributes to the organization, rather than coordinating the work I do with that of others in teams.

_____ 7. I prefer slow change, rather than regular fast changes.

_____ 8. I prefer routine at work, rather than being delegated new tasks to perform.

_____ 9. I prefer doing more simple tasks, rather than more complex tasks that take more time and effort.

_____ 10. I prefer that people get promoted based primarily on seniority, rather than based on performance.

_____ Total

Scoring: To determine your preference, add up the numbers you assigned to the statements (the total will be between 10 and 50) and place your total score on the continuum below:

10	15	20	25	30	35	40	45	50
Organic								Mechanistic

An organization that is minimally or moderately complex, highly formalized, and centralized is a mechanistic organization. Organic organizations are even more complex but lower on formalization and centralization. This exercise tests the type of structure with which you feel most comfortable. You will learn more about mechanistic and organic structures throughout this chapter. The higher your score, the more you prefer to work in a more traditional, mechanistic, stable structure and job design. The lower your score, the more you prefer to work in a more contemporary, organic, changing structure and job design.

Review your answers, knowing that the opening statement applies to mechanistic and the opposite statement (after "rather than") applies to organic organizational structure and job design. Most firms and people prefer organizations somewhere between the two extremes.

The Job Characteristics Model (JCM)

>> LO 4.5 Identify the components of the job characteristics model (JCM).

The **job characteristics model (JCM)** provides _a conceptual framework for designing or enriching jobs based on core job characteristics._[36] As Exhibit 4.2 illustrates, users of the JCM make the job more interesting and challenging based on the job itself (core job dimensions), the characteristics of the employee doing the job (critical psychological states), and the employee's interest in having an enriched job (employee growth-need strength). The JCM increases performance[37] by meeting employee needs to grow and develop on the job, resulting in improved employee engagement and job satisfaction[38] and reduction in absenteeism and job turnover.[39]

Job characteristics model (JCM) A conceptual framework for designing or enriching jobs based on core job characteristics

In the JCM, the five core job characteristics can be fine-tuned to improve the outcomes of a job in terms of employees' productivity and their quality of working life:

1. *Skill variety* is the number of diverse tasks that make up a job and the number of skills used to perform the job.

2. *Task identity* is the degree to which an employee performs a whole identifiable task. For example, does the employee put together an entire television or just place the screen in the set?

3. *Task significance* is an employee's perception of the importance of the task to others—the organization, the department, coworkers, and/or customers.

4. *Autonomy* is the degree to which the employee has discretion to make decisions in planning, organizing, and controlling the task performed.

5. *Feedback* is the extent to which employees find out how well they perform their tasks.

Note that if employees are not interested in enriching their jobs, the job characteristics model will fail.

The first three of the core job characteristics lead collectively to the psychological state (in the second column of Exhibit 4.2) of *experienced meaningfulness of work* to provide workers with a variety of things to do. If the employee can identify what it is that they are accomplishing, and if they think that their job is a significant endeavor, then they will think their work has meaning and thus be more likely to stay in the job and do it well.

The core characteristic of *autonomy* leads to the psychological state of *experienced responsibility for outcomes*. If we give people the ability to make some decisions on their own, it is likely they will feel more responsible for the outcome of the decisions that they make.

Finally, *feedback* leads to the psychological state of *knowledge of results*. However, it is not the knowledge of the result itself that matters. Remember that the second column is *psychological* states! It is the psychological feeling that we get from knowing the results that create the state of, for lack of a better term, satisfaction with the results of our work.

All of the psychological states *collectively* lead to all of the outcomes noted on the right side of the diagram. It is an interesting list. If the job is designed correctly, the model says that the worker will quite possibly be more motivated and more productive and have higher job satisfaction/engagement while also being less likely to be absent or leave the organization. The use of the

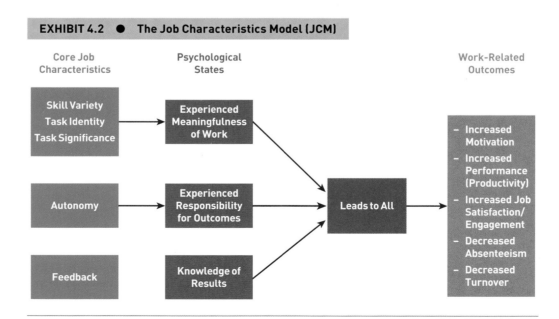

EXHIBIT 4.2 ● The Job Characteristics Model (JCM)

JCM is even more critical for motivating young millennials (rather than older workers) who are looking for meaning in their work; they don't want, and will leave, boring jobs.[40]

4.2 APPLYING THE CONCEPT
JOB DESIGN

Review the list of job design techniques below and write the letter corresponding to each technique before the statement exemplifying that technique.

a. Mechanistic

b. Organic

c. Biological

d. Perceptual-motor

e. Motivational

_____ 5. We are required to wear these special belts when we unload the trucks at **Target**.

_____ 6. We have added enough employees so that we are breaking the human resources function

into its own department. Jack will now focus on compensation and benefits, and Jill will conduct the training. Latoya will be responsible for safety and security.

_____ 7. Here at **Intel**, we are going to change your job so that you can develop new skills and complete entire jobs by yourself. We're doing this to make the job more meaningful to you and so that you can do the job the way you want to and know how you are doing.

_____ 8. I just finished the Casey project. What should I do now?

_____ 9. This is the 30th customer I've checked out at **Stop & Shop** supermarket today.

Designing Motivational Jobs

>> **LO 4.6 Explain the three major tools for motivational job design.**

In addition to the more complex JCM, a variety of other job tools can be used in different circumstances to design or redesign motivational jobs. Our tools include job simplification, job expansion, and flexible work. These are discussed next.

Job Simplification

Job simplification is *the process of eliminating or combining tasks and/or changing the work sequence to improve performance*. Job simplification makes jobs more specialized. Job simplification breaks a job down into steps using a flowchart, [41] and then employees analyze the steps to see if they can do the following:

- Eliminate. Does the task, or do parts of it, have to be done at all? If not, don't waste time on them.

- Combine. Doing similar things together often saves time. Make one trip to the mailroom at the end of the day instead of several trips throughout the day.

- Change sequence. Often, a change in the order of doing things, or designing new systems, results in a lower total time spent on tasks.

Work simplification may be motivational when an individual is overwhelmed by a job because it can allow that employee to understand the job better, and the job therefore becomes more motivational. However, we don't want to simplify the process to the point where the worker becomes bored with the job. So we have to strike the right balance.[42] **GE** has Workout sessions where employees present ideas for eliminating pointless tasks.[43] Companies including **McDonald's** and **Costco** stopped requiring signatures for credit card sales to speed up service.

Job simplification The process of eliminating or combining tasks and/or changing the work sequence to improve performance

Job Expansion

Job expansion allows us to focus on making the work more varied.[44] **Job expansion** is *the process of making jobs broader, with less repetition. Jobs can be expanded through rotation, enlargement, and enrichment.* The trend is toward organic structure, giving employees more job autonomy.[45]

Job Rotation

Job rotation involves performing different jobs in some sequence, each one for a set period of time. Many organizations develop conceptual skills in management trainees by rotating them through jobs in various departments. **Jumpstart:HR** consulting CEO **Joey Price** says you need at least two people trained on every single function to cover for each other when not at work.[46] **(SHRM P:6-g)**

Job Enlargement

Job enlargement involves adding tasks—at the same level—to broaden variety. By broadening the number of tasks for a worker, we are affecting the core job characteristic of skill variety, and we may be helping with task identity and significance. Unfortunately, adding more similar tasks to an employee's job is often not a great motivator.

Job Enrichment

Job enrichment is the process of building motivators into the job itself to make it more interesting and challenging.[47] The goal is to get employees fully engaged at work so they are satisfied and productive.[48] A simple way to enrich jobs is to delegate more authority to employees[49] by making them more autonomous (another core job characteristic) to make some decisions that were reserved for management.[50] An enriched job may also help the employee with the JCM characteristics of task identity and significance in some cases.

▲
Target employees will rotate through a number of positions on the job, giving them a range of skills and experiences.

©Associated Press/Julio Cortez

Flexible Job Design

In addition to the primary tools for designing and redesigning specific jobs, we have another set of tools that can be used in the workplace to improve motivation in entire groups of jobs or maybe even the entire workforce.[51] Flexible job design has become necessary in today's workforce. Flexible work arrangements mean that we can target people with time constraints and as a result have more and better pools of applicants to choose from when we need new workers. These tools include flextime, job sharing, telecommuting, and compressed workweeks.[52]

Flextime allows us to provide workers with a flexible set of work hours. We usually create a set of *core hours* where everyone is at work, *bandwidth* or *work hours* available, and then a set of *flex hours* when people can be at work or can take time off. Individuals have the opportunity to modify their schedule within the work hours as long as they complete a set number of hours per day or week at work. Flextime has the potential to motivate workers because it allows them much greater autonomy with regard to their schedule. However, not every organization can utilize flextime because of customer requirements or production problems that would occur if everyone isn't together to do the work. Take a look at Exhibit 4.3 for a sample flextime schedule.

In *job sharing* (also called work sharing) we allow two (or more) people to share one whole job, including the workload and any benefits that are associated with the job. Job sharing again allows greater autonomy in the individual's job.

Telecommuting allows workers to work from a location other than the corporate office, usually from home. It provides another form of autonomy, but we need to make sure that telecommuters get opportunities to engage with coworkers and receive feedback concerning their work, since an absence of these opportunities are two of the major drawbacks to telecommuting.[53] We may not be able to do telecommuting in all business environments. There have been some well publicized

EXHIBIT 4.3 ● Sample Flextime Work Schedule[54]

Acmemegadyne Corporation Flextime Work Schedule

Normal operating hours: 8:30 a.m.–5:30 p.m. Monday through Friday (1 hour for lunch)

Full-time workers (40 hours per week):

Core hours: 9:00–11:00 a.m.; 1:00–3:00 p.m.

Flexible hours: 7:30–9:00 a.m.; 11:00 a.m.–1:00 p.m.; 3:00–6:30 p.m.

Work hours (bandwidth): 7:30 a.m.–6:30 p.m.

"A flextime arrangement may be suspended or cancelled at any time. Exempt employees must depart from any flextime schedule to perform their jobs. Nonexempt employees may be asked to work overtime regardless of a flextime schedule" (from SHRM flextime policy sample).

incidences of companies doing away with telecommuting because of productivity problems within their business. Both **IBM** and **Yahoo** moved remote employees back to headquarters or at least a hub location where they will work face-to-face with fellow employees.[55,56]

Finally, a *compressed workweek* means that we take the normal 5-day, 40-hour workweek and compress it down to less than 5 days. One common example would be a 4-day, 10-hour per day workweek.

You should be able to see that job simplification, job expansion, and flexible job design can all be part of applying the JCM. Each of these tools allows us to design greater flexibility into our organization in one way or another. As a result, in many cases, we can improve both productivity and job satisfaction and in turn lower rates of absenteeism and turnover, improving engagement at the same time—a win-win for the organization and the employee. The JCM helps provide a comprehensive system for designing and redesigning jobs to make them more motivational.[57] Exhibit 4.4 reviews the job design options we have discussed so far as they relate to JCM.

EXHIBIT 4.4 ● Job Design Options, Processes, and the JCM

Option	Process	Core Characteristics Affected (JCM)
Job simplification	Eliminate tasks	Task identity and significance
	Combine tasks	
	Change task sequence	
Job expansion	Rotate jobs	Skill variety, task identity, and significance
	Enlarge jobs	Possibly feedback
	Enrich jobs	Autonomy, possibly feedback
Flexible job design	Flextime	Autonomy
	Job sharing	Skill variety, autonomy
	Telecommuting	Autonomy
	Compressed workweek	Autonomy

4.3 APPLYING THE CONCEPT
DESIGNING MOTIVATIONAL JOBS

Review the following job design techniques and write the letter corresponding to each technique before the statement exemplifying it.

a. Job simplification

b. Job rotation

c. Job enlargement

d. Job enrichment

e. Flextime

_____ 10. Would you like more job variety? If so, I can add three new tasks to your job to make it less repetitive.

_____ 11. I'm going to teach you to balance the accounts so that you can do it for Carlos while he is on vacation.

_____ 12. Would you like me to delegate a new task to you to make your job more challenging?

_____ 13. **Domino's Pizza** stopped requiring customers to sign a credit card slip for under $25.

_____ 14. I'm creating a new crew with the seven of you. There will not be a formal manager; you will share that responsibility. From now on, you don't have a manager. So share the job together.

HR Forecasting

>> **LO 4.7 Discuss two types of HR forecasting.**

HR forecasting and labor requirements planning are at the core of determining our future employment needs.[58] Through forecasting, we will make determinations—based on both quantitative and qualitative information—of what types of jobs and how many of each type we will need to fill over a particular period of time. If we fail to get it right, we won't get the right people in place at the time when they are needed and will always be chasing the organizational losses created by voluntary and involuntary turnover, which causes lower organizational productivity. **HR forecasting** *identifies the estimated supply and demand for the different types of human resources in the organization over some future period, based on analysis of past and present demand.* (**SHRM N:3-b; Q:3, and I:5**)

Before we get into forecasting, we need to understand a couple of terms. You always need to make sure that any analytical process you use includes *valid* and *reliable* measures. If you don't, then your results will always be suspect and will generally be of very little value. We will discuss these terms in more detail later, but need to briefly introduce them here.

HR forecasting Identifying the estimated supply and demand for the different types of human resources in the organization over some future period, based on analysis of past and present demand

Reliability

Reliability identifies how consistent a particular measure is. In other words, does the measure give a similar result every time it is used? If it does, then it is probably reliable. For instance, if you give a test of comprehension on a set of company terms after teaching those terms in the same manner to several groups of employees, and if the results in each group are similar, then the test is most likely reliable.

Validity

Validity refers to whether or not we measured what we thought we measured. It is not as easy as it sounds for subjective measures. For example, does a motivational test actually, and accurately, measure the level of motivation? If we don't measure what we meant to measure, our test was not valid.

Notice that a measure can be reliable but not valid, but it can't be valid if it is not reliable. For example, if you step on a low-quality home scale and weigh 175, get off and on again several times, and weigh 175 every time, then the scale is reliable. However, if you go to a high-quality scale and weigh 180 repeatedly, then the measurements you got from the home scale are reliable but not valid. So remember validity and reliability as you decide on the tools that you are going to use in the forecasting process.

Forecasting Methods

>> **LO 4.8 Explain the three most common quantitative HR forecasting methods.**

Forecasting should be completed in two distinct steps. First, we complete a quantitative analysis of our workforce using one or more of several methods, and then we adjust the results of the quantitative (math) analysis using qualitative methods. Experience is needed when analyzing situations that are unique or different from what has happened in our business environment in the past, and qualitative analysis looks at the differences between the "historical" and the "now." Let's define each type. **(SHRM K:6)**

Quantitative Forecasting

A **quantitative forecast** *utilizes mathematics to forecast future events based on historical data.* Three common quantitative methods of forecasting are trend analysis, ratio analysis, and regression analysis.[59] Let's take a quick look at each method in Exhibit 4.5. **(SHRM K:7)**

Trend analysis is *a process of reviewing historical items such as revenues and relating changes in those items to some business factor to form a predictive chart.* For example, we could look at historical revenues and relate those revenue volumes to the number of people in the organization for each year, or alternatively, we could analyze historical production levels and relate those levels to the number of people used to accomplish those levels of production. Either of these would give us a historical trend that we could then extend into the future to predict the number of people that would be required for a particular sales or production level.[60] **(SHRM O:2-h)**

Ratio analysis is *the process of reviewing historical data and calculating specific proportions between a business factor (such as production) and the number of employees needed.* It generally gives us very similar results to trend analysis, but it should be a bit more precise because we are computing an exact value for the ratio. **(SHRM K:9)**

Regression analysis is *a statistical technique that identifies the relationship between a series of variable data points for use in forecasting future variables.* We can use statistical software to create the regression diagram (most human resources management systems include this capability). Then it is just a process of looking at the values along the line and applying them to your company's situation in a given year.

Qualitative Forecasting

Qualitative forecasting is *the use of nonquantitative methods to forecast the future, usually based on the knowledge of a pool of experts in a subject or an industry.* We provide our group of experts with the quantitative predictions that we have created and ask for their assessment of the data, taking into account circumstances within our industry and the general economic climate while comparing the present situation with the historical environment on which the quantitative evaluations are based. The experts will then come to a consensus about how to adjust the quantitative data for today's environment. **(SHRM K:1)**

We need to use both quantitative and qualitative analysis to get good forecasts for the future needs of the organization and its human resources. We will look at both forecasting methods and identify whether we expect to have a surplus or a shortage of people in the organization over the next few years. More likely, we will find that we will have a surplus of some types of people and a shortage of others. Regardless of whether we have a shortage or a surplus, we have to attempt to get the right numbers of people with the right skill sets into our organization at the right time. Let's take some time to review the mechanisms to combat either a labor surplus or shortage in the next two sections.

Quantitative forecast Utilizing mathematics to forecast future events based on historical data

Trend analysis A process of reviewing historical items such as revenues and relating changes in those items to some business factor to form a predictive chart

Ratio analysis The process of reviewing historical data and calculating specific proportions between a business factor (such as production) and the number of employees needed

Regression analysis A statistical technique that identifies the relationship between a series of variable data points for use in forecasting future variables

Qualitative forecasting The use of nonquantitative methods to forecast the future, usually based on the knowledge of a pool of experts in a subject or an industry

EXHIBIT 4.5   ●   Quantitative Forecasting Analysis

Trend Analysis

Historical Data	2015	2016	2017	2018	2019
Revenues ($MM)	27.84	29.92	25.48	26.3	30.12
Total # of Employees	225	244	215	214	240

We then estimate the number of employees needed based on the historical trend. In this case, how many total employees would you say we need if we expect 2020 revenues to be $31.8 million? You likely said something around 250 people, because you looked at the historical trend.

Ratio Analysis

Historical Data	2015	2016	2017	2018	2019
Production Levels ($MM)	18.62	20.58	17.44	17.23	19.16
Avg. # Production Workers/Year	62	71	61	55	61
$ Production/Worker (000's)	300	290	286	313	314

The average production per worker for the 5 years listed would be just under $301,000, so $301,000: worker is our ratio. If we expect production requirements to be $20.2MM in 2020, we could divide $20,200,000 by $301,000 and get approximately 67 production workers as an expected complement for 2020. If we had 61 workers at the end of 2019, we would need to recruit 6 more for 2020—assuming no voluntary turnover during the year.

Regression Analysis

A regression diagram of all of the companies in our industry by year for the past 10 years, plotted with the number of employees on the x-axis and revenues on the y-axis, might look like this:

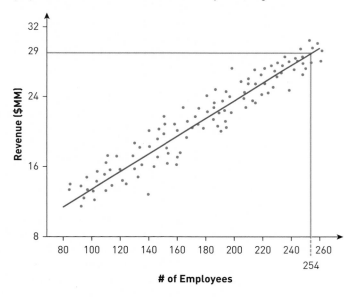

Based on this diagram, if we were expecting to have revenues of $29MM next year, we would need approximately 254 employees.

4.4 APPLYING THE CONCEPT
QUANTITATIVE METHODS

Complete each problem below:

_____ 15. Turn to the Regression Analysis section of Exhibit 4.5. Assume that in 2020, you expect a recession and revenues to drop to $24 million. Around how many employees will you need?

  a. 160   b. 180   c. 210   d. 230

_____ 16. You have 253 employees. Over the past year, there were 26 absences. What is the approximate percentage and ratio of absenteeism?

  a. 9.7%, 1–10   b. 10%, 1–10   c. 10%, 1–100
  d. 12%, 1–12

_____ 17. You have 1,215 employees. Over the past year, 298 left the firm. What is the approximate percentage and ratio of turnover?

  a. 4%, 1–20   b. 40%, 4–10   c. 22%, 22–100
  d. 25%, 1–4

_____ 18. Turn to the Trend Analysis section of Exhibit 4.5. Assume that in 2020, you expect revenues to be $35 million. Around how many employees will you need?

  a. 210   b. 230   c. 250   d. 270

_____ 19. Turn to the Ratio Analysis section of Exhibit 4.5. Assume that in 2020, you expect the production level to increase to $22 million. Around how many employees will you need, and how many new workers do you need to add?

  a. 2 and 11   b. 73 and 12   c. 74 and 13
  d. 75 and 14

Methods for Reconciling a Labor Surplus

>> **LO 4.9 Identify the seven major options for managing a labor surplus.**

If we are predicting a surplus of people going into the future, what can we do about it? We can't usually just hang on to employees that aren't needed, because it is too expensive. However, we don't necessarily have to get rid of a large number of employees, either. How we handle the situation will depend on how soon we are able to predict that there will be a surplus, and it will also depend on our strategy, values, and philosophy. We have to understand the consequences of each option and choose wisely.

Downsizing and Layoffs

Our first option may have to be a layoff, especially if we have large numbers of extra people due to changes in our business or in the competitive environment. A **layoff** is *a process of terminating a group of employees with intent to improve organizational efficiency and effectiveness.* In a layoff, we are generally allowed to terminate the employment of a group of individuals with very little advance warning, and we usually don't have to provide any disciplinary or other justification for what we are doing. We may have to comply with the Worker Adjustment and Retraining Notification Act (WARN Act), which we will discuss in some detail in Chapter 9, but other than that, we have few documentation needs other than ensuring there is no illegal discrimination in a layoff event.[61] We do have to document the method by which we determined who should be in the layoff, and it would be wise not to be arbitrary in our selection of individuals and not to target specific groups of employees.

The most valuable result of a layoff is that the resulting savings are immediately added to bottom-line corporate performance.[62] However, layoffs create many potential problems, including lower employee engagement and job satisfaction.[63] Evidence is also pretty strong that organizations who utilize layoffs tend to have lower overall profitability and growth during the several years following the layoff.[64] So we end up with a lot of stress issues in layoffs, and these create problems for the organization. **(SHRM Q:2, S:5, S:11, S:14, S:2, Q:1, S:8, S:9, S:13, and S:3)**

Layoff A process of terminating a group of employees with intent to improve organizational efficiency and effectiveness

Pay Reduction

A second option for immediately lowering labor costs is a *pay reduction* for all or part of the work-force. Supply and demand for various types of labor drive the market value of the people who provide that labor. If there is an oversupply of people in a particular field, or if new technology has made the job easier, then those employees may not provide as much value as they did 5 or 10 years ago. In other cases, economic conditions may demand a cut in organizational expenses, and labor is the biggest organizational expense in many companies.[65] Again, this option can be accomplished fairly quickly, but it can decrease employee engagement or job satisfaction.

Work Sharing

A third option for lowering labor costs without terminating employees is some form of *job- (or work-) sharing* arrangement. We may cut the hours available to each worker because fewer jobs are available in the company, but instead of cutting workers, we may split one job up among more than one worker. This way, nobody is laid off. However, all of the workers suffer to some extent because of a decrease in income. There is certainly some suffering in the workforce due to a reduction in income, but nobody loses an entire paycheck. Plus, when the firm comes out of a recession, it already has enough skilled workers to meet the increase in business. **(SHRM S:1)**

Natural Attrition

Next, we have the option to allow *natural attrition* to lower organizational numbers without the need for a layoff or pay reduction. We can just allow some positions to stay unfilled as turnover occurs.

Hiring Freezes

Natural attrition, along with the slightly more stringent option of a *hiring freeze* (where we do not bring in any new hires in either new or existing positions), causes our number of employees to drop slowly. Therefore, they can't be used in a situation where speed in reducing expenses is critical, but if we have done our job forecasting, we may have enough time for these two options to work without putting massive stress on our workforce.

Retraining and Transfers

Retraining workers and *transferring* them from one job to another may be options in some circumstances. However, this option will only work if we have too many employees in one type of job and too few in another. If there are no positions where we have a shortage, retraining workers will not work. Again, the process is a little slow due to the fact that each person has to be retrained in a new field. But if we have a good worker who is willing to try a new job, and if a position is available, then using this option can allow us to retain that good employee.

Early Retirement

The last option that we will discuss here is *early retirement*. Early retirement can be a valuable option in some cases. However, there can be many pitfalls to using early retirement to reduce our workforce.[66] In an early retirement offer, employees are given the choice of leaving the company before they would ordinarily do so (reaching the "normal" retirement age of 65, for instance), and in exchange for leaving, the employee will receive benefits of some type in the form of a buy-out from the organization. **(SHRM B:27)**

There are some good reasons to use early retirement as an option to reduce an employee surplus, but it is a slow method of getting rid of people, and we have to be careful in planning for and offering early retirements. Problems with early retirement may include too many or too few people taking the offer, or the perception of being forced out of work due to age, among other issues.[67] In a surplus situation, we want to use the options that we discussed in this section from the bottom up—starting with things like early retirements and attrition, because they are the least disruptive to the workforce and allow us to maintain motivation and job satisfaction levels much better than things like layoffs and pay reductions. This will provide us with the best long-term results.

4.1 ETHICAL DILEMMA: WHAT WOULD YOU DO?

As firms struggle to compete in the global economy, many have downsized, especially since the last recession. In some firms, the positions formerly held by full-time employees are filled by contractors and part-time workers. Using contractors and part-time employees saves companies money because they do not receive any or many benefits (e.g., health insurance) in contrast to full-time employees. **Walmart** and other companies are known for maintaining a high ratio of part-time to full-time employees as a way of keeping costs down. Walmart's policy of using part-time workers at low wages is one of the reasons the chain can offer lower prices.

1. Is downsizing ethical and socially responsible?

2. Is using part-time employees rather than full-time ones ethically and socially responsible?

3. Would you be willing to pay higher prices at stores, such as Walmart, so that more full-time workers could replace part-time workers?

Methods for Reconciling a Labor Shortage

>> **LO 4.10 Identify the seven major options for overcoming a labor shortage.**

What if our forecasts show an expected shortage? What we need to analyze here is not only how fast we can solve the problem but also how quickly we can lower our number of employees again if we need to. The best options here are methods that are really fast in solving the shortage but that also can be reversed quickly if a surplus of employees starts to take form. As opposed to the surplus situation in the last section, we want to work here from the *top down* to the bottom. We would start with asking for or requiring overtime and work down the list as we have to, because again, we want the smallest possible disruption to our workforce.

Overtime

Our first option—the quickest and easiest way to fix a personnel shortage—is *overtime*. Can we force you to work overtime? The answer is yes. No federal law limits the option to require you to work a "reasonable amount" of overtime if you are an employee of the organization.[68] It works until we get to the point where we start to stress our people too much because the overtime becomes excessive. When stress levels get too high, employees' work will suffer.[69] So, if we start to see too much stress among our workforce, we need to do something else to relieve our personnel shortage. What other options do we have?

Temporary or Contract Workers

We can frequently use *temporary or contract workers* to overcome a short-term shortage, but we probably don't want to use temporary employees for more than a year at most, for reasons we will discuss shortly. Since the recession of 2008, many employers are reluctant to hire full-time employees, so firms are using temps and independent contractors and other forms of "gig workers" who are not legally employed by the firm. At an estimated "20–30% of the working-age population" in the United States and Europe,[70] these gig workers are an important and growing segment of the U.S. population and are increasingly prevalent throughout the developed world.[71] **(SHRM N:5)**

Hiring temporary and gig workers is a quick fix for shortages. And the upside is that hiring most forms of temporary help is easy to take back. When we no longer need a "temp," we just release that individual back to the temp agency. For contract workers, independent or otherwise, we allow the contract to lapse in order to release them.

However, there are some common problems. First, most gig workers have little or no loyalty to you and your organization and may not be motivated to work hard because they aren't staying.[72] They may not know the specific jobs in your company, and they generally don't know the company as well as do your permanent workers.[73] There can also sometimes be a clash between gig workers and permanent employees.

Temps and other contractors can also create legal problems for the organization. If an organization classifies a worker as an "independent contractor" and exerts significant control over the actions of that worker, then the organization can be judged guilty of misclassification of the worker.[74] This is becoming a much more significant concern in more progressive states like California, where the state courts recently created a new set of tests for whether or not an individual working with the company is an employee or a contractor.[75] If we misclassify the individual, the government can penalize the organization for not withholding employment taxes on the "employee" and not paying for required overtime wages and benefits, such as workers' compensation insurance and Social Security withholding.

Along the same lines, if the company keeps "temporary" employees longer than a year, then those workers are probably not really temporary, and they may be eligible for full-time employment benefits. **Microsoft** had to pay almost $100 million to about 10,000 workers that it had classified as temporary,[76] and **FedEx** was charged $319 million in unpaid employment taxes and penalties in 2007 because it misclassified drivers as contract workers.[77] **Uber** is fighting the same issue with their drivers as this book is being written. These are just some of the problems with gig workers of all types. However, they are highly revocable if we no longer need them.

Technological Innovation

Today, we may be able to overcome a shortage of personnel through technological innovation. In other words, we may be able to use machinery or robotics that can do the job of a human being. But this is a relatively slow process in many cases, and it cannot be revoked. We can't create or find new equipment, install it, and make it operational overnight. Also, if we create a group of robots that are capable of assembling our product, we are not going to stop using them and hire a bunch of new assembly workers again, are we? However, the cost of technology has come down so much and so fast that this has become a much more common option in resolving a labor shortage.

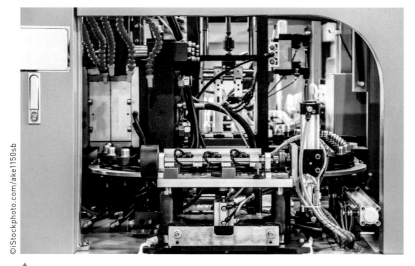

Technological innovations can help a company deal with a labor shortage by automating processes normally performed by people.

©iStockphoto.com/ake1150sb

Retraining Workers

The next three options take a bit longer to put into effect. We can *retrain workers,* but doing so isn't a quick response to a shortage.[78] This option is especially useful if we have a surplus of employees somewhere else. It is moderately fast and generally easy to revoke, because the workers are still trained to do their old jobs.

Outsourcing

Outsourcing may be another option. We can outsource to an outside organization a whole function that we currently do in-house.[79] For instance, we might outsource all of our computer-programming jobs to an outsourcing company that specializes in computer programming. This option is moderately fast, but it is not extremely fast because we have to find a company that can do the job, research the company, negotiate with it, come up with a contract, and then finally get it to do the work when we want it done.

Turnover Reduction

Next is *turnover reduction*. If fewer people voluntarily leave than we have predicted, we can reduce a projected shortage.[80] But how can we reduce turnover? We can improve working conditions or do other things that may cause our workforce to become more satisfied. We can adjust work hours (minimally), make benefits packages better, and maybe make work schedules a little better. As discussed, we can also use job design flexibility. Any of these might cause turnover to go down. But this won't happen overnight because it takes some time to change people's opinions of the organization. In addition, this option is very difficult to take back later.

New Hires

Our next option is to *hire new employees*. But this option takes a while, doesn't it? We have to go through a long process of analyzing the job, recruiting people, selecting employees, training, and working through a learning curve to get them capable of doing the work. We can see that this is a slow method of resolving a worker shortage. It is also not easy to take back.

Trends and Issues in HRM

In this chapter's trends and issues section, we will review Gig Work and the Agile Workforce. Secondly, we will brief you on Automation at Work in modern companies.

Gig Work and the Agile Workforce

Let's take a closer look at the changing shape of the workforce. The last edition of this text, published 3 years ago, noted that gig work was accounting for a little over 7% of the workforce in the United States. The most recent estimates for the various types of gig work—mostly forms of contract or temporary labor—are between 20% and 30%,[81] and that is expected to grow to nearly 50% of the labor force by 2025.[82,83]

Certainly, gig work is not going to overtake regular employment as the primary means of labor engagement any time soon, but as an optional form of work it is increasing at a massive rate. McKinsey Global Institute recently identified four types of independent workers: "free agents," who choose gig work and make a living doing it; "casual earners," who supplement their regular work with gigs; "reluctants," who work primarily through gigs but would rather have a regular job; and the "financially strapped," who do supplemental work because they need the money. McKinsey says that that as many as 162 million people do gig work in the United States and the major countries of the European Union.[84]

The U.S. federal government has taken notice of gig work also. The Bureau of Labor Statistics and the Census Bureau are trying to count how many gig workers there really are in the economy,[85] while the Department of Labor (DOL) and the Equal Employment Opportunity Commission (EEOC) are identifying ways in which gig workers may be misclassified or otherwise treated unfairly by employers. The major concern of the EEOC and the DOL is whether or not companies are misclassifying individuals as contractors when they are really company employees. (We will talk more about classification of employees for pay purposes in Chapter 11.) Regardless of government concern, it appears that gig work is going to continue to increase in areas where it is easy to identify discrete tasks that can be farmed out by the company and can be done quickly and easily by outsiders. Doing so allows companies to remain fairly lean in their number of permanent employees. Remember—companies should only hire new permanent employees as a last option!

Automation at Work

Automation, work that was once done by a person that is now relegated to machines or other technology, is increasing. In a 2017 study, 36% of C-suite and HR leaders had increased their use of artificial intelligence (AI) in the past 12 months as opposed to a year earlier when only 18% had increased AI usage.[86] That is a 100% increase in just one year! It is fairly clear from available information that use of automation in multiple forms—robotics, AI, neural network computers, analytics programs, and others—is increasing at record rates. Why now? The major answer is that we are now able to create computers and other automation with computer components that have the ability to *think, analyze, and learn* at least in some limited circumstances, and this ability is only going to get better—and cheaper—in the future.

Is this going to be a boon or bane for human workers? There are experts on both sides of this argument.[87] Some say new technology is going to create jobs—good jobs in computer engineering, data analysis and analytics, among others. Other experts say that the number of jobs created will be far fewer than the number that are wiped out by technological change in the near future. Experts *do* generally agree that as many as half of all jobs that currently exist are at risk of automation, and the more routine the job, the more likely it will be automated.[88] And the machine results also have fewer defects than their human counterparts.

There are arguments that some of the increase in the use of automation has been as a result of wage battles between employees and employers such as the "Fight for $15" campaign that some food/culinary unions are pushing.[89] Based on the evidence in this situation, it is very hard to say whether or not the automation of low-skilled jobs such as using "order-taking" kiosks or tablet computers is a result of the fight for higher human wages or simply because the technologies have become readily available and inexpensive. Regardless, the end result is going to be that lower skilled workers are going to find it harder to gain employment in the very near future. They will either have to become trained in higher level work that cannot currently be done through automation, or they will be relegated to a lifetime of minimal or no full-time work.[90]

Chapter Summary

4.1 Describe the process of workflow analysis, identifying why it is important to HRM.

We start our workflow analysis by determining the end result. Once we identify the result we expect, we can determine the steps or activities required to create the end result that we've identified. This is basically an analysis of the tasks that are going to have to be performed in order to create the output that we expect. Finally, we can identify the inputs that are going to be necessary to carry out the steps and perform the tasks. The inputs are known as the 4 Ms: machines (tools, equipment, and machines), material (physical resources used in production), manpower (the people needed in a particular production process), and money (the capital that must be spent to perform our processes).

4.2 Discuss the reason for job analysis, stating the expected outcomes of the process.

Job analysis provides the basis for every major HRM function, from selection and development to performance management and compensation. The two main outcomes are the *job description* and the *job specification*.

4.3 Identify the four major methods used for job analysis.

Questionnaires ask questions that help to identify the functions that are a part of a particular job, and then, in most cases, they assign a point value to each of those functions. In the job analysis *interview*, questions are asked verbally, usually of the incumbent, and the answers are compiled into a profile of the job. *Diaries* have the workers maintain a work log, or diary, in which they write down the tasks that they accomplish as they go about their job. This log becomes the document from which we build the description of the job. We can also use *observation* of the worker at work, where an observer shadows the worker and logs tasks that are performed over a period of time.

4.4   Discuss the four major approaches to job design.

Mechanistic job design focuses on designing jobs around the concepts of task specialization, skill simplification, and repetition. *Biological job design* focuses on minimizing the physical strain on the worker by structuring the physical work environment around the way the body works. *Perceptual-motor job design* attempts to make sure that workers remain within their normal mental capabilities and limitations. *Motivational job design* focuses on the job characteristics that affect psychological meaning and motivational potential, and it views attitudinal variables as the most important outcomes of job design.

4.5   Identify the components of the job characteristics model (JCM).

The five core job characteristics include skill variety, task identity, task significance, autonomy, and feedback. The first three lead collectively to the psychological state of *experienced meaningfulness of work,* in which workers believe their work has meaning. The fourth core characteristic of autonomy leads to the psychological state of *experienced responsibility for outcomes.* Finally, feedback leads to the psychological state of *knowledge of results*—the psychological feeling that we get from knowing the results and that in turn creates *satisfaction* with the results of our work.

All of the psychological states *collectively* lead to the outcomes: motivation, performance, job satisfaction/ engagement, absenteeism, and turnover. These can go up or down depending on the design of the job.

4.6   Explain the three major tools for motivational job design.

Job simplification is the process of eliminating or combining tasks and/or changing the work sequence to improve performance. It makes jobs more specialized. However, we might make the job less motivational if we simplify the work to the point where the worker gets bored. *Job expansion,* on the other hand, makes jobs less specialized. Jobs can be expanded through rotation, enlargement, and enrichment. *Flexibility in job design* includes flextime, job sharing, telecommuting, and compressed workweeks, and allows the manager to use these tools to increase worker motivation.

4.7   Discuss two types of HR forecasting.

Forecasting is done through the use of two methods: quantitative and qualitative forecasting. Quantitative forecasting utilizes mathematics to forecast future events based on historical information while qualitative forecasting generally uses the knowledge base of a pool of experts in a subject or industry. These experts will adjust the quantitative forecast based on their expertise.

4.8   Explain the three most common quantitative HR forecasting methods.

The three quantitative methods are the following:

- *Trend analysis* allows the company to look at historical trends—for instance, whether employment went up or down in a given year and how the number of employees related to revenue or productivity—and make judgments based on those trends.

- *Ratio analysis* calculates specific values by comparing a business factor with the number of employees needed.

- *Regression analysis* is a statistical technique in which we use a regression diagram made from historical data points to predict future needs presented with a y- and x-axis.

4.9   Identify the seven major options for managing a labor surplus.

The major options for managing surplus are a *layoff,* terminating a group of employees; *pay reduction,* which lowers the rate of pay for groups of employees; *work sharing,* where we cut hours available to each worker; *natural attrition,* where we lower employee numbers by not refilling jobs when turnover occurs; a *hiring freeze,* where we allow natural attrition, but in addition, we don't create any new jobs, even if they are needed; *retraining and transferring workers* from one job to another; and *early retirement,* where employees are given the choice of leaving the company before they would normally retire.

4.10   Identify the seven major options for overcoming a labor shortage.

Options for a shortage include *overtime,* our best option until we get to the point where we are starting to stress our people too much, and using *temporary workers* of many different types who can be used for short periods. Other options include *retraining workers, outsourcing, using technological innovation, reducing turnover, and hiring new employees.*

Key Terms

biological job design,   90
HR forecasting,   96
job analysis,   85
job characteristics model
    (JCM),   91
job description,   89
job design,   90

job expansion,   94
job simplification,   93
job specification,   89
layoff,   99
mechanistic job design,   90
motivational job design,   90
perceptual-motor job design,   90

qualitative forecasting,   97
quantitative forecast,   97
ratio analysis,   97
regression analysis,   97
trend analysis,   97
workflow analysis,   84

Key Terms Review

Complete each of the following statements using one of this chapter's key terms.

1. _____ is the tool that we use to identify what has to be done within the organization to produce a product or service.

2. _____ is the process used to identify the work performed and the working conditions for each of the jobs within our organizations.

3. _____ identifies the major tasks, duties, and responsibilities that are components of a job.

4. _____ identifies the qualifications of a person who should be capable of doing the job tasks noted in the job description.

5. _____ is the process of identifying tasks that each employee is responsible for completing as well as how those tasks will be accomplished.

6. _____ focuses on designing jobs around the concepts of task specialization, skill simplification, and repetition.

7. _____ focuses on minimizing the physical strain on the worker by structuring the physical work environment around the way the body works.

8. _____ focuses on designing jobs in which the tasks remain within the worker's normal mental capabilities and limitations.

9. _____ focuses on the job characteristics that affect the psychological meaning and motivational potential, and it views attitudinal variables as the most important outcomes of job design.

10. _____ provides a conceptual framework for designing or enriching jobs based on core job characteristics.

11. _____ is the process of eliminating or combining tasks and/or changing the work sequence to improve performance.

12. _____ is the process of making jobs broader, with less repetition.

13. _____ identifies the estimated supply and demand for the different types of human resources in the organization over some future period, based on analysis of past and present demand.

14. _____ utilizes mathematics to forecast future events based on historical data.

15. _____ is a process of reviewing historical items such as revenues, and relating those changes to some business factor to form a predictive chart.

16. _____ is the process of reviewing historical data and calculating specific proportions between a business factor (such as production) and the number of employees needed.

17. _____ is a statistical technique that identifies the relationship between a series of variable data points for use in forecasting future variables.

18. _____ uses nonquantitative methods to forecast the future, usually based on the knowledge of a pool of experts in a subject or an industry.

19. _____ is a process of terminating a group of employees, with intent to improve organizational efficiency and effectiveness.

Communication Skills

The following critical-thinking questions can be used for class discussion and/or for written assignments to develop communication skills. Be sure to give complete explanations for all answers.

1. Think of something you could make or build. Now analyze the workflows to make that item, using the information in the book. Don't forget to identify what you would need in each category of the 4 Ms.

2. Think of a job that you have held or that was held by someone you know. If you were going to analyze that job using one of the methods in the book, which method would you use and why?

3. Can more than one of the four main approaches to job design be used at the same time to design a job? Can you provide an example of how this could work?

4. Are there any situations in which you might design a job using the JCM and yet the job would still not be motivational? What circumstances might cause this to happen?

5. Do you think that using flextime, telecommuting, job sharing, or compressed workweeks is really going to motivate employees? Why or why not?

6. Have you seen job simplification, job rotation, or job expansion being used in your workplace? (If you aren't currently working, use a workplace that you are familiar with.) Did it work to motivate the employees? Why?

7. Which of the three quantitative forecasting methods do you think would give you the most accurate forecast? Explain your choice.

8. Is a layoff, or downsizing, ever the best option to resolve a projected surplus in an organization? Justify your answer.

9. How much overtime is reasonable in a week? How long can the company expect workers to continue to work overtime before they see employee stress levels getting significantly higher than normal?

Case 4.1 Walmart's Everyday Hiring Strategy: Fueling Future Consumer Demand With Passion and Talent[91]

Walmart is the world's largest company by revenue and is the world's top retailer with more than 2.3 million employees. In the United States, Walmart operates more than 5,300 stores, including about 4,570 Walmart stores and 655 Sam's Club warehouses, and a growing number of smaller format stores. The company's faster growing international division (26% of sales) numbers more than 6,100 locations. Walmart is the number one retailer in Canada and Mexico and has operations in Asia (where it owns a 95% stake in Japanese retailer SEIYU), Africa, Europe, and Latin America.[92]

How can Walmart continue to expand successfully in the United States as well as internationally? Walmart's human resource management (HRM) is a critical success factor for the business's growth and influences how Walmart maintains its more than 2 million employees to provide service to an expanding population of consumers. How does human resources (HR) perform such functions? Job analysis and design are implemented through the company's hierarchical functional structure. Walmart uses work-oriented

job analysis and worker-oriented job analysis. The company applies work-oriented job analysis for sales positions in the form of interviews and direct observations. HR uses direct observation of sales personnel's activities while conducting interviews to analyze the jobs of team leaders and supervisors. This method enables HR to establish expectable job outcomes. On the other hand, the worker-oriented job analysis method is used to analyze managerial jobs and provides information on interpersonal, cognitive, and perceptual abilities. A specific application of this method is through the work profiling system. This method enables Walmart's HRM to pinpoint the necessary capabilities of managers, such as store managers and corporate managers.

HR uses the following variables based on job analysis as the criteria for job descriptions: Position, Functions, Duties, Performance Standards, Job Factors, and Job Knowledge. The company uses a wide array of job specifications that are broken down into essential attributes and desirable attributes and included in all job descriptions.

For managerial positions, HR's essential attributes accentuate analytical and problem-solving knowledge, skills, and abilities. In contrast, for sales personnel, HR emphasizes the essential attributes of job knowledge and interpersonal skills. More precisely, HR specifies communication skills, knowledge of the business, and knowledge of products. However, there are also some attributes classified as desirable (preferred but not necessary for a sales employee to fulfill the job). Walmart's HRM specifies desirable attributes as likeable and sociable qualities and multitasking skills.

HR forecasts its workforce needs to ensure they have the capacity to address changes in consumer demand while not being oversized. The three most notable forecasting techniques are the bottom-up approach, trend analysis, and the Delphi method. The bottom-up approach analyzes human resource needs starting at the lowest level of the organizational structure. HR's objective for this approach is to ensure that all levels of the organization have adequate employees based on HR needs at the frontline (e.g., hourly sales employees); forecasting therefore begins with these frontline employees. HR managers then proceed to analyze HR needs at the next higher level of the organizational structure. This approach ensures that all human resource needs at the lowest levels of Walmart's organizational structure are supported through an adequate number of employees at the upper levels of the organizational structure. On the other hand, trend analysis is used to predict future HR needs based on current needs. Walmart's HRM uses trend analysis to determine HR needs along with the company's global expansion. In addition, the Delphi method forecasts future HR needs based on expert opinion. Walmart's HRM uses the Delphi method to ensure adequate human resources in establishing new brands, stores, or other facilities. For example, HR experts can discuss the HR needs in opening a new Walmart store of a certain size. The company's HRM applies the Delphi method to estimate the number of employees needed in each type of job, such as supply chain jobs, inventory jobs, and sales jobs.

Walmart faces minimal concerns about the shortage of employees; however, Walmart experiences HR surplus when aggregate consumption declines. Such surplus is a challenge to HRM because it translates to lower HR cost-effectiveness. Walmart uses the following approaches to determine HR needs and prevent surpluses or shortages: sales performance analysis, turnover rate analysis, and gap analysis.

HR changes recruitment efforts based on changes in sales performance, which is an indicator of HR needs. Turnover, together with the rate of recruitment, is an indicator of changes in the size of the company's workforce. HR ensures that the recruitment rate is commensurate to the turnover rate. An increase in workforce size usually happens when the company expands or opens new stores. In addition, HR uses gap analysis to determine the gap between HR needs and actual HR capacity. A significant gap means reduced HR cost-effectiveness or inadequacy in meeting organizational needs. Gap analysis is used to decide on changing recruitment efforts. The company has a gap allowance or threshold. When the HR gap exceeds the threshold, HR increases or decreases recruitment efforts. HR supply and demand is balanced by adjusting compensation strategy and recruitment efforts. These adjustments are based on trends in internal human resource demand and the rate of applicant entry.

Changes in recruitment are HR's main approach to balance HR supply and demand. HR changes the recruitment rate to address workforce requirements. Recruitment efforts can easily be adjusted without significantly affecting financial performance. In prioritizing changes in recruitment to balance HR supply and demand, HR minimizes changes in the firm's compensation strategy. On the other hand, changes in compensation are also used to prevent an imbalance in HR supply and demand. The compensation strategy is designed to minimize HR expenditures. This strategy agrees with the company's cost leadership generic strategy. When HR supply becomes inadequate, Walmart's last resort is to increase wages. Theoretically, higher wages attract more applicants. Walmart's HRM uses this second approach to compete effectively in the labor market.[93]

Questions

1. How is job analysis performed at Walmart? What job analysis methods are employed?

2. What are the pros and cons of the job analysis methods used for Walmart's salesforce?

3. For which position does Walmart use task- or competency-based job analysis?

4. What are the main differences in job specifications between Walmart's sales force and their managers?

5. What are the methods Walmart uses for HR forecasting? Which are quantitative and which are qualitative?

6. How does Walmart try to prevent labor shortages or surpluses?

Case created by Herbert Sherman, PhD, and Theodore Vallas, Department of Management Sciences, Long Island University School of Business, Brooklyn Campus

Skill Builder 4.1 Job Analysis

Objective

To develop your skill at completing a job analysis; to improve your ability to get ready

Skills

The primary skills developed through this exercise are as follows:

1. *HR management skills*—Technical, business, and conceptual and design skills

2. *SHRM 2018 Curriculum Guidebook*—I: Job Analysis and Job Design

Overview

Your output is to arrive at school or work. Your inputs (4 Ms) are each and every task you perform until you arrive at your destination. Through your job analysis flowchart, improve the efficiency of your inputs so you can get more done in less time, with better results.

Step 1. Make a Flowchart

List step-by-step exactly what you do from the time you get up (or start your routine) until the time you start school or work. Get up or start earlier, say 15 minutes, to allow enough time to complete your flowchart without making you late. Be sure to number each step and list each activity separately with its M (don't just say "go to the bathroom"—list each activity in sequence while in there). For example:

1. **Get up at 7:00—manpower**

2. **Go to bathroom—manpower**

3. **Take shower—material**

4. **Dry hair—material**

   . . .

18. **Drive car—material**

19. **Buy coffee—money**

20. **Walk to school at 8:00—manpower**

Step 2. Analyze the Flowchart

Later in the day, when you have time, do a job simplification analysis of your flowchart of activities to determine if you can do the following:

— Eliminate: Are you doing anything that you don't need to do?

— Combine: Can you multitask any simple tasks, make fewer trips to the bathroom, etc.?

— Change sequence: Will you be more efficient if you rearrange your flowchart of tasks?

Step 3. Develop a New Flowchart

Based on your analysis, make a new flowchart that eliminates, combines, and changes the sequence of tasks you will perform to get ready more efficiently.

Step 4. Change Your Routine

Consciously follow the steps of your new flowchart until it becomes your new habit.

Apply It

What did I learn from this experience? How will I use this knowledge in the future?

_____

_____

Your instructor may ask you to do this Skill Builder in class in a group. If so, the instructor will provide you with any necessary information or additional instructions.

Skill Builder 4.2 Job Characteristics Model (JCM)

Objective

To develop your skill at implementing the JCM

Skills

The primary skills developed through this exercise are as follows:

1. *HR management skills*—Technical, business, and conceptual and design skills

2. *SHRM 2018 Curriculum Guidebook*—I: Job Analysis and Job Design

Preparation

Select a job you have now or have held in the past. Using Exhibit 4.2: The Job Characteristics Model (JCM) and Exhibit 4.4: Job Design Options, Processes, and the JCM, apply these concepts to do a job analysis for your job. Be sure to use the exact terms from the text. The two exhibits provide a good summary of the process and terminology.

Apply It

What did I learn from this experience? How will I use this knowledge in the future?

_____

_____

Would you change your job to make it more motivational? If so, how and why?

_____

_____

Your instructor may ask you to do this Skill Builder in class in a group. If so, the instructor will provide you with any necessary information or additional instructions.

Skill Builder 4.3 O*NET

Objective

To visit O*NET and learn how to use Career Exploration Tools and/or to learn more about a job.

Skills

The primary skills developed through this exercise are as follows:

1. *HR management skills*—Technical, business, and conceptual and design skills

2. *SHRM 2018 Curriculum Guidebook*—I: Job Analysis and Job Design

Preparation

The instructor or student selects one or both options:

a. Select a job you would like to learn more about, visit http://www.onetonline.org, and search for the job. Write a brief report identifying your job search and state what you learned about the job.

b. Complete Self-Assessment 4.1 O*NET Interest Profiler following the instructions on page 87. Write a brief report including your results of the Interest Profile and identifying what you learned about yourself. You may be asked to pass in your answers and/or share them during class or online.

Apply It

What did I learn from this experience? How will I use this knowledge in the future?

_____

_____

Your instructor may ask you to discuss your results in a group or as a class. If so, the instructor will provide you with any necessary information or additional instructions.

©iStockphoto.com/Steve Debenport

Recruiting Job Candidates

Learning Outcomes

After studying this chapter, you should be able to do the following:

5.1 Describe the main external forces acting on recruiting efforts. **PAGE 114**

5.2 Name the five main organizational recruiting considerations. **PAGE 115**

5.3 Identify the major advantages and disadvantages of both internal and external recruiting. **PAGE 117**

5.4 Summarize the major challenges and constraints involved in the recruiting process. **PAGE 121**

5.5 Discuss the basic methods available for evaluating the recruiting process. **PAGE 124**

SHRM HR Content

See Online: *SHRM 2018 Curriculum Guidebook* for the complete list

J. Managing a Diverse Workforce

    7. Generational differences: The multigenerational workforce

K. Metrics and Measurement of HR

    4. Calculating and interpreting yield ratios

N. Staffing (Recruitment and Selection)

    3-a. Determining labor demand and supply—External influences on staffing: labor markets, unions, economic conditions, technology

    4-a. Employment brand—Image advertising

    6. External influences on staffing: Labor markets, unions, economic conditions, technology

    9-a. Online recruiting—Electronic recruiting

    9-b. Online recruiting—Use of social media in recruitment

    11-a. Sources—External recruitment: Recruiters, open vs. targeted recruitment, recruitment sources, applicant reactions, medium (electronic, advertisement)

    11-c. Sources—Internal sources (employee referrals, posting, internal applicants)

Practitioner's Perspective

Cindy describes the day that Angie timidly knocked at her door before she came into her office. Angie said, "I know I just started here last month, but I'm giving you my 2 weeks' notice. I just can't do this anymore."

"What seems to be the problem?" Cindy asked.

"Well, when I accepted the job of quality administrative assistant, I never expected to actually have to go to the units to gather information as part of my work. Being around the patients makes me uncomfortable."

Uh-oh. Angie and Cindy just experienced the fallout from a process breakdown that apparently prevented her from getting a realistic preview of her job duties. Why does an honest exchange of information matter when you are recruiting? How does a high turnover rate impact your company? The factors you need to consider as you endeavor to attract and retain the best qualified candidates are highlighted in Chapter 5.

The Recruiting Process

>> **LO 5.1 Describe the main external forces acting on recruiting efforts.**

Recruiting is important for many businesses,[1] but for **Amazon** in 2018, they were looking to hire as many as 50,000 new people for "HQ2."[2] And this doesn't even count seasonal workers they expected to hire for the Christmas holiday season—about another 100,000 people. The total costs associated with recruiting, selecting, and training new employees often add up to as much as 300% to 400% of their individual annual salaries, according to a series of estimates,[3,4,5] so we need to get it right. Thus, recruiting has become a top priority.[6]

After HR managers have determined our hiring needs through the forecasting process, and after we have done job analyses (providing job descriptions and job specifications), we begin the *talent acquisition process:* We will need to recruit the correct numbers and types of people to fill our job openings, and then select from the recruit pool. We can't select and hire good employees without effectively recruiting them.[7]

Recruiting is *the process of creating a reasonable pool of qualified candidates for a job opening.* Notice that this definition identifies the fact that we need *qualified* applicants.[8] In a recent study, 84% of HR professionals reported candidates having "applied skill deficits (such as problem solving skills)" and 68% were having difficulty in filling jobs.[9] Recruiting isn't effective if the candidates we attract are not qualified to do the work.

If you think about it, you will also realize that if you find too many applicants, it costs the organization too much to go through the selection process. On the other hand, finding too few candidates allows no real *selection* process. Typically, a good rule of thumb might be to recruit about 15 to 25 qualified candidates *for each job opening.* That's just a rule of thumb, but it is probably going to allow a reasonable applicant pool. However, you may get more or less if you don't target your recruiting correctly.

To fill an opening, potential job candidates must generally be made aware that the organization is seeking employees. They must then be persuaded to apply for the jobs. In the talent acquisition process, we want to use a series of tools to show the candidates why they might want to become a part of the organization. We will discuss these tools as we go through the remainder of this chapter.

External Forces Acting on Recruiting Efforts

First, though, we want to identify the forces that affect our ability to successfully recruit new employees. A series of external forces affect our ability to recruit individuals into our organization at a particular point in time.[10] Think about what is happening around you right now. Is the unemployment rate high or low? Are there government incentives to increase hiring, or is government doing very little to increase employment? Is the available supply of people with advanced skills very large, or are there not enough people with high-level skill sets available? Generally, the external forces acting on recruiting fall into two large categories: the available labor market and the social and legal environment.

The Labor Market

The availability of talent to fill our needs depends on several items in the labor market, including labor supply and demand, the unemployment rate, and competition for that labor.[11] The **labor market** is *the external pool of candidates from which we draw our recruits.* **(SHRM N:3-a and N:6)**

First, to evaluate the available labor market, we must consider the *supply and demand* factors in a particular category of jobs. This issue usually ties in directly with the *unemployment rate* in an area. Every business recruits primarily from an identifiable geographic area. So we need to identify our recruiting area, whether that is local, regional, national, or international, and then determine what the unemployment rate is in that area. If unemployment is high, the job of recruiting is generally easier than if unemployment is very low.

Competition will also affect the labor market. If recruiting competition is very strong for available talent such as mechanical engineers—for instance, if there are a significant number of competitors and each competitor needs a large number of engineers—then it will be a more difficult recruiting environment.[12]

Recruiting The process of creating a reasonable pool of qualified candidates for a job opening

Labor market The external pool of candidates from which we draw our recruits

Social and Legal Environment

The *social environment* also affects our ability to recruit people.[13] Generational changes are creating new challenges for recruiting professionals. The millennial generation is now the largest group in the U.S. workforce along with the workforce in most EU nations. However, most companies will have at least four distinct generations in their workforce at the same time: baby boomers (1946–1964); Gen X or the baby busters (1965–1979); Gen Y or the millennials (1980–1994); and just the beginning of Gen Z or the iGeneration (1995–present).[14,15] Each generation has different ways of working. Millennials tend to work better when working in a collaborative environment while the newest Gen Z workers want their own space and their own goals.[16] In many cases, new employees also expect a high level of benefits and good opportunities for training and development.[17] In order for recruiters to be successful, they will need to approach individuals from different generations in different ways. **(SHRM J:7)**

We also have to take into account the *legal environment* that limits the ways in which we can recruit. First and most obviously, we have to abide by all of the equal employment opportunity (EEO) laws that we discussed in Chapter 3, and we must avoid any issues of discrimination in our recruiting efforts. There are also laws in some situations that limit our ability to lure employees away from competitor firms. These anti-poaching and "wage-fixing" laws significantly limit ability to attract talent from competitor companies in some industries.[18] In other cases, labor agreements may limit our ability to recruit, or a union may be able to place limits on our ability to recruit from outside of the union's ranks. We may also choose to recruit more part-timers due to the costs involved with the Affordable Care Act.[19] In addition, states have become much more active in creating employment laws. HR managers must therefore be well versed in the various laws, agreements, and regulations that in any way limit their ability to recruit.

Organizational Recruiting Considerations

>> **LO 5.2 Name the five main organizational recruiting considerations.**

Once we become aware of the limitations that are placed on us externally by the labor market and the social/legal environment, we can start to consider the internal issues that control our recruiting processes. We have to set recruiting policies in order to be consistent, in order to be fair and equitable, and so we can defend our processes legally if it becomes necessary. So, what do we have to think about, and in what level of detail?

What Policies to Set

We have to determine *how* we are going to go through the recruiting process before we start trying to recruit new members into our workforce. The policies we set will determine our actions on the other four major recruiting considerations. Among other things, we have to answer questions concerning when we will recruit new members into the organization, alternatives to new recruits, where we recruit (local, national, global), and how to incorporate technology into our efforts. Let's discuss these four primary items we will need to consider before the recruiting process starts.

When to Recruit

Yes! We recruit when we need someone to fill a job. But it's not that simple. There are alternatives to recruitment to mitigate a worker shortage, and which alternative we choose depends on a number of factors. We need to identify the points at which we would generally go through the process of starting and carrying out a recruitment campaign. We don't want to go through a long recruiting process and then figure out that we didn't need to—we would just be wasting time and money.

Alternatives to Recruitment

Do we have a viable and financially feasible way to solve our shortage other than through recruitment? Is the alternative less expensive or better for our circumstances in some other way?

Remember that alternatives may include using overtime, outsourcing some work, or using temporary or contract workers or other options to mitigate a shortage—at least temporarily. We need to analyze each of these options before deciding on new hires, and we need to create a policy concerning when each of these options is useful.

Reach of the Recruiting Effort

We also need to identify our effective labor market. Do we plan to recruit only from local sources? Should we consider people all over a particular region (e.g., the mid-South or New England)? Do we need to recruit nationally or even globally?[20] The answer, again, is "It depends." Can we find the right number and types of employees if we only recruit locally? If not, we may be forced to recruit from a broader pool of talent. Is the job that we are recruiting for so specialized that we need to recruit from all over the world? We must remember that it is time-consuming and expensive to bring people to the organization from far away. So we only expand our geographic recruiting area when we need to.

However, despite the political debate, the U.S. economy needs foreign workers to fill both low- and high-skilled jobs. Some 27 million workers (about 17% of the labor force) are foreign-born—and 5% of these are unauthorized immigrants.[21] There is also a shortage of highly skilled workers, and major multinational corporations search and recruit from around the world to attract the top candidates, and as a method of hiring for diversity.[22]

©iStockphoto.com/SeanShot

▲

When planning to recruit new employees, an organization needs to decide how it will utilize social media in recruitment efforts.

The Technology Recruiting Revolution

More and more, companies are targeting recruiting efforts to very specific candidates with exacting requirements. The only way we have good reach into the appropriate labor market in such cases is by using technology and specific online platforms to look for the few candidates who match our needs.

Many firms are heavily using social media sites, including **LinkedIn** and **Facebook**, which can provide recruiters with much more reach than they had in the past.[23] However, this reach also brings with it some significant issues for the business—such as having to pour over thousands of résumés in response to a single job opening. So to avoid this problem, you have to understand social media's reach and use it selectively, whether you're a job seeker or a recruiter.

Social media provides a number of valuable recruiting services. For example, in May 2017, Facebook had more than 1.923 billion monthly active users (nearly 2 of every 7 people on earth!), meaning it gives recruiters a huge reach into the global labor market.[24] Especially in higher-level job recruiting, where there will be few individuals with the necessary skills. Social media job sites like **Indeed** (200 million unique visitors per month in 2017), **Jobvite**, or **Monster.com**, and now **Google for Jobs**, can get our message out to a much larger group of potential candidates across the country or even around the world.[25]

Social media sites such as **LinkedIn** can also provide the candidate with information on our company values and culture.[26] This profile information can help individuals make a better decision concerning whether or not they would be comfortable in our organization, which in turn lowers the possibility they will leave shortly after they arrive.

Recruiters are also beginning to heavily use *artificial intelligence (AI)* and other *smart technology* recruiting tools in their jobs. AI is changing the way managers do their jobs—from who gets hired, to how new employees are evaluated, to who gets promoted. A company can provide a job description, and AI will collect and crunch data from a variety of sources to find people that match.[27] Chatbots follow up with active candidates, schedulers set appointments, search programs look for and query passive candidates about interest in open positions, and other tools now take care of many routine tasks for the recruiter. Programs like Mya from **Firstjob**,[28] Olivia by **Recruiting.ai**,[29] and RAI from **HiringSolved**,[30] will continue to take over many of the common tasks in recruiter interactions with candidates and applicants. **(SHRM N:9-a and N:9-b)**

Issues With Technology Recruiting

There *are* problems with technology-based and social media recruiting, and some of them are significant dangers to the company. For instance, there is the potential for discrimination through disparate treatment of individuals because of information posted on their Facebook or LinkedIn sites or on their Twitter feed.[31,32] There can also be bias built in to AI programs, causing the searches done to be biased.[33] Pictures can potentially identify individuals as members of a protected class, and those pictures may cause subconscious bias on the part of some recruiters. AI systems also pose privacy issues.[34] Any privacy invasion or bias, whether intentional or unintentional, is a danger to the organization during the recruiting and hiring process.

Internal or External Recruiting?

>> **LO 5.3 Identify the major advantages and disadvantages of both internal and external recruiting.**

People provide a competitive advantage,[35] so it is critical to use the right recruiting source for the specific job.[36] A general internal recruiting policy like "we promote from within" sounds good, but we also have to recruit externally to fill at least some jobs. So the question is, which jobs do we fill with current employees, and which jobs do we recruit from outside the firm? If we say our policy is to promote from within and we hire an outsider to fill a management position, many of our employees will begin to think that we don't follow our policy and won't trust management. However, if our policies say that we will go outside for recruits when it is unlikely that anyone in the organization would have the skill set necessary to do the job identified in our job specification, then we can provide a legitimate answer to someone who questions our recruiting process.

When we are instituting new processes or we have identified significant resistance to change as an issue in a section of the organization, we may need to bring in new people with new ideas and different skills. We may also identify specific occupations in our organization that will typically be recruited from outside, usually due to the need for a specialized skill set (e.g., nuclear plant operator or corporate attorney). It is unlikely that we would promote from within to these types of positions.

In this section, we discuss internal versus external recruiting efforts and the advantages and disadvantages of each approach.

Internal Recruiting

Internal recruiting involves *filling job openings with current employees or people the employees know*. There are two common types of internal recruiting:

- *Promotions from within.* Many organizations post job openings on physical or electronic bulletin boards, in company newsletters, and so on. Current employees may apply or bid for the open positions. Around 66% of **Wegmans** appointments are filled internally.[37]

- *Employee referrals.* Employees may be encouraged to refer friends and relatives for positions. **Jobvite** notes that about 40% of its client-company new hires are from existing employee referrals.[38] For hard-to-recruit-for jobs, some firms pay a bonus to employees when their referred applicant is hired. **(SHRM N:11-c)**

Internal recruiting Filling job openings with current employees or people the employees know

Advantages and Disadvantages of Internal Recruiting

Is it generally a good idea to recruit from inside the organization? What are the major advantages and disadvantages of internal recruiting?

Advantages include the following:

- There may be increases in organizational engagement and job satisfaction based on the opportunity to advance, with commensurate increases in pay.

- The internal recruit will be able to learn more about the "big picture" in the company and become more valuable.

- The individual also has shown at least some interest in the organization, has knowledge of our operations and processes, and feels comfortable continuing employment within the company.

- The company has existing knowledge of the applicant and a record of that person's previous work.

- The organization can save money by recruiting internally because of both lower advertisement costs and lower training costs.

- Internal recruiting is usually faster than external recruiting.

And here are some of the disadvantages:

- The pool of applicants is significantly smaller in internal recruiting.

- There will still be a job to fill—the employee will move from somewhere else in the organization into the new job, so that employee's old job will need to be filled as well.

- Success in one job doesn't necessarily mean success in a significantly different job, especially if the employee is promoted to supervise former coworkers.

- An external candidate may have better qualifications for the job opening.

- Current employees may feel they are entitled to the job whether or not they are capable and qualified, especially if we have a strong policy of preferring internal candidates.

- And the biggest threat to the company: We may create or perpetuate a strong resistance to change or stifle creativity and innovation because everyone in the organization, even the "new hires," is part of the old organizational culture.

External Recruiting

External recruiting The process of engaging individuals from the labor market outside the firm to apply for a job

Companies commonly recruit people from outside the firm to satisfy their HR needs.[39] **External recruiting** is *the process of engaging individuals from the labor market outside the firm to apply for a job*. To recruit qualified external candidates, we have to look at the type of person we are trying to find and then go to the source or sources that will most likely provide that type of person. Our internal and external recruiting options are listed with a summary of strengths in Exhibit 5.1. Let's briefly review each external option now. **(SHRM N:11-a)**

Walk-Ins

Qualified candidates may come to an organization "cold" and ask for a job. Walk-ins may be good recruits for a couple of reasons. First, they have already selected your organization as an employment target, and second, there are no advertising costs associated with walk-ins. So the process can occur much more quickly than it would with other external recruiting methods. However, candidates seeking professional and management-level positions generally send a résumé and cover letter asking for an interview.

Educational Institutions

Educational institutions are good places to recruit people who have little or no prior experience but have a good general skill set, such as a degree. Do recruiters come to your college to interview and hire graduates?

Employment Agencies

There are three major types of employment agencies: temporary, public, and private.

Temporary agencies, such as **Kelly Services**, provide part- or full-time help for limited periods. They are useful for replacing employees who will be out for a short period of time or for supplementing the regular workforce during busy periods. Some HR experts expect the number

EXHIBIT 5.1 ● Major Recruiting Sources

Internal Sources	Strengths
(A) Promotion from within	Provides current employees new job opportunities within the firm
(B) Employee referral	Inexpensive recruiting based on employee knowledge of the candidate

External Sources	Strengths
(C) Walk-ins	Inexpensive and self-selected
(D) Educational institutions	Good basic skill sets; typically less expensive than others with more experience
Employment agencies	Temporary, public, or private
1. (E) *Temporary agencies*	Prescreened workers; useful in short-term shortage situations
2. (F) *Public agencies*	At least some prescreening; very inexpensive
3. (G) *Private agencies*	Heavy prescreening of recruits, lowering organizational prescreening costs; typically very well targeted; good for experienced recruits
Advertising	Local mass media, specialized publications, or Internet
1. (H) *Local mass media*	Fairly broad reach if searching for many recruits; cost per person is low; good for semiskilled or skilled line employees
2. (I) *Specialized publications*	Good for targeting specific types of recruits; fairly good reach; fairly low cost per person
3. (J) *Internet*	Very broad reach; beginning to be able to target to specific audiences as many professional organizations have sites

of short- and long-term temps to continue to increase.[40] However, make sure your temps are not really full-time employees, like in our **Microsoft** discussion in Chapter 4, or you, too, might face a lawsuit.

Public agencies are state employment services. They generally provide job candidates to employers at no cost or very low cost. Too often, the public agencies get reputations as havens for the hard-core unemployed—those who do not want to work. However, they can be a strong source of good-quality employees, especially in bad economic conditions when many good workers lose their jobs.

Private employment agencies are privately owned and charge a fee for their services of recruiting candidates for you. Private agencies are generally used for recruiting people with prior experience. Here are three different types of private employment agencies you can use:

- *General employment agencies.* Some of them charge job seekers for their services, and others charge the employer. They are generally used for lower-level jobs that require experience.

- *Contingency agencies.* They offer candidates to the employer and are paid when the job candidate is hired by the employer. Contingency agencies frequently work with a more skilled set of clients, such as high-level manufacturing skills or mid-level management experience.

- *Retained search firms or executive recruiters.* They are paid to search for a specific type of recruit for the organization and will be paid regardless of success in their recruiting efforts. Often referred to as "headhunters," they specialize in recruiting senior managers and/or those with specific high-level technical skills, like highly specialized engineers and

©iStockphoto/ablokhin

▲
There are various ways to
advertise for job openings and
to recruit new employees.

information technology (IT)/computer experts. They help ensure the right person is hired.[41] They tend to charge the employer a large fee and will be at least partially paid whether or not there is a successful hire.

Advertising

A simple "Help Wanted" sign in the window is an advertisement. Newspapers are places to advertise positions, but advertising in professional and trade magazines may be more suitable for specific professional recruiting. There are also several online job search websites, such as **Indeed**, **Monster.com**, and **Google for Jobs**, which is partnering with companies such as **LinkedIn**, **Facebook**, **Careerbuilder** and **Glassdoor**. Here are three main ad options:

- *Local mass media.* Is the *Daily Planet* (Thanks, Superman!), Channel 5, or the oldies FM radio station a good option for your recruiting dollars? As usual, it depends on what kind of candidate you are looking for. Local advertising generally works to recruit semiskilled or skilled line employees but may not work as well for highly skilled managers. Ads are especially useful if you need a large number of recruits for a specific type of job.

- *Specialized publications.* These target specific groups—the *Wall Street Journal* and *APICS Magazine* are two examples. There are many types of industry trade and professional publications you can use to recruit the niche candidates you are looking for.

- *The Internet.* Should your company put every job opening up on the Internet? In many cases, companies are discovering they may not want to advertise every job opening on the Internet because of its reach.[42] They just don't have the time to wade through possibly thousands of applications for a single opening. Jobs requiring computer or other high-level technical skills would probably have good potential for Internet recruitment. But you may not find a five-star chef on the Internet because they may use other job search methods.

As you can see, there are a number of options when recruiting externally. Regardless of method, however, external recruiting has gone mobile and agile to a great extent. Technology is finally becoming a valuable time-saver for the recruiter, so you will need to keep in mind the earlier information on AI and other recruiting technologies as you recruit externally.

Advantages and Disadvantages of External Recruiting

So, what are the advantages and disadvantages of external recruiting?

Advantages include the following:

- The first and biggest advantage is the mirror image of the biggest disadvantage in internal recruiting—we *avoid* creating or perpetuating resistance to change, allowing a foothold for innovative new ways of operating.

- We may be able to find individuals with complex skill sets who are not available internally.

- We can lower training costs for skilled positions by externally hiring someone with the requisite skills.

- External hires will frequently increase organizational diversity.

What about disadvantages? There are certainly potential problems in bringing outsiders into the company.

- There may be disruption of the work team due to introducing significantly different ways of operating.

- External recruiting takes much longer, which means it costs more.

- It might adversely affect current employees' motivation and satisfaction due to the perceived inability to move up in the organization.

- External recruiting likely will incur higher orientation and training costs than internal recruiting.

- The candidate may look great on paper, but we have no organizational history on the individual.

5.1 APPLYING THE CONCEPT
RECRUITING SOURCES

Using Exhibit 5.1: Major Recruiting Sources, write the letter (A–J) of which recruiting source is most appropriate in each of the following recruiting situations:

_____ 1. You need a CEO from outside the company.

_____ 2. "We need more employees, Jean. Do you know anyone interested in working for us?"

_____ 3. We need to hire a new history professor.

_____ 4. We need another computer programmer.

_____ 5. A worker got hurt on the job and will be out for a week.

_____ 6. We need an experienced clerical worker, but we don't have any money for ads.

_____ 7. We need a person to perform routine cleaning services, and experience is not necessary.

_____ 8. The VP of finance needs a new administrative assistant.

_____ 9. We have a supervisor retiring in a month.

_____ 10. We like to hire young people without experience in order to train them to sell using a unique approach.

Challenges and Constraints in Recruiting

>> **LO 5.4 Summarize the major challenges and constraints involved in the recruiting process.**

Recruiting is challenging today because it is difficult to attract and retain top talent,[43] making it a top priority.[44] The process of recruiting is time-consuming and expensive.[45] As a result, we want to pay attention to the effectiveness of our recruiting methods. We have budgetary and other constraints, so we face the challenge of balance in finding qualified candidates without spending too much and without recruiting too many or too few candidates. So let's discuss these issues in this section.

Budgetary Constraints

We obviously have to live within our budgets in all cases, and recruiting is no exception. There are times when we would like to fly half a dozen top-notch recruits in from around the world to interview for a position, but such costs add up very quickly. Generally, the more value the recruit brings to the firm, the more we can afford to spend.

Policy Constraints and Organizational Image

There are many *organizational policies* that can affect our recruiting efforts. Whether we have a *promote-from-within* policy or not affects how we recruit. Our policies on *temporary-to-permanent* employees would also affect how we recruit in most cases. Do we have policies concerning *recruiting and hiring relatives* of current employees? If so, this would affect our recruiting efforts. Do we have an *affirmative action policy* in the organization? If so, it will dictate many of our recruiting procedures. We can also have other policies that affect recruiting. **(SHRM N:4-a)**

We are also affected in our recruiting efforts by our *organizational image* in the markets from which we source our recruits.[46] You may know of a company in your local community that you would not apply to because of its bad reputation, and there may be others you want to work for. This is just one of many reasons why we want to maintain a strong reputation in the communities that we serve.

Job Characteristics

Let's face it. Not every job we need to fill is glamorous, and every job has some aspects we'd rather not deal with. We need to realize that not everyone wants, or can get, great jobs. Some people are very happy in low-level jobs you may find boring, and they do a great job. The key is to recruit "qualified" candidates—people that actually want the job and will stay with the company. [47] One mistake companies have made is to make the job sound better than what it really is. They may successfully recruit and hire, but when the employee realizes what the job really is, they leave. This turnover wastes recruiting time and expenses, as well as training costs, which becomes a vicious cycle.

5.1 ETHICAL DILEMMA: WHAT WOULD YOU DO?

Andre Jehan, Pizza Schmizza founder of the Northwest chain, has an unusual way of recruiting and selecting workers. Homeless people are given pizza slices and soda and sometimes a couple of dollars to carry a sign that reads "Pizza Schmizza paid me to hold this sign instead of asking for money." Jehan believes he is helping the homeless, saying that carrying the signs has been a win-win situation, as the homeless, many of whom have mental illnesses or other problems that keep them from being able to hold a job, don't feel embarrassed or exploited; they look forward to the work and food. However, Donald Whitehead, former

executive director of the National Coalition for the Homeless, says Jehan is exploiting the people he recruits to hold his signs.

1. Is Andre Jehan exploiting the homeless?

2. Is it ethical and socially responsible to give homeless people food for carrying signs?

Source: G. Williams, "Will Work for Pizza," *Entrepreneur* (October 2003), http://www.entrepreneur.com/article/65058 (retrieved October 29, 2013).

The Recruiter–Candidate Interaction and the Realistic Job Preview (RJP)

Does the recruiter (or recruiters) affect the job candidates and their willingness to apply for a job in our organization? The obvious answer is yes. The recruiter is one of the primary factors responsible for an applicant showing interest in our organization and our jobs.[48] According to one report, "Recruiters with higher degrees of engagement and job fit dramatically outperform their peers who score lower in those areas. That's measured both in the quality of hires and in productivity."[49] So we have to be sure to hire qualified candidates to be our recruiters; experienced internal people usually work out better than external candidates because knowing the organization helps them give an RJP.

It takes good communication skills for recruiters to accurately assess if job candidates are actually qualified for the job—including whether or not they fit the organizational culture and are likely to stay with the firm. So when hiring recruiters, make sure they have a strong set of communication skills. The recruiter must be able to talk with the recruits "on their level" in order to make them feel comfortable with the process. Recruiters need to learn when to ask probing questions and when to lie back and let a recruit talk. Role-playing training for the recruiter is particularly effective in teaching this skill.[50] Another important communication skill to assess is **active listening**, which is *the intention and ability to listen to others, use the content and context of the communication, and respond appropriately.* This means that recruiters have to want to listen and must have developed their active listening skills so they not only hear the words that recruits are saying but also understand the context of the conversations (what the circumstances are and why the other person is communicating this information) so they can empathize with recruits and visualize why they are providing this information.[51] Empathy in this situation (putting yourself in another's position) allows the recruiter to visualize why something is being communicated and is critical if the recruiter is to respond correctly.

The recruiter's job also includes successfully communicating with the hiring managers in the organization. The same active listening skills that serve recruiters in interactions with an applicant can allow them to more clearly define what the hiring manager wants and needs in the new organizational recruit. So we need to create strong training programs in communication with recruiters in the organization.[52]

We also have to train recruiters in the process of the realistic job preview (RJP). Most companies have come to the conclusion that RJPs are a necessary part of the recruiting process to recruit a qualified candidate that will stay with the firm. A **realistic job preview (RJP)** is *a review of all of the tasks and requirements of the job, both good and bad.* A good job analysis (Chapter 4) with a clear job description should provide a good RJP. We have found that "it's incumbent upon recruiters and hiring managers to paint a clear picture of what will be expected of the candidate in his or her new role and to make sure promises of resources, job structure and reporting relationships are fulfilled."[53] There is strong research evidence that early turnover in a job is directly related to failure to provide an RJP for that job.[54]

The recruiter needs to understand the job in detail so he or she can give honest answers and an RJP of the job to the potential candidate. In many cases today, we may have a recruiting team with one person on the team having the "technical" knowledge of the job (maybe the supervisor of the job) and the other person having the HR-related knowledge that keeps us from inadvertently violating any laws, regulations, or internal policies. This helps us with the RJP because the technical person can explain details that the HR recruiter would generally not know or understand.

So recruiting, selecting, and then training our recruiters is a major factor in our overall recruiting success with both the hiring manager and the candidates.

Active listening The intention and ability to listen to others, use the content and context of the communication, and respond appropriately

Realistic job preview (RJP) A review of all of the tasks and requirements of the job, both good and bad

5.1 SELF-ASSESSMENT

CAREER DEVELOPMENT

Indicate how accurately each statement describes you by placing a number from 1 to 7 on the line before the statement (7 = strong agreement; 1 = strong disagreement).

Describes me						Does not describe me
7	6	5	4	3	2	1

_____ 1. I know my strengths, and I can list several of them.

_____ 2. I can list several skills that I have to offer an employer.

_____ 3. I have career objectives.

_____ 4. I know the type of full-time job that I want next.

_____ 5. I have analyzed help-wanted ads or job descriptions, and I have determined the most important skills I will need to get the type of full-time job I want.

(Continued)

(Continued)

_____ 6. I have, or plan to get, a part-time job, summer job, internship, or full-time job related to my career objectives.

_____ 7. I know the proper terms to use on my résumé to help me get the next job I want.

_____ 8. I understand how my strengths and skills are transferable, or how they can be used on jobs I apply for, and I can give examples on a résumé and in an interview.

_____ 9. I can give examples (on a résumé and in an interview) of suggestions or direct contributions I made that increased performance for my employer.

_____ 10. My résumé focuses on the skills I have developed and on how they relate to the job I am applying for, rather than on job titles.

_____ 11. My résumé gives details of how my college education and the skills developed in college relate to the job I am applying for.

_____ 12. I have a résumé that is customized to each part-time job, summer job, or internship I apply for, rather than one generic résumé.

Add up the numbers you assigned to the statements and place the total on the continuum below:

| 84 | 74 | 64 | 54 | 44 | 34 | 24 | 12 |

| Career ready | In need of career development |

Evaluation of Recruiting Programs

>> **LO 5.5 Discuss the basic methods available for evaluating the recruiting process.**

We need to measure our recruiting processes the same as we measure every other process in the organization. This is another point at which HR analytics skills are becoming significantly more important. As we noted earlier, the recruitment process is expensive, and unless we identify and control those costs, the beneficial results may end up being outweighed by the costs. But recruitment and salary cost are an investment. If you hire the best people, as **Google** does, their productivity will more than pay for itself.

See Exhibit 5.2 for an overview of five evaluation methods that we discuss in this section.

Yield Ratio

Yield ratio A calculation of how many people make it through the recruiting step to the next step in the hiring process

Recruiting is not about getting lots of applications;[55] rather, it's about attracting qualified candidates[56] for jobs and for organizational culture fit.[57] You don't want to waste your time reviewing unqualified applicants' applications.[58] Our first measurement option is the recruiting **yield ratio**—*a calculation of how many people make it through the recruiting step to the next step in the hiring process.* For example, we advertise for a job opening and receive 100 résumés and applications. Of these applicants, 50 are judged to have the basic qualifications for the job. As a result, our yield ratio on the advertisement would be 50% (50 of our 100 applicants made it through the first recruiting step). As with most metrics, we then compare to historical data or to other company benchmarks to see how we are doing in the process. If our historic yield ratio for advertisements is 40%, then our ad was much more effective than average. **(SHRM K:4)**

EXHIBIT 5.2 ● Recruiting Evaluation Methods

Generally, all recruiting evaluation methods are comparisons to historical averages to see whether the organization is improving in its recruiting efforts or is less successful than in the past.

Yield ratio:

Divide the number of qualified applicants by the number of applicants.

An advertisement yielded 40 applications, and 28 have the basic qualifications. The yield ratio is 28:40, or 70%.

Cost per hire:

Divide the total cost by the number of applicants hired.

$60,000/10 = $6,000

Time required to hire:

Count the number of days from a position coming open until a new hire is in place.

A new opening on October 15 was filled on December 5, so our time to hire was 51 days.

New hire turnover:

Divide the number of recruits that left within a specified time frame by the number of new hires.

Last year 84 people were hired, and 13 of those left within 3 months. Our new hire turnover would be 13/84, or 15.5%.

New hire performance:

Divide the difference in performance by new recruits into the average for all employees in the same category to determine the percentage above or below average.

The average of all new hire appraisals last year was 3.1 on a 4-point grading scale. The average of all appraisals in the organization last year was 3.2. Therefore, new recruits are 3.3% below average (3.2 − 3.1 = 0.1; 0.1/3.2 = 3.3%).

Cost per Hire

Another measure you probably want to use is how much it costs to get each person hired, or *cost per hire*—which is calculated based on this formula:[59]

$$\text{Cost per Hire} = \Sigma \ (\text{External Costs}) + \Sigma \ (\text{Internal Costs})$$

External costs include: Advertising; Agency fees; Employee referrals; Candidate travel costs; Relocation costs plus any other cost associated with the recruiting process

Internal costs include: Recruiter pay and benefits; Corporate travel costs; Interviewing and selection costs and other internal items

For example, when needing several new customer service representatives, we were successful in recruiting and hiring 15 fully qualified applicants for the open positions. During the recruiting campaign, the company spent $140,000 on all of the recruiting costs combined. The cost per hire was therefore $140,000/15 = $9,333.33.

Time Required to Hire

Time required to hire is pretty self-explanatory. How many days/weeks/months did it take to get someone hired into an open position? If our company has a new opening on June 10 and we are able to fill the position on August 28, our time to hire was 79 days ([June] 30 − 10 = 20 + [July] 31 + [August] 28 = 79).

New Hire Turnover

Employee retention remains a critical issue for organizations and HR managers.[60] In measuring new-hire turnover, we need to identify a time frame. We would usually look at turnover within the first 3 to 6 months. So we identify our time frame and then measure how many new recruits compared to all hires during that period chose to leave the organization.

If we had 30 new hires in the past year and 2 of them left again within 6 months of being hired (we are identifying our turnover window as 6 months), we can calculate the turnover percentage and then compare it to historical averages: 2/30 = 6.7% new-hire turnover rate. If our historical new-hire turnover is 10%, then we have improved, at least during this annual cycle.

▲
It is important to evaluate the performance of new hires against all employees to understand how they fit in the organization, and make adjustments as necessary.

New Hire Performance

We can also analyze the performance ratings of new hires versus all employees. There are many ways to evaluate employees, but suppose you evaluate employees on an over-all 4.0 scale (as in college). Further, let's assume the average employee in the organization is judged to be a 3.0 on our 4-point scale. If our new hires are performing significantly below the average (say, at 2.4), we may want to analyze where they are not being successful and provide training opportunities to them and all new hires going forward to increase their chances for long-term success.

To make the measure more objective, we can calculate the percentage of new recruits who perform above or below average. You divide the difference in performance by new recruits compared to the average. Let's use the new recruit average of 2.4 compared to the 3.0 average: 3.0 − 2.4 = 0.6; 0.6/3.0 = 0.2 or 20% below average. Don't bother working with negative numbers. You can easily see if the new recruits are above or below average, so just subtract the smaller from the larger number.

5.2 APPLYING THE CONCEPT
RECRUITING EVALUATION METHODS

Do the math.

11. Your company had a new opening on May 5 and you filled the position on June 25. Your time to hire was _____ days.

12. Your company hired 24 people last year, and 14 of those left again within 3 months. Your new hire turnover is _____.

13. The average of all new hire appraisals last year was 4.3 on a 5-point grading scale. The average of all appraisals in the organization last year was 4.1. Therefore, new recruits are _____ % above or _____ % below average.

14. An advertisement for a job opening receives 62 applications. Of these, 48 have the basic qualifications required for the job. The yield ratio would be _____.

15. You hired 7 workers and it cost you $72,000. The cost per hire is _____.

Trends and Issues in HRM

The first issue that we will cover here is the newest generations moving into, and through, the workforce. Then we close out the chapter with a discussion of grit and what it means to companies and recruiters.

Millennial Versus Generation Z: Aren't They All the Same?

We have mentioned generational differences briefly, but millennials in many cases are now in positions of authority in companies around the world, and Gen Zers are not far behind.

Millennials have gained notoriety for some specific characteristics the baby boomers and traditionalists don't share. These previous-generation workers commonly complain that millennials are rude, they don't respect authority, and they are impatient and entitled.[61] However, millennials receive instant answers to many questions using the Internet that earlier generations could not know the answers to, and they have grown up with a "team" mind-set that tends to level out authority. So there are explanations for why differences exist.

What about Gen Z? Certainly they share the understanding of the digital world, and in fact may have better knowledge and more capability in that world than even the millennials, since they literally grew up in a world where there has always been a smart phone or some other instant connectivity to answers at their fingertips. However, it appears that Gen Z is not as team oriented as the millennials, and they are more concerned with stability and rewards for individual performance. Likely because they lived most of their formative years as children in an economy that was in the worst recession since the 1920s, this generation values job security and stability much more than their generation-earlier counterparts. So what is a recruiter to do? Here are some similarities and differences in generations, understanding that obviously not every millennial or Gen Z worker will fall within the stereotype.

For both generations:

- **The digital world matters.** Both expect the latest technology and integration of that technology into daily labor-saving activities at work.

- **Transparency.** Information asymmetry is a foreign concept to generations raised on the Internet and World Wide Web. Whether you want them to know or not, they probably will find out an answer if they have a question.

- **Immediate feedback.** Neither generation feels it is acceptable to receive feedback on their performance only in an end-of-year evaluation process. Feedback needs to be real-time and continuous.

- **Speed.** Business moves today at light speed—literally. Both generations are comfortable with the speed of the Internet and the fact that decisions have to be made quickly in that environment. *And* they are comfortable with making those quick decisions.

Millennials:

- **Teamwork.** Millennials have grown up on teams and with diversity. They expect to be part of a team and that the team be valued as a whole—no individual is a superstar.

- **Flexible schedules.** Millennials, more than earlier U.S. generations, work to live. In one survey, 95% said work–life balance was important in their choice of jobs.[62]

- **Meaningful work.** Millennials look for "purpose" in their work life. Work must mean something and needs to help society in some significant way or it isn't worth doing.

- **Mobility.** Millennials are notoriously willing to leave their current employer with little thought of loyalty. Understandable when you look at the loyalty companies have shown to employees for the past 25 to 30 years.

- **Support and appreciation.** They and the members of their team matter. If the company doesn't show support and appreciation routinely, they will tend to cut the relationship.[63]

Gen Z:

- **Individualism and competitiveness.** Gen Z accepts the fact that there are winners and losers in life—the product of a major recession as they were growing up. The team matters, as does diversity, but some individuals work harder and should receive greater returns.

- **Pay and job security.** Survival and saving for an uncertain future matter. They want to make a difference with their work, but making a living comes first.[64]

- **Stability.** Gen Z is willing to stay with a company. In a survey, 61% said they would be willing to stay at a company more than 10 years as long as they could move up based on merit.[65]

- **You don't own me.** "Side hustles" are a way of life to Gen Z. Many in this generation work on making money from a hobby or hobbies in addition to working for another company. Their time off is theirs to do with as they please.

Look for Grit, Not Just Talent

In a recent book titled *Grit: The Power of Passion and Perseverance,* Dr. Angela Duckworth discusses the issue of talent and what she calls *grit.* Her research on the topic of grit, which she says is "passion and perseverance for long-term goals," is a common topic of conversation within both academic and business communities.[66] She notes that talent alone is not enough when looking for someone who will outperform the average. We need to look for individuals who have grit.

So how do we look for grit, and how do we know that it works better than looking for talent? The Grit Scale, available to you free at https://angeladuckworth.com/grit-scale/, will allow you to test yourself on how gritty you are. Don't lie! It does you no good to fake being gritty. When you look at the scale, though, you should see that perseverance and passion appear to be the keys to success. And it works—at least in some very significant controlled studies so far. New cadets entering West Point Military Academy took the Grit test and it predicted who would succeed and who would drop out better than any other instrument available, including some that had been in used for more than 50 years. The Grit test also worked better with high school juniors in Chicago Public Schools, kids in the National Spelling Bee, Army Rangers, and salespeople at a vacation time-share company.[67]

What is the takeaway we can use in organizations to recruit better candidates? Look for passion and perseverance in candidates more than, or at least equal to, talent. There are many people who have a talent for particular types of work, but not as many have true passion for it. It's not always the "straight A" student or the person with a 145 IQ who will do the best job. Persistent practice in a chosen field shows a dedication to improvement and also most likely shows enjoyment within that chosen field.

Finally, one of the best points to Dr. Duckworth's work is that grit can be improved. We can change our behaviors and learn to be more passionate and persistent, according to her and others who study people in complex and difficult circumstances. So if we don't have that drive that we need, there is help out there.

Chapter Summary

5.1 Describe the main external forces acting on recruiting efforts.

The main external forces are the effective labor market and the social and legal forces that act on us as well as our potential recruits. These forces include (1) supply and demand, meaning whether there are plenty of candidates for the available jobs or whether there are more jobs than candidates; (2) the unemployment rate in the recruiting area; (3) competitors and whether competition for available workers is strong or weak; and (4) the social and legal environments, meaning the social factors that recruits emphasize when weighing whether or not to accept employment in a particular company and what limits are placed on recruiting efforts by laws and regulations.

5.2 Name the five main organizational recruiting considerations.

The five considerations are organizational policies, when we should recruit new employees, alternatives to recruiting, the reach of the recruiting effort, and how to use social media. *Policies* set the other four items. *When to recruit* tells us whether or not we should first mitigate a shortage with other organizational tactics, such as overtime. *Alternatives* include using overtime, outsourcing some work, or using temporary or contract workers or other options to mitigate a shortage. *Reach* determines the geographic locations that we will search for new employees. Finally, we need to determine how we are willing to use *social media* to assist in our recruiting efforts.

5.3 Identify the major advantages and disadvantages of both internal and external recruiting.

The major advantages of internal recruiting include increases in organizational engagement and job satisfaction, the ability to learn more about the "big picture" in the company, the fact that the individual feels comfortable working for the company, the fact that the company knows the individual and that person's work history, lower recruiting costs, and a relatively speedy process compared to external recruiting. Disadvantages include the facts that the pool of applicants is smaller, you will have to fill the old job of the person you hire, success in one job doesn't necessarily mean success in a different job, external candidates may be more qualified, internal candidates may feel they are entitled to the job, and we may perpetuate resistance to change and stifle innovation and creativity.

Advantages of external recruiting are that we avoid perpetuating resistance to change and encourage innovation and creativity, we may be able to find individuals with complex skill sets who are not available internally, there will be lower training costs for complex positions, and we have the potential to increase diversity. Disadvantages include potential disruption of the work team, the fact that it takes longer than internal recruiting and costs more, the fact that it may adversely affect current employees' motivation and satisfaction, higher orientation and training costs, and the fact that the candidate may look great on paper but may not perform after being hired.

5.4 Summarize the major challenges and constraints involved in the recruiting process.

The most obvious constraint is money. We have to avoid spending too much on the recruiting process. Additionally, organizational policies also affect how we recruit. Our organization's image also plays a significant role in our ability to source the people we need from the communities around us. Next is the type of job. Not all jobs are clean or fun. Finally, our selection and training of the recruiter and their delivery of an RJP is a major factor in recruiting success. We have to find an individual who has the ability to actively listen and empathize with the candidate.

5.5 Discuss the basic methods available for evaluating the recruiting process.

The recruiting *yield ratio* calculates how many people make it through the recruiting step to the next step in the hiring process. Another measure is *cost per hire.* You also may want to analyze *time required to hire.* *New-hire turnover* is another measure of success. If we have high rates of turnover immediately after recruitment and selection, we probably need to reevaluate our recruiting and selection process. Finally, we can also analyze *new-hire performance ratings* and compare them to the organizational norms. If our new hires perform at a significantly lower level than the norm, we may want to analyze where they are not being successful and provide training opportunities to increase their chances for long-term success.

Key Terms

active listening,   123
external recruiting,   118
internal recruiting,   117

labor market,   114
realistic job preview (RJP),   123

recruiting,   114
yield ratio,   124

Key Terms Review

Complete each of the following statements using one of this chapter's key terms.

1. _____ is the process of creating a reasonable pool of qualified candidates for a job opening.

2. _____ is the term for the external pool of candidates from which we draw our recruits.

3. _____ involves filling job openings with current employees or people they know.

4. _____ is the process of engaging individuals from the labor market outside the firm to apply for a job.

5. _____ is a review of all of the tasks and requirements of the job, both good and bad.

6. _____ is the intention and ability to listen to others, use the content and context of the communication, and respond appropriately.

7. _____ is a calculation of how many people make it through the recruiting step to the next step in the hiring process.

Communication Skills

The following critical-thinking questions can be used for class discussion and/or for written assignments to develop communication skills. Be sure to give complete explanations for all answers.

1. Should you "shop" for good employees who are out of work in a bad economy, and then should you terminate existing employees who aren't doing their jobs very well after finding a good replacement? What consequences of this course of action can you see?

2. If you were in charge of your company, would you rather recruit new employees, or would you rather use some of the other tools for addressing a shortage of employees that were discussed in this and the last chapter? Why?

3. In your personal experience, do you think that internal recruiting really improves organizational engagement, job satisfaction, and productivity? Why or why not?

4. Do you think targeted or closed recruiting leads to the potential for discrimination in recruiting efforts? Why or why not?

5. When would you definitely use the Internet as a recruiting tool, and when would you definitely not use the Internet to recruit? Why?

6. What could an organization do to improve its image if it has a bad reputation with recruits? Categorize your efforts into immediate-term and longer-term items.

7. If you were in charge of your company, what would you tell recruiters to do or not do to enhance their recruiting efforts? Why?

8. Do you think that you are a good "active listener"? Why or why not, and what could you do to become better?

9. What options do you see as alternatives to recruiting globally for knowledge-based jobs in the coming years?

Case 5.1 Trying to Build When Nobody Wants to Work

The U.S. residential construction contracting industry includes about 160,000 establishments (single-location companies and units of multi-location companies) with annual revenue of about $425 billion. Companies in this industry construct and renovate residential buildings. The industry includes general contractors, who build on land owned by others; operative builders, who build on land they own or control; and specialty trade contractors, such as plumbers and electricians, who often work as subcontractors for residential construction contractors.[68]

Housing demand is driven by population and economic growth. Demand for new residential buildings can change rapidly, depending on the economy and interest rates. From 1986 to 1991, annual U.S. home construction dropped 40%; from 1995 to 2005, it increased 75%; and from 2006 to 2011, it fell 65%. As the economy has recovered from the Great Recession in the United States, demand for housing has strengthened and prices have increased. In local markets, changes in demand can be even more severe.[69]

"Home building is a key driver of the American economy," said Granger MacDonald, chairman of the National Association of Home Builders (NAHB) and a home builder and developer from Kerrville, Texas. "Housing creates new income and jobs, purchases of goods and services, and revenue for local governments."[70]

That's the general industry backdrop as the number of potential homebuyers in the Denver (Colorado) area increases and the supply of homes for sale continues to fall. Fierce competition pushes home prices higher at one of the fastest rates of any local market in the nation. Denver's average sales rate would normally be about 15,000 homes per year, and the market is now operating at just over half that rate.[71] With all of this demand, why is there such a low supply?

Housing industry veteran Gene Myers says he could be adding 50% more homes if he just had the people to build them. After weathering more than one recession, not to mention the worst housing crash in history, Myers says he has never seen anything like this. "Especially the fact that it seems like we're at capacity at such a low level of actual absorption [sales]," said Myers, CEO of Thrive Home Builders, a midsized, privately owned builder in Denver. "In previous recessions, when we've recovered, we tend to see prices go up and labor starting to get tight after we've recovered to at least an average absorption."

Thousands of construction workers left the industry during the recession, many of them heading to the energy sector. The assumption was they would return when energy lagged and homebuilding recovered. Employment of construction laborers and helpers was projected by the Bureau of Labor Statistics to grow 13% from 2014 to 2024, faster than the average for all occupations. Laborers and helpers work in all fields of construction, and demand for these workers would mirror the level of overall construction activity.[72] They did not. The labor shortage in building actually worsened in 2016—a surprise to most analysts.

Labor is the top concern among the nation's builders, according to an NAHB survey, and worry over its cost and availability is growing. "We thought we'd see a flow back of workers from the energy sector," said Rob Dietz, chief economist with the NAHB. "The labor shortage has basically grown and accelerated. It's the top challenge in the building industry right now."

"These jobs, Americans don't want," Myers said. "We have a hard-working Hispanic labor force here in Denver that really is the foundation for the construction industry."

Dietz points to both an immigration and a generational challenge. The workforce is aging, with the typical age of a construction worker now 42. More Americans are going to college now, and so they are less likely to pursue a career in construction. Simply put, young Americans do not want to build houses anymore and would rather have white-collar, college-based, technology-driven employment. That leaves the construction business to immigrant laborers.

Immigrants make up about a quarter of the overall construction workforce, but that share is likely higher for residential homebuilding, partly due to a large number of undocumented workers. Builders say they make sure their contractors are legal to work, but they have less control over the subcontractors who often move from site to site. Even that group is shrinking, as President Donald Trump tries to impose travel bans and threatens to build a wall between the United States and Mexico. "There is a fear to get out into the labor force, I think there is an uncertainty," Myers said. "I had one of our trades who became a citizen last year ask me if that could be taken away from him. Even for the people who are legal and documented, it's a factor that is holding back the labor force." And it's costing builders more money. Wages in the residential building industry are growing at twice the rate of wages in the overall economy.

Charles Kimmel of Kimmel and Associates observed that those employees who were forced out of the industry during the 2007–2009 downturn took their experience with them and are now established in other careers. That leaves the youth of today, the millennials. This group, age 34 and younger, is particularly hard to reach. He recommends the following recruitment tactics:

1. *Change Your Target Market*
   a. High school and college students. Contact schools and let them know you are available for career days, job shadowing, and summer jobs. Consider providing paid internships. Offer a year's tuition as a scholarship to select students. Set up your own on-the-job/

apprenticeship program, or work with a community college to arrange industry-specific training for your company.

b. Veterans. A proven talent pool is hitting the labor market in increasing numbers. Due to military downsizing, many service members, who planned to stay in for 20 years and retire, are being forced out. Bureau of Labor Statistics (BLS) data indicate the highest unemployment rate in the country is among returning vets ages 18 to 24.

2. *Change Your Recruitment Strategies*

Implement employee referral programs for youth, conduct jobsite tours, use social media, reach out with contests, and brag about on-the-job high technology.

3. *Company Branding*

Build your reputation. Millennials are label conscious. They want the best and most popular in everything from headphones to footwear—Beats to Nike! These brand-conscious youth aren't any less aware of their employer of choice. Great branding will help you recruit construction workers.

4. *Enhance and Promote Your Company Culture*

Employees are attracted to companies that have a strong supportive culture. Youth are interested in more than just medical and dental benefits. Young people are looking for jobs that come with perks and a more informal atmosphere. The construction industry is in a unique position to offer work that fits the bill for many millennials. No ties required![73] "Because the building industry is highly decentralized—there are 40,000 homebuilding companies in the country—you do see poaching. There are situations where you can recruit a worker, and they can work for you for a quarter or two, and then they're working for another subcontractor down the road," Dietz said.[74]

What They Do

The *What They Do* section describes the typical duties and responsibilities of workers in the occupation, including what tools and equipment they use and how closely they are supervised. This tab also covers different types of occupational specialties.

Work Environment

The *Work Environment* section includes the number of jobs held in the occupation and describes the workplace, the level of physical activity expected, and typical hours worked. It may also discuss the major industries that employed the occupation. This tab may also describe opportunities for part-time work, the amount and type of travel required, any safety equipment that is used, and the risk of injury that workers may face.

How to Become One

The *How to Become One* section describes how to prepare for a job in the occupation. This tab can include information on education, training, work experience, licensing and certification, and important qualities that are required or helpful for entering or working in the occupation.

Pay

The *Pay* section describes typical earnings and how workers in the occupation are compensated—annual salaries, hourly wages, commissions, tips, or bonuses. Within every occupation, earnings vary by experience, responsibility, performance, tenure, and geographic area. This tab may also provide information on earnings in the major industries employing the occupation.

State and Area Data

The *State and Area Data* section provides links to state and area occupational data from the Occupational Employment Statistics (OES) program, state projections data from Projections Central, and occupational information from the Department of Labor's Career InfoNet.

Job Outlook

The *Job Outlook* section describes the factors that affect employment growth or decline in the occupation and, in some instances, describes the relationship between the number of job seekers and the number of job openings.

Similar Occupations

The *Similar Occupations* section describes occupations that share similar duties, skills, interests, education, or training with the occupation covered in the profile.

Contacts for More Information

The *More Information* section provides the Internet addresses of associations, government agencies, unions, and other organizations that can provide additional information on the occupation. This tab also includes links to relevant occupational information from the Occupational Information Network (O*NET).

2015 Median Pay

The wage at which half of the workers in the occupation earned more than that amount and half earned less. Median wage data are from the BLS Occupational Employment Statistics survey. In May 2015, the median annual wage for all workers was $36,200.

On-the-Job Training

Additional training needed (postemployment) to attain competency in the skills needed in this occupation.

Entry-Level Education

Typical level of education that most workers need to enter this occupation.

Work Experience in a Related Occupation

Work experience that is commonly considered necessary by employers, or is a commonly accepted substitute for more formal types of training or education.

Number of Jobs, 2014

The employment, or size, of this occupation in 2014, which is the base year of the 2014–2024 employment projections.

Job Outlook, 2014–24

The projected percent change in employment from 2014 to 2024. The average growth rate for all occupations is 7%.

Employment Change, 2014–2024

The projected numeric change in employment from 2014 to 2024.

Growth Rate (Projected)

The percent change of employment for each occupation from 2014 to 2024.

Projected Number of New Jobs

The projected numeric change in employment from 2014 to 2024.

Projected Growth Rate

The projected percent change in employment from 2014 to 2024.

Questions

1. What are the external forces acting on the recruitment effort for construction workers?

2. What are some viable alternatives that homebuilders can use in lieu of employee recruitment?

3. Social media recruiting is one of the methods recommended by Charles Kimmel of Kimmel and Associates to reach the millennials. What are the issues involved in using social media, and how can they be overcome?

4. What external recruitment methods are discussed in the case?

5. What are the challenges and constraints in recruiting construction workers?

6. What are the differing methods for evaluating the success of a recruitment program, and what methods are described in the case?

Skill Builder 5.1 Online Job Search

Objectives

To develop your job search skills and to learn more about job descriptions and specifications

To get you thinking about your career

Skills

The primary skills developed through this exercise are as follows:

1. *HR management skills*—Technical, business, and conceptual and design skills

2. *SHRM 2018 Curriculum Guidebook*—N: Staffing (Recruitment and Selection)

Preparation

Study the steps in the job search, which is preparation for the written assignment.

Let's do an exercise related to your professional development. Employers recruit job candidates, so we focus on you.

1. Think about a job or internship you would like to have. You may also get ideas when you go to a job search website.

2. Go to a job search website of your choice. You may use https://education.wsj.com (jobs and tips for new college grads), http://www.collegerecruiter.com (career tests to identify possible jobs, internships, and entry-level jobs), http://www.shrm.org (HR jobs and advice), http://www.monster.com (simply a listing of all types of jobs), and http://www.careerbuilder.com (jobs and advice). You may want to search using other websites and use more than one job search engine. If you are interested in working for a specific business or nonprofit organization, you may also visit its website.

3. Read about the job, job description, and specifications.

4. Your professor may want the URLs you used in your job search.

Written Assignment Instructions

Type the answers to these three questions.

1. What job(s) were you searching for, and which website(s) did you use to search?

2. List three or four things that you learned about job searching.

3. How will you use this information to get a job?

Apply It

What did I learn from this experience? How will I use this knowledge in the future?

_____

_____

_____

_____

Your instructor may ask you to do this Skill Builder in class in a group by sharing your answers. If so, the instructor will provide you with any necessary information or additional instructions.

Skill Builder 5.2 Résumé

Objective

To develop a résumé you can use for internships and part-time, summer, and full-time employment

Skills

The primary skills developed through this exercise are as follows:

1. *HR management skills*—Technical, business, and conceptual and design skills

2. *SHRM 2018 Curriculum Guidebook*—N: Staffing (Recruitment and Selection)

Preparation

Writing the résumé:

You may go to your college's Career Center and/or visit Proven Résumés at http://www.provenresumes.com for help. You should read the tips below before writing your résumé:

Type out your résumé, and keep it to one page, unless you have extensive "relevant" experience. Before finalizing your résumé, improve it by using the résumé assessment below, which may be used to grade your résumé.

Answer these résumé questions with Yes, Somewhat, or No:

• Within 10 seconds, can a recruiter understand what job you are applying for and that you have the qualifications (skills/experience and education) to get the position? You should not use the word *I* or *me* on a résumé.

Objective

• Does your résumé have an objective that clearly states the position being applied for (such as sales rep)? The job applied for affects all sections of your résumé because your résumé needs to state how you are qualified for the job. If you don't list the job you are applying for, your résumé will most likely be tossed out and you will not get a job with the firm.

Education (Describe Relevant Courses)

• If education is your major qualification for the job, is there detail that states the skills developed and courses taken in school that qualify you for the position you're applying for?

- Be sure to state your degree, major, and minor and concentration, if you have them. Don't write Bachelor of Science or Master of Business Administration—use BS and name of degree or MBA. Be sure to list your month and year of graduation.

- Your résumé should do a good job of filling one page. If you don't have extensive experience, list relevant courses that prepared you for the job you are applying for. For relevant courses, don't just include a shopping list. Pick a few "relevant" courses and describe how each course qualifies you for the job listed in your objective. So if you want to be a sales rep, you should state that you are a marketing major (or that you pursued a marketing concentration) and that you have taken the Sales and Selling course. Describe the skills you developed in the sales and other relevant courses.

- If you list computer courses/skills, be sure to list programs such as Microsoft Word, Excel, Access, PowerPoint (it is *one* word, not two), Windows, SPSS, HTML, etc. If you've used them on the job, say so with the program you used.

Experience

- Does your résumé list experience or skills that support the fact that you can do the job stated in your objective?

- Be sure to list names and addresses of employers, with months and years on the job. If you want the company to which you are applying to contact your boss for a reference, list your boss's name and telephone number on your résumé.

- Don't just list activities, such as cutting grass. Focus on general skills that can be applied to the job you want. Try to show skills. Did you do any planning, organizing, leading (influencing others, communicating, and motivating), and controlling? Give examples of your skills.

- For the sales job example, if any of your past jobs don't include sales experience, list sales skills

developed on the job. List communication skills that you used while interacting with customers, and state how you used them. Also state that you enjoy meeting new people and that you have the ability to easily converse with people you don't know.

Accomplishments (NOT Necessarily a Separate Section and Heading)

- Does your résumé clearly list your accomplishments and valuable contributions you made while attaining your education and/or experience?

- If you have a high GPA, you should list it with your education.

- If you are on a college sports team, be sure to list it with any accomplishments (such as Maroon of the Week, captain, MVP, or selection to conference teams). A good place to list sports is in the education section.

- List job accomplishments like "Increased sales by 10% from May to August 2010," "Employee of the Month," and "Earned highest tips based on superior sales skills and excellent communication skills used with customers."

- Is your résumé neat, attractive, and free of errors? Have neat columns and use tables without gridlines. Use high-quality bond paper and ink colors for hard copies.

Apply It

What did I learn from this experience? How will I use this knowledge in the future?

_____

_____

_____

Your instructor may ask you to do this Skill Builder in class in a group by showing others your résumé. If so, the instructor will provide you with any necessary information or additional instructions.

©iStockphoto.com/sturti

Selecting New Employees

Learning Outcomes

After studying this chapter, you should be able to do the following:

6.1 Describe why the selection process is so important to the company. **PAGE 138**

6.2 State the importance of the three main types of "fit" in the selection process. **PAGE 140**

6.3 Summarize the major points in the Uniform Guidelines on Employee Selection Procedures (UGESP). **PAGE 141**

6.4 Discuss the use of applications and résumés as selection tools. **PAGE 144**

6.5 Recall the major types of written testing available as selection tools. **PAGE 144**

6.6 Explain the three primary types of selection interviews by the value they bring to the selection process. **PAGE 150**

6.7 Defend the use of various background checks as tests for employment. **PAGE 153**

6.8 List the two basic methods used to make final selection decisions. **PAGE 156**

SHRM HR Content

See Online: *SHRM 2018 Curriculum Guidebook* for the complete list

D. Employment Law

    8. Fair Credit Reporting Act (FCRA)

    11. Genetic Information Nondiscrimination Act (GINA)

    35. Negligent hiring

I. Job Analysis and Job Design

    2. Employment practices (recruitment, selection, and placement)

L. Organizational Development

    15. Social networking

N. Staffing (Recruitment and Selection)

    1-a. Assessment methods—Ability/job knowledge tests, assessment centers

    1-b. Assessment methods—Contingent assessment methods: Drug testing, medical exams

    1-c. Assessment methods—Initial assessment methods: Résumés, cover letters, application blanks, biographical information, reference/

background checks, genetic screening, initial interviews, minimum qualifications

    1-d. Assessment methods—Noncognitive assessments (e.g., personality assessments, integrity tests, situational judgment tests, interest inventories)

    8. Interviews: situational, structured

    10. Selection decisions: Ranking, grouping/banding, random selection

    10-a. Selection decisions—Measurement concepts: Predictors/criteria, reliability, validity

    10-b. Selection decisions—Job offers: Employment-at-will, contracts, authorization to work

P. Training and Development

    5-c. Needs assessment—Personality tests and inventories

R. Workplace Health, Safety, and Security

    3-h. Safety management—Testing for substance abuse

Practitioner's Perspective

In a discussion of hiring, Cindy notes that the process of moving a person from job candidate to employee is a matching game for both the candidate and the company.

Job candidates want to emphasize their attractive qualities while minimizing any drawbacks. Sometimes, it is hard for an employer to determine if "what you see

(Continued)

(Continued)

is really what you get." Is there a line that shouldn't be crossed in the attempt to gather information about a job candidate?

She says, "When Sacha, our finance manager, started talking about vetting the candidates for her open position by checking their Facebook accounts, I knew we needed to talk. 'But you find out so much about people by looking at their page—mostly whether or not they have done something that would disqualify them,' Sacha said."

Is there real potential to access via the Internet candidate information that an employer should not have prior to offering a position? What are the pitfalls to avoid and legal restrictions that must be respected during hiring? Chapter 6 covers the process one should follow to properly select employees.

The Selection Process

>> LO 6.1 Describe why the selection process is so important to the company.

After completing the recruiting process, we need to select the best person from the pool to fill our job opening.[1] Selection is important because bad hires can be costly.[2] Firms should always seek to hire the most highly skilled employees to maximize their output,[3] but there is often a mismatch when the job and person don't fit together, and productivity suffers as a result.[4] Remember that in most organizations today, at least one of our competitive advantages will be our employees, so if we put the wrong people into the wrong jobs, we can have great difficulty in carrying out our strategic plans. So we need to focus on fit.[5]

The Importance of the Selection Process

Selection The process of choosing the best-qualified applicant who was recruited for a given job

Selection is *the process of choosing the best-qualified applicant who was recruited for a given job.* As with all other employee organizational decisions, we can apply the OUCH test to determine whether or not we should use a particular tool or measure in the selection process. The OUCH test will give us an initial analysis of the measure being used and whether we need to do some more investigation before we decide to use that specific measure in the selection process.

Why is the selection process so critical to the organization? Employees are the most important asset,[6] because the success of any company depends on its employees.[7] There are negative consequences of bad hiring decisions, which are essentially the results of mismatches between jobs and employees. Here are three of those reasons.

Bad Hires Cost Time and Money

First and probably most notably, if we hire someone who is not willing or able to do the job successfully, we will most likely have to go through the whole process again in a very short time. Because the process of recruiting and selection is so expensive, we must work to avoid this.

Bad Hires Result in Lower Productivity

Have you ever seen or worked with a bad employee who did a poor job doing the minimum amount of work, resulting in poor customer service, and creating extra work for you and/or coworkers? Just a few new hires who show this lack of concern for the organization and its customers can be devastating[8] and highly contagious. Pretty soon, others may decide, "If they can do the absolute minimum and still get paid what I get paid, then why should I work so hard?" Once this occurs, morale, employee engagement, and organizational commitment can drop very quickly. You don't want to put yourself and your organization in such a position, so you must give your full attention to making sure you hire only candidates who fit the jobs.

Bad Hires Can Be Negligent Hires

Negligent hire A legal concept that says if the organization hires someone who may pose a danger to coworkers, customers, suppliers, or other third parties, and if that person then harms someone else in the course of working for the company, then the company can be held liable for the individual's actions

Almost every state in America recognizes this legal concept, so HR managers must understand it as well.[9] A **negligent hire** is *a legal concept that says if the organization hires someone who may pose* *a danger to coworkers, customers, suppliers, or other third parties, and if that person then harms someone else in the course of working for the company, then the company can be held liable for the individual's actions.* **(SHRM D:35)**

For example, if you hired a salesperson who had a criminal record for assault and they then assaulted a customer, the company could be held liable for the harm done to the customer who was assaulted. So we have to make every legitimate attempt to find out if candidates have the potential to be a danger to others and weed them out during our selection process.

Steps in the Selection Process

The selection process follows a series of steps that are illustrated in Exhibit 6.1. Hiring can be stressful and expensive,[10] and you want to create equal opportunity for everyone, seeking diversity, without discriminating in violation of the 1964 Civil Rights Act.[11] Note this is a general guide and that one may skip some steps in the process or perhaps not follow them in the exact sequence shown. For example, there may not be any preliminary testing or initial interviewing, and there may not be any drug screening or physical exam.

EXHIBIT 6.1 ● Steps in the Selection Process

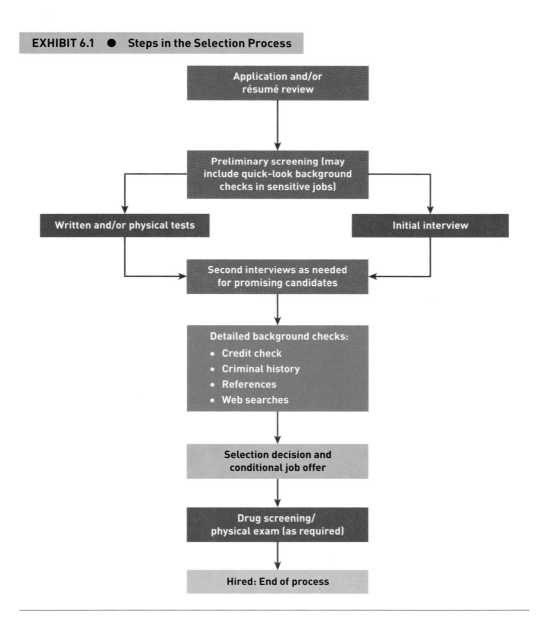

If you think about it for a minute, the process steps make logical sense. People apply for jobs, and the firm screens the job candidates to narrow down the selection. This screening may include a test of some type and an initial interview for the top candidates.

Before we get into those selection steps though, let's discuss the importance of selecting the applicant who best matches the job, or what we call "looking for fit." We also need to discuss the federal Uniform Guidelines on Employment Selection Procedures (UGESP), which affect how we conduct each of the steps in the selection process. Once we have covered these two items, we can go into the actual steps of the selection process.

Looking for "Fit"

>> **LO 6.2 State the importance of the three main types of "fit" in the selection process.**

"We hold these truths to be self-evident, that all men are created equal."[12] Is this a true statement? It is what the U.S. Declaration of Independence says! However, we all know that people are not equal. We also know that as managers, if we treat people equally (the exact same way), then we really aren't doing our job. Managers are supposed to get the best productivity out of their workforce, but not everyone can do everything equally well. So we have to treat people differently *but fairly* in order to be successful in our jobs. We need to attempt to assess three things in this process: personality-job fit, ability-job fit, and person-organization fit. Let's take a look at these items. **(SHRM I:2)**

Personality-Job Fit

Personality is a predictor of job performance.[13] Personality and job fit are so important that companies give job applicants personality tests.[14] Why? Our personality defines to a great extent who we are and how we act and react in certain situations,[15] including how we make decisions.[16] We all have unique personalities. Some of us are strongly extroverted and enjoy "working the crowd" in a social setting, while others may be fairly introverted and feel extremely uncomfortable in such an environment. Some of us desire to try new things constantly, while others don't like change—but employers want people open to learning and adapting to change.[17] Personality affects the things people enjoy doing and even affects the way that they work. So you have to do your best to identify candidates' personality types and put them in positions that will be enhanced by their particular personality traits, such as an outgoing extrovert in sales.[18] This is called *personality-job fit*.[19]

Ability-Job Fit

All of us have a certain set of physical and intellectual skills, and no two people are exactly alike. Some of us are very capable at working with computers, while others are more capable at sales or physical work. Each of us is more skilled at some things than others. However, across industries and jobs, even in tech jobs, employers want employees with people skills[20] and the ability to work in teams.[21]

Managers have to analyze a candidate's abilities and limitations. Using this information, the manager must hire the right people and then assign them to the types of jobs for which they are best suited.[22] Here again, if we assign the wrong person to a job, we can easily frustrate that employee and as a result cause motivation and engagement to drop, which in turn will likely cause losses in productivity and possibly early turnover. So we have to get the ability-job fit right.[23]

Person-Organization Fit

Person-organization fit deals with the cultural and structural characteristics of the organization and how well the candidate will fit within that structure and culture.[24] Employers want culture fit;[25] in fact, most evaluators rank cultural fit as the *most important item* in a job interview, even above analytical thinking.[26] However, one of the major problems in using cultural fit as the primary criterion in selection is that we may end up not getting the best person for a particular job. Certainly, we need to analyze cultural fit as part of the selection process because the better the fit, the more likely the individual will stay in the job for a longer period of time.[27] However, we can't use it as the sole criterion in selection.

If a candidate does not match the company structure and culture reasonably, they will probably be unhappy and more likely to leave as soon as they can find another opportunity that more closely matches their personality. To avoid this turnover, **Netflix** makes its culture very clear to job candidates to help ensure a successful match.[28]

You can see that in each of the situations of personality-job fit, ability-job fit, and person-organization fit, we have the potential to lower productivity and engagement while increasing the likelihood of absenteeism and early turnover—the exact opposite of what we want as a manager. So we have to get this right to gain a competitive advantage.[29] To get a better idea of your personality, job, and organizational fit, see Self-Assessment 6.1.

There is one caveat here though—we are not looking for people *just like us*. That is not what it means to have "fit." This type of hiring can harm the company. Research consistently shows the value of diversity in a business setting, so we don't want to hire all the same type of person.[30] The new HR buzzword being used by companies, including **Pandora** and **Lyft**, is *"Culture Add,"* or hiring for diversity, replacing culture fit.[31]

6.1 SELF-ASSESSMENT
O*NET INTEREST PROFILER REVISITED

Recall back in Chapter 4, Self-Assessment 4.1, that you were asked to take the O*NET Interest Profiler to help you find out what you like to do and help you decide what kinds of careers you might want to explore. In HR terms, it will help you match your interest to jobs. Go back and review your assessment, or complete it now at http://www.onetcenter.org/IP.html following the instructions from Chapter 4, p. 87.

Uniform Guidelines on Employee Selection Procedures

>> **LO 6.3 Summarize the major points in the Uniform Guidelines on Employee Selection Procedures (UGESP).**

The **Uniform Guidelines on Employee Selection Procedures (UGESP)** *provide information that can be used to avoid discriminatory hiring practices as well as discrimination in other employment decisions.* Most often called simply the "Uniform Guidelines," they were created to guide employers in their efforts to comply with the federal laws concerning all employment decisions, and especially the selection process.[32]

What Qualifies as an Employment Test?

Testing helps place people in the right jobs.[33] The UGESP formalize and standardize the way in which the federal government identifies and deals with discriminatory employment practices. They define the concept of "tests for employment" that are used in either the selection process or

> **Uniform Guidelines on Employee Selection Procedures (UGESP)** Guidelines that provide information that can be used to avoid discriminatory hiring practices as well as discrimination in other employment decisions

Part II ● Staffing

142   Part II ● Staffing

other employment actions. But what is a *test for employment?* It is a pretty broad term. The guidelines define it as applying to tests and other selection procedures

> which are used in making employment decisions, such as hiring, retention, promotion, transfer, demotion, dismissal or referral . . . Employee selection procedures include job requirements (physical, education, experience), and evaluation of applicants or candidates on the basis of application forms, interviews, performance tests, paper and pencil tests, performance in training programs or probationary periods, and any other procedures used to make an employment decision whether administered by the employer or by an employment agency.[34]

Although the guidelines specifically say that they "apply only to selection procedures which are used as a basis for making employment decisions,"[35] if we look closely at the Equal Employment Opportunity Commission's (EEOC's) definition of *employment decision* above, pretty much any employment procedure that we would use becomes a test for employment, which means that we need to follow the UGESP during every step of the selection process and all other actions with employees.

Valid and Reliable Measures

The UGESP also discuss the need for any employment test to be valid and reliable. In simple language, **validity** is *the extent to which a test measures what it claims to measure.* The UGESP note that "users may rely upon criterion-related validity studies, content validity studies, or construct validity studies"[36] to validate a particular selection procedure. But what are these validity measures?

Criterion-Related Validity

Criterion-related validity is *an assessment of the ability of a test to measure some other factor related to the test.* For example, SAT scores are designed to be one of the predictors of college success. In employment, criterion-related validity occurs when we can show a strong relationship between job candidates' scores on a test and on-the-job performance of those candidates after they are hired.[37]

Content Validity

Content validity is *an assessment of whether a test measures knowledge or understanding of the items it is supposed to measure.* So we have to show that "the content of a selection procedure is representative of [measures] important aspects of performance on the job."[38] In other words, our test has to be a valid measure of knowledge, skills, or abilities that are directly applicable to the job, such as an essay test that contains intentional English errors to determine how many errors the editor candidate can correct in a set period of time.

Construct Validity

Construct validity *measures a theoretical concept or trait that is not directly observable.* For construct validity to be applicable, we must demonstrate that "(a) a selection procedure measures a construct (something believed to be an underlying human trait or characteristic, such as personality and honesty) and (b) the construct is important for successful job performance."[39] For example, intelligence is a construct that is measured by an IQ test, and research has supported the

▲
Employment tests must be designed to have valid and reliable measures, meaning the test should actually measure what it claims to, and that it tests these measures consistently for all participants. Otherwise, the test may not provide accurate results.

Validity The extent to which a test measures what it claims to measure

Criterion-related validity An assessment of the ability of a test to measure some other factor related to the test

Content validity An assessment of whether a test measures knowledge or understanding of the items it is supposed to measure

Construct validity An assessment that measures a theoretical concept or trait that is not directly observable

IQ test's validity. Intelligence is a major predictor of job performance. However, the UGESP say that this method of validation is far more difficult to demonstrate than are the other two options, so it would be best if you can show that a measure has criterion-related or content validity. Large corporations often use personality, honesty, and IQ types of tests, but the tests are usually developed and tested with supporting validity by consulting firms, and there is a fee for every test given, so it can be expensive.

Reliability

Reliability is *the consistency of a test measurement.* In addition to being valid, for a measure to be useful in any type of employment testing, it needs to be *reliable.*

Reliability The consistency of a test measurement

Reliability means that the measure is consistent in some way—perhaps consistent when used by two different people (called inter-rater reliability) or consistent over time (called test-retest reliability). When we are working with people, we want our measures to be reliable measures, meaning they should be consistent over time and between people.[40]

The Relationship Between Reliability and Validity

Let's put validity and reliability together. If a test is not reliable, it can't be valid. For example, if a job candidate steps on our company scale and weighs 150 pounds, then steps off and on again and weighs 155, the scale is not reliable. How much does the candidate actually weigh? A test can be reliable but not valid, but it can't be valid without being reliable. If a job candidate steps on the company scale and weighs 150 pounds and then weighs 150 pounds three more times, our scale is reliable. However, what if we place the person on a more expensive, better scale and the person weighs 155? Then our scale is reliable but not valid because it doesn't accurately measure a person's weight. **(SHRM N:10-a)**

Now that we understand that we need to select for fit and follow the UGESP, we are ready to discuss the selection steps illustrated in Exhibit 6.1.

6.1 APPLYING THE CONCEPT
VALIDITY AND RELIABILITY

Write the letter corresponding to each of the following before the situation in which it is discussed.

a. Criterion-related validity

b. Content validity

c. Construct validity

d. Reliability

_____ 1. A job candidate failed a job application test, but she claims that the test is not fair and that she can do the job. What type of evidence do you need to ensure that the test is in fact a good predictor of job performance?

_____ 2. You are running a law firm and require all your lawyers to pass the bar exam. What does the bar exam need to do to indicate it is a good test?

_____ 3. You have developed a new system for predicting future company sales. Your boss wants some proof that it works.

_____ 4. An NFL team makes a recruit take an intelligence test. The recruit's score is below the acceptable level, so the team refuses to hire the player. The player complains, stating that his intelligence score has nothing to do with playing football. What evidence do you need to support not hiring the player?

_____ 5. You decided to let the job candidate in situation 1 (above) take the application test again. The next day she took the test again, and the score was within a couple of points of her score on the first test. So you again decide not to hire her. What evidence do you need to support this decision?

Applications and Preliminary Screening

>> **LO 6.4 Discuss the use of applications and résumés as selection tools.**

The first step in the selection process is to get job applicants to fill out an application and/or send in their résumé. Then we do preliminary screening that may include a quick background check, testing, and initial interviewing to narrow down the applicants to the best matches, or fit, for the job. Let's discuss the application and résumé and what you generally can and can't ask during the pre-employment inquiries.

Applications and Résumés

Candidates are typically asked to complete an application form to provide biographical data,[41] to identify basic skill sets, background, work history, education, and other general information. We need data to aid in selecting the best person for the job.[42] Even in cases where résumés are appropriate, many companies today require a completed application in order to be able to compare candidates easier because the information is in a standard format; this is needed for computer scanning of applications, which is commonly used in large organizations. Many recruiters spend some 60% of their time reading résumés, so they are using computer software to take hundreds of résumés and narrow down the applicants to the top 10 candidates.[43] **(SHRM N:1-c)**

Whether it is an application or a résumé, we need to verify the information. There is anecdotal evidence from professional recruiters and background screeners that one half or more of all applications and résumés include significant fictitious information,[44] and 80%[45] to 88% of recruiters said that they had seen "a misrepresentation of some kind on an applicant's resume."[46] Companies have started to check these documents much more thoroughly because they know that many of their applicants will embellish and outright lie.

Application forms and résumés give us valuable information on job candidates' past, but it is difficult to assess motivation to work hard and evaluate future potential.[47] So we move to the next step with the top candidates.

Pre-Employment Inquiries

On a job application or during an interview, no member of an organization should ask any questions that can be used to illegally discriminate against an applicant based on protected group characteristics, unless the questions are bona fide occupational qualifications (BFOQs). Exhibit 6.2 lists some information on what generally can and cannot be asked during the selection process.

It may be hard to memorize the list, but to keep it simple, use the OUCH test. Everyone in the firm that is involved in recruiting and selecting, not just HR, should also follow two major rules of thumb to avoid discrimination:

1. Every question asked should be job related. If the question is not job related, there is no reason to ask it, so don't.

2. Any general question that you ask is one you should ask of all candidates.

Testing and Legal Issues

>> **LO 6.5 Recall the major types of written testing available as selection tools.**

Testing is on the increase as 8 of the top 10 U.S. companies administer testing for some positions.[48] As we noted in Chapter 3, all of the federal equal employment opportunity (EEO) laws apply to "any employment action," so clearly, they apply in all selection tests. Managers must also know that there are some other significant laws dealing with allowable hiring practices. Let's complete a quick review of EEOC rules and various testing options.

EXHIBIT 6.2 ● Pre-Employment Inquiries

Topic	Generally Acceptable	Generally Unacceptable or Risky
Name	Current legal name and whether the candidate has ever worked under a different name	Maiden name or whether the person has ever changed their name
Address	Current residence	Whether the candidate owns or rents their home
Age	Only whether the candidate's age is within a certain range (if required for a particular job); for example, an employee may need to be 21 to serve alcoholic beverages	How old are you? What is your date of birth? Can you provide a birth certificate? How much longer do you plan to work before retiring?
Sex	Candidate to indicate sex on an application only if sex is a BFOQ	Candidate's sexual preference, orientation, or gender identity
Marital and Family Status	None	Specific questions about marital status or any question regarding children or other family issues
National Origin, Citizenship, or Race	Whether the candidate is legally eligible to work in the United States, and whether the candidate can provide proof of status if hired	Specific questions about national origin, citizenship, or race
Language	What languages the candidate speaks and/or writes; can ask candidate to identify specific language(s) if these are BFOQs	What language the candidate speaks when not on the job or how the candidate learned the language
Criminal Record	Whether the candidate has been convicted of a felony; if the answer is yes, can ask other information about the conviction if the conviction is job related	Whether the candidate has ever been arrested (an arrest does not prove guilt) or charged with a crime
Height and Weight	Generally none unless a BFOQ	Candidate's height or weight if these are not BFOQs
Religion	None unless a BFOQ	Candidate's religious preference, affiliation, or denomination if not a BFOQ
Education and Work Experience	Academic degrees or other professional credentials if information is job related	For information that is not job related
References	Names of people who can verify applicant's training and experience	A reference from a religious leader
Military Record	Information about candidate's military service	Dates and conditions of discharge from the military; draft classification; National Guard or reserve unit of candidate
Organizations	About membership in job-related organizations, such as unions or professional or trade associations	About membership in any non-job-related organization
Disabilities	Are you capable of performing the essential tasks of the job with or without any accommodation?	General questions about disabilities or medical condition
Past Salary/Pay	For determining prior employments	How much the candidate was paid on the job

6.2 APPLYING THE CONCEPT
PRE-EMPLOYMENT QUESTIONS

Using Exhibit 6.2 and the general guideline not to ask any questions that are not job related unless they are BFOQs, identify whether each question can or cannot be asked on an application form or during a job interview.

a. Legal (can ask)

b. Illegal (cannot ask during pre-employment)

_____ 6. What languages do you speak?

_____ 7. Are you married or single?

_____ 8. How many children do you have?

_____ 9. So you want to be a truck driver. Are you a member of the Teamsters Union representing truck drivers?

_____ 10. Are you straight or a homosexual?

_____ 11. Have you ever belonged to a union?

_____ 12. What is your date of birth?

_____ 13. Have you been arrested for stealing on the job?

_____ 14. Do you own your own car?

_____ 15. Do you have any form of disability?

_____ 16. Are you a member of the Knights of Columbus?

_____ 17. Can you prove you are legally eligible to work?

_____ 18. Are you currently a member of the military reserve?

_____ 19. What is your religion?

_____ 20. How much do you weigh?

The EEOC and Employment Testing

The UGESP (covered earlier) were created to provide a "uniform federal position in the area of prohibiting discrimination in employment practices on grounds of race, color, religion, sex, or national origin."[49] The guidelines have been formally adopted by the federal EEOC, the Department of Labor, the Department of Justice, and the Civil Service Commission.

As such, the EEOC will use these guidelines any time it is faced with a discrimination-in-hiring complaint. If the EEOC investigates a complaint about employment testing being discriminatory, the company will have to provide evidence to support the validity of the test for the job being filled. If the company can't support that the measure is valid, it is likely that the EEOC will consider the test a discriminatory hiring practice. In 2015, **Target** agreed in conciliation with the EEOC to pay more than $2.8 million over use of tests that were not job related and didn't meet the requirements for business necessity, because those tests had a disparate impact on women and minority applicants.[50]

Polygraphs and Genetic Testing

Polygraph testing can be used only in a few circumstances. The 1988 Employee Polygraph Protection Act (EPPA) made it illegal to use a polygraph to test employee honesty in most circumstances. However, there are two exceptions for corporations and other businesses (there are other exceptions for government and national security).[51] See Exhibit 6.3 for a summary of some of the exceptions. **(SHRM D:11)**

Genetic Testing

As discussed in Chapter 3, the Genetic Information Nondiscrimination Act (GINA) protects people from discrimination by health insurers and employers on the basis of their DNA information.[52] We have to remember that this information is protected and not use it in selection processes.

Written Testing

Written tests can be used to predict job success, as long as the tests meet EEOC guidelines for validity and reliability. Today, written tests are a common part of the selection process.[53] In fact, 80% of midsize and large companies use personality and ability assessments for entry and

EXHIBIT 6.3 ● Exceptions to the EPPA for Polygraph Testing

General Exception	Specific Exception—can request the employee to submit when:
1. For armored car personnel; personnel engaged in the design, installation, and maintenance of security alarm systems; or other uniformed or plainclothes security personnel	1. There is an active investigation involving economic loss or injury to the employer's business.
	2. The employee had access to the property.
2. Use by any employer authorized to manufacture, distribute, or dispense a controlled substance listed in Schedule I, II, III, or IV of Section 202 of the Controlled Substances Act	3. The employer has reasonable suspicion that the employee was involved in the incident or activity under investigation.
	4. The employer executes and maintains a statement of the facts for a period of 3 years and provides a copy of the statement to the employee.

midlevel management positions to help ensure the right fit between the job candidate and the job.[54] Companies have good reason to be seriously concerned that job candidates don't have the skills to match up with their education and degrees. One recent study noted that "millennials are on track to be the best educated generation in U.S. history, but their education level isn't translating into the job skills that most employers seek."[55] And a number of other developed countries are having similar problems.[56] So testing is becoming more common to figure out who can perform and who can't. **(SHRM N:1-d)**

Skills Tests

Skills tests can be either written or done in physical form. A written **skills test** is simply *an assessment instrument designed to determine if you have the ability to apply a particular knowledge set* to do the job you are applying for. Have you ever taken a written test on Microsoft Word or PowerPoint? If so, you have taken a written skills test.

Let's use the OUCH test to find out if we should use a test. Is a skills test *objective?* Can we give you a test on Microsoft Word, for example, and then answer yes or no as to whether you know how to indent and italicize? If so, the test is objective. Is a skills test *uniform in application?* If we give the same test to everyone in the same situation, it is. Is it *consistent in effect?* In general, the answer is yes. However, we can certainly design skills tests that are not consistent in effect, whether we do so intentionally or unintentionally, so we have to validate the test. Does it *have job relatedness*—a direct relationship to the primary aspects of job performance? If the answer is yes, it meets the OUCH test.

Skills test An assessment instrument designed to determine if you have the ability to apply a particular knowledge set

Personality and Interest Tests

Personality tests *measure the psychological traits or characteristics of applicants to determine suitability for performance in a specific type of job.* An estimated 60% to 70% of U.S. applicants take an online personality test.[57] The Myers-Briggs Type Indicator and the Birkman Method are two common personality tests. **Interest tests** are similar, but they *measure a person's intellectual curiosity and motivation in a particular field.* If there is a legitimate reason for having a person with a particular type of personality or certain set of interests in a job, then we need to support the validity and reliability of the test for those personality traits or interests. If we can't support a relationship between these items and the job, then an applicant could potentially take the company to court for discriminatory hiring practices.[58] **(SHRM P:5-c)**

Personality test A test measuring the psychological traits or characteristics of applicants to determine suitability for performance in a specific type of job

Interest test A test measuring a person's intellectual curiosity and motivation in a particular field

Cognitive Ability Tests

Cognitive ability tests are *assessments of general intelligence or of some type of aptitude for a particular job.* Here again, we need to ensure the tests that may be used are professionally developed,

Cognitive ability test An assessment of general intelligence or of some type of aptitude for a particular job

reliable, and valid indicators of a particular ability or knowledge set. Courts have upheld the use of cognitive ability testing, even when such testing had a potential disparate impact, as long as the ability being tested was directly related to a business necessity and was job related.[59] If you can't validate the test, don't use it.

Honesty or Integrity Tests

There are actually two types of honesty tests: pen-and-paper tests and polygraph tests, also known as lie detector tests, which, as stated, have very limited legal use. Dishonest employees can be negligent hires and steal from the company or hurt its image, which can be very costly, so you want to do your best not to hire them. Honesty and integrity tests are certainly not infallible, and they can be faked in some cases. But the evidence supports that they have value in identifying people who may be less honest and allowing the employer to weed some of these individuals out of the selection process.[60]

Physical Testing

Physical test A test designed to ensure that applicants are capable of performing on the job in ways defined by the job specification and description

Physical testing can also help us select the best candidate for certain jobs. **Physical tests** are *designed to ensure that applicants are capable of performing on the job in ways defined by the job specification and description.* Physical testing will generally be valuable where there are significant physical skills required to perform the job or where there is a significant safety risk, creating danger for the employee or others by working in a job for which they are physically unqualified. There are many types of physical testing, but we will limit our discussion to some of the most common forms. **(SHRM N:1-a)**

Physical Skills Tests

Physical skills tests are designed to determine whether you have the skills and abilities to perform a particular set of physical tasks. Physical skills tests may include tests of strength and/or endurance, tests of eye-hand coordination, or other physical abilities. These tests can also be conducted in several different forms, including work sample tests, assessment centers, and simulations.

Work sample A test conducted by providing a sample of the work that the candidate would perform on the job and asking the candidate to perform the tasks under some type of controlled conditions

Let's take a closer look at some of the common forms of physical testing. **Work samples** *provide a sample of the work that the candidate would perform on the job and ask the candidate to perform the tasks under some type of controlled conditions.* A simple example of a work sample test might be asking the candidate to type a particular letter and then judging the speed and accuracy of the results.

Assessment center A place where job applicants undergo a series of tests, interviews, and simulated experiences to determine their potential for a particular job.

An assessment center provides a more rigorous physical testing environment.[61] An **assessment center** is a *place where job applicants undergo a series of tests, interviews, and simulated experiences to determine their potential for a particular job.* These assessments help select the best candidates.[62] For example, at **T-Mobile**, you might have to assist a fictitious customer who is angry about his bill, or you might have to provide customers with information about new company services. So an assessment center used by T-Mobile might give tests designed to make candidates demonstrate how well they can use several different computer systems designed to obtain and communicate the information that customers need.

Simulation A test where a candidate is put into a high-pressure situation in a controlled environment so that the danger and cost are limited

We can also use **simulations**, *tests where a candidate is put into a high-pressure situation, but in a controlled environment so that the danger and cost are limited.* Simulations are very valuable in cases where a real event could be dangerous or emotionally taxing or cost a lot of money.[63] Simulators and even virtual reality environments are used in many situations, such as military training and teaching new doctors how to perform different types of surgery.[64]

Physical Exams

If the job will require heavy physical exertion, there may be a legitimate need to have individuals submit to a physical exam to ensure they are healthy enough for the stress. (Think NFL lineman!) In other cases, we may be required by the state or federal government to have individuals who work in specific fields take a physical exam before they are allowed to work in certain jobs such as driving a heavy truck (DOT physical) or flying a plane (FAA physical). **(SHRM N:1-b)**

However, we have to be very aware of the potential for discrimination based on disability if we require a physical exam as a prerequisite to work in our organization, so make sure any physical test is valid or don't use it.

Drug Testing

Drug testing and drug-free workplaces have become more of an issue for HR and other organization managers in the past few years. By 2018, 29 states had passed medicinal marijuana laws and 9 of those, along with Washington, D.C., also allowed recreational use.[65] This sets up potential conflicts for employers who follow the federal drug-free workplace initiatives, which for federal contractors is mandatory but for most other employers is an optional program. **(SHRM R:3-h)**

The fact is that state marijuana laws do not affect company drug policies—at least not at this time. In each case where an individual has challenged a detrimental employment action (including termination for a positive drug test) in court—from state supreme courts (*Coats v. Dish Network*),[66] all the way up to the U.S. Supreme Court (*Ashcroft v. Raich*)—the decision has been that employers can "safely refuse to accept medical marijuana as a reasonable medical explanation for a positive drug test result."[67] Employers have also not yet been required to accommodate employee use of medical marijuana under the Americans with Disabilities Act (ADA).

Although recreational marijuana is legal in some states, it is against federal law. So organizations need to make their policy clear. Many colleges and universities in all states don't permit the use of marijuana out of fear of losing federal funding. Also, even if the state in which you are applying for a job has legalized the use of marijuana, some multinational corporations follow federal law nationally and will not hire you if you test positive for it during a drug test and you can be legally fired.

But employers need to follow some guidelines to stay within the law in implementation and maintenance of any drug-testing program they choose to implement. In general, testing must be done systematically in one of two forms: either "random" or "universal." Testing can't be selective in most states. In other words, we can't decide we want to test "Amy Jones" because we just want to. Testing can be universal in some situations (e.g., after a workplace accident or on initial offer of employment) and random in others (e.g., quarterly drug testing of a sample of the workforce), but it has to be one or the other and we have to specify which option we use in each situation.

Most states now require prior authorization for drug testing. In the case of applicants, this authorization is usually part of the legal notices on the job application. For existing employees, it will usually be part of the employee handbook. The drug-testing policy must include full disclosure of substance abuse training, when testing will occur, which substances to be detected, and disciplinary action if an employee tests positive. The policy may also require the employer to "reasonably accommodate" employees who voluntarily submit to an alcohol or drug rehabilitation program. Again, a caution: State laws vary and are constantly changing. Always be sure that you are operating within the laws of the state in which you are testing.

Fitness-for-Duty Testing

A significant number of companies today are turning to fitness-for-duty tests in place of more invasive drug testing. A **fitness-for-duty test** simply *identifies whether or not an employee is physically capable at a particular point in time of performing a specific type of work.*[68] Federal law notes that we can use a medical examination "if it is job related and consistent with business necessity."[69] For instance, some trucking firms use fitness-for-duty testing before drivers are allowed to take an 18-wheel truck out of their terminals. Another advantage of this type of testing is that it is much more acceptable to employees than drug testing.

Fitness-for-duty test A test identifying whether or not an employee is physically capable at a particular point in time of performing a specific type of work

To Test or Not to Test

Testing, in all forms, can be time-consuming and expensive. Therefore, testing has to pay for itself through its ability to help you hire applicants who are in fact a good fit for the job and the organization. It may save you time and money by preventing you from hiring and then immediately losing employees who are a bad fit, preventing negligent hires, and improving worker productivity by maximizing the chance of hiring good-fit employees. This justifies the investment in the test. So as an HR manager, you will have to make decisions about whether or not testing is a good investment in your particular industry and for helping you select the best candidate for the specific jobs you need to fill.

6.3 APPLYING THE CONCEPT
TYPE OF TEST

Write before each job situation below the letter corresponding to the type of test described.

a. Genetic

b. Skills

c. Personality and interest

d. Cognitive ability

e. Honesty or integrity—polygraph

f. Physical skills

g. Physical exam

h. Drug

_____ 21. As part of the selection process, you will have to answer questions while being monitored by this machine.

_____ 22. A paper-and-pencil test is administered so that we can determine whether you have the right characteristics to succeed on the job.

_____ 23. You have to undergo an exam by our doctor to determine whether you can handle the job.

_____ 24. To get the drywalling job, you will have to hang, tape, and paste 10 sheets while doing a quality job, all in 3 hours.

_____ 25. Part of the selection process is to take our intelligence test.

_____ 26. Part of the firefighter test is to carry this 50-pound dummy up this ladder in 2 minutes or less.

_____ 27. You have to go in the bathroom now and put a sample of your urine in this cup so we can test it.

_____ 28. You need to take a test so that we can determine if you might get any known illnesses or diseases in the future.

Selection Interviews

>> **LO 6.6 Explain the three primary types of selection interviews by the value they bring to the selection process.**

Remember that during the selection process, some of the usual steps may be skipped or completed out of sequence. While the initial interview may be skipped, rarely will a candidate get a job without being interviewed by at least one person. Many organizations today, such as **Nike**, **PricewaterhouseCoopers**, and **Google**, are using technology to enhance their ability to quickly complete initial screening interviews.[70] Artificial intelligence chatbots, games that must be played before an applicant is allowed to submit a final application, simulations of actual work, video submissions, and other technologies are being used early on in the process to weed out individuals who are a poor fit with organizational needs. We also use technology to keep track of applicants as they go through what can sometimes be a very long selection process—here, again, chatbots can be valuable—to keep the applicant engaged throughout that process.

Interviewing

The interview is usually the most heavily weighted and is one of the last steps in the selection process.[71] To get a job, you need to be able to ace the interview,[72] but as a manager, you will need to know how to conduct a job interview. So this part of the section can help you do both well. You can practice this skill in Skill Builder 6.1.

An important focus of the interview is to assess the applicant's fit (personality-, ability-, and person-organization fit). More than half of HR professionals rank culture fit as the most important criterion at the interview stage.[73] You can also practice your interviewer skills in Skill Builder 6.2.

Types of Interviews and Questions

Exhibit 6.4 shows the various types of interviews and questions, which we discuss in this section, that can help you develop the important skill of interviewing.[74] **(SHRM N:8)**

▲
Many companies now use computers to conduct the first round of interviews.

Types of Interviews

Three basic types of interviews are based on structure. In a structured interview, all candidates are asked the same list of prepared questions. In an unstructured interview, there are no preplanned questions or sequence of topics. In a semistructured interview, the interviewer has a list of questions but also asks unplanned questions. The semistructured interview is generally preferred because it helps avoid discrimination (because the interviewer has a list of prepared questions to ask all candidates), but it also allows the interviewer to ask each candidate questions relating to that person's own situation. The interviewer departs from the structure when appropriate. At the same time, using a standard set of questions makes it easier to compare candidates. The amount of structure you should use depends on your experience as an interviewer. The less experience you have, the more structure you need.

However, we should consider interview validity in predicting who will be a good employee. Recent studies basically say that interviews are not our best selection tool. Testing for "general mental ability," or an intelligence test, holds that honor. A meta-analysis study found strong evidence for the superiority of structured interviews compared to unstructured interviews.[75] Interviews do increase your chance of predicting post-selection performance, but by a maximum of about 18% for a structured interview and 13% for unstructured interviews.[76] Some studies even found evidence that *unstructured* interviews actually had a negative effect on selecting new employees.[77] So you might convince some managers that interviews are not a great selection method and that unstructured interviews are actually poor indicators of future performance because of their potential for bias.

Types of Questions

Developing a set of consistent questions to ask all candidates can help you objectively compare the candidates and select the most qualified.[78] The questions you ask give you control over the interview; they allow you to get the information you need to make your decision. So you need to be prepared to ask and answer questions.[79] Remember, though, that all questions should have a purpose and should be job related.

You may use four types of questions during an interview:

1. *Closed-ended questions* require a limited response, often a yes or no answer, and are appropriate for dealing with fixed aspects of the job. Examples include "Do you have a class-one license?" and "Can you produce it if you are hired?"

2. *Open-ended questions* require detailed responses and are appropriate for determining candidate abilities and motivation, as they test critical thinking instead of pure knowledge.[80] Examples include "Why do you want to be a computer programmer for our company?" and "What do you see as a major strength you can bring to our company?"

EXHIBIT 6.4 ● Common Interview Questions

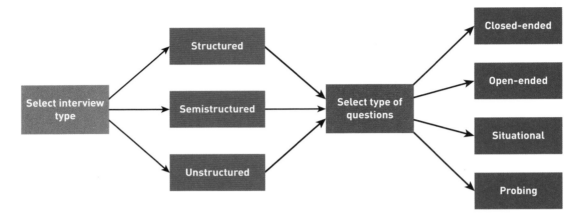

Common Interview Questions

Answering these questions prior to going to a job interview is good preparation that will help you get the job. Written answers are better preparation than verbal ones.

- How would you describe yourself?
- What two or three things are most important to you in your job and career?
- Why did you choose this job and career?
- What do you consider to be your greatest strengths and weaknesses?
- What have you learned from your mistakes?
- What would your last boss say about your work performance?
- What motivates you to go the extra mile on a project or job?
- What have you accomplished that shows your initiative and willingness to work?
- What two or three accomplishments have given you the most satisfaction? Why?
- Why should I hire you?
- What skills do you have?
- What makes you qualified for this position?
- In what ways do you think you can make a contribution to our company?
- Do you consider yourself a leader?
- How do you work under pressure?
- Why did you decide to seek a position in this company?
- What can you tell us about our company?
- What are your expectations regarding promotions and salary increases?
- Are you willing to travel and relocate?
- What are your long-range and short-range goals and objectives?
- What do you see yourself doing 5 years from now? Ten years from now?
- What do you expect to be earning in 5 years?

3. *Situational questions* require candidates to describe what they would do and say in a given situation. These questions are appropriate for assessing capabilities. An example would be "What would the problem be if the machine made a ringing sound?"

4. *Probing questions* require a clarification response and are appropriate for improving the interviewer's understanding. Probing questions are not planned. They are used to clarify

the candidate's response to an open-ended or situational question. Examples include "What do you mean by 'It was tough'?" and "What was the dollar increase in sales you achieved?"

Today, HR interviewers prefer behavior-based questions that ask candidates to describe how they handled specific situations in the past (behavioral descriptive) as well as situational questions of what they would do now in a specific given situation. Laszlo Bock, **Google**'s vice president of people operations, noted in a recent interview that "what works well are structured behavioral interviews, where you have a consistent rubric for how you assess people, rather than having each interviewer just make stuff up." One of his sample behavioral descriptive questions is "Give me an example of a time when you solved an analytically difficult problem".[81]

Preparing for and Conducting the Interview

Completing the interview preparation steps and the interviewing steps shown in Model 6.1 and Model 6.2 will help you improve your interviewing skills. The steps are straightforward and self-explanatory, so we will not discuss them.

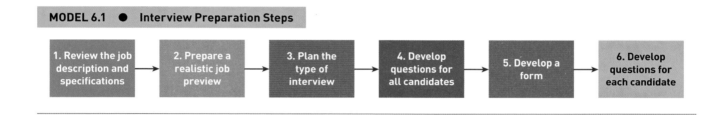

MODEL 6.1 ● Interview Preparation Steps

1. Review the job description and specifications → 2. Prepare a realistic job preview → 3. Plan the type of interview → 4. Develop questions for all candidates → 5. Develop a form → 6. Develop questions for each candidate

MODEL 6.2 ● Interviewing Steps

1. Open the interview → 2. Present the realistic job preview → 3. Ask your questions → 4. Introduce the top candidates to coworkers → 5. Close the interview

Background Checks

>> **LO 6.7 Defend the use of various background checks as tests for employment.**

Recall that résumés commonly contain discrepancies and that job candidates can lie during interviews.[82] So, background checks are needed to help prevent negligent hires and bad employees.[83] Background checks can become rather expensive depending on which checks we do and how often we have to do them, so they are usually left until we have at least narrowed down the list of candidates to a final few, or in some cases even to the final candidate. We may then offer employment to the candidate conditioned on passing various background checks. Remember, though, that you cannot use a background check to discriminate in violation of federal or state laws.[84]

Common background checks include credit checks, criminal background checks, reference checks, and social media and Web searches. In this section, we describe them and provide guidelines on when to use them.

6.2 SELF-ASSESSMENT

INTERVIEW READINESS

Select a professional job you would like to apply for. On a scale of 1 to 7 (1 = not confident, 7 = totally confident), indicate for each question how confident you are that you can give an answer that would make a positive impression on an interviewer.

I am confident that I have an answer				I am not confident that I have an answer		
7	6	5	4	3	2	1

_____ 1. Why did you choose the job for which you are applying?

_____ 2. What are your long-range career goals over the next 5 to 10 years?

_____ 3. What are your short-range goals and objectives for the next 1 to 2 years?

_____ 4. How do you plan to achieve your career goals?

_____ 5. What are your strengths and weaknesses?

_____ 6. What motivates you to put forth your greatest effort? Describe a situation in which you did so.

_____ 7. What two or three accomplishments have given you the most satisfaction? Why?

_____ 8. Why do you want this job?

_____ 9. In what kind of an organizational culture do you want to work?

_____ 10. Why did you decide to apply for a position with our organization?

_____ 11. What do you know about our organization?

_____ 12. In what ways do you think you can make a contribution to our organization?

_____ 13. What two or three things would be most important to you in your job?

_____ 14. Are you willing to relocate for the job? Do you have any constraints on relocation?

_____ 15. Describe a situation in which you had to work with a difficult person (another student, a coworker, a customer, a supervisor, etc.). How did you handle the situation?

_____ Total. Add up the numbers you assigned to each question and place the total on this line and on the continuum below.

105	95	85	75	65	55	45	35	25	15
Ready for the job interview					Not ready for the job interview				

These are common interview questions, so you should be prepared to give a good, confident answer to each of them. For additional interview questions, see Exhibit 6.4 "Common Interview Questions" and answer them. Your career services office may offer mock interviews to help you with your interview skills to help you get the job you are looking for.

Credit Checks

Although several states have recently put limits on its use,[85] one of the most commonly used background checks is the credit check. Credit checks are subject to the Fair Credit Reporting Act (FCRA),[86] which requires that employers disclose to the applicant that they will use credit reports for employment decisions. The act also says that if the information on the credit report results in an adverse employment action, the employer has to give a copy of the report to the person and inform the applicant of rights under FCRA, including the right to dispute the report. FCRA lawsuits have been on the rise over the past few years, with companies such as **Disney**, **Domino's Pizza**, **Kmart**, and **Dillard's** being accused of FCRA violations in hiring.[87] **(SHRM D:8)**

Credit checks will most likely be done if applicants will have access to any money or if they will work with the company's financial information. Credit checks may also be done with other employees to evaluate their personal responsibility—to see if they have a habit of being dishonest in credit transactions.

A history of not paying bills tells the organization that the person is likely to be dishonest in other ways as well. Does something like a bankruptcy on your credit report automatically knock you out of contention for a job? No. In fact, by law, the company can't refuse to hire you solely because of a bankruptcy.[88] However, again, if your credit report shows a pattern of failure to live up to your credit obligations, the company can and probably will use that information to remove you from the applicant pool, as long as state laws allow it.

Criminal Background Checks

All states allow criminal background checks in at least some cases. Can or should a criminal record keep an individual from being hired? It depends on (1) the nature and seriousness of the offense, (2) how long ago it occurred, and (3) what type of job the individual is being considered for. In fact, federal guidance on use of criminal record information requires that we do exactly those three things when considering a criminal offense.[89]

We would have a much easier time defending the use of a conviction for theft with an individual who would have access to products or funds that are easily stolen than we would in the case of someone with no access to anything of significant value in the company. Similarly, we would be more likely to be able to use a violent criminal history to rule out an applicant if the applicant would have access to children or other innocent persons who could easily be harmed by the employee.

We also have to be aware that more than half of the states in the United States and hundreds of cities and other municipalities have passed "Ban-the-Box" legislation that generally makes it illegal to complete a criminal background query of any kind prior to a conditional job offer.[90] Once a job is offered, in most cases the criminal check can be accomplished, keeping in mind the three criteria identified by the EEOC (mentioned earlier in this chapter). And as always, we have to look at all the circumstances and make a decision based on the OUCH test and the defensibility of the selection tool that we are considering.

Reference Checks

Reference checks include not only calls to references that are provided by the applicant but also reference letters from employers, personal letters of recommendation, and possibly cold calls to previous employers and coworkers. But is a reference check going to be of any value, or are the references that the applicant provides going to say only good things about the applicant?

The basic answer is that a reference letter that is requested by the applicant is almost always going to say good things. The applicant will almost never ask anybody to provide a reference unless the applicant knows that the reference will be good. In addition, though, we want to check references that might not have been given to us by the applicant but instead by people such as former employers and coworkers.

What is a previous employer most likely going to tell you if you call for a reference check? The most common HR answer will be in the form of "Yes, he/she worked at this company, from (date) to (date) in (job type) job." This is to protect the company from being sued for providing defamatory information about the former employee—in other words, for hurting the individual's reputation. Over time, company lawyers have found that if companies provide more information than noted above, we can become the target of lawsuits. So most companies won't provide more information than they have to. A phone conversation may get you some useful info, but don't expect it in writing.

Social Media and Web Searches

Finally, with the ability to access very large amounts of information, virtually all organizations are using the Internet to do research on job candidates whenever they are allowed to do so by applicable federal, state, or local laws.[91] "Googling" a candidate's name is becoming a standard practice.[92] And it is truly amazing what the company finds in many cases. **(SHRM L:15)**

Should social media be used as a selection device? HR departments are going to use the tools that they have available to get the best possible people, so social media will most likely continue to be one tool that is used in the recruiting and selection process where, and when, it is allowed by law. However, we need to be very careful to avoid using information that would be illegal in consideration for employment. It would be very easy to find out information on

▲
Web searches should be used carefully in the recruiting process, as the results of a Web search may reveal factors that employers cannot legally consider when making a hiring decision (such as religion, race, gender, marital status, etc.).

someone's religion, race, gender, or other facets of that individual's personal life—factors that would be illegal to consider in the hiring process—that might allow a company representative to make a biased and even discriminatory choice. Most legal opinions seem to favor the employer in cases where there might be a question of violation of privacy if the employer is doing a check of social media to avoid negligent hires, but companies need to make sure they are doing so in an ethical and legally equitable manner, or they can be considered liable for invasions of off-duty privacy.[93]

Two ways that companies have found to avoid illegal bias are to have either an outside agency do the social media search or have a company insider who has no decision authority in hiring do that same search and bring only relevant information to the person or persons doing the selection.[94] This separates the search (and any items found that would be illegal to consider) from the selection process.

On a personal note, as a potential job applicant, make sure that everything on the Web about you is information that you are comfortable with a company discovering in a Web search. You may not be putting negative things about yourself online, but you also need to make sure your friends aren't, either. Employers *will* most likely do a Web search on you as a candidate in today's world. Also, make sure your e-mail address and telephone message are professional for job searching.

6.1 ETHICAL DILEMMA: WHAT WOULD YOU DO?

Several recent state laws and executive orders at the federal level have brought the topic of LGBTQ individuals to the forefront of attention in many businesses, but as of the writing of this text, there is no federal law that currently prohibits workplace discrimination on the basis of sexual orientation.[95] Assume that you are the hiring authority at a company that is not affected by a state law protecting LGBT individuals. You decide to complete a Web search of the two primary candidates for a job opening and find that one of the two is obviously and very publicly transgender. Information on LGBT issues are all over their personal Facebook and other social media pages. They appear to be very much an activist for the cause.

1. Would it be unethical to use this information in your hiring decision? Why or why not?

2. How would you use the information to sway your hiring decision?

3. Would you decide to hire this person if they were the best qualified candidate? Justify your answer.

Selecting the Candidate and Offering the Job

>> **LO 6.8 List the two basic methods used to make final selection decisions.**

Even when you follow all the steps in the selection process, you can't find out everything about a potential job candidate. You may only be able to discover some basics that tell you whether or not the individual is a *really* good fit for the job. These might include the following three things:

1. Does the candidate have the basic qualifications for the job—right personality, ability, and person-organization fit?

2. Does the candidate actually *want* to do the job, or does this person want just *any* job? In other words, will the candidate be satisfied with the job and stay for some time and be a productive hire?

3. Is the candidate basically honest, and is this person telling the truth? If not, you could be looking at a problem employee. **(SHRM N:10)**

The recruiter may know that by finding out these three basic things, the candidate will be a valuable addition to the organization and can be trained to do any specific job that is necessary.

We do now have evidence that by using more statistically valid methods of selection, we gain a much greater likelihood of getting a high-quality candidate. One meta-analysis reviewed two options for evaluating selection data—*mechanical* or *clinical/holistic*. Mechanical approaches "involve applying an algorithm or formula to each applicant's scores," whereas holistic, or clinical, approaches use "individual judgments of data and group consensus meetings."[96] The meta-analysis showed that "the difference between the validity of mechanical and holistic data combination methods translated into an improvement in prediction of more than 50% [for the mechanical approach]."[97] We can apply the mechanical approach to the two methods for final selection decisions discussed below.

The two basic methods that we would generally use to make final selection decisions are the multiple-hurdle model and the compensatory model. The **multiple-hurdle selection model** *requires that each applicant must pass a particular selection test in order to go on to the next test*. If an applicant fails to pass any test in the process, that person is immediately removed from the running. On the other hand, the **compensatory selection model** *allows an individual to do poorly on one test but make up for that poor grade by doing exceptionally well on other tests*. Again, each step in the selection process (interviews and background checks) is a test. Using the compensatory model allows the employer to rank each of the candidates based on their overall score from all of the testing. The employer can also group candidates based on this same information.

Multiple-hurdle selection model Model requiring that each applicant must pass a particular selection test in order to go on to the next test

Compensatory selection model Model allowing an individual to do poorly on one test but make up for that poor grade by doing exceptionally well on other tests

Hiring

After all selection activities are completed, compare each candidate's qualifications to the job specifications, identify whether or not this person really wants to do the job, and analyze whether or not the individual has been basically honest during the selection process. Do all this to determine who would be the best fit for the job. Be sure to get coworkers' impressions of each candidate when appropriate because they will have to work and get along with whomever you hire (person-organization fit), and they can tell you if they think the person fits and if they want the person on their team or not. Diversity should also be considered when selecting a candidate.[98]

To bring the selection process to an end, contact the best candidate and offer that person the job. You will need to consider issues such as what type of employment contract (if any) you will present, whether or not the employment will be "at-will" (we discuss this in Chapter 9), and authorization to work in the country where you are hiring, among other items. Ultimately, if the candidate does not accept the job or accepts but leaves after a short period of time, you can frequently offer the next-best candidate the job. **(SHRM N:10-b)**

Trends and Issues in HRM

Let's take a brief look at the issues of federal regulations limiting selection testing and the global workforce and immigration. Each of these issues has affected the process of selection in a significant way during the past decade, which in turn has caused HR managers to change the way they work.

Federal Regulation Limits Selection Testing

There is good evidence that new employees are coming into the workforce without the skills needed for work. The problem is that we can't just decide to do employment testing without paying attention to the UGESP.

Recall that the UGESP tell us what is a "test for employment," and that is *everything* that we use to determine who to hire and who to remove from our candidate pool. The UGESP also require that *all* tests for employment be *validated and reliable.* In many cases, tests are not being rigorously validated before they are used. You cannot just find a test you like on the Internet and decide to use it, or decide that you need to have candidates take a personality profile test because you think you need to hire extroverts or people with a high need for achievement. For one thing, the test used may not be valid and reliable. For another, remember that any test has to be "job related and consistent with business necessity," according to the UGESP.

The EEOC and the Department of Labor have also issued guidance on employment testing noting that they will be increasing attention on employment testing issues, and there is evidence that this is happening. We mentioned **Target** stores being fined for testing that created disparate impact, and there are others. **Aqualon Company** was charged with hiring discrimination against African-American applicants because of a biased written test. Amsted Rail was charged with using improper physical tests in violation of the ADA. **Fabricut Inc.** settled a lawsuit with the EEOC over ADA and GINA claims. And the list goes on.

But it's easy to fix this problem with technology, right? Not so fast! Technology can test large numbers of people and can do so without any emotional attachment to the people or the process, but technology can't tell us whether or not a test is job related and meets the requirement for business necessity, or whether that test may have a disparate impact on groups of candidates. There are many HR tech companies who will sell us a technology solution to manage testing for all kinds of organizational purposes, but we still have the legal obligation to make sure those solutions don't discriminate illegally.

How do we ensure that we are managing the selection process correctly? First, we need to know the laws and regulations for our area and then we need to manage the actual testing process—not only the tests, but whether or not we even use a certain type of testing in a situation. The best way to ultimately make sure we are in compliance with all of the rules is to apply the OUCH test—Objective facts, Uniformly applied, Consistent across all protected groups, and Has job relatedness. If you do that, you will most likely have met all of the requirements for employment testing.

The Global Workforce and Immigration

Immigration for the purpose of work continues to become a more significant issue. There are several issues of importance when we are selecting individuals from all over the world. The first major issue for HR managers is the process of immigration and work visas. Each country has its own requirements for immigration and for foreign workers who want to gain employment in that country. The HR manager is typically responsible for identifying the requirements and making sure that the individual fulfills them.

The organization, through the HR department, is also typically responsible for assisting the individual with filling out the forms and in many cases for sponsoring the individual's work visa. The HR department generally is required to maintain records of the company's employees showing a legal right to work in the country of operations. So there is a lot of paperwork involved in moving individuals who are citizens of one country to another country in order to work for your organization—and the above paperwork is just the basics. In some circumstances, many other forms are required for entry into a country for the purpose of work.

In addition to immigration and visa requirements, organizations that hire workers in other countries face issues with the selection process itself. How does HR select somebody who we may not be able to meet, interview, or interact with in any direct form? In many cases, the HR representative may never see the individual who's being hired. A large portion of the selection process is now done virtually. Inability to interact directly with the candidate creates an entirely new set of problems for the HR representative. There may also be a language barrier between the candidate and the HR representative, and there are almost certainly cultural differences. Each of these barriers must be overcome, and every company handles them a little bit differently. However, HR managers must understand and be trained to work within today's global hiring environment or their company will be at a significant disadvantage versus competitors.

Chapter Summary

6.1 Describe why the selection process is so important to the company.

Selection is important primarily because we need the best possible person in each job in order to maximize productivity. Unproductive members of the organization can cause lower motivation and employee engagement in all of a company's employees. Second, organizations have a responsibility to avoid negligent hires—people who may pose a danger to others within the organization. The company can incur legal liability if we don't screen potential applicants carefully.

6.2 State the importance of the three main types of "fit" in the selection process.

The three types of fit are personality-job fit, ability-job fit, and person-organization fit. They are important because managers are supposed to get the best productivity out of their workforce. But not everyone can do everything equally well, so managers have to treat people differently, but fairly, in order to put the right person in the right job. They do this by assessing the three types of fit between the person and the company.

6.3 Summarize the major points in the Uniform Guidelines on Employee Selection Procedures (UGESP).

The UGESP are guidelines on how to avoid discriminatory hiring practices. They identify what the federal government considers to be an employment test and how those tests can be used in making employment decisions. The UGESP also identify the acceptable types of validity that can be used to validate employment tests, and they note that these tests must be reliable.

6.4 Discuss the use of applications and résumés as selection tools.

Applications and résumés are used in a fairly interchangeable manner, except that the application gives the company information on the applicant that is in a standard format. This makes it easier to quickly scan and evaluate the different applicants. Applications also typically have some legal language or disclosures that must be agreed to by the applicant. Both documents should be used to review and verify both the work experience and the education of the applicant. This experience and education should always be

verified, though, because evidence shows that a high percentage of people exaggerate or lie on applications and résumés.

6.5 Recall the major types of written testing available as selection tools.

The major types of written tests are *skills tests,* which evaluate the candidates' ability to apply their knowledge to a specific type of problem; *personality tests,* which evaluate the applicants' personal traits or characteristics so that they can be matched up with appropriate types of jobs; *interest tests,* which identify what an applicant is interested in and therefore most likely motivated to learn; *cognitive ability tests,* which are assessments of intelligence or aptitude for a specific type of work; and *honesty or integrity tests,* which evaluate the individual's philosophy concerning theft and other forms of dishonesty.

6.6 Explain the three primary types of selection interviews by the value they bring to the selection process.

The interview gives the manager a chance to make a face-to-face assessment of the candidate, including the person's ability to communicate, and personality, appearance, and motivation. It also gives the candidate a chance to learn about the job and the organization. The three primary types of interviews are the *unstructured interview,* in which the interviewer has no preplanned questions or topics; the *semistructured interview,* where the interviewer may ask both planned and unplanned questions; and the *structured interview,* where all candidates are asked the same set of questions. Most interviewers prefer the semistructured interview.

6.7 Defend the use of various background checks as tests for employment.

Credit checks are one of the most commonly used background checks. They should not automatically disqualify a person for a job, but if a credit report shows a pattern of dishonesty, then it can be valuable as a tool for selection. Criminal background checks may or may not be allowed by state law. Any criminal conviction should have something to do with the essential job functions; otherwise, we should not use it to disqualify an individual. Reference checks will usually not provide a lot of information, but we should complete them anyway in case they do provide valuable information. And, finally, social media and Web searches frequently turn up information on the morals, values, or honesty of potential employees; companies use these when they are allowed under state and local laws.

6.8   List the two basic methods used to make final selection decisions.

There are two basic methods that can be used to make final selection decisions for the organization. The *multiple-hurdle selection model* requires that each applicant must pass a particular selection test in order to go on to the next test. If an applicant fails to pass any test in the process, that person is immediately removed from the running. The *compensatory selection model* allows an individual to do poorly on one test but make up for that poor grade by doing exceptionally well on other tests. Using the compensatory model allows the employer to rank each of the candidates based on their overall score from all of the testing.

Key Terms

assessment center,   148
cognitive ability test,   147
compensatory selection
    model,   157
construct validity,   142
content validity,   142
criterion-related validity,   142
fitness-for-duty test,   149

interest test,   147
multiple-hurdle selection
    model,   157
negligent hire,   138
personality test,   147
physical test,   148
reliability,   143
selection,   138

simulation,   148
skills test,   147
Uniform Guidelines on
    Employee Selection
    Procedures (UGESP),   141
validity,   142
work sample,   148

Key Terms Review

Complete each of the following statements using one of this chapter's key terms.

1. _____ is the process of choosing the best-qualified applicant recruited for a job.

2. _____ is a legal concept that says if the organization selects someone who may pose a danger to coworkers, customers, suppliers, or other third parties, and if that person then harms someone else in the course of working for the company, then the company can be held liable for the individual's actions.

3. _____ provide information that can be used to avoid discriminatory hiring practices as well as discrimination in other employment decisions.

4. _____ is the extent to which a test measures what it claims to measure.

5. _____ is an assessment of the ability of a test to measure some other factor related to the test.

6. _____ is an assessment of whether a test measures knowledge or understanding of the items it is supposed to measure.

7. _____ measures a theoretical concept or trait that is not directly observable.

8. _____ is the consistency of a test measurement.

9. _____ is an assessment instrument designed to determine whether you have the ability to apply a particular knowledge set.

10. _____ measures the psychological traits or characteristics of applicants to determine suitability for performance in a specific type of job.

11. _____ measures a person's intellectual curiosity and motivation in a particular field.

12. _____ is an assessment of general intelligence or of some type of aptitude for a particular job.

13. _____ ensures that applicants are capable of performing on the job in ways defined by the job specification and description.

14. _____ means that we provide a sample of the work that the candidate would perform on the job and ask the candidate to perform the tasks under controlled conditions.

15. _____ is a place where job applicants undergo a series of tests, interviews, and simulated experiences to determine their potential for a particular job.

16. _____ allows us to put a candidate in a high-pressure situation but still control the environment so as to limit the danger and cost.

17. _____ identifies whether or not an employee is physically capable at a particular point in time of performing a specific type of work.

18. _____ requires that each applicant must pass a particular selection test in order to go on to the next test.

19. _____ allows an individual to do poorly on one test but make up for that poor grade by doing exceptionally well on other tests.

Communication Skills

The following critical-thinking questions can be used for class discussion and/or for written assignments to develop communication skills. Be sure to give complete explanations for all answers.

1. Do you agree that selection of a top-quality candidate is a critical process in organizations, or do you think intensive training after the person is selected is more valuable? Explain your answer.

2. Should organizations be held liable by the justice system for negligent hires? Why or why not?

3. In your mind, how critical is the concept of person-organization fit? Why do you think so?

4. Are there cases other than the two instances noted in the chapter when companies should be allowed to use polygraph tests on employees? When and why?

5. Do you feel that it's OK to tell "little white lies" on résumés and applications? Why or why not?

6. Are companies overtesting applicants by using the processes that were discussed in this chapter? Explain your answer.

7. Are background checks—including credit checks, criminal history checks, and looking at a candidate's Facebook page—too invasive? Explain your answer.

8. Is the use of HRMS for narrowing down the list of candidates and sending form letters, including rejection letters, too impersonal? Why or why not?

Case 6.1 A Kink in Links of London's Selection Process

Links of London is an iconic jewelry brand with an international presence that captures the wit, spirit, and heart of London. The design team strives to create exquisite jewelry and statement watches that will captivate our customers worldwide. Passionate about watches and jewelry, Links of London continuously seeks improved techniques and pays special emphasis on quality and design with a British touch.[99] Links of London is a subsidiary of the publicly traded Folli Follie Holdings S.A., selling 18K gold and 925 sterling silver jewelry in Europe, Asia, the Americas, and the Caribbean and with its 650 employees worldwide is considered to be the English equivalent of New York's Tiffany's & Co.[100]

It was the summer and Krissy was perusing LinkedIn when she noticed an advertisement for the assistant store manager position at Links of London for their Madison Avenue, New York, flagship location. She was very excited about the position and working for Links of London for several reasons:

- She had a "passion for fashion" and wanted to work in the "luxury fashion center" of Manhattan—near **Saint Laurent, Chanel,** and **Louis Vuitton.**

- She had recently been accepted to a MBA program in fashion merchandising, felt that with this additional education she could work her way up into corporate headquarters, and apply her acquired knowledge to the firm's best advantage.

- She went to their website, read about their culture and values, and wanted to work for a firm that wanted employees who were accountable and proactive, passionate and innovative, ambitious and driven, knowledgeable and engaging, and respectful and honest.[101]

Krissy continued to surf Link's website and read about their benefits and career development. She was most impressed with their statement:

Our objective is to match the needs of the Company with those who work for us. We believe in training and developing our people and teams to deliver high performance to achieve the Company objectives and demonstrate our People Values, which maximizes job satisfaction for our teams. We are often looking for bright and enthusiastic new people to join our team, whether it is assisting our customers in one of our stores or behind the scenes at one of our offices. Links of London is a great place to work and we are immensely proud of our brand and our people so if you are interested in joining a Company that rewards talent and invests in people then we would love to hear from you.[102]

Krissy immediately hit the "check out our vacancies" tab but hit a small roadblock—the link took her to a website on LinkedIn that said, "Oops, try again." She tried several more times but to no avail. Undaunted, she contacted the Links of London Madison Avenue store directly and was told that there was an opening for an assistant store manager and that she could apply online. Krissy explained the problem with the website and was told they would send her a job application blank via e-mail. She completed the application, attached her résumé but was surprised that they asked

for a head shot photo as well as her date of birth. They also specifically instructed her not to include a cover letter. She found this curious but nonetheless applied. Part of the application included a checkoff allowing the firm to conduct employment verification, examine her personal websites, and run a credit check.

The following day Krissy was directed to a website where she was asked to take what seemed to be a personality test as well as a test of her integrity. She was again a bit surprised that she was not asked to take a cognitive test relative to the job. A few days later Krissy received a phone call from the personnel office describing the job to her in more detail and advising her that, if she were still interested in the job, she could interview with the manager of the store the following week. Krissy immediately took the first available time slot and went online to see if she could research more about the firm and their Madison Avenue store.

Krissy's interview with the store manager seemed like a tale of two cities ("It was the best of times; it was the worst of times"). She came early to the meeting so she could walk around the store and get a feeling for what Links of London was all about. She was intrigued as to the store layout and the staging of the jewelry and was very impressed with how the sales associates were able to, after a question or two, size her up as a "window shopper" and not a buyer. When she actually asked for the store manager, she was sold on the store—it seemed like everything she could have hoped for and she was primed for her interview.

She waited for 15 minutes after the allocated interview time and was then informed that the manager was in a conference call with corporate and thus unavailable. One of the staff members was in fact confirming that personnel had set up the appointment. When Krissy suggested to the staffer that she might come back at a better time, the manager insisted that Krissy wait and that the interview continue. In the interim, Krissy handed the staffer a copy of her résumé in both hard copy and electronic form so that the store manager could look it over while Krissy waited outside her office.

A half an hour later, the manager came out of her office to greet Krissy and escorted her into her office. The interview lasted no more than 15 minutes with the manager, list in hand, asking some very common interview questions while not going into any details of the job responsibilities or even some background about the firm. Most answers to the manager's questions required a yes/no response. She did not receive a tour of the store nor did she meet any of the store employees, including those she dealt with earlier. Krissy tried to ask several of her prepared questions in order to develop a relationship with the manager, yet each was answered in a very curt, perfunctory manner. Krissy walked out of the store feeling that she had the worst interview in the history of job interviews.

Two days later Krissy was astonished when she was asked to have a Skype interview with the regional district manager at Links. This manager was quite positive, emphasizing the importance of the New York store as the "showcase" for Links of London products and services; service had to be "of the highest quality" with the customer always coming first. The regional district manager was supportive of her efforts to obtain a graduate degree and indicated the financial support she would receive from the firm for her continued education. When the job offer came "out of the blue" 3 weeks later to start immediately, Krissy didn't know what to do or what to think. No one had contacted her references throughout the process to verify her abilities. There seemed to be several loose links in the chain of command at Links of London that tarnished their golden image.

Questions

1. What types of "fit" was Links of London looking for in their employees, according to their career services website?

2. What are the steps in the selection process, and where did this process seem to falter with Krissy?

3. What determines if a question is acceptable in a pre-employment inquiry, and what questions might have been deemed unacceptable on Links's job application?

4. Krissy took a personality test as well as a test of her integrity yet not a job-specific cognitive test. What might be the firm's rationale for using the tests they did?

5. What type of interview did the store manager seem to conduct using what type of questions?

6. What steps should have been taken when conducting the interview? Did the store manager miss any of them?

7. If you were Krissy, would you accept the job offer?

Case is derived from a previously published case (see reference 2) and includes fictitious material added to enhance the case solely for instructional purposes.

Adapted from Sherman, Herbert and Tina Tae (July 2016). "'Linking' Expectations and Culture at Links of London." *Journal of Business and Retail Management*, Volume 10, Issue 3, 57–68.

Skill Builder 6.1 Interviewing

Objective

To develop your ability to develop interview questions

To develop your ability to interview and to be interviewed

Skills

The primary skills developed through this exercise are as follows:

1. *HR management skills*—Technical, interpersonal, business, and conceptual and design skills

2. *SHRM 2018 Curriculum Guidebook*—N: Staffing (Recruitment and Selection)

Preparation

Assume you are the HR director and you need to hire a new college grad for an entry-level HR position.

Because you are not a large company, you have a small staff and the new hire will help out in a wide variety of HR functions. Develop a list of at least 10 questions you would ask the candidates during a job interview for the position.

Apply It

What did I learn from this experience? How will I use this knowledge in the future?

_____

_____

_____

Your instructor may ask you to do this Skill Builder in class by breaking into groups of two or three and actually conducting interviews using your questions. If so, the instructor will provide you with any necessary information or additional instructions.

Skill Builder 6.2 Interview Questions for Use When Hiring a Professor to Teach This Course

Objective

To develop your ability to develop interview questions

Skills

The primary skills developed through this exercise are as follows:

1. *HR management skills*—Technical, business, and conceptual and design skills

2. *SHRM 2018 Curriculum Guidebook*—N: Staffing (Recruitment and Selection)

Preparation

Assume you are the dean of your college and you need to hire a professor to teach this course next semester. Develop a list of at least 10 questions you would ask the candidates during a job interview for the position.

Apply It

What did I learn from this experience? How will I use this knowledge in the future?

_____

_____

_____

Your instructor may ask you to do this Skill Builder in class in a group by sharing your interview questions and coming up with a group list of questions. If so, the instructor will provide you with any necessary information or additional instructions. This may be followed by the professor actually being interviewed by answering group questions. One of the coauthors prefers taking one question from each group at a time until all questions (without repeat) are answered or the time is up. Of course, I get the job every time.

Developing and Managing

7 Training, Learning, Talent Management, and Development

8 Performance Management and Appraisal

9 Employee Rights and Labor Relations

PART III

PRACTITIONER'S MODEL

⬆ Productivity
⬆ Engagement
⬇ Absenteeism
⬇ Turnover

PART V: Protecting and Expanding Organizational Outreach How do you PROTECT and EXPAND your Human Resources?		
Chapter 12 Workplace Safety, Health, and Security	Chapter 13 Ethics, Sustainability, Diversity, and Inclusion	Chapter 14 Global Issues for Human Resource Managers

PART IV: Compensating How do you REWARD and MAINTAIN your Human Resources?	
Chapter 10 Compensation Management	Chapter 11 Employee Incentives and Benefits

PART III: Developing and Managing How do you MANAGE your Human Resources?		
Chapter 7 Training, Learning, Talent Management, and Development	Chapter 8 Performance Management and Appraisal	Chapter 9 Employee Rights and Labor Relations

PART II: Staffing What HRM Functions do you NEED for sustainability?		
Chapter 4 Workforce Planning: Job Analysis, Design, and Employment Forecasting	Chapter 5 Recruiting Job Candidates	Chapter 6 Selecting New Employees

PART I: The Human Resource Management Environment What HRM issues are CRITICAL to your organization's long-term sustainability?		
Chapter 1 Today's Human Resource Management Process	Chapter 2 Strategy-Driven Human Resource Management	Chapter 3 The Legal Environment

©iStockphoto.com/kali9

Training, Learning, Talent Management, and Development

Learning Outcomes

After studying this chapter, you should be able to do the following:

7.1 Identify each of the common points in the tenure of employees within the organization where training may be needed. **PAGE 168**

7.2 Describe the interrelationship of the steps in the training process. **PAGE 170**

7.3 Summarize the four methods for shaping behavior. **PAGE 172**

7.4 Compare each of the major training delivery types. **PAGE 175**

7.5 Discuss the four-level evaluation method for assessing training programs. **PAGE 180**

7.6 List some of the individual and organizational consequences that can occur as a result of organizational career planning processes. **PAGE 181**

SHRM HR Content

See Online: *SHRM 2018 Curriculum Guidebook* for the complete list

F. HR Career Planning

1. Balancing work and life
3. Career development
3-a. Career development—Definition of a career

I. Job Analysis and Job Design

8. Training and development
8-b. Training and development—Needs assessment
8-c. Training and development—Career pathing

L. Organizational Development

2. Developing human resources
4. Equipping the organization for present and future talent needs
9. Measurement systems
11. Organizational learning
14. Outsourcing employee development
16. Succession planning
17. Training employees to meet current and future job demands

P. Training and Development

1-b. Business games and studies—Creating a learning environment
2-a. Competency models—Learning theories: Behaviorism, constructivism, cognitive models, adult learning, knowledge management

2-b. Competency models—Training evaluation: Kirkpatrick's model
3. Evaluating training programs
3-a. Evaluating training programs—Determining return on investment (ROI)
4-a. Human/intellectual capital—Role of training in succession planning
5. Needs assessment
5-a. Needs assessment—Employee development: Formal education, experience, assessment
6-d. Selecting training methods—E-learning and use of technology in training
6-e. Selecting training methods—Hands-on methods
6-h. Selecting training methods—On-the-job training (OJT)
6-k. Selecting training methods—Simulations
7. Transfer of training: Design issues, facilitating transfer
8-a. Training resources—Outsourcing

Q. Workforce Planning and Talent Management

7. Succession planning

Practitioner's Perspective

Cindy told the story of Jennifer, who had worked in the same position for 10 years. Jennifer had always been a valuable employee, but lately, her productivity and performance had started to decline. Her supervisor, Mandy, finally called her in to find out what was wrong.

After some hesitation, Jennifer said, "To tell the truth, I feel like I am in a rut. I just don't get the same satisfaction from doing my job that I used to get."

"I wish we'd had this talk sooner," Mandy replied, "but now that I know how you feel, there is something we can do. Let's take a look at some of the training opportunities coming up this quarter. Tell me what training classes you might be interested in taking."

What if Jennifer and Mandy never had that talk? Do you think Jennifer would have remained at her job? Chapter 7 looks at the ins and outs of managing and retaining talent through training and development.

The Need for Training and Development

>> **LO 7.1 Identify each of the common points in the tenure of employees within the organization where training may be needed.**

After we hire new employees, we need to invest in training[1] to teach them about the organization and its routine processes[2] as well as how to do their new jobs. There is a relationship between training, job satisfaction, and employee engagement;[3] it decreases expensive turnover[4] and makes it less likely that employees will engage in neglectful behavior.[5] Therefore, we need to ensure the required onboarding training is completed.[6]

Training is costly,[7] but effective training and development are investments, not expenses, as they pay for themselves through competitive advantage and increased performance.[8] This is why companies worldwide are investing heavily in training and long-term employee development.[9] As managers' skills should also be developed,[10] leadership programs and courses are currently popular.[11] This is why best-practice companies (e.g., **Deloitte, Hyatt**, and **Scripps Health**) provide leadership programs.[12] Let's begin by discussing training and development and the difference between them, followed by when training is needed.

Training and Development

In this chapter, we will discuss both organizational training and employee development. The two are related but separate pieces of the organization's processes involving the management of its employees. **Training** is *the process of teaching employees the skills necessary to perform a job.* We train employees to provide them with the knowledge, skills, and abilities (KSAs) they can put to immediate use.[13] **(SHRM I:8, L:17, L:2)**

Somewhat in contrast to training is the process of employee development. Both colleges and corporations have been criticized for not doing a good job of developing business leaders.[14] Management education needs more emphasis on skills development.[15] This is one of the reasons why this book focuses on developing HR *skills,* not just knowledge. **Employee development** is *ongoing education to improve knowledge and skills for present and future jobs.* So, employee development teaches our workers skills at those tasks that they will need to know to move into higher-level jobs.

To remain competitive in today's dynamic environment, organizations must have employees who maintain up-to-date knowledge and skills, and development plays an important role in this effort.[16] Doing so significantly enhances the firm's stock of human capital, while reducing the costs of recruiting and selecting external new hires.[17] So for people to really be the organization's most valuable resource, they need to be developed.[18]

When Is Training Needed?

Employees have to be taught how to perform a new job and to update skills with changes including technology.[19] If we are considering a potential training opportunity, we should begin by completing a *needs assessment.*[20] We will discuss needs assessments shortly, but let's review some

Training The process of teaching employees the skills necessary to perform a job

Employee development Ongoing education to improve knowledge and skills for present and future jobs

common points at which we should probably complete a needs assessment and at least consider providing training. **(SHRM P:5)**

New Employee Onboarding

Onboarding is *the process of introducing new employees to the organization and their jobs.* Onboarding, also called orientation, introduces the new employee to all of the things that exist within the organizational society in order to be able to go about their daily lives.[21] People are socialized by institutions,[22] and onboarding is about socializing new hires and developing relationships,[23] because if people don't feel like they are accepted into the team, they tend to quit.[24] So firms want to create a sense of belonging for newcomers quickly.[25]

Newcomer socialization done effectively during the onboarding process increases job satisfaction and performance and reduces turnover rates.[26] Onboarding frequently emphasizes corporate values, culture, and strengths.[27] This socialization process is important to both newcomers and organizations, as the new employees learn the ropes and understand what is expected from them as they assimilate into the organization and attempt to become productive members.[28] Thus, job and career orientation have long-lasting effects on new employee job attitudes and satisfaction, behavior, work mastery, and performance.[29]

Onboarding is an introduction of the person to the company.[30] What do we need to think about when we introduce somebody to the company? We need to think about introducing the new employee to all of the things that exist within the organizational "society" they are entering.[31] The process is very similar to someone moving to a different country and having to assimilate into a new culture. What do people need to know in order to be able to go about their daily lives, do the routine things they need to do, and provide for their own personal needs? Onboarding should be designed to answer all of the questions necessary to allow new employees to find their place in the organizational culture.

First, the new employee needs to learn the organization's policies, procedures, rules, and regulations—much like learning the laws in society. The second thing people would probably want to know is how to act and interact with others in the new society. Therefore, in addition to introducing the employee to the job and how to perform it within the organization, we would want to teach the individual about the underlying organizational structure and culture, plus where to go and whom to talk to in order to get certain things done. When they have questions, who do they go to for answers? Safety and security issues will vary with the type of environment, but these also need to be covered.

They would also likely need to fill out paperwork with HR, such as home address and payroll information, and to get an employee ID. We also need to tell them about their pay and benefits, including whom to contact with HR questions.[32]

Part of the problem of high turnover rates today is poor onboarding.[33] Effective onboarding results in lower turnover rates,[34] so orientation to the firm and the new employee's job should "last at least one year to ensure high retention say staffing and HR experts."[35] **Facebook** uses a 6-week boot camp where new hires learn their role and the company culture, **Zappos'** basic onboarding process lasts 4 weeks,[36] and **Honda** has a 6-week onboarding process.

However, in most organizations, the onboarding process is significantly shorter than this and one reason that organizations suffer significant early turnover of new hires. If our new employee is frustrated due to not knowing how to do the job or how to fix an issue that concerns pay, the likelihood of that person leaving the organization goes up drastically. Many organizations could significantly reduce new-hire turnover by modestly increasing the onboarding and socialization period for new hires.[37]

New Job Requirements or Processes

The second common point where training may be necessary occurs when jobs change in some form, either the same job or transferring to a new one. The change may be based on discovery of new techniques or technologies to perform particular work to make the work more efficient.[38] The organization may require new processes or procedures or entirely new jobs. With any major job changes, we should conduct a training needs assessment, and when needed, an appropriate training program can be designed and implemented. Also, having diverse skills enables employees to perform a variety of tasks.[39]

Remediation The correction
of a deficiency or failure in a
process or procedure

Remediation

The third common point at which managers need to investigate the requirement for additional training occurs when there has been some failure of an employee or some employees to perform successfully and meet organizational standards. **Remediation** is *the correction of a deficiency or failure in a process or procedure*. In remediation, we work to correct the actions of the individual or individuals responsible for the process or procedure so they can successfully carry out the action in the future.

Employee Development for Advancement

Finally, we need to develop current employee skills and abilities so employees can move into higher-level jobs within the organization. Offering development opportunities generally decreases turnover.[40] Providing development opportunities and succession planning is the only way the organization can be sustainable over long periods of time. It requires identifying high-potential individuals for development and ultimately advancement into managerial and executive slots. So succession is an important function of the HR department. Organizations that neglect succession processes and employee development can find themselves at a competitive disadvantage when senior personnel leave the firm through either retirement or resignation. Although both training and development are critically important to company success, in this chapter we will focus more on training than development. **(SHRM L:16, Q:7, and P:4-a)**

The Training Process and Needs Assessment

>> **LO 7.2 Describe the interrelationship of the steps in the training process.**

How do we know who needs what training, in what forms, and at what point; if employees are ready for training; and if our training has been effective? We answer these questions in this section, as we plan our training processes very carefully. We need to look at what's currently going on in the organization and how that differs from what needs to happen in the future to accomplish our strategic business goals. Once we do this, we can analyze the types of training that will be necessary to build new knowledge, skills, and abilities for our workforce.

Steps in the Training Process

This chapter is primarily organized to follow the steps in the training process. Let's take a look at how we go through the training process in Exhibit 7.1. Here is a brief description of the steps; we provide more detail of each step throughout the chapter with titles similar to the steps.

> ***Step 1: Assessing needs.*** We conduct a needs assessment to determine what training is necessary to improve performance.
>
> ***Step 2: Selecting how to shape behavior.*** We select a method based on learning theories so that we can change employee behavior to improve performance.
>
> ***Step 3: Designing training.*** We design the training and development based on the needs assessment. We must determine which training methods we will use to shape employee behavior.
>
> ***Step 4: Delivering training.*** Before we actually conduct the training and development, we must select the delivery method.
>
> ***Step 5: Assessing training.*** After we complete the training, our last step is to assess how effective the training was at developing the needed skills to determine our success at shaping behavior.

Interrelationship of the Training Process Steps

Note in Exhibit 7.1 that each of steps 2, 3, 4, and 5 has a double-headed arrow; this is because all the steps are so closely related and based on each other that they are commonly planned together before actually delivering the training. In other words, you are constantly thinking ahead and behind your current step in the training process. If the assessment of the training reveals that the behavior has not been shaped (changed) as needed, we may have to go back to Step 1 and start the training process again.

EXHIBIT 7.1 ● The Training Process

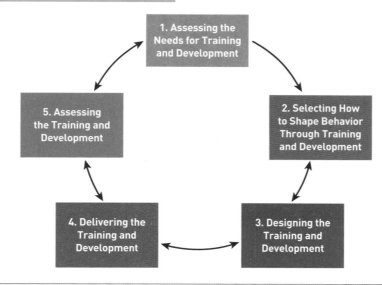

Needs Assessment

The first major step in the training process is the needs assessment.[41] A **needs assessment** is *the process of analyzing the difference between what is currently occurring within a job or jobs and what is required—either now or in the future—based on the organization's operations and strategic goals.* If management does not make the correct diagnosis—like a mechanic working on your car—they may create training solutions that don't solve the existing problem. So if a needs assessment is not done correctly, none of the other steps will be successful. We may not shape the behavior needed, the design and delivery can be wrong, training may not even be needed, and the assessment of training may not measure the desired outcome we wanted to begin with. Only by diligently going through the process of looking at that chain of events in the status quo can a manager identify where the process can be changed to improve organizational productivity and reach the organization's goals. **(SHRM L:4 and I:8-b)**

> **Needs assessment** The process of analyzing the difference between what is currently occurring within a job or jobs and what is required—either now or in the future—based on the organization's operations and strategic goals

Employee Readiness

As part of our needs assessment, the manager needs to evaluate the employees who would be taking part in the training. Employees may feel insecure about their ability to learn, and they may therefore be unwilling to participate in training for new processes. We must also evaluate whether the employees are physically and mentally ready to go through the training process successfully. In other words, are they *able and willing* to learn?[42] Do they have the skills and competencies necessary to succeed in this training process?

Ability

We have to determine whether or not our employees feel they are *able* to participate in the training process—do they believe they can do it. **Self-efficacy** is *whether or not a person believes that they have the capability to do something or attain a particular goal.* As Henry Ford said, if you believe you can or cannot do something—you are correct.

> **Self-efficacy** Whether or not a person believes that they have the capability to do something or attain a particular goal

If employees feel they are unable to learn, then the job of the manager becomes one of upgrading the employees' abilities if necessary and then convincing them of their capabilities. In addition, the manager has to analyze the true abilities and limitations of each of the employees who may participate in the training process. Remember that each of us has physical and intellectual abilities, but at different levels. Managers must match abilities to jobs, so don't put employees in jobs they can't do at the desired level of performance—never set up a person to fail and be demoted or fired.

The training process begins with assessing the needs of the new hire.

Willingness

The second major piece in the employee readiness equation is whether or not employees are *willing* to learn what's being taught in a training program. In other words, we have to determine their motivation to learn. There are many reasons why employees resist change, including if they believe the training is necessary or not. A significant part of willingness to learn is based on the support the individual gets from the people around them, including coworkers, supervisors, and even family members. So managers need to clearly explain why the training is needed and how the employee and organization will benefit.

Learning and Shaping Behavior

>> **LO 7.3 Summarize the four methods for shaping behavior.**

Step 2 of the training process consists of selecting how to shape or change employee behavior. To do this, trainers have to understand how people learn. So in this section, we begin by explaining learning. Then we discuss a common learning theory used to shape employee behavior. Next, we put the theory into practice in Exhibit 7.2 and discuss how to shape or change employee behavior.

EXHIBIT 7.2 ● Shaping Behavior

	Reward	Noxious stimulus
Apply	**(A) Positive Reinforcement** Apply a reward	**(B) Punishment** Apply a noxious stimulus— Give bad consequence
Withdraw	**(C) Punishment** Remove a reward	**(D) Negative Reinforcement** Avoid or remove a noxious stimulus

Extinction (E) = The absence of a response, designed to avoid reinforcing negative behaviors
Shaping (changing) behavior:
A, D = Increasing target behaviors
B, C, E = Decreasing target behaviors

Learning

We hope you aren't thinking, "I can't wait to be done with college studies," because as former **PepsiCo** CEO **Indra Nooyi** says, never stop learning; the strongest leaders are lifelong students.[43] Ongoing learning benefits both employees and firms,[44] but learning can be the result of many different things. In a business, we usually need to *know* that our employees have mastered something that we are trying to train them to do. How do we know they have learned a particular thing, then? We know because of changes in their behavior at work. So in our case, **learning** is *any relatively permanent change in behavior that occurs as a result of experience or*

Learning Any relatively permanent change in behavior that occurs as a result of experience or practice

practice.[45] There is visible evidence that individuals have learned something because they *changed behavior*—the way they act, or what they do and say. **(SHRM L:11 and P:1.b)**

Learning Theories

Let's take some time now to discuss the most common learning theories: classical conditioning, operant conditioning and reinforcement, and social learning. We will then show you how to use operant conditioning to cause employees to do more of the things you need them to do, and do less of other behaviors that lower productivity in the organization. **(SHRM P:2-a)**

Classical conditioning says we will react *involuntarily* to a stimulus in the environment if we associate that stimulus with something else.[46] For example, if you hear a particular sound, it can cause you to be afraid because you realize that the sound indicates danger to you. You have been involuntarily conditioned to the feeling of danger associated with that sound.

Operant conditioning is B. F. Skinner's theory that behavior is based on the consequences received from behaving in a similar way at an earlier point in time.[47] Skinner figured out how to get people to behave based on the reinforcement they receive. In other words, if we acted in a certain way previously and received a reward, we will likely repeat that behavior. If, however, we acted in a particular way and received a negative consequence (punishment), then we will probably not repeat the behavior.

Social learning is experienced through watching the actions of another person and witnessing the consequences of those actions.[48] If you see a person work hard and get a raise, you may also work hard to get a pay increase.

7.1 APPLYING THE CONCEPT
LEARNING THEORIES

Review the three learning theories below and write the letter corresponding to each theory before the statement(s) illustrating it.

a. Classical conditioning

b. Operant conditioning

c. Social learning

_____ 1. My parents continuously told me how to behave properly as I was growing up. Could that be why customers comment on my good manners and social skills?

_____ 2. I got caught smoking in a no-smoking area and was given a verbal warning. I'm not doing it again because I don't want to get into more trouble and possibly end up losing my job.

_____ 3. Shelly is a very hard worker, but I've never even seen her get as much as a thank-you for her performance. So why should I work?

_____ 4. After seeing what happened to Sean, you better believe that I'm keeping my goggles on when I'm on the job.

_____ 5. I completed the project ahead of schedule and did an excellent job. As a result, my boss gave me a sincere thanks and a $100 gift certificate to Amazon.com. I learned that it is worth putting in extra effort for the boss.

Shaping Behavior

We can use Skinner's concept of operant conditioning to shape the behaviors of employees by providing reinforcement (rewards) or punishment or, as a third alternative, provide neither. Take a look at Exhibit 7.2 and the four methods of shaping behavior. We can break these methods down into a process of applying a reward, removing a reward, applying punishment, removing punishment, or providing no response to the actions of the individual. If we understand each of the four methods, we can use them to cause workers to act in ways that are conducive to the improvement and ultimate success of the organization.[49]

You get what you reinforce. One thing you should know is that people will generally do what they are rewarded for doing (good work) and avoid what they are punished for doing (breaking rules). Reinforcement is a motivation theory. Like almost all students, do you only study what the professor says will be on the test, or do you study everything in the text chapters? Do you complete any of the nonassigned and nongraded application or skills exercises in this book? Why? Now, let's discuss each part of Exhibit 7.2.

Positive Reinforcement

Shown in the upper left quadrant A in Exhibit 7.2, **positive reinforcement** is *providing a reward in return for a constructive action on the part of the subject.* For example, if our employees do something that improves productivity, we give them a positive reinforcement bonus (a reward) to encourage repeat performance of more suggested improvements. We should realize that positive reinforcement is the most commonly used method of shaping employee behavior when we train new employees to do their jobs and when existing employees need to learn new job requirements and processes. Reward results rather than looking busy and hours worked.[50] It is generally considered the best form of reinforcement but is not always the best option based on the situation.

Negative Reinforcement

Our second option would be to *avoid or remove* a *noxious stimulus* (the lower right quadrant D in the exhibit), a process called negative reinforcement. **Negative reinforcement** is the *withdrawal of a harmful thing from the environment in response to a positive action on the part of the subject.* Negative reinforcement is commonly based on rules, with punishment being given for breaking the rules.[51] A rule itself is not a punishment; it is a means of getting people to do or avoid a specific behavior, such as coming to work on time. But if the rule is broken, punishment is usually the consequence, such as after coming to work late four times (rule), you get fired (punishment). We certainly don't want to punish employees for breaking a rule that they don't know exists, so during new employee onboarding make sure employees know the expected behaviors and the consequences for breaking rules.

Punishment

In contrast to reinforcement, we may punish bad behaviors. **Punishment** is *the application of an adverse consequence, or the removal of a reward, in order to decrease an unwanted behavior.* One method of punishment would be to remove a reward (the lower left quadrant C in the exhibit) as a result of people doing something that they shouldn't have done. For instance, a company may not provide a normal end-of-year bonus for their employees because of poor productivity during the year.

Alternatively, we can *apply a noxious stimulus* (the upper right quadrant B in the exhibit), which is also considered to be punishment. An example here would be suspending a worker without pay because of excessive absenteeism. By suspending the worker, we're applying a negative response. The negative response received by the worker is designed to cause a decline in the behavior that created such a response. So in other words, punishment can be the application of something bad (a noxious stimulus) or the removal of something good (a reward).

We should realize that punishment is not commonly used during training of employees; rather, it is commonly used when employees know how to do the job but just will not meet the job standards, or when employees break a rule and get disciplined for doing so. We will learn more about when and how to discipline employees in Chapter 9.

Extinction

The last option doesn't fit in the diagram itself, because it's the absence of reinforcement or punishment of any kind. **Extinction** is *the lack of response, either positive or negative, in order to avoid reinforcing an undesirable behavior.*[52] You may have heard the phrase "Ignore it and it will go away." How does a lack of response cause behavior to be shaped in a way that we desire?

Employees will sometimes exhibit problem behavior to cause a reaction from the manager or fellow employees. The employee who exhibits the behavior may delight in causing others concern or consternation. For example, the male employee who continually asks his female manager about organizational sexual harassment policies in front of other workers to cause her discomfort as she explains the policy is most likely *intentionally* acting to cause her embarrassment. In such a case, the female manager may be able to ignore the stimulus behavior and provide no

Positive reinforcement Providing a reward in return for a constructive action on the part of the subject

Negative reinforcement Withdrawal of a harmful thing from the environment in response to a positive action on the part of the subject

Punishment The application of an adverse consequence, or the removal of a reward, in order to decrease an unwanted behavior

Extinction The lack of response, either positive or negative, in order to avoid reinforcing an undesirable behavior

reinforcement. The employee's behavior will most likely decline or go away completely because it is not having the desired negative effect on the manager.

Shaping (Changing) Behavior

If you understand these methods of shaping behavior, they become powerful tools in your managerial toolbox for changing behavior to increase performance. These tools allow you to *cause* your employees to act in ways you want them to and avoid acting in ways that are detrimental to themselves or the organization. Now let's discuss how to increase and decrease behaviors to increase performance.

Increasing Targeted Behavior

If we want to cause the behavior to increase, then we want to use positive or negative reinforcement (quadrant A or D in Exhibit 7.2). Reinforcement, whether positive or negative, is designed to cause an increase in the targeted behavior.

Decreasing Targeted Behavior

If, on the other hand, we want to cause a particular behavior to decrease, we would use punishment (in either of its forms) or extinction (quadrant B, C, or E in Exhibit 7.2). Punishment and extinction are designed to cause a targeted behavior to decrease over time.

7.2 APPLYING THE CONCEPT
SHAPING BEHAVIOR

Review the following methods of shaping employee behavior and write the letter corresponding to each before the situation(s) illustrating it.

a. Positive reinforcement

b. Punishment—give bad consequence

c. Punishment—remove reward

d. Negative reinforcement

e. Extinction

_____ 6. Betty used to give me that intimidating look when I assigned her a task she didn't want to do, and that behavior made me uncomfortable. So I just ignored it and didn't let her make me feel uncomfortable, and she stopped giving me the look.

_____ 7. You know the rules. That behavior is going to cost you $25.

_____ 8. You got that angry lady to calm down and leave the store as a happy customer. This behavior leads to keeping our customers. Thanks, keep up the good work.

_____ 9. If you don't stop breaking the pricing gun, you will have to buy a new one.

_____ 10. I know you like to leave work for a while and get our lunches, but because you mixed up the order today, Santana will go tomorrow.

Design and Delivery of Training

>> **LO 7.4 Compare each of the major training delivery types.**

Recall that back in Chapter 1 we identified four important human resource management (HRM) skills: technical, interpersonal, conceptual and design (decision making), and business skills. Essentially, all of the training methods are used to develop specific skills that can be classified into one of these four skills categories. Once we have completed our needs assessment and selected how we plan to shape behavior, we are ready to complete Steps 3 and 4 of the training process: designing the training by selecting training methods and then delivering the training. So in this section, we will present which training methods to use based on which types of skills we are developing. Exhibit 7.3 presents the type of skills, the training methods appropriate for developing each skill, and descriptions of the training methods.

7.1 SELF-ASSESSMENT

YOUR LEARNING STYLE

Below are 10 statements. For each statement, distribute 5 points between the A and B alternatives. If the A statement is very characteristic of you and the B statement is not, place a 5 on the A line and a 0 on the B line. If the A statement is characteristic of you and the B statement is occasionally or somewhat characteristic of you, place a 4 on the A line and a 1 on the B line. If both statements are characteristic of you, place a 3 on the line that is more characteristic of you and a 2 on the line that is less characteristic of you. Be sure to distribute 5 points between each A and B alternative for each of the 10 statements. When distributing the 5 points, try to recall recent situations on the job or in school.

1. When learning:

   _____ A. I watch and listen.

   _____ B. I get involved and participate.

2. When learning:

   _____ A. I rely on my hunches and feelings.

   _____ B. I rely on logical and rational thinking.

3. When making decisions:

   _____ A. I take my time.

   _____ B. I make them quickly.

4. When making decisions:

   _____ A. I rely on my gut feelings about the best alternative course of action.

   _____ B. I rely on a logical analysis of the situation.

5. When doing things:

   _____ A. I am careful.

   _____ B. I am practical.

6. When doing things:

   _____ A. I have strong feelings and reactions.

   _____ B. I reason things out.

7. I would describe myself in the following way:

   _____ A. I am a reflective person.

   _____ B. I am an active person.

8. I would describe myself in the following way:

   _____ A. I am influenced by my emotions.

   _____ B. I am influenced by my thoughts.

9. When interacting in small groups:

   _____ A. I listen, watch, and get involved slowly.

   _____ B. I am quick to get involved.

10. When interacting in small groups:

    _____ A. I express what I am feeling.

    _____ B. I say what I am thinking.

Scoring: Place your answer numbers (0–5) on the lines below. Then add the numbers in each column vertically. Each of the four columns should have a total number between 0 and 25. The total of the two A and B columns should equal 25.

1. _____ A. _____ B. (5)   2. _____ A. _____ B. (5)
3. _____ A. _____ B. (5)   4. _____ A. _____ B. (5)
5. _____ A. _____ B. (5)   6. _____ A. _____ B. (5)
7. _____ A. _____ B. (5)   8. _____ A. _____ B. (5)
9. _____ A. _____ B. (5)   10. _____ A. _____ B. (5)

Totals: _____ A. _____ B. (25)   _____ A. _____ B. (25)

Style: Observing   Doing   Feeling   Thinking

There is no best or right learning style; each of the four learning styles has its pros and cons. The more evenly distributed your scores are between the As and Bs, the more flexible you are at changing styles. Understanding your preferred learning style can help you get the most from your learning experiences.

Determining Your Preferred Learning Style

The five odd-numbered A statements refer to your self-description as being "observing," and the five odd-numbered B statements refer to your self-description as "doing." The column with the highest number is your preferred style of learning. Write that style here: _____

The five even-numbered A statements refer to your self-description as being a "feeling" person, and the five even-numbered B statements refer to your self-description as being a "thinking" person. The column with the highest number is your preferred style. Write that style here: _____

Putting the two preferences together gives you your preferred learning style. Check it off below:

_____ Accommodator (combines doing and feeling)

_____ Diverger (combines observing and feeling)

_____ Converger (combines doing and thinking)

_____ Assimilator (combines observing and thinking)

EXHIBIT 7.3 ● Skills and Training Methods

Skills Developed	Methods	Description
Technical Skills	a. Written material, lectures, videotapes, question-and-answer sessions, discussions, demonstrations	Questions or problems related to previously presented material are presented to the trainee in a booklet or on a computer screen. The trainee is asked to select a response to each question or problem and is given feedback on the response.
	b. Programmed Learning	Depending on the material presented, programmed learning may also develop interpersonal and communication skills.
	c. Job Rotation	Employees are trained to perform different jobs. Job rotation also develops trainees' conceptual skills.
	d. Projects	Trainees are given special assignments, such as developing a new product or preparing a report. Certain projects may also develop trainees' interpersonal skills and conceptual skills.
Interpersonal Skills	e. Role-Playing	Trainees act out situations that might occur on the job, such as handling a customer complaint, to develop skill at handling such situations on the job.
	f. Behavior Modeling	Trainees observe how to perform a task correctly, by watching either a live demonstration or a videotape. Trainees role-play the observed skills and receive feedback on their performance. Trainees develop plans for using the observed skills on the job.
Conceptual and Design/ Business Skills	g. Cases	The trainee is presented with a simulated situation and asked to diagnose and solve the problems involved. Trainees usually must also answer questions about their diagnosis and solution.
	h. In-Basket Exercises	The trainee is given actual or simulated letters, memos, reports, and so forth that would typically come to the person holding the job. The trainee must determine what action each item would require and must assign priorities to the actions.
	i. Management Games	Trainees work as part of a team to "manage" a simulated company over a period of several game "quarters" or "years."
	j. Interactive Videos	Trainees can view videotapes that present situations requiring conceptual skills or decision making.

Before we actually conduct the training, in Step 4, the HR department or other trainers have to select the methods for training delivery. The choice will depend to some extent on what information is being transferred, as well as on the options that are available to the particular organization.[53] We also need to look at the best type of training to use in order to maximize transfer of knowledge while minimizing the cost of the training process. In the next sections, we discuss our four options: on-the-job, classroom, distance, and simulation training.

On-the-Job Training (OJT)

Most large organizations conduct some training off the job, whereas small companies tend to use OJT.[54] *On-the-job training (OJT)* is done at the work site with the resources the employee uses to perform the job. The manager, or an employee selected by the manager, usually conducts the training one-on-one with the trainee. Teaching by demonstration is supported by evidence-based management.[55] Because of its proven record of success, job instructional training (JIT)—a specific type of on-the-job training—is a popular training type used worldwide.[56] See Model 7.1 for the self-explanatory steps of JIT. (**SHRM P:6-e, P:6-h**)

MODEL 7.1 ● **Job Instructional Training Steps**

1. Preparation of the trainee → 2. Presentation of the task by the trainer → 3. Performance of the task by the trainee → 4. Follow-up

Classroom Training

Our second common training option is classroom training. A training course includes content, instruction methods, lesson plans, and instructor materials—and provides all these materials to a qualified instructor who will teach the class.

Classroom training is generally very good for consistently transferring general knowledge or theories about a topic to a large number of people. It is generally not very good for teaching specific hands-on skills because of the passive nature of learning in a classroom. However, it is effective when using the same equipment that is used on the job.

Distance or E-Learning

Our third option is some form of distance learning—also called e-learning—in either a synchronous or an asynchronous format.[57] *Synchronous distance learning* occurs when all of the trainees sign in to a particular learning management system (LMS) such as Blackboard or Moodle, or a corporate LMS, where their instructor then interacts with them and teaches the topics for the day. In contrast, *asynchronous distance learning* is a process in which the student can sign in to the training site at any point in time and materials are available for their studies. The instructor may or may not be online at the same time as the student, but there's no dedicated connection between the two for the purpose of teaching the information. In many cases today, the student does not have to work through an LMS. They can learn using any number of free or low-cost apps for training in just about any field. (**SHRM P:6-d**)

Distance learning, similar to classroom training, is also valuable for teaching basic concepts and providing general information on the topic. There's typically even less interaction between an instructor and trainees in this form than in classroom training.

Microlearning

With the decline in attention span of many of our employees, one of the trends is to keep lessons short. E-learning companies offer microlearning formats to client organizations for a variety of training needs. Most produce or distribute a mix of video and interactive lessons that take less than 5 minutes to complete and include a quiz. Lessons are available to users whenever they want to access them online or via smart phones.[58]

▲ Organizations are now offering training and development to employees anytime, from anywhere—24/7/365.

7.1 ETHICAL DILEMMA: WHAT WOULD YOU DO?

You are familiar with the traditional internship model, in which a student works at an organization to gain experience and perhaps a full-time job after graduation. With today's technology, more and more companies are hiring virtual interns who work remotely from their college computers. Virtual interns do a variety of tasks, including secretarial work, software and website development, and information technology (IT) projects. Most virtual interns never even set foot inside the organization's facilities.

Entrepreneurs Nataly Kogan and Avi Spivack cofounded Natavi Guides, a New York–based small business, in 2002 to publish guidebooks for students. Natavi hires virtual interns to write stories and recruits people by posting openings with career offices at more than 30 universities nationwide. Kogan

estimates that Natavi saved $100,000 in overhead during the first year in business by not having to furnish office space, computers, and other equipment to interns.

1. What are the benefits of virtual internships to employers and to interns?

2. Should a student be given college credit for a virtual internship, or should he or she receive only pay without credit—a part-time job?

3. Is it ethical and socially responsible to use interns instead of full-time or part-time employees?

4. Will the use of virtual internships become the norm, or will the practice fade?

Simulations

The trend in training is toward having more active involvement of participants and offering online simulation training and development.[59] A simulation is a method whereby we may simulate a real-life situation to teach trainees what actions to take in the event that they encounter the same or a similar situation on the job. Some common examples of simulations are flight simulators, driving simulators, and firefighting simulations. Simulations would typically be used in situations where actually performing an action or set of actions could lead to significant financial cost (because of lost equipment) or could put the trainee in significant danger of injury or death.[60] **(SHRM P:6-k)**

In these types of cases, providing simulations makes much more sense than actually performing a particular task. Asking trainees to perform in a simulation will also generally cause them to go through the same emotions they would go through in the real-life situation being simulated. Training through the use of a simulation allows the trainee to experience these emotions and learn to control them in order to resolve a complex or dangerous situation.

7.3 APPLYING THE CONCEPT
TRAINING METHODS

For each of the training situations below, identify the most appropriate training method. Use the letters a through j from Exhibit 7.3 as your answers.

_____ 11. You want your customer service staff to do a better job of handling customer complaints.

_____ 12. Your large department has a high turnover rate, and new employees need to learn several rules and regulations to perform their jobs.

_____ 13. You need your new employees to learn how to handle the typical daily problems they will face on the job.

_____ 14. You need an employee to conduct an Internet search to find out more about a new product

you want to buy for the department; you want a special report.

_____ 15. You want employees to be able to do each other's job when they take vacations.

_____ 16. You want to improve your employees' ability to sell products to customers in the store so that customers don't end up leaving and buying the products online.

_____ 17. You need to prepare middle managers to advance to upper-level managers. You are considering having them run a simulated company getting quarterly results.

Assessing Training

>> **LO 7.5 Discuss the four-level evaluation method for assessing training programs.**

The fifth and last step of our training process (see Exhibit 7.1) is assessment. No matter what the training covers, we always want to evaluate whether or not it achieved the shaped behavior changes identified through our needs assessment. In this section, we present four assessment methods and how to choose an assessment method. **(SHRM L:9, P:2-b, and P:3)**

Assessment Methods

One of the most common assessment options is called the four-level evaluation method.[61] It measures *reaction, learning, behaviors,* and *results.*

Reaction evaluations measure how the individual responds to the actual training process. Self-reporting measures are quick and common measures of training.[62] Participants say how they feel about the training process, including the content provided, the instructors, and the knowledge that they gained by going through the process. This is the lowest level of training evaluation, and it is frequently discounted due to its subjectivity and because some people overestimate their capabilities.[63] Reaction evaluations provide the organization with valuable feedback concerning the learners' state of mind at the end of the training process as well as their attitude toward the process and instructor at its conclusion. Student course assessments are an example of reaction evaluations.

Learning evaluations are Level 2 measures designed to determine what knowledge the individual gained, whether they learned any new skills because of the training, and whether the person's attitudes toward their knowledge or skill set changed as a result of the training. Learning evaluations are easily done using quizzes, tests, and even topic-based discussions to see whether or not the individual gained knowledge of the subject as a result of the training process.

Behavior evaluations are designed to determine whether or not the trainee's on-the-job behaviors changed as a result of the training. Behavior evaluations usually take the form of observation of the individual on the job, after completion of the training process, to see if the training had a direct effect on the individual's post-training job performance. The behavior evaluation is specifically designed to identify whether or not the individual is able to transfer the knowledge gained into new skills that they then use in their work.

Results evaluation is used to determine whether or not individual behavioral changes have improved organizational results—was the training worth the time, effort, and cost? In other words, we look at the organization's bottom line to determine whether or not productivity has increased. This is the level at which return on investment (ROI) is measured and evaluated to see whether or not the training has paid off for the company. However, ROI is not the only thing that we measure at this level. Other results we may measure include increased quality of work, lower absenteeism and turnover, reductions in rework and scrap, lower on-the-job accident rates, and many others. **(SHRM P:3-a and P:7)**

Why not just evaluate all of our training programs at each of the four levels? The primary reason is that it costs the organization money to go through the evaluation process. In fact, as we go from Levels 1 through 4, the complexity and cost of evaluating the training process increases with each level.

Unfortunately, much of what is taught through development isn't used on the job.[64] Be honest. How many of the developmental skills you have learned through this course are you actually using in your personal and professional lives? It's tough to implement new skills because we don't like to change our habits.

7.4 APPLYING THE CONCEPT
TRAINING ASSESSMENT METHODS

Review the following assessment methods and write the letter corresponding to each one before the situation(s) where it is most appropriate.

a. Reaction evaluation

b. Learning evaluation

c. Behavior evaluation

d. Results evaluation

_____ 18. You are a software sales manager and you want your new sales reps to be able to demonstrate the various features of your software.

_____ 19. You are a restaurant owner who installed a new food-ordering computer system with the objective of speeding up the time it takes to serve meals, so you need to train employees on how to use the new system.

_____ 20. You are the HR manager and want to make sure that your staff understands what questions they

can and can't legally ask during the selection process.

_____ 21. You are the service desk manager at a retail store and need to train employees on how to effectively deal with angry customers when they return merchandise. You want the employees to remain calm and satisfy the customer.

_____ 22. You are the HR manager responsible for diversity, and you develop a training program to help employees better understand each other and not use stereotypes so that they can work well together.

Talent Management and Development

>> **LO 7.6 List some of the individual and organizational consequences that can occur as a result of organizational career planning processes.**

Now let's discuss developing employees. We should realize, however, that development programs also follow the same five steps of the training process listed in Exhibit 7.1. Recall that employee development deals primarily with training workers for *future* jobs, not their current position. In this section, we discuss careers, common methods of employee development, and a model of career development consequences.

Careers

Half a century ago, a large percentage of people would spend their entire work life with one company. This obviously does not happen very often today, as you will likely have several changes in career throughout your work life. **(SHRM F:3 and F:3-a)**

So how do we define a career in the current workforce? "A **career** is *the individually perceived sequence of attitudes and behaviors associated with work-related experiences and activities over the span of the person's life.*"[65] Whew! Let's break this definition down into its subcomponents.

- *"Individually perceived."* This definition of the term *career* relies heavily on the perception of the individual who is making the judgment concerning success or failure of the career. So, success or failure is determined within the individual's own mind. Back to Henry Ford—with either perception, you are correct.

- *"Sequence of attitudes and behaviors."* Attitude is simply a positive or negative individual judgment about a particular situation. A career consists of both attitudes and behaviors, so it is not only *what* you do; it's also the way you *feel* about what you do and how well you think you've done over time. Your career attitudes and behaviors will most likely change over time.

- *"Associated with work-related experiences and activities over the span of the person's life."* So a career also involves all work-related experiences and activities. So, even nonwork activities that are work related, such as training off-site, would be included in our definition of career. We can expand this to say that any interaction of family, friends, and work could help define your career. If you like your job but significant people put your job down, you may change your attitude. **(SHRM F:1)**

Career The individually perceived sequence of attitudes and behaviors associated with work-related experiences and activities over the span of the person's life

Common Methods of Employee Development

There is a series of common methods that organizations use, including outsourcing or internal development through formal education, experience, and assessments.[66] Let's go through a brief description of each. **(SHRM P:8-a and L:14)**

Outsourcing

Based on a recent survey by **ADP**, "91 percent of large companies and 80 percent of midsized companies" say that outsourcing one or more HR functions provides "real value."[67] Outsourcing of the training and development function significantly lags other functions in the HR department, though.[68] Modern organizations must evaluate whether or not outsourcing of the training and development functions makes sense. If the company can reduce costs for training and development as well as improve the quality of the development function, it may make sense for the organization to consider outsourcing of these functions. However, the organization must carefully evaluate all of the information in an analysis for potential outsourcing of the training and development function. Without this careful evaluation, significant mistakes can be made and large amounts of money may be spent without the organization receiving the requisite benefits from the process.

Formal Education

Formal education provides employees with the opportunity to participate in programs that will improve their general knowledge in areas such as finance, project management, or logistics. These formal education opportunities include such things as degree programs at colleges and universities, certificate programs, and short courses of study that are available from many different sources. Formal education courses may be held with any of the training and delivery methods discussed earlier. Many organizations pay part or all of the cost of external formal education for employees. **(SHRM P:5-a)**

Experience

Experience, as a method for developing the individual, would put the person through a number of different types of job-related experiences over time, such as job rotation. This allows the person to see more of what goes on within the organization and how each job ties to others. Experience-based development can also include the use of coaches or mentors for the individual. They work with the person to identify how these different job experiences help the individual to learn and grow within the organization.[69] There's significant evidence that career experience, team experience, and job-related skills are all related to higher levels of team performance.[70]

▲
Exposing employees to a range of experiences on the job is an effective way to develop their skills.

Employee Assessment

Assessment tools provide individuals with information about how they think, how they interact with others, and how they manage their own actions and emotions. These assessments provide information that allows them to better understand how they can manage others within the organization. Some of the more common measures include psychological assessments, emotional intelligence tests, and performance appraisals. Each of these assessments, if properly used, provides individuals with information that can be used to modify the way they interact with others within the organization.

A Model of Career Development Consequences

Because the organization and the individual have joint responsibility for career planning and development, both will suffer significant consequences if the planning isn't done successfully. Individual employees go through a series of career stages as they progress through their work life. Within each of these stages, the employee has different needs that the organization must meet so the relationship between the two can remain stable and the worker will continue to be motivated to produce for the organization. Organizations must respond successfully to the individual employee based on the employee's current career stage. **(SHRM I:8-c)**

Let's discuss the commonly identified stages of career development[71] summarized in the first section of Exhibit 7.4.

EXHIBIT 7.4 ● Career Stages and the Hierarchy of Needs			
Exploration	**Establishment**	**Maintenance**	**Disengagement**
Meet personal needs	Career entry	Personal satisfaction	Lower output
Identify interests	Building skills	Continue advancement	Coach/mentor as desired
Evaluate skills	Security/stabilization	Coach/mentor	Balance between work and nonwork
Tentative work choice	Work relationships	Improve policies and procedures	
	Work contributions		
	Advancement		

Maslow's Hierarchy of Needs

Physiological	**Safety/Security**	**Social**	**Esteem**	**Self-Actualization**
Air, food, water, sleep, etc.	Physical shelter, physical security, financial security, stability, etc.	Friendship, love, relationships, family, belonging to social groups, etc.	Social status, recognition, self-respect, reputation, achievement, etc.	Wisdom and justice—pass knowledge to others because *you* think it is valuable.

Exploration

The *exploration* stage is the period of time during which the individual is identifying the personal needs that will be satisfied by a particular type of work, the types of jobs that interest them, and the skill sets necessary to be able to accomplish those types of jobs. This stage is usually identified as being between the ages of 15 and 24.

Establishment

The *establishment stage* is the period when the individual has entered into a career and becomes concerned with building a skill set, developing work relationships, and advancing and stabilizing their career. The individual starts to make significant personal contributions to their career and begins to create relationships or alliances with coworkers that allow them to become more secure within the organization. This stage is usually identified as age 25 through the mid-40s.

Maintenance

In the *maintenance stage,* the individual typically continues to advance but begins to seek personal satisfaction in the jobs that they perform for the organization. This is the phase where we see individual employees begin to act as mentors or trainers to their younger coworkers and to act to improve the organization and its processes and policies because they see a need to do so. This stage covers the period from the mid-40s to age 60 years old or older.

Disengagement

The fourth stage is the *disengagement* stage. This stage typically shows lower levels of output and productivity as the individual prepares for life after work. During this stage, because of the desire to balance nonwork with work activities, the individual may begin to choose to work only on efforts they feel are necessary or worthy of their attention. They may continue to mentor or sponsor other individuals' progression through their own careers. This stage goes from the early 60s to whenever the individual finally completely disengages from the organization.

Let's take a look now at the second part of Exhibit 7.4 to illustrate why career stages matter so much to managers in the organization, and especially to HR management. We have added Abraham Maslow's Hierarchy of Needs below each of the career stages. It's rather surprising how closely Maslow's needs hierarchy matches up with our career stages.

What are people most concerned with at the earliest career stage or when they have to fall back to a lower level of work? They are typically most concerned with physical and safety/security issues, right? Are they physically able to get the *basic things* that they need in order to live and work—like money for shelter, food to eat, fuel for their car? Are they getting paid enough to *survive and be safe?* Then, as they get into the establishment and maintenance stages, they become more concerned with *social interactions* and then gaining *status and recognition.* Finally, as they move to the disengagement stage, they are more concerned with higher-level esteem needs such as *self-respect, achievement* of personal goals, and being able to do the *things that they think are important.* So, we see people go through these different motivational points in their life as they go through their career.

Now that we understand career stages and how those stages identify what might motivate workers in a particular stage, let's match those up with organizational HR strategies that are available to reinforce employee behavior. This will give us a general working model of how organizational HR strategies can create either positive or negative consequences for both the individual and the organization, depending on how the HR strategies are applied in a particular situation. Take a look at Exhibit 7.5. We have individual career stages identified on the left side of the diagram. On the right side are some of the major organizational HR strategies that are available. Depending on how the HR strategies are applied, and based on the individual's career stage and motivating factors, we end up with either positive or negative consequences to both the individual and the organization.

If we apply the correct HR strategy or strategies to an individual employee based on the factors that motivate the employee, we can improve each of the major organizational dependent

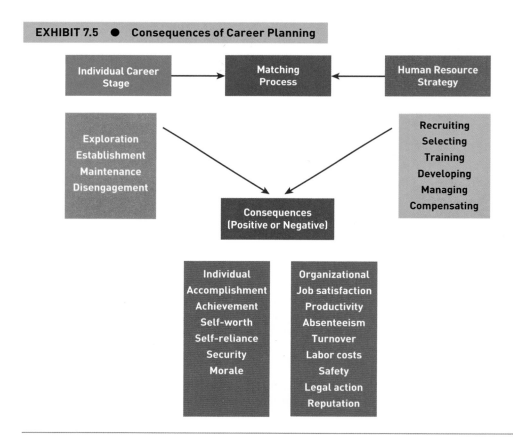

EXHIBIT 7.5 ● Consequences of Career Planning

variables that we identified in Chapter 1—engagement, productivity, absenteeism, and turnover. In addition, there are several other organizational factors that can either improve or decline based on the application (or lack thereof) of the correct HR strategy. These factors include labor costs, organizational safety, employee lawsuits, and organizational reputation, among others. So as you can see, if the organization fails to apply the correct strategy to motivate the employee (based on the employee's current career stage), the consequences can be severe.

On the other side of the diagram, the consequences to the employee are equally significant. If the organization applies the correct types of HR strategies to develop the employee successfully over time, individual feelings of accomplishment and achievement increase, self-worth and self-reliance increase, the employee's sense of security increases, and their morale is likely to increase due to higher individual satisfaction levels. Again, if the strategies applied are unsuccessful, each of these individual consequences can become negative. After looking at the model, it should become obvious that successfully applying HR strategies to individual employees based on their personal motivating factors and career stage is critical to overall organizational success over time.

So now you know why it's so important to create career paths for our employees within the organization and provide employee development opportunities. If we do these things successfully, we end up with a series of positive consequences for both the organization and the individuals involved. We have better productivity, better job satisfaction and employee engagement, and lower absenteeism and turnover. However, if we fail to do these things successfully, a series of negative consequences can occur that ultimately cost both the organization and the individual time and money. Employee development is a critical piece in the organizational puzzle in order to provide long-term success.

Trends and Issues in HRM

The first issue that we will discuss involves the "gamification" of training and development. Then we will briefly look at the issue of employer concerns that their workers don't have necessary skills and what they are doing about it.

Gamification—A Phoenix Rising?

A 2017 article by author Simon Parkin asks "Was Gamification a Terrible Lie?"[72] Gamification continues to be a major trend in organizational training, but it has had its ups and downs. Gamification is the process of designing and utilizing video, social media, and other game technologies to teach the player a business concept. It gained popularity a few years ago, but some early attempts did not provide the learning outcomes that were expected because of poor training design so it fell out of favor with some companies. Technology providers that didn't understand training and learning have now washed out of the market though, and gamification is making a comeback in some circles. It is being used for training in areas such as corporate values training, leadership development, customer service training, technical training, and more. It is also being used by a diverse group of organizations, including **Unilever**, the **Department of Defense, Weight Watchers**, and **Nike**, so you can see that it isn't just useful in technology companies.[73]

What problems do we continue to see in learning using gamification? One issue has been the fact that gamification has been overhyped as a cure—all for training problems. Another common problem is that the player may become wrapped up in playing the game, and not understand *why* a result occurs, and will therefore miss the lesson to be learned. A third issue is poor game design—about 80% of them still fail to meet business objectives because the provider does not understand basic learning theories. However, one of the key challenges with training has always been to get people engaged in the process and the evidence is mounting that gamification can help with engagement and ultimately get people to learn and retain key information for work.

The Corporate Learning Imperative

Employers are concerned that their workers don't have the skills necessary to compete in modern organizations. In a recent Gallup poll, almost 90% of business leaders said that college graduates did not have the necessary skill sets for the workplace.[74] Other studies note that existing employee skill sets go stale at an alarming rate as well. Partially as a result of this lack of confidence in employee skills, U.S. and European companies continue to increase their spending on internal talent development. Each year from 2010 through 2015, companies increased their spending on employee training, and that trend appears to be continuing.[75,76]

A problem with corporate learning environments, however, is that they provide no large blocks of time to learn. The average employee has about 25 minutes a week to "slow down and learn."[77] So companies are exploring various forms of digital learning that can provide just-in-time content that is compact and valuable. *Digital learning,* according to Josh Bersin of Bersin by Deloitte, is "employee-directed, intelligent-machine driven," and brings "learning to where employees are."[78]

Life-long learning will continue to become more necessary.[79] Many times a professor will hear "I'll be glad when I graduate. I'll never have to go to class again" from one of their students and will chuckle. The professor knows their student will be "going to class" constantly for the rest of their work life. Executives note that the average "shelf life" of skills associated with a college degree is 5 years.[80] HR managers will need to understand the new technologies available and the new ways their employees learn, and will have to adapt to each challenge to enable the self-directed training that will become a more important part of the workplace.

Chapter Summary

7.1 Identify each of the common points in the tenure of employees within the organization where training may be needed.

The most common points at which managers should consider workforce training include new-employee *onboarding,* which is used to acculturate new employees to the organization and its culture and to prepare them to do their own job within the organization; when *processes or procedures have changed;* whenever there has been some *failure to perform* successfully (remedial training); or when *employee development* opportunities come up, allowing the company to develop current employees' skills and abilities so that they are able to move into higher-level jobs within the organization.

7.2 Describe the interrelationship of the steps in the training process.

The first step involves conducting a needs assessment to identify the type of training needed. The second step involves selecting how to shape employee behavior. The third step involves designing the training by selecting training methods. The fourth step involves selecting the delivery method and delivering the training. The last step involves assessing the training to determine if employee behavior has changed to improve performance—if not, return to Step 1. The steps are so closely related and based on each other that they are commonly planned together before actually delivering the training.

7.3 Summarize the four methods for shaping behavior.

The four options for shaping behavior include positive reinforcement, negative reinforcement, punishment, and extinction. Positive reinforcement involves the application of a reward in response to a person's behavior in order to increase the chances that that behavior will be repeated. Negative reinforcement involves the withdrawal or avoidance of a noxious stimulus, or a negative thing, in response to a person's positive behavior to increase the chances that the behavior will be repeated. Punishment occurs either when a noxious stimulus is applied or when a reward is taken away in response to a negative behavior. Extinction provides no reinforcement, either positive or negative, to the actions of the subject.

7.4 Compare each of the major training delivery types.

On-the-job training (OJT) is done at the work site with the resources the employee uses to perform the job, and it is conducted one-on-one with the trainee. In *classroom training,* the organization creates a training course and provides a qualified instructor to teach the class in a single location at a specific time. *Distance learning,* also called e-learning, allows the students to sign in to the training site and provides materials to them for their studies. There's typically less interaction between an instructor and trainee than in OJT or classroom training.

7.5   Discuss the four-level evaluation method for assessing training programs.

The four-level evaluation method measures *reaction, learning, behaviors,* and *results.* In *reaction evaluations,* we ask the participants how they feel about the training process, including the content provided, the instructor(s), and the knowledge that they gained. *Learning evaluations* are designed to determine what knowledge was gained by the individual, whether any new skills have been learned, and whether attitudes have changed as a result of the training. *Behavior evaluations* are designed to determine whether or not the trainee's on-the-job behaviors changed as a result of the training. In a *results evaluation,* we try to determine whether or not individual behavioral changes have improved organizational results. This is the level at which ROI will be measured and evaluated.

7.6   List some of the individual and organizational consequences that can occur as a result of organizational career planning processes.

Organizational consequences include all of the major organizational dependent variables that we identified in Chapter 1: employee engagement, productivity, absenteeism, and turnover. In addition, labor costs, organizational safety, employee lawsuits, and organizational reputation can either improve or decline based on the application (or lack thereof) of the correct HR strategy. On the employee side of the diagram, if the organization applies the correct HR strategies, individual feelings of accomplishment and achievement increase, self-worth and self-reliance increase, the employee's sense of security increases, and employee morale is likely to increase due to higher individual satisfaction levels. If the strategies are unsuccessful, each of these individual consequences can become negative.

Key Terms

career, 181	needs assessment, 171	punishment, 174
employee development, 168	negative reinforcement, 174	remediation, 170
extinction, 174	onboarding, 169	self-efficacy, 171
learning, 172	positive reinforcement, 174	training, 168

Key Terms Review

Complete each of the following statements using one of this chapter's key terms.

1. _____ is the process of teaching employees the skills necessary to perform a job.

2. _____ is ongoing education to improve knowledge and skills for present and future jobs.

3. _____ is the process of introducing new employees to the organization and their jobs.

4. _____ is the correction of a deficiency or failure in a process or procedure.

5. _____ is the process of analyzing the difference between what is currently occurring within a job or jobs in comparison with what is required—either now or in the future—based on the organization's operations and strategic goals.

6. _____ is whether people believe that they have the capability to do something or attain a particular goal.

7. _____ is any relatively permanent change in behavior that occurs as a result of experience or practice.

8. _____ is providing a reward in return for a constructive action on the part of the subject.

9. _____ is the withdrawal of a harmful thing from the environment in response to a positive action on the part of the subject.

10. _____ is the application of an adverse consequence or removal of a reward in order to decrease an unwanted behavior.

11. _____ is the total lack of response, either positive or negative, to avoid reinforcing an undesirable behavior.

12. _____ is the individually perceived sequence of attitudes and behaviors associated with work-related experiences and activities over the span of a person's life.

Communication Skills

The following critical-thinking questions can be used for class discussion and/or for written assignments to develop communication skills. Be sure to give complete explanations for all answers.

1. Is the currently available workforce really not sufficiently trained to participate in knowledge-intensive jobs? Why or why not?

2. Think of and then list all of the items that you think should be included in a new employee onboarding. Briefly justify why each item should be included.

3. Briefly describe a job you have or had. If you were promoted, which training method(s) would you use to train the person to do your current job?

4. Which one of the primary delivery of training types would you use to teach basic accounting to a group of employees? Justify your answer.

5. Have you ever filled out an evaluation form for an employee training class? Which type of evaluation was it? What evidence led you to think it was this type?

6. What management tools or processes would you use in order to evaluate your employees for remediation training?

7. Do you agree with the definition of a career presented in the text? Why or why not? How would you change it?

8. Which method of development, formal education, experience, or assessment do you think is most valuable? Justify your choice.

9. Identify and discuss two or three ways in which poor application of HR strategies (Exhibit 7.5) would create negative *employee* consequences.

Case 7.1 Doing Crunches at Nestlé: Continuous Improvement of Human Assets

With instant coffee, baby food, and bottled water in the mix, Nestlé crunches more than just chocolate. The world's number-one food and drinks company in terms of sales, Nestlé is also the world leader in coffee (Nescafé). It also makes coffee for the home-brewing system, Nespresso. Nestlé is one of the world's top bottled water makers (Nestlé Waters), one of the biggest frozen pizza makers (DiGiorno), and a big player in the pet food business (Friskies, Purina). Its well-known global food brands include Buitoni, Dreyer's, Maggi, Milkmaid, Carnation, and Kit Kat. The company also owns Gerber Products. North America is Nestlé's most important market.[81]

Nestlé has over 2,000 brands, which are made in 418 factories located in 86 countries, and employs nearly 330,000 employees selling products in 191 countries.[82] How does one feed this growing concern? Mergers and acquisitions is one answer, yet that does not solve the skills-gap issue faced worldwide. Primarily, Nestlé's success in growing its local companies in each country has been highly influenced by the functioning of its International Training Centre, located near corporate headquarters in Switzerland. For over 30 years, the Rive-Reine International Training Centre has brought together managers from around the world to learn from senior Nestlé managers and from each other. Country managers decide who attends which course, although there is central screening for qualifications, and classes are carefully composed to include people with a range of geographic and functional backgrounds. Typically, a class contains 15 to 20 nationalities. The center delivers some 70 courses, attended by about 1,700 managers each year from over 80 countries. All course leaders are Nestlé managers with many years of experience in a range of countries. Only 25% of the teaching is done by outside professionals, as the primary faculty is the Nestlé senior management. The programs can be broadly divided into two groups:

- **Management courses:** These account for about 66% of all courses at Rive-Reine. The participants have typically been with the company for 4 to 5 years. The intention is to develop a real appreciation of Nestlé values and business approaches. These courses focus on internal activities.

- **Executive courses:** These classes often contain people who have attended a management course 5 to 10 years earlier. The focus is on developing the ability to represent Nestlé externally and to work with outsiders. It emphasizes industry analysis, often asking, "What would you do if you were a competitor?"[83]

An important factor in Nestlé's productivity is the skill set of entry-level workers. Employers invest in the skills of new entrants as an alternative to hiring more experienced people, partly on grounds of cost but also for the opportunity to shape ways of working around specific technologies and processes and particular company values.[84]

The willingness to learn is therefore an essential condition to be employed by Nestlé. Primarily, training is done on-the-job. Guiding and coaching is part of the responsibility of each manager and is crucial to make each person progress in his or her position. Formal training programs are generally purpose-oriented and designed to improve relevant skills and competencies. Therefore, they are proposed in the framework of individual development programs and not as a reward.

Most of Nestlé's people development programs assume a good basic education on the part of employees. However, in a number of countries, they have decided to offer employees the opportunity to upgrade their essential literacy skills. A number of Nestlé companies have therefore set up special programs for those who, for one reason or another, missed a large part of their elementary schooling.

These programs are especially important as they introduce increasingly sophisticated production techniques into each country where they operate. As the level of technology in Nestlé factories has steadily risen, the need for training has increased at all levels. Much of this is on-the-job training to develop the specific skills to operate equipment that is more advanced. However, not only new technical abilities are required. It is sometimes new working practices. For example, more flexibility and more independence among work teams are sometimes needed if equipment is to operate at maximum efficiency.

Two thirds of all Nestlé employees work in factories, most of which organize continuous training to meet their specific needs. In addition, a number of Nestlé operating companies run their own residential training centers. The result is that local training is the largest component of Nestlé's people development activities worldwide, and substantial majorities of the company's employees receive training every year. Ensuring appropriate and continuous training is an official part of every manager's responsibilities and, in many cases, the manager is personally involved in the teaching. For this reason, part of the training structure in every company is focused on developing managers' coaching skills. Additional courses are held outside the factory when required, generally in connection with the operation of new technology.

The variety of programs is very extensive. They start with continuation training for ex-apprentices who have the potential to become supervisors or section leaders, and continue through several levels of technical, electrical, and maintenance engineering as well as IT management. The degree to which factories develop "home-grown" specialists varies considerably, reflecting the availability of trained people on the job market in each country. On-the-job training is also a key element of career development in commercial and administrative positions. Here too, Nestlé trainers deliver most courses in-house but, as the level rises, collaboration with external institutes increases.

Virtually every national Nestlé company organizes management-training courses for new employees with high school or university qualifications. Nevertheless, their approaches vary considerably. In Japan, for example, they consist of a series of short courses typically lasting 3 days each. Subjects include human assessment skills, leadership and strategy, and courses for new supervisors and new key staff. In Mexico, Nestlé set up a national training center in 1965. In addition to those following regular training programs, some 100 people follow programs for young managers there every year. These are based on a series of modules that allows tailored courses to be offered to each participant. Nestlé India runs 12-month programs for management trainees in sales and marketing, finance and human resources, as well as in milk collection and agricultural services. These involve periods of fieldwork, not only to develop a broad range of skills but also to introduce new employees to company organization and systems.

The scope of local training is expanding. The growing familiarity with information technology has enabled distance learning to become a valuable resource, and many Nestlé companies have appointed corporate training assistants in this area. It has the great advantage of allowing students to select courses that meet their individual needs and do the work at their own pace, at convenient times. In Singapore, to quote just one example, staff is given financial help to take evening courses in job-related subjects. Fees and expenses are reimbursed for successfully following courses leading to a trade certificate, a high school diploma, university entrance qualifications, and a bachelor's degree.[85]

Questions

1. For what purposes does Nestlé train and develop employees?

2. What challenges does Nestlé face in conducting their training programs?

3. Which skill sets does Nestlé focus on in their training programs?

4. What on-the-job training methods does Nestlé utilize in their training programs?

5. What forms of off-the-job training are available at Nestlé?

6. What are some of the ways that Nestlé's training programs address career development?

7. What trends in training and development are Nestlé utilizing, and what trends could they benefit from?

Case created by Herbert Sherman, PhD, and Theodore Vallas, Department of Management Sciences, Long Island University School of Business, Brooklyn Campus

Skill Builder 7.1 The Training Process

Objective

To develop your ability to conduct a needs assessment, to select how to shape employee behavior, to design a training program by selecting training methods, to select a method to deliver training, and to choose an assessment method

Skills

The primary skills developed through this exercise are as follows:

1. *HR management skills*—Conceptual and design skills

2. *SHRM 2018 Curriculum Guidebook*—P: Training and Development

Assignment

As an individual or group, select a job and write out your answers. Follow the steps in the training process below to train a person to do the job.

Step 1: Needs assessment. Conduct a needs assessment for the job by developing a competency model identifying the knowledge, skills, and abilities needed to do the job successfully.

Step 2: Select how you will shape behavior. Be sure to specify if you will use positive reinforcement, punishment, negative reinforcement, or extinction. State the rewards and/or punishment.

Step 3: Design the training. Select and describe in detail the training method(s) you will use to shape the behavior.

Step 4: Deliver the training. Select one of the four methods of delivery that you will use to conduct the actual training and describe how you will deliver the training.

Step 5: Assessment of training. Select one of the four assessment methods and describe in detail how you will determine if the training did in fact shape the behavior.

Apply It

What did I learn from this experience? How will I use this knowledge in the future?

_____

_____

_____

Your instructor may ask you to do this Skill Builder in class by breaking into groups of four to six and doing the preparation. If so, the instructor will provide you with any necessary information or additional instructions.

Skill Builder 7.2 Career Development

Objective

To begin to think about and develop your career plan

Skills

The primary skills developed through this exercise are as follows:

1. *HR management skills*—Conceptual and design skills

2. *SHRM 2018 Curriculum Guidebook*—P: Training and Development

Assignment

Write out your answers to the following questions.

1. Do you now, or do you want to work in human resource management (HRM)? Why? If not, what career do you want to pursue, and why?

2. If you want to work in HR, based on your self-assessment back in Chapter 1 or other knowledge, list your highest levels of interest in HR disciplines. If not, what are your highest levels of interests, functions, or disciplines within your chosen career?

3. What methods of employee development (formal education, experience [e.g., internships and jobs], and assessment) are you using to prepare for your career?

Apply It

What did I learn from this exercise? How will I use this knowledge in the future?

_____

_____

_____

Your instructor may ask you to do this Skill Builder in class by breaking into groups of two to three and discussing your career plans. If so, the instructor will provide you with any necessary information or additional instructions.

©iStockphoto.com/JohnnyGreig

Performance Management and Appraisal

Learning Outcomes

After studying this chapter, you should be able to do the following:

8.1 Discuss the difference between performance management and performance appraisals. **PAGE 194**

8.2 Explain the purposes of performance appraisals. **PAGE 198**

8.3 Discuss the options for what to evaluate in a performance appraisal. **PAGE 198**

8.4 List the commonly used performance measurement methods and forms. **PAGE 201**

8.5 Discuss the available options for determining the rater/evaluator. **PAGE 205**

8.6 Name some of the common problems encountered with performance appraisals and provide a method used to avoid each. **PAGE 208**

8.7 Briefly discuss the differences between evaluative performance reviews and developmental performance reviews. **PAGE 212**

SHRM HR Content

See Online: *SHRM 2018 Curriculum Guidebook* for the complete list

C. Employee and Labor Relations

   7. Cognitive biases

I. Job Analysis and Job Design

   7. Performance management (performance criteria and appraisal)

L. Organizational Development

   1. Coaching

   5. Improving organizational effectiveness

  13. Ongoing performance and productivity initiatives

M. Performance Management

   1. Approaches to measuring performance

 1-a. Approaches to measuring performance—Performance measure criteria

 1-b. Approaches to measuring performance—Performance standards/goals

 1-c. Approaches to measuring performance—Rater errors in performance measurement

 1-d. Approaches to measuring performance—Reliability (interrater reliability)

 1-e. Approaches to measuring performance—Validity

   2. Identifying and measuring employee performance

 2-a. Identifying and measuring employee performance—Forced distribution

 2-b. Identifying and measuring employee performance—Graphic rating scales

 2-c. Identifying and measuring employee performance—Paired comparison

 2-d. Identifying and measuring employee performance—Ranking

   3. Performance appraisals

 3-a. Performance appraisals—Appraisal feedback

 3-c. Performance appraisals—Electronic monitoring

 3-d. Performance appraisals—Managing performance

 3-f. Performance appraisals—Process of performance management

 3-g. Performance appraisals—Sources of information (e.g., managers, peers, clients)

Practitioner's Perspective

Cindy remarks that although performance evaluation can be uncomfortable for both managers and employees, failure to accurately and honestly evaluate performance is never a good choice. She recalls the time that a supervisor, Annette, came to see her.

"I want to fire Christine," Annette said angrily. "She entered the wrong invoice numbers again, and now I have to stay and correct her mistakes—again!"

"Is this common?" Cindy asked. "Have you expressed your concerns or initiated a performance improvement plan?"

(Continued)

(Continued)

"She does it all the time, but I usually don't catch it until after she is off for the day," Annette replied. "By morning, it doesn't seem worth my time go over it with her."

"How about her performance evaluation?" she asked next. "Have you brought Christine's poor performance to her attention at her annual evaluation?"

"Well, no, I always give all my employees a satisfactory rating—it's easier that way," answered Annette.

Without ever bringing Christine's unacceptable performance to her attention and thus giving her a chance to change, firing or otherwise severely disciplining Christine at this point would be questionable. How can this problem be avoided? In Chapter 8, you will learn how to create and utilize a performance evaluation process that works.

Performance Management Systems

>> **LO 8.1 Discuss the difference between performance management and performance appraisals.**

"In a knowledge economy, organizations rely heavily on their intangible assets to build value. Consequently, performance management at the individual employee level is essential and the business case for implementing a system to measure and improve employee performance is strong."[1] Committing management time and effort to increase performance not only meets this goal but also decreases turnover rates.[2] Therefore, an important responsibility of the human resource management (HRM) department is to oversee the performance management and appraisal processes.[3] It is critical to evaluate how well our newly trained employees perform their jobs. Therefore, performance appraisal is an important part of the jobs of managers[4] and HRM staff.[5] We need to figure out how to manage employees' performance over time to ensure they remain productive and hopefully become even more capable as they progress in their careers. So, the primary purpose of performance appraisal should be to help employees to continuously improve their performance.[6]

In this section we will discuss the difference between performance management and performance appraisal, and present the performance appraisal process.[7] But first, let's review a popular debate—the push to modify or discontinue annual performance ratings.

Is It Time to Delete the Annual Appraisal Process?

It is worth noting that many people do not like performance appraisal systems and do not think these systems have the ability to improve employee performance. One study even noted that 95% of managers are dissatisfied with their performance management system and 90% of HR managers believe the system does not yield accurate performance information![8] Routinely, there are calls to do away with performance appraisal processes.[9] **Netflix** is one company that has completely stopped doing *formal* performance appraisals, even though the CEO noted that "excellent colleagues trump everything else."[10] (Netflix still does *informal* 360-degree appraisals. We will introduce you to these shortly.)

In addition to Netflix, a list of **Fortune 500** companies like **Deloitte, Adobe Systems, GE, PwC,**[11] **SAP,**[12] **Accenture, IBM,** and **Gap**[13] have trashed their annual appraisal approaches. Why? Many companies don't believe the old-school annual reviews, by themselves, work for employers or employees.[14]

Looking at the articles written about dumping appraisals, the natural question would be "Why are we studying this if it is going away?" The quickest answer is that it isn't quite gone yet and probably won't be for some time—if ever. Based on a number of different surveys, around 10% to 15% of companies have decided to stop using annual reviews. The numbers were about 6% of Fortune 500 companies in 2015[15] and about 12% to 15% in 2017,[16] which leaves around 85% of those companies and many smaller firms still using annual evaluations.

Why hasn't the rest of the business world let go of this relic of the industrial age if it doesn't work? Again, the quick answer is that there is valuable information gained from the process and the latest online, app-based, and/or social options have not gotten to the point yet where they can provide all of the same valuable information. "The documentation that traditional appraisals produce is a business necessity. The data collected . . . allows the organization to make important decisions in a whole host of business areas."[17] So, if we don't have that information, decisions become more difficult and dangerous. In addition, at least some research shows that deleting the performance appraisal does not automatically make the organization better and may make it worse. "At firms where reviews had been eliminated, measures of employee engagement and performance dropped by 10% . . . Managers actually spent less time on conversations, and the quality of those conversations declined."[18]

There is certainly a trend to *supplement* the annual appraisal with more frequent feedback in technology-driven forms like 360-degree pulse surveys and other instant feedback mechanisms—even if most companies are not completely doing away with annual reports. Millennial and post-millennial employees certainly desire this instant feedback as well, so these immediate forms of work evaluation will likely continue to become more common over the next few years.

Performance Management Versus Performance Appraisal

The most common part of the performance management process, and the one with which we are most familiar, is the performance appraisal, or evaluation. (In this chapter, we will use the terms *performance evaluation, performance appraisal,* and just *appraisal* interchangeably.) However, the performance appraisal process is not the only part of performance management. **Performance management** is *the process of identifying, measuring, managing, and developing the performance of the human resources in an organization.* So it is a systematic analysis and measurement of worker performance (*and* communication of that assessment to the individual) that we use to improve performance over time. Through performance management,[19] people need to be evaluated for current performance and potential promotions.[20] **(SHRM L:5)**

Performance appraisal, on the other hand, is *the ongoing process of evaluating employee performance.* Performance appraisal should not be simply a once- or twice-a-year formal interview. It should be *an ongoing process.* Employees need regular feedback on their performance,[21] so give routine and candid assessments.[22] Assessment apps that provide ongoing feedback have only been around for a few years, so it is too early to know if they will help or hurt corporate culture.[23]

Although we will spend most of the chapter discussing performance appraisals, there are several other significant pieces to performance management that we already covered in past chapters and will cover in future chapters. **(SHRM I:7 and L:13)**

We discussed strategic planning, which provides inputs into what we want to evaluate in our performance management system, in Chapter 2, and the major method of identifying performance requirements in a particular job when we went through job analysis and design in Chapter 4. In Chapter 7, we discussed training and development. Additionally, we will discuss motivating employees, coaching and counseling, employee relations, compensation, and other pieces in Chapters 9 through 14. Now that we understand the difference between performance management and performance appraisal, let's look at the performance appraisal process. **(SHRM L:1, M:3-f, and M:1-b)**

The Performance Appraisal Process

Exhibit 8.1 illustrates the performance appraisal process. Note the connection between the organization's mission and objectives and the performance appraisal process. Here we briefly discuss each step of the process.

Step 1: Job analysis. If we don't know what a job consists of, how can we possibly evaluate an employee's performance in that job? We learned how to do a job analysis in Chapter 4.

Step 2: Develop standards and measurement methods. We can't assess performance without standards and measuring to see if standards are met.[24] We will discuss performance appraisal methods in the next part of this section, and in the section "How Do We Use Appraisal Methods and Forms?" we will discuss these topics in more detail.

Step 3: Informal performance appraisal—Coaching and disciplining. As its definition states, performance appraisal is an ongoing process. While a formal evaluation may only take place once or twice a year, people need regular feedback on their performance to know how they are doing,[25] so use coaching.[26] Coaching involves giving praise for a job well done to maintain and improve performance or taking corrective action when standards are not met.[27]

Step 4: Prepare for and conduct the formal performance appraisal. The formal performance appraisal review with the boss usually occurs once or sometimes twice a year, using measurement forms. We will discuss them later in this chapter along with the steps of preparing for and conducting the performance appraisal.

Performance management The process of identifying, measuring, managing, and developing the performance of the human resources in an organization

Performance appraisal The ongoing process of evaluating employee performance

EXHIBIT 8.1 ● The Performance Appraisal Process

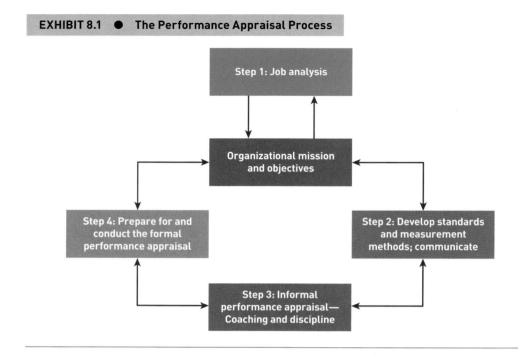

8.1 ETHICAL DILEMMA: WHAT WOULD YOU DO?

ACADEMIC STANDARDS

The academic credit-hour system was set up many years ago to ensure there would be some standardization across colleges throughout the country and that academics and employers had the same understanding of the workload a college student carried to earn a degree. The credit-hour system was based on the assumption that a student would spend 2 hours of preparation for each hour of in-class time. So a student taking five classes should spend 15 hours per week in classes and about 30 hours preparing for classes, or a total of about 45 hours a week—which is a full-time schedule.

1. How many hours outside of class, on average, do you and other students you know spend preparing for class each week?

2. Are college professors today assigning students 2 hours of preparation for every hour in class? If not, why do you think they have dropped this standard?

3. Are students who are essentially doing part-time work (i.e., attending classes but doing little academic work outside of class) during college being prepared for a career after graduation (with a 40- to 60-hour workweek)?

4. Is it ethical and socially responsible for professors to drop standards and for colleges to award degrees for doing less work than students did 5, 10, or 20 years ago?

5. Are professors who inflate grades being ethical and socially responsible?

Accurate Performance Measures

To effectively assess performance, we need to have clear expectation standards[28] and methods to objectively measure performance.[29] We need both to effectively assess performance and to let employees know where they can improve.[30] This in turn should lead to training employees to develop the skills they need to improve their performance.[31]

Also, to be an accurate measure of performance, our measure must use effective reinforcement, be valid and reliable, acceptable and feasible, specific, and based on the mission and objectives. Let's discuss each of those requirements here.

You Get What You Reinforce

Recall from Chapter 7 that we can shape behavior through reinforcement. People will generally do what they are rewarded for doing (good work) and avoid what they are punished for doing (breaking rules). Real-time specific feedback is highly useful in reinforcing positive behavior and helps people correct problematic behavior.[32] The key is to make sure you are measuring the critical success factors that result in high levels of performance for the job.

Valid and Reliable

We have to create valid and reliable measurement to be accurate. Recall that we discussed reliability and validity in Chapter 4 and Chapter 6. *Valid* means that a measure accurately measures what you wanted to measure. *Reliable* means the measure is consistent each time we use it. **(SHRM M:1-d and M:1-e)**

Acceptable and Feasible

Acceptability means that the use of the measure is satisfactory or appropriate to the people who must use it. To be acceptable, an evaluation tool must also be feasible.[33] Is it possible to reasonably apply the evaluation tool in a particular case, or is it too complex or lengthy to work well? As an example, if the manager must fill out a 25-page form that has very little to do with the job being evaluated, the manager may not feel the form is acceptable or feasible, at least partially due to its length, even if the employees do. Conversely, if the manager fills out a two-page evaluation and feels it is a true measure of performance in an employee's job, but the employee feels the evaluation leaves out large segments of what is done in the work routine, the employee may not feel the form is acceptable and feasible. If either management or employees feel the form is unacceptable, it most likely will not be used successfully.

Specific

The evaluation measure must be specific enough so that everyone involved completely understands what is going well and what needs to be improved.

Based on the Mission and Objectives

Finally, as with everything else we do in HR, we need to ensure that the performance management process guides our employees toward achievement of the company's mission and objectives. For some examples of inaccurate measures of performance, complete Applying the Concept 8.1.

8.1 APPLYING THE CONCEPT
MEASUREMENT ACCURACY

Before each of the situation descriptions below, write the letter corresponding to the accuracy criterion for a measure that is NOT met in the situation.

a. Valid
b. Reliable
c. Accepted
d. Feasible
e. Specific
f. Based on the mission and objectives

_____ 1. My boss is on my case because I'm not producing as much as I used to. But it's not my fault that the machine jams more often and then I have to stop working to fix it.

_____ 2. My boss said I have to evaluate all 25 of my employees four times a year instead of only once. I told her I don't have the time to do it that many

(Continued)

(Continued)

times. It's just not possible to do a good review that often without cutting back on other things that are more important.

_____ 3. My boss said I have a bad attitude and gave me a lower overall performance rating. I questioned what my attitude had to do with my performance because I get all my work done well, and by the deadline.

_____ 4. My boss asked me to complete a self-evaluation form rating my performance. But I didn't do it because it is her job—I let her do it.

_____ 5. My boss told me that I was not doing a very good job. But when I asked him why, he never gave me any details to support his assessment.

Why Do We Conduct Performance Appraisals?

>> **LO 8.2 Explain the purposes of performance appraisals.**

Let's discuss three major reasons (communicating, decision making, and motivating) why performance evaluations are completed, and why they are so critical to continually improving organizations' performance.[34] **(SHRM M:3-d)**

Communication (Informing)

The first major reason for performance appraisal is to provide an opportunity for formal communication between management and the employees concerning how the supervisor believes each employee is performing. "Organizations can prevent or remedy the majority of performance problems by ensuring that two-way conversation occurs between the manager and the employee, resulting in a complete understanding of what is required, when it is required, and how everyone's contribution measures up."[35] Within this two-way interaction, the process requires that we provide the opportunity for the employee to speak to us concerning factors that inhibit their ability to successfully perform to expectations.

Factors in a job that management may not know about can include lack of training, poorly maintained equipment, lack of necessary resources, conflict within work groups, and many other things that management may not see on a daily basis. We can only resolve problems when we know about them. So you need two-way communication with your employees to find out when issues within the work environment are causing a loss of productivity so they can be fixed.

Decision Making (Evaluating)

Accurate information is necessary for management decision making and is absolutely critical to allow the manager to improve organizational productivity.[36] We use information from performance appraisals to make evaluative decisions concerning our workforce, including such things as pay raises, promotions, training, and termination. When we have valid and reliable information concerning each individual we supervise, we have the ability to make administrative and performance decisions that can enhance productivity for the firm.

Motivation (Engaging)

We need to motivate our employees to improve the way they work, which in turn will improve organizational productivity overall.[37] But what is motivation, and are performance appraisals normally motivational? We define **motivation** here as *the willingness to achieve organizational objectives*. We need to increase this willingness to achieve the organization's objectives, which will in turn increase organizational productivity.

Motivation The willingness to achieve organizational objectives

What Do We Assess?

>> **LO 8.3 Discuss the options for what to evaluate in a performance appraisal.**

Our next step is to figure out what needs to be evaluated in our performance appraisal. In HRM terms, the performance appraisal should be based on our job analysis.[38] However, we can't evaluate everything, so we have to choose what we will focus on because what gets measured and evaluated gets done.[39] Our three primary options for what to evaluate are traits, behaviors, and results, so let's discuss them in this section. **(SHRM M:1-a)**

Trait Appraisals

Traits are *the physical or psychological characteristics of a person.* Traits of an individual can be part of the performance appraisal process. There is evidence that traits, including inquisitiveness, conscientiousness, and general cognitive ability, are valuable in jobs that require management and leadership skills.[40] However, we must ensure we focus on traits that have a direct relationship to the essential success functions of the job, that are within the control of the individual, and that are accurate measures.[41]

Traits The physical or psychological characteristics of a person

Give Traits the OUCH Test

When measuring traits, it's difficult to meet the *objective* requirement of the OUCH test because it is difficult to create a quantifiable and factual link between characteristics like height or job enthusiasm and job performance. If we utilized these measures in all cases in employee evaluations, we would be able to meet the *uniform in application* requirement of the OUCH test. The third test—*consistent in effect*—would be extremely difficult to meet due to the fact that different racial, ethnic, social, and gender groups tend to have different physical and personality characteristics. Remember, reliability is a measure of consistency. Physical and personality characteristics have less to do with success in the job than certain behaviors do. So it's difficult to meet the *has job relatedness* test in most cases. Finally, it would be very difficult to get different supervisors to evaluate subjective traits the same because of their own personality traits.

Should We Measure Traits?

Author **Ken Blanchard** said there are too many evaluation items that can't be objectively measured—such as attitude, initiative, and promotability. Therefore, it's important to ask whether both managers and employees will agree with the measured rating as being accurate. The bottom-line test (we will call it the Blanchard test) is this: Does everyone understand why they are assessed at a specific level (evaluation) and what it takes to get a higher rating (development)?[42] We should only assess traits that meet the bottom-line test of having a direct and obvious objective measureable relationship between the trait and success in the job.

Behavioral Appraisals

Our second option in the assessment process is to evaluate employees based on behaviors. You will recall that **behaviors** are simply *the actions taken by an individual*—the things they do. Behavioral appraisals measure what individuals *do* at work, not their personal traits and characteristics. Behaviors can be directly observed and, as a result, are more likely to be a valid assessment of the individual's performance than are traits.

Behaviors The actions taken by an individual

Give Behavior the OUCH Test

Let's take a look at a behavioral evaluation using the OUCH test. In general, directly observing and evaluating an action is significantly more *objective* than making an attempt to judge a trait like individual effort. If we applied the same evaluation of behaviors to all of the individuals in the same type of job, we would have a reasonable certainty that we were being *uniform in application.* The same thing would be true here in evaluating the concept of *consistent in effect.* To meet the test of *has job relatedness,* we would need to make sure that we chose behaviors that were necessarily a part of successfully accomplishing a task; the behaviors need to be directly related to the essential functions of the job. So the behavioral evaluation process is generally more *valid and reliable.*

Should We Measure Behavior?

The most useful and therefore most acceptable feedback to employees is feedback on specific job-related behaviors.[43] As managers, though, we still need to be cognizant of the fact that a behavioral evaluation can be a poor measure of work performance if the behaviors chosen are not directly applicable to being successful in the job, and **Blanchard** says it happens more often than you may think. So, as with traits, the Blanchard test asks whether employees understand why they are assessed at a specific level (evaluation) and what it takes to get a higher rating (development).[44]

Results Appraisals

Our final option is to evaluate the results, or outcomes, of the work process. **Results** are simply *a measure of the goals achieved through a work process.* Using results as an evaluation measure provides management with an assessment of the goals that were achieved in a particular job over time. **Ryan LLC** says to reward results, not looking busy, and hours worked.[45] Done correctly, results provide the company with its return on investment—its investment in the people in the organization. So, organizations measure results.

Give Results the OUCH Test

Results are a very *objective* measure of performance. If we apply the same results-based measure to each similar job, then our measure is *uniform in application*. The measure of results would almost certainly be consistent across different groups of employees, so we would also meet the *consistency in effect* requirement of the OUCH test. And of course, if we are measuring the results of what happens in a job, we are certainly providing a measure that *has job relatedness*. So with a quick scan, we can see that a results-based performance appraisal meets the requirements of the OUCH test better than traits and behavior options.

Should We Measure Results?

Results-based evaluations, like behavior-based evaluations, are typically very acceptable to both the employee and the manager. We can better defend results appraisals than we can defend the other two options, even in court. It tends to be very easy for the organization to go into a courtroom and show that an individual's results were objectively lower than those achieved by others in the same or similar jobs, if necessary. The results-based evaluation would most likely be valid and would usually be reliable, assuming that we were able to take into account factors outside the individual's control that nonetheless affect job performance. So again, the Blanchard test asks: Does everyone understand why they are assessed at a specific level (evaluation) and what it takes to get a higher rating (development)?[46]

8.2 APPLYING THE CONCEPT
ASSESSMENT OPTIONS

Write the letter corresponding to each of the following assessment options for measuring performance before the situation describing it.

a.   Traits

b.   Behavior

c.   Results

_____ 6.   On the assessment form question number 7, "willingness to take responsibility," I'm giving you an average rating.

_____ 7.   You have to stay calm and stop yelling at your coworkers.

_____ 8.   You only sold 25 units 3 weeks in a row. You know the standard is 35, so I'm giving you a formal warning that if you don't get up to standard in 2 weeks, you will be fired.

_____ 9.   When you promote one of the women, make sure she is attractive.

_____ 10.   I'm pleased with your performance. It is only your second week on the job, and you are already producing the standard 10 units per day. I don't think it will be long before you exceed the standard and get bonus pay.

How Do We Use Appraisal Methods and Forms?

>> **LO 8.4 List the commonly used performance measurement methods and forms.**

The formal performance appraisal usually involves the use of a standard form, selected or developed by the HR department, to measure employee performance.[47] Employees need to know the standards and understand what good performance looks like, and they need to be able to measure their own performance. If you are stuck with a form that has subjective sections, work with your employees to develop clear, accurate standards. **(SHRM M:1, M:2, and M:3)**

Exhibit 8.2 lists the commonly used performance appraisal measurement methods and forms and displays them on a continuum based on their use in evaluative and developmental decisions. In this section, we discuss each of the measurement methods and forms, starting with the developmental methods and working toward the evaluative ones.

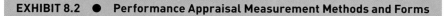

EXHIBIT 8.2 ● Performance Appraisal Measurement Methods and Forms

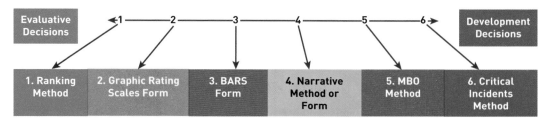

Critical Incidents Method

The **critical incidents method** is *a performance appraisal method in which a manager keeps a written record of the positive and negative performance of employees throughout the performance period.* There is no standard form used, so it is a method. Every time an employee does something very well, like beating a tough deadline or keeping an angry customer from terminating a business relationship with the firm, a note goes in the employee's file. Notes also go into the file every time the employee's behavior hurts performance. Most of us can't remember events that happened more than a few weeks ago, so we record significant critical incidents over the entire period in order to do a good assessment.

Although critical incidents are commonly used for developmental decisions, they are also used for evaluative decisions. For legal purposes, a list of documented critical incidents is especially important to have leading up to the evaluative decision of firing employees. We will discuss discipline and documentation in Chapter 9.

One error managers tend to make in critical incidents evaluation is focusing on the negative actions of employees. Remember that a good, balanced evaluation includes both positive and negative feedback, so look for good performance, not just poor performance, and praise it when you see it.[48] **Robert Graham** CEO **Michael Buckley** does it the old-fashioned way with a file folder for each of his direct reports,[49] but there are software program apps to track performance that should be used during the formal review.[50]

Management by Objectives (MBO) Method

The **management by objectives (MBO) method** is *a process in which managers and employees jointly set objectives for the employees, periodically evaluate performance, and reward employees according to the results.* MBO is a three-step process, discussed next.

Critical incidents method A performance appraisal method in which a manager keeps a written record of the positive and negative performance of employees throughout the performance period.

Management by objectives (MBO) method A process in which managers and employees jointly set objectives for the employees, periodically evaluate performance, and reward employees according to the results

Step 1: Set Individual Objectives and Plans

The manager sets objectives jointly with each individual employee.[51] The objectives are the heart of the MBO process and should be accurate measures of performance results. To be accurate, objectives should be SMART: specific, measurable, attainable, relevant, and time based.[52] We developed a model based on the work of **Max E. Douglas**, and we have provided two examples in Model 8.1 that we can use when setting objectives for ourselves or others.

MODEL 8.1 ● Setting Objectives Model			
(1) To +	(2) Action Verb +	(3) Specific and Measurable Result +	(4) Target Date
To +	produce +	20 units + per day	

To increase widget productivity 5% by December 31, 2020

Step 2: Give Feedback and Continually Evaluate Performance

Communication is the key factor in determining MBO's success or failure, and employees should continually critique their own performance.[53] Thus, the manager and employee must communicate often to review progress.[54]

Step 3: Reward According to Performance

Employees' performance should be measured against their objectives, again jointly by both manager and employee. Employees who meet their objectives should be rewarded through recognition, praise, pay raises, promotions, and so on.[55] Employees who do not meet their goals, so long as the reason is not out of their control, usually have rewards withheld and are even given punishment when necessary.

Narrative Method or Form

Narrative method or form Method in which the manager is required to write a statement about the employee's performance

Graphic rating scale form A performance appraisal checklist form on which a manager simply rates performance on a continuum such as excellent, good, average, fair, and poor

The **narrative method or form** *requires a manager to write a statement about the employee's performance.* A narrative gives the manager the opportunity to give the evaluative assessment in a written form that can go beyond simply checking a box to describe an assessment item. Narratives can be used alone, but they often follow an objective part of the form. Although the narrative is ongoing, it is commonly used during the formal review. A letter of recommendation is often a narrative method.

©iStockphoto.com/Yuri_Arcurs

▲ Managers and employees can set objectives together.

Graphic Rating Scale Form

The **graphic rating scale form** is *a performance appraisal checklist form on which a manager simply rates performance on a continuum such as excellent, good, average, fair, and poor.* The continuum often includes a numerical scale, for example, from level 1 (lowest performance level) to 5 (highest). Self-Assessment and Skill Builder 8.1 use a graphic rating scale form. **(SHRM M:2-b)**

The graphic rating scale form is probably the most commonly used form during the formal performance appraisal because it can be used for many different types of jobs, making this a kind of one-size-fits-all (or none) form that requires minimal time, effort, cost, and training. But on the negative side, graphic rating scales are not very accurate measures of performance because the selection of one rating over another, such as an excellent versus good rating, is very subjective.

Behaviorally Anchored Rating Scale (BARS) Form

A **behaviorally anchored rating scale (BARS) form** is *a performance appraisal that provides a description of each assessment along a continuum*. As with graphic rating scales, the continuum often includes a numerical scale that runs from low to high. However, BARS forms overcome the problem of subjectivity by providing an actual description of the performance (behavior) for each rating along the continuum, rather than one simple word (*excellent, good,* etc.) that graphic rating scales provide. A description of each level of performance makes the assessment a more objective, accurate measure. You can see an example of both the graphic rating scale and the BARS form in Exhibit 8.3.

Behaviorally anchored rating scale (BARS) form A performance appraisal that provides a description of each assessment along a continuum

---

EXHIBIT 8.3 ● Graphic Rating Scale Versus Behaviorally Anchored Rating Scale

Employee work habits:

(GRS)–Daily work habits within his or her team

5	4	3	2	1
Excellent	Above average	Average	Below average	Poor

(BARS)–Teamwork

Excellent—5	Above Average—4	Average—3	Below Average—2	Poor—1
Actively participates with the team, providing insights and thought-provoking ideas when appropriate	Generally participates in meetings while occasionally providing detailed analysis of situational factors of importance	Participates in meetings but is mostly passive, without providing detailed thought and analysis of the problem	Sometime participates in meetings, but little to no interaction with other team members and no major analysis of problems	Generally passive in meetings with no interaction or nearly none, and no contribution to problem solving

Writing skills:

(GRS)–Writing skills, including organization, grammar, and spelling.

5	4	3	2	1
Outstanding	Excellent	Average	Needs work	Unskilled

(BARS)–Writing skills

Outstanding-5	Excellent—4	Average—3	Needs Work—2	Unskilled—1
No significant grammar or syntax errors, with minimal (1–2 per page) or no spelling and word usage mistakes	Minor grammar or syntax errors that do not affect readability with few spelling and word usage errors (average 3–4 per page)	Moderate grammar or syntax errors that affect readability and/or significant spelling and word usage errors (average more than 5 per page)	Significant grammar, syntax, spelling. and/or word usage errors throughout the document that make it difficult to understand the information being presented	Written documents or major portions thereof are unreadable due to grammar, spelling, and other writing mistakes

---

Why are BARS forms less commonly used than graphic rating scales? It's partly economics and partly expertise. The graphic rating scale can be used for many different jobs, but BARS forms have to be customized to every different type of job. And developing potentially hundreds of different BARS forms takes a lot of time, money, and expertise. Even when a firm has an

HR staff, the question becomes "Is developing BARS forms the most effective use of our time?" Obviously, the answer depends on the types of jobs being evaluated and the resources available to complete the evaluation process.

In education, the trend is to require teachers to develop BARS, called grading rubrics, so that subjective grading of essays and case studies is more objective. Students use the rubric to do the work by meeting the written descriptive of how each part will be graded. When getting it back with a grade, students better understand why they got the grade they did and how to improve in the future. Have you seen and used one?

Ranking Method

Ranking *A performance appraisal method that is used to evaluate employee performance from best to worst*

Ranking is *a performance appraisal method that is used to evaluate employee performance from best to worst.* There often is no actual standard form used, and we don't always have to rank all employees. This method can be contentious, as evidenced by changes at **GE,** which until about 2015 was the king of the "rank and yank" companies that was notorious for terminating the lowest-ranked performers each year. GE has been working to reinvent their employee review process, providing routine feedback from managers *and* coworkers during the year, but also doing a brief review with each employee at the end of the period.[56] **Dell** says when they tried forced-ranking, it turned good employees into politicians, bad employees into backstabbers, colleagues into enemies, and destroyed collaboration—so **Dell** dropped it.[57] **(SHRM M:2-a, M:2-c, and M:2-d)**

Under the ranking method, and in a similar method called paired comparison, the manager compares an employee to one or more similar employees, rather than to an objective standard. Another offshoot of ranking is the *forced distribution method,* which is similar to grading on a curve. Predetermined percentages of employees are placed in various performance categories—for example, excellent, 5%; above average, 15%; average, 60%; below average, 15%; and poor, 5%. The employees ranked in the top group usually get the rewards (a raise, a bonus, or a promotion), those not in the top tend to have rewards withheld, and the ones in the bottom group sometimes get punished. In Skill Builder 8.1, you are asked to rank the performance of some of your peers.

Which Option Is Best?

Using a combination of the methods and forms is usually superior to using just one. For developmental objectives, the critical incidents, MBO, and narrative methods work well. Alternately, you can't decide who gets the promotion or merit raise without an evaluative method. So for administrative decisions, a ranking method based on the evaluative methods, and especially graphic rating scales or BARS forms, works well.

Remember that the success of the performance appraisal process does not just lie in the formal method or form used once or twice a year. It depends on the manager's interpersonal skills in ongoing critical incidents coaching, and it also depends on effective measures of performance that are accurate enough to let everyone know why they are rated at a given level (evaluative) and how they should improve (developmental) for the next assessment.[58]

8.3 APPLYING THE CONCEPT
APPRAISAL METHODS AND FORMS

State which of the following assessments is being described in each of the given situations, writing each assessment's corresponding letter before the situation(s) in which it is described.

a. Critical incidents method

b. MBO method

c. Narrative method and forms

d. BARS forms

e. Graphic rating scale forms

f. Ranking method

_____ 11. Hank is not doing a good job, so you decided to talk to him about it and keep track of his performance regularly.

_____ 12. Your employees perform different tasks. You want to create a system for developing each of them.

_____ 13. Sara is moving, has applied for a job at another company, and has asked you for a letter of recommendation.

_____ 14. You started a new business a year ago, and you are extremely busy focusing on sales, but you want to develop a performance appraisal form you can use with all 14 of your employees, who do a variety of jobs.

_____ 15. You have been promoted, and you have been asked to select your replacement.

Who Should Assess Performance?

>> **LO 8.5 Discuss the available options for determining the rater/evaluator.**

Now that we've learned the why, what, and how of the performance appraisal process, we need to discuss the options for choosing a rater or evaluator. There are a number of different options concerning who should evaluate the individual employee, and the decision needs to be based on a series of factors. The trend is to provide apps that offer real-time feedback from bosses, peers, and subordinates.[59] Let's take a look at six options for deciding who may evaluate an employee based on their jobs. **(SHRM M:3-g)**

Supervisor

The most commonly used evaluator is the immediate supervisor because supervisors are supposed to know the level of performance of their employees. However, this is not always the case due to problems with supervisor performance assessments.

Problems With Supervisor Evaluations

Let's face it, most managers dread performance evaluations because they are time consuming to prepare and nerve-racking to give. Employees often get upset during the interview,[60] for a least a couple of reasons.

1. Many supervisors are not good coaches that don't give honest ongoing feedback to employees regarding their performance. They don't say anything about being average or how to improve, so employees think they are doing a good job. So when it comes time for the formal evaluation and the supervisor gives an average rating, the employee is surprised and disappointed.

2. Many times today, supervisors have little or no direct contact with their employees because they may be in a different building, city, state, or even country. Virtual teams, Internet-linked offices, telecommuting, and other factors cause supervisors to not be in constant touch with their employees. What if the supervisor doesn't even know what you're supposed to be doing in your job? What if there's a personality conflict?

Avoiding Supervisor Review Problems

A way to overcome the lack of coaching is to train managers to be coaches and to require regular (say monthly) ongoing reviews in place of, or in preparation for, the annual review. Another way to help overcome both of these problems is to have others in addition to (or in place of) the supervisor assess performance. Also, multiple measures can make a performance assessment more accurate—valid and reliable. Using other evaluators and multiple measures can help overcome personal bias and provide information that supervisors don't always know about.

Peers

In addition to, or in place of, supervisors, the trend is to use more teams, and teams commonly evaluate each member's performance,[61] as is done at **Zappos**.[62] Why? Peers often know the job of the individual employee better than the supervisor does, and they are more directly affected by the employee's actions, either positive or negative. In addition, peers can evaluate the ability of the individual to interact with others successfully in a group or team setting—something that may be very difficult for the supervisor to see unless they are intimately involved with the group. Employees at **Netflix** and **Facebook** are expected to give each other open, candid verbal feedback.[63]

Problems With Peer Reviews

Peer evaluations can cause problems because the process can become less objective. Also, the validity of peer evaluations is really unclear.[64] Personality conflicts and personal biases can affect how individual employees rate their peers, so they probably should not be used for administrative purposes because they don't hold up well in court.

Avoiding Peer Review Problems

Because we know that problems can occur within a peer evaluation, the manager can take the issues into account and adjust rating values as necessary. For example, if a personality conflict has occurred between two group members that caused them to lower each other's grades, those grades can be adjusted based on feedback from other group members. Some research shows that as peers evaluate each other more, their ability to provide relevant and valuable feedback increases, as does their personal confidence. So giving employees practice in peer evaluations can improve the validity and reliability of such evaluations.[65] Even with the potential for personality conflicts and bias, peer evaluations can give us good insight into the inner workings of a group or team when the supervisor has infrequent contact with the team.

Subordinates

We may also have employees evaluate their boss. Subordinate evaluations can give us good insight into the managerial practices and potential missteps of people who oversee others. As a result, subordinate evaluations may give us valuable information that we would be unable to find out using any other means. Have you filled out a form that assesses professors?

Problems With Subordinate Reviews

There is potential for bias here, especially from subordinates who have been disciplined by their supervisor. So here again, we should probably not use them for administrative purposes because of having to explain how we avoided such bias if we have to go to court. Obviously, the subordinates may try to get back at their supervisor for giving them tasks they did not want to perform or for disciplining them for failure in their jobs. There may also be a personality conflict, or some subordinates may be biased against their supervisor or manager for other reasons—recall perception problems.

On the other end of the scale, the subordinates may inflate the capabilities of their manager, at least partly because of a lack of understanding of all the tasks and duties required of the manager. In fact, in a recent survey, about two thirds of employees rated their managers higher than the managers rated themselves.[66]

Avoiding Subordinate Review Problems

In many cases, as we go through a group of subordinate evaluations, we will see one or two outliers providing either very high or very low marks for the supervisor. In such a case, we should probably throw those outliers out of the calculation when determining overall marks for the supervisor. It's surprising how often these outliers are extremely easy to spot in a subordinate evaluation process. Another significant issue in the case of subordinate evaluations is confidentiality. Subordinate evaluations *must* be anonymous or it is unlikely that the subordinates will provide an honest evaluation of their supervisor. Despite potential problems, subordinate evaluations can provide us with valuable information about the supervisor's capabilities.

Self

Ever done a self-assessment at work? Virtually all of us have informally evaluated how we perceive we are doing on the job, and it can also be part of the formal performance appraisal process.

As you know, every chapter of this book has one or more self-assessments, and in one for this chapter—Self-Assessment and Skill Builder 8.1 at the end of the chapter—you will assess your performance on a group project. If you want to, you can do the skill builder now.

Problems With Self-Assessments

Let's face it, we tend to be biased in our self-perception because we all want to view ourselves positively. A significant portion of the research evidence seems to show that individuals with lower overall levels of knowledge and skills tend to inflate the self-assessment of their abilities.[67] Conversely, as individuals become more knowledgeable and more skilled, the evidence tends to show that they will either accurately estimate or even underestimate their capabilities in their jobs.[68]

Avoiding Self-Assessment Problems

Here again, if we know that self-evaluations tend to be skewed, we can most likely adjust for that. In addition, receiving information from the individual concerning their perception of their skill set is extremely valuable in a number of management processes—including plans for training and development opportunities, providing work assignments, and counseling and disciplinary measures.[69] As stated in the Blanchard test, both the manager and employee need to agree on the level of performance and what it takes to get to the next level—it's called *perception congruence*.[70]

Customers

We may want to use customers as evaluators when the individual being evaluated has frequent contact with internal or external customers. It does not matter what else we do successfully if our customers are uncomfortable with their interactions with our employees because they can usually take their business elsewhere. And even *internal* customers can create significant problems within the firm due to conflict between departments or divisions. So we may want to ask internal and external customers to evaluate the individuals with whom they come into contact.

©iStockphoto.com/asiseeit

▲
Employees who frequently interact with customers may be evaluated based on customer evaluations, but this method may present issues of subjectivity.

Problems With Customer Assessments

One problem with customer evaluations is that they commonly use simple graphic rating scales, which we discussed as being very subjective. Also, customers are usually not trained to do an accurate assessment, so bias is a problem. For these and other reasons, the popular opinion is that customer evaluations are negatively skewed. However, research shows that in some situations, customer evaluations actually exceed internal evaluations.[71]

Avoiding Customer Assessment Problems

Regardless of problems, customer evaluations provide us with valuable information concerning our employees who have direct customer contact. And we can always adjust the evaluation process knowing that customer evaluations may be biased. Haven't we all been on the phone and heard something like "This conversation will be recorded and used for training purposes"? This is true, but it's also usually an evaluation and employees are rewarded or punished based on how they deal with customers.

360-Degree Evaluations

In some cases, the evaluation is expanded to everyone that an employee comes into contact with through 360-degree feedback.[72] The **360-degree evaluation** *analyzes individuals' performance from all sides—from their supervisor's viewpoint, from their subordinates' viewpoint, from their customers (if applicable), from their peers, and from their own self-evaluation.* The 360-degree evaluation would generally give us the most accurate analysis of performance.

360-degree evaluation An evaluation that analyzes individuals' performance from all sides—from their supervisor's viewpoint, from their subordinates' viewpoint, from their customers (if applicable), from their peers, and from their own self-evaluation

Problems With 360-Degree Evaluations

Although considered the best, 360-degree evaluations are not the most popular method because of the time, effort, and money needed to use them and they can be a distraction. There can be abuse, especially in a strained, toxic, or politicized workplace.[73] Also, some employees have little contact with others, making them unnecessary anyway.

Avoiding 360-Degree Evaluation Problems

Unfortunately, there really is no simple way to avoid these problems besides what is commonly done—simply not using 360-degree evaluations. The 360-degree evaluation format tends to be most valuable if it is used for purposes of individual development, rather than to make administrative evaluative decisions.[74] A good 360-degree feedback system can provide specific suggestions about how to improve individual competencies."[75] It can also go a long way toward minimizing some of the most common problems with the performance appraisal process, which we will review in the next section.

Performance Appraisal Problems

>> **LO 8.6 Name some of the common problems encountered with performance appraisals and provide a method used to avoid each.**

During the performance appraisal process, we face some common problems. However, we can take measures to avoid them if we know about them. So in this section, we discuss the problems first with simple ways to avoid each of them as an individual. Then we discuss what the organization can do to overcome these problems on an organization-wide basis. We can actually overcome multiple problems with the same method. **(SHRM M:1-c and C:7)**

Common Problems Within the Performance Appraisal Process

Let's briefly discuss each of the common problems during the performance appraisal process listed in Exhibit 8.4.

EXHIBIT 8.4 ● Performance Appraisal Problems and Avoiding Them

Common Problems	How to Avoid Problems
Bias	Develop accurate performance measures
Stereotyping	Use multiple criteria
Halo error	Minimize the use of trait-based evaluations
Distributional errors	Use the OUCH and Blanchard tests
Similarity	Train your evaluators
Proximity	Use multiple raters
Recency	
Contrast	

Bias

Bias is simply *a personality-based tendency, either toward or against something*. Performance appraisal bias is toward or against an individual employee. We all have biases, but supervisors especially cannot afford to allow their biases to enter into their evaluation of subordinates. This is easier said than done. Biases make the performance appraisal process subjective rather than objective, and they certainly provide the opportunity for a lack of consistency in effect on different groups of employees. So we need to be objective and not let our feelings of liking or disliking an individual influence our assessment of that person.

Stereotyping

Stereotyping is *mentally classifying a person into an affinity group and then identifying the person as having the same assumed characteristics as the group*. Making any assumptions about individual employee characteristics based on their supposed membership in a group, rather than explicitly identifying the performance of the individual, creates the potential for significant error in evaluations. So we need to get to know each employee as an individual and objectively evaluate actual performance.

Halo Error

This occurs when the evaluator forms a *generally* positive impression of an individual and then artificially extends that general impression to an overall evaluation of the individual.[76] (Alternatively, the evaluator can form a negative initial impression and extend it to form an overall negative evaluation—this is sometimes called the "horns error.") So we need to remember that employees are often strong in some areas and weaker in others, and we need to objectively evaluate their actual performance for each and every item of assessment.

Distributional Errors

These errors occur in three forms: severity or strictness, central tendency, and leniency. They are based on a standard normal distribution, or the bell curve that we are all so familiar with. In *severity* or *strictness* error, the rater evaluates just about everyone as below average. *Central tendency* error occurs when just about everyone is rated average. Finally, *leniency* error occurs when just about everyone is rated as above average—like grade inflation. So we need to give a range of evaluations because we really aren't all equal in our level of performance, and everyone can't be the worst or the best.

Similarity Error

This error, also called "like me," occurs when the rater gives better evaluations to subordinates whom they consider more similar to themselves and poorer evaluations to subordinates whom they consider to be different from themselves. We all have a tendency to feel more comfortable with people who we feel are more similar to ourselves,[77] and if we are not careful, we can allow this feeling of comfort with similar individuals to be reflected in the performance appraisal process. So we need to evaluate all employees based on their actual performance, even if they are different from us and don't do things the same way that we do.

Proximity Error

This error states that similar marks may be given to items that are near (in other words, proximate to) each other on the performance appraisal form, regardless of differences in performance on those measures. For instance, if we mark the first three items as "meets expectations," we tend to continue marking the same way on down the form. So we need to be objective in evaluating employees' actual performance on each and every item on the assessment form, and having *reverse item scales* really helps.

Recency Error

This occurs when the rater uses only the last few weeks of a rating period as evidence when putting together performance ratings. For instance, if a warehouse worker has been a strong performer for most of the appraisal period, but right before his annual evaluation he accidentally set a fire, he may be rated poorly due to recency error. So we need to evaluate the employee based on their performance during the entire assessment period. Using the critical incident evaluation method really helps avoid recency error.

Contrast Error

Here the rater compares and contrasts performance between two employees, rather than using absolute measures of performance to assess each employee. For example, the rater may contrast a good performer with an outstanding performer; then, as a result of the significant contrast, the good performer seems to be "below average." So we need to evaluate the individual based on their actual performance against an objective standard.

Avoiding Performance Appraisal Problems

As discussed, performance appraisal can fail to provide an accurate assessment of the capabilities and behaviors of individual employees. Thus far, we have only provided simple solutions to help us overcome these problems as individuals. But how can a firm avoid these problems on an organization-wide basis? Let's discuss how the firm can limit the potential for the appraisal process to go astray by developing accurate performance measures, training evaluators, and using multiple raters.

Develop Accurate Performance Measures

As discussed, if the performance appraisal methods and forms are not accurate measures, then the entire process will have problems. Therefore, the organization should have its own HR specialist or hired consultants develop an objective assessment process and measures. Let's discuss three things HR specialists commonly do to help ensure accurate measures.

Use Multiple Criteria

HR must ensure we focus on more than one or two criteria to evaluate an individual's performance. We should generally have at least one evaluation criterion for each major function within an individual job so that we have the ability to lower the incidence of halo, recency, and contrast errors, and we may even be able to affect bias and stereotyping because of the fact that many criteria, not just one or two, are being analyzed.

Minimize the Use of Trait-Based Evaluations

As noted, trait-based evaluations tend to be more subjective than behavior and results-based evaluations, and as a result, they should generally not be used unless there is a *specific reason* why employees must exhibit a particular trait to be successful in a job. By eliminating traits, we lower the incidence of bias, stereotyping, and similarity errors.

Give the Measures the OUCH Test

We already stated this, but it is so important that it bears repeating here. With the OUCH test, the measure has to be objective, uniform in application, consistent in effect, and have job relatedness.

Train Evaluators

Next, we should train our evaluators to avoid the common errors and problems that occur in performance assessment and in how to use the various methods and forms.

Train Evaluators to Overcome the Common Problems of Assessment Through training, the evaluator becomes aware that the common errors occur with some regularity, so they can guard against them. Most employees want to do a good job, and once they know these errors are routinely made, they will make attempts to correct them.

Train Evaluators to Use the Measurement Methods and Forms Evaluators should also be trained to use the various performance appraisal methods and forms. Because the critical incident method is not commonly used as a formal assessment method, evaluators should be taught to use it to help overcome recency error. Evaluators also need training to effectively use MBO and to write a good narrative. When using a graphic rating scale, the organization should provide some training for the raters so they better understand the differences between the word descriptors along the continuum (excellent, good, etc.). BARS forms and ranking are fairly straightforward, but supervisors need to realize that they too are subject to common problems when selecting each rating.

Use Multiple Raters

At least in some cases, we can have multiple raters evaluate an individual. As we noted earlier, this becomes expensive very quickly, so we must decide whether or not the value inherent in using multiple evaluators overcomes the cost of the process. However, if it does, using multiple evaluators can conquer some significant problems in the appraisal process, including bias and stereotyping. In addition, halo, similarity, and contrast errors become less likely, and distributional errors tend to even out among multiple raters. It is for these reasons that 360-degree evaluations have gained favor in many organizations.

Effective Ongoing Coaching

The success of performance appraisal does not lie in the method or form used; it depends on your interpersonal coaching skills using critical incidents. An important part of your job is to make sure your employees know what the standards are and how they are performing through ongoing coaching. If you give an employee an average rather than a good rating, you should be able to clearly explain why. The employee should understand what exactly needs to be done during the next performance period to get the higher rating. With clear standards and coaching, you can minimize disagreements over performance during the formal performance appraisal debriefing.

8.4 APPLYING THE CONCEPT
AVOIDING APPRAISAL PROBLEMS

Review the list of common problems or errors and then write the letter corresponding to each one before the statement describing or involving it.

a. Bias

b. Stereotyping

c. Halo error

d. Distributional error

e. Similarity error

f. Proximity error

g. Recency error

h. Contrast error

_____ 16. I got a lower rating than I deserve because I'm not afraid to speak my mind to the boss, and she doesn't like it.

_____ 17. I'm sick and tired of hearing how many units Sally produces and that I should be more like her.

_____ 18. I told my boss that I thought I deserve an excellent rating, but she said that she gives everyone a good rating.

_____ 19. I tend to take it easy during the year, but I make sure to really push and do a good job for the month of December, and that's why I got a good performance review.

_____ 20. I attended all the classes and participated in the class discussions, so the professor gave me an A even though my final average on my test scores was a B.

Debriefing the Appraisal

>> **LO 8.7 Briefly discuss the differences between evaluative performance reviews and developmental performance reviews.**

The debriefing process is where we communicate to individuals our analysis of their performance. Most managers dislike debriefing because of the time it takes to prepare for the formal interview, and it's nerve-racking to deliver them.[78] But it's an important part of the manager's job, and if you follow the guidelines throughout this chapter, you can improve your debriefing skills. Recall that there are two major reasons for assessing performance: for evaluative decisions and for development. The evaluative performance appraisal focuses on the past, whereas the developmental performance appraisal focuses on the future. They are related because a developmental performance appraisal is always based on an evaluative performance appraisal. Employees need to be evaluated for current performance and to continuously improve their performance for potential promotions.[79]

We also suggested breaking the formal performance appraisal debriefing into two separate interviews. Why? When a developmental and an evaluative performance appraisal are conducted together (which they commonly are), the appraisal is often less effective as evaluation crushes development, especially when the employee disagrees with the evaluation.[80] Most managers are not good at being a judge and a coach at the same time. Therefore, separate meetings make the two uses clear and can help you be both a judge and a coach.

In this section, we will briefly describe how to conduct both reviews.

The Evaluative Performance Appraisal Interview

When preparing for an evaluative interview, follow the steps outlined in Model 8.2. Our evaluation should be fair (meaning ethically and legally not based on any of the problems discussed).[81] If we have had regular coaching conversations with our employees, they know where they stand,[82] and our preparation is mostly done except for filling out the form. So our relationship with the employee will directly affect the outcome.[83] Employees should also critique their own performance through a self-assessment using the same form as the evaluator prior to the meeting.[84] **(SHRM M:3-a)**

MODEL 8.2 ● The Evaluative Performance Appraisal Interview

Preparation for the Appraisal Interview

1. Make an appointment → 2. Have the employee perform a self-assessment → 3. Assess the employee's performance → 4. Identify strengths and areas for improvement → 5. Predict the employee's reactions and plan how to handle them

Conducting the Appraisal Interview

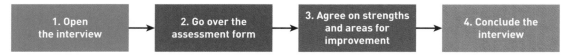

1. Open the interview → 2. Go over the assessment form → 3. Agree on strengths and areas for improvement → 4. Conclude the interview

---

Conducting an Evaluative Interview

During the interview, encourage the employee to talk and also listen to the critique of their performance.[85] Model 8.2 lists the steps for conducting an evaluative performance appraisal interview. In Step 1, we open the meeting with some small talk to put the person at ease. Then in Step 2, we go over our evaluation of the items on the assessment form. In Step 3, we identify the employee's strengths and weaknesses, discuss them, and agree on them. Finally, in Step 4, we conclude the interview, which may involve making the appointment for the developmental interview.

The Developmental Performance Appraisal Interview

After the employee's performance evaluation is completed, you should prepare for the developmental interview based on targeting areas for improvement you already discussed in the evaluative interview. Yes, as a manager you are busy, and you may question the need for coaching and the cost of separate formal developmental interviews, but the benefit of spending time developing employees will lead to increased performance and lower turnover in your organization.[86]

Conducting a Developmental Interview

The steps for conducting a developmental performance appraisal interview are listed in Model 8.3. Again, Step 1 starts with small talk to open the interview. In Step 2, it is important to agree on developmental objectives. As part of Step 3, the employee needs to be made aware of exactly what he or she must do to improve and increase the rating on the next review. For employees not performing up to the standard, you need clear performance goals that must be met to avoid being fired.[87] You must also let the employee know that follow-up progress feedback is essential for changing behavior.[88] So Step 4 is to set up a follow-up meeting to review the employee's progress. When conducting Steps 3 and 4, we don't want the employee working on too many things at once, so we should keep the number of objectives down to three or fewer related issues. We can always add new objectives later. We end in Step 5 by concluding the interview with some positive encouragement to reach the objectives.

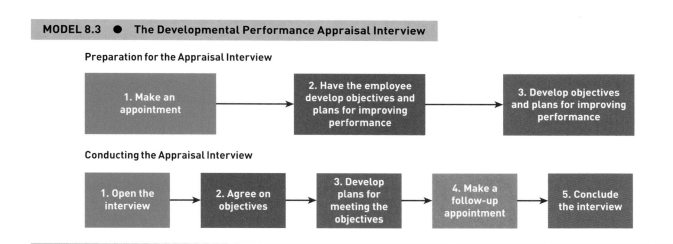

MODEL 8.3 ● The Developmental Performance Appraisal Interview

Preparation for the Appraisal Interview

1. Make an appointment → 2. Have the employee develop objectives and plans for improving performance → 3. Develop objectives and plans for improving performance

Conducting the Appraisal Interview

1. Open the interview → 2. Agree on objectives → 3. Develop plans for meeting the objectives → 4. Make a follow-up appointment → 5. Conclude the interview

Being Evaluated

On a personal note, you may not agree at all with your boss's assessment, but your supervisor's evaluation will affect your pay raises and promotions. But when you get evaluated by your boss, here is some good advice of things not to do.[89] Try not to get angry and raise your voice, because your boss will become angry and mistrustful of you. Don't deny mistakes and not meeting the boss's performance expectations, especially when your boss has a critical incidents file, because your boss will doubt your credibility. Don't make excuses and blame others, because your boss will lose respect for you.

What can you do? Take responsibility for not meeting your boss's expectations. The best thing to do is calm down and have a separate developmental session with your boss. During the meeting, tell your boss you want to improve and get a higher-level assessment the next time. Get your boss to very clearly state exactly what needs to be improved, develop a plan to improve, and agree that if you meet the expectations you will get a higher assessment the next time. Document your agreement in writing, and both of you sign it.

If you don't want to follow this advice, or it doesn't work, you can find another job that may better utilize your skills and provide greater job satisfaction. Here is a warning that some people learned the hard way. If you complain to your boss's supervisor about your boss (going over your boss's head), remember that the higher-level manager most likely promoted your boss because he or she meets the supervisor's expectations, and you will most likely only cause your boss to dislike and distrust you all the more. Some people are vengeful, and your boss can make your life even more miserable at work.

©iStockphoto.com/milanvirijevic

▲
Developmental performance appraisals can be time consuming but will ultimately lead to increased performance and lower turnover.

Trends and Issues in HRM

The first item in this trends and issues section asks whether performance appraisals can improve engagement. Then we discuss the implementation of electronic performance monitoring.

Building Engagement Through Performance Management

Recall that performance management is a broad process of analysis and measurement of worker performance *and* communication of that assessment to the individual over time. But can performance management actually create a more highly engaged workforce? There is evidence that it can when performance management is done as we discussed during the body of the chapter.

Going back to Chapter 1, employee engagement is a combination of job satisfaction, ability, and a willingness to perform for the organization at a high level and over an extended period of time. Job satisfaction alone isn't enough, and neither is annual or more frequent performance appraisal. You're probably getting the feeling by now that good people management processes are always a combination of things—there is no simple solution.

So how do we increase engagement by managing performance? It starts with orientation/onboarding where the new employee learns about the company culture. High-quality onboarding processes allow us to socialize the new employee into the work environment. Through the socialization process, the employee learns how to function successfully in their new environment by participating in conversations with others, including their future supervisor, concerning how things are done in the organization.[90] These conversations have to endure though. The manager/supervisor needs to provide frequent feedback about how well the job is being done as well as taking the time to listen during these feedback sessions to what issues are confronting the employee.[91]

The ultimate goal here is to increase employee engagement through continuing performance management, and there is real evidence that this does occur. One research study identified five performance management activities that influence engagement: setting performance goals, providing ongoing feedback and recognition, managing employee development, conducting appraisals, and creating a climate of trust and empowerment.[92] If we can do these things, performance management can "have a positive and direct influence on employee engagement," as well as individual attitudes, behaviors, and, ultimately, organizational outcomes.[93]

Electronic Performance Monitoring

Electronic performance monitoring (EPM) is the process of observing ongoing employee actions using computers or other nonhuman methods. The number of employees monitored through EPM continues to increase. In the early 1990s, about one third of employees were being monitored electronically. By 2001, approximately 78% were being monitored electronically,[94] and that percentage has likely increased ever since. The reason for this steep increase is that using EPM apparently is an effective means of increasing productivity.[95] EPM allows management to know if employees are actually working or doing personal things during paid work hours. The biggest upside to EPM seems to be that it provides information for concrete, results-based performance evaluations. **(SHRM M:3-c)**

However, some researchers and practitioners argue against EPM because of a number of factors, including ethical questions concerning such monitoring, legal concerns over employee privacy, and potential increases in stress due to constant monitoring of performance. Stress research provides an interesting dichotomy. If the monitoring is done for employee development and involves more communication between the employee and manager, stress is generally reduced. If, however, monitoring is done as a means of giving rewards and administering punishment, stress appears to generally increase.[96] So, should organizations use EPM systems, and if so, how?

There's no simple answer. Again, EPM has been shown to increase productivity, and organizations need to maximize employee productivity. However, when stress levels become too great, productivity decreases. So there's an obvious tradeoff between more employee monitoring and controlling stress levels in our workforce. Management must understand this tradeoff to successfully improve productivity in the organization overall.

Finally, as these programs are rolled out, managers must be acutely aware of the potential downside effects of increased stress levels and employees feeling that their privacy is being invaded. These could lead to decreases in productivity and higher rates of turnover.[97] In other words, management must work to overcome the potential problems and costs associated with EPM to gain the benefits.

Chapter Summary

8.1 Discuss the difference between performance management and performance appraisals.

Performance management is a continual process that identifies, measures, manages, and develops the performance of people in the organization. It is designed to improve worker performance over time. Performance appraisal is the part of the performance management process that identifies, measures, and evaluates the employee's performance and then discusses that performance with the individual. This should also be on an ongoing basis.

8.2 Explain the purposes of performance appraisals.

Communication is the first purpose. Appraisals need to provide an opportunity for formal two-way communication between management and the employee concerning how the organization feels the employee is performing. The second purpose is to gain information for evaluative decisions. We need good information on how employees are performing so that we can take fair and equitable actions with our workforce to improve organizational productivity. Providing motivation for development is the last major purpose. Used correctly, appraisals can motivate by providing opportunities for the employees to improve their performance over time.

8.3 Discuss the options for what to evaluate in a performance appraisal.

Our three primary options for what to evaluate are traits, behaviors, and results. There is *some* evidence that particular types of traits are valuable in jobs that require management and leadership skills, but many traits have been shown to have very little bearing on job performance, meaning they are not valid measures of performance. We can also use behaviors to evaluate our workers. Measuring behaviors is usually a much better appraisal option because physical actions or behaviors can be directly observed, and as a result, they are more likely to be a valid assessment of the individual's performance. Finally, we can evaluate performance based on results. Results are a concrete measure of what has happened in the organization. However, results may be skewed based on factors that are outside the control of the individual who is being evaluated.

8.4 List the commonly used performance measurement methods and forms.

The *critical incidents* method utilizes records of major employee actions over the course of the appraisal period to complete the employee evaluation. *MBO* uses objectives jointly set by the manager and employee to gauge employee performance during the evaluation period. In the *narrative method,* the manager writes either a structured or unstructured paragraph about the employee's performance. *Graphic rating scales* provide a numerical scale so that the manager can check off where an employee falls on the continuum. BARS forms provide a description of the behaviors that make up acceptable performance at each level on the scale. Finally, *ranking* creates a hierarchy of employees, from best to worst.

8.5   Discuss the available options for determining the rater/evaluator.

It is logical to choose *supervisors* as evaluators when they have ongoing contact with the subordinate and know the subordinate's job. When the supervisor may not spend lots of time with the individual employee, *peers* may make better evaluators because they may know the job of the individual employee better than the supervisor does and may be more directly affected by the employee's actions. *Subordinate* evaluations can give us good insight into the managers who control employees in our organization. We may want to use *customers* as evaluators when the individual being evaluated has frequent contact with those customers, because we need to know how customers feel about their interactions with our employees. *Self-evaluation* is valuable in a number of management processes, from training and development to counseling and disciplinary measures, among others.

8.6   Name some of the common problems encountered with performance appraisals and provide a method used to avoid each.

Personal biases and stereotyping are two of the most significant appraisal problems. Other problems include halo error, distributional errors (either the grading is too harsh or too lenient, or everyone is judged to be average), similarity error, proximity error, recency error, and contrast error.

There are several ways to avoid these problems. The first option would be to develop *accurate performance measures*. Accurate performance measures use *multiple criteria, minimize trait-based evaluations,* and can be analyzed *using the OUCH test and the Blanchard test.* Next, we should *train the evaluators,* because as soon as they know some of the common errors, those errors will become less pronounced. We can also *use multiple raters* to mitigate any potentially biased evaluations and minimize other errors such as similarity, contrast, and attribution errors.

8.7   Briefly discuss the differences between evaluative performance reviews and developmental performance reviews.

The *evaluative interview* is a review of the individual employee's performance over a certain period. The evaluation needs to be fair and equitable, not based on bias. The employee must be given the opportunity to talk as well as listen to the critique of their performance. The *developmental interview,* on the other hand, focuses on areas for improvement over time. You should have employees come up with their own objectives and strategies for improvement, and you should develop your own objectives for them.

Key Terms

behaviorally anchored rating scale (BARS) form,   203
behaviors,   199
bias,   209
critical incidents method,   201
graphic rating scale form,   202

management by objectives (MBO) method,   201
motivation,   198
narrative method or form,   202
performance appraisal,   195
performance management,   195

ranking,   204
results,   200
stereotyping,   209
360-degree evaluation,   207
traits,   199

Key Terms Review

Complete each of the following statements using one of this chapter's key terms.

1. _____ is the process of identifying, measuring, managing, and developing the

performance of the human resources in an organization.

2. _____ is the ongoing process of evaluating employee performance.

3. _____ is the willingness to achieve organizational objectives.

4. _____ identify the physical or psychological characteristics of a person.

5. _____ are the actions taken by an individual.

6. _____ is a measure of the goals achieved through a work process.

7. _____ is a performance appraisal method in which a manager keeps a written record of positive and negative performance of employees throughout the performance period.

8. _____ is a process in which managers and employees jointly set objectives for the employees, periodically evaluate performance, and give rewards according to the results.

9. _____ requires a manager to write a statement about the employee's performance.

10. _____ is a performance appraisal checklist on which a manager simply rates performance on a continuum such as excellent, good, average, fair, and poor.

11. _____ is a performance appraisal that provides a description of each assessment along a continuum.

12. _____ is a performance appraisal method that is used to evaluate employee performance from best to worst.

13. _____ analyzes individual performance from all sides—from the supervisor's viewpoint, from the subordinates' viewpoint, from customers' viewpoints (if applicable), from peers, and using the employee's own self-evaluation.

14. _____ is a personality-based tendency, either toward or against something.

15. _____ consists of mentally classifying a person into an affinity group and then identifying the person as having the same assumed characteristics as that group.

Communication Skills

The following critical-thinking questions can be used for class discussion and/or for written assignments to develop communication skills. Be sure to give complete explanations for all answers.

1. Other than giving an annual evaluation, what would you do to manage the performance of your employees? Explain why.

2. What would you do as the manager in order to make sure that your employees knew the standards that they would be evaluated against? Explain your answer.

3. Do you really think that it is possible for a performance appraisal to be motivational? Why or why not?

4. Can you think of a situation in which a trait-based evaluation would be necessary? Explain your answer.

5. You are in charge and you want to evaluate a group of assembly workers. Who would you choose as the evaluator(s)? What about evaluating the director of operations—who would you choose to do that? Explain your answer.

6. How would you minimize the chances that stereotyping could affect the evaluation process in your company?

7. Which of the solutions to performance appraisal problems would you implement first if you were in charge? Second? Why?

8. What would you do to make the performance appraisal debriefing more comfortable and less confrontational for your employees? How do you think this would help?

9. Do you agree that annual performance appraisals should be discontinued in companies? Defend your answer.

Case 8.1 Not Spilling the Beans at Jelly Belly: Developing a More Accurate Performance Appraisal System

Candy making is a fun business, and so it is no surprise that it is fun to work at the Jelly Belly Candy Company of Fairfield, California. Although this company has cheesecake, buttered popcorn, orange sherbet, and jalapeño on the menu, they are most known for making jelly beans—fifty "official" flavors, with new and sometimes startlingly flavored (and named) versions introduced periodically, such as Chili Mango. The company's other products include gumballs, gummies, and sour candies in Jelly Belly flavors. Its more than 100 confections also include candy corn, sour candies, jellies, novelty candy, chocolates, chocolate-covered nuts, cinnamon confections, and licorice, along with seasonal offerings. Jelly Belly's candy is sold in more than 70 countries worldwide. In addition to making candy, the company dabbles in retail. It operates half a dozen retail Jelly Belly candy stores in California, as well as a visitor center/warehouse (with tours) in Pleasant Prairie, Wisconsin.[98]

Jelly Belly Candy Company is dedicated to producing the highest-quality confections, delivering superior customer service and creating a reliable and enjoyable product line to the consuming public. They seek to be a responsible corporate citizen and to ensure high quality and safety standards. They expect their consumers and business partners to have confidence in the products bearing their name and that their products are manufactured in accordance with a guiding code of conduct. Jelly Belly is committed to conducting business with ethical business standards and asks its vendors, suppliers, and licensees to conduct themselves in the same manner.[99]

Given this family firm's commitment to maintaining high operating and ethical standards, there is no "sugar coating" employee performance and job satisfaction. Like almost every smart company, Jelly Belly also recognized that employees are more likely to stay with their employer when they feel connected and recognized for their efforts. Programs for managing and evaluating employee performance are critical to aligning corporate and employee values and priorities. Therefore, when Jelly Belly decided to overhaul and automate its antiquated employee performance and talent management process, it was looking for a serious solution to help give its employees across the United States fair, accurate performance appraisals.

Jelly Belly's search for a new employee performance and talent management system began when two branches of the family business were reunited into a single company. One branch was using an outdated performance management software program. The other was doing its employee performance appraisals manually, using paper forms. The task of updating and consolidating the performance management process fell to Margie Poulos, HR manager of Jelly Belly's Midwest operations. She and a small team of Jelly Belly HR staff were charged with finding a single automated system that could be used for all of Jelly Belly's 600 employees in three locations.

The driving factor behind Jelly Belly's performance management was the belief that thorough, accurate reviews help employees to better understand what is expected of them, so they can set clear, measurable objectives. That translates into higher employee satisfaction, said Jeff Brown, Jelly Belly's director of human resources. "When employees feel they have gotten a thorough and accurate review, it boosts their morale," Brown said. It also leads to improved talent management and makes it easier to retain valuable employees, which management experts know is a key factor in corporate growth and market leadership.

Under Jelly Belly's old system, employees conducting reviews started from scratch once a year with new performance journals. They wanted a new system that would let them log notes throughout the year and regularly update their online appraisals. Employees could then use one consistent employee evaluation form to add comments and to sign their appraisals. A Web-based product would help remote and traveling managers maintain access to the forms and the data they needed to evaluate their staff. "In our old system, a few folks in Chicago would have access to the system. However, we have managers in California with Chicago subordinates. It is important that they can share the same forms across the board. And we have folks who are on the road a lot or are working out of home offices, so having them be able to access this is a huge point for us," Brown explained.

To meet their strategic goals, Poulos and her team drew up a list of the criteria that a new system had to meet. Top on the list was ease of use. "We didn't want to end up with a system that is so complicated that the managers wouldn't use it," Poulos said. A new system also had to save time and had to be flexible, easily incorporating core competencies into different forms.

Once the software was selected, about 50 managers received a crash course in using the software and then used it to complete annual employee evaluations. Jelly Belly's HR team then customized the software to include competencies that are more relevant and to respond to comments from managers and staff on the new system. The new automated employee appraisal system completely formalized and organized Jelly Belly's employee evaluation process. "It allows us to standardize competencies across job classifications, add signature and comment sections to make our process more interactive, and increase accessibility for remote managers," Brown said. Organizing and automating the appraisal process results in performance appraisals that are more accurate and fair, Brown noted. "This is important because, after all, an employee appraisal is a legal document," he said.

The new system is helping Jelly Belly track training requirements and development in its staff, Poulos added. "We've always had a separate training manual. Now we can go in to the evaluations and more easily monitor employees' skills development, see what training individuals need and check the due dates for training and renewal. That makes it much easier for us to keep track," Poulos noted.

The new employee performance and talent management system has proven to be a big time-saver for Jelly Belly's HR team. "Since this year was the first time using the new system, it took us a little longer than it will next year. But the process was a whole lot faster," Poulos said. "It has already saved us a lot of time, and we got everybody's appraisals done in one shot." The new system is also helping Jelly Belly to better align employee goals with the company's business objectives.

"The feedback has been really positive, from both managers and employees as well. Some staff said this was the best appraisal they've had," Poulos said, "They felt the evaluations were fair and realistic, and supervisors had the scope to provide more relevant and legitimate comments than they could before. Rather than just clicking on a bunch of canned comments, they were accurately reviewing the employee."[100]

Questions

1. What is performance management, and what is the driving force behind Jelly Belly Candy Company's performance management approach?

2. What is performance appraisal, and what are the key features Jelly Belly Candy Company wanted in their new appraisal system?

3. What is the performance appraisal process, and how does Jelly Belly Candy Company's new appraisal system incorporate those processes?

4. How did the question of performance accuracy affect the development of Jelly Belly Candy Company's automated appraisal system?

5. Why did Jelly Belly Candy Company redesign their performance appraisal system?

6. What does Jelly Belly Candy Company evaluate when they conduct employee appraisals, and why are they using that approach?

7. Who is assessing training performance at Jelly Belly Candy Company?

8. What trends in performance appraisal are affecting Jelly Belly Candy Company's appraisal system?

Self-Assessment and Skill Builder 8.1 Peer and Self-Assessments

This exercise includes the usual self-assessment for each chapter, plus an evaluation of peers and developing measures of performance.

Objective

To develop your skill at assessing your performance and that of your peers

To develop your skill at developing measures of performance

Skills

The primary skills developed through this exercise are as follows:

1. *HR management skills*—Conceptual and design skills

2. *SHRM 2018 Curriculum Guidebook*—M: Performance Management

Assignment Part 1—Self-Assessment

During your college courses, you most likely had to do some form of group assignments, and you've also done group assignments in this course. Select one group you worked with, and based on your performance in that group, do a self-evaluation using the rating scale form that follows.

Evaluator (you) _____ (Self-Evaluation)

	A A– Always	B+ B B– Usually	C+ C C– Frequently	D+ D D– Sometimes	F Rarely
Did a "good" analysis of project					
Developed "good" questions to ask					
Actively participated (truly interested/involved)					
Made "quality" effort and contributions					
Got along well with group members					
Displayed leadership					
List at least three of your own measures of performance here					
Class attendance—number of absences	0–1	2	3	4	5+
Attendance at group meetings to prepare group project—number of absences	0	1	2	3	4+
Managed the group's time well					

This exercise can stop with just a self-assessment, or it can continue to also include peer evaluations.

Assignment Part 2—Peer Review

1. Part 2 begins by conducting a peer evaluation using the above form for each of the other members in your group, but using this heading for the form:

Group Member _____ (Peer Evaluation)

Either copy the above form for each group member, do your assessment on any sheet without using the form, or have your instructor provide you with multiple forms that you can complete for each group member.

2. Below, rank each group member (including yourself) based on their performance. The first person you list should be the best performer, and the last person you list should be the least effective performer, based on the performance

appraisal above. If members are close or equal in performance, you may assign them the same rank number, but you must list the better one first.

3. To the right of each group member (including yourself), place the overall letter grade (A–F) you would assign to that member based on the performance appraisal. You may give more than one member the same grade if those individuals deserve the same grade. You may also use plus and minus grades.

Rank	Name	Grade
_____	_____	_____
_____	_____	_____
_____	_____	_____
_____	_____	_____
_____	_____	_____

Skill Builder 8.2 Debriefing the Appraisal

Note: This exercise is designed for groups that have been working together for some time as part of the course requirements. It is a continuation of Skill Builder 8.1. Based on your peer evaluations, you will conduct performance appraisals for your group members.

Objective

To develop a plan to improve your team performance, and to develop your skills in conducting performance appraisals

Skills

The primary skills developed through this exercise are as follows:

1. *HR management skills*—Conceptual and design skills

2. *SHRM 2018 Curriculum Guidebook*—M: Performance Management

Assignment

You will be both evaluator and evaluatee. Get together with group members and have each member select a letter, beginning with the letter A. Pair off as follows: A and B, C and D, E and F, etc. If the group consists of an odd number of people, each member will sit out one round. A should conduct the evaluation interview for B, C should conduct the evaluation interview for D, etc., using the form in Skill Builder 8.1. The evaluators should follow up the evaluation interview with the developmental interview to give suggestions on improving B, D, and F's performance. (Be sure to follow the evaluative and developmental interview steps in Models 8.1 and 8.2.) Make sure you are evaluators and evaluatees; do not be peers having a discussion. When you finish, or when the instructor tells you time is up, reverse roles of evaluators and evaluatees. B, D, and F will become the new evaluators for A, C, and E.

When the instructor tells you to, or when time is up, form new groups of two and decide who will be the evaluators first. Continue changing groups of two until every group member has appraised and been appraised by every other group member.

Apply It

What did I learn from this experience? How will I improve my group performance in the course? How will I use this knowledge in the future?

_____

_____

9

©iStockphoto.com/TennesseePhotographer

Employee Rights and Labor Relations

Learning Outcomes

After studying this chapter, you should be able to do the following:

9.1 Explain the value of trust and communication in employee relations. **Page 224**

9.2 Discuss the primary reason why measuring job satisfaction is so difficult. **Page 227**

9.3 Identify the best tool for getting employees to tell the truth about their level of satisfaction. **Page 227**

9.4 Identify the commonly accepted individual rights in the workplace. **Page 230**

9.5 List some rights that management has in modern organizations. **Page 232**

9.6 Contrast the coaching, counseling, and discipline processes used in organizations. **Page 233**

9.7 Describe the major labor relations laws in the United States, including the main reasons why we have each law. **Page 239**

9.8 Discuss what management cannot do in attempting to limit union organizing efforts. **Page 241**

SHRM HR Content

See Online: *SHRM 2018 Curriculum Guidebook* for the complete list

A. Change Management
- 2. Building trust
- 3. Coaching
- 4. Commitment

C. Employee and Labor Relations
- 5. Attitude surveys
- 6. Closed shops
- 8. Collective bargaining issues
- 9. Collective bargaining process
- 10. Communication
- 13. Contract negotiation
- 14. Disciplinary actions: Demotion, disciplinary termination
- 18. Employee records
- 20. Fairness
- 22. Grievance management
- 26. Investigations
- 28. Managing union organizing policies and handbooks
- 30. Measuring and monitoring job satisfaction
- 34. National Labor Relations Act (NLRA)
- 37. Principles of justice
- 41. Right-to-work laws
- 43. Strikes, boycotts, and work stoppages
- 44. Unfair labor practices
- 45. Union decertification and deauthorization
- 46. Union membership
- 47. Union organizing

- 48. Union shops
- 49. Union/management relations
- 50. Union-related labor laws

D. Employment Law
- 14. Labor Management Relations Act of 1947 (LMRA)
- 17. National Labor Relations Act of 1935 (NLRA)
- 20. Railway Labor Act of 1926 (RLA)
- 24. Worker Adjustment and Retraining Notification Act of 1988 (WARN Act)
- 30. Employee privacy
- 31. Employer unfair labor practices
- 32. Employment contracts
- 33. Employment-at-will doctrine

M. Performance Management
- 3-b. Diagnosing problems
- 3-e. Performance improvement programs

N. Staffing (Recruitment and Selection)
- 10-b. Job offers: Employment-at-will, contracts, authorization to work

P. Training and Development
- 6-b. Selecting training methods—Coaching

Q. Workforce Planning and Talent Management
- 4. Retention: Involuntary turnover, outplacement counseling, alternative dispute resolution
- 5. Retention: Voluntary turnover, job satisfaction, withdrawal, alternatives

V. Sustainability/Corporate Responsibility
- 2. Employee relations and employment practices

Practitioner's Perspective

Cindy says, "If it isn't documented, it didn't happen."

That's a common expression in health care settings, and it stresses the importance of record keeping for patient care. The same holds true for management of personnel issues.

"I've had it with Jeremy!" Leonard exploded when Cindy returned his phone call one morning. "I've told him a million times how to run this report, and he won't follow my instructions! If he makes one more mistake, that's it—he's out of here."

"Whoa, Leonard," Cindy soothed. "You know our policy advises progressive discipline. Are you documenting your issues with Jeremy? Have you tried nondisciplinary counseling or a written warning?"

"I don't have time for all that nonsense," scoffed Leonard. "I should be able to fire any employee I want!"

"If you haven't been keeping records to back up your management of Jeremy's performance issues, discharge is not your first option," Cindy cautioned.

For the sake of due process in disciplinary matters, supervisors must document that an employee was informed of performance issues and given an opportunity to improve. You will find helpful information on employee versus management rights and related legal requirements in Chapter 9.

Managing and Leading Your Workforce

>> LO 9.1 Explain the value of trust and communication in employee relations.

Organizations need effective management and employee relations.[1] Managers and employees have to work together to accomplish sets of goals.[2] For this to happen successfully, people in organizations must be able to communicate with each other.[3] Open communications are needed for the organization to be successful,[4] and good managers are good communicators.[5] **Communication** is *the process of transmitting information and meaning.* This meaning can be transferred verbally, nonverbally, and/or in writing between a sender and receiver of the message. It's your job to make communications easier for the other person. **(SHRM C:10)**

Communications is the foundation of interpersonal skills[6] (Chapter 1), and it is a transferable skill.[7] HR professionals rated interpersonal-communication skills as the most valuable knowledge, skill, or ability for career success.[8] However, companies say that communication and other soft skills are difficult to find in job applicants.[9] Think about the jerks you have to deal with. Well, a major reason you think they are jerks is their poor communication skills. In this section, we begin with an overview of trust and communication and then provide details of effective listening skills when communicating. **(SHRM V:2)**

Trust and Communication

Whenever people communicate to accomplish a goal, the sender and receiver must establish trust to avoid creating barriers in the communication process.[10] We need others to trust us when we communicate with them. In any communication, receivers consider the trust they have in the senders, as well as the senders' credibility.[11] When receivers do not trust senders, or do not believe senders know what they are talking about, then the receivers are reluctant to accept the message.[12] If you think about creating trust, open communication is a necessary part of the equation of "doing what you say you will."

Trust is simply *faith in the character and actions of another.* In other words, it is a belief that another person will do what they say they will do—every time. There is evidence of a "crisis of trust" in business today.[13] So how do we get others to trust us? We must do what we say we will do consistently, over a period of time. **(SHRM A:2)**

Happiness and success in our personal and professional lives are based on our relationships. Good relationships are based on trust.[14] Do you have good relationships with people you can't trust? A survey revealed that 74% of engaged employees trust their manager, while only 14% don't trust their boss.[15] Would you go above and beyond what is expected (work harder) for a boss you don't trust?

Communication The process of transmitting information and meaning

Trust Faith in the character and actions of another

In turn, managers need to be able to trust employees.[16] Trust is absolutely necessary to strong management-labor relations, and research shows that companies that have the trust of their employees have stronger organizational commitment, "lower turnover [and] higher revenue, profitability, and shareholder returns."[17] As soon as trust goes, loyalty to the company goes with it.[18] **(SHRM A:4)**

Trust takes a while to create, but it only takes an instant to lose if we don't come through for the other person. So if we want to improve others' level of trust in us, we need to be open and honest.[19] If people catch you in a lie, they may never trust you again. To gain and maintain trust and credibility, always get the facts straight before you communicate, and then send clear, complete messages.[20] When receivers do not trust senders, or do not believe senders know what they are talking about, then the receivers are reluctant to accept the message.

Listening Skills

Ever hear the advice that we should listen more and talk less and you learn more when your mouth is closed and your ears are open? Serial entrepreneur **Norm Brodsky** put it bluntly: "Shut up and listen."[21]

If someone were to ask us if we are good listeners, most of us would say yes. However, unfortunately we are naturally poor listeners.[22] A recent survey found that the number one thing lacking in new college graduates is listening skills.[23] Find out how good a listener you are by completing Self-Assessment 9.1, and focus on developing your listening skills.

9.1 SELF-ASSESSMENT

LISTENING SKILLS

For each statement, select the response that best describes how often you actually behave in the way described. Place the letter A, U, F, O, or S on the line before each statement to indicate your response.

A = almost always   U = usually   F = frequently   O = occasionally   S = seldom

_____ 1. I like to listen to people talk. I encourage others to talk by showing interest, smiling, nodding, and so forth.

_____ 2. I pay closer attention to people who are similar to me than to people who are different from me.

_____ 3. I evaluate people's words and nonverbal communication ability as they talk.

_____ 4. I avoid distractions; if it's noisy, I suggest moving to a quiet spot.

_____ 5. When people interrupt me when I'm doing something, I put what I was doing out of my mind and give them my complete attention.

_____ 6. When people are talking, I allow them time to finish. I do not interrupt, anticipate what they are going to say, or jump to conclusions.

_____ 7. I tune out people who do not agree with my views.

_____ 8. While another person is talking or a professor is lecturing, my mind wanders to personal topics.

_____ 9. While another person is talking, I pay close attention to that person's nonverbal communication so I can fully understand what they are trying to communicate.

_____ 10. I tune out and pretend to understand when the topic is difficult for me to understand.

(Continued)

(Continued)

_____ 11. When another person is talking, I think about and prepare what I am going to say in reply.

_____ 12. When I think there is something missing from or contradictory in what someone says, I ask direct questions to get the person to explain the idea more fully.

_____ 13. When I don't understand something, I let the other person know I don't understand.

_____ 14. When listening to other people, I try to put myself in their position and see things from their perspective.

_____ 15. During conversations, I repeat back to the other person, in my own words, what the other person says; I do this to be sure I understand what has been said.

If people you talk to regularly answered these questions about you, would they have the same responses that you selected? To find out, have friends answer the questions using your name rather than "I." Then compare answers.

To determine your score, do the following:

For statements 1, 4, 5, 6, 9, 12, 13, 14, and 15, give yourself 5 points for each A, 4 for each U, 3 for each F, 2 for each O, and 1 for each S. Focus on doing these things to improve your listening skills.

For statements 2, 3, 7, 8, 10, and 11, give yourself 5 points for each S, 4 for each O, 3 for each F, 2 for each U, and 1 for each A. Focus on not doing these things to improve your listening skills.

Write your score for each letter response on the line next to the letter. Now add up your total number of points. Your score should be between 15 and 75. Note where your score falls on the continuum below. Generally, the higher your score, the better your listening skills. But regardless of your score, we can all improve.

Poor Listener												**Good Listener**
15	20	25	30	35	40	45	50	55	60	65	70	75

9.1 APPLYING THE CONCEPT
COMMUNICATIONS

Identify whether each strategy listed below is an effective or ineffective aid to communications.

a. Effective

b. Ineffective

_____ 1. When listening to instructions, if you don't understand something being said, you should not do or say anything until you have received the entire set of instructions.

_____ 2. You should repeat back what the other person said word-for-word.

_____ 3. After you finish giving instructions, you should ensure understanding by asking the person, "Do you have any questions?"

_____ 4. When giving instructions, you should tell the receiver your communication objective before giving the details of what is to be done to complete the task.

_____ 5. We should multitask while receiving messages face-to-face so that we can get more than one thing done at a time.

Job Satisfaction

>> **LO 9.2 Discuss the primary reason why measuring job satisfaction is so difficult.**

>> **LO 9.3 Identify the best tool for getting employees to tell the truth about their level of satisfaction.**

Remember that job satisfaction is important to us because it affects many other factors, including our dependent variables from Chapter 1—productivity, absenteeism, and turnover.[24] Almost half of all U.S. employees are unsatisfied with their jobs.[25] So we need to know how satisfied our workforce is at any point in time.[26] Also, job satisfaction can affect our satisfaction off the job, as we tend to take our jobs home with us.[27]

Measuring Job Satisfaction

Job satisfaction can be measured through an organizational development survey, but we have to remember that a survey is an indirect measurement. Since job satisfaction is an attitude, we can't directly see or measure it—we have to *ask* employees about their attitudes. **(SHRM C:30, Q:5, and C:5)**

Because of questions of trust between employees and management, it's always a good idea to ensure that any job satisfaction surveys are administered in a completely *anonymous* format. There are two common types of job satisfaction surveys or questionnaires, with a fairly new method that can be used for either of the two. Let's briefly review each of them.

The Faces Scale of Job Satisfaction Measurement

The first and simpler survey is called the "faces scale."[28] All the employee is asked to do is circle the face that most closely matches their overall satisfaction with their job. Exhibit 9.1 shows an example of the faces scale.

The Questionnaire Job Satisfaction Measurement

Take a look at Exhibit 9.2, which shows some of the questions from the Job Satisfaction Survey (JSS). There are many different surveys of this type. Some firms develop their own, but the JSS is one of only a few that have been shown to be valid and reliable.[29]

Pulse Surveys

This short survey method—sometimes as short as a single question—is now being used by many companies.[30] We can use a pulse survey to gain either a general picture of employee satisfaction or to spot problem areas, so it can supplement either the faces scale or a job satisfaction survey. Because millennial and post-millennial employees are used to continual feedback, pulse surveys are catching on with companies that need to routinely engage these employees.

EXHIBIT 9.1 ● Female Faces Scale

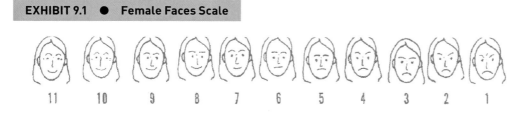

Source: R. B. Dunham, J. B. Herman, "Development of a female faces scale for measuring job satisfaction" by Randall B. Dunham and Jeanne B. Herman, *Journal of Applied Psychology*, 60(5), October 1975, 629–631.

EXHIBIT 9.2 ● Sample of Job Satisfaction Survey (JSS) Questions[31]

	Disagree very much	Disagree moderately	Disagree slightly	Agree slightly	Agree moderately	Agree very much
People get ahead as fast here as they do in other places.	1	2	3	4	5	6
My supervisor shows too little interest in the feelings of subordinates.	1	2	3	4	5	6
The benefits package we have is equitable.	1	2	3	4	5	6
There are few rewards for those who work here.	1	2	3	4	5	6
I have too much to do at work.	1	2	3	4	5	6
I enjoy my coworkers.	1	2	3	4	5	6

P. Spector, "Measurement of human service staff satisfaction: Development of the Job Satisfaction Survey", *American Journal of Community Psychology* (1985) Vol. 13, No. 6, pp. 693–713.

Regardless of analytical method, job satisfaction affects many other factors within an organization. Employers who keep tabs on their employees' levels of job satisfaction may see higher rates of productivity and engagement and lower rates of absenteeism and turnover.

Determinants of Job Satisfaction

Although compensation (pay and benefits) is important to job satisfaction, research historically has not strongly supported the idea that pay is the primary determinant of job satisfaction or that people in high-paying jobs are more satisfied than those in low-paying jobs.[32] According to recent studies, the top reasons for job *dissatisfaction* are that employees don't like their supervisor, they feel powerless, they don't have any say in their work, and they don't feel like they get recognition for their work.[33] Millennials will not work for a bad boss.[34]

Seven major determinants of job satisfaction are presented in Self-Assessment 9.2: Job Satisfaction. Complete it to find out what is important to you and your own level of job satisfaction. You *can* have an overall high level of job satisfaction and still not like some aspects of your job; this is common.

Oftentimes, it's the small hassles that throw us off and cause us to develop negative attitudes.[35] And complaining about things you can't change anyway only leads to more dissatisfaction. So don't focus on the negative part of your job. Let it go and focus on the positive, optimistic side of what you like about your job to maintain your job and life satisfaction.

9.2 SELF-ASSESSMENT

JOB SATISFACTION

Select a present or past job. Identify your level of satisfaction with that job by placing a check at the appropriate position on the continuum for each determinant of job satisfaction.

1. Personality

I have positive self-esteem.	6	5	4	3	2	1	I have negative self-esteem.

2. Work Itself

I enjoy doing the tasks I perform.	6	5	4	3	2	1	I do *not* enjoy doing the tasks I perform.

3. Compensation

I am fairly compensated (with pay and benefits).	6	5	4	3	2	1	I am *not* fairly compensated (with pay and benefits).

4. Growth and Upward Mobility

I have the opportunity to learn new things and get promoted to better jobs.	6	5	4	3	2	1	I have *no* opportunity to learn new things and get promoted to better jobs.

5. Coworkers

I like and enjoy working with my coworkers.	6	5	4	3	2	1	I do *not* like and enjoy working with my coworkers.

6. Management

I believe that my boss and managers are doing a good job.	6	5	4	3	2	1	I do *not* believe that my boss and managers are doing a good job.

7. Communication

We have open and honest communication.	6	5	4	3	2	1	We do *not* have open and honest communication.

Overall Job Satisfaction

When determining your overall job satisfaction, you cannot simply add up a score based on the above seven determinants because they are most likely of different importance to you. Rank your top three factors below:

1. _____

2. _____

3. _____

Now, think about your job and the above factors, and rate your overall satisfaction with your job below:

I am satisfied with my job (high level of job satisfaction).	6	5	4	3	2	1	I am dissatisfied with my job (low level of job satisfaction).

9.2 APPLYING THE CONCEPT
JOB SATISFACTION

Correctly match each statement with its determinant of job satisfaction, writing the letter corresponding to each determinant before the statement associated with it.

a. Personality

b. Work itself

c. Compensation

d. Growth

e. Coworkers

f. Management

g. Communications

_____ 6. There is a job opening in the metal fusion shop, and I am going to apply for the position.

_____ 7. I really enjoy fixing cars to help people get around.

_____ 8. I'm mad at my manager because he didn't give me the good performance review that I deserved.

_____ 9. Of course I can do that task for you.

_____ 10. The thing I like best about my job is the people I work with.

Commonly Accepted Employee Rights

>> LO 9.4 Identify the commonly accepted individual rights in the workplace.

Providing employees with reasonable rights in the organization helps them to remain satisfied with their work. In this section, we discuss six common employee rights; see Exhibit 9.3 for a list.[36] Let's break down each of the six rights individually in separate sections.

Right of Free Consent

Individuals in a modern organization have the *right of free consent,* which is the right of the individual to know what they're being asked to do and the consequences of that action for the individual or others. The organization's duty is to ensure that the individual *voluntarily agrees* to do a particular job or task for the organization, making them fully aware of everything involved.

Organizations have a duty to provide their employees a right to life and safety on the job.

Right to Due Process

We have due process so that employees are not punished arbitrarily.[37] If the organization contemplates a disciplinary action, the employee has a right to know what they are accused of, to know the evidence or proof thereof, and to tell their side of what happened. We will review due process and the seven tests for Just Cause shortly, but due process is basically the concept of providing fair and reasonable disciplinary actions as consequences of an employee's behavior.

Right to Life and Safety

Every employee within the organization has a right to be protected from harm, to the best of the organization's ability. In 1948, the United Nations declared that every individual has a right to life, liberty, and security of person.[38] Security of person basically means personal safety. So the organization has a general duty to see that every employee is protected from harm when working within the organization because the individual has a right to life and safety.

Right of Freedom of Conscience (Limited)

Employees generally should not be asked to do something that violates their personal values and beliefs, *as long as these beliefs generally reflect commonly accepted societal norms.* A person's conscience determines what that person considers to be right and wrong. The organization has a general duty to avoid forcing an individual to do something that they consider to be wrong, either morally or ethically, and the individual has a right to avoid doing things within the organization that would violate their personal values and beliefs.

Right to Privacy (Limited)

This right protects people from unreasonable or unwarranted intrusions into their personal affairs. This general right to privacy would include the employee's right to have their personnel files, other employee records, and/or private areas of their workplace (such as a personal locker) kept private, *to an extent.* However, if the employer feels there might be a hazard to others, in keeping with all employees' right to life and safety, a locker or other personal space (e.g., a desk) could be searched. **(SHRM C:18 and D:30)**

Right to Free Speech (Limited)

The First Amendment to the U.S. Constitution guarantees the right to freedom of speech.[39] What most people don't understand, though, is that the First Amendment only applies to the government not being allowed to control free speech. In the workplace, individual freedom of speech is limited, based on many years of case law.

Within the organization itself, individuals should be free to express concerns or discontent with organizational policies without fear of harm. However, many types of speech have no protection. If the individual employee exercises the right to freedom of speech, and if, in the course of that action, the employee harms the organization or other employees, then the organization has a right to discipline the employee based on the harm that the employee did to others.

EXHIBIT 9.3 ● Employee Rights

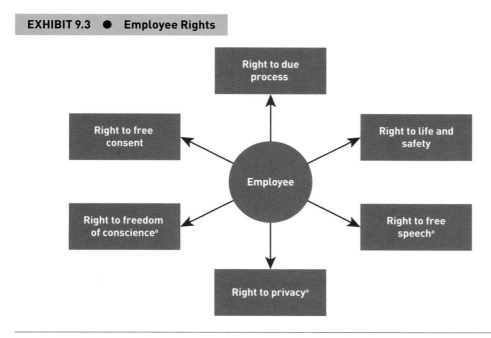

[a]Note that these three rights have limitations.

9.3 APPLYING THE CONCEPT
EMPLOYEE RIGHTS

Review the list of rights below and write the letter corresponding to each right before the statement involving that right.

a. Free consent

b. Due process

c. Life and safety

d. Freedom of conscience

e. Privacy

f. Free speech

_____ 11. The HR manager made me sign this form before I could start the job, stating that she had told me about the possible side effects from the lead paint removal.

_____ 12. I enjoy writing negative comments online about my boss and company.

_____ 13. I'm going to teach you how to use the rifle. Rule number one is to always make sure this lever is down so you don't fire the gun by accident.

_____ 14. You can't discipline me for this minor safety violation. I'm going to the labor union to stop you from doing it.

_____ 15. Let me keep working in security. I don't want to work in the bar, even though it pays better, because drinking is against my religion.

_____ 16. Get out of my locker now. You have no right to search it without my permission.

Management Rights

>> **LO 9.5 List some rights that management has in modern organizations.**

Organizations, like individuals, have rights within the larger society. Organizational rights tend to be based on the necessity for the organization to protect itself and its employees from persons that might do them harm, whether intentionally or unintentionally. In cases where such harm may occur, the organization has the right to limit individual employee rights. Let's briefly discuss two additional significant management rights.

Codes of Conduct

Managers of organizations have a right to create and require compliance with a code of employee conduct. The code of conduct is the organization's mechanism for identifying the ethics and values of the firm, and it serves as a guide to individual action.[40] Employees are more unethical when they believe they will not get caught and punished.[41] A code of conduct gives an employee a practical tool for determining whether or not an action that they are contemplating is within the acceptable boundaries of conduct within their organization.

Employment-at-Will

Employment-at-will Concept allowing the company or the worker to break the work relationship at any point in time, with or without any particular reason, as long as in doing so, no law is violated.

Currently, under common law, "employment relationships are presumed to be 'at will' in all US states except Montana."[42] The legal concept of **employment-at-will** *allows the company or the worker to break the work relationship at any point in time, with or without any particular reason, as long as in doing so, no law is violated.* This means the employer does not have to have *cause* (reasons) to terminate an employment relationship with an individual worker. **(SHRM D:33 and N:10-b)**

However, employment-at-will is in reality a fairly weak law because courts in many jurisdictions in the United States have for years ruled that employment-at-will is limited. Courts in various jurisdictions have specifically noted three standard *exceptions* to employment-at-will.[43]

Public policy exceptions include such things as being terminated for filing a legitimate worker's compensation claim, refusing to campaign for a particular political candidate just because your boss likes the candidate, or refusing to violate a professional code of ethics. Such exceptions could also be based on the organization violating the law. For instance, if the company terminated a pregnant woman because she was pregnant (a violation of the Pregnancy Discrimination Act), but claimed that the termination was at will, the termination would violate the public policy exception.

Evidence of an *implied contract* between the employee and the employer is another exception. For instance, if the company were to note in its employee handbook that "our organization values hard work, and many of our employees who perform well have been with us for many years," that *might* be considered an implied contract stating, "If you work hard, we will continue to employ you." This implication of a contract could negate the employment-at-will rights of the employer.

A *lack of good faith and fair dealing* is the third exception. If the employer does something that will benefit them but will significantly harm the individual employee, that action would create a lack of good faith and fair dealing. For instance, we might release a 38-year-old employee citing employment-at-will shortly before they become eligible for a company-sponsored retirement plan in order to hire a younger (and cheaper) employee in the same position and thus not have to pay the retirement benefits. This would be lack of good faith and fair dealing, even though it would not be a violation of age discrimination laws.

Coaching, Counseling, and Discipline

>> **LO 9.6 Contrast the coaching, counseling, and discipline processes used in organizations.**

Managing people is important,[44] and as a manager, it's your job to have employees meet standards[45] and follow the rules.[46] Your most valuable resource is your employees, and you want them to meet their full potential,[47] so how you manage people will determine your success.[48] So this section discusses how to coach, counsel, and discipline employees to maintain and increase their performance, and if necessary, how to terminate employment.

Coaching

As discussed in Chapter 8, managers need to continually coach because engaging employees leads to high performance,[49] and organizations with strong coaching cultures have higher engagement and performance.[50] **Coaching** is *the process of giving motivational feedback to maintain and improve performance.* Feedback is the central part of coaching,[51] and it should be immediate, continuous, and motivational.[52] Feedback is intended to praise progress and celebrate success, to redirect inappropriate behavior, and to guide employees on how to improve.[53] **(SHRM M:3-e, A:3, and P:6-b)**

Coaching The process of giving motivational feedback to maintain and improve performance

The Coaching Model

Managers need to play the role of coach,[54] because coaching improves performance.[55] However, ask managers what they tend to put off doing, and they'll likely say that they put off advising weak employees that they must improve their performance. Procrastinating managers often hope the employees will turn around on their own, only to find—often too late—that the situation just continues to get worse. Don't cover for them or do their work; you need to confront and coach them to improve.[56] Part of the problem is that managers don't know how to coach or are not good at coaching.[57] Model 9.1 provides a simple four-step coaching model you can use to improve performance.[58]

Management Counseling

When you are coaching, you are fine-tuning performance. But when you are counseling and disciplining, you are dealing with an employee who is not performing to organizational standards.

MODEL 9.1 ● Coaching Model

| 1. Describe current performance. | → | 2. Describe desired performance. | → | 3. Get a commitment to change. | → | 4. Follow up. |

The number of employees with depression and anxiety disorders and alcohol and substance use is on the rise; this increase costs more than $1 trillion in lost productivity to the global economy annually.[59] So organizations realize the need to help employees with problems.[60]

When most people hear the term *counseling,* they think of psychological counseling or psychotherapy. That type of sophisticated help should not be attempted by a noncounseling professional such as a manager.[61] Instead, **management counseling** is *the process of giving employees feedback (so they realize that a problem is affecting their job performance) and referring employees with problems that cannot be managed within the work structure to the organization's employee assistance program.*

Problem Employees

Problem employees have a negative effect on performance.[62] Good human resource management skills can help you avoid hiring problem employees,[63] but even so, you will most likely have to confront problem employees as a manager.[64] Problem employees do poor-quality work, they don't get along with coworkers, they display negative attitudes, and they frequently come in late or don't show up for work.[65]

HR and managers' first obligation is to the organization's performance rather than to individual employees.[66] Not taking action with problem employees—because you feel uncomfortable confronting them, because you feel sorry for them, or because you like them—does not help you or the employee.[67] Not only do problem employees negatively affect their own productivity, but they also cause more work for managers and other employees.[68] Problem employees also lower morale, as others resent them for not pulling their own weight. Thus, it is critical to take quick action with problem employees.[69]

Disciplining

You should try coaching, then counseling, in dealing with a problem employee. However, if an employee is unwilling or unable to change or a rule has been broken,[70] discipline is necessary.[71] **Discipline** is *corrective action designed to get employees to meet standards and the code of conduct.* The major objective of coaching, counseling, and disciplining is to change behavior.[72] Secondary objectives may be to let employees know that action will be taken when standing plans or performance requirements are not met, and to maintain authority when challenged. **(SHRM M:3-b and C:37)**

But how do we know as managers that we are being fair in applying discipline? Let's take a look at one mechanism for determining whether or not to discipline an errant employee and what level of discipline is appropriate—Just Cause. **(SHRM C:20)**

Just Cause

Just Cause is *a set of standard tests for fairness in disciplinary actions; these tests were originally utilized in union grievance arbitrations.* However, many other companies have adopted the tests for Just Cause in their own nonunion disciplinary processes to try to ensure fairness.

The seven tests for Just Cause are as follows:

1. Did the company give the employee forewarning or foreknowledge of the possible or probable disciplinary consequences of the employee's conduct?

   With this test, we basically want to determine whether or not the employee was given any knowledge beforehand that the action was prohibited.

Management counseling The process of giving employees feedback (so they realize that a problem is affecting their job performance) and referring employees with problems that cannot be managed within the work structure to the organization's employee assistance program

Discipline Corrective action designed to get employees to meet standards and the code of conduct

Just Cause A set of standard tests for fairness in disciplinary actions; these tests were originally utilized in union grievance arbitrations

2. Was the company's rule or managerial order reasonably related to (a) the orderly, efficient, and safe operation of the company's business and (b) the performance that the company might properly expect of the employee?

    Here we want to find out whether the rule was reasonable. We also look at whether or not the employee should be expected to act in a certain manner in order to follow the rule or order.

3. Did the company, before administering discipline to an employee, make an effort to discover whether the employee did in fact violate or disobey a rule or order of management?

©iStockphoto.com/shironosov

▲
Employers may use a set of standard tests—a mechanism called Just Cause—for providing disciplinary action.

    Test 3 deals with investigation of the alleged infraction. If, upon investigating, the supervisor finds that there is reasonable evidence the individual did violate the rules, then we've passed the third test.

4. Was the company's investigation conducted fairly and objectively?

    Are we utilizing facts, figures, and knowledge of the events (the OUCH test), or is the supervisor basing the investigation on some emotional reaction to the supposed infraction?

5. Upon investigation, was there substantial evidence or proof that the employee was guilty as charged?

    Substantial evidence (some companies refer to the legal term "clear and convincing evidence" which means "substantially more likely to be true than untrue")[73] is a large body of circumstantial information showing that the individual probably committed the offense. In a disciplinary action, we don't have to meet court standards of proof of guilt. If we have *proof,* then we meet this test, but if we have substantial evidence, we *still* meet the requirements of Test 5.

6. Has the company applied its rules, orders, and penalties evenhandedly and without discrimination to all employees?

    Test 6 tries to identify whether or not the rule is applied in an equitable manner. If the company punishes one person for an infraction with a written reprimand and punishes another person for the same infraction with a disciplinary discharge, then the company may not have been evenhanded in its disciplinary action. Does this mean that we have to punish every person in the exact same way for the exact same infraction? The answer is no—and that is where we get into Test 7.

7. Was the degree of discipline administered by the company in a particular case reasonably related to (a) the seriousness of the employee's proven offense and (b) the record of the employee's service with the company?

    Test 7 is where we are allowed to provide a different punishment to different people *based on past history.* So if we have two employees who have committed the same infraction and one of the employees has never been in trouble while the other has repeatedly committed the same infraction, then we have the flexibility to provide a different punishment for the two different offenders. **(SHRM C:26)**

Guidelines for Effective Discipline

Exhibit 9.4 lists eight guidelines for effective discipline.

EXHIBIT 9.4 ●	Guidelines for Effective Discipline

A.   Clearly communicate the standards and code of conduct to all employees.

B.   Be sure that the punishment fits the crime.

C.   Follow the standing plans yourself.

D.   Take consistent, impartial action when the rules are broken.

E.   Discipline immediately, but stay calm and get all the necessary facts before you discipline.

F.   Discipline in private.

G.   Document discipline.

H.   When the discipline is over, resume normal relations with the employee.

Progressive Discipline

Progressive discipline A process in which the employer provides the employee with opportunities to correct poor behavior before terminating them

If discipline is deemed necessary after going through the Just Cause standards, what type of discipline is warranted? Many organizations have a series of progressively more severe disciplinary actions.[74] **Progressive discipline** is *a process in which the employer provides the employee with opportunities to correct poor behavior before terminating them.* It is typically only used in cases of minor behavioral infractions such as arriving late to work or insubordination with a superior.[75] Punishment usually varies with the severity of the violation.[76]

The progressive disciplinary steps are (1) informal coaching talk, (2) oral warning, (3) written warning, (4) suspension, and (5) dismissal. In some *limited* cases, we may add a sixth option between suspension and dismissal. Be sure to document each step.[77] Let's briefly discuss each step in progressive discipline.

Step 1: Informal Coaching Talk. As we noted, the first step in progressive discipline is an *informal coaching talk.* In an informal talk, the supervisor may see an employee coming in late to work and just ask them what is going on and why they are late. Typically, the manager won't even write down a recording of such conversations for their own use, although they can do so in the critical incident file (Chapter 8). They're just in an information gathering and recognition mode at this point, and they hope to avoid any further disciplinary problems.

Step 2: Oral Warning. In the second step, the supervisor formally tells the employee that their behavior is currently unacceptable and also tells them what they need to do to correct the behavior. In this situation, even though the supervisor does not write a report for the individual to sign, they will keep a formal record in their own files of this conversation. The oral warning is the first of our formal methods of disciplining an employee.

Step 3: Written Warning. The third step is a *written warning.* In this situation, the supervisor writes up the facts of the situation. They identify the unacceptable behavior for the individual and identify ways to correct the behavior. The supervisor then speaks with the employee using the written document to assist the employee in correcting their actions. Typically here, we ask the employee to sign the written warning, acknowledging that their actions are under review and not currently acceptable. This signed paper (documentation) is then put into the employee's permanent file.[78]

Step 4: Disciplinary Suspension. As a fourth step, we may move on to a *disciplinary suspension* of the employee for a period of from one day to typically a maximum of one week. Most companies use an unpaid suspension, but some companies have experimented with a paid day off as time for the employee to figure out whether or not they wish to continue working for the organization. There is *some* evidence that these paid suspensions work, although the conclusions are slightly mixed.

Other Options Before Termination. Next, we have a couple of limited options we noted at the top of this section—options that would typically not be used but might be valuable in certain cases.

We can sometimes *demote* an individual to a lower position in the organization. In some cases, this may be valuable because the employee may be overwhelmed at the higher-level position. In general, however, demotion creates even more job dissatisfaction within the individual employee, and we may see their performance deteriorate even further.

Alternatively, we may choose in some cases to *transfer* an employee from one part of the organization to another. The only time you should use a transfer as a progressive discipline measure is when you know there is a personality conflict between the employee and another employee or their supervisor. Transfers should never be used simply to get rid of a problem employee from your department or division. Instead, you should correct the problem behavior. **(SHRM C:14 and Q:4)**

Step 5: Termination. The last resort is *discharge*. If an employee's behavior does not improve over time as a result of verbal and written warnings, suspensions, demotions, or a transfer, we may be forced to let the employee go. As a manager, if an employee is not producing, you have the right and an obligation to fire them.[79] If we documented following the progressive discipline process, we will have sufficient evidence to limit the employee's opportunity to bring an unlawful termination lawsuit against us.[80]

9.1 ETHICAL DILEMMA: WHAT WOULD YOU DO?
DISCIPLINING ETHICAL BEHAVIOR

Unfortunately, some managers are unfair/unethical in coaching, counseling, and/or disciplining employees. Also, some employees are rewarded for being unethical, while others are disciplined for being ethical. For example, some auto repair shops pay a commission for work done, so mechanics are paid more if they get customers to buy parts and services they don't need. Mechanics who have a below-average number of repairs may be considered underachievers and may be pressured, through discipline, to perform unneeded repair work. Similarly, those in the medical field may push unnecessary tests or even treatments.

1. Has a manager ever been unfair/unethical in coaching, counseling, or disciplining where you work or have worked? If so, explain the situation.

2. Have you ever been in or known of a situation in which people were rewarded for being unethical and disciplined for being ethical? If so, describe the situation.

3. Is it ethical and socially responsible for firms to establish controls that reward unethical behavior and discipline ethical behavior to make more money?

4. Has anyone you know of been unfairly/unethically terminated? If so, explain the situation.

The Discipline Model

Model 9.2 is a simple five-step discipline model that works very well. You should follow the steps of the discipline model each time you must discipline an employee.

MODEL 9.2 ● The Discipline Model

| 1. Refer to past feedback. | → | 2. Ask why the undesired behavior was used. | → | 3. Give the discipline. | → | 4. Get a commitment to change and develop a plan. | → | 5. Summarize and state the follow-up. |

Causes of Immediate Termination

Termination, or dismissal, is the most serious form of disciplinary action. Let's quickly look at some of the offenses that might be cause for dismissal immediately upon completion of an investigation of the facts.

Organizations are generally allowed to set up their own rules, listing violations that are grounds for immediate termination without progressive discipline. For example, many firms list stealing money or other assets from the organization as cause for immediate dismissal.

Two of the more common situations in which we might immediately dismiss employees would be in cases of gross negligence or serious misconduct. **Gross negligence** is *a serious failure to exercise care in the work environment*. It is a reckless disregard for circumstances that could cause harm to others—a lack of concern for safety or life.[81] So, if in the course of work, someone failed to exercise care in a way that would be likely to harm or kill others, then they would be guilty of gross negligence.

Serious misconduct is a little different from gross negligence. Where negligence is a failure to take care, *misconduct* is intentionally doing something that is likely to harm someone or something else. So, **serious misconduct** is *intentional behavior that has the potential to cause great harm to another or to the company*. An example of serious misconduct is bringing a weapon to work.[82] These types of incidents could be cause for termination of the individual responsible. Of course, termination would happen only after an investigation to ensure that they actually did what they are accused of.

Gross negligence A serious failure to exercise care in the work environment

Serious misconduct Intentional behavior that has the potential to cause great harm to another or to the company

9.4 APPLYING THE CONCEPT
GUIDELINES FOR EFFECTIVE DISCIPLINE

Identify which guideline is being followed—or not being followed—in the following statements. Use the guidelines in Exhibit 9.4 as the answers, writing the letter of the guideline (A–H) on the line before the statement involving it.

_____ 17. "Are you kidding me? Can you really fire me just for being late for work once?"

_____ 18. "I didn't know that I'm not supposed to make a personal call while I'm working. Can't you let it go this one time?"

_____ 19. "Some days, my boss comments about my being late, but other days, she doesn't say anything about it."

_____ 20. "Let's get back to the way things were before I had to discipline you, OK?"

_____ 21. "Let's go to my office so that we can discuss your rule violation now."

_____ 22. "I missed it. Why was the boss yelling at Rita?"

_____ 23. "The boss comes back from break late all the time and nothing happens to him; so why do I get in trouble for being late?"

_____ 24. "When I come to work late, the manager reprimands me. But when Latoya is late, nothing is ever said."

_____ 25. "The boss gave me a written warning for being late for work and placed it in my permanent record file."

Legal Issues in Labor Relations

>> LO 9.7 Describe the major labor relations laws in
the United States, including the main reasons why we have each law.

As with most management processes, a number of laws and regulations affect labor relations. In this section, we will introduce you to the major labor laws in the United States. To successfully do their job, *all* managers need to understand the constraints set by these labor laws. See Exhibit 9.5 for a brief overview of the four major labor laws that we will discuss. **(SHRM C:50)**

The Railway Labor Act (RLA) of 1926

The Railway Labor Act was originally enacted to significantly limit the potential for railroad strikes to affect interstate commerce by hindering the general public's ability to procure goods and services. Railroads were the primary means of moving the U.S. mail as well as goods from one state to another in 1926. Airlines were added to the act in 1936 because much of the U.S. mail was beginning to be delivered with the help of airlines, and an airline disruption would affect the delivery of the mail. **(SHRM D:20 and C:43)**

The act also provides protection for workers' right to join a union,[83] and it requires that in so-called *major disputes*—disputes involving rates of pay, work rules, or working conditions— management and labor must participate in a negotiation and mediation process before a labor strike may be called. A **strike** is *a collective work stoppage by members of a union that is intended to put pressure on an employer.* This negotiation process is designed to force the two parties to come to an agreement without resorting to a strike, in almost all cases.

Strike A collective work stoppage by members of a union that is intended to put pressure on an employer

The National Labor Relations Act (NLRA) of 1935 (Wagner Act)

The National Labor Relations Act (NLRA; frequently called the Wagner Act) was the first major modern law to deal with the legal issue of workers' employment rights in the general workforce (workers who were not covered by special laws such as the Railway Labor Act) in the United States. In part, the act states, **(SHRM C:34, D:17, D:31, and C:44)**

> *Employees shall have the right to self-organization, to form, join, or assist labor organizations, to bargain collectively through representatives of their own choosing, and to engage in other concerted activities for the purpose of collective bargaining or other mutual aid or protection.*[84]

EXHIBIT 9.5 ● Major Labor Laws

The Railway Labor Act of 1926 (RLA)	The act was passed to significantly limit the potential for railroad strikes to affect interstate commerce; it was later expanded to include airlines.
	In an amendment to the law, the National Mediation Board (NMB) was established to mediate between management and labor to help them come to agreement.
National Labor Relations Act of 1935 (NLRA—Wagner Act)	The act gave employees the right to unionize without fear of prosecution, as it listed unfair employer practices.
	The law also established the National Labor Relations Board (NLRB) to enforce the provisions of the act and conduct elections to determine whether employees will unionize and who will be their representative in collective bargaining.
Labor Management Relations Act of 1947 (LMRA—Taft-Hartley Act)	The act was passed to offset some of the imbalance of power given to labor by previous laws. It amended the Wagner Act (NLRA) to include a list of unfair practices by unions.
Worker Adjustment and Retraining Notification Act of 1988 (WARN)	The act was passed to give employees 60 days' advance notice in cases of plant closings or large-scale layoffs.

The NLRA was considered to be very one-sided by employers when it originally passed because it identified "unfair labor practices" (prohibitions) for employers but identified no unfair labor practices for employee unions or labor organizations.

Some *employer* unfair labor practices identified by the NLRA include the following:

1. Interfering with, restraining, or coercing employees in the exercise of the rights guaranteed in the NLRA

2. Dominating or interfering with the formation or administration of any labor organization, or contributing financial or other support to it

3. Discriminating in regard to hiring or tenure of employment or any term or condition of employment to encourage or discourage membership in any labor organization (with some specific exceptions)

4. Discharging or otherwise discriminating (retaliating) against an employee because that person has filed charges or given testimony under the NLRA

5. Refusing to bargain collectively with the legitimate representatives of employees

The NLRA is enforced by the **National Labor Relations Board (NLRB)**, which was created by the act. The NLRB has five primary functions: conducting elections, investigating charges, facilitating settlements, deciding cases, and enforcing orders.[85] For more information about the NLRB, visit its website at http://www.nlrb.gov.

The Labor Management Relations Act (LMRA) of 1947 (Taft-Hartley Act)

The Labor Management Relations Act (LMRA), also called the Taft-Hartley Act, was passed as an amendment to the NLRA. Whereas the NLRA identified a series of employee rights and employer unfair labor practices, the LMRA attempted to rebalance employer and employee rights by identifying unfair labor practices on the part of unions and labor organizations. Unfair *union/labor* practices include the following:[86] **(SHRM D:14)**

1. Restraining or coercing (a) employees in the exercise of their rights guaranteed in the NLRA or (b) an employer in the selection of his representatives for negotiations

2. Causing or attempting to cause an employer to discriminate against an employee who is not a union member

3. Refusing to bargain collectively with an employer, provided the union is the elected representative of its employees

4. Requiring dues that the NLRB finds excessive or discriminatory

5. Picketing or threatening to picket an employer for the purpose of forcing the employer to bargain with the labor organization, unless the labor organization is certified as the employees' representative

LMRA also outlawed several types of union actions that had been used since passage of the Wagner Act. These included *jurisdictional strikes*,[87] which union members used to push companies to provide them with certain types of jobs; *wildcat strikes*,[88] where individual union members participated in strikes that were not authorized by the union; *secondary boycotts*,[89] in which a union participating in a strike against a company would pressure other unions to boycott organizations that did business with that company; and *closed shops*, which provided for "the hiring and employment of union members only."[90] In addition, the law limited *union shops*,[91] where every employee was required to become a member of the union within a certain time period. Finally, the LMRA provided that supervisors had no right to be protected if they chose to participate in union activities, so if a supervisor participated in unionizing activities, the company was allowed to terminate them. **(SHRM C:6, C:41, and C:48)**

In addition to the limitations on unions and labor, the LMRA created mechanisms for decertifying unions through an election process, and it allowed the states to pass a right-to-work law. *Right-to-work laws* work directly against union shops by declaring that every employee in a company has a right to work, even if they choose not to join the union representing the shop.[92] Union shops cannot be set up in states that pass right-to-work laws.

The Worker Adjustment and Retraining Notification Act of 1988 (WARN Act)

The Worker Adjustment and Retraining Notification Act was designed to protect workers in the case of a plant closing or large-scale layoff. The act requires management to give employees notice of a plant closing or layoff at least 60 days ahead of time if more than 50 people will be laid off and if there are more than 100 full-time employees at the workplace. All workers are entitled to notice under WARN, including hourly and salaried workers as well as managers.[93] **(SHRM D:24)**

The penalty provision of the act says that an employer who fails to provide notice "is liable to each aggrieved employee for an amount including back pay and benefits for the period of violation, up to 60 days," plus a fine of up to $500 per day of violation.[94] So, if we lay people off with less than 60 days' notice (e.g., to avoid the possibility of sabotage), we have to pay them as if they were still employed for the 60 days anyway.

9.5 APPLYING THE CONCEPT
LABOR LAWS

Identify each statement by the law it is discussing, writing the letter corresponding to each law before the statement discussing it.

a. RLA of 1926

b. NLRA of 1935

c. LMRA of 1947

d. WARN of 1988

_____ 26. Featherbedding is illegal. The union can't put in the contract that we have to pay for services that we really don't get. We should call in the National Labor Relations Board to investigate.

_____ 27. I think we should call in the National Labor Relations Board to investigate the action that management is taking to stop us from unionizing.

_____ 28. The company can't give us a notice today, with our paychecks, that our factory is being closed next week and all 500 of us will be without a job.

_____ 29. As pilots, we shouldn't go on strike. Let's get the National Mediation Board to help us.

Unions and Labor Rights

>> **LO 9.8 Discuss what management cannot do in attempting to limit union organizing efforts.**

Workers in the United States enjoy more rights and freedoms than do workers in many other countries, including the right to form and become members of unions. A labor union is simply a group of workers in an organization who come together to collectively bargain with their employer for their common welfare—issues like improved safety, fair wages, reasonable working conditions, and other benefits. Let's take a brief look at unions and their impact on organizations.

Union Organizing

Around 12% of the total U.S. workforce is unionized.[95] More than one third of government employees are unionized, whereas only 6.5% of the private sector is unionized.[96] Union membership has been steadily declining in the United States for several decades.[97] A major reason for the decline in union membership is that companies are working together with employees to treat them well to attract and retain top talent, which leads to profits.[98] **(SHRM C:46 and C:47)**

The NLRA is the federal law governing union organizing and elections,[99] and the NLRB is an independent federal agency that protects the rights of private sector employees to join together, with or without a union, to improve their wages and working conditions.[100] If employees decide they want to join a union, they will go through a union organizing process (see Exhibit 9.6). In this process, employees will select a union to represent them and then ask for a vote of employees concerning whether or not they desire to be represented by the union. The primary method for union elections is a secret ballot.

EXHIBIT 9.6 ● The Union Organizing Process

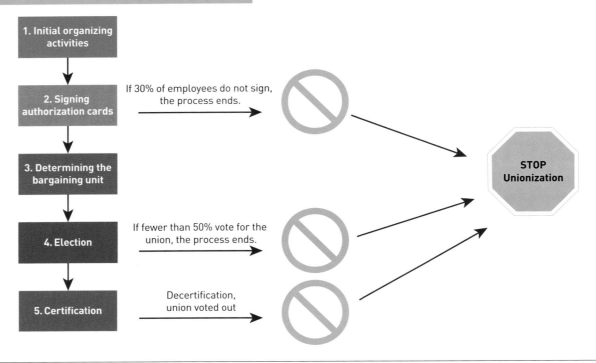

An election is authorized if at least 30% of the employees in an appropriate bargaining unit sign authorization cards allowing a union to negotiate employment terms and conditions on the employees' behalf. The union then presents these cards to the NLRB as an election petition. Once this happens, the NLRB sharply limits what management can say and do without being accused of an unfair labor practice.

The NO TIPS Rules

What practices are prohibited after providing the authorization cards to the NLRB? A lot of organizations use the acronym NO TIPS to identify what the company and its managers can't do. NO TIPS stands for no *t*hreats, no *i*nterrogations, no *p*romises, and no *s*pying.[101] There is also one final limitation on actions by the organization and its managers in the last 24 hours prior to the union authorization election. Management is prohibited from holding group meetings with employees who will vote on unionization during this 24-hour period.

Once the election is held, a simple majority of those voting determines the success or failure of the campaign. In other words, if only 51 workers in a bargaining unit of 200 vote, and if 26 of the voters desire union membership, then membership in the union will be authorized.

Labor Relations and Collective Bargaining

Labor relations The interactions between management and unionized employees

Collective bargaining The negotiation process resulting in a contract between union employees and management that covers employment conditions

Labor relations are *the interactions between management and unionized employees.* Because there are many more nonunionized than unionized employees, most organizations don't have to manage labor relations as part of their human resources systems.[102] **(SHRM C:28, C:13, C:49, D:32)**

Collective bargaining is *the negotiation process resulting in a contract between union employees and management that covers employment conditions.* The most common employment conditions covered in contracts are compensation, hours, and working conditions, but a contract can include almost any condition that both sides agree to. Job security continues to be a major bargaining issue for many unions.[103] **(SHRM C:8 and C:9)**

Grievances

A **grievance** is *a formal complaint concerning pay, working conditions, or violation of some other factor in a collective bargaining agreement.* Grievance procedures help protect employees against arbitrary decisions by management regarding discipline, discharge, promotions, or benefits. They also provide labor unions and employers with a formal process for enforcing the provisions of their contracts. The "tests for Just Cause" mentioned earlier are used if a grievance involves questions of fairness in disciplinary actions. **(SHRM C:22)**

Today, employee relations often focus on limiting company liability. So, a growing trend in nonunionized private sector firms is to force employees into mandatory arbitration agreements to settle complaints. This contractual agreement, which is speedier and cheaper than litigation, prohibits employees from filing lawsuits in public court, and some agreements prohibit employees from even talking to anyone (especially the press) about their grievance.[104]

As a manager, when you have an employee come to you with a complaint, you can follow the steps in Model 9.3: The Employee Complaint Resolution Model. Note that in Step 2, you don't have to agree and implement the recommendation, and in Steps 4 and 5, unless the employee is totally wrong or in violation of company policy in the complaint, you should try to resolve the complaint.

> **Grievance** A formal complaint concerning pay, working conditions, or violation of some other factor in a collective bargaining agreement

Decertification Elections

Decertification elections can be held to remove a union as the representative of company workers. This cannot happen within a year of a previous failed attempt at decertification, and management of the company cannot bring a decertification petition up on its own. Management cannot even directly encourage this action on the part of the employees, but it can provide information to employees regarding decertification processes if they request it, "as long as the company does so without threatening its employees or promising them benefits."[105] **(SHRM C:45)**

What happens in a decertification process? First, 30% of covered employees must sign a petition for decertification of the union. Once this happens, the election process proceeds in pretty much the same way as the process for voting *for* union representation.

Trends and Issues in HRM

It's time to take a look at this chapter's trends and issues. Our first issue for this chapter concerns the importance of giving feedback to employees about their performance. Secondly, we will review some more issues concerning employee use of social media.

Good Feedback Makes a Good Manager

As you can easily see by reading this chapter, feedback is one of the most critical managerial obligations. So, let's explore the general process of providing feedback and give you some hints for providing feedback in difficult situations. You probably noticed a pattern in the *corrective feedback* process in each of the sections in this chapter where it was discussed: Identify what is happening and what is wrong with the current performance, provide information on desired performance,

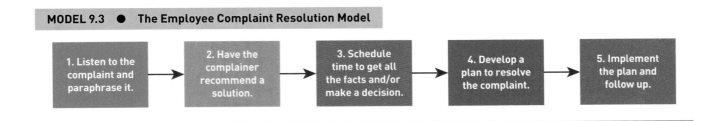

MODEL 9.3 ● The Employee Complaint Resolution Model

1. Listen to the complaint and paraphrase it. → 2. Have the complainer recommend a solution. → 3. Schedule time to get all the facts and/or make a decision. → 4. Develop a plan to resolve the complaint. → 5. Implement the plan and follow up.

get a commitment to change, and follow up. Let's look at how to use these in a little more depth, because giving corrective feedback is not easy the first few times you do it.

You, as the manager or supervisor, will be the one tasked with starting the feedback conversation. *Do not* go into the act of providing feedback by accusing the employee of intentionally failing to do what they needed to. Talk with them, see what is going on, ask about issues or problems that you may not know about. Initiate this conversation *as soon as possible* after you notice something is wrong. Once the conversation starts, you may be faced with a number of reactions, from crying, to anger, to denial that they are at fault and attempting to deflect blame, or just refusing to listen. How should these and other negative responses be handled?

First, as we noted earlier, stick with the facts. Don't allow your emotions to control your response to the employee. Second, remember that feedback is an attempt to make the employee better at what they do, not an attempt to belittle them. Explain the issues clearly and make sure the employee knows that you are working to help. Third, do not allow the employee to deflect responsibility because of their emotional reaction to the feedback. For instance, if the employee cries, provide emotional support, but do not back off from the facts of the situation.

The ktey to good feedback is control. You have to control your emotions. You have to control the message to the employee. And you have to control their response so that they do not avoid taking responsibility for their actions. So preparation for the meeting is key. Good-quality feedback is an absolute necessity if you are going to get the best performance out of your employees, and that is why you are there as a manager!

Social Media and the Web Continue to Create Managerial Nightmares

Employee use, and employer monitoring, of social media continues to be an issue for many organizations. Nearly every person who has an e-mail account, much less a social media account, has at some point sent something they almost immediately regretted. One columnist noted, "People were snapping at each other long before the Internet. Email and texting have only made it easier: We can now respond instantaneously, much faster than our rational brain can intervene."[106] This is a problem we have never faced before. In an age of instant communication, we don't always think about the damage we may be doing to ourselves or others when we rip off what we consider to be a witty zinger, or a heartfelt complaint—and then the repercussions start rolling in. We can also communicate with thousands or even millions of people (think of any viral video you have seen) whom we don't know and who don't know us, and that may also do harm that we didn't intend.

The problem for the organization comes when—in the eyes of the employer—the individual employee does potential or actual harm to the company or other employees within it. In one well-publicized case, employees of a **DirecTV** contractor (**MasTec** in Coral Gables, FL) were given incentives to push customers to pay for phone installations they felt were unnecessary in an attempt to deceive those customers. When the company ignored them, they contacted the local TV news and were interviewed by a reporter. And then the company fired them.[107]

The actions the company can or cannot take are not always clear based on law and existing precedent. In the MasTec case, the employees filed an unfair labor practice charge with the National Labor Relations Board[108] claiming they were engaged in "protected concerted activity" in connection with the company's policies. The employees initially lost, but when they appealed to a federal circuit court, the court agreed that their treatment had violated labor laws. But in other cases, companies have prevailed in disciplinary actions.

So managers have to continue to make judgment calls on when and how to intervene when employees have done potential harm to the company. Management is also responsible for keeping up with changing regulatory guidance and legal changes. And, most of all, managers are responsible for the protection of the company and all of the employees therein. If you as a manager were to come across evidence that one employee was harassing others—whether the reason is religion, race, sexual, or anything else—you would be obligated to act to protect those individuals and the organization.

Chapter Summary

9.1 Explain the value of trust and communication in employee relations.

Trust is absolutely necessary to strong management-labor relations. Research shows that companies that have the trust of their employees have lower turnover, higher revenue, more profitability, and higher shareholder returns. As soon as trust goes, loyalty to the company goes with it. Open communications are needed for the organization to be successful because we can't do what we say we will unless we communicate.

9.2 Discuss the primary reason why measuring job satisfaction is so difficult.

Job satisfaction is an attitude, not a behavior. We can experience behaviors directly, while we can measure attitudes only indirectly. Because of this, we must use some form of survey and ask the employees about their job satisfaction level.

9.3 Identify the best tool for getting employees to tell the truth about their level of satisfaction.

When using job satisfaction surveys, we have to ensure that they are anonymous or employees will most likely not tell the truth about their satisfaction levels.

9.4 Identify the commonly accepted individual rights in the workplace.

The commonly accepted rights of individuals within the workplace include the following:

Right of free consent—the right of the individual to know what they are being asked to do, and the consequences of doing it

Right to due process—a right to not be punished arbitrarily or without reason. Generally, we use the seven tests for Just Cause to protect this right.

Right to life and safety—the right of everyone in the organization to be protected from harm while working

Right of freedom of conscience—a general right to not be forced to violate the individual's personal values and beliefs on the job

Right to privacy—a right to protection from unreasonable searches or intrusions into their personal space at work

Right to free speech—freedom to express their opinions or concerns within the organization, without fear of harming their work relationship

9.5 List some rights that management has in modern organizations.

We discussed two major management rights. Management first has a right to create and enforce an employee *code of conduct*. The organization can also identify the relationship with workers as one of *employment-at-will*, which basically allows either party to break the relationship at any time, even without stating a reason. These rights are offered based on the need for managers to be able to protect the organization and the employees from unnecessary danger or harm.

9.6 Contrast the coaching, counseling, and discipline processes used in organizations.

Coaching is designed to give employees feedback to improve their performance over time. This feedback in general should be designed to improve the employee's motivation to perform for the organization. The management counseling process is designed to provide employees with feedback so that they understand that their performance is not currently at an acceptable level, and it's designed to provide them with guidance on how to improve their performance over time. In cases where an employee is unwilling or unable to change or a rule has been broken, discipline is necessary. Discipline is corrective action applied in order to get employees to meet organizational standards.

9.7 Describe the major labor relations laws in the United States, including the main reasons why we have each law.

1. The Railway Labor Act of 1926 was enacted to force negotiation between labor and management, first in railroads and later in the airlines, to prevent shutdown of these critical services.

2. The National Labor Relations Act of 1935 was the first major law to deal with the rights of labor to form unions in the general workforce and collectively bargain with employers. It identified unfair labor practices for management in negotiating with labor organizations.

3. The Labor Management Relations Act of 1947 was an amendment to the NLRA that focused on unfair labor practices on the part of unions

and other labor organizations. It outlawed or restricted a variety of strikes and boycotts, and it also allowed the states to pass right-to-work laws.

4. The Worker Adjustment and Retraining Notification Act of 1988 required that organizations with certain qualifying characteristics should provide 60 days' notice when laying off more than 50 people or closing a plant.

9.8 Discuss what management cannot do in attempting to limit union organizing efforts.

NO TIPS is an acronym that stands for no *t*hreats, no *i*nterrogations, no *p*romises, and no *s*pying.

This means first that employers cannot threaten to terminate employees from their jobs, threaten to close the plant, or threaten employees in any other manner during the period prior to a labor election. Second, employers cannot call the individual employees in to question them about union organizing activities on either their part or the part of others within the organization. Third, management cannot promise that if employees vote against unionization, the organization will provide them with benefits because of their votes. Finally, management cannot spy on individual employees taking part in union organizing events, either through planting individuals in such meetings or through electronic or other means.

Key Terms

coaching, 233
collective bargaining, 242
communication, 224
discipline, 234
employment-at-will, 232

grievance, 243
gross negligence, 238
Just Cause, 234
labor relations, 242
management counseling, 234

progressive discipline, 236
serious misconduct, 238
strike, 239
trust, 224

Key Terms Review

Complete each of the following statements using one of this chapter's key terms.

1. _____ is faith in the character and actions of another.

2. _____ is the process of transmitting information and meaning.

3. _____ allows the company or the worker to break their work relationship at any point in time, with or without any particular reason, as long as in doing so, no law is violated.

4. _____ is the process of giving motivational feedback to maintain and improve performance.

5. _____ is the process of (a) giving employees feedback so they realize that a problem is

affecting their job performance and (b) referring employees with problems that cannot be managed within the work structure to the organization's employee assistance program.

6. _____ is corrective action to get employees to meet standards and the code of conduct.

7. _____ is a set of standard tests for fairness in disciplinary actions; these tests were originally utilized in union grievance arbitrations.

8. _____ is a process whereby the employer provides the employee with opportunities to correct poor behavior before the individual is terminated.

9. _____ is a serious failure to exercise care in the work environment.

10. _____ is intentional employee behavior that has the potential to cause great harm to another or to the company.

11. _____ is a collective work stoppage staged by members of a union that is intended to put pressure on an employer.

12. _____ consists of the interactions between management and unionized employees.

13. _____ is the negotiation process resulting in a contract between union employees and management that covers employment conditions.

14. _____ is a formal complaint concerning pay, working conditions, or violation of some other factor in a collective bargaining agreement.

Communication Skills

The following critical-thinking questions can be used for class discussion and/or for written assignments to develop communication skills. Be sure to give complete explanations for all answers.

1. What actions would you consider taking, other than increasing pay, if job satisfaction survey data showed that your employees' satisfaction level was dropping significantly?

2. Do you think that organizations should provide more rights or fewer rights to employees than those listed in the chapter? If more, what would you add? If fewer, which rights do you think are unimportant?

3. Should companies make a strong attempt to never violate the privacy rights of an employee? Why or why not?

4. Do you think codes of conduct have any effect on employees' activities? What would make them more or less effective in an organization?

5. Is employment-at-will fair, or should companies have to have a legitimate reason to discharge their employees? Justify your answer.

6. Should coaching, counseling, and discipline processes be utilized by the firm, or should we just terminate the employment of workers who are not doing their job? Explain your answer.

7. Do you feel that progressive discipline processes actually work to improve employee performance in most cases? Why or why not?

8. Do you think it is ever okay for employees to strike against an employer? If so, in what circumstances? If not, why?

9. Assume that you are a fairly high-level manager in your company and that one of your employees comes to you to tell you that other employees are attempting to unionize the company. What would your initial actions be, and why?

Case 9.1 Willful Violation, or a Problem That Can Be Corrected?

Sandy Clark has worked for Healthy Meals Company for 10 years in a facility that cooks and packages prepared, frozen meals. Sandy is part of a crew that provides cleaning and sanitation services for the equipment used to prepare the meals. She has always sustained an excellent work record with no complaints about her work performance. She was recently assigned to the night shift to clean and sanitize the equipment used to mix and dispense sauce for the meals. The equipment consists primarily of a large vat and a rotating paddle with wooden blades driven by an electrical motor to continuously stir the sauce. After the meal preparation crew finishes production for the day shift, Sandy's work begins cleaning and sanitizing the equipment for production the next day.

Sandy was trained to clean and sanitize the equipment by observing an experienced member of the sanitizing crew who had been performing the work for the past 3 years. During her training, she was instructed to use a high-pressure water hose, bleach, and sanitizing cleaner on the paddle blades and the lower part of the vat, then use a sponge pad to scrub the top part of the vat. Her trainer explained the best way to get the wooden paddles thoroughly clean was to spray them while the machine was running, then turn off the equipment and lock it out before she used the sponge pad to clean the inside of the vat. After 2 days of training, Sandy demonstrated to the person who trained her that she could satisfactorily perform all the duties of cleaning the equipment.

During her second week of working alone cleaning the vat and the wooden paddles of sauce residue, she was spraying the paddles using the high-pressure water hose while the machine was running with the paddles turning in the vat. While holding the sponge pad in one hand and holding the hose nozzle in the other hand, she finished spraying the moving paddles and accidently dropped the pad from her hand into the vat. She reached to grab the sponge pad as a reflex action and the fingertips of her rubber gloves were caught between the wall of the vat and the paddle. The paddle pulled her right hand further into the hopper up to her knuckles. Immediately, a nearby coworker turned off the equipment and freed Sandy's hand. Fortunately, she only suffered minor injuries to her hand. She later stated that she reacted to reach for the pad and catch it to avoid damage to the equipment. After an investigation was conducted by a safety inspector, the company's management stated that Sandy did not follow the proper procedure for cleaning the equipment by first unplugging the power cord for the motor, then locking out the electrical

source to ensure that no one started the motor. This procedure was to be followed before any cleaning of the equipment was started.

During her rebuttal, Sandy claimed that discharge was too severe a punishment in light of her 10 years of service to the company and that she was never told by any management official that her job performance was unacceptable. According to two other employees who previously held this job, training for these duties was typically done with instruction and observation by someone who had previously carried out the tasks. Sandy pointed out that she followed the procedure for cleaning and sanitizing that she was taught by another employee during her training and no one had ever instructed her otherwise. She added that she learned from her mistake and that she would not make that mistake again. She believed that progressive discipline should be used in this particular case. Sandy was subsequently fired for "willfully violating the company's proper safety procedures."

Written by Robert F. Wayland, University of Arkansas at Little Rock

Questions

1. Do the facts in this case indicate that Sandy Clark was guilty of a willful violation of the company's safety rules? Explain your answer.

2. What possible corrective action could the company take as an alternative to discharge?

3. If Sandy is represented by a labor union with a current labor agreement or contract stating that "employees shall only be discharged for Just Cause," how could this affect her termination?

4. What particular mitigating factors or circumstances in this case should be considered in determining whether or not her termination is for "Just Cause?"

Skill Builder 9.1 Coaching

Objective

To develop coaching skill using the coaching model

Skills

The primary skills developed through this exercise are as follows:

1. *HR management skills*—Conceptual and design

2. *SHRM 2018 Curriculum Guidebook*—P: Training and Development

Procedure 1 (2–4 minutes)

Break into groups of three. Make some groups of two, if necessary. Each member selects one of the following three situations in which to be the manager and a different one in which to be the employee. In each situation, the employee knows the standing plans; the employee is not motivated to follow them. You will take turns coaching and being coached.

Three Problem Employee Situations

1. Employee 1 is a clerical worker who uses files, as do the other 10 employees in the department. The employees all know that they are supposed to return the files when they are finished so that others can find them when they need them. Employees should have only one file out at a time. The supervisor notices that Employee 1 has five files on the desk, and another employee is looking for one of them.

2. Employee 2 is a server in an ice cream shop. The employee knows that the tables should be cleaned up quickly after customers leave so that new customers do not have to sit at dirty tables. It's a busy night. The supervisor finds dirty dishes on two of this employee's occupied tables. Employee 2 is socializing with some friends at one of the tables.

3. Employee 3 is an auto technician. All employees know that they are supposed to put a paper mat on the floor of each car so that the carpets don't get dirty. When the service supervisor got into a car Employee 3 repaired, the car did not have a mat and there was grease on the carpet.

Procedure 2 (3–7 minutes)

Prepare for coaching to improve performance. Each group member writes an outline of what they will say when coaching Employee 1, 2, or 3, following the steps below:

1. Describe current performance.

2. Describe desired performance. (Don't forget to have the employee state why it is important.)

3. Get a commitment to the change.

4. Follow up.

Round 1 (5–8 minutes)

Role-playing. The manager of Employee 1, the clerical worker, coaches that employee as planned.

(Use the actual name of the group member playing Employee 1.) Talk—do not read your plan. Employee 1 should put themselves in the worker's position. Both the manager and the employee will have to ad lib. The person not playing a role is the observer. This person makes notes as the observer for each step of the coaching model listed above. The manager should coach the employee and try to make positive comments and point out areas for improvement. The observer should give the manager alternative suggestions about what could have been said to improve the coaching session.

Feedback. The observer leads a discussion of how well the manager coached the employee. (This should be a discussion, not a lecture.) Focus on what the manager did well and how the manager could improve. The employee should also give feedback on how they felt and what might have been more effective in motivating change. Do not go on to the next interview until you are told to do so. If you finish early, wait for the others to finish.

Round 2 (5–8 minutes)

Same as Round 1, but change roles so that Employee 2, the server, is coached. The job is not much fun if you can't talk to your friends. As the supervisor, coach Employee 2. Again, the observer gives feedback after the coaching.

Round 3 (5–8 minutes)

Same as Rounds 1 and 2, but change roles so that Employee 3, the auto technician, is coached. As the supervisor, coach Employee 3. Again, the observer gives feedback after the coaching.

Apply It

What did I learn from this exercise? How will I use this knowledge in the future?

_____

_____

_____

Skill Builder 9.2 Disciplining

Objective

To develop your ability to discipline an employee using the discipline model

Skills

The primary skills developed through this exercise are as follows:

1. *HR management skills*—Conceptual and design

2. *SHRM 2018 Curriculum Guidebook*—P: Training and Development

Note that this is a continuation of Skill Builder 9.1. Coaching didn't work, and you have to discipline the employee.

Procedure 1 (2–4 minutes)

Break into groups of three. Make some groups of two, if necessary. Each member selects one of the three problem employee situations from Skill Builder 9.1. Decide who will discipline Employee 1, the clerical worker; Employee 2, the ice cream shop server; and Employee 3, the auto technician. Also select different group members to play the employee being disciplined and the observer.

Procedure 2 (3–7 minutes)

Prepare for the discipline session. Write a basic outline of what you will say to Employee 1, 2, or 3; follow the steps in the discipline model below.

1. Refer to past feedback. (Assume that you have discussed the situation before, using the coaching model.)

2. Ask why the undesired behavior occurred. (The employee should make up an excuse for not changing.)

3. Administer the discipline. (Assume that an oral warning is appropriate.)

4. Get a commitment to change, and develop a plan.

5. Summarize and state the follow-up.

Round 1 (5–8 minutes)

Role-playing. The manager of Employee 1, the clerical worker, disciplines that employee as planned. (Use the actual name of the group member playing the employee.) Talk—do not read your plan. Both the manager and the employee will need to ad lib. As the supervisor, discipline Employee 1.

The person not playing a role is the observer. This person makes notes on the five steps of the discipline model above. For each of the steps, try to make a statement about the positive aspects of the discipline and a statement about how the manager could have improved. Give alternative things the manager could have said to improve the discipline session. Remember, the objective is to change behavior.

Feedback. The observer leads a discussion of how well the manager disciplined the employee. The employee should also give feedback on how they felt and what might have been more effective in motivating change. Do not go on to the next interview until you are told to do so. If you finish early, wait until the others finish or the time is up.

Round 2 (5–8 minutes)

Same as Round 1, but change roles so that Employee 2, the ice cream server, is disciplined. As Employee 2, put yourself in the worker's position. As the supervisor, discipline Employee 2. As the observer, give feedback.

Round 3 (5–8 minutes)

Same as Rounds 1 and 2, but change roles so that Employee 3, the auto technician, is disciplined. As Employee 3, put yourself in the worker's position. As the supervisor, discipline Employee 3. As the observer, give feedback.

Apply It

What did I learn from this exercise? How will I use this knowledge in the future?

_____

_____

Compensating

10 Compensation Management

11 Employee Incentives and Benefits

PRACTITIONER'S MODEL

| ↑ Productivity |
| ↑ Engagement |
| ↓ Absenteeism |
| ↓ Turnover |

PART V: Protecting and Expanding Organizational Outreach
How do you PROTECT and EXPAND your Human Resources?

Chapter 12	Chapter 13	Chapter 14
Workplace Safety, Health, and Security	Ethics, Sustainability, Diversity, and Inclusion	Global Issues for Human Resource Managers

PART IV: Compensating
How do you REWARD and MAINTAIN your Human Resources?

Chapter 10	Chapter 11
Compensation Management	Employee Incentives and Benefits

PART III: Developing and Managing
How do you MANAGE your Human Resources?

Chapter 7	Chapter 8	Chapter 9
Training, Learning, Talent Management, and Development	Performance Management and Appraisal	Employee Rights and Labor Relations

PART II: Staffing
What HRM Functions do you NEED for sustainability?

Chapter 4	Chapter 5	Chapter 6
Workforce Planning: Job Analysis, Design, and Employment Forecasting	Recruiting Job Candidates	Selecting New Employees

PART I: The Human Resource Management Environment
What HRM issues are CRITICAL to your organization's long-term sustainability?

Chapter 1	Chapter 2	Chapter 3
Today's Human Resource Management Process	Strategy-Driven Human Resource Management	The Legal Environment

©iStockphoto.com/ronstik

Compensation Management

Learning Outcomes

After studying this chapter, you should be able to do the following:

10.1 Identify the components of a compensation system. **Page 254**

10.2 Describe how expectancy and equity theories apply to compensation. **Page 255**

10.3 Identify the seven basic issues that make up the organizational compensation strategy. **Page 257**

10.4 Discuss the three major provisions of the Fair Labor Standards Act (FLSA). **Page 259**

10.5 Name the three types of job evaluations by describing whether they are more objective or subjective in form. **Page 264**

10.6 Briefly describe the concept of job structure, pay levels, product market competition, and labor market competition. **Page 266**

10.7 Briefly describe the concept of a pay structure, including broadbanding and delayering. **Page 266**

SHRM HR Content

See Online: *SHRM 2018 Curriculum Guidebook* for the complete list

B. Compensation and Benefits

Compensation

1. Compensation of special groups (e.g., executives, sales, contingent workers, management)
2. Determining pay increases
3. Development of a base pay system
4. Developing pay levels
5. External competitiveness strategies
6. Fair Labor Standards Act (FLSA)
8. Internal alignment strategies
9. Job evaluation point factor system
10. Labor market competition
11. Legal constraints on pay issues
12. Market compensation surveys
13. Market pressures
14. Minimum wage/overtime
15. Monitoring compensation costs
16. Motivation theories: Equity theory, reinforcement theory, agency theory, expectancy theory
17. Pay discrimination and dissimilar jobs

18. Pay grades
20. Prevailing wage
21. Role of job analysis/job design/job descriptions in determining compensation
22. Skill-based pay
24. Union role in wage and salary administration

D. Employment Law

9. Fair Labor Standards Act of 1938 (FLSA)

I. Job Analysis and Job Design

1-b. Compliance with legal requirements—Equal pay (skill, effort, responsibility, and working conditions) and comparable worth

1-c. Compliance with legal requirements—Overtime eligibility (exempt vs. nonexempt work)

3. Job evaluation and compensation (grades, pay surveys, and pay setting)

K. Metrics and Measurement of HR

3. Benchmarking

N. Staffing (Recruitment and Selection)

4. Employment brand

Practitioner's Perspective

Cindy tells the story of when Drew walked dejectedly into her office and flopped down in the nearest chair.

"I hear they hired a new payroll clerk—the same job I've been doing for 5 years—and this new person is going to be paid more than I make! I've been a loyal employee for years and haven't had a real raise since I started. Is that fair?"

Cindy couldn't fault Drew for his feelings, and she knew it was past time the company examined its compensation guidelines.

Once you have an established pay scale, is it really important to reexamine your compensation levels? What is the solution when the going market rate for a position outdistances your set pay scale? Chapter 10 answers these questions and more as it demonstrates the reasons why compensation management is so vital to attracting and retaining your best employees.

Compensation Management

>> **LO 10.1 Identify the components of a compensation system.**

Employees are the most important company asset,[1] so we have to recruit and train the best people,[2] and minimizing turnover improves job and financial performance.[3] So how do we retain our good employees? Meeting employee needs helps,[4] and an important factor is compensation.[5] **Compensation** is *the total of an employee's pay and benefits*. How important is compensation to you?

A business designs and implements a compensation system to focus worker attention on the specific efforts the organization considers necessary to achieve its desired goals.[6] According to recent research by Payscale, "Compensation has officially expanded from 'just a human resources issue' to a C-suite issue," with about 57% of respondents saying that compensation is becoming more important to executives and that it has strategic value to the firm.[7]

One reason for C-suite concern is that compensation costs are frequently the largest part of total production costs at today's firms. Thus, management must continually monitor and manage total organizational compensation. Compensation costs also continue to rise as companies face shortages of skilled talent as world economies continue to expand.[8] According to the U.S. Bureau of Labor Statistics, average total compensation costs rose from $31.93 to $36.22 per hour from March 2014 to June 2018.[9]

Compensation also affects the process of both attracting and retaining employees.[10] Pay is now identified by employees as the top reason for job satisfaction, overtaking job security as the top driver of satisfaction in 2013. In fact, pay is second in importance overall (respectful treatment is number one) to all four generations of employees currently in the workforce—veterans, baby boomers, Generation X, and millennials—so HR must pay attention to fair and equitable compensation for company employees.[11]

Compensation The total of an employee's pay and benefits

The Compensation System

The **compensation system** of an organization includes *anything an employee may value and desire and that the employer is willing and able to offer in exchange*. This includes the following:

Compensation system Anything an employee may value and desire and that the employer is willing and able to offer in exchange

1. *Direct compensation components.* All rewards that can be classified as monetary payments and in-kind payments constitute the direct compensation component. In-kind means that we exchange something of value (in this case our work time) for other things of value, instead of getting cash payments. So, for instance, free company-paid housing and free meals at work would be in-kind payments, because providing housing and meals provides value to the employees.

2. *Nonmonetary compensation components.* All rewards other than monetary and in-kind payments constitute the nonmonetary compensation component, even if the company pays money to others (e.g., a health insurer) on behalf of the employee.

Types of Compensation

There are four basic parts of a compensation system:

1. *Base pay.* This is typically a flat rate, either as an hourly wage or salary. Many employees consider this to be the most important part of the compensation program, and it is therefore a major factor in their decision to accept or decline the job.

2. *Wage and salary add-ons.* This includes overtime pay, shift differential, premium pay for working weekends and holidays, and other add-ons.

3. *Incentive pay.* Also called variable pay, *incentive pay* is pay for performance, and it commonly includes items such as piecework, merit pay, and commissioned sales. We will discuss incentives in detail in Chapter 11.

4. *Benefits.* This is compensation that provides something of value to the employee. Some benefits are part of in-kind payments (the company-paid housing mentioned earlier, for

instance), and therefore part of direct compensation. Others are in the nonmonetary compensation component (life insurance, being allowed to take pets to work, or vacation time would be examples). Benefits may include health insurance; payments to employees if they are unable to work because of sickness or accident; retirement pay contributions; and provision of a wide variety of desired goods and services such as cafeteria service, tuition reimbursement, and many other items. We will also discuss benefits in detail in Chapter 11.

In for-profit businesses, we want to design the mix of direct and nonmonetary compensation that provides us with the best productivity return for the money spent. However, to do that, we need to understand something about the motivational value of our compensation system. Let's take a look at a few theories that help us understand how compensation systems can motivate our workers to perform to the best of their ability.

10.1 APPLYING THE CONCEPT
TYPES OF COMPENSATION

Review the types of compensation and then write the letter corresponding to each one before the statement(s) describing it.

a. Base pay

b. Wage and salary add-ons

c. Incentive pay

d. Benefits

_____ 1. I'd like to work for a firm that will help pay for me to get my master of business administration (MBA) degree.

_____ 2. I only get paid $11 an hour, so I'm looking for a better job.

_____ 3. I like getting paid the same each week. It helps me to budget my expenses.

_____ 4. I like being paid for every sale I make, but my pay does vary from week to week.

_____ 5. I like working nights because it pays more.

Motivation and Compensation Planning

>> **LO 10.2 Describe how expectancy and equity theories apply to compensation.**

When we look at designing compensation programs, we need to remember that we are trying to motivate the employee to do the things we need them to do, consistently, over a period of time. However, "while 73 percent of employers say they pay their workers fairly, only 36 percent of employees agree."[12] Why does this result exist? Probably the most significant theories that help you to understand compensation planning and employee motivation are *expectancy theory* and *equity theory*.[13] **(SHRM B:16)**

Expectancy Theory

Expectancy theory is a process theory of motivation. This means that we go through a cognitive process to evaluate something or a situation. **Expectancy theory** *proposes that employees are motivated when they believe they can accomplish a task and that the rewards for doing so are worth the effort.* Expectancy theory is based on Victor Vroom's formula: Motivation = Expectancy × Instrumentality × Valence.[14]

For compensation purposes, we have intentionally simplified the theory to show how it affects a person's motivation to perform. *Expectancy* is the person's perception of their ability to accomplish or probability of accomplishing an objective. Generally, the higher one's expectancy, the

Expectancy theory A theory proposing that employees are motivated when they believe they can accomplish a task and that the rewards for doing so are worth the effort

better the chance for motivation. *Instrumentality* is the perception that a particular level of performance is likely to provide the individual with a desired reward. *Valence* refers to the value a person places on the outcome or reward, because not all people value the same reward. So, it helps to let employees have a voice in the rewards they get.[15] One thing we need to remember here is that the three components of the theory—valence, instrumentality, and expectancy—are multiplicative, so if any one of the three is near zero, the motivating potential is low, and the individual has almost no motivation to perform![16] For an illustration of expectancy in action, see Exhibit 10.1. Therefore, as managers, if we help employees get what they want, they will give us the work we want to help meet the organizational goals.[17]

EXHIBIT 10.1 ● Expectancy Theory and Compensation

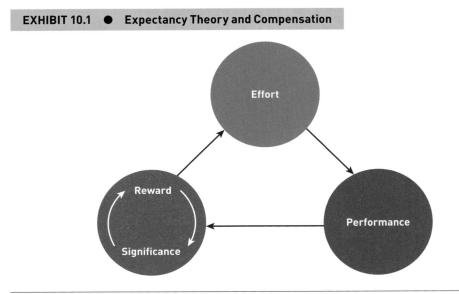

Equity Theory

We all apply equity theory constantly.[18] Equity theory, particularly the version developed by J. Stacy Adams, proposes that people are motivated to seek social equity in the rewards they receive (outcomes) in exchange for their performance (input).[19] So in general, **equity theory** *proposes that employees are motivated when the ratio of their perceived outcomes to inputs is at least roughly equal to that of other referent individuals.* Employees are more motivated to achieve organizational objectives when they believe they are being treated fairly,[20] especially regarding pay equity.[21]

According to equity theory, people compare their inputs (effort, loyalty, hard work, commitment, skills, ability, experience, seniority, trust, support of colleagues, etc.), their financial rewards (pay, benefits, and perks), and intangible outcomes (praise, recognition, status, job security, sense of advancement and achievement, etc.) to those of relevant others.[22] A *relevant other* could be a coworker or a group of employees from the same or different organizations.[23] **(SHRM B:8 and B:5)**

Notice the definition says that employees compare their *perceived* (not actual) inputs and outcomes.[24] Equity may actually exist, but if employees believe there is inequity, they will change their behavior to create what they consider to be equity. Employees must perceive that they are being treated fairly, relative to others. Managers can also help control employee perceptions of fairness through honest discussion of compensation.[25] Perceptions of inequity hurt attitudes, commitment, and cooperation, thereby decreasing individual, team, and organizational performance.[26] This perceived inequity is often used as a justification for unethical behavior.[27] When employees perceive inequity, they are motivated to reduce it by decreasing input or increasing outcomes or they leave for another job.[28]

Remember this: We want to be treated fairly,[29] with mutually beneficial relationships.[30] Employees' perception of being treated fairly affects their attitude and performance.[31] People are generally not really motivated to work harder by equity; rather, they are demotivated if it doesn't exist. So HR managers need to understand that people will be demotivated if they feel (perceive) that they are not being treated fairly. Unfair and abusive managers demotivate employees and hurt performance.[32] We need to be honest and fair to develop trusting relationships to motivate others,[33] especially regarding compensation.[34] As a result, we have to use this information when we begin to structure our compensation plan. We need to "build in" *and* advertise equity to minimize the problems associated with equity theory. Companies like Nike are working on equity compensation, [35] especially for women and minorities.[36]

Compensation Strategy

>> **LO 10.3 Identify the seven basic issues that make up the organizational compensation strategy.**

In addition to understanding our compensation options and how they motivate employees, we need to identify what our overall compensation strategy will be. Let's discuss some of these major organizational issues that we will need to evaluate before we can set up our compensation system.

Ability to Pay

Probably the first thing we need is an honest assessment of how much we can afford, or are willing to afford, to pay our employees. This means we need to complete an assessment of estimated revenues from business operations and determine what percentage of revenues can or should realistically go toward compensation costs over the long term. Why? Because if we have to cut compensation, employees may believe we broke our promises to them, and that will most likely lead to intense demotivation and high rates of turnover.[37]

At, Above, or Below the Market?

The next item we must determine, based on our ability to pay, is whether we will pay *above market, at market,* or *below market.* We will need to know the market compensation offered by our competitors. Competitors will sometimes advertise job salaries, and you can use pay calculators including Glassdoor.com, PayScale.com, and others for free.[38] **(SHRM N:4)**

We might decide to pay above market to attract better workers and enhance our employment brand. We want good employees to have a strong incentive to work for us, and one way to enhance our employment brand is to pay above the market rate.[39] We also want better productivity out of our workforce if we pay more for employees. But do better workers generally have higher levels of productivity? *Efficiency wage theory* says that if a company pays higher wages, it can generally hire better people who will in turn be more productive.[40] Because we have higher-quality employees, we get a productivity increase that more than offsets the higher cost of employing them.[41]

Would we necessarily get lower productivity from our workforce if we paid *below* the market? In general, yes, but not always. If our firm is in an industry where unemployment is high, it is easy to find replacement workers, and if most positions require a low-level skill set, we may be able to get away with paying less than average.

Highly successful companies like Google, Facebook, Starbucks, and Costco pay above average to hire the best, whereas most companies shoot for average, and companies like Walmart and McDonald's with lower-skilled workers have historically paid below average compared to other industries but generally have to pay close to the same compensation as direct competitors to attract and retain employees.

A strong economy with high employment gives workers the incentive to seek better positions and higher pay.[42] You may have heard that restaurant employees and other low-paid service workers continue to press for a minimum wage of $15 an hour, and some companies including Amazon are now paying that rate.[43] But at the same time the higher wages give some companies like McDonald's and Amazon the incentive to use technology/machines to replace employees who perform simple repetitive jobs.

What Types of Compensation?

We noted earlier in the chapter that we have four basic components to compensation—base pay, wage add-ons, incentives, and benefits. We need to determine how to divide the funds available between each of the components. **(SHRM B:15)**

▲
Starbucks pays their employees above-average rates. This could be to motivate employees to work harder or to create a reputation for valuing their employees.

There are some legal requirements for certain mandatory benefits such as Social Security, so these legal requirements have to be dealt with "off the top"—they have to be subtracted from the available funds. Once this is done, we need to determine how much direct compensation will be in the form of base pay and how much will be incentive pay.

Finally, we need to consider voluntary benefits. We need to analyze competition within the labor market and what benefits each of our close competitors provides because we will most likely have to approximately match the benefits that are provided by those competitors.[44]

Pay for Performance or Pay for Longevity?

In breaking down base pay versus incentives, we will need to look at whether our organization is going to have a *performance philosophy* or a *longevity philosophy*. Some companies pay people more for *longevity* or *seniority,* meaning accumulating years of service with the firm, by providing promotions and raises over time (assuming that we meet minimal organizational standards) regardless of performance because we have been a loyal member of the organization. Other companies, however, pay more for *performance*—for completing certain tasks or doing certain things faster or better than average, not just for being there and being loyal to the firm.[45] **(SHRM B:22)**

Skill-Based or Competency-Based Pay?

If we decide to *use skill-based* or *competency-based* pay, we will pay members of the workforce for individual skills or competencies that they bring to work, whether or not those skills are necessary for the individuals to do their current job. *Competencies* involve the individual's level of knowledge in a particular area, while *skills* involve the ability to apply that knowledge set in that field. Examples of competencies include such things as an understanding of negotiation and collaboration, or problem-solving and decision-making expertise. Examples of skills related to these competencies would include the ability to actually negotiate contract agreements, apply principles of physics to a new equipment design, or make a high-quality decision based on good analysis of a situation. With either method, we are paying our employees for knowledge, skills, and abilities that they may not necessarily ever use in the organization, so we have to ask whether it is valuable to have people with these extra skill sets.

Wage Compression

Wage compression When new employees require higher starting pay than the historical norm, causing narrowing of the pay gap between experienced and new employees

Another concern is wage compression. **Wage compression** occurs *when new employees require higher starting pay than the historical norm, causing narrowing of the pay gap between experienced and new employees.*[46] We bring workers into the organization in both good economic times and bad. When the economy is doing poorly and wages are depressed, people will generally accept jobs for less than they would if the economy were doing well and higher-wage jobs were available. Since raises are frequently based on an employee's initial salary or pay rate, those who start at lower pay than others may stay that way over time, and pay inequality for the same work may increase over time as well.

We may create a situation where workers with less time on the job might be paid nearly as much as, or more than (called *wage inversion*), employees who have worked for us for many years. This wage compression or inversion can weaken or destroy the desired link between pay and performance (expectancy theory), creating significant dissatisfaction on the part of long-term employees because of the pay differential.[47] Most companies and organizations don't set out to do this—they just fall into it.[48] If we understand wage compression when creating a pay structure for the organization, we can avoid at least some of the dissatisfaction associated with the pay differentials between short-term and long-term employees.

Pay Secrecy

Recall our discussion of equity theory earlier in the chapter. One of the things some companies have historically done to avoid equity issues is demand *pay secrecy,* which means requiring employees to not disclose their pay to anyone else. But the National Labor Relations Board (NLRB) has consistently ruled that companies may not discipline workers who reveal information about their pay and other work conditions as long as the workers are participating in "protected, concerted activity," and the NLRB views this activity very broadly. In addition, President Obama signed an Executive Order in 2014 (EO 13665) prohibiting pay secrecy policies in federal government contractors, with potential loss of government contracts as punishment for failure to comply. Several states in the United States have also passed laws specifically prohibiting pay secrecy policies. So, creating and enforcing pay secrecy clauses is becoming more dangerous to companies and is likely not worth the danger in today's employment environment.

Legal and Fairness Issues in Compensation

>> **LO 10.4 Discuss the three major provisions of the Fair Labor Standards Act (FLSA).**

Several federal and state laws directly or indirectly affect pay and compensation systems. Virtually every equal employment opportunity (EEO) law identifies compensation as one of the employment actions where discrimination is prohibited if it is based on a protected characteristic. So we have to keep these laws in mind as we set up our pay system. See Exhibit 10.2 for a list of the major EEO laws and legal concepts that cover compensation.

Fair Labor Standards Act of 1938 (Amended)

Besides the Equal Pay Act and the other EEO laws, there are laws that deal with specific compensation issues. The grandfather of these laws is the Fair Labor Standards Act (FLSA). The major

EXHIBIT 10.2 ● Major EEO Laws and Legal Concepts

Antidiscrimination Legislation
1. Equal Pay Act of 1963 (EPA)
2. Title VII of the Civil Rights Act of 1964 (CRA)
3. Age Discrimination in Employment Act of 1967 (ADEA)
4. Vietnam Era Veteran's Readjustment Act of 1974
5. Americans with Disabilities Act of 1990 (ADA)
6. CRA of 1991
7. Lilly Ledbetter Fair Pay Act of 2009 (LLFPA)

Legal Concepts Linking Employment Discrimination and Pay Discrimination
1. Disparate impact
2. Disparate treatment
3. Bona fide occupational qualification (BFOQ)

provisions of the FLSA cover minimum wage, overtime issues, and child labor rules for most US-based businesses.[49] Let's complete a quick review of the FLSA. **(SHRM B:6 and D:9)**

Minimum Wage

The first major provision of the FLSA concerns the federal minimum wage. The **minimum wage** is *the lowest hourly rate of pay generally permissible by federal law.* The federal minimum wage in 2018 for most employees in the United States was $7.25 per hour.[50] This is adjusted periodically by Congress, but the FLSA sets the minimum wage provision. Many states, and even cities, have set the minimum wage higher than the federal rate. You may have heard that Seattle, Washington, set the city's minimum wage at $15 per hour, and several other large cities around the United States have now followed suit for at least some workers, including San Francisco and New York City.[51] In addition, in 2014 Executive Order 13658 raised the minimum wage for federal contract workers, which stands at $10.60 per hour as of January 2019.[52] So an HR manager needs to know, and keep up with changes to, the laws in their state and city. **(SHRM B:14)**

Exempt or Nonexempt

Does everyone get paid at least the minimum wage for their area? Not exactly. There are some exemptions to the rules.[53] If someone is *exempt,* by the definitions in the FLSA, they are exempt from the minimum wage requirement, overtime provisions, child labor rules, or possibly all three. People not meeting any of the requirements for an exemption are called *nonexempt* and must be paid minimum wage, overtime, and so forth.

As an example, workers who most people know are commonly exempt include restaurant servers. The current minimum wage for servers is $2.13 per hour.[54] Servers normally expect to get a large portion of their wages in tips. The FLSA says we can pay tipped employees a minimum of $2.13 per hour as long as their tips make up the difference. So, if somebody in a restaurant works 20 hours in a week and does not make an average of $5.12 an hour in tips, it is illegal to pay that person $2.13. There are also other exemptions for individuals who are live-in child care providers, newspaper carriers, seasonal workers, among others. In fact, there are hundreds of exemptions. If you would like to review some of the exemptions in the FLSA, you can go to the Department of Labor website at http://www.dol.gov, and search for FLSA.

A set of quick guidelines can be used to determine exempt and nonexempt persons at work. If you make under $455 per week, or an annual salary of $23,660, you are pretty much guaranteed to be nonexempt under the provisions of the FLSA as of October 2018.[55] "Highly compensated employees" paid $100,000 or more (*and* at least $455 per week) are pretty much automatically exempt from the minimum wage and overtime rules if they regularly perform at least one of the duties of an exempt executive, administrative employee, or professional employee identified in the standard tests for exemption.[56] If an individual is paid more than $23,660 but less than $100,000, then the employee usually must meet a set of specific "duties tests" in order to fall within an exemption category (see Exhibit 10.3). There was a proposal by the Department of Labor to increase the minimum for exempt workers to approximately $970 per week, or around $50,000 annually, and the amount for highly compensated employees to roughly $122,000 per year, but the Department of Labor pulled the proposed regulation back for further work and comments. **(SHRM B:1)**

Overtime

Overtime is *a higher than minimum, federally mandated wage, required for nonexempt employees if they work more than a certain number of hours in a week.* Overtime is set by the FLSA as 150% of the individual's normal wages for all hours in excess of 40 hours worked in a calendar week. With few exceptions, if a nonexempt employee works more than 40 hours in a week, that employee is eligible for overtime. **(SHRM I:1-c)**

Contrary to what many people think, the FLSA has no requirement for paying anything more than time-and-a-half for any overtime work.[57] Employers are also not required to provide paid holidays, vacation, or extra pay for working on weekends or on holidays under federal law, although many states now have rules covering these situations.

EXHIBIT 10.3 ● Duties Tests for General Employee Exemptions

Executive Exemption

To qualify for the *executive employee* exemption, the employee must meet **all of the following criteria**:

- The employee must be compensated on a salary basis (as defined in the regulations) at a rate of not less than $455 per week;

- The employee's primary duty must be managing the enterprise or managing a customarily recognized department or subdivision of the enterprise;

- The employee must customarily and regularly direct the work of at least two or more other full-time employees or their equivalent; and

- The employee must have the authority to hire or fire other employees; or the employee's suggestions and recommendations as to the hiring, firing, advancement, promotion, or any other change of status of other employees must be given particular weight.

Professional Exemption—Learned or Creative

To qualify for the *learned professional employee* exemption, the employee must meet **all of the following criteria**:

- The employee must be compensated on a salary or fee basis (as defined in the regulations) at a rate not less than $455 per week;

- The employee's primary duty must be the performance of work requiring advanced knowledge, defined as work that is predominantly intellectual in character and that requires the consistent exercise of discretion and judgment;

- The employee's advanced knowledge must be in a field of science or learning; and

- The employee's advanced knowledge must be customarily acquired by a prolonged course of specialized intellectual instruction.

- To qualify for the *creative professional* employee exemption, the employee must meet **all of the following criteria**:

- The employee must be compensated on a salary or fee basis (as defined in the regulations) at a rate not less than $455 per week;

- The employee's primary duty must be the performance of work requiring invention, imagination, originality, or talent in a recognized field of artistic or creative endeavor.

Administrative Exemption

To qualify for the *administrative employee* exemption, the employee must meet **all of the following criteria**:

- The employee must be compensated on a salary or fee basis (as defined in the regulations) at a rate not less than $455 per week;

- The employee's primary duty must be the performance of office or nonmanual work directly related to the management or general business operations of the employer or the employer's customers; and

- The employee's primary duties must include the exercise of discretion and independent judgment with respect to matters of significance.

Outside Sales Exemption

To qualify for the *outside sales employee* exemption, the employee must meet **all of the following criteria**:

- The employee's primary duty must be making sales (as defined in the FLSA) or obtaining orders or contracts for services or for the use of facilities for which a consideration will be paid by the client or customer; and

- The employee must be customarily and regularly engaged away from the employer's place or places of business.

- The salary requirements of the regulation do not apply to the outside sales exemption.

Computer Employee Exemption

To qualify for the *computer employee* exemption, the employee must meet **all of the following criteria**:

- The employee must be compensated either on a salary or fee basis at a rate of not less than $455 per week or, if compensated on an hourly basis, at a rate of not less than $27.63 an hour;

(Continued)

EXHIBIT 10.3   ●   (Continued)

Computer Employee Exemption

- The employee must be employed as a computer systems analyst, computer programmer, software engineer, or other similarly skilled worker in the computer field performing the duties described in the next bullet point;

- The employee's primary duty must consist of one of the following:

  1. The application of systems analysis techniques and procedures, including consulting with users to determine hardware, software, or system functional specifications;

  2. The design, development, documentation, analysis, creation, testing, or modification of computer systems or programs (including prototypes), based on and related to user or system design specifications;

  3. The design, documentation, testing, creation, or modification of computer programs related to machine operating systems; or

  4. A combination of the aforementioned duties, the performance of which requires the same level of skills.

Source: U.S. Department of Labor, Wage and Hour Division, "Fact Sheet #17A: Exemption for Executive, Administrative, Professional, Computer & Outside Sales Employees Under the Fair Labor Standards Act (FLSA)," https://www.dol.gov/whd/overtime/fs17a_overview.htm (retrieved October 31, 2018).

10.2 APPLYING THE CONCEPT
EMPLOYEE EXEMPTIONS

Identify each job as generally being considered exempt or not from minimum wage or overtime pay (write *a* or *b* before each job type).

a. Exempt

b. Nonexempt

_____ 6. Auto mechanic

_____ 7. Fruit picker

_____ 8. Worker on a foreign-flag cruise ship

_____ 9. Librarian

_____ 10. Taxi driver

_____ 11. Real estate agent

_____ 12. Bellperson at a hotel

_____ 13. Computer programmer (paid more than $27.63 per hour)

_____ 14. Hairdresser

_____ 15. Bank teller

Child Labor

The FLSA also has rules on the use of *child labor,* meaning workers under 18 years old. If individuals are 18 or older, we can use them in any normal employment situation. However, we can employ 16- and 17-year-olds only in *nonhazardous* jobs, although their work hours are unrestricted, and there are significantly different rules for 14- and 15-year-olds.

Minors age 14 and 15 may work outside school hours for no more than "three hours on a school day, 18 hours in a school week, eight hours on a nonschool day, and 40 hours in a nonschool week."[58] They can't start work before 7:00 a.m. or work after 7:00 p.m., except from June 1 through Labor Day, when they can work until 9:00 p.m. Jobs they can work are limited to retail, food service, and gasoline service at establishments specifically listed in the FLSA regulations. Employees 14 and 15 years old may not work overtime. While there are some exceptions to these rules for businesses such as family businesses or family farms, these are the general guidelines for child labor.

Employee Misclassification Under the FLSA

Misclassification of employees as exempt from minimum wage or overtime is one of the most common areas where companies get into serious trouble. Just paying an employee a "salary" and then working that person for unlimited hours is obviously illegal under the general exemption FLSA rules listed in Exhibit 10.3.

So why does misclassification occur? Obviously, companies want to save money. Many employers think that if they put you on salary, they don't have to pay overtime—so they put you on a salary and work you 70 hours per week. Another company might say, "All my people are professionals, so they are all exempt." But this is rarely possible in reality, if you look at the FLSA rules for exemption. Breaking FLSA law can result in costly civil penalties, and repeated offenses can even land you in jail.

Pay Equity and Comparable Worth

One of the more controversial issues in compensation is comparable worth. *Comparable worth* is the principle that when jobs are distinctly different but entail similar levels of ability, responsibility, skills, and working conditions, they are of equal value and should have the same pay scale. According to the U.S. Census Agency, women earn an average of about 80 cents for every dollar that men earn.[59] This is one of the major reasons that comparable worth continues to be an issue in both business and government. While equal pay for equal work is the law (EPA of 1963), comparable worth is not currently federal law except in some very limited cases. **(SHRM B:17 and I:1-b)**

Comparable worth is simply "similar pay for similar work." Although this sounds almost like the equal pay for equal work stipulated by the Equal Pay Act, the doctrine of comparable worth says that if we can compare your job with that of another person, and if the two jobs are *similar but not the same,* then we should pay you a similar wage but not necessarily exactly the same wage. So this concept is much broader than equal pay.

As we noted, though, there are a few exceptions where comparable worth is law. A number of states—with California in the lead—have passed fair pay laws that are designed to require comparable pay in at least most work environments and that shift to the employer the burden of showing that any pay differences are due to valid, legal reasons.[60] But in most cases these laws have not passed yet, at least partially because of the market value factor for jobs. Let's face the facts that measurement, reliability, and validity issues exist. It is very difficult to compare a factory job to an office job. And as discussed, many companies are working to get more women and minorities into better paying jobs rather than trying to figure comparable worth.

©iStockphoto.com/eli_asenova

▲
Comparable worth dictates that jobs with similar levels of ability, responsibility, skills, and working conditions should offer the same pay scale.

Other Legal Issues

A number of other federal laws place controls on pay and benefits. Recall from Chapter 9 that the National Labor Relations Act (NLRA) allows collective bargaining on the part of workers who join a union. Since the NLRA allows employees to bargain collectively with their employers for wages, benefits, and working conditions, in limited cases the workers can agree to a workweek that is longer than 40 hours. The wages paid must be significantly higher than the minimum wage, and other conditions apply, but it is possible for the collective bargaining unit to agree to more than a 40-hour workweek.[61] Some union contracts also require mandatory overtime with pay. **(SHRM B:11 and B:24)**

Mandatory employee *pension and benefits legislation* affecting overall compensation also includes the following:

- Social Security

- Workers' compensation

- Unemployment insurance

- Family and Medical Leave Act (FMLA)

- Patient Protection and Affordable Care Act (ACA)

- Employee Retirement Income Security Act (ERISA—mandatory for employers who offer pension plans)
- Health Insurance Portability and Accountability Act (HIPAA—mandatory for employers who offer health insurance)

We will discuss each of these laws further in Chapter 11.

Job Evaluation

>> **LO 10.5 Name the three types of job evaluations by describing whether they are more objective or subjective in form.**

Deciding how much each job is worth in a company is difficult. There are two approaches to this—internal and external—though they may be used together. First we discuss the external method, followed by three internal methods. **(SHRM B:12)**

External Versus Internal Methods

An *external approach* involves finding out what other organizations pay for the same or similar jobs through available pay surveys, and setting pay levels based on market pricing. In a recent survey, about 95% of companies said they use at least one source of pay survey data or other external information to determine market pricing for their jobs.[62] On the other hand, an *internal approach* uses job evaluation. **Job evaluation** is *the process of determining the worth of each position relative to the other positions within the organization.* Organizations commonly group jobs into pay levels or grades, and the higher the grade of the job, the higher the pay. A common example of this type of grouping is the federal government's general schedule (GS) ratings. **(SHRM I:3 and B:21)**

How do we accomplish a job evaluation? There are several ways, but methods usually involve ranking jobs, or assigning points to activities that occur within a job and totaling the points for the job.[63] Once this is done, we can place the job in a hierarchy, called a *job structure,* and create our pay grades.

Job evaluation The process of determining the worth of each position relative to the other positions within the organization

Job Ranking Method

Job ranking is simply the process of putting jobs in order from lowest to highest, in terms of value to the company. When doing job ranking, we utilize the job descriptions we discussed in Chapter 4 to identify the factors in each job and then rank those jobs based on their content and complexity. We usually do job ranking without assigning points to different jobs. So we might start at the top of the organization with the CEO as the highest-ranking person and then work all the way down to the lowest-skilled housekeeping job.

But if you look at this method for a second, you will see that somebody has to decide the value of each job and do so without any quantitative factors. Therefore, this determination requires judgment and is highly subjective. This means it is difficult to defend if we have to do so in court.

Point-Factor Method

A second type of job evaluation is the point-factor method, which attempts to be completely objective in form. This method breaks a job down into components like particular skills or abilities and then assigns a number of points to each component based on its difficulty. These components are usually referred to as *compensable factors.* **(SHRM B:9)**

Many of the compensable factors will be common among a number of different jobs, so once we have identified the number of points the factor is worth, we can then transfer that same value to all other jobs where the factor is present. The value of the point-factor job evaluation method is that we can differentiate jobs based on the difficulty or intensity of each factor, so it becomes easier to determine the total value of the job in a quantitative form.

Factor Comparison Method

The factor comparison method combines the job ranking and point-factor methods to provide a more thorough form of job evaluation.[64] This model is somewhat similar to the point-factor method in that it assigns points to compensable factors. However, the factor comparison method first identifies a group of benchmark jobs—positions that are identified and evaluated in a large number of organizations and that can generally be found in most pay surveys.

Examples of benchmark jobs include "Training Specialist I," "Accountant II," "Lending Officer I," and "Hotel Registration Clerk." These benchmark jobs are then analyzed in some detail based on their compensable factors. We then rank the benchmark jobs in order, and we finally compare all other jobs in the organization to the benchmark jobs to determine where each one fits in the rankings. Here again, the primary method of determining the monetary value of a job is through the analysis of the compensable factors.

10.1 ETHICAL DILEMMA: WHAT WOULD YOU DO?
EXECUTIVE COMPENSATION

In 2017, the CEO-to-worker pay ratio was about 361:1.[65] Oracle's co-CEOs made about $25.3 million each in 2018.[66] A minimum wage full-time employee at Walmart would have to work more than 1,500 hours to earn as much as the Walmart CEO makes in 1 hour.[67] Some say top executives are being overpaid; Fortune 500 CEOs all make millions.

However, not everyone agrees. In capitalist countries, talented CEOs, like in pro sports, are entitled to fetch their price. Top executives should be paid multimillion-dollar compensation packages; after all, if it weren't for effective CEOs, companies would not be making the millions of dollars of profits they make each year. CEOs deserve a piece of the pie they help create.

1. Do executives deserve to make 300 times more than the average worker?

2. Is it ethical for managers to take large pay increases when laying off employees?

3. Is it ethical for managers to get pay raises when their companies lose money?

4. Are companies being socially responsible when paying executives premium compensation?

Sources: Information from AFL-CIO, "Executive Paywatch," https://aflcio.org/paywatch (retrieved March 30, 2019); https://www.bloomberg.com/graphics/ceo-pay-ratio/ (retrieved October 31, 2018). https://www.marketwatch.com/story/walmart-ceos-salary-is-1188-times-the-median-employees-2018-04-23(retrieved October 31, 2018); R. Lowenstein, "Is Any CEO Worth $189,000 per hour?" *Businessweek* (February 20–26, 2012), pp. 8–9; R. Fisman, T. Sullivan, "In Defense of the CEO," *Wall Street Journal* (January 12–13, 2013), pp. C1–C2.

10.3 APPLYING THE CONCEPT
JOB EVALUATION

Review the list of job evaluation methods and then write the letter corresponding to each method before each statement below.

a. External

b. Job ranking

c. Point-factor

d. Factor comparison

_____ 16. I use two methods together to determine how much to pay each position because I'm an HR professional.

_____ 17. I look at the job and determine the specific skills needed to do the job, and then I add up the total point value of the skills to set the pay.

_____ 18. To figure out how much to pay the data entry person, I'm checking the SHRM data.

_____ 19. I placed all the jobs in rank order, from the one that was worth the most to the one that was worth the least, in order to determine how much to pay for each position.

_____ 20. All of the companies in our industry pay essentially the same hourly wage.

Developing a Pay System

>> LO 10.6 Briefly describe the concept of job structure, pay levels, product market competition, and labor market competition.

>> 10.7 Briefly describe the concept of a pay structure, including broadbanding and delayering.

Well, we have finally gotten to the point where we can start to develop our pay structure. Remember, though, all of the things that we had to review and decide on first. Take a look now at Exhibit 10.4 to see how each of those items comes together to allow us to create a *pay structure* and *individual pay rates* for each job. **(SHRM B:3)**

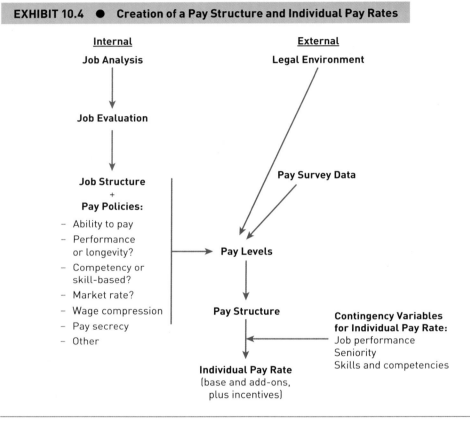

EXHIBIT 10.4 ● Creation of a Pay Structure and Individual Pay Rates

Job Structure and Pay Levels

Pay structure A hierarchy of jobs and their rates of pay within the organization

A **pay structure** is *a hierarchy of jobs and their rates of pay within the organization.*[68] It allows us to identify what the pay range is for each job. Once we have completed the process of creating a pay structure, we will have the pay range for every job in the hierarchy. From that, managers can determine individual compensation levels based on the employee's performance, seniority, skills, and any other significant factors.

A pay structure is composed of both a job structure and pay levels.[69] The *job structure* is what gives us our job hierarchy. As we noted in the job evaluation section of this chapter, the job structure is the stacking up of the jobs in the organization, from the lowest to the highest level. Each of the jobs within the job structure will end up at a particular pay level. On the other hand, a *pay level* (frequently called a pay grade) can be made up of many different jobs, and each pay level has a maximum pay rate and a minimum pay rate. **(SHRM B:18)**

Creation of Pay Levels

To establish pay levels and determine the maximum and minimum pay rates for particular jobs, we will have to look at some market factors. We look at product market competition and labor market competition because if we don't pay attention to external equity or fairness, we are going to have trouble filling many of our jobs. **(SHRM B:4)**

Product Market Competition and Labor Market Competition

To set the minimum value for a particular pay level, we have to look at the applicable *labor market competition,* meaning labor supply versus demand for labor. If we graph compensation for a given type of work versus the number of workers in the labor market who can do that type of work, the place where the two lines cross is the average pay for that work. As shown in Exhibit 10.5, when the supply of labor equals the demand for that labor in the workforce, we have equilibrium. The market will pay close to what the workers demand to be paid, or workers who have the necessary skills won't be willing to fill the job. **(SHRM B:10 and B:13)**

What happens in bad economic times, when there are more workers available than jobs? The market can get some of them to work for less than the normal rate (where the lines cross in Exhibit 10.5) because those workers need to work and earn a living. So the average compensation will most likely go down because we will have an oversupply situation. Conversely, if we have more jobs available than we have workers, we will usually have to pay more to attract the limited number of workers with the skill sets that we require. In either case, labor market competition will set the minimum pay that a worker will require in order to come to work for us—but it can be a moving target that we have to track.

On the other hand, how do we determine the top of the pay level? We have to look at something called *product market competition.* This is basically a function of the value of the product or service that we sell to the customer.[70] An example will help make it clear. Let's say we manufacture utility trailers (see Exhibit 10.6). The public will pay about $500 for our 5- by 8-foot utility trailers. To make the problem simple, we will pretend that we only have a couple of components that go into making that trailer: labor and materials. Let's assume that all of the materials are going to cost $250.

What do we have left for labor? Do we have $250? No! We also have some other indirect costs like overhead, don't we? And we would like to make a profit, right? So if we estimate all of our other costs at $50, we now have $200 left. We can pay labor $200 if we only want to break even. However, if we want to make any money, we have to pay less than $200 for labor. Assume that our person who makes the trailer makes $20 per hour and it takes that person 8 hours to build a trailer—$160 for the 8 hours of labor costs. So we have a $40 profit left, or about 8% before-tax profit.

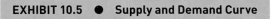

EXHIBIT 10.5 ● Supply and Demand Curve

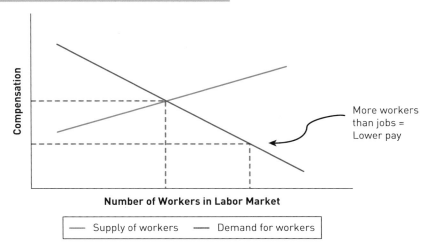

EXHIBIT 10.6 ● Product Market Competition Limits

Utility Trailer Manufacturing

$500 Sale price

−$250	Material costs
$250	= Remainder

− $50	Overhead costs
$200	= Remainder

−$160	Labor (maximum cost of labor)
$40	= Before-tax profit (8%)

Your assembler comes to you and says, "Boss, I need a raise." What do you just about have to tell the employee? "We can't pay you more." If our trailer is priced at $800 and a competitor's trailer is $500, almost everyone will buy the competitor's trailer. We can't charge much more than the normal rate for a product or service. The labor is only worth so much money, because the sale price of the good or service has to cover the cost of the labor. So, *product market competition* sets the top of the pay level for most types of jobs in the company.

Exhibit 10.7, then, shows that we have a maximum and a minimum level of pay for a particular class of jobs, with labor market competition setting the bottom of the range and product market competition setting the top of the range. Remember, though, that this is a simplified example—there may be other factors involved as well.

EXHIBIT 10.7 ● Pay Levels

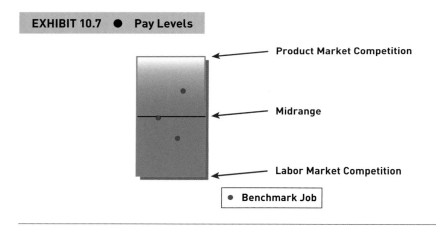

- Product Market Competition
- Midrange
- Labor Market Competition
- ● Benchmark Job

Benchmarking Pay Survey Data

Next, we look at benchmarks from the pay survey data that we reviewed earlier and put those benchmark jobs into the pay level where they belong (the **blue** dots in Exhibit 10.7). Once we place some benchmark jobs in a plot of our pay levels, we can get a *market pay line* (sometimes called a *pay curve*)—a line that shows the average pay for various jobs at different levels in a particular industry (see Exhibit 10.8). We use the benchmarks to see whether or not what we are doing is OK. If the range is correct, we have successfully created a pay level; if not, we have to figure out what is wrong with our range. **(SHRM K:3 and B:20)**

Rate range The maximum, minimum, and midpoint of pay for a certain group of jobs

After going through this process for a particular pay level, we end up with a **rate range**, which provides *the maximum, minimum, and midpoint of pay for a certain group of jobs*. Once the range is created, we can go in and add to the range any other jobs that are at approximately the same level based on our earlier job evaluations.

Pay Structure

So we have figured out our first pay level. What do we do now? We start to lay pay levels out next to each other, creating a pay dispersion.[71] Again, look at Exhibit 10.8. We take our first pay level and put it down: bottom, midpoint, and top. The bottom of the range for the first level will probably be near minimum wage in most cases. Then our second tier will start, and beyond that will be the third and the fourth, and so on.

Notice that the ranges overlap each other. Why do they overlap? Take a look at the market pay line. It would have to go exactly through the corners of each pay level if the levels didn't overlap. That doesn't give us much wiggle room on which to base people's pay rates, does it? So the major reason for the overlap is to give the company some flexibility in each person's pay within a particular pay level.

Once we set up our pay levels, we can plot the actual pay for people in the organization. These are indicated in Exhibit 10.8 as black dots. We identify where these actual pay levels fall within the pay structure, and we will sometimes see that we have someone plotted outside our pay level ranges—either too high or too low. Individual pay rates that fall outside the pay range on the high side are called *red-circle rates* (**red** dots in Exhibit 10.8), and those that are lower than the bottom of the pay range are *green-circle rates* (**green** dots in Exhibit 10.8). If we find a green-circle rate for an individual, the correct thing to do is to raise the individual's pay to at least the minimum for that pay level, because we are not paying them fairly for their skill set.[72]

But what should we do about a red-circle rate? We probably won't cut someone's pay, but we will not be able to pay them any more unless they move up to a higher skill level, and therefore

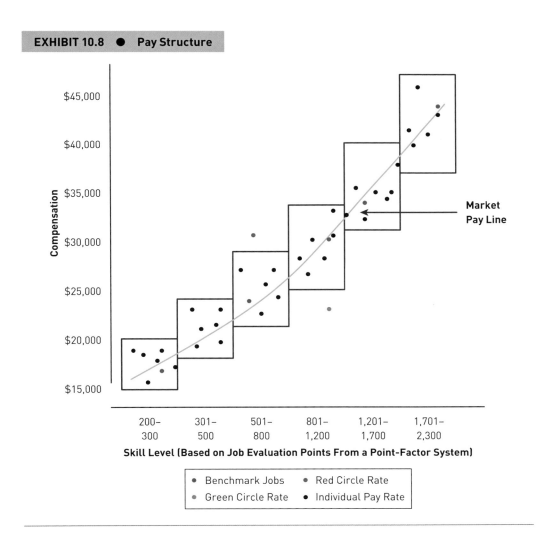

a higher pay level. For instance, if our assembler is making $24 per hour, the maximum for his pay level is $20, but he wants a pay raise and hasn't had one in several years, we will have to tell him no. However, we can also tell him that if he is willing to become a supervisor, he can get the chance to raise his pay rate because the skill level for a supervisor is higher than that of an assembler. **(SHRM B:2)**

Understanding pay levels and pay structure allows us to provide good answers to employees about why their pay is set at a certain level. If a worker decides to become a supervisor, that employee is worth more and we can pay more. So we are able to tell the employee, "*The job* isn't worth any more than what you are being paid," instead of saying, "*You* are not worth any more than that."

Delayering and Broadbanding

Delayering The process of changing the company structure to get rid of some of the vertical hierarchy (reporting levels) in an organization

Broadbanding Combining multiple pay levels into one

A trend for many years now has been to lower the number of pay levels using one of two options—either delayering or broadbanding. **Delayering** is *the process of changing the company structure to get rid of some of the vertical hierarchy (reporting levels) in an organization.*[73] On the other hand, **broadbanding** is accomplished by *combining multiple pay levels into one.*[74] When we lower the number of pay levels that we have to deal with, managing the pay process is simpler. It takes a long time to create, maintain, and evaluate 20 pay levels, when instead we can have just 5 broadbands. It also allows more capacity to reward outstanding performers. Because we have taller and wider levels, there is more pay flexibility while staying within the boundaries of the pay level.

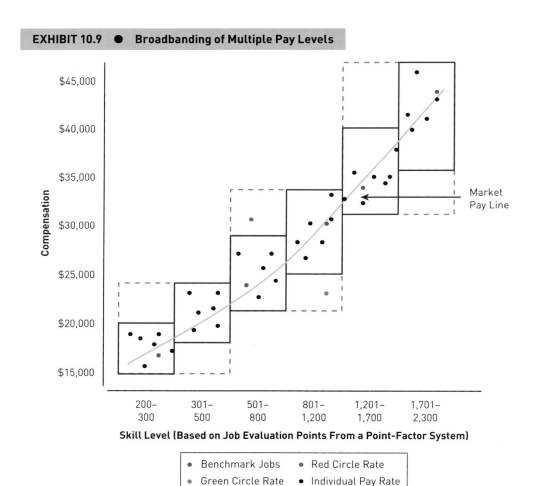

EXHIBIT 10.9 ● Broadbanding of Multiple Pay Levels

Take a look at what happens to the pay structure in Exhibit 10.9 when we convert it into a broadband pay structure. The new broadband pay structure combines the first two pay levels, the third and fourth level, and finally the fifth and sixth, making three levels instead of six. This causes our red- and green-circle rates to disappear. It also creates greater ability to adjust the pay of people based on their performance and ability. Finally, it lowers the administrative burden of maintaining the compensation system.

So when we are done with the pay structure, we will have created that hierarchy of jobs that we mentioned earlier—from lowest to highest. And as you have probably already guessed, much of this work is now done using computers. Once the human resources management system (HRMS) has the necessary data, we can create most of our pay structure using existing company information. In many cases, the HRMS can identify the market pay line and provide other compensation information, too.

We should realize that developing a pay system is not a one-time task. Achieving pay equity requires monitoring and addressing pay as you hire, promote, and try to retain key employees.[75] Most large companies don't start from scratch or make huge overhauls, they do things little by little to see how the changes are working.[76] Thus, compensation management is an important function within HR management. As we bring this chapter to a close, complete the self-assessment to determine your compensation management satisfaction.

10.1 SELF-ASSESSMENT

COMPENSATION MANAGEMENT SATISFACTION

This exercise is also a good review of the chapter, as it uses most of the important concepts discussed in this chapter. Select an organization that you work for, or have worked for, and select your level of satisfaction with each of the following parts of the compensation management system, on a scale of 1 to 5.

1	2	3	4	5
Not satisfied				**Satisfied**

_____ 1. Base pay

_____ 2. Wage and salary add-ons

_____ 3. Incentive pay

_____ 4. Benefits

_____ 5. Meeting expectancy theory

_____ 6. Meeting equity theory

_____ 7. What the firm actually pays based on its ability to pay

_____ 8. Pay for performance vs. longevity

_____ 9. What the firm pays based on being below, at, or above market-level pay

_____ 10. Wage compression

_____ 11. Pay secrecy

_____ 12. Meeting the Fair Labor Standards Act

_____ 13. Pay equity and comparable worth

_____ 14. The system used for job evaluation

_____ 15. Job structure

_____ 16. Pay levels

_____ 17. Benchmarking

_____ 18. Pay structure

_____ 19. Pay raises

_____ 20. Benefit increases

_____ Total the points and place the score on the continuum below.

20	30	40	50	60	70	80	90	100
Not satisfied								**Satisfied**

The higher the score, the greater your level of satisfaction with the compensation management system of the organization. However, to most employees, what really matters most is answers to questions regarding their own pay and benefits (compensation), and we all are more satisfied when these increase.

Think about the people you worked with as a group. You can select the group's level of satisfaction with each question. Would their answers vary from yours? Would the satisfaction level vary by the level in the organization—among executives versus nonmanagers, by department, or among other groupings?

Trends and Issues in HRM

What trends are we seeing in the compensation of our current workforce? One trend is more independent contractors working with companies over the long term. Second, we look at that continuing stubborn gender wage gap.

Designation of Independent Contractors Continues to Be an Issue

More on-demand workers, more independent contractor relationships, and fewer employer-employee relationships is the new normal. Why are companies moving toward these independent contractor relationships? One reason is to maximize organizational flexibility. In many cases, the relationship with independent contractors can be severed much more easily than those with employees. If there is no long-term contract, the company can release the contractor immediately on completion of whatever job is currently being done. Another reason for this type of arms-length relationship is that it can save the company from significant costs. Compensation of an independent contractor is much simpler than compensation of employees. In the contract relationship, the company pays the agreed-upon amount on the contract, and there is no need to calculate hours, minimum wage, overtime, benefits costs, health care insurance eligibility, or any other compensation factors. They also do not have to pay federal (social security and other) taxes or state mandated (unemployment, workers' compensation, etc.) taxes among other costs. All of those requirements fall to the contractor to manage.

Employers may think it is easy to make an employee into a contractor, but independent contractors must be truly independent of the company's control. According to the IRS website, "The general rule is that an individual is an independent contractor if the payer has the right to control or direct only the result of the work and not what will be done and how it will be done."[77] The U.S. Supreme Court identified a "total activity" test to help determine whether or not a case is dealing with an employer-employee relationship:[78]

1. The extent to which the services rendered are an integral part of the principal's business

2. The permanency of the relationship

3. The amount of the alleged contractor's investment in facilities and equipment

4. The nature and degree of control by the principal

5. The alleged contractor's opportunities for profit and loss

6. The amount of initiative, judgment, or foresight in open market competition with others required for the success of the claimed independent contractor

7. The degree of independent business organization and operation

Uber and the federal government disagree concerning whether or not Uber drivers are independent contractors. In one case, a federal judge rejected a proposed settlement for $100 million because the deal "undervalued" potential claims.[79] However, several other federal judges have ruled that Uber drivers are not employees.[80] Employers need to be aware of, and concerned with, their use of such identifications, because of the current confused nature of the rulings. Intentionally misclassifying employees as contractors is also very dangerous to the company. It is unethical and illegal to intentionally misclassify individuals to avoid paying them what would reasonably and ordinarily be due them in their relationship with the company, and it carries the same penalties as other FLSA violations should the employer get caught.

The Stubborn Gender Wage Gap—Can It Be Fixed?

According to *Fortune* magazine, "Gender parity in wages still has a long way to go."[81] Research backs this up. Sex differences in total rewards in the workplace were 14 times larger than sex differences in performance evaluations[82] according to one study, and even though the pay gap is likely the smallest it has been since about 1960, evidence still shows that women make only 80% of what men do on average across all industries in the United States.[83] Why is this wage gap so stubborn?

Some of the gap can be explained away based on a number of factors other than discrimination. For instance, it is true that women leave the workforce more often than men and that women tend to be absent more when employed compared with their male counterparts. There are logical reasons for these facts, including the fact that women tend to still be the primary caregiver to children in a family, but they are still fact. However, at least some of the difference appears to still be an inherent bias toward male employees. Some states have passed laws that limit the ability for companies to exhibit such biases, and companies are taking notice. According to *HR Magazine,* "Pay equity has become a top-of-mind concern for employers nationally as a result of California's new gender pay equity law and similar legislation in New York and elsewhere."[84] Pay equity is not just a U.S. issue either. Countries as varied as Iceland, New Zealand, and Singapore are discussing the issue and passing gender equity laws.[85] But not enough seems to be getting done.

So what can be done? Government rulemaking can only go so far. In some cases, it appears there has been some overreach on the part of federal—and maybe state—agencies, which will probably not help the situation either. Google pushed back when the Department of Labor demanded information that the company claimed would cost more than $1 million to gather on a contract that only paid them $600,000.[86] But good companies, including Google, say they want to do something to minimize the gap. The monitoring of the problem and enforcement of solutions will almost always fall to HR. Leaders can maintain records of initial salary negotiations and ultimately of offers, manage and evaluate any compensation increases over time, and complete pay audits on a periodic basis. If unexplainable disparities are found during the various analysis efforts, HR needs to make recommendations to senior management to correct any problems by adjusting compensation components as needed. Pay disparity is a fact. Consistent vigilance is the only way to combat this stubborn issue.

Chapter Summary

10.1 Identify the components of a compensation system.

Components of compensation include the following four items:

1. *Base pay, either an hourly wage or salary.* Base pay is frequently a major decision factor for most employees in deciding to accept the job.

2. *Wage and salary add-ons.* These include overtime pay, shift differential, premium pay for working weekends and holidays, and other add-ons.

3. *Incentive pay for performance.* Incentives give workers strong reasons to perform above the standard.

4. *Benefits.* This provides something of value to the employee. Benefits cost the company money even though they aren't direct compensation.

10.2 Describe how expectancy and equity theories apply to compensation.

Expectancy theory (Motivation = Expectancy × Instrumentality × Valence) says that employees *expect* to put forth some form of effort at work and believe they can accomplish the task or objective (expectancy). This effort is expected to result in some level of performance resulting in some type of reward (instrumentality). The reward has to be *significant* (*valence*) to the individual, and as long as it is, the employee will continue to put out effort to get the reward.

In equity theory, people compare their inputs (the things they *do* in the organization) and outcomes (the things that they *receive* from the organization) to those of relevant others. But it's their and others' *perceived* inputs and outcomes that employees compare, not necessarily actual inputs and outcomes. If employees believe that there is inequity, they will change their work behavior to create equity.

10.3   Identify the seven basic issues that make up the organizational compensation strategy.

1. *Ability to pay.* This is an honest assessment of how much we can afford, or are willing to afford, in order to compensate our employees.

2. *At, above, or below the market.* What will our general pay structure look like, and why?

3. *Types of compensation.* This refers to the mix of the four basic components of compensation—base pay, wage add-ons, incentives, and benefits—that we employ. We must divide available funds among the components.

4. *Pay for performance or longevity.* Will we pay people based on organizational loyalty/tenure, or will we pay based on performance in their jobs?

5. *Skill or competency-based pay.* Competencies involve the individual's level of knowledge in a particular area, while skills involve the ability to apply that knowledge set.

6. *Wage compression.* This lowers the pay differential between long-term and newly hired employees.

7. *Pay secrecy.* Will we utilize pay secrecy clauses in employment contracts? Pay secrecy may allow us to hide actual wage inequities from employees, but it has the potential to create dissatisfaction and demotivation.

10.4   Discuss the three major provisions of the Fair Labor Standards Act (FLSA).

1. Minimum wage rates identify the lowest hourly rate of pay generally allowed under the FLSA. There are many exemptions, but if a person is *nonexempt,* minimum wage will apply.

2. Overtime rates are also required for persons who are nonexempt. However, there are different exemptions for overtime than there are for minimum wage, so HR managers must check the law to determine who will have to be paid overtime.

3. Child labor requirements within the FLSA identify the jobs and allowable working hours for individuals between 14 and 18 years old. Sixteen- and 17-year-olds can only be employed in nonhazardous jobs, but their work hours are unrestricted. However, 14- and 15-year-olds can only work outside school hours, and the jobs that they are allowed to do are limited to retail and other service positions; also, they may not work overtime.

10.5   Name the three types of job evaluations by describing whether they are more objective or subjective in form.

1. The job ranking method is simply the process of putting jobs in order from lowest to highest or vice versa, in terms of value to the company. However, it has limited usefulness because it is subjective.

2. The point-factor method attempts to be completely objective in form. It breaks a job down into component skills or abilities, known as factors, and then applies points to each factor based on its difficulty.

3. The factor comparison method combines the ranking and point-factor methods to provide a more thorough form of job evaluation. It identifies benchmark jobs and then analyzes and rank-orders them. We then compare all other jobs in the organization to the benchmark jobs to determine where each one fits in the rankings.

10.6   Briefly describe the concepts of job structure, pay levels, product market competition, and labor market competition.

- The *job structure* is what gives us a job hierarchy. The *job hierarchy* is the stacking of the jobs in the organization from the lowest (simplest) to the highest (most complex) levels.

- A *pay level* (frequently called a pay grade) will be made up of several different jobs. Pay levels provide a framework for the minimum and maximum pay for a particular group of jobs in the organization. Pay levels are then laid out one next to another in order to create the entire pay structure for the company.

- *Product market competition* sets the top of a pay level. We can only pay someone as much as we can recover from a customer when we sell our goods or services. We can't pay more than the value added to the product or service by the labor. Together, product market and labor market competition identify the maximum and minimum rates of pay for a particular group of jobs in a pay level.

- *Labor market competition sets the bottom of a pay level.* We have to compete with other companies to attract labor, and if we don't pay enough, we will be unable to attract the workers we need. So we compete in the labor market for available workers.

10.7 Briefly describe the concept of a pay structure, including broadbanding and delayering.

A *pay structure* is created by laying out our pay levels, one next to the other. The entire group of pay levels creates the pay structure. Benchmark jobs can be plotted on the pay structure to get a *market pay line*—a line that shows the average pay at different levels in a particular industry. Once pay levels are set, we can actually plot employee rates of pay on the pay structure to see if any are plotted outside our pay level ranges, either high or low. Individuals who fall outside our pay range to the high side are paid *red-circle rates,* and those who fall outside low are paid *green-circle rates.* Each of these rates should be reviewed and corrected if necessary.

Broadbanding lowers the number of pay levels that a company administers by combining multiple pay levels into one. Lowering the number of pay levels makes the process simpler. It takes a long time to create, maintain, and evaluate many pay levels, but instead, we can have just a few broadbands. Because pay bands are wider and taller under broadbanding, the company also has more flexibility in pay rates for individuals who are overperforming or underperforming. Broadbanding may also cause most red- and green-circle rates to disappear. *Delayering* also lowers the number of pay levels, but it does so by getting rid of layers of vertical hierarchy in the organizational structure.

Key Terms

broadbanding,   270
compensation,   254
compensation system,   254
delayering,   270

equity theory,   256
expectancy theory,   255
job evaluation,   264
minimum wage,   260

overtime,   260
pay structure,   266
rate range,   268
wage compression,   258

Key Terms Review

Complete each of the following statements using one of this chapter's key terms.

1. _____ is the total of an employee's pay and benefits.

2. _____ includes anything that an employee may value and desire and that the employer is willing and able to offer in exchange.

3. _____ proposes that employees are motivated when they believe they can accomplish a task and the rewards for doing so are worth the effort.

4. _____ proposes that employees are motivated when the ratio of their perceived outcomes to inputs is at least roughly equal to that of other referent individuals.

5. _____ occurs when new employees require higher starting pay than the historical norm, causing narrowing of the pay gap between experienced and new employees.

6. _____ is the lowest hourly rate of pay generally permissible by federal law.

7. _____ is a higher than minimum, federally mandated wage, required for nonexempt employees if they work more than a certain number of hours in a week.

8. _____ is the process of determining the worth of each position relative to the other positions within the organization.

9. _____ is a hierarchy of jobs and their rates of pay within the organization.

10. _____ provides the maximum, minimum, and midpoint of pay for a certain group of jobs.

11. _____ is the process of changing the company structure to get rid of some of the vertical hierarchy (reporting levels) in an organization.

12. _____ is accomplished by combining multiple pay levels into one.

Communication Skills

The following critical-thinking questions can be used for class discussion and/or for written assignments to develop communication skills. Be sure to give complete explanations for all answers.

1. Do you believe it is always necessary to provide incentives as part of a pay structure? Why or why not?

2. As the HR manager, would you pay more attention to expectancy theory or equity theory in designing your compensation system? Why?

3. If your company had promised an incentive program right before the recession of 2007–2008, and if the recession made it impossible for the company to pay employees what they had been promised, then how would you explain this to your workforce to keep them motivated?

4. Would you rather have higher pay or better benefits? Why?

5. Would you ever consider paying below the market rate for employees if you had control of wages? Why or why not?

6. How would you approach a CEO or company president who insisted on classifying nonexempt workers as exempt? What would you say to get the CEO to stop this practice?

7. Do you think that comparable worth should be made federal law? Why or why not?

8. If you were the lead HR manager in your company, would you ever consider setting pay levels by just using external pay surveys and no internal analysis? What are the advantages and disadvantages of this?

9. As the head of HR, would you rather change narrow pay levels into broadbands? Can you think of any disadvantages to doing so?

Case 10.1 Discounting Everything but Compensation at Costco

Only Costco as a physical retailer can go toe-to-toe with Walmart in the wholesale market and come out on top. Operating more than 715 membership warehouse stores, Costco is the nation's largest wholesale club operator (ahead of Walmart's Sam's Club). Primarily under the Costco Wholesale banner, it serves more than 71 million members in 44 U.S. states, Washington, D.C., and Puerto Rico, as well as in Canada, Mexico, the United Kingdom, Japan, South Korea, Taiwan, and Spain. Stores offer discount prices on an average of about 3,700 products (many in bulk packaging), ranging from alcoholic beverages and appliances to fresh food, pharmaceuticals, and tires. Certain club memberships also offer products and services, such as car and home insurance, mortgage and real estate services, and travel packages.[87]

How can Costco beat other retailers, such as Walmart, BJ's, and Target, who sell similar products and services? By looking for ambitious, energetic employees who enjoy a fast-paced team environment filled with challenges and opportunities. Their successful employees are service-oriented people with integrity and commitment toward a common goal of excellence. More important, Costco offers, in their own words, "great jobs, great pay, great benefits and a great place to work."[88]

Their benefits package not only provides their employees with a full spectrum of benefits (medical, dental, pharmacy, vision, 401K matching, short- and long-term disability, life insurance, and others), but employees also may elect coverage for their spouses, children, and domestic partners. The company pays a larger percentage of the premiums than do most other retailers, and employee-paid premiums are withheld pre-tax, which means employees get to keep more of their hard-earned money.

U.S. BENEFIT-ELIGIBILITY REQUIREMENTS ARE AS FOLLOWS:

- **Hourly employees** (full-time) are benefit-eligible on the first of the month after working 450 hours or 90 days, whichever comes first.

- **Hourly employees** (part-time) are benefit-eligible on the first of the month after working 600 hours or 180 days, whichever comes first.

- **Salaried employees** are benefit-eligible on the first of the month after date of hire.

HEALTH CARE

Full-time and part-time benefit-eligible Costco employees are offered generous health care coverage with low biweekly payroll contributions.

DENTAL CARE

Full-time benefit-eligible Costco employees may choose from two different dental plans: a core dental plan and a premium dental plan. Part-time benefit-eligible employees may elect a core dental plan.

PHARMACY PROGRAM

Most Costco warehouses have pharmacies in-house, making it easy to pick up prescriptions at work. Benefit-eligible employees' co-payments can be as little as $3 for generic medications, and a 15% co-pay applies to other types of medications.

VISION PROGRAM

Most Costco warehouses have in-house optical centers, which make it easy to access this benefit. For benefit-eligible employees and covered dependents, the program pays up to $60 toward a refraction eye exam and $175 for the purchase of prescription glasses and contact lenses.

401K PLAN

Costco matches employee contributions 50 cents on the dollar for the first $1,000 each year to a maximum company match of $500 a year ($250 a year for West Coast Union employees).

DEPENDENT CARE ASSISTANCE PLAN

This allows you to pay for day care for children under age 13, as well as adult day care, with pre-tax dollars.

CARE NETWORK

Care Network's professional counselors are dedicated to Costco employees and trained to help resolve personal, work, or family challenges. They also can provide guidance, information, and/or referrals to local service providers, including lawyers, debt resolution services, and behavioral health professionals.

VOLUNTARY SHORT-TERM DISABILITY

Where disability coverage isn't mandated by their state, all hourly employees who pass their 90-day probationary period and are working at least 10 hours a week will be automatically enrolled in short-term disability insurance.

LONG-TERM DISABILITY

Coverage is at no cost for benefit-eligible employees who are enrolled in a medical plan. This policy pays up to 60% of their earnings if they are out past 180 days.

LIFE INSURANCE

Benefit-eligible employees enrolled in a medical plan also receive basic life insurance and accidental death and dismemberment policies provided at no cost.

EMPLOYEE STOCK PURCHASE PLAN

New employees are immediately eligible to enroll in this plan, which allows them to purchase Costco stock by payroll deduction.

HEALTH CARE REIMBURSEMENT ACCOUNT

Benefit-eligible employees can arrange to have pre-tax contributions automatically deducted from their paychecks and placed into a Health Care Reimbursement Account.

LONG-TERM CARE INSURANCE

Designed to pay for nursing home care, Costco provides a basic policy for employees with 10 or more years of service.[89]

According to a 2014 report published by glassdoor.com, Costco is the number two company to work for based on compensation and benefits (Google is number one).[90] The Glassdoor ranking is based on employees' opinions of their employer's benefit and compensation package. The company received a 4.4 out of a possible 5 for compensation and benefits, and 3.8 out of 5 for total employee satisfaction. In addition, 82% of Costco employees would recommend the company to a friend. CEO Craig Jelinek has a 92% approval rating among employees. Reviews posted on the site by employees praising the Costco work environment said, "The best incentive at Costco is the benefits, whether you are working full time or part time. I paid 20 bucks a month for a $500 deductible with no co-pay. The hourly compensation is more than fair, and I got the sense very quickly that management was eyeing the most competent workers for advancement." "Great wages, benefits . . . and working for a great company that really truly cares about their members and employees."[91]

Questions

1. What organizational processes does compensation affect, and what is Costco's rationale for having an exceptional compensation plan?

2. What are the parts of a compensation system, and what component(s) does Costco's compensation system focus on?

3. What are the four basic types of compensation, and which are evident at Costco?

4. What is expectancy theory, and how does or does not Costco employ this theory within their compensations system?

5. What are the differing types of basic wage classifications, and how does Costco categorize their workforce by basic wage?

6. What is Costco's philosophy about employee compensation?

7. Costco lists numerous benefits that the firm provides employees above their basic salary. What pay rate and benefits must Costco provide their employees as required by federal labor laws?

Case created by Herbert Sherman, PhD, and Theodore Vallas, Department of Management Sciences, School of Business Brooklyn Campus, Long Island University

Skill Builder 10.1 Job Evaluation

Objective

To develop a better understanding of the job evaluation process

Skills

The primary skills developed through this exercise are as follows:

1. *HR management skills*—Technical, conceptual and design, and business skills

2. *SHRM 2018 Curriculum Guidebook*—B: Compensation and Benefits

Assignment

Step 1. You decided to open a restaurant and pub, and you have five job categories:

- *Owner/manager:* You are the owner, performing all the management functions and also greeting and seating people as you oversee all activities.

- *Wait staff:* They take food orders and bring food to customers.

- *Cook:* They prepare the food.

- *Helpers:* They bus tables, wash dishes, help in food preparation, and bring food to some customers.

- *Bartenders:* They make the drinks for both the dining and bar areas.

Rank the jobs from 1 to 5, with 5 being the highest-ranking job and 1 being the lowest.

Job	Mental Requirements (education, intelligence, and specialized knowledge)	Physical Requirements (effort such as standing, walking, and lifting)	Skill Requirements (specific job knowledge/ training to do work)	Responsibilities (for equipment, money, public contact, and supervision)	Working Conditions (safety, heat, ventilation, and coworkers)
Manager					
Wait Staff					
Cook					
Helper					
Bartender					
Factor Rank (1–5) Weight (100%)					

Step 2. Using the table, rank each job for each of the five factors commonly used in job evaluations.

Step 3. The five factors are commonly weighted since some are more important than others.

(A) In the table in the row with the heading "Factor Rank," rank the five factors from 1 to 5, with 5 being the most important and 1 being the least important.

(B) The five factors can also be weighted as percentages. For example, based on a total of 100%, the highest-rated factor could be weighted at 40%, then the next-highest could be rated at 30%, followed by 20%, and the other two at 5% each. Also include your percentage-based weights for each factor, as in the example.

People generally will not agree on all the rankings, and that is a major reason why there is virtually always a committee that conducts job evaluations.

Step 4 (optional due to difficulty). Assign pay values to each of the five factors and weight them to determine pay levels for each job.

Apply It

What did I learn from this experience? How will I use this knowledge in the future?

_____

_____

_____

Skill Builder 10.2 Product Market Competition Limits

Objective

To develop a better understanding of product market competition limits

Skills

The primary skills developed through this exercise are as follows:

1. *HR management skills*—Technical and business skills

2. *SHRM 2018 Curriculum Guidebook*—B: Compensation and Benefits

Assignment

Complete the math problems below.

_____ 1. Your product sells for $1,000. Materials cost $300, labor costs $300, and overhead costs $200. What is your profit in dollars and as a percentage?

_____ 2. Your product sells for $750. Materials cost $250, labor costs $300, and overhead costs $150. What is the profit in dollars and as a percentage?

_____ 3. Your product sells for $1,000. Materials cost $300 and overhead costs $200. What is the maximum amount you can pay labor to make a $100 profit with a 10% return?

_____ 4. Your product sells for $750. Materials cost $250 and overhead costs $150. What is the maximum amount you can pay labor to make a 10% profit return on the sales price?

_____ 5. Your product sells for $800. Materials cost $300 and overhead costs $200. What is the maximum amount you can pay labor to make a 15% profit return on the sales price?

©iStockphoto.com/YinYang

Employee Incentives and Benefits

Learning Outcomes

After studying this chapter, you should be able to do the following:

11.1 Identify the advantages and disadvantages of individual incentives. **Page 282**

11.2 Identify the advantages and disadvantages of group incentives. **Page 284**

11.3 Discuss the issue of whether or not executive compensation is too high. **Page 287**

11.4 Summarize the major statutory benefits required by federal law. **Page 289**

11.5 Name the main statutory requirements that must be followed if organizations choose to provide health care or retirement plans for their employees. **Page 292**

11.6 Describe the main categories of voluntary benefits available to organizations. **Page 294**

11.7 List the organization's options when providing flexible benefit plans to employees. **Page 299**

SHRM HR Content

See Online: *SHRM 2018 Curriculum Guidebook* for the complete list

B. Compensation and Benefits

Compensation

19. Pay programs: Merit pay, pay-for-performance, incentives/bonuses, profit sharing, group incentives/gainsharing, balanced scorecard

23. Team rewards

Employee Benefits

25. Cost-benefit analysis

26. Domestic partner benefits

28. Educational benefits

30. Family-oriented benefits

32. Family and Medical Leave Act (FMLA)

33. Federal insurance programs (Old-Age, Survivor, and Disability Insurance [OASDI], Medicare)

34. Financial benefits (gainsharing, group incentives, team awards, merit pay/bonuses)

36. Health care cost containment

36-a. Health care cost containment—Managing employee benefits (cost control, monitoring future obligations, action planning, strategic planning)

37. Health care plans (multiple payer/single payer, universal health care systems, HMOs, PPOs, fee-for-service, consumer-directed HSAs)

37-a. Health care plans—Affordable Care Act (2010)

38. Life insurance

42. Paid leave plans

44. Regulation of health insurance programs (COBRA, HIPAA, Health Maintenance Organization Act of 1973)

45. Regulation of retirement plans (FLSA, ERISA, Pension Protection Act of 2006)

48. Statutory vs. voluntary benefits

49. Survivor's benefits

50. Social Security

51. Time off and other benefits

52. Types of retirement plans (defined benefit, defined contribution, hybrid plans)

53. Unemployment Insurance

55. Workers' compensation

D. Employment Law

1. Affordable Care Act (2010)

4. COBRA: Consolidated Omnibus Budget Reconciliation Act of 1985

5. Employer Retirement Income Security Act of 1974 (ERISA)

10. Family and Medical Leave Act of 1993 (FMLA)

12. Health Insurance Portability and Accountability Act (HIPAA) of 1996

Practitioner's Perspective

Cindy reflects: Whether the economy is up or down, your star employees can always find another job. This keeps HR departments looking for ways to keep their best employees motivated and engaged in their positions.

One of Cindy's colleagues, Terry, is a big advocate of incentive pay and good benefits packages. "We need to look at ways to reward our exceptional employees now without expanding our base labor costs into future years," Terry said at one of their strategy meetings. "I've seen evidence to support the case that employees work harder if they know they have a fair chance of being rewarded for that extra effort."

"Well, I've heard lots of complaints against incentive pay," says Bill, another member of their department. "I'm not sure we want to open our compensation program to those issues."

Are strong incentive and benefits packages a good idea? The pros and cons plus the methods of implementation are detailed for your consideration in Chapter 11.

The Strategic Value of Incentives and Benefits

We discussed the basic pay system and how our core wages or salaries are set in Chapter 10. Recall for a moment the motivation theories we discussed in that chapter because they boost productivity[1] and they decrease turnover.[2] Incentive compensation takes advantage of both expectancy theory (where the employee expects a reward that matches their effort and performance) and equity theory (where an individual employee evaluates their rewards against others based on the amount of "input" effort they provide). Incentives allow us to vary the reward[3] based on the *individual* (or group) *effort* put into the work process.

In addition to incentive pay, employees tend to pay close attention to company benefits packages in today's workforce.[4] And their companies pay attention to benefits as well—benefits are expensive![5] According to the U.S. Bureau of Labor Statistics (BLS), benefits for all groups of workers average roughly 32% of total employee compensation cost.[6] So it makes sense that companies pay significant attention to benefits[7] and track their total cost. Because people are demanding more and better benefits, companies add new benefits to what they have historically offered,[8] which requires HR to spend more time monitoring the cost as well as the value provided. But it also provides an incentive to employees to continue with us,[9] due to the fact that they feel as if they are being cared for by the company.[10] So the strategic value is that we increase job satisfaction and engagement because when employees are taken care of, they work harder and take good care of our customers and the organization.[11]

Because incentives and benefits provide strategic value to companies, we must carefully manage them. Poorly structured programs can actually backfire and hurt performance.[12] Let's take a little closer look at both of these compensation components. **(SHRM B:25)**

Individual Incentives, or Variable Pay

>> **LO 11.1 Identify the advantages and disadvantages of individual incentives.**

Variable pay Compensation that depends on some measure of individual or group performance or results in order to be awarded

Let's get into some detail now on variable pay, also known as incentives. **Variable pay** is *compensation that depends on some measure of individual or group performance or results in order to be awarded*. People respond to incentives,[13] and rewards and recognition are combined to create motivational incentive systems.[14] The use of pay for performance rather than hours worked is a strongly increasing trend today.[15]

There are two basic choices in incentive pay—individual or group-based incentives. Individual incentives reinforce a person's performance with a reward that is significant to that person.[16] They are based on operant conditioning and reinforcement theory and are designed to motivate the individual employee to do more than the minimum while on the job. We want to be able to reward our best employees so they feel that they are being recognized,[17] and individual incentives allow us to do that.

Advantages and Disadvantages of Individual Incentives

Take a look at Exhibit 11.1 for a brief list of advantages and disadvantages of individual incentive plans.

Individual Incentive Options

There are five common options for individual financial incentives. Let's review each of these options. Remember you can also give nonfinancial awards. Personal praise and recognition from managers can cost nothing and be a more effective motivator than cash.[18] However, watch out for problems with any awards. If the same person(s) consistently wins an award, such as top sales or employee of the month, it can result in envy and destructive behaviors. Be careful to avoid employees gaming the program or concentrating efforts on meeting the award criteria at the expense of less measurable tasks, such as collaborating and teamwork. Watch for faking performance or manipulating the measures to win the awards.[19]

Bonus

Bonus pay is *a lump sum payment, typically given to an individual at the end of a time period.*[20] Giving bonuses does help retain employees.[21] A bonus does not carry over from one period to the next. How would a bonus program have to be designed in order to motivate increased performance? We would need to identify specific and measurable goals that the individual could affect.[22] If they then reached the measurable goal, they would receive the bonus. Companies, including **Nike**, are rethinking pay and bonus practices,[23] and several employers choose bonuses over raises.[24] But at the same time, companies, such as **Amazon**, that are being pressured to raise wages to $15 an hour, are eliminating stock awards and bonuses for some hourly employees.[25]

Bonus pay A lump sum payment, typically given to an individual at the end of a time period

Commissions

Commissions are well-known incentive tools for sales professionals. A commission is a payment typically provided to a salesperson for selling an item to a customer and is usually paid as a percentage of the price of an item that is sold. If you sell a $100 product and you are on a 10% commission, you would receive $10 for that sale. Salespeople sometimes work on straight commission, where they only get paid when they sell an item, or they can be paid a salary plus commission.

EXHIBIT 11.1 ● Individual Incentive Plan Advantages and Disadvantages

Advantages	Disadvantages
Promotes the link between performance and results; pay is based on performance.	Many jobs have no direct output; measuring performance to reward is difficult.
Offers the ability to match rewards to employee desires; individuals want different rewards.	May motivate undesirable employee behaviors; individuals can use unethical behavior to achieve rewards.
Makes it easy to evaluate individual employees; individuals perform at different levels.	Record-keeping burden is high; it takes more time to evaluate and record individual performance than group performance.
May motivate less productive employees to work harder; individuals may perform at higher levels to get rewards.	May not fit organizational culture; incentives can hurt team effort of collaboration.

Merit Pay

The next incentive option is called merit pay. **Merit pay** is *a program to reward top performers with increases in their annual wage that carry over from year to year.* Merit pay works as follows: The company announces a "merit pool" available for pay increases in a given period, usually annually. The merit raises will be given to the top performers in the company based on performance evaluations. Frequently, individuals who receive either outstanding or excellent marks will get merit increases above the average, while average performers will get a lower raise and those who receive below-average marks will get no raise at all. **(SHRM B:19)**

Piecework Plans

Piecework or piece-rate plans are one of the simplest forms of compensation, and they can act as an incentive to produce at a higher level because the more workers produce, the more they get paid. In a "straight piece-rate" compensation system, the employee gets paid for every "piece" they complete.[26] A "differential piece-rate" system provides the employee with a base wage to complete a certain amount of work, and if they produce more than the standard, a differential wage is paid for the extra pieces produced.

Standard Hour Plans

In a standard hour plan, each task is assigned a "standard" amount of work time for completion.[27] The individual doing the job will get paid based on the standard (expected) time to complete the job, but good workers can frequently complete the work in less than the standard amount of time. If they do, they can get paid for an hour of work while working less than an hour of time.

11.1 APPLYING THE CONCEPT
INDIVIDUAL INCENTIVE OPTIONS

Place the letter of the individual incentive on the line next to the scenario illustrating it.

a. Bonus

b. Commissions

c. Merit pay

d. Piecework

e. Standard hour

f. Nonmonetary awards

_____ 1. I'm an auto mechanic at a dealership, and we have a set amount of time to complete each type of repair work. I complete a job before a stated time so that I can go on to the next car and get paid extra for being faster than the average mechanic.

_____ 2. I just sold that top-of-the-line BMW M3. I can't wait to get my pay this week.

_____ 3. I'm the top producer in the entire department, so I will get an extra raise for high performance this year.

_____ 4. The boss gave me a plaque and check for $5,000 in front of the entire company at our annual meeting.

Group Incentives

>> **LO 11.2 Identify the advantages and disadvantages of group incentives.**

Individual incentive programs obviously work well in some cases. However, group incentives tend to work better in a number of other situations. In fact, one study found that group incentives, combined with policies to empower employees, increase employee intent to stay with a company, lower voluntary turnover, and increase return on equity (ROE).[28] **(SHRM B:23)**

Advantages and Disadvantages of Group Incentives

What are the basic advantages and disadvantages of group incentive plans? See Exhibit 11.2 for a list. As with individual incentives, be careful to avoid employees gaming the program or concentrating efforts on meeting the award criteria at the expense of less measurable tasks, faking performance, or manipulating the measures to win the awards.[29]

EXHIBIT 11.2 ● Group Incentive Plan Advantages and Disadvantages

Advantages	Disadvantages
Promotes better teamwork; it promotes collaboration to work together to achieve the goal.	Social loafing can occur; *social loafers avoid providing their maximum effort in group settings because it is difficult to pick out individual performance.*
Broadens individual outlook; employee better understands the relationship among jobs and departments.	Individual output may be discounted; Some individuals may feel as if they are providing most of the group's effort and are not equitably rewarded for it.[30]
Requires less supervision; the members will enforce accepted standards of behavior and performance.	Outstanding performers may slacken efforts; faster employees may hold back performance to lower group standard level.
Is easier to develop than individual incentive programs; one incentive for a department of 20 is easier than 20 individual incentives.	Group infighting may arise; conflict can hurt group results.

Social loafers Individuals who avoid providing their maximum effort in group settings because it is difficult to pick out individual performance

11.2 APPLYING THE CONCEPT
GROUP ADVANTAGES AND DISADVANTAGES

Identify each statement by its group advantage or disadvantage.

	Advantages		Disadvantages
a.	Promotes better teamwork	e.	Social loafing can occur
b.	Broadens individual outlook	f.	Individual output may be discounted
c.	Requires less supervision	g.	Outstanding performers may slacken efforts
d.	Is easier to develop than individual incentive programs	h.	Group infighting may arise

_____ 1. What happened? Latoya and Katie used to get along so well. Now they are constantly bickering.

_____ 2. Katrina, you are not being fair to the rest of us by not doing your fair share of the work.

_____ 3. Now that we use a team-based process, the manager doesn't check up on us like she used to.

_____ 4. By assembling the product as a team, we actually increased production by 20%.

_____ 5. I know I'm the best, but none of the department members work very hard, so why should I?

Group Incentive Options

We can use group incentives to motivate higher levels of performance from groups. Let's take a look at some of the more common group incentive options.

Profit Sharing Plans

Profit sharing programs Programs that provide a portion of company proceeds over a specific period of time (usually either quarterly or annually) to the employees of the firm through a bonus payment

Profit sharing programs *provide a portion of company proceeds over a specific period of time (usually either quarterly or annually) to the employees of the firm through a bonus payment.* The programs are designed to cause everyone in the company to focus on total organizational profitability.[31]

One major issue with profit sharing as a motivator is that it is focused on total organizational performance and profitability. If the employee doesn't know what to do in order to increase profits, what will they do differently in their job? The answer is "absolutely nothing." So profit sharing in some cases may not provide the company with the expected boost in productivity.[32]

Gainsharing Plans

An alternative to profit sharing is a gainsharing program. Gainsharing is similar to profit sharing because the "gain" is shared with the employees who helped to create the gain. However, gainsharing can be accomplished using any organizational factor that makes, or costs, the company money and that can be analyzed and modified for performance improvement.[33] Some of the more common gainsharing options are increased revenues, increased labor productivity or lower labor costs, improved safety (fewer lost-time accidents), return on assets or investment, and increased customer satisfaction. **(SHRM B:34)**

Employee Stock Plans

There are also stock ownership plans that may work well as group incentives as they do help retain employees.[34] The first is an *employee stock ownership plan* (ESOP). An ESOP ultimately allows at least part of the stock in the company to be earned by the employees over a period of time based on some formula.[35] For example, if you work for the company for a year, you might get 10 shares of stock, and for every additional year of employment, you would receive 10% more than the year before. An ESOP has the potential to be an incentive to the company's employees, because they become part owners of the firm.

Second, *stock options* may be offered to an employee to allow them to buy a certain number of shares of stock in the company at a specified point in the future, but at a price that is set when the option is offered.[36] The intent here is to motivate the employees to work to improve the value of the company so that when the option to buy the stock comes up at the agreed upon future date, the price of the stock has increased, giving the employee more value than what they paid for.

Lastly, *stock purchasing plans* are similar to stock options, but instead of giving you the option to buy stock in the future, they let qualifying employees buy the stock essentially anytime, usually at a discount. ESOPs, stock options, and stock purchasing give employees ownership in the company, with the intent that the employees will act more like owners of the company than simply employees.

11.1 ETHICAL DILEMMA: WHAT WOULD YOU DO?
ACADEMIC GRADES AND INCENTIVES

Grades are not actually pay, but they are meant to be an incentive to do well academically in college. Grade reports are based on individual performance, but in some courses part of the grade is based on group work.

Recall the Ethical Dilemma about academic standards in Chapter 8. Successful managers establish and maintain high expectations for all their employees. As **Lou Holtz** said, we need to set a higher standard. Today, it is generally agreed that students are doing less work while getting higher grades (grade inflation) than 10 or 20 years ago, based on a continuing trend of lowering of standards.

1. As an incentive, what affect do you believe grades have on performance, and does grade inflation affect the incentive to do well?

2. Has group work been part of your grade in any of your courses? If so, how did it affect your performance?

3. Do you believe group work should increase as part of student grading? Why or why not?

4. Do you find consistency among your professors' standards in terms of the work required in their courses and the grades given, or do some professors require a lot more work and some give lots of As and others lots of lower grades? Should colleges take action to improve consistency among professors' standards? If so, what should they do?

5. Are students who are putting in less time and getting higher grades being well prepared for a career with high standards after graduation?

6. Is it ethical and socially responsible for professors to drop standards and for colleges to award higher grades today than they did 10 or 20 years ago?

7. Should colleges take action to raise standards? If so, what should they do?

11.3 APPLYING THE CONCEPT
GROUP INCENTIVE OPTIONS

Place the letter of the group incentive option on the line next to the matching description.

a. Profit sharing

b. Gainsharing

c. ESOP

d. Stock options

e. Stock purchasing

_____ 10. Our group incentive option gives us a bonus at the end of the year based on how profitable we were for the year.

_____ 11. Our group incentive option plan allows me to get stock and put it in my retirement account without paying anything for it.

_____ 12. Our group incentive option plan worked like this. The manager told us that if we could cut cost in our department by 5%, as a group we would get 5% of the savings to the company distributed evenly among us.

_____ 13. Our group incentive option allows me to buy company stock for 10% less than the market value.

_____ 14. Our group incentive option plan allows me to buy $50 shares of the company stock for only $13 apiece next year.

Executive Compensation

>> **LO 11.3 Discuss the issue of whether or not executive compensation is too high.**

No modern discussion of compensation is complete without at least touching on the topic of executive compensation. Executives drive organizational performance more than any other employee. CEOs like the late **Steve Jobs** of **Apple** have the power to make or break a company.[37] When **Jobs** retired in August of 2011 and died shortly thereafter, Apple stock lost nearly a third of its market value (about $120 billion!) in a year.[38] Research clearly links managerial leadership to consequences for both the individual and organizations, including financial performance. So like the few that have the skills to get paid millions as professional athletes, it makes sense that executives are well paid for their managerial and decision-making skills.

But has executive pay gotten out of line? To even attempt to answer such a question, we need to look at what executives are paid to do. Executives are paid to make decisions for the organization and to guide it toward its goals. And the decisions that executives are paid to make are not easy decisions, such as what products to sell and where to sell them. Successful executive leadership requires a high level of inherent intelligence, knowledge, and skills to analyze so much information, as well as significant experience in making decisions of similar types and consequences.

11.1 SELF-ASSESSMENT

COMPENSATION OPTIONS

Answer each question based on how well it describes you.

1	2	3	4	5	6
Not like me				Describes me	

_____ 1. I enjoy competing and winning.

_____ 2. I usually work faster than others.

_____ 3. I like working alone more than being part of a group.

_____ 4. I don't need to have approximately the same pay every week; varying income is fine.

_____ 5. I enjoy meeting new people and can strike up a conversation with most people.

_____ 6. I take risks.

_____ 7. I would prefer to get a large sum of money all at once rather than many smaller payments.

_____ 8. I'm thinking long term for my retirement.

_____ 9. I like working toward a set of goals and being rewarded for achieving them.

_____ 10. I like knowing that I am one of the best at what I do (merit pay and praise).

There is no simple sum to add up here. Although we would all love to have a high wage or salary with lots of incentive pay on top of it, this is not the reality in most jobs today. In general, the higher your number of "describes me" statements, the more open you are to incentives versus wages/salaries. Below is an explanation of each statement.

Item 1: If you don't like competing and winning, you may be more comfortable in a job with a wage or salary; you usually have to compete for incentives like merit raises. Item 2: If you are not faster than others, piecework and standard hour incentives may not be your best option. Item 3: Commissions, piecework, and standard hours are often based on individual performance. Item 4: Wages and salaries give you a fixed income, whereas incentives provide a variable income. Item 5 is characteristic of commission salespeople. Item 6: If you don't like risk, incentives can be risky. Item 7: Getting a large sum at once tends to involve a bonus, profit sharing, or gain-sharing incentives. Item 8: ESOPs are retirement plans, and stock purchases can be, too. Item 9 reflects gainsharing and bonuses. Item 10 reflects merit pay and praise.

Because labor is always at least partly priced based on supply and demand, and there are very few executives with the high-level skills necessary to run large firms, these individuals are always going to be worth quite a bit of money to the firm. However, this is not to say that there have not been some serious excesses in executive pay, especially when CEO pay has increased while employees were taking pay cuts and getting laid off.[39] According to the AFL-CIO, in 2017, CEOs of S&P 500 companies received, on average, $13.94 million in total compensation. America's production and nonsupervisory workers earned $38,613, on average. So, the CEO-to-worker pay ratio is 361 to 1.[40]

One result of excessive executive compensation resulted in federal legislation on executive compensation—the Dodd-Frank Wall Street Reform and Consumer Protection Act.

The Dodd-Frank Wall Street Reform and Consumer Protection Act of 2010

The Dodd-Frank Act placed new limits on executive pay in public corporations and also added requirements for reporting of both compensation and shareholder involvement with executive compensation.[41] Let's look at the major provisions of the act.

Shareholder "Say on Pay" and "Golden Parachute" Votes

Among the most significant requirements is that shareholders must be allowed to vote on compensation packages for their executive officers at least once every three years. This provision is called "say on pay." While the vote is nonbinding, it can still put pressure on executives to maintain compensation in line with organizational performance.

Shareholders also have a vote on what's called "golden parachutes" for executives. **Golden parachutes** are *a provision for executives who are dismissed from a merged or acquired firm of typically large lump sum payments on dismissal.* This tool is used to discourage a takeover of the firm, because the cost of the takeover becomes much higher due to the high payout to these executives.

Golden parachutes Provision for executives who are dismissed from a merged or acquired firm of typically large lump sum payments on dismissal

Executive Compensation Ratios

Other provisions in Dodd-Frank include a requirement that every public company disclose the total compensation of the CEO and the total median compensation of all employees and provide a ratio of these two figures.[42] For a listing of ratios, visit the AFL-CIO website https://aflcio.org,and search for "pay ratios."[43] It also requires companies to provide information on the ratio between executive compensation and the total shareholder return of the company each year, which allows shareholders to more easily evaluate the performance of firms in which they hold stock.

The act also requires that public companies establish policies to "claw back" incentives if the company has to restate financial information that is detrimental to the firm's value.[44] In other words, if the company paid an executive incentive based on its financial statements and then had to disclose later that those statements were not accurate, company policy would require that any incentives paid out to the executives be given back to the company.

Executive Incentives

Some of the most common incentives used in executive compensation are *stock incentives.*[45] They are supposed to cause the executive to act to increase the value of the company over time, because if this is done, the executive's stock becomes more valuable.

Although used less than in years past, *short-term and long-term bonuses* attached to company performance goals are another popular incentive for executives.[46] Finally, executives generally receive compensation in the form of *perquisites* or "perks." **Perquisites** are *extra financial benefits usually provided to top employees in many businesses.* While perks are not technically incentive pay (they are generally classed as benefits), they do serve to entice top-level executives to consider accepting jobs within an organization in some cases.

Perquisites Extra financial benefits usually provided to top employees in many businesses

Statutory Benefits

>> **LO 11.4 Summarize the major statutory benefits required by federal law.**

Incentives are important to employee performance,[47] but many employees pay close attention to company-provided benefits.[48] Some benefits are statutory (mandatory), due to federal and state laws, but some are optional, based on the desires of the firm. There are also laws that apply if the company chooses to provide certain nonmandatory benefits. Let's do a review of statutory benefits first. **(SHRM B:48, B36-a, B;30, B:49, and B:50)**

Social Security and Medicare

By far the largest of the statutory programs, in both size and cost to employers (and employees), are Social Security and Medicare. The combined cost to the U.S. Treasury of the Old-Age, Survivors, and Disability Insurance (OASDI) and Medicare programs was over $1.66 trillion in 2017,[49] or approximately half of all revenue received by the Treasury Department during that year. Since these programs are so complex, the best we can do in this introductory text is to provide some general information on the programs.

The employer and employee jointly pay into Social Security through withholdings from the employee's paycheck and a mandatory employer payment. Each of them pays a 7.65% tax on the employee's total pay per pay period, with 6.2% going into OASDI and 1.45% of the employee's pay into the Medicare fund. If you are self-employed, you pay both parts for yourself.

Retirement

Once an employee becomes eligible and meets the retirement age requirements, they can receive a monthly check. At what age are you eligible for Social Security retirement? If you were born in 1937 or earlier, you are eligible for retirement at age 65. If you were born in 1960 or later, your retirement age is 67. For those born between 1937 and 1960, it is based on a sliding scale between age 65 and 67.

Disability and Survivor Benefits

These components are really basically the same benefit. If an employee becomes disabled or dies and is otherwise eligible, the person, or their survivors, will get payments each month roughly equal to what the employee would have gotten in retirement based on their historical earnings.

Medicare

Finally, there is the Medicare component of Social Security. Individuals generally become eligible for health care through Medicare at age 65.[50] Medicare is not completely free to the retiree though. The covered person has to pay copayments and deductibles, and there are other out-of-pocket costs involved with Medicare. **(SHRM B:33)**

Workers' Compensation

The next mandatory benefit (in nearly all states in the United States) is workers' compensation, an insurance program designed to provide medical treatment and temporary payments to employees who cannot work because of an employment-related injury or illness. "Employment-related" means the illness or injury had to do with the worker's actions for the company, although the injury or illness didn't have to happen while the person was actually at work. **(SHRM B:55)**

The workers' compensation program is paid for by employers and is a type of "no-fault" insurance, which means that no matter which party—the employer or the employee—was at fault in an accident- or illness-related situation, the insurance will be paid out to the party harmed. Rates are primarily determined by three factors:

1. *Occupations.* Some occupations are much riskier than others. For instance, it costs a lot more to insure firefighters, police officers, or construction workers than it does to cover office workers.

2. *Experience ratings.* An **experience rating** is *a measure of how often claims are made against an insurance policy.* It is calculated on the frequency and severity of injuries that occur within that particular company. The more frequent and severe the claims are, the higher the cost of insurance will be. Experience ratings can significantly affect a company's workers' compensation costs.

3. *Level of benefits payable.* Injured workers will get compensated based on their state's workers' compensation rating manual. Individual states set the rates for injuries within the state's boundaries, and these rates affect the cost of workers' compensation insurance.

Experience rating A measure of how often claims are made against an insurance policy

Unemployment Insurance

The third statutory benefit is unemployment insurance (UI). UI provides workers who lose their jobs with payments from UI funds for a specified period of time. The basic federal tax rate is 6% of wages earned (in 2019) for the first $7,000 in individual wages but can be reduced if the employer pays state unemployment taxes on time and avoids tax delinquencies. **(SHRM B:53)**

Here again, as in workers' compensation, the tax rate is affected by the company's "experience rating." Employers who tend to terminate more employees have a higher experience rating and, as a result, a higher UI tax rate.[51] So within the same state, some employers will pay much more in UI taxes than other employers will.

An individual becomes eligible for UI if they were terminated from employment—either through downsizing, layoff, or other processes—and in most cases if they worked in four of the last five quarters and met minimum income guidelines in each of those quarters.

What will make them *ineligible* for UI?

- The individual quit voluntarily.

- They fail to look for work.

- They were terminated "for cause" (because they did something wrong).

- They refuse suitable work (work comparable to what they were doing prior to being terminated).

- They, as a member of a union, participate in a strike against the company (in most states).

- They become self-employed.

- They fail to disclose any monies earned in a period of unemployment.

Family and Medical Leave Act of 1993 (FMLA)

The next mandatory benefit is Family and Medical Act leave (FMLA). FMLA requires that the employer provide unpaid leave for an "eligible employee" when they are faced with any of the following situations:[52] **(SHRM B:32 and D:10)**

Leave of 12 workweeks in a 12-month period for . . .

- The birth of a child and to care for the newborn child within 1 year of birth

- The placement with the employee of a child for adoption or foster care and to care for the newly placed child within 1 year of placement

- To care for the employee's spouse, child, or parent who has a serious health condition

- A serious health condition that makes the employee unable to perform the essential functions of their job

- Any qualifying exigency arising out of the fact that the employee's spouse, son, daughter, or parent is a covered military member on "covered active duty"

or . . .

> *Leave of 26 workweeks during a single 12-month period* to care for a covered service member with a serious injury or illness if the eligible employee is the spouse, son, daughter, parent, or next of kin to the employee (military caregiver leave)

Any private sector employer is covered under the act if they have 50 or more employees who worked at least 20 weeks during the year, working within a 75-mile radius of a central location. The act exempts "salaried eligible employee(s) . . . among the highest paid 10% of the employees employed by the employer within 75 miles of the facility at which the employee is employed"[53] from job protections if they take FMLA leave, though, because loss of these individuals for as much as 12 weeks could be significantly disruptive to the company. Take a look at the U.S. Department of Labor FMLA webpage (http://www.dol.gov, search for "FMLA") for more information on managing FMLA leave.

Even though FMLA requires only *unpaid* leave, the costs to the company are significant. It puts a significant financial strain on businesses, especially small businesses. The HR department usually bears a large part of the burden of monitoring and curbing abuses of FMLA leave as well as having responsibility for documentation of FMLA cases, and HR managers must be aware of the rules and regulations in order to apply the law correctly.

The Family and Medical Leave Act of 1993 provides unpaid leave for certain "eligible employees" to care for family issues such as births, adoptions, illnesses, and injuries.

The Affordable Care Act of 2010 (ACA)

The last mandatory benefit is the Affordable Care Act of 2010. In general, this act requires that all employers with more than 50 employees provide their *full-time employees* with health care coverage or face penalties for failing to do so.[54]

One lesser-known provision of the law was that employees not covered by a health care plan at work were *required* to go to the state health exchange where they could purchase individual coverage. Individuals who failed to gain coverage were fined until 2019, when the penalty no longer applied. However, several states have passed laws that reinstate the fines within their state borders.[55] You can find out more about the ACA by going to the official site at http://www.hhs.gov, and search for "ACA." **(SHRM B;37-a, D:1, and B:44)**

Statutory Requirements When Providing Certain Voluntary Benefits

>> **LO 11.5 Name the main statutory requirements that must be followed if organizations choose to provide health care or retirement plans for their employees.**

Let's take a look now at some legal requirements that apply *if* we choose to provide certain benefits to our employees. These requirements may apply if we provide our employees with health insurance or company-sponsored retirement plans.

Consolidated Omnibus Budget Reconciliation Act of 1985 (COBRA)

COBRA A law that requires employers to offer to maintain health insurance (for a period of time) on individuals who leave their employment

If employers choose to provide health insurance, we have to abide by the Consolidated Omnibus Budget Reconciliation Act (COBRA). **COBRA** is *a law that requires employers to offer to maintain health insurance (for a period of time) on individuals who leave their employment*. The individual former employee has to pay for the full cost of the insurance (plus up to 2% for administration of the program), but the employer is required to keep the former employee on their group insurance policy. **(SHRM D:4)**

COBRA applies to companies with 20 or more full-time equivalent employees. It must be offered to both terminated employees and those who voluntarily quit, in most cases.

Health Insurance Portability and Accountability Act of 1996 (HIPAA)

The Health Insurance Portability and Accountability Act (HIPAA) is another health insurance law that applies if the company provides health insurance to its employees. What are the general provisions of HIPAA? **(SHRM D:12)**

First, health insurance is *"portable."* This means that if we had group health insurance at our previous employer and *if* our new employer has health care coverage for their employees, they are required to provide us with the opportunity to participate in their health insurance plan.

Second is *accountability*. HIPAA protects "the privacy of individually identifiable health information" from being disclosed to unauthorized individuals.[56] It also provides that employers are accountable to ensure the security of personal health information. So COBRA and HIPAA are mandatory if we as an employer offer health insurance to our employees.

Employee Retirement Income Security Act of 1974 (ERISA)

The first two government mandates discussed were contingent on firm actions in companies that choose to provide *group health insurance* to their employees. However, ERISA covers employers who provide a group retirement plan and/or group health and welfare plans of basically any type, including medical, dental, vision, life insurance, and others. Here are the major provisions of ERISA. **(SHRM D:5 and B:45)**

Eligibility

If the company provides an employee retirement plan, the guidelines in ERISA say that the plan has to be available to all employees over 21 years of age who have worked in the company for 1 year.

Vesting

A second major provision of ERISA is vesting. **Vesting** provides for *a maximum amount of time beyond which the employee will have unfettered access to their retirement funds, both employee contributions and employer contributions*. ERISA identifies the maximum amount of time that the company can retain company contributions to the employee's retirement account. If the employer puts money into the employee's retirement account, that employer must vest the employee in all employer contributions by one of two optional deadlines:

Vesting A maximum amount of time beyond which the employee will have unfettered access to their retirement funds, both employee contributions and employer contributions

100% of employer contributions at the end of 5 years of contributions to the plan; or

20% of employer contributions from the end of Year 3 through the end of Year 7.

Portability

The portability rule allows us to take our retirement fund and move it from one employer to another qualified fund. The employer cannot require that we keep the funds with them, or under their control.

Fiduciary responsibility

ERISA also requires that administrators and managers of retirement, or health and welfare plans meet certain fiduciary standards of conduct. Fiduciary responsibility simply means that the person has an obligation to provide sound and reasonable financial advice to the clients (employees) of these plans.

PBGC

The last big provision of ERISA is the creation of the Pension Benefit Guarantee Corporation (PBGC). The **PBGC** is *a governmental corporation, established within the Department of Labor, whose purpose is to insure "defined benefit" retirement funds* (which we will cover shortly) *from failure* if employers go

PBGC A governmental corporation, established within the Department of Labor, whose purpose is to insure "defined benefit" retirement funds from failure

---

11.4 APPLYING THE CONCEPT
STATUTORY BENEFIT LAWS

Place the letter of the relevant statutory benefit law on the line next to the statement below.

a. FMLA

b. ACA

c. COBRA

d. HIPAA

e. ERISA

_____ 15. I don't trust my company's financial future, so I like this law because it will allow me to move my funds out of my company fund to a new account with the stockbroker of my choice.

_____ 16. I like this law because it will allow me to take time off from work to take care of my sick mother.

_____ 17. I'm going quit and look for a new job, so I like this law because I need to continue to have health insurance while I search for a new job.

_____ 18. I currently have health insurance and medical problems, but when I change jobs, the new company can't refuse to give me insurance based on any medical problems I have when I join the firm.

_____ 19. I'm out of school and almost 25, so I like this law that allows me to continue on my parents' insurance plan.

bankrupt or are for other reasons not able to provide promised retirement benefits. The PBGC may not fund 100% of what was promised in the specific retirement plan, but it "guarantees 'basic benefits' earned before the plan's termination date" or the employer's date of bankruptcy.[57]

Voluntary Benefits

>> **LO 11.6 Describe the main categories of voluntary benefits available to organizations.**

In addition to mandatory benefits, almost all employers provide some group of voluntary benefits to their employees. Companies evaluate their workforce and the funds available to the company and choose the voluntary benefit packages that will best allow them to maintain a satisfied and engaged workforce.[58] They are also offering more perks, like dog-friendly offices and free snacks[59] to attract and retain employees.[60] Let's discuss some of the more common voluntary benefits.

Group Health Insurance

While the ACA requires certain employers with more than 50 full-time employees to provide health insurance to their full-time workforce, all other organizations generally have the choice of whether or not to offer this benefit. The annual premium for an employer-provided family health insurance plan in 2018 was almost $20,000 ($19,616).[61] The U.S. Bureau of Labor Statistics reported that 67% of private-industry workers receive medical care benefits and that employers offering health insurance paid an average of 80% of the cost of premiums for single coverage and 68% of the cost for family coverage in 2017.[62] Health costs continue to rise, and employers have increased health insurance coverage faster than they've increased pay.[63] Health care is a very expensive benefit, and many people make it a major factor in considering an employer. Let's look at the major types of group health insurance. **(SHRM B:37)**

Traditional Plans (Also Called Fee-for-Service)

Traditional health care plans Plans that cover a set percentage of fees for medical services—for either doctors or in-patient care

Traditional health care plans typically *cover a set percentage of fees for medical services—for either doctors or in-patient care.* The most common percentage split between the insurance plan and the individual is 80/20. In other words, if the employee has to go to the hospital and is charged $10,000 for services, the insurance would pay $8,000 and the individual would be responsible for the other $2,000. Traditional plans typically do not cover preventive care, such as an annual physical exam. They do, however, give the employee a lot of choice of health care providers, but there are some serious issues with potential out-of-pocket costs, so this type of plan isn't used much anymore.

Health Maintenance Organizations (HMOs)

Health maintenance organizations (HMOs) A health care plan that provides both health maintenance services and medical care as part of the plan

Health maintenance organizations (HMOs) are *a health care plan that provides both health maintenance services and medical care as part of the plan.* HMOs are a managed care program. This provides the patient with routine preventive care but requires that a review of specific circumstances concerning the individual and their health condition be completed before any significant medical testing, medical procedures, or hospital care is approved. Managed care plans generally require that the employee and their family use doctors and facilities that are in the managed care network.

Preferred Provider Organizations (PPOs)

Preferred provider organizations (PPOs) A kind of hybrid between traditional fee-for-service plans and HMOs

Preferred provider organizations (PPOs) are *a kind of hybrid between traditional fee-for-service plans and HMOs.* They have some of the advantages and disadvantages as well as some of the requirements of both. PPOs have networks of physicians and medical facilities, just like HMOs. PPOs act like HMOs in that they *prefer* (but do not require) that you have a primary care physician within their medical network and that you go to that doctor before going elsewhere for medical care. Similar to HMOs, they also provide preventive care services to their insured members and have similar copayments and annual deductibles.

However, PPOs are more similar to traditional plans in that they do not require that you have a referral from the primary care physician to see a specialist. They will also allow you to see any provider of care either in or outside the network, although you may be required to pay a larger percentage of the cost of care if you choose to go beyond the network of physicians and facilities.

Health or Medical Savings Accounts (HSAs/MSAs) and Health Reimbursement Accounts (HRAs)

Health or medical savings accounts and health reimbursement accounts are savings accounts for health care services. An **HSA or MSA** *allows the employer and employee to fund a medical savings account from which the employee can pay medical expenses each year with pretax dollars.* The money in this account is used to pay for medical services for the employee (and their family, if desired) over the course of that year. One of the big advantages of HSAs and MSAs is that money remaining in the account at the end of the year can usually be rolled over to future years without paying a tax penalty.[64] In an HSA, you pay the full cost of medical services used from the HSA account. There are no copayments; there are no deductibles.

HSAs are also portable, so we can take our HSA balance with us if we change employers. One of the benefits to companies using an HSA or MSA is that it causes the employee to understand the full cost of providing health care for the year because the full cost of care is coming out of the employee's pocket through the use of the HSA debit card. It is thought they might pay more attention to unnecessary medical expenses, such as going to the doctor's office when they have a cold or cut a finger.

One of the biggest differences between HRAs and HSAs is the portability of the account.[65] HRAs do not go with an employee who leaves the company. Another difference is that the HRA is not funded with real dollars until the employee provides a claim against the HRA. So HRAs provide more control to the employer than does an HSA. The HRA also does not carry over from year to year, unless the employer decides that they want it to, and it is not treated as a retirement account. Finally, there is no *requirement* that an HRA is tied to a high-deductible health plan,[66] which we will discuss next. **(SHRM B:36)**

HSA or MSA A plan allowing the employer and employee to fund a medical savings account from which the employee can pay medical expenses each year with pretax dollars

High-Deductible Health Plan (HDHP)

One of the problems that you can quickly see with an HSA is that medical services in a particular year could cost much more than a few thousand dollars, especially if you had surgery. However, federal rules on HSAs and MSAs require that employees who have these accounts also participate in an HDHP. A **high-deductible health plan (HDHP)** *is a "major medical" insurance plan that protects against catastrophic health care costs and in most cases is paid for by the employer.* A very common HDHP would pay for medical costs in any given year that total more than $10,000. So if an individual exceeded the amount of money in their HSA, they would be responsible for out-of-pocket costs up to $10,000, at which time the HDHP would take over and pay all of the remaining costs of the individual's health care for the year. One of the big advantages of HSAs and MSAs is that the individual can go to any physician or medical facility. There are no HMO networks and no preferred providers.

High-deductible health plan (HDHP) A "major medical" insurance plan that protects against catastrophic health care costs and in most cases is paid for by the employer

11.5 APPLYING THE CONCEPT
GROUP HEALTH INSURANCE

Place the letter of each type of health insurance option offered on the line next to the statement describing it.

a. Traditional
b. HMO
c. PPO
d. HSA
e. MSA

_____ 20. I don't like the new insurance plan because I can only go to doctors and hospitals that are approved by the plan. I have to stop seeing my doctor and start with a new one that I'm assigned to.

_____ 21. I have expensive health problems, and my insurance plan requires me to pay 20% of my health care costs, making it very expensive for me.

_____ 22. I like my insurance plan because I'm healthy and pay the full cost, but I don't use it all every year and it has accumulated in case I need it someday.

_____ 23. I do have copays and deductibles, but at least I can go to any doctor or hospital I want to at an extra cost.

Retirement Benefits

According to the Bureau of Labor Statistics, employer-provided retirement plans are available to 77% of all full-time workers and 38% of part-time workers in private industry.[67] Retirement benefits are categorized into two types.

Defined Benefit Versus Defined Contribution Plans

Defined benefit plan A plan providing the retiree with a specific amount and type of benefits that will be available when the individual retires

A **defined benefit plan** *provides the retiree with a specific amount and type of benefits that will be available when the individual retires.* For instance, a simple defined benefit plan might provide that employees who work in the company for 25 years will get 60% of the average of their two highest years of pay. In addition, they will receive 1% more for every additional year that they work. So if the same employee worked for 35 years, they would receive 70% of the average of their two highest years of pay. Because it is a defined benefit retirement plan, the employee knows exactly what their retirement payment will be.

Defined contribution plan A plan providing only the amount of funds that will go into a retirement account, not what the employee will receive upon retirement

Unlike a defined benefit plan, under a defined contribution plan the employee does not know what their retirement benefit will be. A **defined contribution plan** *provides only the amount of funds that will go into a retirement account, not what the employee will receive upon retirement.* If those retirement funds are invested successfully, growing significantly over time, the individual's retirement account will be able to pay much higher benefits than if the funds are not invested successfully and don't grow very much.

Shift From Defined Benefit to Defined Contribution Plans

Defined benefit plans used to be the most common type of retirement plan, but they have been overtaken by defined contribution plans—some would say for legitimate business reasons. Providing a defined contribution retirement plan to employees shifts the investment risk from the company to the individual employee. Let's look at a couple of common defined contribution retirement programs.

©iStockphoto.com/PeopleImages

▲ Employer-provided retirement plans give workers a financial cushion after they retire.

401(k) Plans

The best-known retirement plan in U.S. companies today is the 401(k). 401(k) accounts, or 403(b) accounts for nonprofits, are available to nearly all employees of corporations as well as most self-employed persons. A *401(k) retirement plan* is a savings investment account. **(SHRM B:52)**

Both the employee and the employer are allowed to contribute funds each year to the employee's 401(k) account, with the *employee* allowed to contribute up to a maximum of $19,000 (for an employee under 50 years of age in 2019).[68] Contributions are made on a "pretax basis." This means that when funds are put into the account, they do not count as taxable income for the individual. Once the individual retires and begins to remove funds from the account, they pay income taxes on the distributions from the account.

Matching contributions. Many employers that offer a 401(k) provide a matching contribution up to a set maximum. For example, an employer might allow a 100% match of employee contributions up to a $2,000 maximum. So if the employee put $2,000 of their salary into the retirement account over the course of the year, this plus the employer's matching funds would total $4,000 a year to the individual's retirement account.

IRAs and Roth IRAs

Under U.S. law, any person who pays taxes can contribute to an individual retirement account (IRA), and the contributions are tax-free (subject to a maximum annual income limit). In other words, they reduce your taxable income by the full amount of the contribution in the year in which they are contributed to the account.

Both IRAs and Roth IRAs can supplement the amount that an individual is contributing to a company-sponsored 401(k) account, because you are allowed to contribute to both. An individual can contribute a maximum of 100% of their income up to $6,000 per year (in 2019) into a traditional IRA or a Roth IRA.[69]

The Roth IRA is basically the same type of account as a traditional (regular) IRA, with the exception that the Roth IRA "front-loads," or requires that we pay the taxes immediately for funds put into the retirement account. If we put $4,000 into a Roth IRA in 2019 and were in the 25% federal tax bracket, we would pay $1,000 in tax for 2019, but when we withdrew these funds upon retirement, they would be tax-free. With the traditional IRA, you pay no tax on the funds when you contribute them, but you pay taxes at your current tax rate when those funds are withdrawn.

Paid Time Off

Paid time off (PTO) benefits include a group of options such as vacation time/annual leave, severance pay, personal time off, sick days, and holidays. Some companies provide an all-encompassing PTO plan allowing the employee to use their paid time off in any way they wish, whether for sick days or vacation, holidays, or for any other purpose. Others apportion the available days for vacation, sick time, holidays, and others.[70] The average cost of paid time off is $1 for every $10 in direct wages. None of the PTO benefits is mandatory based on federal law in the United States, but be aware that some states have passed, or are currently attempting to pass, mandatory sick leave and even in some cases annual leave laws. Let's do a quick review of the most common types of PTO. **(SHRM B:51 and B:42)**

Vacation or Annual Leave

The majority of U.S. firms provide paid vacations to their employees, according to the U.S. Bureau of Labor Statistics. In fact, about 95% of employers provide paid vacation in some form—either as a stand-alone benefit or as part of a PTO plan—to their full-time workforce.[71] The average time provided was about 10 days after 1 year of service in 2018, and 17 days after 10 years of service.[72] Employers are increasing vacation and paid leave at a faster pace than they are salaries.[73]

Sick Leave

The next most popular PTO is sick leave. Approximately 78% of employers in the United States provide sick leave of some type to their employees.[74] Paid sick leave can offer employees relief from loss of income associated with having to miss work due to an illness.

Holiday Pay

Nearly all employers provide for at least some paid holidays with their workforce. Companies can be subject to charges of discrimination if there is cultural or religious diversity in the firm and the company does not have flexibility on days available for holiday pay. Because of these issues, some companies provide "floating" holidays so that the employee can pick which days they will observe as holidays during the work year.

Paid Personal Leave

Finally, many companies today provide time off for a variety of personal needs. Personal leave is an effort on the part of the organization to maintain or improve job satisfaction and organizational commitment on the part of their employees.

Other Employee Benefits

Health insurance, retirement accounts, and PTO are three of the most significant, and most expensive, benefits provided by organizations. But there are many other benefits that can be offered to a company's employees. Let's look at a few of those now.

Employee Insurance Options

Life Insurance. Many firms will provide group term life (GTL) insurance policies to provide for survivors of an employee who dies while employed by the company. GTL provides for a survivor payment to occur only if the employee dies during the term that is covered by the insurance policy. It is also a valuable benefit to the employer because they receive a tax deduction for up to $50,000 in coverage if it complies with IRS regulations.[75] A fairly standard benefit here would be 1 to 2 times the individual's annual compensation. **(SHRM B:38)**

Disability Insurance. The other large-scale insurance benefit in many companies is disability insurance. This insurance can be either short- or long-term in nature, and some companies offer both options.

Short-term disability is insurance against being unable to work for up to 6 months due to illness or injury. This is valuable because most *long*-term disability policies do not provide replacement income until the employee completes a 180-day "elimination period" (a period during which they are unable to work). Short-term coverage closes this 6-month gap.

Long-term disability policies cover employees who are unable to work for more than 6 months due to illness or injury. Long-term disability is designed to replace a portion of the disabled employee's income (*typically* about 60%) for extended periods of time, or even permanently.[76]

Employee Services

Companies may provide a wide variety of employee services as benefits for their workforce. *Educational (or tuition) assistance* is one common benefit in this group. In 2018, roughly 50% of all companies provided some form of educational assistance to their employees,[77] including Wegmans[78] and Walmart.[79] **(SHRM B:28)**

Other common employee services include on-site child care or child care vouchers, elder care assistance, executive coaching, company-provided fitness facilities or vouchers for memberships outside the business, organization-sponsored sports teams, services to mitigate commuting costs or public or private transportation vouchers, cafeterias or meal vouchers, plus too many others to name.

Employee services are provided in order to minimize disruptions to the employee's work life and help work/life balance.[80] If employees aren't worried about their children (because the company has a day care facility on site), they can concentrate on work. If they don't have to deal with figuring out where they can park downtown, they are less stressed when they start their day. Other services that help work/life balance include flexible work schedules[81] and telecommuting.[82] Companies don't provide these services because they like to give money away; rather, they provide employee services to lower stress and allow employees to concentrate on their jobs.

Before we go on to discuss how to administer and communicate benefits, let's review the list of benefits discussed so far (see Exhibit 11.3). Note that there are an unlimited number of voluntary benefits, but only some major ones are listed here.

EXHIBIT 11.3 ● Employee Benefits

Statutory Benefits	Voluntary Benefits
Social Security and Medicare	**Paid time off**
Workers' compensation	Group health insurance
Unemployment Insurance	Retirement benefits
Family and Medical Leave Act (FMLA)	Employee insurance coverage
The Patient Protection and Affordable Care Act (ACA)	Employee services
	Educational (or tuition) assistance
Statutory requirements when providing certain voluntary benefits	On-site child care or child care vouchers
	Elder care assistance
Consolidated Omnibus Budget Reconciliation Act (COBRA)	Company-provided fitness facilities or vouchers for memberships
Health Insurance Portability and Accountability Act (HIPAA)	Organization-sponsored sports teams
Employee Retirement Income Security Act (ERISA)	Services to mitigate commuting costs, including work shuttles, company-provided or paid parking, "green" vehicle allowances, public or private transportation vouchers
	Free or low-cost meals

11.2 SELF-ASSESSMENT

SELECTING EMPLOYEE BENEFITS

Assume you are graduating with your college degree and getting your first or a new full-time job. The organization gives you the list below and asks you to rank-order the list of employee benefits from 1 (the most important to you) to 11 (the least important to you).

1. _____ Paid time off (vacations, sick and personal days, holidays)

2. _____ Health insurance (traditional, HMO, PPO, HSA/MSA)

3. _____ Retirement benefits (401[k] or 403[b], IRA or Roth IRA)

4. _____ Employee insurance coverage (life, disability, others)

5. _____ Educational (or tuition) assistance (getting your MBA or other degree or some type of certification or license like the PHR and SPHR, CPA, or FICF)

6. _____ Child care (on-site or vouchers)

7. _____ Elder care (on-site or vouchers)

8. _____ Fitness (organization-provided fitness facilities or vouchers for memberships)

9. _____ Organization-sponsored sports teams (softball, basketball, bowling, golf, etc.)

10. _____ Commuting (work shuttles, company-provided or paid parking, "green" vehicle allowances, public or private transportation vouchers)

11. _____ Meals (free or low-cost meals on site or meal vouchers)

There is no scoring as this is a personal choice. Think about your selection today. Will your priority ranking change in 5, 10, 15, or 20 years?

Flexible Benefit (Cafeteria) Plans

>> **LO 11.7 List the organization's options when providing flexible benefit plans to employees.**

We need to allow at least some flexibility in our benefits system so it can be partially tailored to the needs of the worker. In fact, employees who were placed on a flexibility program were both happier at work and less prone to burnout and psychological stress than their colleagues who were not on the program.[83] What is a flexible benefits plan, commonly known as a *cafeteria* plan? Most cafeteria plans fall into one of three categories—each with its own advantages and disadvantages.

Modular Plans

The employee has several basic modules from which they can choose to provide a set of benefits that match their life and family circumstances. Each module has a different mix of insurance, employee services, and retirement options. The employee chooses a module that most closely meets their needs. There may be a module for young single employees that maximizes work flexibility with more time off for personal activities but has minimal or no benefits in areas such as family health plans, child care, or dental. Another module might be designed for families with young children, while a third might be set up for older workers whose children are grown.

Core-Plus Plans

In a *core-plus plan,* we have a base set of benefits, called the *core,* that are provided to everyone, and then employees are allowed to choose other options to meet personal needs and desires. The core benefits provide basic protection for all of the company's employees in areas such as health and life insurance, and maybe a minimum amount of retirement funding. The remaining benefits are available for the employee to pick and choose other options that match their personal needs.

Full-Choice Plans

The full-choice plans provide complete flexibility to the organizational member. Each employee can choose exactly the set of benefits they desire, within specified monetary limitations. This is truly a cafeteria plan in that employees can choose any offered benefit they want without a modular or core set of benefits. However, there are some significant problems with full-choice plans for both the individual and the organization. Employees may choose the wrong mix of benefits, or they may try to manipulate the system by only choosing a benefit, such as dental care, in a year when they know they will have a significant expense in that area. Through this manipulation of the benefits system, the overall cost to the organization for providing these benefits can go up significantly.

The bottom line is that flexible plans are really gaining ground because our workforce is much more diverse than it used to be. Benefits need to match the needs of our workers, but we have to remember that the more flexible the plan is, the more expensive it is.

11.6 APPLYING THE CONCEPT
FLEXIBLE BENEFIT PLANS

Place the letter of the type of flexible plan on the line next to statement that describes it.

a. Modular

b. Core-plus

c. Full-choice

_____ 25. I don't think our benefit plan is fair because I use my spouse's health insurance plan and I just lose the benefit. To be fair, I should be able to use the money for other benefits I want.

_____ 26. I sure wish we got more of our compensation in benefits, but at least with my benefit package, I can choose any benefit I want each year.

_____ 27. My benefit plan has five packages, and I get to pick any one of them that I want each year. But it's difficult to select one.

_____ 28. I definitely want to get health care and retirement benefits, and it's nice to have the option of selecting a few other benefits with a set dollar value.

_____ 29. The hard part about my benefit plan is that there are so many options to choose from that I have a hard time selecting the ones I may really need.

Trends and Issues in HRM

Here we explore whether or not incentive pay improves employee performance and the trend toward benefits for domestic partners.

Does Incentive Pay Actually Improve Performance?

We would be remiss in discussing incentive pay if we did not mention the fact that there is an ongoing argument that incentive pay actually causes demotivation. Although we can't go into all of the details in this section, we need to briefly lay out the issues. An article in the *Journal of Business Research* makes the argument that incentives don't work.[84] It says one study "found it makes better business sense to reward team performance rather than provide bonuses to the top-performing individuals," and that "McKinsey consultants found that shareholder returns were no higher when management had incentive plans" (emphasis added).[85] However, if you follow the guidelines we provided earlier, you know we never want to incentivize only managers (we should provide incentives to all) and that we take team performance into account through a number of the guidelines, from creating SMART goals, which make sure there is a link between performance and payout, to making the program part of a comprehensive approach to managing people that ensures that all organizational goals are met, not just the individual goals that are incentivized.

The same study also notes that "financial incentives can create pay inequality, which in turn can cause turnover and harm performance."[86] But in fact, isn't turnover of nonperformers or low performers part of what we want in the organization? If they self-select out of the company, we have the opportunity to bring in people better suited to do the job. Remember back in Chapter 1, we said that some turnover is necessary in order for the organization to improve over time.

There are also many studies of incentives that back up variable pay, despite the detractors. One recent meta-analysis on the effectiveness of incentives identified 146 studies of financial incentives and concluded that the "overall effect size of individual incentives was positive" and the studies "indicated a positive effect regarding team-based rewards on performance" as well.[87] The study also noted that equitably distributed rewards created higher performance levels than equally distributed rewards, which is what equity theory predicts.

So there are arguments concerning the value of incentives. However, if you look at business research, the evidence seems to strongly favor providing equitable (fair, but not equal) incentives to all in order to get maximum productivity in return. Although research indicates team incentives seem to be more valuable, they are much more difficult to implement successfully. So organizations have to choose what type of programs to implement, knowing there are potential flaws with every option. Using the guidelines to creating motivational incentives will help you work through the issue and come up with an incentive program that can work for your company.

Benefits for Domestic Partners

One of the more significant recent issues in benefits management has been the question of providing benefits for domestic partners. Sometimes called "significant others," **domestic partners** are *individuals who are not legally married but who are in a one-to-one living arrangement similar to marriage,* whether that arrangement is same-sex or opposite-sex. About 25% of companies offered some benefits to domestic partners in 2017,[88] but should we treat such domestic partners the same as spouses for the purpose of providing company benefits? **(SHRM B:26)**

Domestic partners
Individuals who are not legally married but who are in a one-to-one living arrangement similar to marriage

Our purpose here is not to discuss the validity of domestic partner arrangements and whether or not they are morally right or wrong. That is up to the individuals, the organization, and the state and country in which they operate. Our analysis has to look at the costs as well as any organizational advantages that might be gained by providing domestic partner coverage. Organizations may choose to provide domestic partner benefits in order to support a more diverse workforce, to recruit the best talent possible, or just to provide equity to all of their employees.

Benefits that are affected by the employee's marital status include Social Security survivor benefits, workers' compensation survivor payments, access to FMLA, and coverage under COBRA and ERISA. Each of these laws has at least some language that provides for benefits only to legal spouses of employees, not to domestic partners. In some cases, federal law requires the employer to tax any benefits provided to an employee's unmarried domestic partner, because the tax code says that to receive favorable tax treatment for benefits, such as a health savings account, the coverage has to go to the employee and their immediate family members, not to domestic partners. Employers have to be aware of the language of the laws so that they don't unintentionally violate such laws. One significant recent change has been the recognition of same-sex marriage at the federal level in the United States, which is different in the eyes of the law from domestic partnerships. The Treasury Department and the IRS have ruled that legally married same-sex couples must be treated the same as other married couples for federal tax purposes.

In addition, companies have to be aware that providing domestic partner benefits may cost them significant amounts of money. Allowing domestic partners to be covered under company insurance and other benefit policies will almost always add to the cost of the benefits program. We must weigh the value of the loyalty and satisfaction gained by such actions against the direct monetary cost of this type of coverage. Companies are taking a hard look at the cost of domestic partner benefits and, in some cases at least, deciding that the cost is too high to cover the added value to their employee base.

Chapter Summary

11.1 Identify the advantages and disadvantages of individual incentives.

Individual incentives make it easy to evaluate each individual employee. They provide the ability to choose rewards that match employee desires, they promote a link between performance and results, and they may motivate less productive workers to work harder. Disadvantages include the fact that many jobs have no direct outputs, making it hard to identify individual objectives; we may motivate undesirable behaviors; there is a higher record-keeping burden than in group incentives; and individual rewards may not fit in the organizational culture.

11.2 Identify the advantages and disadvantages of group incentives.

Group incentives help foster more teamwork, and they broaden the individual's outlook by letting them see how they affect others. They also require less supervision and are easier to develop than individual incentives. Disadvantages include the potential for social loafing, the possibility that we will discount individual efforts and output, the fact that outstanding performers may lessen their efforts, and the potential for group infighting.

11.3 Discuss the issue of whether or not executive compensation is too high.

There is no doubt that in some cases, executive compensation has gotten out of control. There is evidence that there have been some serious excesses in executive pay, especially when CEO pay has increased while employees were taking pay cuts and getting laid off. However, executives drive organizational performance more than any other employee. Since labor is always at least partly priced based on supply and demand, and there are very few executives with the high-level skills necessary to run large firms, these individuals are always going to be worth quite a bit of money to the firm. This means that as a general rule, executive pay is probably not out of line, considering the pressure on executives to perform at the highest level all the time.

11.4 Summarize the major statutory benefits required by federal law.

Social Security and Medicare—Social Security is composed of Old-Age, Survivors, and Disability Insurance (OASDI) programs, and Medicare is the national health care program for the elderly or disabled.

Workers' compensation is a program to provide medical treatment and temporary payments to employees who are injured on the job or become ill because of their job.

Unemployment insurance is a federal program managed by each state to provide payments for a fixed period of time to workers who lose their jobs.

FMLA is leave that must be provided by the employer to eligible employees when they or their immediate family members are faced with various medical issues. The leave is unpaid, but the employer must maintain health coverage for the employee while they are on leave.

ACA requires that all employers with more than 50 employees provide health insurance for their full-time employees or face significant penalties levied by the federal government.

11.5 Name the main statutory requirements that must be followed if organizations choose to provide health care or retirement plans for their employees.

COBRA is a law that requires employers to offer continuation of health insurance, for up to 18 to 36 months, on individuals who leave their employment if the employee is willing to pay the premium cost of the insurance policy.

HIPAA requires that, if the employee had health insurance at their old job and the new company provides health insurance as a benefit, it must be offered to the employee. In other words, the individual's health insurance is "portable." HIPAA also requires that companies take care to protect the health information of employees from unauthorized individuals.

ERISA lays out requirements that must be followed if the employer provides a retirement or health care plan. ERISA determines who is eligible to participate and, when they are eligible, provides rules for "vesting" of the employee's retirement funds, requires portability of those funds, and requires that the funds are managed "prudently" by the fiduciary that maintains them.

11.6 Describe the main categories of voluntary benefits available to organizations.

Major voluntary benefits include group health insurance, retirement plans, other insurance coverage, paid time off, and employee services. Paid time off comes in various forms, such as sick leave, vacation time, holidays, and personal days. Group health insurance provides employees with health care coverage, and retirement plans allow them to save for their own retirement, sometimes with some help from the organization. Other insurance includes group term life insurance, short- and long-term disability policies, dental and vision insurance, group automobile and homeowners insurance, and many more. Finally, employee services can include a massive range of options from educational assistance to child or adult day care, gyms, cafeterias, and too many others to list.

11.7 List the organization's options when providing flexible benefit plans to employees.

Companies can choose modular plans, core-plus plans, or full-choice plans. Modular plans provide several basic modules from which each employee chooses. There is no other option outside one of the modules. Core-plus plans provide a base set of benefits to all employees (the core) and then other options that the employee can choose from freely to meet their personal desires and needs. Full-choice plans allow the employee complete freedom of choice, but they come with some potential problems such as "moral hazard," "adverse selection," and high management costs.

Key Terms

bonus pay,   283
COBRA,   292
defined benefit plan,   296
defined contribution plan,   296
domestic partners,   301
experience rating,   290
golden parachutes,   289

health maintenance
   organizations (HMOs),   294
high-deductible health plan
   (HDHP),   295
HSA or MSA,   295
merit pay,   284
PBGC,   293
perquisites,   289

preferred provider organizations
   (PPOs),   294
profit sharing programs,   286
social loafers,   285
traditional health care plans,   294
variable pay,   282
vesting,   293

Key Terms Review

Complete each of the following statements using one of this chapter's key terms.

1. _____ is compensation that depends on some measure of individual or group performance or results in order to be awarded.

2. _____ is a program to reward top performers with increases in their annual wage that carry over from year to year.

3. _____ are individuals who avoid providing their maximum effort in group settings because it is difficult to pick out individual performance.

4. _____ provide a portion of company proceeds over a specific period of time (usually either quarterly or annually) to the employees of the firm through a bonus payment.

5. _____ provide executives who are dismissed from a merged or acquired firm of typically large lump sum payments on dismissal.

6. _____ are extra financial benefits usually provided to top employees in many businesses.

7. _____ is a measure of how often claims are made against an insurance policy.

8. _____ is a law that requires employers to offer to maintain health insurance (for a period of time) on individuals who leave their employment.

9. _____ provides for a maximum amount of time beyond which the employee will have unfettered access to their retirement funds, both employee contributions and employer contributions.

10. _____ is a governmental corporation established within the Department of Labor whose purpose is to insure retirement funds from failure.

11. _____ are plans that cover a set percentage of fees for medical services—for either doctors or in-patient care.

12. _____ are health care plans that provide both health maintenance services and medical care as part of the plan.

13. _____ are a kind of hybrid between traditional fee-for-service plans and HMOs.

14. _____ allows the employer and employee to fund a medical savings account from which the employee can pay medical expenses each year with pretax dollars.

15. _____ is a "major medical" insurance plan that protects against catastrophic health care costs and in most cases is paid for by the employer.

16. _____ provide the retiree with a specific amount and type of benefits that will be available when the individual retires.

17. _____ identify only the amount of funds that will go into a retirement account, not what the employee will receive upon retirement.

Communication Skills

The following critical-thinking questions can be used for class discussion and/or for written assignments to develop communication skills. Be sure to give complete explanations for all answers.

1. Would you rather be given the opportunity to receive incentives based on individual performance or group performance? Does it depend on the situation? Why?

2. Would you rather work on a commission basis if you were in sales, or would you rather have a salary—or a combination of both? Why?

3. Would you personally rather participate in a profit sharing plan or a gainsharing plan? Why?

4. Do you think incentive programs in general really work? Why or why not?

5. Would you rather have better benefits and a modest salary or a high salary and lower levels of benefits? Why?

6. Based on what is in the chapter, should the ACA federal health care legislation remain in its current form, or should we rescind the requirement that employers and/or employees have to pay a fine if the employee is not covered by a health care plan? Explain your answer.

7. Is the vesting requirement in ERISA too long, too short, or just about right? Why did you answer the way that you did?

8. Should the United States mandate a certain amount of paid time off per year as many other countries currently do? Why or why not?

9. Do you think that in today's workforce it is becoming necessary to have a "full-choice" flexible benefits plan? Why or why not?

Case 11.1 Best Buy or Best Scam? Trying to Get Commission Results on So-Called Non-Commission Pay

Best Buy is one of the largest consumer electronics outlets in the United States and across the world. Its stores sell a variety of electronic gadgets and wearables, tablets, movies, music, computers, mobile phones, and appliances. On the services side, it offers installation and maintenance, technical support, and subscriptions for mobile phone and Internet services. Best Buy's operations consist of its domestic and international segments. The domestic segment, which made up 92% of the retailer's total sales in fiscal 2016 (ended January), focuses on the U.S. market, where Best Buy Mobile (mobile sales and service), Geek Squad (technology support services), and Pacific Sales (kitchen appliance sales and installation) can be found in U.S. Best Buy stores using the store-within-a-store format. Some also operate as stand-alone stores. Struggling from declining sales amid stiff competition from retailers (such as Amazon and Walmart), Best Buy reiterated that it would look for ways to optimize store space, renegotiate leases, and selectively open and close locations to support the company's long-term transformation.[89]

One way that Best Buy has tried to increase store revenues is by focusing on providing customers product knowledge and services over direct sales. The Best Buy Code of Ethics is very clear on how customers should be treated.

> Customers are at the core of our success and must be treated with respect. Every customer. Every situation. Every day. On the Responsibility to Our Business Partners page, we noted how important Best Buy's reputation is to the long-term success of our Company. For this reason, every employee is obligated to: • Treat all customers fairly and honestly • Communicate with customers in a respectful and helpful manner • Provide prompt and accurate customer service. . . . Our customers rely on us to price and present our products and services fairly and accurately. . . . We do not condone any behavior that would violate their trust in us. Ever.[90]

Best Buy's point of pride is that their employees are not paid on commission. Employees are trained to make non-commission statements, informing customers they are simply paid a flat rate in an attempt to gain customer trust and increase sales.[91]

This can be a great benefit to the customer, but according to one self-proclaimed employee veteran, this is not the whole story. It is true that most customer-facing employees (like Geek Squad agents or sales staff) are not paid on commission. However, sales are still incentivized in ways that create a commission-like atmosphere. For example, managers have the opportunity to make big bonuses based off revenue/margin goals. Lower-level employees can hit Blue Crew Bucks (a bonus tacked onto a paycheck). Some employees (like Best Buy for Business) receive commission on sales. None of these practices is unethical, but giving customers the impression that sales performance is not rewarded seems to this employee to be misleading and wrong. The data below from Payscale indicates that sales associates earn bonuses plus commission.[92]

Sales Associate at Best Buy Salary Range[93]

Bonus	$199.11–$2,970
Commission	$122.82–$16,650
Total Pay	$19,262–$28,070

In an attempt to increase in-store sales to combat increased online competition, Best Buy implemented a new sales tracking system. Now, each sales employee's performance is closely tracked, as it would be in a commission pay system. Employees are tracked on multiple metrics, including sales per hour, protection plans sold, margin and gross revenue per sale, payments made on a Best Buy credit card, and accessory attach rate. By implementing this tracking system, Best Buy has promptly and profoundly changed the work climate within the stores. They have created all of the problems of a commission system, like competitive relationships between employees and in-fighting for sales—both of which damage the customer relationship and defy their claims. It clearly hurts the work culture.

Best Buy understands that such a tracking system has the potential to have a negative effect on the culture, so they instruct management to use the metrics only as a coaching tool. Unfortunately, there is a big difference between the theory espoused and the theory in use. These sales metrics are being used in performance appraisals and to promote and demote employees.[94] An employee blog reported the following:

> One of the store managers was demoted recently because his department wasn't meeting the sales numbers all the time even though he was the best manager in the store. He would be constantly running

around from department to department helping any customer he could while the rest of the "leaders" stand around or sit in the back of geeksquad and talk, usually personal conversations.[95]

Is Best Buy getting the best they can from their sales associates given their current compensation system? Working 50 weeks a year, 40 hours a week, sales associates earn between $9.50 and $14 an hour. Is this a "Best Buy"? for the employees, their customers, and, ultimately, their stockholders?

Questions

1. What is the definition of an incentive pay system? Given this definition, does Best Buy have a pay for performance system?

2. Why would any firm (including Best Buy) use an "incentive-like" pay system?

3. Of the two basic choices in incentive pay, which one(s) does Best Buy appear to utilize in their compensation plans and "tracking systems"?

4. The veteran employee claims that by using their "tracking system," Best Buy has created all of the problems of a commission system. What are the advantages and disadvantages of this system in general and more specifically for Best Buy?

5. The veteran employee's perception was that Best Buy's metric system, which focused on individual employees' behaviors, decreased their job performance. What would be the pros and cons of Best Buy using a group incentive system?

6. Best Buy seems to use bonuses and commissions as part of their pay system. What are the effective and ineffective uses of each system?

7. What group incentive do you think might work best for Best Buy?

8. In light of Best Buy's code of ethics and the opinions reported in this case, do you believe that it is ethical for sales associates to tell customers that they are simply paid a flat rate?

Case created by Herbert Sherman, PhD, and Theodore Vallas, Department of Management Sciences, School of Business Brooklyn Campus, Long Island University

Skill Builder 11.1 Developing a Compensation With Incentive Plan

Objective

To develop a better understanding of creating motivational incentives

Skills

The primary skills developed through this exercise are:

1. *HR management skills*—Technical, conceptual and design, and business skills

2. *SHRM 2018 Curriculum Guidebook*—B: Compensation and Benefits

After a few years of selling new cars, you managed to get the funding to start your own small new car dealership as a sole proprietorship. Your starting staffing of 10 employees will be as follows:

- **You** are the **owner manager** and will oversee everything. You will also be the **sales manager** and do some selling.

- **Sales staff**. Three sales people reporting directly to you.

- **Service and parts manager**. You will have one person supervise the mechanics and detailer.

- **Mechanics**. Three mechanics to work on the cars.

- **Detailer**. One person to clean the cars, help out the mechanics, and work in parts.

- **Office staff**. Two people to answer phones, greet customers, make up the bills and collect money from sales and service, and do other paperwork including bookkeeping. They will report to you.

Preparing for Exercise 11.1—Develop an Incentive System

1. What type of compensation will each classification of employee receive for their work? Will you give them a wage, salary, or incentive pay (commissions, piecework, or standard hour)?

2. Will you give incentives (recognition and other nonmonetary incentives, merit pay, bonuses, profit sharing, gainsharing, ESOPs, stock option and/or stock purchase plans)?

3. As the only executive, what will your compensation package include?

Skill Builder 11.2 Developing Flexible Employee Benefit Plans

Objective

To develop your skill at designing flexible benefits

Skills

The primary skills developed through this exercise are:

1. *HR management skills*—Technical, conceptual and design, and business skills

2. *SHRM 2018 Curriculum Guidebook*—B: Compensation and Benefits

Assignment

1. Using Exhibit 11.3: Employee Benefits, the "Voluntary Benefits" column, as the HR benefits manager, select the benefits to be offered in three different modular plans. Be sure to identify the target group for each of the three modules.

2. Again using Exhibit 11.3, as the HR benefits manager, develop a core-plus benefits plan.

Skill Builder 11.3 Selecting Flexible Employee Benefit Plans

Objective

To develop your skill at selecting flexible benefits

Skills

The primary skills developed through this exercise are:

1. *HR management skills*—Technical, conceptual and design, and business skills

2. *SHRM 2018 Curriculum Guidebook*—B: Compensation and Benefits

Assignment

As an employee, rank-order the voluntary benefits from 1 being most important to 9 being the least important to you in Self-Assessment Exercise 11.2.

Protecting and Expanding Organizational Outreach

12 Workplace Safety, Health, and Security

13 Ethics, Sustainability, Diversity, and Inclusion

14 Global Issues for Human Resource Managers

PRACTITIONER'S MODEL

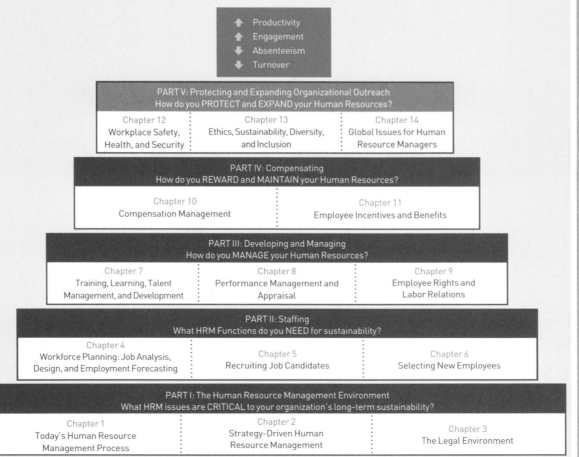

- ⬆ Productivity
- ⬆ Engagement
- ⬇ Absenteeism
- ⬇ Turnover

PART V: Protecting and Expanding Organizational Outreach
How do you PROTECT and EXPAND your Human Resources?

Chapter 12 Workplace Safety, Health, and Security	Chapter 13 Ethics, Sustainability, Diversity, and Inclusion	Chapter 14 Global Issues for Human Resource Managers

PART IV: Compensating
How do you REWARD and MAINTAIN your Human Resources?

Chapter 10 Compensation Management	Chapter 11 Employee Incentives and Benefits

PART III: Developing and Managing
How do you MANAGE your Human Resources?

Chapter 7 Training, Learning, Talent Management, and Development	Chapter 8 Performance Management and Appraisal	Chapter 9 Employee Rights and Labor Relations

PART II: Staffing
What HRM Functions do you NEED for sustainability?

Chapter 4 Workforce Planning: Job Analysis, Design, and Employment Forecasting	Chapter 5 Recruiting Job Candidates	Chapter 6 Selecting New Employees

PART I: The Human Resource Management Environment
What HRM issues are CRITICAL to your organization's long-term sustainability?

Chapter 1 Today's Human Resource Management Process	Chapter 2 Strategy-Driven Human Resource Management	Chapter 3 The Legal Environment

©iStockphoto.com/Thossaphol

Workplace Safety, Health, and Security

Learning Outcomes

After studying this chapter, you should be able to do the following:

12.1   Identify the responsibilities of both employers and employees under the general duties clause of the OSH Act. **Page 312**

12.2   Briefly describe what OSHA does in a worksite inspection, specifying the types of violations OSHA looks for. **Page 313**

12.3   Identify employer rights during an OSHA inspection. **Page 313**

12.4   Discuss EAPs, EWPs, and ergonomics, specifying the value of each of these to companies and employees. **Page 318**

12.5   Briefly discuss the causes of stress and how it can be managed. **Page 319**

12.6   Identify the top concerns for security in the workplace today, specifying what can be done to make the workplace more secure. **Page 324**

SHRM HR Content

See Online: *SHRM 2018 Curriculum Guidebook* for the complete list

B. Compensation and Benefits

Employee Benefits

   29.   Employee assistance/wellness programs

   54.   Wellness programs

D. Employment Law

   18.   The Occupational Safety and Health Act of 1970 (OSHA)

E. Globalization

I. Job Analysis and Job Design

   1-d.   Compliance with legal requirements—Ergonomics and workplace safety (work hazards and mitigation)

R. Workplace Health, Safety, and Security

   1.   Creating a healthy work environment

   1-a.   Creating a healthy work environment—Communicable diseases

   1-b.   Creating a healthy work environment—Corporate wellness programs

   1-c.   Creating a healthy work environment—Employee health

   1-d.   Creating a healthy work environment—Job stress and burnout

   1-e.   Creating a healthy work environment—Protection from retaliation

   1-f.   Creating a healthy work environment—Reducing workplace violence

   1-g.   Creating a healthy work environment—Work-life balance

   2.   OSHA citations and penalties

   2-a.   OSHA citations and penalties—Data security

   2-b.   OSHA citations and penalties—Inspection

   2-d.   OSHA citations and penalties—Material Safety Data Sheets (MSDSs)

   2-f.   OSHA citations and penalties—Security concerns at work

   3.   Safety management

   3-a.   Safety management—Alcoholism, drug abuse

   3-b.   Safety management—Crisis management teams

   3-c.   Safety management—Disaster preparation, continuity, and recovery planning

   3-e.   Safety management—Enforcing safety rules

   3-f.   Safety management—Ergonomics

   3-g.   Safety Management—Proactive safety programs

Practitioner's Perspective

Describing her workplace, Cindy says: We believe a safe and healthy workplace is a right—whether you work in a factory or an office. Is it also an employer's responsibility to provide for their employees' mental health? Not everyone may see it as an obligation, but there is great benefit in assisting an employee whose personal issues may be impacting their job performance.

"I think I am going to have to take time off," Nancy confessed the other day. "I just can't seem to manage everything going on in my life, and I can't concentrate at work."

(Continued)

(Continued)

"I know things are tough with the divorce—but can you really afford to miss work right now?" her coworker Chloe queried. "Have you seen the information HR posted about the employee assistance program? Let's get the contact information. It's completely confidential and available to you and your family. Perhaps they can help. In the meantime, you can talk to your supervisor about the new flexible work hours until things are better."

Could this level of support "save" a good employee? Learn more about the issues and ethics behind workplace health, safety, and security in Chapter 12.

Workplace Safety and OSHA

>> **LO 12.1 Identify the responsibilities of both employers and employees under the general duties clause of the OSH Act.**

We now have a workforce that is fairly compensated, well trained, and productive. The next major management concern is to keep them safe and healthy so they can continue to perform at high levels. Employees are concerned about safety.[1] The HR department commonly has responsibility for ensuring the health and safety of employees and needs to develop policies and rules to provide a safe environment for all groups. It works closely with the other departments to enforce safety rules and maintains health and safety records.[2] This chapter will first focus on federal workplace safety laws and regulations as well as the governing agencies for industrial safety and health. Later in the chapter, we will cover employee health issues—including employee assistance and employee wellness programs, and stress—and how they affect our employees. Finally, we cover the increasingly important topics of workplace security and violence.

The Occupational Safety and Health Act (OSH Act)

Workplace safety The physical protection of people from injury or illness while on the job

Workplace safety is a concern for all companies, but especially in more dangerous industries with higher death rates ranked as construction; transportation and warehousing; agriculture, forestry, fishing, and hunting; professional and business services; and manufacturing.[3] Most accidents such as plane crashes,[4] and 98% of truck accidents,[5] are caused by human error. To help protect employees, the Occupational Safety and Health Act (OSH Act) of 1970 requires employers to pursue workplace safety. **Workplace safety** deals with *the physical protection of people from injury or illness while on the job*. Employers must meet all Occupational Safety and Health Administration (OSHA) safety standards, maintain records of injuries and deaths due to workplace accidents, and submit to on-site inspections when notified. Those who do not comply are subject to citations and penalties, usually in the form of fines.[6] **(SHMR D:18 and R:3-e)**

Did you know that employers can go to prison for willfully failing to maintain safe work environments? You may have heard that the walls of a building that was being demolished in Philadelphia in 2013 caved in on a Salvation Army store, killing six people. The company in that case, **Campbell Construction**, was cited for *willful violations* (we will discuss this term shortly) of the OSH Act, and the general contractor, Griffin Campbell, was convicted of involuntary manslaughter and aggravated assault in that case and received a sentence of 15 to 30 years in prison for failing to follow a series of safety procedures. Willful violations of the OSH Act that cause a death are directly punishable with a fine of up to $500,000 for the organization and $250,000 and up to 6 months in prison for an individual who is found culpable.

It is critical that you know the safety rules, be sure your employees know them, and that you and other managers enforce them to prevent accidents.[7] In addition to many specific requirements in the act, the *general duties clause* in OSHA that *covers all employers* states that each employer

1. shall furnish a place of employment that is free from recognized hazards that are causing or are likely to cause death or serious physical harm to employees;

2. shall comply with occupational safety and health standards and all rules, regulations, and orders issued pursuant to this Act which are applicable to his own actions and conduct.[8]

The general duties clause also states that *each employee* has a *duty to comply* with occupational safety standards, rules, and regulations.

In 1970, the year the OSH Act was passed, job-related accidents accounted for more than 14,000 worker deaths in the United States.[9] The good news is that the rate of fatal work injuries has fallen, but the bad news is that in 2016 (the latest records at time of writing), there were still 5,190 fatalities[10] and about 2.8 million injuries or illnesses in 2017, half of which required time away from work.[11] This is a rate of almost 2.8 per 100 equivalent full-time workers. Recall from Chapter 1 that absenteeism is one of the major concerns of all managers, and by allowing injuries and occupational illnesses to occur, we are contributing to absenteeism. So, losing this many workdays, as well as nearly 5,200 lives, has to be a concern to all of us.

The Occupational Safety and Health Administration (OSHA)

>> **LO 12.2 Briefly describe what OSHA does in a worksite inspection, specifying the types of violations OSHA looks for.**

>> **LO 12.3 Identify employer rights during an OSHA inspection.**

OSHA is the division within the Department of Labor that is charged with overseeing the OSH Act. It was created to "assure safe and healthful working conditions by setting and enforcing standards and by providing training, outreach, education and assistance."[12] OSHA has broad authority to investigate complaints and impose citations and penalties on employers who violate the OSH Act.

What Does OSHA Do?

OSHA is responsible for setting federal safety and health standards and promulgating those standards to employers. OSHA is also responsible for occupational safety and health inspections. Inspections are made *without any advance notice* to the employer and are done based on the following issues (in priority order):[13]

- Imminent danger

- Catastrophes (fatalities or hospitalizations)

- Worker complaints and referrals

- Targeted inspections (particular hazards, high injury rates)

- Follow-up inspections

Inspectors must identify themselves and tell the employer the reason for the inspection upon arrival at the worksite. The employer can decide not to allow the inspection without an *inspection warrant* (a court order establishing OSHA's probable cause for the inspection).

Employer and Employee Rights and Responsibilities Under OSHA

General rights of employers and employees are shown in Exhibit 12.1. We want to make sure that company management always stays within their rights in interactions with OSHA.

Employer Rights

During an inspection, the employer has a right to get the inspector's credentials, including their name and badge number, and to receive information on the reason for the inspection—either the employee complaint or the program inspection information. The employer also has the right to refuse to allow the inspection without a warrant being provided, but this is generally not a very

EXHIBIT 12.1 ● Employer and Employee Rights and Responsibilities Under OSHA	
Employer Rights[14]	**Employee Rights[15]**
OSHA inspections should be conducted "reasonably"	Working conditions free from unnecessary hazards
Have an opening conference/know the reason for inspection visits	Receipt of information and training on workplace hazards
Accompany inspectors when on site	File a complaint about hazardous working conditions and request an inspection
Contest OSHA citations	Maintain anonymity when filing a complaint
Know the names of employees interviewed in an inspection	Use their rights without fear of retaliation or discrimination
Take notes on what is inspected and any discrepancies	Object to the time frame for correction of discrepancies
Employer Responsibilities	**Employee Responsibilities**
General Duty Clause	Follow employer safety and health rules and keep the workplace free from hazards
Find and correct safety/health hazards	Comply with OSHA standards and regulations
Inform and train employees about existing hazards in the workplace	Report hazardous conditions to their supervisor
Notify OSHA within 8 hours if a fatality occurs or if three or more workers are hospitalized	Report job-related injuries or illnesses to their supervisor
Provide personal protective equipment necessary to do the job at no cost to workers	Tell the truth if interviewed by an OSHA inspector
Keep accurate records of work-related injuries or illnesses	
Avoid retaliation against workers who exercise their rights under the OSH Act	

Source: OSHA.

good idea on a number of levels. Besides making it look like the company might have something to hide, it wastes time, and the inspector will be less likely to assist the employer in immediately correcting discrepancies that might be found during the inspection—*which will ultimately occur anyway* after the warrant is provided. In general, it makes more sense to allow the inspection to go on, in accordance with OSHA rules.[16] **(SHRM R:2-b)**

So assuming the inspection is allowed, we need to be aware of some things that we have a right to and should do during the inspection. If the inspection is being conducted due to a worker complaint, we have the right to get a copy of the complaint (without the employee's name), and we want to do so because we want to know what is being alleged. Second, we have a right to have a company representative accompany inspectors as they go through their site visit, and we, as the HR representative, want to accompany them.

There are a few reasons to accompany the inspector. First, we want to understand any violations the inspector finds and notes because sometimes, no matter how hard a person tries to describe a problem, it will be unclear unless we see it ourselves. Second, in many cases we can immediately fix a discrepancy such as loose lines or hoses strung across a workspace. Although the discrepancy will almost surely still be noted, the inspector will see that we are willing to comply with the law and OSHA regulations quickly and to the best of our ability. This willingness can keep minor infractions from becoming major infractions. Third, we want to make sure the inspection stays within the scope noted in the complaint or the program inspection guidelines.

We don't really want the OSHA representative wandering all over the worksite, and we have a right to limit their movements to cover only the inspection scope.

An employer representative also has a right to be present when the inspector is interviewing employees (unless the interview is private by request of the employee being interviewed) and the right to stop interviews that are becoming confrontational or disturbing the work environment.

The employer also has a right to inform the employees of their rights during the inspection. The inspector will provide the employer with a list of discrepancies upon completion of their inspection. After an inspection, employers have a right to contest any citations they receive through OSHA.

12.1 APPLYING THE CONCEPT
EMPLOYER RIGHTS AND RESPONSIBILITIES UNDER OSHA

Respond yes or no to each question regarding employer rights and responsibilities.

a. Yes

b. No

_____ 1. Is it permissible to ask the inspector the reason for the inspection?

_____ 2. Henry got us into trouble with OSHA, so is it OK to demote him?

_____ 3. Is it OK to take some notes during the OSHA inspection?

_____ 4. Does OSHA require us to inform and train employees about existing hazards in the workplace?

_____ 5. Does OSHA require us to keep records of work-related injuries or illnesses?

_____ 6. Does a member of the HR staff have to accompany the OSHA inspector during the site visit?

_____ 7. Can we require employees to buy their own safety equipment?

Employee Rights

Employee rights during inspections include the right to refuse to be interviewed, or if an employee agrees to an interview, they can request that an employer representative be present *or* that the interview be held in private. The employee also has the right to legal representation during the interview if they request it, and they can end the interview at any point in time just by requesting the interview be discontinued. Finally, employees have a right against company retaliation for taking part in an interview with the inspector and telling the truth. **(SHRM R:1-e)**

12.2 APPLYING THE CONCEPT
EMPLOYEE RIGHTS AND RESPONSIBILITIES UNDER OSHA

Respond yes or no to each question regarding employee rights and responsibilities.

a. Yes

b. No

_____ 8. Is it OK to object to the time frame for correction of discrepancies of OSHA standards?

_____ 9. Can OSHA make my employer maintain working conditions free from any hazards?

_____ 10. If I see hazardous conditions, does OSHA state that I have to tell my supervisor?

_____ 11. Do I have to wear this back brace? It is heavy and uncomfortable, and I can't move as well with it on.

_____ 12. If I report hazardous conditions to HR, do I have to tell them who I am?

_____ 13. If an OSHA inspector interviews me, can I cover up for the company and say we followed OSHA guidelines so we don't get into trouble?

_____ 14. Do I have to tell my supervisor I just got hurt? I don't want him to be mad at me for making him do all the paperwork.

Hazard Communication Standards

OSHA requires all employers maintain information at each worksite that describes any chemical hazards that may be present on site. A new set of hazard communication standards was established in 2012 and can be found on the OSHA website (http://www.osha.gov). Under federal law, "All employers with hazardous chemicals in their workplaces are required to have a hazard communication program, including container labels, safety data sheets, and employee training."[17] **Safety data sheets** (SDSs) are *documents that provide information on a hazardous chemical and its characteristics*. The OSHA-required SDS format is provided in Exhibit 12.2 (Sections 12–15 are nonmandatory). The SDS provides employees with a quick reference to the hazards of working with a particular chemical compound. Electronic versions of SDSs are acceptable, as long as there are no barriers to immediate access at the worksite. **(SHRM R:2-d)**

Safety data sheets
Documents that provide information on a hazardous chemical and its characteristics

---

EXHIBIT 12.2 ● **Safety Data Sheets (SDS) Format**[18]

OSHA now requires that hazard communication SDSs follow the following 16-section format.

Section 1, Identification, includes product identifier; manufacturer or distributor name, address, phone number; emergency phone number; recommended use; restrictions on use.

Section 2, Hazard(s) identification, includes all hazards regarding the chemical.

Section 3, Composition/information on ingredients, includes information on chemical ingredients.

Section 4, First-aid measures, includes important symptoms/effects (acute, delayed) and required treatment.

Section 5, Fire-fighting measures, lists suitable extinguishing techniques, equipment; chemical hazards from fire.

Section 6, Accidental release measures, lists emergency procedures; protective equipment; proper methods of containment and cleanup.

Section 7, Handling and storage, lists precautions for safe handling and storage.

Section 8, Exposure controls/personal protection, lists OSHA's permissible exposure limits (PELs); threshold limit values (TLVs); appropriate engineering controls; personal protective equipment (PPE).

Section 9, Physical and chemical properties, lists the chemical's characteristics.

Section 10, Stability and reactivity, lists chemical stability and possibility of hazardous reactions.

Section 11, Toxicological information, includes routes of exposure; related symptoms, acute and chronic effects.

Section 12, Ecological information, includes ecotoxicity (aquatic and terrestrial); persistence and degradability; bioaccumulative potential; mobility in soil.

Section 13, Disposal considerations, includes description of waste residues and information on their safe handling and methods of disposal.

Section 14, Transport information, includes transport hazard class(es); environmental hazards; special precautions which a user needs to be aware of, or needs to comply with, in connection with transport.

Section 15, Regulatory information, includes safety, health, and environmental regulations specific for the product in question.

Section 16, Other information, includes the date of preparation or last revision.

Source: OSHA.

Violations, Citations, and Penalties

OSHA violations include the following:[19]

- *Willful*—a violation in which the employer knew that a hazardous condition existed but made no effort to eliminate the hazard

- *Serious*—a violation where the hazard could cause injury or illness that would most likely result in death or significant physical harm

- *Other than serious*—a violation where any illness or injury likely to result from the hazard is unlikely to cause death or serious physical harm, but the violation does have a direct impact on employees' safety and health

- *De minimis*—violations that have no direct or immediate safety or health danger. This does not result in citations or penalties.

- *Failure to abate*—violations where the employer has not corrected a previous violation for which a citation was issued and the settlement date has passed

- *Repeated*—violations where the employer has been previously cited for the same type of violation within the previous 5 years **(SHRM R:2)**.

Willful and/or repeated violations could present the employer with up to a $129,336 fine for each violation in 2018, even without a serious injury occurring because of the violation. *Failure to abate* violations could also cost the employer as much as $12,934 per day while the violation continues to exist, and *serious* violations can also cost the employer a $12,934 fine.

National Institute of Occupational Safety and Health (NIOSH)

NIOSH works under the umbrella of the Centers for Disease Control and Prevention (CDC). NIOSH was also created as part of the 1970 OSH Act, and its mission is global in scope. "[NIOSH] is the federal agency that is tasked with ensuring that "every man and woman in the nation safe and healthful working conditions and to preserve our human resources."[20] NIOSH notes three major goals in its strategic plan:[21]

- Conduct research to reduce work-related illnesses and injury, and to advance worker well-being.

- Promote safe and healthy workers through interventions, recommendations, and capacity building.

- Enhance worker safety and health through global collaborations.

NIOSH routinely works with worldwide government health laboratories and other member nations in the World Health Organization (WHO) to identify workplace issues that can cause illness or injury and to create standards for the WHO member countries. NIOSH also works hand in hand with OSHA to identify workplace illnesses and to track communicable diseases in the work environment. It does research on occupational safety and health topics from ergonomics (we will discuss this shortly) to MRSA (methicillin-resistant *Staphylococcus aureus*) infections and workplace violence. NIOSH research frequently provides the data that OSHA uses to create new workplace standards and regulations. **(SHRM R:1-a)**

©NationalInstituteforOccupationalSafetyandHealth(NIOSH)/ CreativeCommons/Wikimedia Commons

▲ The National Institute of Occupational Safety and Health (NIOSH) works on a global scale to understand and preserve workplace safety by conducting research and providing recommendations on workplace safety measures.

Employee Health

>> **LO 12.4 Discuss EAPs, EWPs, and ergonomics, specifying the value of each of these to companies and employees.**

Employee health The state of physical and psychological wellness in the workforce

Meeting OSHA requirements is necessary, but there are many other aspects to maintaining good employee health. **Employee health** is *the state of physical and psychological wellness in the workforce.* We have to consider both physical *and* psychological health in order to have a strong workforce. We need to provide our employees with the ability to maintain both because they affect performance and the bottom line. Roughly 18% of American adults have some form of mental illness, and depression alone costs more than $210 billion per year.[22] In this section, we are going to complete a quick review of some of the physical and psychological issues in today's workplace. **(SHRM R:1 and R:1-c)**

Employee Assistance Programs (EAPs) and Employee Wellness Programs (EWPs)

Two significant employee services that can assist with employee mental and physical health are employee assistance programs (EAPs) and employee wellness programs (EWPs), also known as workplace wellness programs (WWPs). EAPs and EWPs continue to grow in popularity in the United States and other countries around the world, most likely because companies are seeing benefits from the use of such programs.[23] **(SHRM B:29 and B:54)**

EAPs

EAP A set of counseling and other services provided to employees that help them to resolve personal issues that may affect their work

An **EAP** is *a set of counseling and other services provided to employees that help them to resolve personal issues that may affect their work.* In 2018, about three-quarters of private sector workers (78%) had access to an EAP.[24] An EAP is designed to assist employees in confronting and overcoming problems in their personal lives, such as marital problems or divorce, financial problems, alcohol and drug abuse and addictions, emotional problems, and many other issues. Employers pay for these services because they help retain valuable employees and, as a result, save the company money.[25] **(SHRM R:3-a)**

EAPs are confidential services. The employee can contact the EAP and receive counseling and/or treatment. In some cases, EAPs may be regulated by federal laws, including the requirements of ERISA and COBRA, so HR personnel need to be aware of this fact.

EWPs

EWP Plan designed to cater to the employee's physical, instead of psychological, welfare through education and training programs

An **EWP** is *designed to cater to the employee's physical, instead of psychological, welfare through education and training programs.* Wellness programs offer health education, training and fitness, weight and lifestyle management, and health risk assessment services to employees. The obvious goal is improving the health of our workforce, but why? There is strong evidence that Americans (and people in most other countries) do not exercise enough. Nearly 40% of Americans are obese, with many more overweight.[26] Excess weight creates all kinds of health problems, and we are seeing the effects of overweight employees at work. Many employees have health problems such as diabetes, high blood pressure, and heart disease that are brought on by excess weight. EWPs work to help our employees become more healthy and fit and to lower the incidence of these types of health problems. EWPs can return from $2 to $6 in lower health care and lost productivity costs for every dollar spent.[27] Another interesting effect of EWPs appears to be lower turnover: "Healthy employees stay with your company."[28] So wellness programs provide employers with high return on investment and help with productivity, absenteeism, and turnover. No wonder companies continue to institute these programs. **(SHRM R:1-b)**

Ergonomics and Musculoskeletal Disorders (MSDs)

Ergonomics According to OSHA, "the science of fitting workplace conditions and job demands to the capabilities of the working population"

According to OSHA, **ergonomics** is *"the science of fitting workplace conditions and job demands to the capabilities of the working population."*[29] The CDC identifies the goal of ergonomics as being to "reduce stress and eliminate injuries and disorders associated with the overuse of muscles, bad posture, and repeated tasks."[30] Workplace ergonomics focuses on design of jobs and workspaces to limit the repetitive stresses that employees face in doing their daily work. OSHA provides employers with a set of voluntary guidelines on ergonomics in the workplace. These voluntary guidelines took the place of an earlier set of more rigid rules from OSHA on ergonomics that were rescinded by Congress in 2001. **(SHRM I:1-d and R:3-f)**

Several industries still have specific sets of guidelines provided by OSHA though. Other industries have the general set of voluntary guidelines published by OSHA.[31] It is wise for the organization to know OSHA's voluntary guidelines for your industry, even though the earlier ergonomics rule was rescinded, because "under the OSH Act's General Duty Clause, employers must keep their workplaces free from recognized serious hazards, including ergonomic hazards. This requirement exists whether or not there are voluntary guidelines."[32] It just makes sense to pay attention to ergonomics. Musculoskeletal disorders (MSDs) "affect the body's muscles, joints, tendons, ligaments, and nerves"[33] and can occur in many different work environments. They can take a toll on employee productivity when workers suffer from these issues. MSDs include a commonly known *repetitive stress injury* called *carpal tunnel syndrome* where the nerves in the wrist become inflamed and painful, making movement difficult.

But a large number of other problems fall under the MSD category, including other repetitive stress injuries such as rotator cuff syndrome, tennis elbow, Guyon canal syndrome, and many others.[34] All of these problems have the potential to cost the organization money in the form of lost productivity as well as workers' compensation claims. So paying attention to ergonomics at work can both improve productivity and save the company money.

You may want to review the OSHA Ergonomics pages if you have an interest in musculoskeletal disorders and repetitive stress injuries. You can find them beginning at https://www.osha.gov/SLTC/ergonomics/. There are several links to information on various hazards in the workplace on the primary page.

Safety and Health Management and Training

HR managers need to understand OSHA rules and standards in order to make the workplace as safe as possible, and offering EAPs and EWPs and stress management training (our next section) is part of safety and health management. **(SHRM R:3-g)**

By keeping the number of accidents and incidents low, we lower absenteeism plus increase job satisfaction. By improving two of our four most important variables at work—absenteeism and job satisfaction—we are almost assured of increasing employee engagement and productivity over time. This is yet another way HR management can assist in reaching organizational goals while using the least amount of organizational resources possible.

Stress

>> **LO 12.5 Briefly discuss the causes of stress and how it can be managed.**

People often have internal reactions to external environmental stimuli. **Stress** is *the body's reaction to environmental demands*. This reaction can be emotional and/or physical and can be caused by a lack of work-life balance.[35] According to *Forbes*, 35% of Americans have thought about leaving a job because of stress at work, and 42% have *actually done so!*[36] As stated in Chapter 1, absenteeism is costly, and there is a significant relationship between absenteeism and workplace stress.[37] In this section, we discuss functional and dysfunctional stress, how to manage it, and the stress tug-of-war. **(SHRM R:1-g)**

Stress The body's reaction to environmental demands

Functional and Dysfunctional Stress

What's the difference between functional and dysfunctional stress and the consequences of dysfunctional stress?

Functional Stress

Stress is *functional* (also called *eustress*[38]) when it helps improve performance by challenging and motivating people to meet objectives. People perform best under some pressure. When deadlines are approaching, adrenaline flows and people rise to the occasion. Stress actually provides greater strength and focus than we think we are capable of—so long as we are in control of it.[39]

Dysfunctional Stress

Stressors Factors that may, if extreme, cause people to feel overwhelmed by anxiety, tension, and/or pressure

Burnout Constant lack of interest and motivation to perform one's job

On the other hand, too much stress is dysfunctional because it decreases performance. **Stressors** are *factors that may, if extreme, cause people to feel overwhelmed by anxiety, tension, and/or pressure.* Stress that is constant, chronic, and severe can lead to burnout over a period of time.[40] **Burnout** is *a constant lack of interest and motivation to perform one's job.* Burnout results from too much stress. [41] Stress that is severe enough to lead to burnout is dysfunctional stress.[42]

Causes of Stress

Here are six common reasons for workplace stress: (1) personality (complete Self-Assessment 12.1 to determine if you are a Type A or Type B), (2) organizational culture (highly competitive cultures are stressful), (3) organizational change (change is stressful), (4) management (a bad boss can stress employees), (5) type of work (some jobs are more stressful), and (6) interpersonal relationships (jerks can cause you stress). The causes of stress are also listed later, in Exhibit 12.4.

12.1 SELF-ASSESSMENT

PERSONALITY TYPE A OR B AND STRESS

Identify how frequently each item applies to you at work or school. Place a number from 1 to 5 on the line before each statement.

5 = Usually   4 = Often   3 = Occasionally   2 = Seldom   1 = Rarely

_____ 1. I enjoy competition, and I work/play to win.

_____ 2. I skip meals or eat fast when there is a lot of work to do.

_____ 3. I'm in a hurry.

_____ 4. I do more than one thing at a time.

_____ 5. I'm aggravated and upset.

_____ 6. I get irritated or anxious when I have to wait.

_____ 7. I measure progress in terms of time and performance.

_____ 8. I push myself to work to the point of getting tired.

_____ 9. I work on days off.

_____ 10. I set short deadlines for myself.

_____ 11. I'm not satisfied with my accomplishments for very long.

_____ 12. I try to outperform others.

_____ 13. I get upset when my schedule has to be changed.

_____ 14. I consistently try to get more done in less time.

_____ 15. I take on more work when I already have plenty to do.

_____ 16. I enjoy work/school more than other activities.

_____ 17. I talk and walk fast.

_____ 18. I set high standards for myself and work hard to meet them.

_____ 19. I'm considered a hard worker by others.

_____ 20. I work at a fast pace.

_____   Total. Add up the numbers you assigned to all 20 items. Your score will range from 20 to 100. Indicate where your score falls on the continuum below.

Type A								Type B
100	90	80	70	60	50	40	30	20

The higher your score is, the more characteristic you are of the Type A personality. The lower your score is, the more characteristic you are of the Type B personality.

The *Type A personality* is characterized as fast-moving, hard-driving, time-conscious, competitive, impatient, and preoccupied with work. The Type B personality is pretty much the opposite of Type A. In general, people with Type A personalities experience more stress than people with Type B personalities. If you have a Type A personality, you could end up with some of the problems associated with dysfunctional stress.

Negative Consequences of Dysfunctional Stress

HR managers need to understand and be able to recognize the symptoms of stress, and especially dysfunctional stress, because it causes mental and physical health problems.[43] More than 80% of Americans said they were less productive at work because of stress. Excess stress costs an estimated $300 billion a year in absenteeism; decreased productivity; employee turnover; accidents; and medical, legal, and insurance fees.[44] **(SHRM R:1-d)**

Burnout can cause mental and physical health problems, including colds; weight gain; sleep dysfunction; heart disease; depression; ulcers and other stomach problems; and back, neck, and shoulder pain.[45] Stress also weakens our immune system, it makes us sick more often, it ages us so we look older, it makes us fatter, it decreases our sex drive, it ruins our sleep, and it can even kill us.[46] At its extremes, stress can cause even more serious problems. For instance, an **Uber** engineer was said to have suffered so much stress on the job due to overwork that he committed suicide.[47] We should always be aware that extreme stress can cause extreme reactions.

Stress Management

When we continually feel pressured and fear that we will miss deadlines or fail, we are experiencing stress. We *can* limit job stress,[48] and many firms are making wellness a top priority through training employees in stress management because it affects the bottom line.[49] EWPs frequently provide stress management programs for employees. *Stress management* is the process of reducing stress and making it functional. Here are seven stress management techniques that have proven valuable in stress reduction.[50]

Time Management

Generally, people with good time management skills experience less job stress.[51] **Vince Lombardi**, the famous football coach, said, "Plan your work and work your plan." Remember that procrastinating gives us more time to think about what we have to do and to get stressed before starting, so starting earlier lowers stress. It's a huge relief when we finish the task.[52] If we are perfectionists, we may do a high-quality job, but perfectionism stresses us as we perform the work, so sometimes it's OK to define what is "good enough" and stop there.

Relaxation

Relaxation is an excellent stress management technique, and we should relax both on and off the job. *Laughter* releases stress-reducing endorphins that lower blood pressure, relax muscles, stimulate our brain, improve our mood, and increase our oxygen intake—so laugh it up.[53] In addition, understand that each of us has our own way of relaxing. It doesn't matter *how* you relax, as long as you relax in a way that is soothing to you. Exhibit 12.3 lists muscle relaxation exercises that we can do almost anywhere.

EXHIBIT 12.3 ●   Relaxation Exercises

Forehead: Wrinkle forehead by trying to make eyebrows touch hairline; hold for 5 seconds.

Eyes, nose: Close eyes tightly for 5 seconds.

Lips, cheeks, jaw: Draw corners of the mouth back tightly in a grimace; hold for 5 seconds.

Neck: Drop chin to chest, slowly rotate head without tilting it back.

Shoulders: Lift shoulders up to the ears and tighten for 5 seconds.

Upper arms: Bend elbows and tighten upper arm muscles for 5 seconds.

Forearms: Extend arms out against an invisible wall and push forward with hands for 5 seconds.

(Continued)

EXHIBIT 12.3   ●   (Continued)

Hands: Extend arms to front; clench fists tightly for 5 seconds.

Stomach: Suck in and tighten stomach muscles for 5 seconds.

Back: Lie on back on the floor or a bed and arch back up off the floor, while keeping shoulders and buttocks on the floor; tighten for 5 seconds.

Hips, buttocks: Tighten buttocks for 5 seconds.

Thighs: Press thighs together and tighten for 5 seconds.

Feet, ankles: Flex feet with toes pointing up as far as possible and hold position for 5 seconds; then point feet down and hold for 5 seconds.

Toes: Curl toes under and tighten for 5 seconds; then wiggle toes to relax them.

Nutrition

Good health is essential to everyone's performance, and nutrition is a major factor in health.[54] Underlying stress can lead to overeating and compulsive dieting, and being overweight is stressful on the body. Unfortunately, about 40% of Americans are obese, while another 32% are overweight.[55] Obesity costs U.S. businesses about $73 billion a year in medical expenses and lost productivity.[56]

We should watch our intake of junk foods, which contain fat (fried meat and vegetables, including French fries and chips), sugar (pastry, candy, fruit drinks, and soda), too much caffeine (coffee, tea, soda), and salt. Eat more fruits and vegetables and whole grains, and drink water and pure juices. Realize that poor nutrition; overeating; and the use of tobacco, alcohol, and drugs to reduce stress often create other stressful problems over a period of time.

12.1 ETHICAL DILEMMA: WHAT WOULD YOU DO?
OBESITY AND SMOKING

Being overweight and smoking places stress on the body, and poor nutrition contributes to obesity. Obesity is on the increase, and it is a major contributor to the rising cost of health care, as is smoking. Health officials are trying to persuade Americans to quit smoking and lose weight. The government has released public service ads to convince people to stop smoking and get in shape and eat right.

1. Is there prejudice and discrimination against obese people and/or smokers at work?

2. Is it ethical and socially responsible for the government to try to get people to stop smoking and lose weight through ads and other methods?

3. Should tax money be spent on ads to promote not smoking, exercise, and healthy eating?

4. What is the reason for the increase in obesity in the United States? Some people blame restaurant owners (like **McDonald's** and its prior super-size it) and other food marketers (**Coke** and **Pepsi, Frito-Lay**) for the obesity problem. Some say consumers love junk food, just want to overeat, don't care about being obese, and are too lazy to exercise. What do you think?

5. Should the government pass laws to require junk food to be healthier? If so, what should the laws require?

6. Should the government pass laws to restrict where people can smoke and/or prevent people from smoking? If so, what should the laws require?

Exercise

Contrary to the belief of many people, proper exercise increases our energy level rather than depleting it. Physical exercise is an excellent way to improve health while releasing stress.[57] Staying fit can reduce the production of stress hormones.[58] If we are stressed for any reason, the fastest way to tame our anxiety can be physical activity. In fact, exercise is usually more effective than antidepressants in making moderate depression disappear.[59]

Aerobic exercise, in which we increase the heart rate and maintain it for 30 minutes, is generally considered the most beneficial type of exercise for stress reduction. Fast walking or jogging, biking, swimming, and aerobic dance or exercise fall into this category. Playing sports and weight lifting are also beneficial and can be aerobic if we don't take many breaks and we cross-train by mixing weights with other aerobic exercises.

Positive Thinking

People with an optimistic personality and attitude generally have less stress than pessimists[60] because thoughts of gloom and doom (which are often distorted anyway) lead to stress.[61] Once we start having doubts about our ability to do what we have to do, we become stressed. Make statements to yourself in the affirmative, such as "This is easy" and "I will do it." Repeating positive statements while doing deep breathing helps us relax and increase performance.

Support Network

Reaching out to supportive family, friends, and colleagues in our network can help reduce stress.[62] So we can find a confidant at work, or people outside of the workplace, and talk things through.[63] Being out of work-life balance is stressful, so cultivate a supportive network of family, friends, and colleagues to help maintain that critical work-life balance.[64]

Cut Back Smart Phone Checking

Stop your addiction to constantly looking at your smart phone. Set a time limit of frequency of checking it (such as every half hour), or better yet shut it off for an extended period when you can; especially when you have a high priority task to complete. When looking at it, hold it higher to help avoid neck and shoulder stress.[65] Also, place your other screens (computer monitor, TV) higher so you look up a bit to help offset your downward pressure.

The Stress Tug-of-War

Think of stress as a tug-of-war with you in the center, as illustrated in Exhibit 12.4. On the left are causes of stress trying to pull you toward burnout. On the right are stress management techniques you use to keep you in the center. If the stress becomes too powerful, it will pull us off center to

EXHIBIT 12.4 ● The Stress Tug-of-War

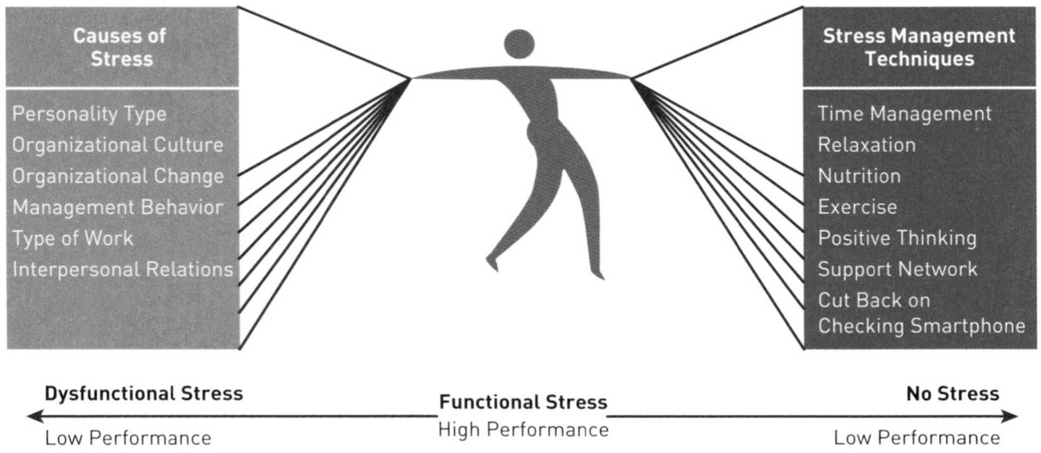

Causes of Stress
Personality Type
Organizational Culture
Organizational Change
Management Behavior
Type of Work
Interpersonal Relations

Stress Management Techniques
Time Management
Relaxation
Nutrition
Exercise
Positive Thinking
Support Network
Cut Back on Checking Smartphone

Dysfunctional Stress
Low Performance

Functional Stress
High Performance

No Stress
Low Performance

the left, and we may suffer burnout and dysfunctional stress with low performance. If there is no stress, we tend to move to the right and just take it easy and perform at low levels. The stress tug-of-war is an ongoing game. Our main objective is to stay in the center with functional stress, which leads to high levels of performance.[66]

If we try stress management but still experience long-term burnout, we should seriously consider getting out of the situation. Ask yourself two questions: Is my long-term health important? Is this situation worth hurting my health? If you answer yes and no respectively, a change of situations may be advisable. Career changes are often made for this reason.

12.3 APPLYING THE CONCEPT
STRESS MANAGEMENT TECHNIQUES

Put the letter of the technique being used on the line next to the corresponding statement.

a. Time management

b. Relaxation

c. Nutrition

d. Exercise

e. Positive thinking

f. Support network

_____ 15. "I've been stressed out, so I have been praying more lately."

_____ 16. "I've been working on positive affirmations, so I have been repeating to myself that 'I can meet the deadline.'"

_____ 17. "I'm not too organized, so I've started using a to-do list."

_____ 18. "I've been taking a walk at lunchtime with Latoya."

_____ 19. "I've been getting up earlier and eating a healthy breakfast."

_____ 20. "I have a bad boss, so I've been talking to my colleague Tom about her."

Workplace Security

>> **LO 12.6 Identify the top concerns for security in the workplace today, specifying what can be done to make the workplace more secure.**

Workplace security The management of personnel, equipment, and facilities in order to protect them

Workplace security is *the management of personnel, equipment, and facilities in order to protect them.* Whereas workplace safety deals with the issue of minimizing occupational illness and injury, workplace security covers topics such as violence in the workplace, bomb threats, management of natural and manmade disasters, risk to company computer systems and intranets, and many other issues. Workplace security is concerned with mitigating these risks to the organization and its members. **Securitas Security Services USA**, a large security firm, identified Internet/intranet security, workplace violence, active shooter threats, business continuity planning, and mobile security as the top security threats to businesses.[67] Prior to 2010, workplace violence had been the number one concern for more than 10 years, but cyber security in several forms replaced it as the number one concern in 2010.[68] Let's take a brief look at some of these major workplace security issues in order of concern. **(SHRM R:2-f)**

Cyber Security

Cyber security The use of tools and processes to protect organizational computer systems and networks

Let's do a quick review of some of the issues companies face today with cyber security in the form of both Internet/intranet and mobile systems security. **Cyber security** is *the use of tools and processes to protect organizational computer systems and networks.* This topic has been in the news constantly for the past several years, with concerns that amateur and professional hackers, hacktivists, terrorist organizations, and even some governments are working to break into company computer systems and mobile devices for a variety of purposes. The U.S. attorney general accused hackers working for the Chinese government of hacking U.S. companies, including

Westinghouse, **Alcoa**, and the **United Steel Workers Union**.[69] More recently, the Russian government was accused of being complicit in hacking various political institutions to try to sway the 2016 presidential election.[70] Every company has to be concerned with this issue and do what it can to prevent becoming a victim. **(SHRM R:2-a)**

Many companies are not focused on the potential danger of information security.[71] For effective security, there needs to be strong attention and support from top management and a clearly designated manager and team responsible for developing, supporting, and sustaining a cyber security culture.[72] HR managers must work with security managers to put up strong roadblocks to outsiders who seek to enter systems to access medical records, payroll and banking data, and other personal information.

In addition, we need to secure private information from employees who can sell the data and from those who don't follow security initiatives that allow hackers access to information, such as downloading software not approved by the IT department and e-mail attachments that can lead to hacking and viruses.[73] Although there are no foolproof systems, we have to do the best that we can to make it as hard as possible for hackers or other unauthorized users to find and exploit employee and company data.

Workplace Violence

There were 500 workplace homicides in 2016, the last annual report from the FBI. While this is serious, and we need to take precautions to respond if such incidents happen, we should also understand that workplace homicides are still extremely rare and that we should not panic over such statistics. These 500 homicides took place in an environment with tens of millions of businesses,[74] and the largest number occurred during robberies, not as the result of employee violence. But for now, let's focus on anger in the workplace that can lead to violence and how to prevent it.

HR managers report increased violence between employees, stating it can happen anywhere. Both men and women may become violent. There has also been an increase in violence between outsiders and employees, with issues such as domestic disputes that boil over into the workplace,[75] and customers shooting employees or other customers. The key to preventing workplace violence is to recognize and handle suspicious behavior before it turns violent.[76] **(SHRM R:1-f)**

Signs of Potential Violence

Workplace violence is rarely spontaneous; it is more commonly passive-aggressive behavior in rising steps, related to an unresolved conflict. Employees do give warning signs that violence is possible, so it can be prevented if we look for these signs and take action to defuse the anger before it becomes violent.[77] The starting point to violence is commonly rudeness. Some 98% of workers experience incivility on the job, and 50% reported engaging in rude exchanges at least weekly, resulting in lost productivity.[78] So, you have to prevent and stop incivility quickly before it escalates to the point of violence. Some actions to prevent violence are listed here.[79]

- Watch nonverbal communication. Behavior such as yelling, gestures, or other body language that conveys anger can also indicate a threat of violence. Talk to the person to find out what's going on.

- Take verbal threats seriously. Most violent people make a threat of some kind before they act. If we hear a threat, or hear about a threat from someone else, talk to the person who made the threat and try to resolve the issue.

- Watch for stalking and harassment. It usually starts small, but it can lead to violence. Put a stop to it.

- Watch for damage to property. If an employee kicks a desk or punches a wall, for example, talk to the person to understand the reason for the behavior. People who damage property can become violent to coworkers.

- Watch for indications of alcohol and drug use. People can be violent if under their influence. Get them out of the workplace and get them professional help from the EAP if it's a recurring problem.

- Include the isolated employee. It is common for violent people to be employees who don't fit in, especially if they are picked on or harassed by coworkers. Reach out to this employee and help them fit in or get them to a place where they do.

- Look for the presence of weapons or objects that might be used as weapons. You may try talking to the person if you feel safe, but get security involved if you feel the least bit unsafe.

Organizational Prevention of Violence

The number one preventive method is to train all employees to deal with anger and prevent violence,[80] which is what you are learning now. However, the starting place is with a written policy addressing workplace violence, and a zero-tolerance policy is the best preventive policy.

From the HR manager's perspective, it is very important to take quick disciplinary action against employees who are violent at work. Otherwise, aggression will spread in the organization, and it will be more difficult to stop. Managers especially need to avoid using aggression at work because employees more readily copy managers' behavior than the behavior of other employees.

As discussed in Chapter 9, the organization should have a system for dealing with grievances, and it should also track incidents of violence as part of its policy. Organizations can also screen job applicants for past or potential violence so that they are not hired. They should also develop a good work environment addressing the issues listed above as signs of potential violence. Demotions, firing, and layoffs should also be handled in a humane way, following the guidelines to deal with anger. Outplacement services can help employees find new jobs, thus helping to cut down on violence.

▲
Security is of concern to organizations today.

©iStockphoto/Andrey Popov

Social Media for Workplace Safety and Security

Organizations around the world are establishing security alert systems like **Rave Guardian** and **AlertMedia** to be used in the case of a company emergency of any type, including a violent individual or group on organization property. The systems use existing technology such as **Twitter** and text messaging to provide immediate warnings to all persons who are signed up to receive alerts. They can even provide information on what steps to take to remain safe in such situations. These systems have already undoubtedly saved lives during violent incidents in many companies, and it's not that expensive, so any company without such a system should probably look at installing the capability as soon as feasible.

Employee Selection and Screening

We discussed tools concerning employee selection and screening in Chapter 6, but we need to be reminded of some of them again here because of their importance to company security. The first tool we want to make sure that we use in employee screening is background checks. Recall that we can be held liable for monetary damages if we are guilty of a "negligent hire." One way to guard against such a hire is through the consistent use of criminal background checks that specifically look for a history of violent actions or threats of violence on the part of an applicant or employee.

Web searches can sometimes turn up negative information on an applicant that may show that they are a potential security risk, even when criminal checks do not. In addition, credit checks might show evidence of a history of unethical behavior that would make it more likely that an applicant might be unscrupulous and might even intentionally harm other employees if hired. So we do have some tools available, as long as the state in which the company is located allows such checks.

In addition to background checks, substance abuse testing can provide us with a tool to minimize the security dangers in our company. As we noted in Chapter 6, "Most employers have the right to test for a wide variety of substances in the workplace,"[81] and the former head of the White House Office of National Drug Control Policy has said that the "issue of drugs in the workplace is an understated crisis that results in $200 billion in lost productivity annually."[82] According to the Society for Human Resource Management (SHRM), "Substance abuse prevention is an essential element of an effective workplace safety and security program. Properly implemented preventive programs—including drug and alcohol testing—protect the business from liability."[83] The U.S. Department of Justice also noted that "the link between drug use and crime has been well-documented in recent years."[84] Screening out substance abusers in the applicant stage can minimize security threats to the organization because there is strong evidence that at least *some* substance abusers will commit crimes, including violent crimes at work.

General Security Policies, Including Business Continuity and Recovery

Common disasters and emergencies might include such events as fires, floods, earthquakes, severe weather, tsunamis, terrorist attacks, bomb threats, and many others. Some are dependent on the company's geographic location, while others are universal possibilities. One thing is sure, though—disasters and emergencies happen without warning, creating a situation in which the normal organizational services can become overwhelmed or even disappear. You may remember the nuclear crisis in Fukushima, Japan, when a tsunami wiped out electrical power to a nuclear plant and then, because there was no power to pump water, several of the reactors melted down.

During such a crisis, companies require a set of processes that address the needs of emergency response and recovery operations. The Japanese power company **TEPCO** did not have sufficient processes for such a disaster. To address these types of emergencies, the company should establish an emergency response plan, which provides guidelines for immediate actions and operations required to respond to an emergency or disaster, and these guidelines need to take into consideration *everything* that a company can think of in order to provide the appropriate plan. **(SHRM R:3-c, E:6-e, R:3-b)**

The overall *priorities* of any plan in any emergency or disaster should be these:

- Protect human life; prevent/minimize personal injury.

- Preserve physical assets.

- Protect the environment.

- Restore programs and return operations to normal.

HR managers should be part of the management team that determines the goals of the plan. Once the goals are determined, HR can again help operational management to staff the various key positions in the disaster recovery teams by understanding the types of people that are necessary to do these jobs under crisis circumstances.

Additionally, HR is typically responsible for the training function in the company, and everyone in the organization needs to be trained on the plan and its processes. The training should also become part of the new employee orientation (Chapter 7) so that all personnel are aware of the correct responses to potential emergencies. There are many examples of good emergency response and business recovery plans out there on the Internet for free. All the company needs to do is find a good sample and modify it for their particular circumstances and the likely disasters that would occur based on their geographic locations.

One final thing that HR management needs to determine is where extra assistance might come from if needed because of a disaster or emergency. For instance, if severe weather were to kill and injure a number of company employees, grief counseling services might become necessary. Most companies don't routinely have grief counselors on hand, but in this type of situation quick access to such counselors may be needed. HR managers can think of likely situations and their aftermaths and determine where these services might be procured if the need presents itself. One potential provider in at least some cases might be the vendor that services the company EAP. Recall that EAPs are services for the psychological well-being of our employees. Therefore, they may have the needed personnel to handle the psychological aftermath of a disaster.

Trends and Issues in HRM

What are some of the significant trends and issues in workplace safety and health? First, we are going to review a recent OSHA rule change concerning drug testing. Then we will show you a medical benefit that has really expanded in the past few years by introducing you to **eDocAmerica**.

OSHA Changes Rules on Post-Incident Drug Testing

In late 2018, OSHA announced a new interpretation of their current rules on workplace drug testing programs. While rule-making by OSHA is not unusual, the memorandum again includes significant changes to OSHA's workplace drug and alcohol testing policies. A 2016 interpretation of the rule—29 CFR 1904.35—had basically made it illegal to do *blanket* post-accident drug and alcohol testing. However, the new memorandum changes that guidance. It states, "Action taken under a safety incentive program or post-incident drug testing policy would only violate 29 C.F.R. § 1904.35(b)(1)(iv) if the employer took the action to penalize an employee for reporting a work-related injury or illness rather than for the legitimate purpose of promoting workplace safety and health."[85]

This is a significant departure from previous guidance on the 29 C.F.R. 1904 regulation. OSHA had said in that earlier guidance that workplace drug testing policies should be limited to cases *in which drug use likely contributed to the accident* to prevent these policies from having a punitive effect (emphasis added). OSHA also said that it "considers injury-free incentive programs may also deter reporting of injuries."[86] So if the company provides an incentive for "zero workplace accidents for the quarter," OSHA considered that to be a deterrent to reporting, and it would violate their safety regulations.

What can companies do under the new memorandum? OSHA notes that most instances of workplace drug testing are permissible under 1904.35(b)(1)(iv), including[87]

- Random drug testing.

- Drug testing unrelated to the reporting of a work-related injury or illness.

- Drug testing under a state workers' compensation law.

- Drug testing under other federal law, such as a U.S. Department of Transportation rule.

- Drug testing to evaluate the root cause of a workplace incident that harmed or could have harmed employees. If the employer chooses to use drug testing to investigate the incident, the employer should test all employees whose conduct could have contributed to the incident, not just employees who reported injuries.

This knowledge should keep you from going afoul of federal regulations. However, remember to always check your state laws regulating drug testing at work to ensure that your program meets those requirements as well.

eDocAmerica—Health and Wellness Online

One example of a new kind of online provider of occupational and employee health-related services is eDocAmerica, found at http://www.edocamerica.com. **eDocAmerica** is a health care service provider that "gives individuals and their family members unlimited email access to board certified physicians, psychologists, pharmacists, dentists, dietitians and fitness experts who provide personal answers to all health-related questions."[88] **eDocAmerica** was started by a physician at the University of Arkansas for Medical Sciences to provide outreach services to employees of client businesses.

The services of **eDocAmerica**, and other similar providers, make it much easier and quicker for employees of client firms to get answers to most of their routine health questions. This has two major benefits. First, it allows the employee to take more control of their personal and family health, and second, it takes some pressure off of the health care system because employees are not running to the doctor's office every time they need a simple question answered.

As a side benefit for the organization, it appears that companies may save money on their group health insurance plans because of the lower utilization rates made possible by quick and easy e-mail access to expertise. **eDocAmerica** has so far been quite successful in creating a more open and accessible health care system with their client company employees. This is just one of the new breed of Web-based providers of safety and health services to companies and employees. We will likely continue to see more companies with similar services come on line in the near future.

Chapter Summary

12.1 Identify the responsibilities of both employers and employees under the general duties clause of the OSH Act.

Employers have to provide employees with a place of employment free from recognized hazards that are causing or are likely to cause death or serious physical harm and are required to comply with occupational safety and health standards identified in the act.

Employees also have a duty to comply with occupational safety standards, rules, and regulations in all cases while at work.

12.2 Briefly describe what OSHA does in a worksite inspection, specifying the types of violations OSHA looks for.

OSHA can inspect a worksite without advance notice. The inspector will identify themselves and provide the reason for the inspection when they arrive. The inspector has the right to interview employees during the inspection and may do so unless the interview becomes confrontational or disruptive of the work environment. The inspector will provide the employer with a list of discrepancies upon completion of the inspection.

Violations include the following:

Willful—where the employer knew that a hazardous condition existed but made no effort to eliminate the hazard

Serious—where the hazard could cause injury or illness that would most likely result in death or significant physical harm

Other than serious—where any illness or injury incurred is unlikely to cause death or serious physical harm, but the violation does have a direct impact on safety and health

De minimis—violations that have no direct or immediate safety or health danger

Failure to abate—where the employer has not corrected a previous violation for which a citation was issued and the settlement date has passed

Repeated—the employer has been cited for the same type of violation within 5 years

12.3 Identify employer rights during an OSHA inspection.

The employer has a right to ask for identification from the OSHA inspector. The employer also has a right to know the reason for the inspection. Employers can refuse to allow the inspector into the worksite, unless they have a court order, but this is usually not a very good idea. The employer also has a right to have a representative accompany the inspector and has the right to tell employees their rights in the inspection process. The employer can also have a representative in any interviews unless the employee specifically requests that the interview be private, and the employer can stop interviews if they become disruptive. Finally, the employer has the right to contest any citations that they receive.

12.4 Discuss EAPs, EWPs, and ergonomics, specifying the value of each of these to companies and employees.

Both EAPs and EWPs help employees with their work-life balance. EAPs provide confidential counseling and other personal services to employees to help them cope with stress created by personal issues related to either work or home life. EWPs help employees with their physical wellness. They provide programs to employees such as health education, training and fitness programs, weight management, and health risk assessments.

Ergonomics is the science of fitting workplace conditions and job demands to the capabilities of the working population. The goal of ergonomics is to reduce stress and limit injuries caused by overuse of muscles, bad posture, and repetitive tasks. OSHA provides guidelines on ergonomics in the workplace that are voluntary but that can be assessed during an inspection based on the general duties clause of the OSH Act. OSHA also has specific ergonomic guidelines for a number of different industries, so HR representatives should check to make sure that they are following OSHA guidelines based on the industry that they are a part of.

12.5 Briefly discuss the causes of stress and how it can be managed.

The major causes of stress include personality type, organizational culture, organizational change, management behavior, type of work, and interpersonal relationship issues. Type A personalities, weak organizational cultures, rapidly changing organizations, bad management, jobs that employees don't enjoy, and poor interpersonal relations all make stress more prevalent in the workplace. Stress management techniques include good time management skills, the ability to relax once in a while (in whatever form you choose), good nutrition, moderate amounts of exercise, positive thinking skills, and a strong personal support network. All of these tools help us cope with stress successfully.

12.6 Identify the top concerns for security in the workplace today, specifying what can be done to make the workplace more secure.

The five biggest concerns of employers today are Internet/intranet security, workplace violence, active shooter threats, business continuity planning, and mobile security. Cyber security in the form of both Internet/intranet and mobile security deals with the company's computers and network security, including how mobile devices connect to those company systems. Workplace violence is another major issue because of the continuing rise in such incidents. Active shooter threats, while uncommon, must be taken seriously, and companies should take precautions to respond if such an incident happens to them. Business continuity planning has become a much more significant issue to most employers in the past 10 years, partly because of terrorism threats but also because of a number of large-scale environmental and natural disasters worldwide.

Key Terms

burnout, 320	ergonomics, 318	stressors, 320
cyber security, 324	EWP, 318	workplace safety, 312
EAP, 318	safety data sheets, 316	workplace security, 324
employee health, 318	stress, 319	

Key Terms Review

Complete each of the following statements using one of this chapter's key terms.

1. _____ is the physical protection of people from injury or illness while on the job.

2. _____ are documents that provide information on a hazardous chemical and its characteristics.

3. _____ is the state of physical and psychological wellness in the workforce.

4. _____ is a set of counseling and other services provided to employees that help them to resolve personal issues that may affect their work.

5. _____ is designed to cater to the employee's physical, instead of psychological, welfare through education and training programs.

6. _____ is the science of fitting workplace conditions and job demands to the capabilities of the working population.

7. _____ is the body's reaction to environmental demands.

8. _____ are factors that may, if extreme, cause people to feel overwhelmed by anxiety, tension, and/or pressure.

9. _____ is a constant lack of interest and motivation to perform one's job.

10. _____ is the management of personnel, equipment, and facilities in order to protect them.

11. _____ is the use of tools and processes to protect organizational computer systems and networks.

Communication Skills

The following critical-thinking questions can be used for class discussion and/or for written assignments to develop communication skills. Be sure to give complete explanations for all answers.

1. Is some number of occupational illnesses and injuries an acceptable part of doing business? Why or why not? Explain your answers.

2. Do you foresee a situation in which you would ever refuse to allow an OSHA inspector on your worksite? Why or why not?

3. What actions would you take if you were the company representative accompanying an OSHA inspector who found a serious violation in your company? Explain your answer.

4. Do you think the OSHA and NIOSH occupational safety and health requirements generally make sense? Why or why not?

5. If you were in charge, would you put an EAP into place at your company? How about an EWP? Why or why not?

6. Do you think that you suffer from too much stress? Name a few things that you could do to minimize the dysfunctional stress in your life.

7. Go through the process of how you would train your employees on a new business continuity and disaster recovery plan. What do you think the most important part of the training would be? Why?

8. Should smoking be banned in all buildings where smokers and nonsmokers have to work together? Why or why not?

9. What programs would you put into effect as a leader in order to make your employees understand that occupational safety and health are critical to a modern company?

Case 12.1 You Are Not Hurt? Good—You're Fired!

ActioNet was founded in 1998 by president and CEO **Ashley Chen**. Key customers have included **Qwest**, the Department of Energy, and the Department of Labor. ActioNet provides information technology services such as custom software development, computer security assessment, network design, consulting, project management, systems integration and design, and training. Customers come from industries such as manufacturing, retail, transportation, telecommunications, financial services, and the public sector.[89]

ActioNet's core values include instilling integrity in everything they do, innovating to enable their mission, making their customers and each other successful, achieving service delivery excellence, and partnering for success.

At **ActioNet**, we are committed to conducting our business with integrity, not only doing things right, but also doing the right things. We believe in transparency and accuracy with open and honest communication. Being fair and ethical are an integral part of how we do business and strengthens our relationships.[90]

Core values aside, in *Yowan Yang v. ActioNet, Inc.* (Case 2:14-cv-00792-AB-PJW) lawyers obtained a $2.4 million verdict plus $5 million in punitive damages on behalf of their client against **ActioNet** when it was determined that their client was the victim of workplace violence and wrongful termination. How is this possible given the firm's core values and their belief in open and honest communications?

Yang began his employment with **L-3 National Security Solutions**, a federal contractor providing technical support to the Federal Aviation Administration in September 2008. In April 2010, **ActioNet** took over the contract and employed Yang. Yang's employment history included consistent strong performance reviews and merit raises, including a raise just 2 months prior to his termination. **ActioNet** hired Cy Tymony in the same capacity as Yang. Tymony was placed on the same team and in a cubicle 4 feet away.[91]

Yang said he and Tymony had several public incidents in the workplace, including some where Tymony was publicly upset because Yang had either stored cans of soda in the office freezer or was eating candy during a staff meeting, according to the complaint. Toward the end of the meeting, Tymony pounded his fist against a cubicle, told Yang that he had no respect for others and cursed several times, the later filed complaint said. On July 24, 2012, both Tymony and Yang met individually with supervisors to see who would be willing to move to another cubicle, according to the complaint. After Tymony left the meeting, he loudly complained that Yang was an "asshole" who chews ice. After Yang suggested that Tymony move his cubicle, Tymony grabbed him by the neck and threatened his life.[92] Tymony continued screaming profanity-laced threats, including that he was going to kill Yang, and destroyed Yang's workstation.

In response, **ActioNet** terminated the employment of Yang and Tymony, without performing an investigation. In spite of receiving an investigation report from federal investigators 2 days after the incident revealing that Yang was a "complete victim," no corrective action was taken by **ActioNet** to investigate further, to communicate with Yang the findings of the investigation, or to rehire him. In fact, **ActioNet** ignored Yang's pleas for an explanation as to why he was terminated as well as his request for reinstatement.

Mr. Yang then filed a civil legal complaint that said that rather than properly investigate the incident,

ActioNet simply moved to quickly fire him and the other employee, causing him emotional harm and making it difficult for him to find a new job. "After being fired 'for cause,' Mr. Yang applied unsuccessfully for hundreds of jobs," says DeSimone, his lawyer. "Mr. Yang lost his career, his apartment, his independence, his self-worth, and his self-esteem."[93] **ActioNet** argued in the case that it should not be held responsible because of any violent tendencies of Tymony, because he was fit to perform his job, because there is no evidence that the company tolerated Tymony's conduct, and because Tymony was not acting in the "course and scope" of his job during the altercation.[94]

The jury compensated Mr. Yang and punished **ActioNet** for what it regarded as callous disregard of Mr. Yang's rights. "The jury sent a loud and clear message via this case to companies that harassment, workplace violence and termination would not be tolerated. **ActioNet** never took responsibility for its wrongful conduct and the jury held them accountable."[95]

Questions

1. The **ActioNet** case was a civil case; how might it have become a federal case under OSHA's charge?

2. How might **ActioNet** have not upheld their OSHA responsibilities?

3. The federal investigators revealed that Yang was a complete victim, that no corrective action was taken by **ActioNet** to investigate further and to communicate with Yang the findings of the investigation. If these were OSHA investigators, under what category of violation might **ActioNet** be subject to?

4. Stress might have been the cause of Tymony's intolerable conduct. Which cause(s) of stress might have accounted for his inexcusable behavior?

5. What are the causes of workplace violence, and how might it help us better understand this case?

6. What are the signs of potential violence, and were any exhibited in this case?

7. What trends or issues in workplace safety apply to this case?

Case created by Herbert Sherman, PhD, and Theodore Vallas, Department of Management Sciences, School of Business Brooklyn Campus, Long Island University

Skill Builder 12.1 Developing a Stress Management Plan

Objective

To develop your skill at managing stress

Skills

The primary skills developed through this exercise are as follows:

1. *HR management skills*—Conceptual and design

2. *SHRM 2018 Curriculum Guidebook*—R: Workplace Health, Safety, and Security

Assignment

Write out the answers to these questions:

1. Identify your major causes of stress.

2. How do you currently manage stress?

3. Select stress management techniques you will use to help overcome the causes of your stress.

©iStockphoto.com/laflor

Ethics, Sustainability, Diversity, and Inclusion

Learning Outcomes

After studying this chapter, you should be able to do the following:

13.1 Discuss the term *ethics* by stating the common elements of the definition. **Page 336**

13.2 Identify each factor required in a good code of ethics. **Page 341**

13.3 Contrast the concepts of equal employment opportunity, affirmative action, diversity, and inclusion. **Page 345**

13.4 Describe the "business case" for corporate social responsibility (CSR). **Page 349**

13.5 Review the concept of sustainability in a business context. **Page 351**

SHRM HR Content

See Online: *SHRM 2018 Curriculum Guidebook* for the complete list

D. Employment Law

    7. Executive Order 11246 (1965)

F. HR Career Planning

    8. Ethical decision-making

J. Managing a Diverse Workforce

    1. Affirmative action (AA)

    2. Aging workforce

    3. Business case for diversity

    6. Gay, lesbian, bisexual, transgender (GLBT)/sexual orientation issues

    11. Racial/ethnic diversity

    13. Reverse discrimination

V. Sustainability/Corporate Responsibility

    1. Corporate philanthropy

1-a. Corporate philanthropy—Accountability and transparency

1-b. Corporate philanthropy—Business case for CSR

1-c. Corporate philanthropy—Community/employee (engagement)

1-d. Corporate philanthropy—Ethics

1-e. Corporate philanthropy—Linking organizational culture and corporate values

1-f. Corporate philanthropy—Management commitment to CSR

1-g. Corporate philanthropy—Reputation and brand enhancement

    6. Sustainability practices

6-a. Sustainability practices—Green management

Practitioner's Perspective

Reflecting on ethics, Cindy says there are many definitions of *ethics* and many shades of gray in their interpretations. Some decisions may be legal but not "fair," justifiable but not "correct," and sometimes it is hard to determine who should even be setting the standards. I prefer to compare ethical behavior to behaving with integrity. My definition is C. S. Lewis's observation: "Integrity is doing the right thing, even when no one is watching." Business does not always behave with integrity, as we know from scandals since the turn of the century. In 2002, a lack of integrity was exemplified by **Enron** and its accounting misrepresentations; in 2007, it was the banking industry and the subprime mortgage morass. Each time, new rules and regulations are put into place to prevent such ethical abuses from ever happening again. But it takes more than reactive rules and regulations. To really make a difference in business behavior, we need to begin with ourselves—we can chart the course for a better future. Chapter 13 takes an in-depth look at what you need to know about business ethics.

Ethical Organizations

>> **LO 13.1 Discuss the term *ethics* by stating the common elements of the definition.**

Does it pay to be ethical? The simple answer is yes. Research shows a positive relationship between ethical behavior and leadership effectiveness.[1] Most highly successful people are ethical.[2] Being ethical may be difficult, but it has its rewards.[3] It actually makes you feel better.[4] Honest people have fewer mental health and physical complaints, less anxiety and back pain, and better social interactions.[5] On the reverse side, unethical behavior is costly; take, for example, its contribution to the 2007–2008 financial crisis, which resulted in the world's economies going into recession.[6] It has long-term negative consequences for companies, including loss of reputation, legal fees, and fines.[7] Also, sales declines, increasing cost of capital, market share deterioration, and network partner loss can all be the result of unethical corporate behavior.[8] Some companies have even gone out of business.

Thus, there have been strong and recurring calls for more ethical business practices globally. To improve ethics, business schools have doubled the number of ethics-related courses to help students prepare to face ethical dilemmas during their careers.[9] But what is ethics, and which business practices are, or should be, considered "ethical"?

Corporate Philanthropy—Ethics Defined

Before we define ethics, complete Self-Assessment 13.1 to determine how ethical your behavior is.

Ethics has been defined in many books and articles. Let's do a quick review here of some of the common definitions of *ethics* and then see if we can apply those definitions to business ethics. **(SHRM V:1-d)**

- "Ethics is a reflection on morality, that is, a reflection on what constitutes right or wrong behavior."[10]

- "[Ethics is] the principles, values and beliefs that define right and wrong decisions and behavior."[11]

- "Ethics is a set of moral principles or values which is concerned with the righteousness or wrongness of human behavior and which guides your conduct in relation to others."[12]

Ethics The application of a set of values and principles in order to make the right, or good, choice

You might notice these definitions all have some common elements: morals, values, beliefs, principles of conduct. So for our purposes, **ethics** is *the application of a set of values and principles in order to make the right, or good, choice.* So ethics also must include personal integrity and trust in the character and behavior of others. *Integrity* means being honest. So lying, cheating, and stealing are unethical behaviors. If you are not honest, the truth will eventually catch up with you.[13] And when it does, you will lose the trust of people and hurt your relationships for a very long time before you will be able to earn their trust back—if you ever can.[14] Remember the common elements among the various definitions of *ethics* as we review some factors contributing to unethical behavior and learn about a few ethical approaches.

13.1 SELF-ASSESSMENT

HOW ETHICAL IS YOUR BEHAVIOR?

For this exercise, you will respond to the same set of statements twice. The first time you read them, focus on your own behavior and the frequency with which you behave in certain ways. On the line before each statement number, place a number from 1 to 4 that represents how often you do that behavior (or how likely you would be to do it) according to the following scale:

Frequently			Never
1	2	3	4

The numbers allow you to determine your level of ethics. You can be honest, as you will not tell others in class your score. *Sharing ethics scores is not part of the exercise.*

Next, go through the list of statements a second time, focusing on other people in an organization that you work for now or one you have worked for. Place an *O* on the line after the number of each statement if you have observed someone doing this behavior; place an *R* on the line if you reported this behavior within the organization or externally: *O* = observed, *R* = reported.

In College

_____ 1. _____ Cheating on homework assignments

_____ 2. _____ Cheating on exams

_____ 3. _____ Submitting as your own work papers that were completed by someone else

On the Job

_____ 4. _____ Lying to others to get what you want or to stay out of trouble

_____ 5. _____ Coming to work late, leaving work early, taking long breaks/lunches and getting paid for them

_____ 6. _____ Socializing, goofing off, or doing personal work rather than doing the work that you are getting paid to do

_____ 7. _____ Calling in sick to get a day off when you are not sick

_____ 8. _____ Using an organization's phone, computer, Internet access, copier, mail, or car for personal use

_____ 9. _____ Taking home company tools or equipment without permission for personal use

_____ 10. _____ Taking home organizational supplies or merchandise

_____ 11. _____ Giving company supplies or merchandise to friends or allowing friends to take them without saying anything

_____ 12. _____ Applying for reimbursement for expenses for meals, travel, or other expenses that weren't actually incurred

_____ 13. _____ Taking a spouse or friends out to eat or on business trips and charging their expenses to the organizational account

_____ 14. _____ Accepting gifts from customers/suppliers in exchange for giving them business

_____ 15. _____ Cheating on your taxes

_____ 16. _____ Misleading a customer to make a sale, such as promising rapid delivery dates

_____ 17. _____ Misleading competitors to get information to use to compete against them, such as pretending to be a customer/supplier

_____ 18. _____ Taking credit for another employee's accomplishments

_____ 19. _____ Selling more of a product than the customer needs in order to get the commission

_____ 20. _____ Spreading rumors about coworkers or competitors to make yourself look better, so as to advance professionally or to make more sales

_____ 21. _____ Lying for your boss when asked or told to do so

_____ 22. _____ Deleting information that makes you look bad or changing information to make yourself look better

_____ 23. _____ Allowing yourself to be pressured, or pressuring others, to sign off on documents that contain false information

_____ 24. _____ Allowing yourself to be pressured, or pressuring others, to sign off on documents you haven't read, knowing they may contain information or describe decisions that might be considered inappropriate

_____ 25. _____ If you were to give this assessment to a coworker with whom you do not get along, would she or he agree with your answers? If your answer is yes, write a 4 on the line before the statement number; if your answer is no, write a 1 on the line.

After completing the second phase of the exercise (indicating whether you have observed or reported any of the behaviors), list any other unethical behaviors you have observed. Indicate if you reported the behavior, using *R*.

26. _____

27. _____

28. _____

Note: This self-assessment is not meant to be a precise measure of your ethical behavior. It is designed to get you thinking about ethics and about your behavior and that of others from an ethical perspective. All of these actions are considered unethical behavior in most organizations.

Another ethical aspect of this exercise is your honesty when rating your behavior. How honest were you?

Scoring: To determine your ethics score, add up the numbers for all 25 statements. Your total will be between 25 and 100. Place the number that represents your score on the continuum below. The higher your score, the more ethical your behavior.

25	30	40	50	60	70	80	90

Unethical   Ethical

Contributing Factors to Unethical Behavior

Let's discuss some of the reasons why unethical behavior occurs—or why do good people do bad things?

Personality Traits and Attitudes

You probably already realize that some people have a higher level of ethics than others, as integrity is considered a personality trait. Unfortunately, a culture of lying and dishonesty is infecting American business and society as these behaviors have become more common and accepted.[15] Some people lie deliberately, based on the attitude that lying is no big deal; other people don't even realize that they are liars.[16]

Moral Development

Moral development refers to distinguishing right from wrong and choosing to do the right thing.[17] Our ability to make ethical choices is related to our level of moral development.[18] There are three levels of personal moral development. At the first level, the *preconventional* level, a person chooses right and wrong behavior based on self-interest and the likely consequences of the behavior (reward or punishment). In this preconventional level, a person thinks, "It's all about me—I'll take advantage of you to get what I want." Those whose ethical reasoning has advanced to the second, *conventional,* level seek to maintain expected standards and live up to the expectations of others. Most people are on this level and do as the others in their group do—they easily give in to peer pressure to act ethically or unethically. Those at the third level, the *postconventional* level, make an effort to define moral principles for themselves; regardless of leaders or group ethics, they do the right thing. People can be on different levels for different issues and situations.[19]

13.1 APPLYING THE CONCEPT
LEVEL OF MORAL DEVELOPMENT

Place the letter of the level of moral development on the line next to the statement that illustrates it.

a. Preconventional level

b. Conventional level

c. Postconventional level

_____ 1. I lie to customers to sell more products because the other sales reps do it, too.

_____ 2. I lie to customers so that I can sell more products and get larger commission checks.

_____ 3. I don't lie to customers because it is unethical to lie.

_____ 4. Carl says to John, "You're not selling as much as the rest of us. You really should lie to customers like we do. If the boss asks why you aren't selling as much as the rest of us, you'd better not tell him we lie, or you will be sorry."

_____ 5. Karen says to John, "Telling lies to customers is no big deal—we're helping them buy a good product."

The Situation

In certain situations, it can be tempting to be unethical,[20] such as when you are negotiating.[21] Unsupervised people in highly competitive situations are more likely to engage in unethical behavior. Unethical behavior occurs more often when there is no formal ethics policy or code of ethics and when unethical behavior is not punished. In other words, people are more unethical when they believe they will not get caught.[22] Unethical behavior is also more likely when performance falls below aspirational levels. People are also less likely to report unethical behavior (blow the whistle) when they perceive the violation as not being serious or when they are friends of the offender. It takes high moral responsibility to be a whistle-blower.

Justification of Unethical Behavior

Most people understand right and wrong behavior and have a conscience. So why do good people do bad things? Most often, when people behave unethically, it is not because they have some type of character flaw or were born bad. Just about everyone has the capacity to be dishonest.[23] We respond to "incentives" and can usually be manipulated to behave ethically or unethically, if we find the right incentives.[24] The incentive can be personal gain or to avoid getting into trouble.[25]

Few people see themselves as unethical. We all want to view ourselves in a positive manner. Therefore, when we do behave unethically, we justify the behavior to protect our *self-concept* so we don't have to feel bad.[26] If we only cheat a little, we can still feel good about our sense of integrity.[27] Take a look at some common justifications for our unethical behavior:

- Everyone else does it. We all pad the expense account.

- I did it for the good of others or the company. I cooked the books so the company looks good.

- I was only following orders. My boss made me do it.

- I'm not as bad as the others. I only call in sick when I'm not sick once in a while.

- Disregard or distortion of consequences. No one will be hurt if I inflate the figures, and I will not get caught. And if I do, I'll just get a slap on the wrist anyway.

13.2 APPLYING THE CONCEPT
JUSTIFYING UNETHICAL BEHAVIOR

Place the letter of the justification given for engaging in unethical behavior on the line next to the statement exemplifying it.

a. Everyone else does it.

b. I did it for the good of others or the company.

c. I was only following orders.

d. I'm not as bad as the others.

e. Disregard or distortion of consequences.

_____ 6. Don't blame me. It was the boss's idea to do it. I just went along with it.

_____ 7. It's no big deal that I lie to customers because no one gets hurt. In fact, I'm helping them buy a good product.

_____ 8. I changed the numbers so the department will look good on our quarterly report to top management.

_____ 9. Yes, I do lie to customers, but it's the way we do business here.

_____ 10. I do take some of the company product home, but I take a lot less than the others.

Ethical Approaches

Several common ethical approaches, or guidelines, exist to help you make ethical choices. Understanding some of the common approaches will help you resolve ethical dilemmas that you will certainly face at work. Let's discuss four guides to ethical behavior. **(SHRM F:8)**

Golden Rule

"Do unto others as you would have them do unto you." Most successful people live by the golden rule.[28] This is a moral principle in virtually every religious text in the world. Following the golden rule will help you to be ethical. The world could literally be changed overnight if people would follow this simple rule.

Four-Way Test

Rotary International uses a four-way test to determine ethical behavior:[29] (1) Is it the truth? (2) Is it fair to all concerned? (3) Will it build goodwill and better friendship? (4) Will it be beneficial to all concerned? If the answers are yes, then the action is probably ethical.

Stakeholders' Approach to Ethics

The stakeholders' approach tries to create win-win results for all stakeholders affected by the decision. This is the approach put forth by **Warren Buffett** at **Berkshire Hathaway**, known as one of the most ethical organizations in business today. Exhibit 13.1 gives the statement taken from **Berkshire**'s code of business conduct and ethics.

So, if you are comfortable telling people who are affected by your decision what you have decided, it is probably ethical. But if you keep rationalizing the decision and try to hide it from others, it is quite likely unethical—at least to some of the affected stakeholders. You can't always create a win for everyone, but you can try.

EXHIBIT 13.1 ● Berkshire Hathaway Code of Business Conduct and Ethics[30]

When in doubt, remember **Warren Buffett**'s rule of thumb:

"I want employees to ask themselves whether they are willing to have any contemplated act appear the next day on the front page of their local paper—to be read by their spouses, children and friends—with the reporting done by an informed and critical reporter."

Discernment and Advice

Research shows that making a decision without using an ethical guide leads to less ethical choices.[31] Using ethical guides at the point of making a decision helps keep you honest.[32] If you are unsure whether a decision is ethical, you can check the company code of ethics/conduct and talk to your boss, higher-level managers, and other people with high ethical standards. If you are reluctant to ask others for advice on an ethical decision because you may not like their answers, the decision may not be ethical.

Each of the previously discussed approaches to making ethical decisions should cue you to think about some concepts that we have previously discussed in this text—trust, integrity, and consistency. If you recall our conversation about trust in Chapter 9, you will remember that trust is "faith in the character and actions of another." Does that sound familiar when you take a look at the definitions of *ethics* mentioned earlier? Without trust, we cannot successfully manage in the organization for very long, so we have to do what we said we would do *consistently* over time in order to get our stakeholders to trust us—the OUCH test helps.

Integrity (honestly doing what you say you will do) and trust (the expectation that you will continue to do so) are important to managers in the firm because research shows that companies who have the trust of employees have lower turnover and higher revenue, profitability, and shareholder returns. Rewarding personal relationships are also based on integrity and trust. But how do we get others to be trustworthy and make decisions based on principles, values, beliefs, and character? Most organizations (like **Buffett's Berkshire Hathaway**) today use a *code of ethics,* sometimes called a *code of conduct,* to project the values and beliefs of the organization to their employees.

13.3 APPLYING THE CONCEPT
ETHICAL APPROACH

Place the letter of the approach to making ethical decisions on the line next to the statement that illustrates it.

a. Golden rule

b. Four-way test

c. Stakeholders' approach

d. Discernment and advice

e. Code of ethics

_____ 11. I'm a member of Rotary International, and I use its approach when I make decisions.

_____ 12. When I make decisions, I follow the guidelines the company gave all of us to use to make sure I'm doing the right thing.

_____ 13. I try to make sure that everyone affected by my decisions gets a fair deal.

_____ 14. I try to treat people the way I want them to treat me.

_____ 15. Hi, Latoya. What do you think of my decision about how to handle this customer's complaint?

Codes of Ethics

>> **LO 13.2 Identify each factor required in a good code of ethics.**

Every culture endorses an ethical way to live.[33] Following the code of ethics is actually an ethical approach. The *Houston Chronicle* provides a good template on their http://chron.com website for an organizational code of ethics that includes values, principles, management support, personal responsibility, and compliance.[34]

Values are *our basic concepts of good and bad, or right and wrong.* Values come from our society and culture. Every culture has concepts of right and wrong, although these values vary from culture to culture (we will discuss this further in Chapter 14). The *Chronicle* article notes that "a primary objective of the code of ethics is to define what the company is about and make it clear that the company is based on honesty and fairness."[35]

Principles are a *basic application of our values.* We *apply* principles to specific situations in order to come up with a set of actions that we consider to be ethical. An example would be to *maintain personal integrity*. This is obviously based on the application of the values of honesty and integrity. Another example would be the principle to *treat all employees fairly*, which would match up with the value of equality.

Management support, and especially top management support, is absolutely critical to a successful code of ethics. If senior managers pay no attention to the code of ethics, subordinate managers and employees will pay no attention either. In addition, we need to encourage reporting of unethical behavior to management. The open-door policies and processes that allow the anonymous reporting of ethics issues should be included in the code. These processes help management maintain and uphold the code across the organization. **(SHRM V:1-e)**

Personal responsibility is the concept that everyone in the organization, and not just the boss, is responsible for the ethical conduct of business. Personal responsibility also refers to accountability for one's own actions, so we need to identify the consequences to an employee if they violate the code of ethics. We have a personal responsibility to report others' violations of the code to the appropriate authority.

Compliance identifies applicable laws or industry regulations that must be adhered to as part of the code of ethics. Certainly, the OSH Act, the Sarbanes-Oxley Act, and the Dodd-Frank Act would apply to pretty much all public companies, but other laws and regulations apply to certain industries and groups, so we need to note them in the code as well. This is just another reinforcement of the annual training that we have to do regarding each law or regulation that covers our business and industry.

Remember that the code of ethics is important because a culture of misconduct can result in higher turnover and lower productivity and profitability,[36] as well as costly legal problems. Management always has to take the lead in being ethical, or employees will not perform.

Values Our basic concepts of good and bad, or right and wrong

Principles Basic application of our values

Creating and Maintaining Ethical Organizations

The code of ethics is a first strong step in maintaining an ethical organization, but as already noted, managers must lead ethically. However, is the right (ethical) choice always the obvious choice? Unfortunately, it is not that easy. People that we interact with continually give us the opportunity to be unethical by providing us with personal advantages that help us but do not help the organization—for instance, by offering us gifts. To understand what managers should do in such situations, we need to look at what they can do, based on authority, responsibility, and accountability. Let's look at these concepts in the context of an organizational setting.

Authority

Authority The right to give orders, enforce obedience, make decisions, and commit resources toward completing organizational goals

Authority is *the right to give orders, enforce obedience, make decisions, and commit resources toward completing organizational goals.* So authority allows managers to tell people who work for them what to do and how to use organizational resources.

Responsibility

Responsibility The obligation to answer for something/ someone—the duty to carry out an assignment to a satisfactory conclusion

Responsibility is *the obligation to answer for something/someone—the duty to carry out an assignment to a satisfactory conclusion.* So responsibility means that, when we are given authority, we have to accept a position-based obligation to use those resources that we are given to help the organization meet its goals.

Accountability

Accountability The personal duty to someone else (a higher-level manager or the organization itself) for the effective use of resources to complete an assignment

Accountability is *the personal duty to someone else (a higher-level manager or the organization itself) for the effective use of resources to complete an assignment.* In other words, the manager can be held personally liable for failing to use resources in the way that they should to help the organization. Unethical behavior often has personal negative consequences,[37] such as getting into trouble at work, being fired, and even going to jail. If you get away with unethical behavior, it can be contagious and lead to more and larger transgressions.[38] **(SHRM V:1-a)**

People who cook the books often start by believing that it is no big deal, they will hit the numbers the next quarter/year and make it up and no one will ever know (we will not get caught), and no one will get hurt. But in most cases, as happened at **Enron**, you never catch up. So be careful not to start down the road using unethical behavior because you may not be able to make a U-turn. You will most likely eventually get caught, and you, too, can end up fired and even in jail.

Peter Drucker, the noted management author, said, "Whoever claims authority thereby assumes responsibility."[39] To be *allowed to use* the authority given, the person must *accept* responsibility. Both of these concepts are tied to the *position* of the manager in the organization. In other words, if you have the position of HR manager, you may be given some types of authority (e.g., authority to require annual equal employment opportunity [EEO] and sexual harassment training programs). However, you have to accept the responsibility to carry out these training programs—the buck stops here, with you. If you do not accept the responsibility for doing so, then the authority needs to be rescinded (you need to be taken out of the position of HR manager).

Authority and responsibility always need to be balanced. This is one of the most common failures in organizations. An example would be a chief executive officer (CEO) who requires subordinate managers to take responsibility for their department's expenditures but doesn't give them authority to veto purchases. This is requiring the subordinate to accept responsibility without commensurate authority. Or consider the sales manager who uses their authority to require subordinates to complete minor tasks that take up large amounts of time and then provides these subordinates with a poor evaluation for failure to sell. This is using positional authority without taking responsibility. So we have to try to make sure that these factors are balanced and that the person accepts their responsibilities.

If you accept responsibility, you become accountable (personally liable) for the effective completion of the action. In the previous case of the HR manager and training, you would have *personal accountability* even if someone else who works for you does the training. Accountability goes beyond an obligation to do something for the organization. It now requires that the person be held to account for their actions—that they give reasons why they did or did not do a certain thing and justify how their actions helped the organization reach its goals. So authority and responsibility give managers rights and obligations based on their job in the company, but accountability concerns when they can be punished—in some cases even go to prison—if they do not exercise their authority in a responsible manner.

As we noted earlier, we constantly have the opportunity to make decisions that will benefit us as an individual but do harm to the organization, peers, or our subordinates. If you apply the concept of responsibility to the situation (an obligation to use those resources to benefit the organization), then it is easy to see that you are being unethical. If you then continue anyway, the consequences of your actions might cause you to be held accountable by the organization and potentially disciplined or even fired if you misuse resources to a great extent.

Managers Face Ethical Questions on a Daily Basis

Should you choose a favorite employee to do overtime work instead of the employee who is best for the job because you know your favorite needs extra money? Should you tell the manager of another department a lie because you haven't completed a project yet? We have to learn to apply the concepts of authority, responsibility, and accountability constantly in order to avoid unethical actions, and in doing so, we will gain the trust of others in the organization. We have to know the appropriate use of company assets and what constitutes misuse of those assets as well. What are some of the most *common ethical issues* that both managers and their companies have to deal with on an ongoing basis?

Bribery

A bribe is a payment meant to cause someone to make decisions that may help a person or an organization but do significant harm to other organizations or other stakeholders in the decision. In a recent case in which a U.S. company was determined to be acting illegally, clothing company **Ralph Lauren** agreed to pay a $1.6 million fine for bribing Argentinian officials from 2005 to 2009.[40]

13.1 ETHICAL DILEMMA: WHAT WOULD YOU DO?
BRIBES

An American businessperson working in a foreign country complained to a local telephone manager that the technician showed up and asked for a bribe before installing the phone. The businessperson refused, so the telephone worker left without installing the phone. The telephone company manager told the businessperson that the matter would be investigated, for a fee (bribe).

1. Is it ethical and socially responsible to pay bribes?
2. Should the businessperson have paid the bribe to get the phone installed?
3. Are you aware of any bribes in the workplace? If so, describe the situation without listing the real names of people and companies to protect their identity.

Corrupt Payments to Government Officials

This type of payment is designed to allow the company to avoid scrutiny of their actions by government agencies or to facilitate a desired company action, such as building a new factory in an environmentally sensitive area. Corruption at the highest government levels was common for many years under the regime of President Suharto of Indonesia; if you were going to do business in Indonesia, you had to pay bribes to government officials and members of the Suharto family. This situation has since been cleaned up, to a significant extent, by the leaders that have followed him.

Employment and Personnel Issues

Who to fire, hire, or promote, and changes in compensation and working conditions all can be affected by managerial decisions, which in turn will affect productivity, absenteeism, and turnover in the company. **Walmart** is a good example of a company that has been identified as having managers that use bias in making personnel decisions.[41] In addition, in many countries, practices such as the use of child labor and forced labor by convicts are common, and many other discriminatory labor practices occur, but many of these practices are not only unethical but illegal in other countries.

Marketing Practices

Dishonest marketing practices can ruin corporate reputations and even cause corporations to fail.[42] **Countrywide Financial** is an excellent example of a company that made billions of dollars by unethical marketing of low-documentation and no-documentation loans to individuals during the housing boom of the early 2000s, and it was still in danger of bankruptcy, even after being purchased by **Bank of America,** as late as 2013.[43] **(SHRM V:1-g)**

Impact on the Economy and Environment

Unethical practices on the part of many financial firms (including **Countrywide**) are thought to be the main cause of the massive recession that started in late 2007. In addition, past practices in many industries have had a long-lasting (if not permanent) effect on the environment around the world. Examples include the use of asbestos long after we knew the health hazards, strip-mining leading to massive flooding in many countries, or recent concerns that some pesticide producers are possibly creating "superbugs" that will be pesticide resistant.[44]

©iStockphoto.com/gradyreese

▲
It may be company policy to monitor any employee communication on any company device.

Employee and Customer Privacy

Due to advancements in technology, the ability to gather and maintain large amounts of personal data has become common in organizations. Use of such data must be for legitimate business purposes only. You may recall that **Facebook** received a huge number of complaints when they decided to experiment on their users by showing them happier or sadder newsfeeds on their personal pages.[45] Many of these customers felt as though this was not done for a legitimate business purpose. There are also many companies who now monitor all employee communication on company computers and other devices. Is this universal monitoring ethical, or is it an invasion of employee privacy?

Of course, all of the information that we have discussed does no good unless and until the manager makes the choice to do the right thing—makes the ethical decision. And this is not always easy. In many cases, there is no single right or wrong decision—it is *shades of gray.* One decision may be more ethical, but it still harms some stakeholders, while the other decision harms more people and has fewer beneficiaries. Here is the simplest takeaway that we can provide you: If you don't think about making the ethical decision *before* a situation arises that requires you to have integrity, you will probably make the expedient decision (the decision that gives you the greatest benefit or does you the least personal harm) and not the ethical decision, and you will *know* this because you rationalize the decision and will not be willing to tell others what is going on and what decision you have made.

So following the ethical approaches including the code of ethics does help us make ethical decisions.

The HR department is nearly always the organizational department responsible for helping to ensure that all employees follow the law and are ethical. As we go through the remainder of this chapter, we will discuss two areas needing legal and ethical considerations. First, we discuss diversity and inclusion. Then we discuss being socially responsible and sustainable, both legally and ethically.

Diversity and Inclusion

>> **LO 13.3 Contrast the concepts of equal employment opportunity, affirmative action, diversity, and inclusion.**

You need to understand the terms *equal employment opportunity* (EEO), *affirmative action, diversity,* and *inclusion.* These are different concepts and should not be used interchangeably. In this section, we will also discuss how to manage diversity through HR initiatives. Before we get into the details of diversity, complete Self-Assessment 13.2.

13.2 SELF-ASSESSMENT

IMPLICIT ASSOCIATION TEST (IAT)

To complete this diversity self-assessment, go to the Project Implicit website at https://implicit.harvard.edu/implicit/demo. From there, under "Project Implicit Social Attitudes," you can select a "language/nation" and hit "Go"; then click "I wish to proceed" and select 1 of 14 tests to take, based on our diversity types with a breakdown of several races, or your professor will select one for you to complete. Simply follow the instructions at the site to complete a test and get interpretations of your attitudes and beliefs about the diversity group you selected. It's free, and you can take as many as you want to.

Equal Employment Opportunity and Affirmative Action

Recall from Chapter 3 that the Equal Employment Opportunity Commission (EEOC) enforces federal and state employment laws and regulations. All organizations must obey the employment laws and regulation. However, affirmative action, and diversity and inclusion initiatives are generally voluntary, as we discuss the differences in this section.

Equal employment opportunity (EEO) is the term that deals with a series of laws and regulations put in place at the federal and state government level over the past 45 years. As such, as already discussed, EEO is very specific and narrowly defined within federal and state laws.

On the other hand, affirmative action was created in the 1960s through a series of policies at the presidential and legislative levels in the United States. Affirmative action, except in a few circumstances, does not have the effect of law.[46] Therefore, affirmative action is a much broader concept based on policies and executive orders (orders from the president) to help legally protected groups. Affirmative action plans have increased the number of women and minorities in several occupations and advancement in management and thus helps promote diversity at work.[47]

The terms *diversity* and *inclusion* are often used interchangeably, but they are different.[48] *Diversity* is a very broad set of concepts that deal with the acceptance of differences among people and getting diverse employees to work well together. *Inclusion* is a practice of ensuring that all employees feel they belong as valued members of the organization.[49] An inclusive value system creates a sense of belonging: a feeling of being respected and being valued for who you are, and feeling a level of supportive energy and commitment from others so that everyone can do their best work.[50]

Having covered EEO in Chapter 3, let's take a closer look at affirmative action, diversity, and inclusion. Exhibit 13.2 provides a summary of the four concepts. **Affirmative action** is *a series of policies, programs, and initiatives that have been instituted by various entities within both government and the private sector that are designed to prefer hiring of individuals from protected groups in certain circumstances, in an attempt to mitigate past discrimination.* There are only two specific cases in which affirmative action can be mandated or required within an organization.[51] In all other cases affirmative action is strictly voluntary. The two situations where affirmative action is mandatory are defined federal contractors under Executive Order 11246 and by federal court order. **(SHRM J:1)**

Affirmative action A series of policies, programs, and initiatives that have been instituted by various entities within both government and the private sector that are designed to prefer hiring of individuals from protected groups in certain circumstances, in an attempt to mitigate past discrimination

EXHIBIT 13.2	● Equal Employment Opportunity, Affirmative Action, Diversity, and Inclusion	

Topic	Governance	Concept
EEO	Federal (and state) law	Narrow, specific requirements and prohibitions
Affirmative action	Executive orders, federal court orders, or voluntary	Policies that broadly define situations in which actions should be taken to balance a workforce with its surroundings
Diversity	Organizational voluntary policies	Designed to get a diversity of people to work well together and better serve a more diverse customer base
Inclusion	Organizational voluntary policies	Designed to ensure that all employees feel they belong as valued members of the organization

Source: OSHA

Executive Order 11246 Defined Federal Contractor

If the company is a contractor to the federal government and receives more than $10,000 per year, they are required by presidential order (Executive Order 11246) to maintain an affirmative action program. Exemptions from this order include the following: **(SHRM D:7)**

- "(A) Government contractor or subcontractor that is a religious corporation, association, educational institution, or society, with respect to the employment of individuals of a particular religion to perform work connected with the carrying on by such corporation, association, educational institution, or society of its activities . . . "[52]

- " . . . facilities of a contractor that are in all respects separate and distinct from activities of the contractor related to the performance of the (federal government) contract."[53]

Federal Court Orders for Affirmative Action Programs

If an organization is presented with a federal court order to create an affirmative action program to correct past discriminatory practices, it must comply. This is usually only done when there is a history of past discriminatory practices in the organization.

Reverse Discrimination

Reverse discrimination
Discrimination against members of the majority group by an organization, generally resulting from affirmative action policies within an organization

Diversity The existence of differences—in HRM, it deals with different types of people in an organization

Inclusion A practice of ensuring that all employees feel they belong as valued members of the organization

The *Bakke v. California* decision of 1978 is the basis for the concept of **reverse discrimination**, which is *discrimination against members of the majority group by an organization, generally resulting from affirmative action policies within an organization.* There have been a number of other recent affirmative action rulings in federal courts. For example, the Supreme Court ordered a lower court to reconsider a "race-conscious" admissions plan at Texas state universities,[54] and it also upheld a voter-backed affirmative action ban in Michigan's universities.[55] **(SHRM J:13)**

Diversity and Inclusion in the Workforce

Diversity is simply *the existence of differences—in HRM, it deals with different types of people in an organization.* **Inclusion** is *a practice of ensuring that all employees feel they belong as valued members of the organization.* Diversity and creating inclusion provides opportunities, but at the same time, increasing diversity in the workforce also poses one of the most challenging HR and organizational issues of our time.[56] So, let's discuss why many organizations value diversity and inclusion and are choosing to promote them.[57]

Demographic Diversity

Is diversity really all that important? Yes![58] The United States has cultural diversity at home as a country populated by immigrants. With the popularity of an American education and potential for higher incomes, you will likely interact with people on campus and at work from other countries.[59]

According to the U.S. Census Bureau,[60] the U.S. population continues to grow slowly, with around 328 million people in 2018, and it is rapidly diversifying. The Caucasian population is decreasing, as there are more deaths than births. The population growth is coming from minorities, and Hispanics are now the largest minority group. Today, minority births are now the majority.

By around 2040, less than half of the total U.S. population will be Caucasian. By 2060, Caucasians are estimated to be 43% of the population, and one in three people (33%) will be Hispanic. What does this shift mean to organizations? It means that employee diversity will continue growing and we will have to become better at managing that diversity than we have been in the past. Companies, including **Travelers Insurance** and **Airbnb,** say diversity is a business imperative, and they are training employees to be inclusive.[61]

Many employee stakeholder subgroups are also beginning to receive much more attention than has historically been the case. Among these groups are older workers, women and minorities in management and the executive suite, lesbian/gay/bi/transgender (LGBT) employees, and a more racially and ethnically diverse employee pool. Public pressure has contributed to the interests of these and other groups in organizations, and therefore companies are having to figure out how to meet the needs of these stakeholders in the organization.

Like it or not, diversity is going to continue to grow, and the better you can work with diverse people, the greater are your chances of having a successful business career. So, develop your global mind-set.[62] Are you willing to commit to offering inclusion to diverse people into your homogeneous groups? **(SHRM J:2, J:6, J:11, and J:3)**

Benefits of a Diverse and Inclusive Workforce

Diversity helps increase sales, revenues, and profits—in other words, embracing diversity and inclusion creates business opportunities.[63] If employees don't feel included, they generally will not place a high value on organizational membership and will not be as productive as those who do.[64]

There is evidence that companies who practice diversity and inclusion gain tangible benefits from their employees and customers, including the following:[65]

1. Cost savings due to lower turnover, absenteeism, and increased productivity

2. An increase in workers that fill the current shortage of skilled employees

3. Winning the competition for diverse talent by being more attractive to women, minority groups, and diverse workforce members

4. An increase in customers as a result of having diverse employees with cultural sensitivity to a diverse customer base

5. Improved corporate image

In addition to these valuable outcomes,[66] there is evidence that other, less tangible returns accrue to companies that practice inclusion in the broadest sense.[67] For these, and other reasons, we will continue to discuss the value of diversity and inclusion as we go through the remainder of this book.

Creativity and Innovation

In addition to the five benefits of a diverse workforce discussed that tend to focus on current business operations, diversity also affects the ability to develop creative and innovate products and processes.

Creativity A basic ability to think in unique and different ways and apply those thought processes to existing problems

Innovation The act of creating useful processes or products based on creative thought processes

Divergent thinking The ability to find many possible solutions to a particular problem, including unique, untested solutions

Conflict The act of being opposed to another

Cohesiveness An intent and desire for group members to stick together in their actions

A wealth of evidence shows that diversity helps teams and organizations perform better in terms of creativity, innovation, revenue, and profits.[68] **Creativity** is *a basic ability to think in unique and different ways and apply those thought processes to existing problems,* and **innovation** is *the act of creating useful processes or products based on creative thought processes.* Being creative and implementing those ideas on improving how the business processes work to improve productivity and by offering new products through innovation results in increased revenue and profits.

A diverse group looking at a problem will analyze the problem from different directions and in different ways, and will discover more of the aspects of the problem than would a single person or a more homogeneous work group.[69] This ability, called divergent thinking, is necessary in order to come up with creative solutions to a problem.[70] **Divergent thinking** is *the ability to find many possible solutions to a particular problem, including unique, untested solutions.*

By introducing diversity into our workforce, we assist the process of divergent thinking. Different people think differently because they have different backgrounds and have solved problems differently in the past, so this has the effect of increasing the creativity and innovation in the organization without the individual having to relearn the ability to be highly creative.

Challenges to Diversity and Inclusion

Several things can cause diversity to break down the organization instead of allowing it to become better and more creative.[71] The first issue is conflict. **Conflict** is simply *the act of being opposed to another.* Conflict occurs in interactions between individuals. There are many reasons for conflict, but it is typically greater when people are significantly different from each other, which means that if we create a more diverse workforce, there's a greater likelihood for more conflict.

The second big issue is group cohesiveness. **Cohesiveness** is *an intent and desire for group members to stick together in their actions.* In organizations, we have learned that in order for a work group to become as good as it possibly can be, the group has to become cohesive. The members have to learn to *want* to be part of the group and want to interact with other members of the group in order for the group to perform at a high level. However, the more diversity there is within the group, the more difficult it is to create the cohesiveness necessary for high performance. So, more diverse groups tend to be less cohesive—not always, but as a general rule.[72]

Managing Diversity

Managing diversity so that we gain the benefits available is one of the most critical jobs today and into the future as the world becomes more diversified as the white population continues to decline globally. The European Union is currently dealing with major diversity issues that the United States will face in the near future.

Although effective management of diversity and inclusion is difficult,[73] here we present initiatives that are being used successfully by major corporations. As the foundation, HR must develop and initiate diversity and inclusion policies and practices. **Microsoft** will spend $55.4 million a year on diversity initiatives through 2020.[74]

Inclusive Equal Opportunity for All

A primary HR goal in managing diversity is to create an inclusive equal opportunity organizational culture (Chapter 2) for all that recognizes the value of each individual.[75] Inclusion must be part of every manager's job starting with the CEO down.[76] CEO **Lip-Bu Tan** says diversity is a top priority at **Cadence**, where 95% of its 6,500 employees state that **Cadence** is an inclusive workplace.[77]

Diversity Recruiting and Promoting

HR should recruit and promote minorities to increase and retain minorities in its diverse workforce. Records of diverse group hiring and promoting should be kept, and efforts should be made to help these groups succeed in the workplace, often called a *diversity audit.* **Twitter** set targets for minority and women representation within the firm and by types of jobs.[78] We discussed staffing in Chapters 4, 5, and 6 and how to avoid illegal discrimination.

Diversity Training

HR can offer diversity training to teach people how to get along better with diverse workers through inclusion. It helps people to talk about bias and better understand each other by becoming aware of and more empathetic toward people different from themselves.[79] **Starbucks** closed thousands of stores for an afternoon to conduct antibias training.[80]

Mentor Programs

Companies can offer mentoring programs, as no one gets to the top alone.[81] Most large corporations, including **Sun Microsystems, Intel,** and **Microsoft** offer several internally developed formal mentoring programs for employees.[82] Mentoring is especially recommended for women and minorities who want to advance to top-level positions because it can help them break into the "good old boy" networks that often make the selections for these jobs.[83] **LinkedIn** offers a new service connecting mentors with mentees for career-advice sessions.[84]

Network Diversity Groups

HR can offer network diversity groups to promote equality.[85] They have employees throughout the organization from a diverse group whose members share information about how to succeed in the company and how to help the company succeed. For instance, **Frito-Lay** has a Latino employee network that provides management with very valuable feedback on marketing products to the Latino community.[86]

All these diversity and inclusion initiatives take time and money. But they have been shown to be HR investments rather than expenses (productivity centers vs. cost centers; see Chapter 1) because they can increase effectiveness and efficiency, which increase revenue and profits.[87] Unfortunately, the HR department always has to compete for limited resources. So, the better you can measure and calculate a return on investment (see Chapter 2), the greater funding HR will get.

Corporate Social Responsibility (CSR)

>> **LO 13.4 Describe the "business case" for corporate social responsibility (CSR).**

Ethics, diversity, and corporate social responsibility (CSR) are closely related, as being socially responsible means going beyond legal and economic obligations to do the right things by acting in ways that benefit society.[88] *CSR is an umbrella term for exploring the responsibilities of business and its role in society.*[89] CSR is in the news constantly. Many of the business problems that have occurred, from the early-2000s financial crisis to the sexual assault and sexual harassment exposed by the #MeToo movement,[90] have been caused at least in part by a lack of CSR. Let's review this concept and then take a look at some of the stakeholders that are affected by CSR.

CSR Defined

The concept of corporate social responsibility is based on the belief that "companies have some responsibilities to society beyond that of making profits for the shareholders."[91] So **corporate social responsibility** is *the concept that organizations have a duty to all societal stakeholders to operate in a manner that takes each of their needs into account.* In other words, companies need to look at their effects on society and all corporate stakeholders, not just shareholders.

They must provide *employees* with safe working conditions and with adequate pay and benefits. Companies must provide safe products and services to customers. For society, the company should improve the quality of life, or at least not destroy the environment. The company must compete fairly with competitors and work with suppliers in a cooperative manner. It must abide by the laws and regulations of government. At the same time, the company must provide shareholders with a reasonable profit. Without profits, it is difficult to be socially responsible. Unfortunately, businesses can't always create a win-win for all their multiple stakeholders because they often have conflicting objectives.[92]

Corporate social responsibility The concept that organizations have a duty to all societal stakeholders to operate in a manner that takes each of their needs into account

The Business Case for CSR

Does it pay to be socially responsible? The answer is yes. With a choice of two products of similar price and quality, 80% of surveyed customers said they are willing to buy the more sustainable option.[93] Being socially irresponsible also has negative consequences, as it gives the company a negative reputation that leads to more difficulty in attracting customers, investors, and employees, and it can lead to costly lawsuits.[94] If CSR didn't benefit the company in some way, why would virtually all large public corporations have CSR programs? Money can be made again, but a negative reputation can take years to improve, and a good reputation may be lost forever.[95] Some companies are using CSR as a strategy to increase profits.[96] Although it is difficult to measure the actual financial impact of CSR, a study by *Forbes* showed that companies considered to be highly socially responsible (including **American Express, F5 Networks, Ford, PepsiCo, Southwest**) had an average return of 13.6% compared with 9.9% for those with lower ratings of CSR.[97] **(SHRM V:1-b, V:1-f, and V:1-c)**

Visit your favorite large corporation's website and you will most likely find a link stating how the firm engages in CSR; it is even included in most companies' annual reports, where it is often called a *social audit* because it is a measure of social behavior.

Stakeholders, Laws, and CSR

In addition to being good public practice, CSR is also being codified more often in law in the United States and in other countries. There are a number of corporate compliance laws written by state and federal government stakeholders, many of which we have already discussed. The Dodd-Frank Wall Street Reform and Consumer Protection Act (Chapter 11), the OSH Act (Chapter 12), the Fair Labor Standards Act (Chapter 10), and many others have already been covered, and we will briefly review another significant compliance law in Chapter 14 called the U.S. Foreign Corrupt Practices Act. You will have to become familiar with each of the major compliance laws as well as compliance regulations in your state or country as you begin your career.

Levels of Corporate Social Responsibility

Clearly, in today's society, the question is not whether business should be socially responsible and take all stakeholder groups into account. Instead, the question is, *at what level of CSR should the business operate?* Businesses vary greatly in their social responsibility activities based on the overall level of CSR at which they decide to operate. Managers can choose to operate the business at one of three levels of CSR. However, the firm can be at different levels for various stakeholders and issues. See Exhibit 13.3 for an illustration of the three levels.

1. *Legal CSR* focuses on maximizing profits while obeying the law; it focuses on increasing sales and cutting costs to maximize returns to stockholders. In dealings with market stakeholders, these firms meet all of their legal responsibilities, such as fulfilling contract obligations and providing legally safe products while honoring guarantees and warranties. They do what it takes to beat the competition legally. In dealing with nonmarket stakeholders (society and government), they obey all the laws and

EXHIBIT 13.3 ● Levels of Corporate Social Responsibility

3. **Benevolent CSR**. Focus on profitability and helping society through philanthropy.

2. **Ethical CSR**. Focus on profitability and going beyond the law to do what is right, just, and fair.

1. **Legal CSR**. Focus on maximizing profits while obeying the law.

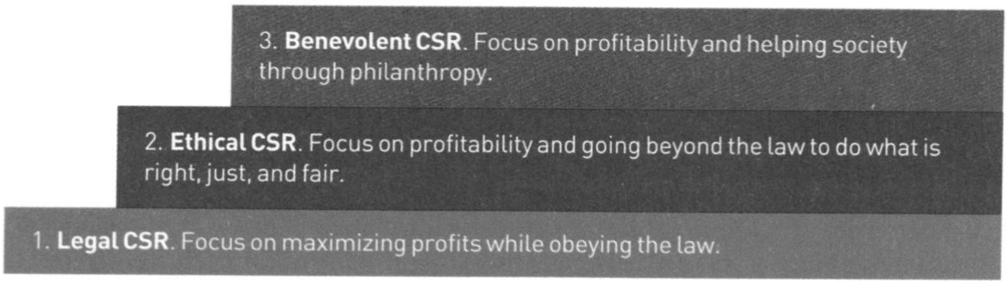

regulations, such as not polluting more than the legal limits and meeting all OSHA standards. **Philip Morris** and **Remington** and other brands sell cigarettes and guns that are legal, but some question the ethics of the business.

2. *Ethical CSR* focuses on profitability and doing what is right, just, and fair. Providing ethical leadership and avoiding questionable practices mean doing more than is required in dealing with market stakeholders, such as treating employees right and paying them fair wages, providing safer products, not squeezing suppliers, and competing to win business ethically. These companies meet reasonable societal expectations and exceed government laws and regulations to be just and fair to stakeholders. **CVS** voluntarily gave up selling legal cigarettes, a decision that cost the company an estimated $2 billion a year.[98]

3. *Benevolent CSR* focuses on profitability and helping society through philanthropy, often referred to as "giving back."[99] This highest level of CSR is also called "good corporate citizenship." Benevolent firms are philanthropic, giving gifts of money, or other resources, to charitable causes. Employees are expected, encouraged, and rewarded for being active volunteers in the community, often on company time. In addition to giving corporate money, many rich entrepreneurs set up foundations and give their own money. **Facebook** founder **Mark Zuckerberg** plans to give away 99% of his Facebook stock.[100]

Sustainability

>> **LO 13.5 Review the concept of sustainability in a business context.**

Sustainability practices are part of CSR. **Sustainability** involves *meeting the needs of the current generation without compromising the ability of future generations to meet their needs.*[101] Sustainability is now a business buzzword,[102] and based on the gravity of environmental problems, it is an important topic for all countries,[103] as is recognized by the AACSB[104] and the Society for Human Resource Management (SHRM). Corporations are accepting the environment as an important external stakeholder.[105] The use of renewable energy is on the increase,[106] and sustainability standards are becoming the standard.[107]

Society expects sustainability and for managers to use resources wisely and responsibly; protect the environment; minimize the amount of air, water, energy, minerals, and other materials found in the final goods we consume; recycle and reuse these goods to the extent possible rather than drawing on nature to replenish them; respect nature's calm, tranquility, and beauty; and eliminate toxins that harm people in the workplace and communities.[108] Thus, including sustainability in managing the business is being socially responsible.

Many corporations are addressing sustainability changes, and an important part of the reason is that it can pay to do so.[109] Some people even refer to the triple bottom line: concern for profit, society, and the environment. **Southwest Airlines** takes environmental awareness seriously and considers it part of its triple bottom line: profits, people, planet.[110] **(SHRM V:6)**

> **Sustainability** Meeting the needs of the current generation without compromising the ability of future generations to meet their needs

HR and Organizational Sustainability

What does business need to do in order to be considered sustainable? Organizations use up resources in the course of their operations. Any resource that is used must be replenished or it disappears forever. In years past, it was thought that resources were so abundant that we could never use them up, but we now know better. There are already shortages of some critical items necessary for the survival of people, and other species, over the long term—shortages of good drinking water in some areas, for instance.

Organizations have to practice sustainability in today's business environment. We cannot afford to waste resources that are difficult to replace.

Sustainability Practices and Green Companies

Sustainability issues influence activities in the business world.[111] A *green company* acts in a way that minimizes damage to the environment. With the current worldwide environmental problems, many new ventures have been created in green management.[112] Social entrepreneurs are taking advantage of sustainability for new businesses. Large corporations are also engaging in sustainability practices in a big way. **(SHRM V:6-a)**

Walmart is a leader in sustainability. It is saving billions in costs by reducing its environmental footprint.[113] Back in 2010, it stated that it would cut some 20 million metric tons of greenhouse gas emissions from its supply chain by the end of 2015—and did it![114] Walmart's requirements of reduced waste from packaging have created industry-wide reforms.[115] It essentially pressures all of its thousands of suppliers to meet its sustainability standards. Even the greenest companies tout their close ties to Walmart in their promotional materials.[116]

Amazon is also a green company that has reduced packaging and makes sure it is made from recycled materials that can be recycled again, and its headquarters was built to have eco-friendly buildings with **LEED (Leadership in Energy and Environmental Design)**–certified interiors and exteriors. **Pratt Industries** makes corrugated boxes using 100% recycled paper, saving an estimated 50,000 trees a day, with an estimated company value of $3.4 billion.[117] With the trend toward online shopping and boxed delivery, **Pratt** is making an environmental impact for **Amazon** and others.

▲ Ben & Jerry's has a long-term reputation for being concerned with sustainability and CSR issues.

The Need for Management Commitment

Sustainable practices require a strong commitment by companies in order to create the necessary follow-through at all levels of the company. As with any other ethical issue, we have to get the most senior level of management to commit to sustainability and walk the talk. A new corporate title has emerged—chief sustainability officer (CSO). CSOs are in charge of the corporation's environmental programs. Nearly all of the 150 world's largest companies have a sustainability officer with the rank of vice president or higher.[118] The process of sustainable design requires that everyone think about what resources are being used in every action that the company takes.

Sustainability goals and objectives tied to the company strategy are an essential part of the efforts to "green the company," and HR must play its part in these efforts. Performance evaluations of all managers should contain items relating to their sustainability efforts, and in many cases part of their incentive compensation may be tied to those efforts. It takes tenacity to make any program take hold in an organization, and the effort to become sustainable is no different than with any other program. HR managers also need to implement sustainability training to inform and guide all employees in their sustainability efforts. Let's take a look at sustainability training now.

Sustainability Training

Just a few years ago, very few sustainability training programs could be found in major corporations. Fortunately for all of us, this is no longer the case. Whereas a very small number of organizations have been concerned with CSR and sustainability for many years (e.g., **Ben & Jerry's Ice Cream**, founded in 1978), most larger businesses didn't become concerned with sustainability programs until about the turn of the 21st century, when they realized their importance[119] and profitability.[120]

A successful initiative needs to be based on the organization embedding the concept of CSR and sustainability throughout the firm. Strong organizational cultures can create a collective commitment to CSR and sustainability within the entire workforce. (For a review of how to develop corporate culture, see Chapter 2.)

In conjunction with the culture, training, and code of conduct, the organization must measure the impact of their sustainability programs to allow modifications to those programs if necessary. Changes in company policies and procedures, as well as organizational structure, may also assist in improving sustainability within the organization. Again, though, *training* on the changes in policies, procedures, and structure must occur in order to modify those employees' behaviors. If the organization succeeds in these training efforts, corporate sustainability efforts will likely improve significantly over time.

The Sustainable Organization

Evidence shows that customers are concerned with sustainability and that more of them today are willing to avoid doing business with companies who do not pay attention to their CSR and sustainability. So, today's sustainable organization has a culture that supports and implements green company initiatives that help meet the triple bottom line. But what can your company do if it has not yet jumped on the transparency bandwagon?

The World Economic Forum provides a reasonably compact set of takeaways in its "Action 2020" document:[121]

1. Get business to buy into long-term goals for sustainability.

2. Change the nature of the debate from attacks and counterattacks on company sustainability initiatives to the science behind the need for sustainable business practices.

3. Speak the right language—the language of business. This means putting the information into the business cycle of "plan, do, check, act."

4. Work toward building partnerships and collaboration, because that is the only way to have a large-scale effect on the environment.

5. Make solutions "open source," and allow all entities who can benefit from them to use them.

Where can you go for more information? There are many good sources for data and information on corporate environmental impact and sustainability. Exhibit 13.4 provides you with information on some of the major sites hosting this information.

EXHIBIT 13.4 ● Internet Resources for Corporate Sustainability

World Business Council for Sustainable Development (WBCSD): http://www.wbcsd.org

Provides a platform for business collaboration around the "Vision to Action" model for sustainable business.

International Organization for Standardization (ISO): http://www.iso.org

The ISO 14000 series of standards address environmental management in organizations, providing "practical tools for companies . . . looking to identify and control their environmental impact."[122]

International Institute for Sustainable Development (IISD): http://www.iisd.org

The IISD champions sustainability development around the world through innovation, partnerships, research, and communications.

United Nations Global Compact: http://www.unglobalcompact.org

Provides "supply chain sustainability" information based on 10 principles that drive the Global Compact efforts.[123]

International Organization for Sustainable Development (IOSD): http://www.iosd.org

A United Nations registered site, IOSD provides a number of white papers on sustainability issues around the world.

World Economic Forum (WEF): http://www.weforum.org

The World Economic Forum is an international institution committed to improving the state of the world through public-private cooperation. It provides sustainability information on everything from climate to food insecurity at https://www.weforum.org/about/sustainability-world-economic-forum.

National Association of Environmental Management (NAEM): http://www.naem.org

NAEM is a membership organization that focuses on environmental health and safety, including sustainability as part of its environmental health mission.

Corporate Social Responsibility Newswire (CSRwire): http://www.csrwire.com

CSRwire is a newswire service that provides "the latest news, views and reports in corporate social responsibility (CSR) and sustainability."[124] This is a very good site that gathers news and information on CSR and sustainability issues.

Now that you have some working knowledge of ethics, diversity and inclusion, CSR, and sustainability and where to find more information, let's move on to this chapter's trends and issues.

Trends and Issues in HRM

Let's take a look at some sustainability-based benefits available in organizations today, followed by a look at the value of diversity training.

Sustainability-Based Benefits

One area that has seen recent interest is sustainability-based benefit programs. A number of companies are looking at options for providing benefits to their employees that assist with improving environmental stability and sustainability over the long term. These programs range from providing "credits" to employees for riding bicycles or public transportation to work to sharing the costs of cars or home appliances that lower energy usage.

Benefits that will lower the employee's individual "carbon footprint" help the environment and help the employee because such benefits almost always lower the employee's cost of living. An example is a program called Home Energy Affordability Loan (HEAL) Arkansas. This program was started by the **Addison Shoe Factory** when they learned that many of their employees spent *up to half of their income* on energy bills.[125] The HEAL program is now offered through the Clinton Foundation **Clinton Climate Initiative** to selected businesses and provides facility audits and zero interest retrofit financing of energy efficiency improvements for their facilities.[126] The companies in turn must use part of their energy savings to help employees with home audits and retrofitting of appliances, windows, and other energy-saving items by providing the employees with zero-interest loans for such improvements.

Companies may also provide a variety of other "green" subsidies so that employees can help the environment. These might include assistance to employees with purchasing renewable energy options for their homes such as solar cells or hybrid, electric, or alternative fuel vehicles. Even telecommuting can be a sustainability benefit because it lowers the number of employees commuting to work. So employers just need to use a bit of imagination and a good search engine to find ways in which they can encourage sustainable practices on the part of their employees as well as practices that they can put into effect within the company.

Does Diversity Training Work?

Competitive organizations always need to work to maximize the talent pool from which they can draw recruits. If, in fact, the organization arbitrarily limits the number and types of recruits through artificial limits on organizational diversity, it restricts its ability to draw on the best talent available from the at-large workforce. However, most organizations today accept the fact that unmanaged diversity can decrease employee commitment and engagement, lower job satisfaction, increase turnover, and increase conflict. Organizations must create a cultural change in order for diversity training to be successful. But because cultural change is very difficult, many organizations try to shortcut the process and as a result end up with failed programs.[127]

©iStockphoto.com/Rawpixel Ltd

▲ It is important for organizations to manage workplace diversity, but taking shortcuts in diversity training is not the answer.

How can organizations create and deliver a diversity training process that has a chance of being successful? Common diversity initiatives include diversity recruitment, diversity training, and formal mentoring programs. However, plugging these programs into organizational training without providing a process by which they can be integrated into the daily activities of the members of the organization will likely lead to minimal, if any, success.

Diversity training has been around in some form since the 1960s. In its earlier days, diversity training primarily focused on organizational *compliance* with equal opportunity laws. Later on, diversity training moved through a sequence of options—from attempting to *assimilate* different individuals into an organizational culture; through attempting to make employees sensitive to others and their differences; and, more recently, to trying to create *inclusion* of all individuals, from all backgrounds, into the organization.[128]

Throughout each phase of diversity training's existence, its effectiveness has been questioned by many organizations and researchers. Evidence, though, appears to be growing that diversity training does add value to the organization, both sociologically and economically.[129] The bottom line is that most major corporations believe that diversity adds significant value to their organizations, by providing different viewpoints and solutions to problems and by providing the organization with a larger talent pool in a period when qualified applicants are becoming less and less available in the at-large workforce.[130]

Chapter Summary

13.1 Discuss the term *ethics* by stating the common elements of the definition.

There are many definitions of *ethics,* but they all have some common elements. The common elements include the concepts of morals, values, beliefs, and principles. These in turn lead to the need for personal integrity and trust in the character of another, or we won't believe that they will act ethically if they have an opportunity for self-enrichment at the expense of others.

13.2 Identify each factor required in a good code of ethics.

Values are the first factor. They "define what the company is about and make it clear that the company is based on honesty and fairness."[131] *Principles* apply our values to specific situations to identify actions that we consider ethical. *Management support* is critical because if senior managers do not pay attention to the code, others will not either. *Personal responsibility* identifies the fact that everyone is personally accountable for their own behavior and is expected to act ethically. Finally, *compliance* identifies applicable laws and regulations that guide ethical behavior in specific industries.

13.3 Contrast the concepts of equal employment opportunity, affirmative action, diversity, and inclusion.

Equal employment opportunity deals with a series of laws and regulations put in place at the federal and state government levels that must be obeyed. *Affirmative action,* except in a few circumstances, does not have the effect of law. Therefore, affirmative action is a much broader concept based on

policy than is EEO, which is more narrowly based on law.

Diversity and inclusion are not law, nor necessarily even policy within organizations. *Diversity* initiatives are designed to get diverse people to work well together and better serve diverse customers. *Inclusion* initiatives focus on ensuring that all employees feel they belong as valued members.

13.4 Describe the "business case" for corporate social responsibility (CSR).

CSR says that organizations have a duty to all stakeholders to operate in a manner that takes each of their needs into account. All stakeholders means *all*—not just shareholders or executives. The business case for CSR is based on the ability of the organization to help or harm various stakeholder groups and of those stakeholder groups in turn to help or harm the company. Each stakeholder group has different—and sometimes competing—interests, but the organization must balance these "social responsibilities" among all of the groups in order to succeed.

13.5 Review the concept of sustainability in a business context.

Sustainability means meeting the needs of the current generation without compromising the ability of future generations to meet their own needs. Business must practice sustainability today because so many resources are being overused to the point where they cannot be replenished and will ultimately disappear unless we quickly change our practices. Sustainability goals must be created and managed like any other organizational goal in order to improve business sustainability.

Key Terms

accountability, 342
affirmative action, 345
authority, 342
cohesiveness, 348
conflict, 348
corporate social
    responsibility, 349

creativity, 348
divergent thinking, 348
diversity, 346
ethics, 336
inclusion, 346
innovation, 348

principles, 341
responsibility, 342
reverse discrimination, 346
sustainability, 351
values, 341

Key Terms Review

Complete each of the following statements using one of this chapter's key terms.

1. _____ is the application of a set of values and principles in order to make the right, or good, choice.

2. _____ are our basic concepts of good and bad, or right and wrong.

3. _____ are a basic application of our values.

4. _____ is the right to give orders, enforce obedience, make decisions, and commit resources toward completing organizational goals.

5. _____ is the obligation to answer for something/someone or the duty to carry out an assignment to a satisfactory conclusion.

6. _____ is the personal duty to someone else for the effective use of resources to complete an assignment.

7. _____ is a series of policies, programs, and initiatives that have been instituted by various entities within both government and the private sector to create preferential hiring of individuals from protected groups in certain circumstances, in an attempt to mitigate past discrimination.

8. _____ is discrimination against members of the majority group by an organization, generally resulting from affirmative action policies within an organization.

9. _____ is the existence of differences—in HRM, it deals with different types of people in an organization.

10. _____ is a basic ability to think in unique and different ways and apply those thought processes to existing problems.

11. _____ is the act of creating useful processes or products based on creative thought processes.

12. _____ is the ability to find many possible solutions to a particular problem, including unique, untested solutions.

13. _____ is the act of being opposed to another.

14. _____ is an intent and desire for group members to stick together in their actions.

15. _____ is the concept that organizations have a duty to all societal stakeholders to operate in a manner that takes each of their needs into account.

16. _____ involves meeting the needs of the current generation without compromising the ability of future generations to meet their needs.

Communication Skills

The following critical-thinking questions can be used for class discussion and/or for written assignments to develop communication skills. Be sure to give complete explanations for all answers.

1. Do you think the term *ethics* is overused in today's business environment? Justify your answer.

2. Will applying the golden rule always result in a decision that you can defend as "ethical"? Why or why not?

3. Can you think of situations where someone might violate the code of ethics in a company but should not be punished for it? Give examples.

4. Using the concepts of authority, responsibility, and accountability, can you explain what should happen to an individual who misuses company resources for personal gain? Provide an example.

5. Has affirmative action gone too far in creating a preference for historically underrepresented groups over other employees and applicants instead of treating everyone equally?

6. Do you agree that companies have a duty to stakeholders other than their shareholders? If so, justify who else they are obligated to and why.

7. Can you identify one case where you think the government (state or federal) is the most important stakeholder of a firm? (Do not use the government as a customer but as another external stakeholder.) Explain your answer.

8. Is sustainability just a marketing tool to get people to "think green," or is it a necessary business tool? Defend your answer.

9. How would you motivate people in your organization to practice sustainability? Be specific with the managerial tools that you would use.

Case 13.1 CEO Compensation: Do They Deserve Rock Star Pay?

It really does pay to be a CEO of a Fortune 500 firm, according to the AFL-CIO. The average S&P 500 chief executive made $13.1 million in 2016, 347 times more than the average U.S. worker did, up from 335 times as much in the previous year. For this study, the AFL-CIO analyzed available filings from 419 companies in the S&P 500 index. It found the average pay of these CEOs was roughly $13.1 million in 2016, a 6% increase over the prior year. In contrast, the average annual pay of production and non-supervisory workers in the United States was $37,632, a 2% increase, the labor group said, citing figures from the Bureau of Labor Statistics, a Department of Labor agency. The AFL-CIO said that when adjusted for inflation, U.S. workers' wages have been stagnant for 50 years. Adjusted for inflation, production and non-supervisory workers averaged $41,473 a year in 1967, for instance.

The widening pay gap reflects a growing income inequality, according to the AFL-CIO, the largest federation of U.S. labor unions, which posted the latest figure on its website. The group used the survey release to highlight slow U.S. wage growth and the outsourcing of jobs to countries with lower wages. The labor group's annual study often draws notice as a measure of how U.S. workers largely are not sharing the economic gains of those at the top of the income scale, even as official unemployment remains at near all-time lows.

Why such a high salary given the fact that the U.S. economy has grown (at most) 2% per year over the past few years, one third of the growth of CEO salaries? U.S. CEO pay is often high because of the widespread practice of using "peer group" averages to set pay, AFL-CIO officials said in a conference call with reporters. One improvement could be to make share-holder votes on pay binding, as they are for British companies, they said. Yet, at the same time, U.S. investors do not seem upset with the situation. In the advisory votes that S&P 500 companies held for their shareholders on executive pay last year, they received average support of 91%, according to consulting firm Semler Brossy. Only six companies received less than 50% support in the advisory votes.[132]

The public certainly feels that CEOs are overpaid. In 2016 the Rock Center for Corporate Governance at Stanford University conducted a nationwide survey of 1,202 individuals—representative by gender, race, age, political affiliation, household income, and state residence—to understand public perception of CEO pay levels among the 500 largest publicly traded corporations. Key takeaways are that, according to most Americans, CEOs are vastly overpaid, most Americans support drastic reductions, yet the public is divided on government intervention.

Among those polled, 74% believe that CEOs are not paid the correct amount relative to the average worker while 16% believe that they are. Although responses vary across demographic groups (e.g., political affiliation and household income), overall sentiment regarding CEO pay remains highly negative. "There is a clear sense among the American public that CEOs are taking home much more in compensation than they deserve," says Professor David F. Larcker of Stanford Graduate School of Business. "While we find that members of the public are not particularly knowledgeable about how much CEOs actually make in annual pay, there is a general sense of outrage fueled in part by the political environment."

Nearly two thirds (62%) of Americans believe that there is a maximum amount that CEOs should be paid relative to the average worker, regardless of the company and its performance. Interestingly, a majority of all political groups believe CEO pay should be capped in some manner, although Republicans are somewhat less likely to hold this opinion (52%) than are Democrats (66%) or Independents (64%). Those who believe in capping CEO pay relative to the average worker would do so at a very low multiple. The typical American would limit CEO pay to no more than 6 times that of the average worker. These figures are significantly below current pay multiples.

Those who favor government intervention support a range of possible actions, although none alone receives majority or even close to near-majority support. Among respondents who advocate government intervention, 28% would substantially increase taxes on CEO compensation above a certain amount, 25% would set a strict limit on the dollar amount a CEO can receive relative to the average worker, and 17% would limit the absolute dollar amount that a CEO can receive. Furthermore, 17% would require more performance-based compensation, 9% would ban the use of stock options in executive compensation contracts, and 8% would ban the use of all equity compensation in CEO pay packages.[133]

However, many experts do not agree with the public and would argue the public does not have all of the facts. Jannice Koors, managing director of Pearl Meyer & Partners in Chicago, has a different perspective on CEO compensation.

> I think most companies are on the right track with their [executive] pay programs. Yes, CEO pay increased this year—because average company profits and share prices grew. Compensation is more closely tied to performance than ever before, which is exactly what shareholders have been pushing for. Today, only a very small percentage of a typical CEO pay package is in the form of a guaranteed annual salary.[134]

Donald Delves, director of Towers Watson in Chicago, justifies CEO pay this way:

> CEOs are paid about three times as much as the next level of executives. . . . In my experience, it is a very rare person who has the skills and experience required to run a huge global corporation. And their average tenure continues to decline. There is not a lot of patience shown by shareholders and boards when a company underperforms.[135]

Anthony Smith, author of The Taboos of Leadership, noted,

> The reality is that the free market is alive and well, and is the true dictator of CEO pay. While what one's peers are making is still a legitimate barometer, critics should look at the macroeconomics of "stars" in

all fields (after all, CEOs are the "stars" of the business world), and not just the *micro* economics of CEO pay, if they are serious about understanding the calculus in determining compensation. Such valuation analysis must factor in the track record of the CEO; his or her potential; competing job offers; personal enticements; what he or she is leaving behind; their reputation on the "street"; and the team of other executives he or she is likely to bring or attract. . . . only a handful of people are capable of leading major multinational corporations with 100,000+ employees and $50+ billion in annual revenue. Bottom line: true stars are in short supply and high demand. It's pure Economics 101.[136]

Whether you agree or disagree with the fairness of CEO pay, CEOs make as much in 1 day as the average worker makes in 1 year.

Questions

1. How does ethics apply to this case?

2. What factors might contribute to what some perceive as unethical behavior concerning CEO pay?

3. What are the differing ethical approaches, and how might they apply to this case?

4. How might the issue of CEO compensation be dealt with in a firm's code of ethics?

5. How might the issue of CEO compensation be used by a firm to create and maintain an ethical organization?

6. What is your own opinion about CEO compensation? Provide facts and arguments supporting your position from this case.

Case created by Herbert Sherman, PhD, and Theodore Vallas, Department of Management Sciences, School of Business Brooklyn Campus, Long Island University

Skill Builder 13.1 Ethics and Whistle-Blowing

Objective

To determine your level of ethics

Skills

The primary skills developed through this exercise are as follows:

1. *HR management skills*—Conceptual and design skills

2. *SHRM 2018 Curriculum Guidebook*—V: Sustainability/Corporate Responsibility

Assignment

For this exercise, first complete Self-Assessment 13.1, earlier in this chapter.

Discussion Questions

1. Who is harmed and who benefits from the unethical behaviors in Items 1 through 3?

2. For Items 4 to 24, select the three (circle their numbers) you consider the most unethical. Who is harmed by, and who benefits from, these unethical behaviors?

3. If you observed unethical behavior but didn't report it, why didn't you report the behavior? If you did blow the whistle, what motivated you to do so? What was the result?

4. As a manager, it is your responsibility to uphold ethical behavior. If you know employees are doing any of these unethical behaviors, will you take action to enforce compliance with ethical standards?

5. What can you do to prevent unethical behavior?

6. As part of the class discussion, share any of the other unethical behaviors you observed and listed.

You may be asked to present your answers to the class or share them in small groups in class or online.

Skill Builder 13.2 Code of Ethics and Corporate Social Responsibility

Objective

To better understand a business's ethics and CSR

Skills

The primary skills developed through this exercise are as follows:

1. *HR management skills*—Conceptual and design skills

2. *SHRM 2018 Curriculum Guidebook*—V: Sustainability/Corporate Responsibility

Assignment

Select a specific business. It can be one you work for or, better yet, one you would like to work for in the future. Make sure the company you select meets the following criteria: It must have a written code of ethics and operate at the benevolent level of CSR.

Go online to the company's website and get a copy of its code of ethics and its report on its corporate social responsibility programs. Be sure to identify any of its sustainability practices—this information may be at a separate link.

Be prepared to make a report on your company's code of ethics and CSR to the entire class or in a small group.

Skill Builder 13.3 Diversity Training

Objective

To become more aware of and sensitive to diversity

Skills

The primary skills developed through this exercise are as follows:

1. *HR management skills*—Interpersonal skills

2. *SHRM 2018 Curriculum Guidebook*—P: Training and Development

Answer the following questions:

Race and Ethnicity

1. My race (ethnicity) is ____.

2. My name, ____, is significant because it means ____. [or]

   My name, ____, is significant because I was named after ____.

3. One positive thing about my racial/ethnic background is ____.

4. One difficult thing about my racial/ethnic background is ____.

Religion

5. My religion is ____.

6. One positive thing about my religious background is ____.

7. One difficult thing about my religious background is ____.

Gender

8. I am ____ (male/female/other).

9. One positive thing about being (male/female) is ____.

10. One difficult thing about being (male/female) is ____.

Age

11. I am ____ years old.

12. One positive thing about being this age is ____.

13. One difficult thing about being this age is ____.

Other

14. One way in which I am different from other people is ____.

15. One positive thing about being different in this way is ____.

16. One negative thing about being different in this way is ____.

Prejudice, Stereotypes, and Discrimination

17. Describe an incident in which you were prejudged, stereotyped, or discriminated against. It could be something minor, such as having a comment made to you about your wearing the wrong type of clothes/sneakers or being the last one picked when selecting teams.

Apply It

What did I learn from this experience? How will I use this knowledge in the future?

_____

_____

Your instructor may ask you to do this Skill Builder in class in a group. If so, the instructor will provide you with any necessary information or additional instructions.

©iStockphoto.com/metamorworks

Global Issues for
Human Resource Managers

Learning Outcomes

After studying this chapter, you should be able to do the following:

14.1 Discuss the reasons for increasing business globalization. **PAGE 364**

14.2 Describe the five dimensions of Hofstede's model of culture. **PAGE 367**

14.3 Name the advantages and disadvantages of parent-country, host-country, and third-country nationals for international assignments. **PAGE 371**

14.4 Explain the two major types of training you should generally provide before expatriate assignments. **PAGE 373**

14.5 Define the options for compensation of expatriate workers. **PAGE 376**

SHRM HR Content

See Online: *SHRM 2018 Curriculum Guidebook* for the complete list

A. Change Management

    7. Culture

B. Compensation and Benefits

Compensation

    7. Geographic location

Employee Benefits

    35. Global employee benefits

    41. Outsourcing

E. Globalization

    1. Cross-border HR management

  1-a. Cross-border HR management—Current issues in global HRM

  1-c. Cross-border HR management—Family concerns related to cross-border assignment

  1-d. Cross-border HR management—Host-country nationals (HCNs)

  1-e. Cross-border HR management—Managing personal and family life for expatriates

  1-f. Cross-border HR management—Parent-country nationals (PCNs)

  1-g. Cross-border HR management—Third-country nationals (TCNs)

    2. Cross-cultural effectiveness

  2-a. Cross-cultural effectiveness—Cultural sensitivity

  2-b. Cross-cultural effectiveness—Cultural training

  2-c. Cross-cultural effectiveness—Hofstede's cultural dimensions

    6. Global benefits

  6-a. Global benefits—Compensation (balance-sheet approach; home-based pay, host-based pay, localization)

  6-b. Global benefits—Global business environment

    7. Managing expatriates in global markets

  7-b. Managing expatriates in global markets—Effective repatriation

  7-c. Managing expatriates in global markets—Inshoring, offshoring, outsourcing

  7-d. Managing expatriates in global markets—Repatriating employees post international assignment

    9. North American Free Trade Agreement (NAFTA)

J. Managing a Diverse Workforce

    4. Cultural competence

    10. Language issues

L. Organizational Development

    8. Managing remote staff

Practitioner's Perspective

Cindy says: One of the biggest changes in business has been the explosion of the global marketplace. Business doesn't compete across the country, but around the world. Americans tend to be Eurocentric (the viewpoint that Western civilization is superior). We must recognize that foreign cultures deserve to be valued in the same manner as a diverse workforce is valued, and that what is acceptable behavior in the United States may not be acceptable in another country.

(Continued)

(Continued)

Zac is an assistant manager for Kawasaki Heavy Industries, a global company with U.S. manufacturing plants. After escorting U.S. employees to company meetings in Japan, Zac has some amusing stories to tell. His favorite is about the fellow who went around waving and saying "Hi" to everyone. Hi in Japanese means yes, so imagine how strange this literal "yes-man" appeared.

Another interesting difference is giving and receiving business cards. In the United States, one would usually put a business card away after receiving it, but in Japan, that would be considered extremely rude. In Japan, one must leave the card lying on the table until all business is concluded.

What will you discover about global issues in Chapter 14?

Globalization of Business and Human Resource Management

>> **LO 14.1 Discuss the reasons for increasing business globalization.**

Globalization is one of the most vital business trends of the past 50 years,[1] as large corporations draw employees from, and conduct business, all over the globe.[2] It is important to realize that no matter where you are, you live in and are affected by the global environment. Globalization may require you to interact effectively as a member of society with people from many different cultural backgrounds:[3] as a consumer in a local store, as a student in college, and with family and friends. You may work for a foreign-owned company. You may work with diverse coworkers, suppliers, and customers at home, and there is a chance that you will work with employees and conduct business in other countries.[4]

Think about the complexity of **FedEx**'s environment, delivering to more than 220 countries and territories.[5] Therefore, it has to follow the rules and regulations of different governments in countries with different economies, labor forces, societies, and so on. There are significant cultural differences between countries and regions. In fact, in many cases, there are multiple cultures in a single country. All of this makes global business more challenging. Clearly, to be successful, companies need global leaders.[6] Today's managers—and students of management—cannot afford to underestimate the importance of the global environment to business.[7] Let's take a look at how human resource management (HRM) has to be handled differently in global firms.

Reasons for Business Globalization

Over the past 40+ years, our environment has conspired to make it easier to move both goods and people, along with abstract ideas and concrete knowledge, across borders and around the world. In turn, business must adapt to this new environment. There are many reasons why business is having to adapt to globalization on a scale never seen before. Let's quickly review some of the major reasons for this. **(SHRM E:6-b)**

Find New Customers

Let's face it: Most large corporations want to continue to grow. If you are a major corporation like **Coca-Cola**, is there any place in America to expand? No, the market is saturated. Also, the U.S. population is approximately 329 million, a small fraction of the world's population of 7.56 billion.[8] Emerging markets (primarily China and India) are still the future as some 3 billion people will continue to enter the middle class, almost all of them in the developing world.[9]

So, if large corporations want to grow, they have to globalize. However, businesses of all sizes also have more growth potential if they go global, so many smaller businesses are conducting international business. You probably haven't heard of Thai Lee or the small company she cofounded. But **SHI International** grew to become the largest minority- and woman-owned business enterprise in the United States. It's made Thai Lee one of just 18 self-made female billionaires in the United States.[10]

Declining Barriers of Distance and Culture

In the 1950s, it was difficult to transport goods across country borders and over oceans. It was also difficult to communicate between one location and another. But—things have changed! Communication to most parts of the world is nearly instantaneous. You can dial up your friend in China, or get on the Internet and use a webcam to see exactly what is wrong with your production equipment in Shanghai, China, and provide instructions on how to fix it in a few minutes. If you need to send experts to the plant, they can be anywhere in the world in about a day.

The Global Village

The **global village** refers to *companies conducting business worldwide without boundaries*. The word *village* implies something small and emphasizes that the world, although very large, is becoming smaller through technology. Technology and the Internet have changed the way business is conducted in the global village. In its first 30 days, **Amazon.com** went global, recording sales in all 50 U.S. states and 45 other countries.[11]

Global village Companies conducting business worldwide without boundaries

Declining Trade Barriers and the WTO

The World Trade Organization's (WTO's) "primary purpose is to open trade for the benefit of all."[12] It is a forum for governments to negotiate trade agreements as the WTO enforces a system of trade rules among its 164 member governments.[13] Visit http://www.wto.org for updated information about the WTO. Because the WTO and its predecessors have been so effective at lowering trade barriers, international trade has opened up to businesses that would not have been able to compete internationally before these organizations and agreements existed.

Despite the 2018 Trump administration engaging in what is called a trade war by increasing barriers with tariffs on imports to the United States, the general trend continues to be to increase global trade by decreasing trade barriers worldwide. The WTO continues to help open trade for the benefit of all.

The Rise of Trade Blocs

Trade blocs are *groups of countries who form an association for the purpose of facilitating movement of goods across national borders*. These trade blocs allow free, or low-cost, passage of goods among member nations to encourage companies to specialize in certain types of goods to become more efficient and therefore lower the cost of those goods to all member countries. The North American Free Trade Agreement (NAFTA) is the bloc that is best known to people in the United States. It has recently been in process of being renegotiated under a new name, the United States–Mexico–Canada Trade Agreement (USMCA), which has been signed by the U.S. and Mexican presidents and the Canadian prime minister but not ratified by legislators in any of the three countries (as of late 2018).[14] So for now, NAFTA is still in existence about 30 years after it was first signed. **(SHRM E:9)**

Trade blocs Groups of countries who form an association for the purpose of facilitating movement of goods across national borders

If you are not part of the bloc, trade barriers tend to be significant, and they will raise your cost of doing business with the countries in the bloc. One method of getting around the barriers is to become part of the bloc. This is usually accomplished by having business operations in at least one country within the bloc, which will make your company a de facto member of the bloc and reduce or eliminate this barrier. So companies will frequently build factories, assembly facilities, component plants, or other facilities within the bloc in order to overcome the trade barrier associated with that trade bloc.

To Remain Competitive!

The last, and most significant, reason for business globalization is simple:

Global corporations vs. Domestic organizations = One-sided competition

In many cases, if a domestic firm is competing head-to-head with a global firm, the competition is seriously one-sided. The global firm will source all of its resources from wherever they are the most efficient. If the global company sources raw materials from one country for half the cost, component production in another country for 75% of the cost, and labor from a third country for 25% of the cost of the domestic competitor, who is going to win the battle for the customers? The domestic firm is at an absolute cost disadvantage versus the global firm. The customer *will not* pay double the price for the same good of the same quality, no matter where it is made! "Buy American products" is a good slogan, but most people don't even know the country of ownership of most products. Complete Self-Assessment 14.1 to find out how knowledgeable you are.

14.1 SELF-ASSESSMENT

PRODUCTS BY COUNTRY OF ORIGIN

For each item, determine the country of origin. If your answer is the United States, place a check in the left-hand column. If it's another country, write the name of the country in the right-hand column.

	Product	United States	Other (list country)
1.	Shell gasoline		
2.	Nestlé hot cocoa		
3.	Unilever Dove soap		
4.	Spotify music-streaming		
5.	L'Oréal cosmetics		
6.	Johnson & Johnson baby powder		

	Product	United States	Other (list country)
7.	Burger King fast food		
8.	Samsung televisions		
9.	Bayer aspirin		
10.	Anheuser-Busch beer		
11.	Volvo cars		
12.	AMC theaters		

1. Shell is owned by Royal Dutch Shell of the Netherlands. 2. Nestlé is headquartered in Switzerland. 3. Unilever is British. 4. Spotify is Swedish. 5. L'Oréal is French. 6. Johnson & Johnson is a U.S. company. 7. Burger King is Brazilian owned. 8. Samsung is South Korean. 9. Bayer is German. 10. Anheuser-Busch InBev is Belgian owned. 11. Volvo and 12. AMC are both Chinese owned.

How many did you get correct?

14.1 ETHICAL DILEMMA: WHAT WOULD YOU DO?

BUY AMERICAN

You most likely have heard the slogan "Buy American." Many labor unions urge Americans to buy products made in the United States because that helps retain jobs for American workers. On the other hand, some Americans ask why they should buy American products if they cost more or their quality or style is not as good as that of foreign-made products. But as you've seen, it isn't always easy for consumers to know the country of ownership of many products they buy.

1. Is it ethical and socially responsible to ask people to buy American?

2. Is it ethical and socially responsible to buy foreign products?

3. Do you attempt to buy American? Why or why not?

Is HRM Different in Global Firms?

"To function effectively in a multicultural global business environment, individuals and organizations must be capable of adapting smoothly and successfully across cultural boundaries."[15] This means that as the organization expands beyond its original borders, employees need to learn to change their personal perceptions from a local focus toward a broader concept of society. They need to become capable cultural chameleons—able to change on the fly as necessary in order to interact with other employees, customers, vendors, and any other stakeholders—to manage the business. Yet, the evidence shows this is one of the most significant weaknesses of individuals who have a business degree but have little work experience.[16]

Companies nearly always start out small and local—they have one shop or store in one town in a single country. When managing this "simple" organization structure, the complexity is minimal. Generally, all decisions are made by the boss. As we get larger and more complex, management in the organization has to change and adapt to that complexity by loosening up on centralized authority so that things can get done in a reasonable time frame.

Ultimately, in many industries at least, the company will consider international operations of some type to gain an advantage over its competitors. And along with the creation of an international presence, the complexity of the firm goes up even more. This is the point at which HR must become a different and more multifaceted department. International operations require us to rethink every major function in HRM, including the following:

- *Staffing.* Home-country, host-country, and third-party employees all require different sourcing, training, disciplinary actions, and compensation and may require many other differences in management.

- *Training.* From orientation to culture and religion, to language problems and managing infrastructure, training will need to be modified. For instance, safety training will need to be provided in multiple languages in many cases, and it will have to be accomplished so as to comply with multiple country laws and regulations.

- *Employee and labor relations.* Different countries' laws concerning employee relations require HR to become competent in legal issues where the company operates. Many countries' labor laws are strongly oriented toward protection of the individual employee—much more so than in the United States—and the HR manager must become competent in all of these legal differences. In addition, cultural attitudes and national laws also affect when and how employees are disciplined.

- *Compensation.* Should the company pay local average wages, home-country average wages, or other wage levels? How do incentives work with employees from different cultures? **(SHRM E:1-a)**

These are just a few of the many issues that must be taken into account as we move from a single-country business to a global firm. Throughout the rest of this chapter, you will learn more about global HRM functions.

Legal, Ethical, and Cultural Issues

>> **LO 14.2 Describe the five dimensions of Hofstede's model of culture.**

Legal, ethical, and especially cultural issues also have to be examined by companies considering global operations. The HR department has responsibility for many of these issues, including international labor laws, organizational ethics policies, and cultural training—for both national culture adaptation and corporate culture orientation.

International Labor Laws

As the company begins to operate in more than one country's market, the managers, including HR managers, have to ensure that the company complies with each country's legal requirements. The major HR laws tend to be in the areas of staffing, labor relations, and disciplinary action/termination. Employment and labor law in different countries is highly complex. Your organization will need to do significant research before moving any operations into another country to avoid violating that country's labor laws.

Some people question, is diversity really important? Yes! Discrimination is illegal in some countries, and promoting diversity and inclusion creates opportunities for all employees, so it is the right thing to do.[17] But it is also beneficial to business. There is a wealth of evidence that diversity helps teams and organizations perform better in terms of creativity, innovation, revenue, and profits.[18]

U.S. Law

You know that most organizations within the United States are subject to a variety of equal employment opportunity (EEO) laws. But are employees of foreign companies working in the United States subject to the same laws, and are employees of U.S. companies operating in other countries subject to these laws? Again, the Equal Employment Opportunity Commission (EEOC) gives us guidance on these situations.

According to the EEOC,

> All employees who work in the U.S. or its territories . . . are protected by EEO laws, regardless of their citizenship or work authorization status. Employees who work in the U.S. or its territories are protected whether they work for a U.S. or foreign employer.[19]

So if you are in the United States or a U.S. territory, you are covered by U.S. EEO laws.

But what about Americans working outside the United States? According to the EEOC, "U.S. citizens who are employed outside the U.S. by a U.S. employer—or a foreign company controlled by a U.S. employer—are protected by Title VII, the ADEA, and the ADA." However, "U.S. employers are not required to comply with the requirements of Title VII, the ADEA, or the ADA if adherence to that requirement would violate a law of the country where the workplace is located."[20] Finally, if you are employed by a foreign company in a country other than the United States, the laws of that country would apply, so you would not have the protection of U.S. EEO laws in such a case.

The United States also has a law specifically addressing corruption and bribery by U.S. national companies while operating in other countries. The **Foreign Corrupt Practices Act** (FCPA) *bars U.S.-based or U.S.-listed companies from bribing foreign officials in exchange for business.* The FCPA also requires companies to keep accurate books and records concerning their foreign operations. However, it is sometimes hard to tell the difference between a legitimate business expense and a bribe.[21] So global companies need to clarify the difference in their code of ethics, top managers must set a good example, and penalties for unethical and illegal behavior must be enforced.

Remember that different countries have different employment laws—based on that country's values, principles, and ethics—which must be obeyed. So think about the complexity facing the HR executive working for a multinational company doing business in more than 100 countries! Thus, multinationals need HR legal specialists in each country.

Foreign Corrupt Practices Act Law barring U.S.-based or U.S.-listed companies from bribing foreign officials in exchange for business

National Culture

Recall that we discussed organizational culture in Chapter 2. All of that information also applies to national culture, but national culture is even more powerful in many cases. It is what people have known their entire lives, and like the old adage about a fish in water not knowing that there *is* any other possible environment, people who have lived their lives in one culture many times don't even realize that there *are* other options for values, beliefs, and culture. This view of the world is called **parochialism**—*a narrow-minded view of the world with an inability to recognize individual differences.* Managers in global organizations cannot survive with a parochial view of the world.

Parochialism A narrow-minded view of the world with an inability to recognize individual differences

Cultural Differences and Management

Let's face it; like it or not, global diversity continues to grow. The better you can work with diverse people, the greater are your chances of having a successful career. So avoid parochialism and develop your global mind-set.[22] Are you willing to commit to offering inclusion to diverse people into your homogeneous groups?

Employees from different countries do not see the world in quite the same way because they come from different national cultures.[23] Understanding national culture is important because it affects nearly every aspect of human behavior,[24] making cultural sensitivity an important skill.[25] For the multinational corporation (MNC), all the normal workplace diversity exists, plus national culture as well.[26] Therefore, capability to manage such cultural diversity has become one of the most important skills global leaders can have.[27]

Differences in national culture influence the effectiveness of different managerial behaviors. These cultural differences require responses that are based on the country in which you are doing business. For instance, singling out and praising an individual worker in Japan is tantamount to yelling at an American employee on the shop floor. Japan, as a highly collectivist culture (we will discuss this momentarily), does not single out the individual for either praise or discipline in a public setting. **(SHRM J:4 and E:2-a)**

In another context, would you manage female employees the same way in a Muslim country such as Iraq as you would in the United States? Would female managers lead others in the same way as male managers in this case? Would they manage male subordinates in the same way as their U.S. counterparts? It's necessary for managers (in all countries and all organizations) to understand the need to adjust their methods and their style to the region/country/community in which they will be operating.

So if you are going to have to manage in an international setting, you will need to understand the cultures you are dealing with. Organizations are placing a top priority on recruiting people who can work with and manage a diversity of employees.[28] But how do expatriate employees know how to act in another culture?

Hofstede's Model of National Culture

Let's look at a way we can classify country cultures in order to determine how to train managers to successfully work with employees in that culture—*Hofstede's model of national culture*. First, though, a disclaimer. You need to understand that Hofstede's cultural model is a model of *average* cultural characteristics. Every person in every culture will vary in some ways from the average. However, the model does allow us to identify common values and beliefs in a culture that can inform the type of culture training we need to do when sending employees into a culture that is foreign to them. Now, let's take a look at Hofstede's dimensions. **(SHRM E:2-b, E:2-c, A:7)**

In the 1960s Geert Hofstede identified five dimensions, each of which allows a country culture to be plotted along a continuum. Each dimension was measured on a scale of 0 to 100, with 100 being the highest exhibition of that dimension. (More countries were added to Hofstede's model in later years, resulting in some scores moving above 100.) Exhibit 14.1 shows the dimensions of the model. Cross-cultural comparisons demonstrate differences,[29] especially between East and West cultures.[30]

EXHIBIT 14.1 ●   Hofstede's Model of National Culture[31]

1. *Power-Distance (low vs. high)*—The degree to which societies accept that inequalities in power and well-being among members of the society are the result of differences in their individual abilities, both physical and intellectual, and their social status. In societies where these inequalities are allowed to continue or even grow, we consider the society to be a high power-distance culture. In societies where the differential value of rich and poor, intelligent and less intelligent, manager and employee is not an accepted part of the culture, we say that they exhibit low power-distance.

2. *Individualism (vs. Collectivism)*—The basis of this dimension is the degree to which individuals are integrated into groups. Individualist cultures value individual freedom and self-expression and believe that people should be judged on their personal achievements. Collectivist cultures believe that the group is the primary unit of value, and the individual only has value insofar as he or she assists the group in reaching its overall goals.

3. *Masculinity (vs. Femininity) or Assertiveness (vs. Nurturing)*—Hofstede used the terms *masculinity* versus *femininity* back in the 1960s. However, these terms have since been changed to *assertiveness* versus *nurturing*. Masculine or assertive societies value performance/winning, assertiveness, competition, and success. Masculine societies value heroes and material rewards. Feminine or nurturing cultures, on the other hand, value relationships with others, interaction over winning, quality of life, and concern for others. So in a masculine society, you might see a sign saying, "He who dies with the most toys wins," but a feminine option might be "The best things in life are free."

4. *Uncertainty Avoidance (high vs. low)*—Societies, like individuals, differ in their tolerance of risk. The uncertainty avoidance dimension "expresses the degree to which the members of a society feel uncomfortable with uncertainty and ambiguity." Societies that are high in uncertainty avoidance will make attempts to avoid uncertainty—at least as much as possible. Cultures with low uncertainty avoidance can tolerate significant risk within their society and will not spend as much societal effort to protect their citizens.

(Continued)

EXHIBIT 14.1 ● (Continued)

5. *Long-Term Orientation (vs. Short-Term Orientation)*—This dimension was not part of the original Hofstede model, but he added it after it became apparent that different cultures had differing concepts of past, present, and future. Cultures with a long-term orientation value saving, thrift, and persistence in working toward and reaching future goals. In cultures with a short-term orientation, we will see little intent to save for the future and a focus on immediate, or at least relatively quick, results.

Hofstede's dimensions with country examples:[32]

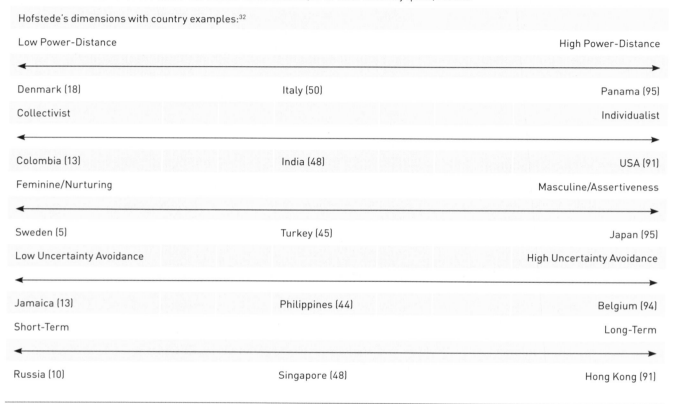

Low Power-Distance		High Power-Distance
Denmark (18)	Italy (50)	Panama (95)
Collectivist		Individualist
Colombia (13)	India (48)	USA (91)
Feminine/Nurturing		Masculine/Assertiveness
Sweden (5)	Turkey (45)	Japan (95)
Low Uncertainty Avoidance		High Uncertainty Avoidance
Jamaica (13)	Philippines (44)	Belgium (94)
Short-Term		Long-Term
Russia (10)	Singapore (48)	Hong Kong (91)

Source: Adapted from "The 6 dimensions of national culture" and "Country Comparison" by Hofstede Insights, The Hofstede Centre.

What is the value in knowing that Russian culture is oriented toward the short term, Japan is highly masculine, and India is moderately collectivist? The *value* in the model is in knowing how significant the differences are between two countries' commonly held cultural beliefs and norms. The greater the difference in the two cultures on each of Hofstede's dimensions, the more difficult it is to bring employees from one culture into the other to work together effectively.

Similarly, putting employees from these two cultures together to accomplish any task is likely to fail unless they are given cultural training before working together. The HR department is typically charged with cross-cultural training of employees who will be working outside their native culture.

14.1 APPLYING THE CONCEPT
HOFSTEDE DIMENSIONS

Place the letter of the Hofstede dimension of cultural diversity on the line next to the statement exemplifying it.

a. Power-Distance (low vs. high)

b. Individualism (vs. Collectivism)

c. Masculinity (vs. Femininity) or Assertiveness (vs. Nurturing)

d. Uncertainty Avoidance (high vs. low)

e. Long-Term Orientation (vs. Short-Term Orientation)

_____ 1. The people seem to prefer sports such as soccer and basketball to sports such as golf and track-and-field.

_____ 2. Managers place great importance on status symbols such as the executive dining room, reserved parking spaces, and big offices.

_____ 3. Managers provide poor working conditions to maximize profits.

_____ 4. Employees get nervous and stressed when changes are made.

_____ 5. Managers focus on quarterly and annual earnings to meet analysis expectations.

Global Staffing

>> **LO 14.3 Name the advantages and disadvantages of parent-country, host-country, and third-country nationals for international assignments.**

As you can see, operating a business on a global scale requires some complex skills. How are we going to staff the organization with people who have both the ability and the desire to work in this type of environment? We will need to recruit people with specific skills. We will also have to make some choices about what types of employees we are going to recruit, and from which countries. Then we will have to determine what training is necessary for them to be successful. These choices by the chief human resources officer (CHRO) or other HR manager can determine the success or failure of our global organization.

Skills and Traits for Global Managers

Going back to Chapter 1, you probably remember that all "managers require a mix of technical, interpersonal, conceptual and design, and business skills in order to successfully carry out their jobs." In international assignments, all of these skill sets can differ from what a manager or employee would typically learn in order to do their job. The way work is carried out—for instance, in a high power-distance culture where employees expect to receive and carry out orders without question—may affect the way a manager does their job, so an American manager going into a high power-distance culture would need different technical skills. Certainly with multiple cultures, probably speaking multiple languages, managers will need very strong interpersonal skills, and even conceptual and design skills may need to vary from what the manager would consider "normal" in different cultures. Finally, as we have already noted, business skills can be significantly different due to the variance in laws, regulations, and business structures in different countries (think of the *keiretsu* and *chaebol* partnerships in Japan and South Korea, respectively).

Cultural values and beliefs are often unspoken and taken for granted; even with a common language, accurate communication can be difficult.[33] We tend to expect people to behave as we do. But you need to be flexible and adapt to other ways of behaving; you cannot expect others to change for you.[34] However, to be successful in the global village, you need to be sensitive to other cultures[35] as you interact with people whose values and behaviors differ from your own.[36] You need to get along with others,[37] and to do so you need to have a global mind-set.[38] In fact, companies seek employees who have intercultural competences[39] and those with multicultural backgrounds.[40]

But what else do we need to take into account before sending someone to another country to work with or manage others? Companies may want *previous international experience* in the employees they are considering sending on assignments outside of their home country. The feeling is that people who have made the adjustment before will have an easier time adjusting to yet another environment. This is not always true, but it can help to have a history of living in different cultures. Culture shock (we will discuss this shortly) is thought to decrease as people are exposed to, and live in, multiple different cultures. This can be advantageous to both the individual and the organization because the individual can settle in and become more productive sooner if they do not have to learn how to behave within the culture.

We noted in Chapter 8 that it is sometimes necessary to evaluate *individual traits* when evaluating our employees. This is one of those cases where it is indeed necessary. "Personality traits have been widely regarded as among the most important potential factors leading to expatriate adjustment,"[41] so a global assignment is one situation in which we will need to attempt to assess the traits of the people we are considering sending to another country to live. Some very strong evidence says that expatriates will fit into a culture better if their personality traits

©iStockphoto.com/XavierArnau

▲

When staffing a global organization, managers need to look for candidates with specific skills that lend themselves to operating on an international scale.

match up well with the culture's most significant characteristics.[42]

Suitability of immediate family who will accompany the employee is also important. We have to consider the entire family when making an international assignment unless the assignment will be "unaccompanied," or without the family. If they do accompany the employee, they will need to be assessed for suitability and disposition as well as being trained right along with the employee. **(SHRM E:1-c and E:1-e)**

All of the assessment that we will accomplish prior to sending an individual on an international assignment is designed to identify the "fit" of the individual, and potentially their family members, with the assignment. Remember that we also discussed *personality-job fit* and *person-organization fit* along with ability-job fit in Chapter 6. Personality-job fit and person-organization fit will need to be measured and analyzed in conjunction with a potential international assignment just as if we were hiring the person into the organization from the outside world. They will have to adapt to the organization and the job in a very different environment from the one they are coming from, and there is a high risk of failure in the job if we don't do the analysis successfully.

Finally, *language ability* is something that may need to be taken into consideration. This will depend on the assignment, the difficulty of learning the language, the benefits of language training, and other considerations, but we do have to at least identify the possible need for the employee to speak the native language of the people in the assignment location. **(SHRM J:10)**

Staffing Choice: Home-, Host-, or Third-Country Employees

Our next consideration is where we will source the individual from for an international assignment. We have three generic options, each of which may be the best in some circumstances:

- *Parent- (home-) country nationals*—People who work for the organization who are from the country where the organization is headquartered

- *Host-country nationals*—People who live in a different country where a work assignment will take place

- *Third-country nationals*—People who happen to have a skill set needed for an international assignment but who are not citizens of either the home or host country

Each of the three staffing options has advantages and disadvantages.[43] Exhibit 14.2 shows what you might need to know to consider each option. **(SHRM E:1-d, E:1-f, and E:1-g)**

Outsourcing as an Alternative to International Expansion

Outsourcing The process of hiring another organization to do work that was previously done within the host organization

As an alternative to expanding the home organization, outsourcing is one way in which organizations can manage work without creating a direct international subsidiary. **Outsourcing** is *the process of hiring another organization to do work that was previously done within the host organization.* In quite a few cases, the organization to which we outsource a particular process will be located in another country. In this case, the outsourcing is often referred to as *offshoring,* and it is expected to increase.[44] **Nike** outsources making all of its products, as it doesn't own any manufacturing facilities. **(SHRM B:41)**

Onshoring The process of shuttering operations in other countries and bringing work back to the home country

On the other hand, in the United States and many other developed countries, there has been a governmental push to return jobs that have been offshored to the home country. This is called onshoring (you may also see the terms *inshoring* and *reshoring*). **Onshoring** is *the process of shuttering operations in other countries and bringing work back to the home country* to increase employment there. In some cases, this onshoring makes sense, but in others it may

EXHIBIT 14.2 ● Advantages and Disadvantages of Parent-, Host-, and Third-Country Nationals

	Parent-country	Host-country	Third-country
Advantages	• Generally have a better understanding of the organization, strategy, structure, and culture of the business	• Minimizes language and culture problems	• Can hire the best talent from wherever they are located
	• Allows managers to gain international experience	• Compensation is generally easier and is based on local pay scale	• May be less expensive than either parent- or host-country managers
	• More effective communication with parent-country management	• Less expensive than moving someone to the country	• May be more advantageous than parent-country managers due to similar culture and/or language with host
		• Better understanding of local business laws, culture, and customs	
Disadvantages	• Language differences may be a problem	• Company culture and ways of doing business may create problems	• Still may have company culture and business process issues
	• Compensation may be more of a problem than with host-country nationals	• May create more problems communicating with the parent office	• Host-country government may create barriers to third-party managers
	• Country culture may create barriers to success for employee and family	• Loyalty to the country may outweigh loyalty to the company	• Income and other tax rules can be complex
	• Income and other tax rules can be complex		

Source: C. Dörrenbächer, J. Gammelgaard, F. McDonald, A. Stephan, H. Tüselmann, "Staffing Foreign Subsidiaries With Parent Country Nationals or Host Country Nationals? Insights From European Subsidiaries," *Working Papers of the Institute of Management Berlin at the Berlin School of Economics and Law* (2013), 74.

not. However, it is also an ethical question in the minds of a significant number of home-country citizens. **(SHRM E:7-c)**

The ethical question in each of these cases first involves the potential for job loss or gain within the home organization because of shipping jobs overseas. In the case of offshoring, the firm may cut entire divisions' worth of employees and send that work to the offshore organization. Many U.S. firms did this with customer service operations in the early 2000s, but you may also recall that several high-profile failures occurred in offshoring, such as **Dell** moving several thousand jobs back to the United States after significant customer complaints about support. Secondarily, companies have to be concerned with doing what is best for their shareholders and in fact have a fiduciary responsibility to do so.

As a result, even when there is pressure from governments to reshore jobs, companies have to consider this option very carefully before taking that step because making some products at home costs too much to compete globally. President Trump was pressing for more production in America, but in late 2018 **General Motors (GM)** announced plans to close several U.S. factories to save $6 billion in costs by 2020, and Trump threatened to cut **GM** subsidies over layoffs.[45]

Developing and Managing Global Human Resources

>> **LO 14.4 Explain the two major types of training that you should generally provide before expatriate assignments.**

Once we have determined that we are going to expand internationally, we need to ensure that our employees will be able to successfully integrate into another country culture and complete

©iStockphoto.com/izusek

▲
Because hiring an expatriate employee comes with significant cost to the organization, it is important to provide expatriates with cultural and communication training so they are able to do their jobs well because it can be difficult to adjust to a different language, culture, and society.[48]

their assignments. We need to select the right types of individuals, train them appropriately, and support them during their international assignments. Finally, we will have to make sure that they reintegrate into the home-country operations once they return from the assignment. Let's look at some details on how we can do that. **(SHRM E:1)**

Recruiting and Selection

We mentioned the problems with finding knowledge workers in Chapter 1. This continuing issue is causing more and more companies to source employees, including managers, from wherever they can find them. If they have to build a facility in another country to find enough of these workers, then that is what they will do. In today's world economy, where low-skilled jobs are going away and we are constantly searching for knowledge workers, we have seen a shift to sourcing skilled employees from any country where they can be found and moving them to the locations where they are most needed. Many of the "lesser-developed economies" are now developing at a rapid rate and have become *sources* of talented knowledge workers.[46]

Expatriate Training and Preparation

Individuals who must manage in cultures other than their home culture face a daunting task. "The main reason for this is that [national] cultures differ in their *implicit theories of leadership,* the lay beliefs about the qualities that individuals need to display to be considered leaders. Depending on the cultural context, your typical style and behavioral tendencies may be an asset or a weakness."[47] These managers have to learn to manage within the cultural norms and expectations of the country to which they are assigned.

You need to think globally but adapt to local cultures in specific countries.[49] "You have to know how to motivate people who speak different languages, who have different cultural contexts, who have different sensitivities and habits. You have to get prepared to deal with teams who are multicultural, to work with people who do not all think the same way as you do."[50] It's very difficult; therefore, capability to manage such cultural diversity has become one of the most important skills for global leaders.[51]

With increasing globalization and workforce mobility, there is a chance that you will be sent to another country to conduct business.[52] It may be a brief visit, or it can be an international assignment as an expatriate. An **expatriate** is *an employee who leaves their home country to go work in another country.* As discussed, they can be home-, host-, or third-country employees. The cost of training and assigning expatriates is very high, so we have to carefully select and develop these employees.[53] **(SHRM E:7)**

Expatriate An employee who leaves their home country to go work in another country

Cultural Training

Preparing employees for expatriate assignments will primarily be a training process, and the biggest training issue will usually be cross-cultural training. *Culture shock* can occur when we move from one culture to another. This culture shock can cause significant problems for the expatriate employee, and in fact, there is evidence that up to 50% of employees absolutely fail to complete their international assignment and have to be removed, with the major reason being an inability (on the part of the employee or family members) to adapt to cultural differences.[54] This inability to adapt may be because the parent company does not support the employee and family members in learning the culture that they will have to live in for an extended period of time.[55] Alternately, it may be due to a bad selection process, as we noted earlier in our discussion of personality traits.[56] Regardless, culture shock is one of the main reasons for early termination of an international assignment. But what is culture shock? The diagram in Exhibit 14.3 helps explain.

EXHIBIT 14.3 ● Culture Shock

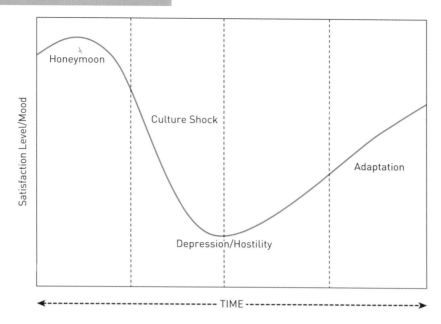

Honeymoon phase (approximately the first 1–3 weeks). Everything is interesting and new. It is exciting to be in a new country, and you feel like you are on an adventure.

Culture shock (month 1–3, or longer). The initially interesting and new things that you recently saw are now annoying. Why can't they do things the same way as they are done at home? You are frustrated by simple everyday things like going to the store or the bank, driving or commuting rules and procedures— and *what's that smell?*

Depression or hostility (month 4–7+). You are frustrated constantly with how different things are. You may even be depressed and not want to go outside and interact with people. You may avoid doing anything that requires that you involve yourself in the culture of the country.

Adaptation (month 7+). You start to accept the cultural norms and can interact with others successfully. You are now accustomed to the way things are done and the normal way to act in common situations. You feel "normal" in your everyday activities.

If people know what to expect and have some training in how to adapt, the problems associated with hostility and depression (which set in from month 4 to 7 and possibly beyond) can be lessened. They will *not* go away, but they can be lessened, and this lessening may be enough to allow employees to ultimately adapt and finish their assignment. "Effective pre-departure training is essential to support the employee to adapt to a new culture and country—as well as a new job."[57] **(SHRM E:2 and L:8)**

Communication Training

Expatriates, also known as "Expats," frequently require both language training and other communication training (verbal, nonverbal, and symbolic). Communication can be difficult even when everyone is speaking the same language.[58] It becomes much more difficult when there is more than one language being spoken and also when you have different nonverbal and symbolic cues based on different cultures. So individuals need to be trained on how to manage their body language and other nonverbal cues.

Symbolic communication is using items that we surround ourselves with to tell a story. It can be a type of clothing or hat; it can be a crucifix necklace; it can be jewelry or body piercings, or even the type of vehicle that you drive. Everything we surround ourselves with that then conveys meaning to others is part of symbolic communication, and it can have very different meanings in different cultures. You would not want to have a visible crucifix in many Muslim countries. If you drive a large SUV in other countries, you may be considered to be a drug dealer or may become a kidnapping target because people may assume you must be rich. So our employees need training on the various forms of symbolic communication.

Repatriation After Foreign Assignments

Would you care to guess what is likely to happen after a lengthy international assignment when an individual (and possibly their family, too) returns to their home country? They are going to go through another culture shock. The same adjustment will be necessary as they return home because they have adapted to another culture and other ways of doing everyday things. So reacculturation training will most likely be necessary. **(SHRM E:7-d and E:7-b)**

Repatriation should include a series of steps that need to occur in order to get the employee back into the home-country work routine. These items include the following:[59]

- Reentry training, including cultural training (things change in several years—even if you are moving back to your home culture!)[60]

- Job placement into a position commensurate with the employee's level of expertise and that will use their knowledge, skills, and abilities developed during their assignment in the host country

- Possibly mentoring assistance and other support to help the returning employee reintegrate quicker and more successfully

- A show of appreciation for the employee's international service and facilitation of knowledge transfer to others who may benefit from a better understanding of the host country and its culture

Repatriation is a critical activity because there is strong evidence that there are high levels of voluntary turnover of repatriates once they complete their international assignments and return home. Because the process of preparing expatriates and sending them to another country is a significant expense for the organization, we need to improve the odds that our newly returned employees will stay with the firm once they do return.

Compensating Your Global Workforce

>> **LO 14.5 Define the options for compensation of expatriate workers.**

The obvious first question about compensation in a global environment is whether compensation in various countries needs to be different and, if so, why and how we compensate a global workforce fairly. In this section, let's discuss the components of a compensation system we discussed in Chapters 10 and 11 (pay, incentives, and benefits) as they relate to a global workforce.

Pay

We need to compensate differently in different countries or regions because each of them has a different standard and cost of living and different labor laws, which vary greatly across countries and must be adhered to. We leave the discussion of the various labor laws to a global HRM course. Here we focus on expatriate pay.

If we want to keep high-quality managers and workers in our organization while asking them to work in countries around the world, we need to compensate them fairly. But what is fair? Is it fair to take a manager from a high-cost country and send them to a location that has a lower cost of living (e.g., United States to China), and once there, we then lower their pay to match the local norm? If you were the manager, would you accept this? **(SHRM B:7 and E:6-a)**

Conversely, if we bring a manager from a low-cost economy to a higher-cost environment, we probably need to increase their pay to match the country or region in which they will be working. However, if we return them to their home country or location, should we lower their pay back to the original rate? Another question concerns the currency in which the employee will be paid. Should we pay our employees in their home currency, or should we pay them in the local currency where they are assigned?

As you can see, compensation of a global workforce becomes pretty complex very quickly. Let's discuss some common options for paying expatriates.

Balance Sheet Approach

Using the *balance sheet* approach, the organization continues to pay the individual at a rate equivalent to their home-country salary while providing allowances during an overseas assignment to enable that employee to maintain their normal standard of living. Obviously, this is only necessary when an individual is moving to a higher-cost environment and out of their home country.

Split-Pay Approach

A variant on the balance sheet approach is to use *split pay.*[61] In fact, about half the organizations in a recent survey said that they use split pay as at least part of their compensation strategy.[62] Split pay is a process where the organization pays the individual partly in home-country currency and partly in the currency of their work location. This allows the individual to lower currency exchange rate risks in moving money from one location to another and to pay obligations in both their home location and their work location much easier than if all their pay were in one currency.

Other Approaches

Other options for compensating employees on international assignments include a *negotiation approach,* where the employer and employee mutually agree on a compensation package; a *localization approach,* where the expatriate's compensation is based on local (host-country) norms; and a *lump sum option,* which pays the expatriate a lump sum of money to use on items such as taxes, vehicles, housing, and similar items during their assignment.[63]

Where workers are operating all over the world, the compensation function is a very difficult process. However, HR must play a part in the analysis and implementation of a compensation system that will allow the company to attract and retain high-quality managers and employees for their facilities. The only way to do this, based on our discussions of operant conditioning and reinforcement as well as equity and expectancy theories, is to provide reasonable and fair returns to those employees for the job that they do.

Incentives in Global Firms

Effective global leaders are a vital asset that can offer a competitive advantage within organizations today.[64] So, a major challenge is to continue to develop the leadership talent to grow the company around the world.[65] But do incentive programs work the same worldwide? The answer, briefly, is "No, but they are becoming more similar over time." In fact, in some emerging-market countries, variable pay is a higher proportion of overall compensation than in most developed markets.[66] However, in other countries, variable pay still has negative connotations, especially as an *individual* incentive. Many countries' cultures do not mesh well with individual incentive programs, and some do not readily accept even group incentive programs.[67]

14.2 APPLYING THE CONCEPT
GLOBAL COMPENSATION

Place the letter of the type of compensation on the line next to the corresponding example.

a. Balance sheet

b. Split-pay

c. Negotiation

d. Localization

e. Lump sum

(Continued)

(Continued)

_____ 6. I'm going overseas for a 6-month assignment, and they are giving half the money in U.S. dollars and half in euros.

_____ 7. I'm going overseas for a 6-month assignment, and they are paying me in the other country's currency, the euro.

_____ 8. I'm going overseas for a 6-month assignment, and they are continuing to pay me in euros, but

they are also giving me a U.S. dollar allowance for the higher cost of living in New York.

_____ 9. I'm going overseas for a 6-month assignment, and we are having a meeting to discuss my compensation for while I'm away.

_____ 10. I'm going overseas for a 6-month assignment, and they are giving me one check to pay for the entire time I'm away.

The main thing that compensation professionals need to understand is that we cannot provide the same types of incentives to employees regardless of the organizational and country culture and structure. We have to understand the function of "significance" in expectancy theory and always make sure that our system rewards are significant and acceptable to our employees.

Benefit Programs Around the World

Company benefit programs must also adapt to the part of the world in which our employees work and live. For one thing, some countries mandate certain benefits that are not required in other countries, and we have no choice but to offer them. In other cases, the living conditions may be such that different benefit packages just make sense. Let's take a look at some examples of differences we might see in benefit programs in various parts of the world. **(SHRM B:35 and E:6)**

Due to government laws, companies in many of the European Union countries have to provide more benefits than do companies in the United States. Retirement benefits vary among countries, with some governments providing a strong centralized retirement system (Australia is a good example) and others providing very little in the way of centralized retirement planning and savings. Even in countries where there is a strong central government plan, most employees are concerned that they have not saved enough for retirement. One reason for this is that people are living longer today than ever before—all across the globe. Another issue is that in most countries, the population is planning on retiring at an earlier age than has historically been the case. This combination of living longer and retiring earlier is creating the potential for a gap in retirement plan funding. More and more companies are working with employees to narrow this gap through a series of options.

A significant trend is the move by companies toward offering more, and a larger variety of, voluntary benefits that are fully paid by the employee, instead of the employer providing at least part of the money to cover the cost of such benefits. In Brazil, for example, almost a third of female employees expressed interest in accident and pension funds for which they would pay 100% of the cost. Likewise, in Mexico, 56% of workers said that they would like a wider choice of voluntary benefits, and about one fourth said that they would pay the _full cost_ for life, disability, and health insurance.[68] Even if there are some significant differences in benefit plans around the world due to differing government policies, the consensus is that a good benefit package is a powerful force in employee satisfaction and retention—and employees globally like flexible benefits so that they can choose the benefits they want and need the most. Employers worldwide would be well served to start formal communications with their employees to find out what types of benefits will best serve to improve satisfaction and retention in their organizations.

Trends and Issues in HRM

In this section, we will take a look at a couple of globalization issues. The first issue is whether or not globalization is a fading trend and what managers need to do about it. The second is how labor organizations are increasingly affecting employee relations in the global environment.

Globalization of Business Continues as a Trend!

The world appears to be moving more toward protectionist trade policies at the present time—restructuring or even breaking up trade blocs.[69] So is it really all that important to be concerned with globalization in the companies that *you* will be working for? The evidence says that it is. *Forbes* magazine noted that "the major cause of [business model] disruption is the rapid advancement of technology and globalization, which allows new business models to be introduced at an ever-increasing rate and with rapidly declining costs."[70] A recent Brookings Institute report also noted, "On two of the three measures, the degree of globalization is continuing to rise based on the most recent available data, contrary to the claim that globalization is receding. And on two of our three measures, the global economy is more globalized today than during the peak of the early 20th century."[71] So globalization of production of both goods and services continues to move forward, despite current rhetoric by country governments.

At the same time, though, evidence is also pretty strong that some developed countries are retrenching a bit when it comes to international operations. Governments continue to pressure business to reshore some of their operations. In fact, in a 2013 survey, a majority of large manufacturers said they are planning to reshore at least some production jobs back to the United States.[72] But don't think global business is going to go away anytime soon. Even with retrenchment of businesses in the developed economies after the 2007–2009 recession, the World Trade Organization (WTO) expected merchandise trade to grow at 2.4% in 2017.[73]

So the bottom line is that while companies may retrench some jobs back to their home countries, it appears that some production and service jobs will continue to be moved out of home countries to other locations around the world to take advantage of capital cost savings. This means that managers, including HR managers, must improve their skills related to training and preparing employees for international assignments.

The Worldwide Labor Environment

In the global village, developing-country unionization is just beginning, and it is expanding quickly. Let's take a quick look at two countries—Brazil and South Korea—and how unions can affect their work processes.

Brazil

Brazil's labor regulations tend to favor the employee over the employer and provide strong protection for unions. Brazil saw a significant increase in unionized workers in the early years of the 21st century. The number of unionized workers stood at 18.35% in 2005, up from 16.73% in 2001.[74] However, the rate of unionization has fallen in the past several years from 16.2% in 2012 to 14.4% in 2017.[75] Labor is guaranteed the right to strike in the constitution, and labor agreements can either be in writing "or may be implied from the relationship between an individual and the company."[76] Labor laws in Brazil also require any disputes between management and workers "to be settled in labor tribunals rather than in the companies involved, so little space is left for direct negotiations between employers and employees."[77]

South Korea

South Korea's laws concerning labor relations are similar to those in the United States. The South Korean Trade Union Act allows workers to organize, collectively bargain, and act in concert to achieve labor goals. However, for many years the government had direct control of the major labor union in the country. This is not so any longer, and as a matter of fact, South Korea passed legislation that allows multiple unions to represent different workers within the same organization. South Korean employers are concerned that relations with employees will deteriorate due to this multiple unions system.[78]

As we can see from the Brazilian and South Korean examples, union influence affects relationships between labor and management in significantly different ways in different countries. For those working in a business that operates in multiple countries, these differences in labor laws will be significant. You may have to become well informed on the differing laws concerning labor relations and union representation in each of the countries in which your firm works.

Chapter Summary

14.1 Discuss the reasons for increasing business globalization.

The main reason for increasing globalization is to increase business, which is aided by the world becoming a global village where goods, ideas, services, and knowledge flow freely across national borders, creating greater demand for products. Barriers to trade have been minimized compared to historical norms, even though there is a series of trade blocs that operate in multiple countries. Barriers to transportation, communication, and culture have also lessened. But the biggest reason for globalization is to remain competitive.

14.2 Describe the five dimensions of Hofstede's model of culture.

Power-distance is the degree to which societies accept that people will have different power because of their abilities and social status. Individualist cultures believe in the value of the individual and judge the individual, while collectivist cultures believe that the group is the unit of value in society, not the individual. Masculine (or assertive) societies value performance, winning, competition, and success, while feminine (or nurturing) societies value relationships between members and quality of life more than winning. High-uncertainty avoidance cultures will do whatever they can to minimize risks to members of the society, and low-uncertainty avoidance cultures will not try to mitigate these risks nearly as much. Finally, short-term societies focus on immediate or short-term outcomes, while long-term societies focus on saving for the future, thrift, and persistence.

14.3 Name the advantages and disadvantages of parent-country, host-country, and third-country nationals for international assignments.

Parent-country members usually know the organization better, know the strategy and structure, and communicate better. However, language, compensation issues, cultural barriers, and national laws on income may be disadvantages. Host-country nationals present advantages with respect to the language, culture, compensation issues, and local laws and regulations, but they may not have the company knowledge that is needed, may be less loyal to the firm, and could have problems communicating with the home office. Third-country nationals allow us to hire the best person for a job and may be less expensive in some cases. They may also share a language or similar culture with the host-country office. Disadvantages include host-country laws concerning third-party employees, income and other tax rules, and potential lack of knowledge of company procedures and culture.

14.4 Explain the two major types of training that you should generally provide before expatriate assignments.

The two types of training are cultural training and communication training. Cultural training shows the employee what culture shock is and how to manage it during an expatriate assignment. Inability to adapt to another culture is one of the major reasons that employees fail to complete foreign assignments. Communication training, including language training if necessary, helps employees overcome some of the problems associated with international assignments. Training in nonverbal and symbolic communication is especially important.

14.5 Define the options for compensation of expatriate workers.

The *balance sheet* approach is one of the most common methods. This is where the employee is paid their home salary, but allowances are provided to "balance" the different costs associated with the overseas assignment. Another option is *split pay,* where part of the compensation is paid based on the home-country norm and part is paid in the assignment-country currency to minimize exchange rate risk. We can also use a straight *negotiation* approach, where the compensation package is agreed to upfront; a *localization* approach, where compensation is based on the host-country standards; or a *lump sum* approach, where a set amount of money is given to the employee to use on unique expenses associated with an assignment to a particular country.

Key Terms

expatriate,   374
Foreign Corrupt Practices
    Act,   368

global village,   365
onshoring,   372
outsourcing,   372

parochialism,   368
trade blocs,   365

Key Terms Review

Complete each of the following statements using one of this chapter's key terms.

1. _____ refers to companies conducting business worldwide without boundaries.

2. _____ are groups of countries who form an association for the purpose of facilitating movement of goods across national borders.

3. _____ bars U.S.-based or U.S.-listed companies from bribing foreign officials in exchange for business.

4. _____ is a narrow-minded view of the world with an inability to recognize individual differences.

5. _____ is hiring another organization to do work that was previously done within the host organization.

6. _____ is the process of shuttering operations in other countries and bringing work back to the home country.

7. _____ is an employee who leaves their home country to go work in another country.

Communication Skills

The following critical-thinking questions can be used for class discussion and/or for written assignments to develop communication skills. Be sure to give complete explanations for all answers.

1. Do you expect that globalization of business will continue to expand? Why or why not?

2. Is it fair to utilize the least expensive "capital resources," no matter where they come from? Why?

3. Should tariffs and other trade barriers be increased in order to protect jobs in the home country? Why or why not?

4. Do you believe that Hofstede's culture model is accurate? If not, what would you change to make it more useful in training people to work in a different culture?

5. Is knowing the local language always necessary when working internationally? Why?

6. Who would you rather assign to manage a foreign office of *your* business? Would you rather have a home-country, host-country, or third-country national? Why?

7. Should companies reshore more jobs that have been moved overseas? What are the pros and cons of doing so?

8. If you were the HR manager, would you ever consider sending someone to work in another country without providing them with cultural training? If so, in what circumstances?

9. Which option for compensation would you want if you were assigned by your company to work in another country? Why?

Case Study 14.1 The Great Singapore Sale at Jurong Point: Finding and Retaining Bargain Employees

Singapore is an island of 646 square kilometers, about the size of Chicago. It is located at one of the crossroads of the world. Singapore's strategic position has helped it grow into a major center for trade, communications, and tourism. In just 150 years, Singapore has grown into a thriving center of commerce and industry.[79] Shopping is second to eating as a national pastime in Singapore. The island has an outstanding range of products that are available in shopping malls, department stores, boutiques, and bargain stores. Avid shoppers love the annual Great Singapore Sale, which usually falls in June to July. It has become a legendary annual event for both Singaporeans and visitors alike. Wide ranges of goods, including designer products, are marked down to present a mighty shopping extravaganza. The bargains are genuine and definitely give value for money. Shoppers can also expect private events that are hosted by the distinguished Sotheby's, Christie's, Tresors, and Glerums & Bonhams and feature exclusive items, such as works of art and jewelry. Antique rugs and carpets can also be bought at a cheaper price during the Great Singapore Sale.[80]

Jurong Point Shopping Centre ("Jurong Point") is a leading suburban retail mall situated in the western part of Singapore. Strategically located next to Boon Lay MRT Station and Bus Interchange, Jurong Point serves as the gateway to the Jurong West industrial estate, Singapore's key educational institutions, and the residential population in the west. Jurong Point in 2014 is the largest suburban mall in Singapore, housing about 450 retailers and showcasing their products and services to 6 million visitors a month. The revamped Jurong Point houses a range of retail zones—expanded and revamped Ginza Delights, Mongkok, Rackets & Track, Korean Street, Malaysia Boleh, Takeaway Alley, Gourmet Garden, and many more. In addition, there are also a 67-bay air-conditioned bus interchange, 11 civic community tenants, and to top it all off, a 610-unit condominium nestled above the retail podium.

Jointly owned by Guthrie GTS Limited and Lee Kim Tah Limited, Jurong Point is poised to take a leap forward to be the "heart of a vibrant community, abuzz with activity and a passion for life, offering WOW experiences for one and all."[81] Jurong Point Shopping Centre has an HR staff of 3 employees who oversee 160 in-house staff with an additional 2,500 employees working for the mall's tenants. Singapore is seeing a growing number of mall projects as more foreign retailers enter the local market, with 13 new malls in the works and scheduled to open between 2014

and 2017. As competition heats up, existing retailers are seeking new and innovative ways to engage and retain their employees.[82]

HR at Jurong Point has launched a number of initiatives to attract the right talent into its fold. One of the most effective means has been the organization's in-house staff referral program, shares Sally Yap, senior HR and administration manager at Jurong Point Shopping Centre. "They receive cash incentives if the employee is confirmed after three months." Recruitment efforts do not stop at in-house and operational roles but extend to the tenants. The mall launched its own job portal in 2012 to help its tenants look for staff. It also runs regular recruitment fairs to attract suitable candidates. This additional help is especially valued by the mall's smaller shops that have resource constraints, shares Yap.

Jurong Point has also beefed up its service levels to keep its customers coming for more. One of the ways it achieves this is by conducting training programs for its tenants. Employees from the mall's various outlets are taken through bite-sized modules that focus on areas such as how to serve people better, personal grooming, and basic conversational English. The latter can be a barrier for some staff, so courses like these help them perform their daily tasks better, says Yap. "We treat our tenants like family. We won't be strong if they are not strong." The mall is also partnering with Singapore Polytechnic (SP) to offer a service training program for its retail and food-and-beverage staff. In this program, employees undergo 30 hours of training focusing on areas such as retail strategies and operations, visual merchandising, restaurant management and challenges, and menu design and pricing. Upon completion, course participants receive a joint certificate from SP and Jurong Point. "It's a sweetener that will encourage them to stay at Jurong Point," Yap says. "It adds value and enhances their employability."

Jurong Point is fully absorbing the cost of training and hopes to put 500 to 700 service staff through the program's 2-year pilot phase. It plans to extend it to the mall's full staff within the next 5 years. According to Yap, the customized training will focus on improving the productivity, emotional intelligence, and entrepreneurial mind-set of in-house and tenant staff.

Once employees are recruited and trained, an employee empowerment program sets the culture for the firm. A bottom-up team approach gives employees the freedom to work out the operational details with their teams. This makes decisions less hierarchical, and employees are also happier as they are not micro-managed, says Yap. Employees are not limited to the roles that they initially signed up for. If an employee in the operations department is interested in a marketing role, they can get a transfer when the right opportunity arises. This flexibility is appreciated by the organization's younger employees in particular. "They are more restless and don't want to be stuck at the computer doing mundane things. We are very open to doing things differently," says Yap.

The HR team at Jurong Point follows this ethos and takes a nontraditional approach to its role. It works very closely with other departments to push out new ideas and programs. It also serves as the umbrella HR organization for the mall's tenants and is actively involved in ensuring a consistent culture across the property. Interaction between departments is also encouraged through activities such as overseas trips. "Every department is represented by a team member, and it allows employees to bond outside of work," says Yap. Quarterly buffet lunches are organized to encourage employees to eat and mingle together while exchanging updates on the latest happenings. "We don't work in silos and like to come together to support each other," says Yap.[83]

Questions

1. Taubman Centers Inc. (TCO) is the owner, manager, and/or lessor of regional, super-regional, and outlet shopping centers in the United States and Asia. They are looking to extend their expertise to booming markets in China and South Korea. Assuming they wanted to break into the Singapore market, what international expansion strategies might they have relative to Jurong Point?

2. Assuming Taubman was to purchase Jurong Point, what legal and cultural issues must they address in order to facilitate a smooth ownership transition?

3. Given your answer to question 2, what global staffing issues would Taubman have to immediately address? Longer-term issues?

4. Human resources play a critical role in Jurong Point's competitive strategy. What HR functions does the small HR staff focus on? Why?

5. Jurong Point's HR staff outsources some of its functions to its tenants. What are those functions, and how does this HR strategy fit Jurong Point's generic strategy?

6. Organizational culture seems to be a distinctive competency for Jurong Point. What is their culture, and what HR policies nurture that culture? How might this culture change if Jurong Point were acquired by Taubman?

Case created by Herbert Sherman, PhD, and Theodore Vallas, Department of Management Sciences, School of Business Brooklyn Campus, Long Island University

Skill Builder 14.1 The Global HRM Environment

Objective

To develop your global HRM awareness

Skills

The primary skills developed through this exercise are as follows:

1. *HR management skills*—Conceptual and design, and business skills

2. *SHRM 2018 Curriculum Guidebook*—Parts of multiple guides, including Question 3—D: Employment Law, Question 4—J: Managing a Diverse Workforce, Question 5—N. Staffing: Recruitment and Selection, Question 6—P: Training and Development, Questions 7 and 8—E: Globalization, Question 9—C: Ethics

Assignment

For this exercise, select a company that conducts business as a multinational corporation or a transnational global corporation, preferably one you work for or would like to work for. You will most likely need to conduct some research to get the answers to the following questions, such as visiting the company's website and talking to HR professionals.

1. Explain the stage of corporate globalization.

2. List at least five countries it conducts business in and the trade agreements these countries participate in.

3. Identify some of the key differences in laws among the five countries.

4. Compare the company's five dimensions (from Hofstede's model of national culture) for the five countries it does business in.

5. Explain how it recruits and selects expatriate employees.

6. Describe how it trains its expatriates and families.

7. Discuss the method(s) of compensation for its expatriates.

8. Compare the compensation (pay, incentives, and benefits) among the five countries.

9. Does the company have any specific code of ethics for conducting business in other countries, and, if so, describe the code.

Your professor may or may not require you to answer all nine questions. You may be asked to pass in this assignment, present your answers to the class, and/or discuss your answers in small groups or online.

Skill Builder 14.2 Cultural Diversity Awareness

Objective

To develop your global cultural awareness

Skills

The primary skills developed through this exercise are as follows:

1. *HR management skills*—Interpersonal skills

2. *SHRM 2018 Curriculum Guidebook*—F: Managing a Diverse Workforce

Assignment

Procedure 1 (4–6 minutes)

You and your classmates will share your international experience and nationalities. Start with people who have lived in another country, then move to those who have visited another country, and follow with discussion of nationality (e.g., "I am half French and half Irish but have never been to either country"). The instructor or a recorder will write the countries on the board until several countries/nationalities are listed or the time is up.

Procedure 2 (10–30 minutes)

You and your classmates will share your knowledge of cultural differences between the country in which the course is being taught and those listed on the board. This is a good opportunity for international students and those who have visited other countries to share their experiences. You may also discuss cultural differences within the country.

Skill Builder 14.3 The Most Important Things I Got From This Course

Objective

To review your course learning, critical thinking, and skill development

Skills

The primary skills developed through this exercise are as follows:

1. *HR management skills*—Conceptual and design

2. *SHRM 2018 Curriculum Guidebook*—The guide will vary with student answers

Assignment

Think about and write/type the three or four most important things you learned or skills you developed through this course and how they are helping or will help you in your personal and/or professional life.

You may be asked to pass in this assignment, present your answers to the class, and/or discuss your answers in small groups or online.

• Glossary •

absenteeism: The failure of an employee to report to the workplace as scheduled.

accountability: The personal duty to someone else (a higher-level manager or the organization itself) for the effective use of resources to complete an assignment.

active listening: The intention and ability to listen to others, use the content and context of the communication, and respond appropriately.

adverse employment action: Any action such as firings, demotions, schedule reductions, or changes that would harm the individual employee.

affirmative action: A series of policies, programs, and initiatives that have been instituted by various entities within both government and the private sector that are designed to prefer hiring of individuals from protected groups in certain circumstances, in an attempt to mitigate past discrimination.

assessment center: A place where job applicants undergo a series of tests, interviews, and simulated experiences to determine their potential for a particular job.

authority: The right to give orders, enforce obedience, make decisions, and commit resources toward completing organizational goals.

behaviorally anchored rating scale (BARS) form: A performance appraisal that provides a description of each assessment along a continuum.

behaviors: The actions taken by an individual.

bias: A personality-based tendency, either toward or against something.

biological job design: Designing jobs by focusing on minimizing the physical strain on the worker by structuring the physical work environment around the way the body works.

bona fide occupational qualification (BFOQ): A qualification that is absolutely required in order for an individual to be able to successfully do a particular job.

bonus pay: A lump sum payment, typically given to an individual at the end of a time period

broadbanding: Combining multiple pay levels into one.

burnout: Constant lack of interest and motivation to perform one's job.

business necessity: When a particular practice is necessary for the safe and efficient operation of the business and when there is a specific business purpose for applying a particular standard that may, in fact, be discriminatory.

business skills: The analytical and quantitative skills—including in-depth knowledge of how the business works and its budgeting and strategic planning processes—that are necessary for a manager to understand and contribute to the profitability of the organization.

career: As defined by Douglas Hall, the individually perceived sequence of attitudes and behaviors associated with work-related experiences and activities over the span of the person's life.

centralization: Degree to which decision making is concentrated within the organization.

coaching: The process of giving motivational feedback to maintain and improve performance.

COBRA: A law that requires employers to offer to maintain health insurance (for a period of time) on individuals who leave their employment.

cognitive ability test: An assessment of general intelligence or of some type of aptitude for a particular job.

cohesiveness: An intent and desire for group members to stick together in their actions.

collective bargaining: The negotiation process resulting in a contract between union employees and management that covers employment conditions.

communication: The process of transmitting information and meaning.

compensation: The total of an employee's pay and benefits

compensation system: Anything that an employee may value and desire and that the employer is willing and able to offer in exchange.

compensatory damages: Monetary damages awarded by the court that compensate the injured person for losses.

compensatory selection model: Model allowing an individual to do poorly on one test but make up for that poor grade by doing exceptionally well on other tests.

complexity: Degree to which different parts of the organization are segregated from one another.

conceptual and design skills: The ability to evaluate a situation, identify alternatives, select a reasonable alternative, and make a decision to implement a solution to a problem.

conflict: The act of being opposed to another.

construct validity: An assessment that measures a theoretical concept or trait that is not directly observable.

constructive discharge: When an employee is put under such extreme pressure by management that continued employment becomes intolerable and, as a result, the employee quits, or resigns from, the organization.

content validity: An assessment of whether a test measures knowledge or understanding of the items it is supposed to measure.

corporate social responsibility: The concept that organizations have a duty to all societal stakeholders to operate in a manner that takes each of their needs into account.

cost center: A division or department that brings in no revenue or profit for the organization—running this function only costs the organization money.

creativity: A basic ability to think in unique and different ways and apply those thought processes to existing problems.

criterion-related validity: An assessment of the ability of a test to measure some other factor related to the test.

critical incidents method: A performance appraisal method in which a manager keeps a written record of the positive and negative performance of employees throughout the performance period.

cyber security: The use of tools and processes to protect organizational computer systems and networks.

data analytics: Process of accessing large amounts of data in order to analyze those data and gain insight into significant trends or patterns within organizations or industries.

defined benefit plan: A plan providing the retiree with a specific amount and type of benefits that will be available when the individual retires.

defined contribution plan: A plan providing only the amount of funds that will go into a retirement account, not what the employee will receive upon retirement.

delayering: The process of changing the company structure to get rid of some of the vertical hierarchy (reporting levels) in an organization.

disability: A physical or mental impairment that substantially limits one or more major life activities, a record of having such an impairment, or being regarded as having such an impairment.

discipline: Corrective action designed to get employees to meet standards and the code of conduct.

discrimination: The act of making distinctions or choosing one thing over another; in HR, it is making distinctions among people.

disparate impact: When an officially neutral employment practice disproportionately excludes the members of a protected group; it is generally considered to be unintentional, but intent is irrelevant.

disparate treatment: When individuals in similar situations are intentionally treated differently and the different treatment is based on an individual's membership in a protected class.

divergent thinking: The ability to find many possible solutions to a particular problem, including unique, untested solutions.

diversity: The existence of differences—in HRM, it deals with different types of people in an organization.

domestic partners: Individuals who are not legally married but who are in a one-to-one living arrangement similar to marriage

EAP: A set of counseling and other services provided to employees that help them to resolve personal issues that may affect their work.

economic value added (EVA): Measure of profits that remain after the cost of capital has been deducted from operating profits.

effectiveness: A function of getting the job done whenever and however it must be done.

efficiency: A function of how many organizational resources we used in getting the job done.

empathy: Being able to put yourself in another person's place—to understand not only what that person is saying but why the individual is communicating that information to you.

employee development: Ongoing education to improve knowledge and skills for present and future jobs.

employee engagement: A combination of job satisfaction, ability, and a willingness to perform for the organization at a high level and over an extended period of time.

employee health: The state of physical and psychological wellness in the workforce.

employment-at-will: Concept allowing the company or the worker to break the work relationship at any point in time, with or without any particular reason, as long as in doing so, no law is violated.

equity theory: Theory that employees are motivated when the ratio of their perceived outcomes to inputs is at least roughly equal to that of other referent individuals.

ergonomics: According to OSHA, "the science of fitting workplace conditions and job demands to the capabilities of the working population."

essential functions: The fundamental duties of the position.

ethics: The application of a set of values and principles in order to make the right, or good, choice.

EWP: Plan designed to cater to the employee's physical, instead of psychological, welfare through education and training programs.

expatriate: An employee who leaves their home country to go work in another country.

expectancy theory: A theory proposing that employees are motivated when they believe they can accomplish a task and that the rewards for doing so are worth the effort.

experience rating: A measure of how often claims are made against an insurance policy.

external recruiting: The process of engaging individuals from the labor market outside the firm to apply for a job.

extinction: The lack of response, either positive or negative, in order to avoid reinforcing an undesirable behavior.

fitness-for-duty test: A test identifying whether or not an employee is physically capable at a particular point in time of performing a specific type of work.

Foreign Corrupt Practices Act: Law barring U.S.-based or U.S.-listed companies from bribing foreign officials in exchange for business.

formalization: Degree to which jobs are standardized within an organization, meaning the degree to which we have created policies, procedures, and rules that "program" the jobs of the employees.

Four-Fifths Rule: A test used by various federal courts, the Department of Labor, and the EEOC to determine whether disparate impact exists in an employment test.

global village: Companies conducting business worldwide without boundaries

golden parachutes: Provision for executives who are dismissed from a merged or acquired firm of typically large lump sum payments on dismissal.

graphic rating scale form: A performance appraisal checklist form on which a manager simply rates performance on a continuum such as excellent, good, average, fair, and poor.

grievance: A formal complaint concerning pay, working conditions, or violation of some other factor in a collective bargaining agreement.

gross negligence: A serious failure to exercise care in the work environment.

health maintenance organizations (HMOs): A health care plan that provides both health maintenance services and medical care as part of the plan.

high-deductible health plan (HDHP): A "major medical" insurance plan that protects against catastrophic health care costs and in most cases is paid for by the employer.

high performance work practices (HPWPs): Practices that have been shown to improve an organization's capacity to effectively attract, select, hire, develop, and retain high-performing personnel

hostile work environment: Harassment that occurs when someone's behavior at work creates an environment that is sexual in nature and that makes it difficult for someone of a particular sex to work in that environment.

HR forecasting: Identifying the estimated supply and demand for the different types of human resources in the organization over some future period, based on analysis of past and present demand.

HSA or MSA: A plan allowing the employer and employee to fund a medical savings account from which the employee can pay medical expenses each year with pretax dollars.

human resource management systems (HRMS): Interacting database systems that aim at generating and delivering HR information and allow us to automate some human resource management functions.

human resources (HR): The people within an organization.

illegal discrimination: The act of making distinctions that harm people and that are based on those people's membership in a protected class.

inclusion: A practice of ensuring that all employees feel they belong as valued members of the organization

Information Age: An era that began around 1980, in which information became one of the main products used in organizations; it is characterized by exponential increases in available information in all industries.

innovation: The act of creating useful processes or products based on creative thought processes.

interest test: A test measuring a person's intellectual curiosity and motivation in a particular field.

internal recruiting: Filling job openings with current employees or people the employees know.

interpersonal skills: The ability to understand, communicate, and work well with individuals and groups through developing effective relationships.

job analysis: The process used to identify the work performed and the working conditions for each of the jobs within our organizations.

job characteristics model (JCM): A conceptual framework for designing or enriching jobs based on core job characteristics.

job description: Identification of the major tasks, duties, and responsibilities that are components of a job.

job design: The process of identifying tasks that each employee is responsible for completing, as well as identifying how those tasks will be accomplished.

job evaluation: The process of determining the worth of each position relative to the other positions within the organization.

job expansion: The process of making jobs broader, with less repetition. Jobs can be expanded through rotation, enlargement, and enrichment.

job relatedness: When a test for employment is a legitimate measure of an individual's ability to do the essential functions of a job.

job simplification: The process of eliminating or combining tasks and/or changing the work sequence to improve performance.

job specification: Identification of the qualifications of a person who should be capable of doing the job tasks noted in the job description.

Just Cause: A set of standard tests for fairness in disciplinary actions—tests that were originally utilized in union grievance arbitrations.

knowledge workers: Workers who "use their head more than their hands" and who gather and interpret information to improve a product or process for their organizations.

labor market: The external pool of candidates from which we draw our recruits.

labor relations: The interactions between management and unionized employees.

layoff: A process of terminating a group of employees with intent to improve organizational efficiency and effectiveness.

learning: Any relatively permanent change in behavior that occurs as a result of experience or practice.

line managers: The individuals who create, manage, and maintain the people and organizational processes that create whatever it is that the business sells.

management by objectives (MBO) method: A process in which managers and employees jointly set objectives for the employees, periodically evaluate performance, and reward employees according to the results.

management counseling: The process of giving employees feedback (so they realize that a problem is affecting their job performance) and referring employees with problems that cannot be managed within the work structure to the organization's employee assistance program.

marginal job functions: Those functions that may be performed on the job but need not be performed by all holders of the job.

mechanistic job design: Designing jobs around the concepts of task specialization, skill simplification, and repetition.

merit pay: A program to reward top performers with increases in their annual wage that carry over from year to year.

minimum wage: The lowest hourly rate of pay generally permissible by federal law.

mission statement: A statement laying out our expectations of what we're going to do in order to become the organization that we have envisioned.

motivation: The willingness to achieve organizational objectives.

motivational job design: Designing jobs by focusing on the job characteristics that affect the psychological meaning and motivational potential of the job; this approach views attitudinal variables as the most important outcomes of job design.

multiple-hurdle selection model: Model requiring that each applicant must pass a particular selection test in order to go on to the next test.

narrative method or form: Method in which the manager is required to write a statement about the employee's performance.

needs assessment: The process of analyzing the difference between what is currently

occurring within a job or jobs and what is required—either now or in the future—based on the organization's operations and strategic goals.

negative reinforcement: Withdrawal of a harmful thing from the environment in response to a positive action on the part of the subject.

negligent hire: A legal concept that says if the organization hires someone who may pose a danger to coworkers, customers, suppliers, or other third parties, and if that person then harms someone else in the course of working for the company, then the company can be held liable for the individual's actions.

objectives: Statements of what is to be accomplished in singular, specific, and measurable terms, with a target date.

onboarding: The process of introducing new employees to the organization and their jobs

onshoring: The process of shuttering operations in other countries and bringing work back to the home country.

organizational culture: The values, beliefs, and assumptions about appropriate behavior that members of an organization share.

organizational structure: The way in which an organization groups its resources to accomplish its mission.

OUCH test: A rule of thumb rule used whenever you are contemplating any employment action, to maintain fairness and equity for all of your employees or applicants.

outsourcing: The process of hiring another organization to do work that was previously done within the host organization.

overtime: A higher than minimum, federally mandated wage, required for nonexempt employees if they work more than a certain number of hours in a week.

parochialism: A narrow-minded view of the world with an inability to recognize individual differences.

pattern or practice discrimination: When a person or group engages in a sequence of actions over a significant period of time that is intended to deny the rights provided by Title VII of the 1964 CRA to a member of a protected class.

pay structure: A hierarchy of jobs and their rates of pay within the organization.

PBGC: A governmental corporation, established within the Department of Labor, whose purpose is to insure "defined benefit" retirement funds from failure.

perceptual-motor job design: Designing jobs with tasks that remain within the worker's normal mental capabilities and limitations.

performance appraisal: The ongoing process of evaluating employee performance.

performance management: The process of identifying, measuring, managing, and developing the performance of the human resources in an organization.

perquisites: Extra financial benefits usually provided to top employees in many businesses.

personality test: A test measuring the psychological traits or characteristics of applicants to determine suitability for performance in a specific type of job.

physical test: A test designed to ensure that applicants are capable of performing on the job in ways defined by the job specification and description.

positive reinforcement: Providing a reward in return for a constructive action on the part of the subject.

preferred provider organizations (PPOs): A kind of hybrid between traditional fee-for-service plans and HMOs.

principles: Basic application of our values.

productivity: The amount of output that an organization gets per unit of input, with human input usually expressed in terms of units of time.

productivity center: A revenue center that enhances the profitability of the organization through enhancing the productivity of the people within the organization.

profit sharing programs: Programs that provide a portion of company proceeds over a specific period of time (usually either quarterly or annually) to the employees of the firm through a bonus payment.

progressive discipline: A process in which the employer provides the employee with opportunities to correct poor behavior before terminating them.

punishment: The application of an adverse consequence, or the removal of a reward, in order to decrease an unwanted behavior.

punitive damages: Monetary damages awarded by the court that are designed to punish an injuring party that has intentionally inflicted harm on others.

qualitative forecasting: The use of nonquantitative methods to forecast the future, usually based on the knowledge of a pool of experts in a subject or an industry.

quantitative forecast: Utilizing mathematics to forecast future events based on historical data.

quid pro quo harassment: Harassment that occurs when some type of benefit or punishment is made contingent upon the employee submitting to sexual advances.

race norming: When different groups of people have different scores designated as "passing" grades on a test for employment.

ranking: A performance appraisal method that is used to evaluate employee performance from best to worst.

rate range: The maximum, minimum, and midpoint of pay for a certain group of jobs.

ratio analysis: The process of reviewing historical data and calculating specific proportions between a business factor (such as production) and the number of employees needed.

realistic job preview (RJP): A review of all of the tasks and requirements of the job, both good and bad.

reasonable accommodation: An accommodation made by an employer to allow someone who is disabled but otherwise qualified to do the essential functions of a job to be able to perform that job.

reasonable person: The "average" person who would look at the situation and its intensity to determine whether the accused person was wrong in their actions.

recruiting: The process of creating a reasonable pool of qualified candidates for a job opening.

regression analysis: A statistical technique that identifies the relationship between a series of variable data points for use in forecasting future variables.

reliability: The consistency of a test measurement.

remediation: The correction of a deficiency or failure in a process or procedure.

responsibility: The obligation to answer for something/someone—the duty to carry out an assignment to a satisfactory conclusion.

results: A measure of the goals achieved through a work process.

retaliation: A situation where the organization takes an "adverse employment action" against an employee because the employee brought discrimination charges against the organization or supported someone who brought discrimination charges against the company.

return on investment (ROI): Measure of the financial return we receive because of something that we do to invest in our organization or its people.

revenue centers: Divisions or departments that generate monetary returns for the organization.

reverse discrimination: Discrimination against members of the majority group by an organization, generally resulting from affirmative action policies within an organization.

right-to-sue: A notice from the EEOC, issued if it elects not to prosecute an individual discrimination complaint within the agency, that gives the recipient the right to go directly to the courts with the complaint.

safety data sheets: Documents that provide information on a hazardous chemical and its characteristics.

selection: The process of choosing the best-qualified applicant who was recruited for a given job.

self-efficacy: Whether or not a person believes that they have the capability to do something or attain a particular goal.

serious misconduct: Intentional behavior that has the potential to cause great harm to another or to the company.

sexual harassment: "Unwelcome sexual advances, requests for sexual favors, and other verbal or physical conduct of a sexual nature constitutes sexual harassment when submission to or rejection of this conduct explicitly or implicitly affects an individual's employment, unreasonably interferes with an individual's work performance or creates an intimidating, hostile or offensive work environment."

simulation: A test where a candidate is put into a high-pressure situation in a controlled environment so that the danger and cost are limited.

skills test: An assessment instrument designed to determine if you have the ability to apply a particular knowledge set.

social loafers: Individuals who avoid providing their maximum effort in group settings because it is difficult to pick out individual performance.

Society for Human Resource Management (SHRM): The largest and most recognized of the HRM advocacy organizations in the United States.

staff managers: Individuals who advise line managers in some field of expertise.

stereotyping: Mentally classifying a person into an affinity group and then identifying the person as having the same assumed characteristics as the group.

strategy: A plan of action designed to achieve a particular set of objectives.

stress: The body's reaction to environmental demands.

stressors: Factors that may, if extreme, cause people to feel overwhelmed by anxiety, tension, and/or pressure.

strike: A collective work stoppage by members of a union that is intended to put pressure on an employer.

sustainability: Meeting the needs of the current generation without compromising the ability of future generations to meet their needs.

technical skills: The ability to use methods and techniques to perform a task.

360-degree evaluation: An evaluation that analyzes individuals' performance from all sides—from their supervisor's viewpoint, from their subordinates' viewpoint, from their customers (if applicable), from their peers, and from their own self-evaluation.

trade blocs: Groups of countries who form an association for the purpose of facilitating movement of goods across national borders.

traditional health care plans: Plans that cover a set percentage of fees for medical services—for either doctors or in-patient care.

training: The process of teaching employees the skills necessary to perform a job.

traits: The physical or psychological characteristics of a person.

trend analysis: A process of reviewing historical items such as revenues and relating changes in those items to some business factor to form a predictive chart.

trust: Faith in the character and actions of another.

turnover: The permanent loss of workers from the organization.

undue hardship: When the level of difficulty for an organization to provide accommodations, determined by looking at the nature and cost of the accommodation and the overall financial resources of the facility, becomes a significant burden on the organization.

Uniform Guidelines on Employee Selection Procedures (UGESP): Guidelines that provide information that can be used to avoid discriminatory hiring practices as well as discrimination in other employment decisions.

validity: The extent to which a test measures what it claims to measure.

values: Our basic concepts of good and bad, or right and wrong.

variable pay: Compensation that depends on some measure of individual or group performance or results in order to be awarded.

vesting: A maximum amount of time beyond which the employee will have unfettered access to their retirement funds, both employee contributions and employer contributions.

vision: What we expect to become as an organization at a particular point in time in the future.

wage compression: When new employees require higher starting pay than the historical norm, causing narrowing of the pay gap between experienced and new employees.

work sample: A test conducted by providing a sample of the work that the candidate would perform on the job and asking the candidate to perform the tasks under some type of controlled conditions.

workflow analysis: The tool that we use to identify what has to be done within the organization to produce a product or service.

workplace safety: The physical protection of people from injury or illness while on the job.

workplace security: The management of personnel, equipment, and facilities in order to protect them.

yield ratio: A calculation of how many people make it through the recruiting step to the next step in the hiring process.

• Notes •

Chapter 1

1. R. Hogan, T. Chamorro-Premuzic, R. B. Kaiser, "Employability and Career Success: Bridging the Gap Between Theory and Reality," *Industrial and Organizational Psychology* (2013), 6(1), pp. 3–16.

2. J. C. Santora, "Quality Management and Manufacturing Performance: Does Success Depend on Firm Culture?" *Academy of Management Perspective* (2009), 23(2), pp. 103–105.

3. P. M. Wright, R. Coff, T. P. Moliterno, "Strategic Human Capital Crossing the Great Divide," *Journal of Management* (2014), 40(2), pp. 353–370.

4. G. Colvin, "Ignore These Insights at Your Peril," *Fortune* (October 28, 2013), p. 85.

5. R. E. Ployhart, A. J. Nyberg, G. Reilly, M. A. Maltarich, "Human Capital Is Dead; Long Live Human Capital Resources!" *Journal of Management* (2014), 40(2), pp. 371–398.

6. I. S. Fulmer, R. E. Ployhart, "Our Most Important Asset: A Multidisciplinary/Multilevel Review of Human Capital Valuation for Research and Practice," *Journal of Management* (2014), 40(1), pp. 161–192.

7. A. Bryant, "Google's Quest to Build a Better Boss," *New York Times* (March 13, 2011), p. BU-1.

8. S. Pleiter, "Engaging Employees," *Smith Magazine* (Winter 2014), https://smith.queensu.ca/magazine/winter-2014/features/engaging-employees (retrieved June 5, 2018).

9. A. Edmans, "Does the Stock Market Fully Value Intangibles? Employee Satisfaction and Equity Prices," *Journal of Financial Economics* (September 2009), 101(3), pp. 621–640.

10. R. Grossman, E. Salas, D. Pavlas, M. A. Rosen, "Using Instructional Features to Enhance Demonstration-Based Training in Management Education," *Academy of Management Learning & Education* (2013), 12(2), pp. 219–243.

11. R. Rubin, E. Dierdorff, "Building a Better MBA: From a Decade of Critique Toward a Decennium of Creation," *Academy of Management Learning and Education* (2013), 12(1), pp. 125–141.

12. G. Elliott, "Critical Practice Leadership in Post-Compulsory Education," *Educational Management Administration & Leadership* (2015), 43(2), pp. 308–322.

13. K. W. Mossholder, H. A. Richardson, R. P. Settoon, "Human Resource Systems and Helping in Organizations: A Relational Perspective," *Academy of Management Review* (2011), 36(1), pp. 33–52.

14. E. Fry, C. Zillman, "HR Is Not Your Friend," *Fortune* (March 1, 2018), pp. 99–108.

15. J. R. Horne, "The Nine Critical Questions Managers Should Ask—A Proposal for Evaluating Organizational Efficiency," *Journal of Strategic Innovation and Sustainability* (2016), 11(1), pp. 20–32.

16. "5 Ways Chief HR Officers Can Impact the Bottom Line," *Forbes* (April 10, 2014), http://www.forbes.com/sites/oracle/2014/04/10/5-ways-chief-hr-officers-can-impact-the-bottom-line/#486cbada5bc4 (retrieved June 5, 2018).

17. http://www.successfactors.com/en_us/company/press-releases/2013/companies-with-chief-hr-officers-consistently-outperform-peers.html (retrieved January 20, 2014).

18. E. Dunn, "Performance Anxiety," *Entrepreneur* (May 2018), pp. 18–19.

19. E. Fry, C. Zillman, "HR Is Not Your Friend," *Fortune* (March 1, 2018), pp. 99–108.

20. Ibid.

21. Ibid.

22. "Business and Human Capital Challenges Today and in the Future," SHRM Research Report (December 9, 2015), https://www.shrm.org/hr-today/trends-and-forecasting/research-and-surveys/Documents/15-0502%20Bus_HC_Challenges_Report_FINAL.pdf (retrieved December 23, 2016).

23. Ibid.

24. D. Teece, M. A. Peteraf, S. Leih, "Dynamic Capabilities and Organizational Agility: Risk, Uncertainty and Entrepreneurial Management in the Innovation Economy," Tuck School of Business Working Paper No. 2771245 (April 7, 2016).

25. M. Toosi, E. Torpey, "Older Workers: Labor Force Trends," Bureau of Labor Statistics (May 2017), https://www.bls.gov/careeroutlook/2017/article/older-workers.htm (retrieved June 6, 2018).

26. "Women as a Percent of Total Employed in Selected Occupations, 2011," *Economics Daily,* Bureau of Labor Statistics (May 1, 2012), http://www.bls.gov/opub/ted/2012/ted_20120501.htm (retrieved January 24, 2014).

27. E. E. Gordon, *The 2010 Meltdown: Solving the Impending Jobs Crisis* (Westport, CT: Praeger, 2005).

28. C. Folz, "Why Millennials Are Who They Are–and What Employers Can Learn From Them," SHRM (July 20, 2016), https://www.shrm.org/resourcesandtools/hr-topics/global-hr/pages/millennials-.aspx (retrieved January 15, 2017).

29. T. H. Davenport, J. Harris, J. Shapiro, "Competing on Talent Analytics," *Harvard Business Review* (October 2010), http://www.harvardbusiness.org/competing-talent-analytics# (retrieved December 23, 2016).

30. J. G. Proudfoot, P. J. Corr, D. E. Guest, G. Dunn, "Cognitive-Behavioural Training to Change Attributional Style Improves Employee Well-being, Job Satisfaction, Productivity, and Turnover," *Personality and Individual Differences* (2009), 46(2), pp. 147–153.

31. A. J. Nyberg, R. E. Ployhart, "Context-Emergent Turnover (CED) Theory: A Theory of Collective Turnover," *Academy of Management Review* (2013), 38(1), pp. 109–131.

32. M. S. Christian, A. J. Ellis, "Examining the Effects of Sleep Deprivation on Workplace Deviance: A Self-Regulatory Perspective," *Academy of Management Journal* (2011), 54(5), pp. 913–934.

33. https://www.shrm.org/Publications/hrmagazine/EditorialContent/2011/0911/Pages/0911grossman.aspx (retrieved January 20, 2014).

34. D. Witters, S. Agrawal, "Unhealthy U.S. Workers' Absenteeism Costs $153 Billion," Gallup (October 17, 2011), http://www.gallup.com/poll/150026/unhealthy-workers-absenteeism-costs-153-billion.aspx (retrieved January 20, 2014).

35. H. Nguyen, M. Groth, A. Johnson, "When the Going Gets Tough, the Tough Keep Working: Impact of Emotional Labor on Absenteeism," *Journal of Management* (2013), published online. doi:10.1177/0149206313490026

36. R. Rubin, E. Dierdorff, "On the Road to Abilene: Time to Manage Agreement About MBA Curricular Relevance," *Academy of Management Learning & Education* (2011), 10(1), pp. 148–161.

37. E. Fry, C. Zillman, "HR Is Not Your Friend," *Fortune* (March 1, 2018), pp. 99–108.

38. H. J. Walker, T. Bauer, M. Cole, J. Bernerth, H. Feild, J. Short, "Is This How I Will Be

Treated? Reducing Uncertainty Through Recruitment Interactions," *Academy of Management Journal* (2013), 56(5), pp. 1325–1347.

39. Definition developed by the Brundtland Commission. Cited from Colvin Interview of Linda Fisher, *Fortune* (November 23, 2009), pp. 45–50.

40. R. S. Rubin, E. C. Dierdorff, "On the Road to Abilene: Time to Manage Agreement About MBA Curricular Relevance," *Academy of Management Learning & Education* (2011), 10(1), pp. 148–161.

41. "SHRM Competency Model," https://www.shrm.org/learningandcareer/career/pages/shrm-competency-model.aspx (retrieved February 17, 2019).

42. D. R. Laker, J. L. Powell, "The Differences Between Hard and Soft Skills and Their Relative Impact on Training Transfer," *Human Resource Development Quarterly* (2011), 22(1), pp. 111–122.

43. A. C. Cosper, "How to Be Great," *Entrepreneur* (March 2010), p. 12.

44. E. M. Wong, M. E. Ormiston, P. E. Tetlock, "The Effects of Top Management Team Integrative Complexity and Decentralized Decision Making on Corporate Social Performance," *Academy of Management Journal* (2011), 54(6), pp. 1207–1228.

45. K. W. Huang, J. H. Huang, G. H. Tzeng, "New Hybrid Multiple Attribute Decision-Making Model for Improving Competence Sets: Enhancing a Company's Core Competitiveness," *Sustainability* (2016), 8(2), p. 175.

46. http://www.shrm.org/about/pages/default.aspx (retrieved December 30, 2013).

47. Association for Talent Development, "About Us," www.td.org/About (retrieved December 23, 2016).

48. Association for Talent Development, "ATD Certification," https://www.td.org/Certification (retrieved December 23, 2016).

49. HR Certification Institute, "About HRCI," https://www.hrci.org/about-hrci/overview (retrieved January 21, 2017).

50. WorldatWork, www.worldatwork.org (retrieved May 28, 2018).

51. E. Fry, C. Zillman, "HR Is Not Your Friend," *Fortune* (March 1, 2018), pp. 99–108.

52. S. Sorenson, "How Employee Engagement Drives Growth," Gallup (June 20, 2013), http://www.gallup.com/businessjournal/163130/employee-engagement-drives-growth.aspx (retrieved December 26, 2016).

53. A. Mann, J. Harter, "The Worldwide Employee Engagement Crisis," Gallup (January 7, 2016), http://www.gallup.com/businessjournal/188033/worldwide-employee-engagement-crisis.aspx (retrieved December 26, 2016).

54. S. Sorenson, "How Employee Engagement Drives Growth," Gallup (June 20,

2013), http://www.gallup.com/businessjournal/163130/employee-engagement-drives-growth.aspx (retrieved December 26, 2016).

55. K. Gurchiek, "Survey: Respect at Work Boosts Job Satisfaction," (April 18, 2016), https://www.shrm.org/resourcesandtools/hr-topics/employee-relations/pages/2016-job-satisfaction-and-engagement-survey.aspx?_ga=1.173552672.2014756516.1480617151 (retrieved December 26, 2016).

56. T. Lytle, "The Engagement Challenge," *HR Magazine* (October 2016), 61(8), pp. 52–58.

57. J. Lowe, *Jack Welch Speaks: Wit and Wisdom From the World's Greatest Business Leader* (New York: John Wiley & Sons, 2008), p. 109.

58. T. Lytle, "The Engagement Challenge," *HR Magazine* (October 2016), 61(8), pp. 52–58.

59. G. Vaynerchuk, "Employees are More Important Than Clients," *INC.* (June 2016), p. 74.

60. K. Gurchiek, "Survey: Respect at Work Boosts Job Satisfaction," (April 18, 2016), https://www.shrm.org/resourcesandtools/hr-topics/employee-relations/pages/2016-job-satisfaction-and-engagement-survey.aspx?_ga=1.173552672.2014756516.1480617151 (retrieved December 26, 2016).

61. J. Phillips, A. Verjovsky, "How to Outmaneuver the Competition," SHRM (April 13, 2016), https://www.shrm.org/hr-today/news/hr-magazine/pages/how-to-outmaneuver-the-competition.aspx (retrieved December 27, 2016).

62. D. Brin, "Digital Cultures Must Be Agile," SHRM (November 14, 2016), https://www.shrm.org/resourcesandtools/hr-topics/technology/pages/digital-cultures-must-be-agile.aspx (retrieved December 27, 2016).

63. D. Zielinski, "Few HR Tech Platforms Untouched by Mobile Trend," SHRM (December 6, 2016), https://www.shrm.org/resourcesandtools/hr-topics/technology/pages/few-hr-tech-platforms-untouched-by-mobile-trend.aspx (retrieved December 27, 2016).

64. J. Phillips, A. Verjovsky, "How to Outmaneuver the Competition," SHRM (April 13, 2016), https://www.shrm.org/hr-today/news/hr-magazine/pages/how-to-outmaneuver-the-competition.aspx (retrieved December 27, 2016).

65. K. Skrzypinski, "SHRM Talent Symposium: HR Must Continue to Disrupt—or Be Disrupted," SHRM (July 21, 2016), https://www.shrm.org/resourcesandtools/hr-topics/talent-acquisition/pages/shrm-talent-symposium-disrupt-or-be-disrupted.aspx (retrieved December 27, 2016).

66. M. Nijssen, J. Paauwe, "HRM in Turbulent Times: How to Achieve Organizational Agility?" *The International Journal of Human Resource Management* (2012), 23(16), pp. 3315–3335.

67. Wethe, D. (March 7, 2017). "Why $80,000 jobs are going unfilled in shale country." Bloomberg. Retrieved from http://www.msn.com/en-us/money/markets/the-shale-industry-is-scrambling-to-catch-up-to-its-own-boom/ar-AAnXLz3?srcref=rss, March 21, 2017.

68. Ibid.

69. Bureau of Labor Statistics (March 10, 2017). "THE EMPLOYMENT SITUATION -- FEBRUARY 2017" USDL-17-0300. Retrieved from https://www.bls.gov/news.release/pdf/empsit.pdf, March 21, 2017.

70. Wethe, D. (March 7, 2017). "Why $80,000 jobs are going unfilled in shale country." Bloomberg. Retrieved from http://www.msn.com/en-us/money/markets/the-shale-industry-is-scrambling-to-catch-up-to-its-own-boom/ar-AAnXLz3?srcref=rss, March 21, 2017.

71. Ibid.

72. Ibid.

Chapter 2

1. Staff, "Controllers," *Entrepreneur* (November 2015), p. 63.

2. R. N. Lussier, C. E. Halabi, "A Three-Country Comparison of the Business Success Versus Failure Prediction Model," *Journal of Small Business Management* (2010), 48(3), pp. 360–377.

3. M. L. Verreynne, D. Meyer, P. Liesch, "Beyond the Formal-Informal Dichotomy of Small Firm Strategy-Making in Stable and Dynamic Environments," *Journal of Small Business Management* (2016), 54(2), pp. 420–444.

4. E. Fry, C. Zillman, "HR Is Not Your Friend," *Fortune* (March 1, 2018), pp. 99–108.

5. Ibid.

6. Staff, "How to Win at the Hiring Game," *INC.* (June 2018), p. 62.

7. T. Lee, D. Wilkie, "How to Earn the Trust of Your CEO," SHRM website (March 19, 2018), https://www.shrm.org/resourcesandtools/hr-topics/employee-relations/pages/hr-is-losing-the-confidence-of-the-c-suite-.aspx (retrieved June 8, 2018).

8. R. Maurer, "The C-Suite Lacks Confidence in HR Data Analytics. But Why?" SHRM website (March 23, 2018), https://www.shrm.org/resourcesandtools/hr-topics/technology/pages/hr-data-analytics-trust-leaders-kpmg.aspx (retrieved June 8, 2018).

9. T. S. Liao, J. Rice, J. C. Lu, "The Vicissitudes of Competitive Advantage: Empirical Evidence from Australian Manufacturing SMEs," *Journal of Small Business Management* (2015), 53(2), pp. 469–481; W. McKinley, S. Latham, M. Braun, "Organizational Decline and Innovation: Turnarounds and Downward Spirals," *Academy of Management Review* (2014), 39(1), pp. 88–110.

10. C. Tkaczyk, "How Google Works," *Fortune* (September 24, 2014), p. 103.

11. D. Korschun, "Boundary-Spanning Employees and Relationships With External Stakeholders: A Social Identity Approach," *Academy of Management Review* (2015), 40(4), pp. 611–629.

12. M. Kibbeling, H. van der Bij, A. van Weele, "Market Orientation and Innovativeness in Supply Chains: Supplier's Impact on Customer Satisfaction," *Journal of Product Innovation Management* (2013), 30(3), pp. 500–515.

13. S. Droege, M. Lane, M. Casile, "A Tumultuous Decade in Thailand: Competitive Dynamics Among Domestic Banks and Multi-national Entrants in an Emerging Market," *International Journal of Business and Emerging Markets* (2013), 5(4), pp. 371–387.

14. R. King, "War for Tech Talent Heats Up," *Wall Street Journal* blog (July 23, 2012), http://blogs.wsj.com/cio/2012/07/23/war-for-tech-talent-heats-up.

15. K. D. Dea Roglio, G. Light, "Executive MBA Programs: The Development of the Reflective Executive," *Academy of Management Learning & Education* (2009), 8(2), pp. 156–173.

16. H. R. Huhman, "As War for Talent Heats Up, So Does Employee Poaching," *Business Insider* (March 11, 2011).

17. Y. Kubota, "Honda CEO Rethinks Car Maker's Priorities," *Wall Street Journal* (December 3, 2014), pp. B1, B2.

18. "Facebook to Add Thousands of Workers to Review Violent Posts and Other Offensive Content," *Mercury News* (May 3, 2017), http://www.mercurynews.com/2017/05/03/facebook-to-add-thousands-of-workers-to-review-violent-posts-and-other-offensive-content (retrieved May 16, 2017).

19. J. P. Doh, N. R. Quigley, "Responsible Leadership and Stakeholder Management: Influence Pathways and Organizational Outcomes," *Academy of Management Perspectives* (2014), 28(3), pp. 255–274.

20. M. J. Canyan, "Executive Compensation and Incentives," *Academy of Management Perspectives* (2006), 20(1), pp. 25–44.

21. D. Chandler, "Morals, Markets, and Values-Based Business," *Academy of Management Review* (2014), 39(3), pp. 396–397.

22. "A Timeline of the Dakota Access Oil Pipeline," Associated Press (February 22, 2107), https://www.usnews.com/news/north-dakota/articles/2017–02–22/a-timeline-of-the-dakota-access-oil-pipeline (retrieved May 16, 2017).

23. A. McWilliams, D. Siegel, "Corporate Social Responsibility: A Theory of the Firm Perspective," *Academy of Management Review* (2001), (26)1, pp. 117–127.

24. A. H. Bowers, H. R. Greve, H. Mitsuhashi, J. A. C. Baum, "Competitive Parity, Status Disparity, and Mutual Forebearance: Securities Analysts' Competition for Investor Attention," *Academy of Management Journal* (2014), 57(1), pp. 38–62.

25. R. Ackoff, *Creating the Corporate Future* (New York: Wiley, 1981).

26. G. F. Keller, "The Influence of Military Strategies on Business Planning," *International Journal of Business and Management* (May 2008), p. 129.

27. C. Wolf, S. Floyd, "Strategic Planning Research: Toward a Theory-Driven Agenda," *Journal of Management*, published online (March 26, 2013). doi:10.1177/0149206313478185

28. P. M. Wright, G. C. McMahan, "Exploring Human Capital: Putting 'Human' Back Into Strategic Human Resource Management," *Human Resource Management Journal* (2011), 21(2), pp. 93–104.

29. I. Ugboro, K. Obeng, O. Spann, "Strategic Planning as an Effective Tool of Strategic Management in Public Sector Organizations: Evidence From Public Transit Organizations," *Administration and Society* (2011), 43(1), pp. 87–123.

30. J. Welch, S. Welch, "Inventing the Future Now," *Businessweek* (May 11, 2009), p. 76.

31. W. Bennis, "Acting the Part of a Leader," *Businessweek* (September 14, 2009), p. 80.

32. University of Arkansas Little Rock, http://ualr.edu/cob/about-us/mission/ (retrieved March 1, 2014).

33. *American Heritage College Dictionary* (New York: Houghton Mifflin, 1993).

34. University of Arkansas Little Rock, http://ualr.edu/cob/about-us/mission/ (retrieved March 1, 2014).

35. R. Karlgaad, "Vivid Vision for Success," *Forbes* (January 19, 2015), p. 26.

36. Y. Koh, K. Grind, "Twitter CEO Costolo Struggles to Define Vision," *Wall Street Journal* (November 7, 2014), pp. B1, B2.

37. S. F. Collins, "Success Steps," *Costco Connection* (January 2016), p. 29.

38. C. Hann, "Always Be Closing," *Entrepreneur* (August 2015), p. 30.

39. Staff, "CEO Survey," *INC.* (September 2014), p. 78.

40. G. Hirst, D. Van Knippenberg, J. Zhou, "A Cross-Level Perspective on Employee Creativity: Goal Orientation, Team Learning Behavior, and Individual Creativity," *Academy of Management Journal* (2009), 52(2), pp. 280–293.

41. Staff, "No. 6 McDonald's," *Entrepreneur* (January 2016), p. 106.

42. D Wakabayashi, "Apple Sets 2019 Goal to Build An Auto," *Wall Street Journal* (September 22, 2015), p. A1.

43. Staff, "Trending," *Forbes* (February 8, 2016), p. 52.

44. T. Mickle, "AB InBev Sets Lofty Goal," *Wall Street Journal* (April 2–3, 2016), p. B1.

45. D. Hull, "Testla," *Businessweek* (August 31–September 6, 2015), pp. 20–21.

46. C. Rogers, "Ford Sets Plans for Cars Without Steering Wheels," *Wall Street Journal* (August 17, 2016): B1.

47. J. Chaussee, "Briefs," *Businessweek* (August 3–9, 2015), p. 25.

48. Burger King website, www.burgerking.com (retrieved January 5, 2015).

49. M. Porter, *Competitive Strategy: Techniques for Analyzing Industries and Competitors* (New York: Free Press, 1980).

50. G. Anderson, "Can Walmart Beat Dollar Stores on Their Own Turf?" *Forbes* blog (May 14, 2013), http://www.forbes.com/sites/retailwire/2013/05/14/can-walmart-beat-dollar-stores-on-their-own-turf/.

51. L. Lorenzetti, "Southwest Airlines Is Flying High," *Fortune* (October 27, 2014), p. 38; J. Bachman, "Southwest Hangs Up Its Low-Cost Jersey," *Businessweek* (September 15–21, 2015), 27–28.

52. J. Bachman, "Southwest Hangs Up Its Low-Cost Jersey," *Businessweek* (September 15–21, 2015), pp. 27–28.

53. M. Cerne, C. G. L. Nerstad, A. Dysvik, M. Skerlavaj, "What Goes Around Comes Around: Knowledge Hiding, Perceived Motivational Climate, and Creativity," *Academy of Management Journal* (2014), 57(1), pp. 172–192.

54. C. Clifford, "My Advice," *Fortune* (August 11, 2014), p. 32.

55. H. L. Smith, R. Discenza, K. G. Baker, "Building Sustainable Success in Art Galleries: An Exploratory Study of Adaptive Strategies," *Journal of Small Business Strategy* (2005/2006), 16(2), pp. 29–41.

56. H. Ibarra, "The Way to Become a Strategic Executive," *Wall Street Journal* (February 23, 2015), p. R7.

57. N. Byrnes, "Why Dr. Pepper Is in the Pink of Health," *Businessweek* (October 26, 2009), p. 59.

58. Y. H. Hsieh, H. M. Chen, "Strategic Fit Among Business Competitive Strategy, Human Resource Strategy, and Reward System," *Academy of Strategic Management Journal* (2011), 10(2).

59. Ibid.

60. Agency for Healthcare Research and Quality, "High-Performance Work Practices in CLABSI Prevention Interventions" (August 2015), https://www.ahrq.gov/professionals/quality-patient-safety/cusp/clabsi-hpwreport/clabsi-hpwpap.html (retrieved May 29, 2018).

61. B. Kroon, K. Van De Voorde, J. Timmers, "High Performance Work Practices in Small Firms: A Resource-Poverty and Strategic Decision-Making Perspective," *Small Business Economics* (2013), 41(1), pp. 71–91.

62. J. H. Marler, "Strategic Human Resource Management in Context: A Historical and Global Perspective," *Academy of Management Perspectives* (2012), 26(2), pp. 6–11.

63. M. S. Wood, "Does One Size Fit All? The Multiple Organizational Forms Leading to Successful Academic Entrepreneurship," *Entrepreneurship Theory and Practice* (2009), 33(4), pp. 929–947.

64. P. Fiss, E. Zajac, "The Symbolic Management of Strategic Change: Sensegiving via Framing and Decoupling," *Academy of Management Journal* (2006), 49(6), pp. 1173–1193.

65. B. R. Spisak, M. J. O'Brien, N. Nicholson, M. Van Vugt, "Niche Construction and the Evolution of Leadership," *Academy of Management Review* (2015), 40(2), pp. 291–306.

66. G. Fisher, S. Kotha, A. Lahiri, "Changing With the Times: An Integrated View of Identity, Legitimacy, and New Venture Life Cycles," *Academy of Management Review* (2016), 41(3), pp. 383–409.

67. B. R. Spisak, M. J. O'Brien, N. Nicholson, M. Van Vugt, "Niche Construction and the Evolution of Leadership," *Academy of Management Review* (2015), 40(2), pp. 291–306.

68. R. Adhikari, "Nadella Begins Microsoft Leadership Transformation," *E-Commerce Times* (March 3, 2014), http://www.ecommercetimes.com/story/80075.html.

69. M. K. Fiegener, "Matching Business-Level Strategic Controls to Strategy: Impact on Control System Effectiveness," *Journal of Applied Business Research* (2011), 10(1), pp. 25–34.

70. Ibid.

71. M. Guadalupe, H. Li, J. Wulf, "Who Lives in the C-Suite? Organizational Structure and the Division of Labor in Top Management," *Management Science* (November 22, 2013).

72. P. M. Figueroa, "Risk Communication Surrounding the Fukushima Nuclear Disaster: An Anthropological Approach," *Asia Europe Journal* (2013), 11(1), pp. 53–64.

73. B. Gates, "The Best Advice I Ever Got," *Fortune* (July 6, 2009), p. 43.

74. P. Drucker, *Management: Tasks, Responsibilities, Practices* (Oxford, UK: Butterworth-Heinemann, 1999), p. 546.

75. M. Berman, "The No-Boss Company," *Wall Street Journal* (October 27, 2015), p. R3.

76. A. Murray, "The Pinnacles and Pitfalls of Corporate Culture," *Fortune* (March 15, 2016), p. 14.

77. E. Fry, C. Zillman, "HR Is Not Your Friend," *Fortune* (March 1, 2018), pp. 99–108.

78. D. West, lecture at Springfield College (November 23, 2009).

79. E. Fry, C. Zillman, "HR Is Not Your Friend," *Fortune* (March 1, 2018), pp. 99–108.

80. Staff, "How to Win at the Hiring Game," *INC.* (June 2018), p. 62.

81. M. J. Culnan, P. J. McHugh, J. I. Zubillaga, "How Large U.S. Companies Can Use Twitter and Other Social Media to Gain Business Value," *MIS Quarterly Executive* (2010), 9(4), pp. 243–259.

82. M. W. DiStaso, T. McCorkindale, D. K. Wright, "How Public Relations Executives Perceive and Measure the Impact of Social Media in Their Organizations," *Public Relations Review* (2011), 37(3), pp. 325–328.

83. K. Steinmetz, "Obama Asks Celebs to Tweet About ObamaCare," *Time* (October 2, 2013), http://swampland.time.com/2013/10/02/obama-asks-celebs-to-tweet-about-obamacare/.

84. M. Lim, "Clicks, Cabs, and Coffee Houses: Social Media and Oppositional Movements in Egypt, 2004–2011," *Journal of Communication* (2012), 62(2), pp. 231–248.

85. C. Skrzypinski, "SHRM Talent Symposium: HR Must Continue to Disrupt—or Be Disrupted" (July 21, 2016), https://www.shrm.org/resourcesandtools/hr-topics/talent-acquisition/pages/shrm-talent-symposium-disrupt-or-be-disrupted.aspx (retrieved May 20, 2017).

86. E. Fry, C. Zillman, "HR Is Not Your Friend," *Fortune* (March 1, 2018), pp. 99–108.

87. D. Gage, "What Do Scientists Do All Day at Work?" *Wall Street Journal* (March 14, 2016), p. R6.

88. B. Simmons, "Data Wimps," *Forbes* (February 9, 2015), p. 34.

89. Staff, "The Meaning of Big Data," *Fortune* (June 16, 2014), p. 232.

90. Teradata, Ad, *Forbes* (February 9, 2015), p. 24.

91. J. Ma, "CEO Wisdom," *Businessweek* (October 19–25, 2015), p. 31.

92. R. Charan, "The Algorithmic CEO," *Fortune* (January 22, 2015), pp. 45–46.

93. V. Harnish, "5 Ways to Turn Precision Into Profits," *Fortune* (July 1, 2015), p. 32.

94. D. Gage, "What Do Scientists Do All Day at Work?" *Wall Street Journal* (March 14, 2016), p. R6.

95. S. Cleland, "Google's 'Infringenovation' Secrets," *Forbes* (October 3, 2011), http://www.forbes.com/sites/scottcleland/2011/10/03/googles-infringenovation-secrets/.

96. S. Lohr, "Big Data, Trying to Build Better Workers," *New York Times* (April 21, 2013), p. BU4.

97. J. Manyika, M. Chui, B. Brown, et al., "Big Data: The Next Frontier for Innovation, Competition, and Productivity," McKinsey Global Institute report (June 2011), p. 23.

98. S. Lohr, "Big Data, Trying to Build Better Workers," *New York Times* (April 21, 2013), p. BU4.

99. McAfee, E. Brynjolfsson, "Big Data: The Management Revolution," *Harvard Business Review* (October 2012), p. 4.

100. Ibid.

101. J. Schramm, "Future Focus: The Trouble With Algorithms," *HR Magazine* (November 2013), 58(11), p. 80.

102. M. L. Brosnan, C. S. Farley, D. Gartside, H. Tambe, "How Well Do You Know Your Workforce?" *Accenture* (October 2013), http://www.accenture.com/us-en/outlook/Pages/outlook-journal-2013-how-well-do-you-know-your-workforce-analytics.aspx.

103. Chartered Institute of Personnel and Development, *Talent Analytics and Big Data—The Challenge for HR* (London, UK: CIPD, 2013), p. 2, http://www.oracle.com/us/products/applications/human-capital-management/talent-analytics-and-big-data-2063584.pdf.

104. S. Lohr, "Big Data, Trying to Build Better Workers," *New York Times* (April 21, 2013), p. BU4.

105. Ibid.

106. "The Insperity Guide to HR Technology," *Insperity* (October 2016), 6, http://www.insperity.com/magazine/derailed-by-data-the-insperity-guide-to-hr-technology-issue-6 (retrieved May 20, 2017).

107. "HR Seeking to Tap High Potential of Talent Analytics," SHRM website, http://www.shrm.org/hrdisciplines/staffingmanagement/articles/pages/tapping-talent-analytics-potential.aspx (retrieved March 15, 2014).

108. Boston Consulting Group, "People Management Translates Into Superior Economic Performance," [press release] (August 2, 2012), http://www.bcg.com/media/PressReleaseDetails.aspx?id=tcm:12–110525/.

109. K. W. Mossholder, H. A. Richardson, R. P. Settoon, "Human Resource Systems and Helping in Organizations: A Relational Perspective," *Academy of Management Review* (2011), 36(1), pp. 33–52.

110. D. Mueller, S. Strohmeier, C. Gasper, "HRIS Design Characteristics: Towards a General Research Framework," *3rd European Academic Workshop on Electronic Human Resource Management* (May 2010).

111. S. Pande, P. Khanna, "Leveraging Human Resource Information Systems: Alignment of Business With Technology," *International Journal of Computer Applications* (2012), p. 56.

112. D. Zielinski, "An HRMS for Everyone," *HR Magazine* (October 2016), pp. 47–50.

113. M. Flester, A. Collis, N. Cossack, "Job Rotations, Total Rewards, Measuring Value," SHRM *HR Magazine* (August 1, 2008), http://www.shrm.org/Publications/hrmagazine/EditorialContent/Pages/0808hrsolutions.aspx (retrieved July 7, 2010).

114. "2018 Global Capital Trends," *Deloitte Insights,* https://www2.deloitte.com/

us/en/pages/human-capital/articles/introduction-human-capital-trends.html?id=us:2ps:3gl:confidence:eng:cons:111215:em:dup1179:7Rjr6jJJ:881105247:184494606203:b:Human_Capital_Trends:Human_Capital_Trends_BMM:nb (retrieved May 20, 2017).

115. This is a real field-based case, but the organization name and individuals' names have been changed to protect their anonymity. This is an abridged version of the case by Amanda DiResto and Herbert Sherman (2017). "The 'Mad' Hatter: Catalya Hats" under review at *Management and Organizational Studies*.

Chapter 3

1. E. Fry, C. Zillman, "HR Is Not Your Friend," *Fortune* (March 1, 2018), pp. 99–108.

2. S. Nkomo, J. Hoobler, "A Historical Perspective on Diversity Ideologies in the United States: Reflections on Human Resource Management Research and Practice," *Human Resource Management Review* (April 2014), p. 24.

3. J. Hendon, "Hiring and the OUCH Test," *Arkansas Business* (May 3, 2010).

4. Adoption of Questions and Answers to Clarify and Provide a Common Interpretation of the Uniform Guidelines on Employee Selection Procedures, https://www.eeoc.gov/policy/docs/qanda_clarify_procedures.html (retrieved June 24, 2018).

5. https://uniformguidelines.com/uniformguidelines.html#18/ (retrieved June 24, 2018).

6. "Employment Tests and Selection Procedures," U.S. Equal Employment Opportunity Commission, https://www.eeoc.gov/policy/docs/factemployment_procedures.html (retrieved June 24, 2018).

7. The Equal Pay Act of 1963, https://www.eeoc.gov/laws/statutes/epa.cfm (retrieved June 20, 2018).

8. Ibid.

9. U.S. Census data, www.census.gov (retrieved June 6, 2018).

10. H. Olen, data from Economic Policy Institute, "Mapping the Gender Wage Gap," *INC.* (June 2018), p. 58.

11. L. Weber, R. L. Ensign, "Promoting Women Is Crucial," *Wall Street Journal* (September 28, 2016), p. B1.

12. H. Olen, data from Economic Policy Institute, "Mapping the Gender Wage Gap," *INC.* (June 2018), p. 58.

13. Staff, "Gender and GDP," *Businessweek* (October 5–11, 2015), p. 20.

14. Title VII of the Civil Rights Act of 1964, U.S. Equal Employment Opportunity Commission website, https://www.eeoc.gov/laws/statutes/titlevii.cfm (retrieved June 24, 2018).

15. "Employment Tests and Selection Procedures," U.S. Equal Employment Opportunity Commission website, https://www.eeoc.gov/policy/docs/factemployment_procedures.html (retrieved June 24, 2018).

16. Ibid.

17. Title VII of the Civil Rights Act of 1964, https://www.eeoc.gov/laws/statutes/titlevii.cfm (retrieved June 21, 2018).

18. https://www3.ce9.uscourts.gov/jury-instructions/node/182/ (retrieved June 24, 2018).

19. Title VII of the Civil Rights Act of 1964, https://www.eeoc.gov/laws/statutes/titlevii.cfm (retrieved June 24, 2018).

20. Ibid.

21. "Regulations Implementing the Vietnam Era Veterans' Readjustment Assistance Act," U.S. Department of Labor, https://www.dol.gov/ofccp/regs/compliance/vevraa.htm (retrieved June 24, 2018).

22. "Facts About Pregnancy Discrimination," U.S. Equal Employment Opportunity Commission, https://www.eeoc.gov/facts/fs-preg.html (retrieved June 24, 2018).

23. Americans with Disabilities Act of 1990, as Amended, https://www.ada.gov/pubs/adastatute08.htm (retrieved June 24, 2018).

24. Ibid.

25. "The Americans with Disabilities Act: Applying Performance and Conduct Standards to Employees with Disabilities," U.S. Equal Employment Opportunity Commission, https://www.eeoc.gov/facts/performance-conduct.html (retrieved June 24, 2018).

26. Americans with Disabilities Act of 1990, as Amended, https://www.ada.gov/pubs/adastatute08.htm (retrieved June 24, 2018).

27. ADA Amendments Act of 2008, Public Law 110–325, https://www.eeoc.gov/laws/statutes/adaaa.cfm (retrieved June 20, 2018).

28. "Charge Statistics (Charges File with EEOC) FY 1997 Through FY 2017," https://www.eeoc.gov/eeoc/statistics/enforcement/charges.cfm (retrieved June 24, 2018).

29. Civil Rights Act of 1991, Public Law 102–166.

30. "Remedies for Employment Discrimination," EEOC, https://www.eeoc.gov/employers/remedies.cfm (retrieved June 24, 2018).

31. An Act to Amend the Civil Rights Act of 1964, https://www.eeoc.gov/eeoc/history/35th/thelaw/cra_1991.html (retrieved June 24, 2018).

32. https://www.dol.gov/vets/usc/vpl/usc38.htm#4301/ (retrieved June 24, 2018).

33. "USERRA Advisor," U.S. Department of Labor, https://www.dol.gov/elaws/vets/userra/userra.asp (retrieved June 24, 2018).

34. https://www.dol.gov/vets/usc/vpl/usc38.htm#4301/ (retrieved June 24, 2018).

35. A. Smith, "Have Workers in the Military? The 4 USERRA Requirements You Should Know" (March 9, 2017), SHRM, https://www.shrm.org/resourcesandtools/legal-and-compliance/employment-law/pages/4-userra-requirements.aspx (retrieved May 22, 2017).

36. https://www.dol.gov/vets/regs/fedreg/final/2005023960.htm#regs/ (retrieved June 24, 2018).

37. The Genetic Information Nondiscrimination Act of 2008, https://www.eeoc.gov/laws/statutes/gina.cfm (retrieved June 24, 2018).

38. Ibid.

39. "Overview," U.S. Equal Employment Opportunity Commission, https://eeoc.gov/eeoc/ (retrieved June 24, 2018).

40. Ibid.

41. https://www.eeoc.gov/employers/ee01survey/faq.cfm (retrieved June 24, 2018).

42. https://www.eeoc.gov/eeoc/newsroom/release/4-4-06.cfm (retrieved June 24, 2018).

43. "Fiscal Year 2013 Performance and Accountability Report Highlights," U.S. Equal Employment Opportunity Commission, https://www.eeoc.gov/eeoc/plan/2013parhigh_discussion.cfm (retrieved June 24, 2018).

44. "Systemic Discrimination," U.S. EEOC, https://www.eeoc.gov/eeoc/systemic/ (retrieved June 24, 2018).

45. Ibid.

46. E. Fry, C. Zillman, "HR Is Not Your Friend," *Fortune* (March 1, 2018), pp. 99–108.

47. Title VII of the Civil Rights Act of 1964, https://www.eeoc.gov/laws/statutes/titlevii.cfm (retrieved June 24, 2018).

48. "Charge Statistics (Charges File with EEOC) FY 1997 Through FY 2017," http://eeoc.gov/eeoc/statistics/enforcement/charges.cfm (retrieved May 28, 2018).

49. *Pennsylvania State Police v. Suders* (03–95), 542 U.S. 129 (2004), 325 F.3d 432.

50. E. Fry, C. Zillman, "HR Is Not Your Friend," *Fortune* (March 1, 2018), pp. 99–108.

51. E. O. Wright, J. Baxter, "The Glass Ceiling Hypothesis: A Reply to Critics," *Gender & Society* (2000), 14, pp. 814–821.

52. J. Adamy, P. Overberg, "Pay Gap Widest for Elite Jobs," *Wall Street Journal* (May 18, 2016), pp. A1, A10.

53. E. Fry, C. Zillman, "HR Is Not Your Friend," *Fortune* (March 1, 2018), pp. 99–108.

54. U.S. Equal Employment Opportunity Commission, "Facts About Sexual Harassment," http://www.eeoc.gov/facts/fs-sex .html (retrieved March 25, 2019).

55. "Policy Guidance on Current Issues of Sexual Harassment," EEOC, https://www .eeoc.gov/policy/docs/currentissues.html (last modified June 21, 1999; retrieved June 24, 2018).

56. http://www.law.cornell.edu/supct/ html/96–568.ZO.html (retrieved June 24, 2018).

57. Ibid.

58. Ibid.

59. E. Fry, C. Zillman, "HR Is Not Your Friend," *Fortune* (March 1, 2018), pp. 99–108.

60. http://www.law.cornell.edu/supct/ html/96–568.ZO.html (retrieved June 24, 2018).

61. "Weinstein Co. Says It Will File for Bankruptcy," *Wall Street Journal* (February 26, 2018), https://www.wsj.com/articles/we instein-co-says-it-will-file-for-bank ruptcy-1519631884 (retrieved June 20, 2018).

62. https://www.shrm.org/resourcesand tools/tools-and-samples/toolkits/pages/ employeedressandappearance.aspx (retrieved June 24, 2018).

63. Ibid.

64. Ibid.

65. A. Smith, "Appeals Court Rules Sexual Orientation Discrimination Is Not Prohibited," SHRM (March 17, 2017), https://www.shrm.org/resourcesand tools/legal-and-compliance/employ ment-law/pages/11th-circuit-title-vii -.aspx (retrieved May 23, 2017).

66. "Corporate Equality Index 2017. Rating American Workplaces on Lesbian, Gay, Bisexual and Transgender Equality." Human Rights Campaign Foundation. http://www.hrc.org/campaigns/corpo rate-equality-index (retrieved May 23, 2017).

67. https://www.shrm.org/resourcesand tools/tools-and-samples/toolkits/pages/ employeedressandappearance.aspx, retrieved June 24, 2018

68. M. Freeman, "Qualcomm Enters $19.5 Million Gender Bias Settlement," *San Diego Tribune* (July 26, 2016), http://www .sandiegouniontribune.com/business/ technology/sdut-qualcomm-lawsuit-gen der-bias-women-stem-2016ju126-story .html (retrieved May 23, 2017).

69. H. Clancy, "HP Inc., Hewlett Packard Enterprise Face Claims of Age Discrimination," *Fortune* (August 29, 2016), http:// fortune.com/2016/08/29/hp-inc-hewlett -packard-enterprise-face-claims-of-age -discrimination/ (retrieved May 23, 2017).

70. T. Jan, "How Racial Bias Could Be Hurting Silicon Valley's Bottom Line," *Washington Post* (February 24, 2017), https://www.washingtonpost.com/news/ wonk/wp/2017/02/24/how-racial-bias -could-be-hurting-silicon-valleys-bot tom-line/?utm_term=.504ee6a7c747 (retrieved May 23, 2017).

71. A. Glaser, R. Molla, "A Not-So-Brief History of Gender Discrimination Lawsuits in Silicon Valley," *Recode* (April 10, 2017), https://www.recode.net/2017/4/ 10/15246444/history-gender-timeline -discrimination-lawsuits-legal-silicon -valley-google-oracle (retrieved May 23, 2017).

72. R. Maurer, "Candidate Personas Focus Search and Save Time," SHRM (September 8, 2016), https://www.shrm.org/resources andtools/hr-topics/talent-acquisition/ pages/candidate-personas-focus-search -save-time.aspx (retrieved May 23, 2017).

73. "'Rogue Algorithms' and the Dark Side of Big Data" [book review of Cathy O'Neil's *Weapons of Math Destruction*] Wharton School, University of Pennsylvania (September 21, 2016), http://knowledge .wharton.upenn.edu/article/rogue -algorithms-dark-side-big-data/ (retrieved May 23, 2017).

74. A. J. King, M. J. Mrkonich, "The Legal Risks of Big Data," SHRM (October 7, 2016), https://www.shrm.org/resources andtools/legal-and-compliance/employ ment-law/pages/legal-risks-of-big-data .aspx (retrieved May 23, 2017).

Chapter 4

1. R. L. Dipboye, "Bridging the Gap in Organizations Behavior," *Academy of Management Learning & Education* (2014), 13(3), pp. 487–491.

2. L. Jia, J. D. Shaw, A. S. Tsue, T. Y. Park, "A Social-Structural Perspective on Employee-Organization Relationships and Team Creativity," *Academy of Management Journal* (2014), 57(3), pp. 869–891.

3. A. Chatterji, A. Patro, "Dynamic Capabilities and Managing Human Capital," *Academy of Management Perspectives* (2014), 28(4), pp. 395–408.

4. V. Di Stasio, "Who Is Ahead in the Labor Queue? Institutions' and Employers' Perspective on Overeducation, Undereducation, and Horizontal Mismatches," *Sociology of Education* (2017), 90(2), pp. 109–126.

5. Staff, "How to Win at the Hiring Game," *INC.* (June 2018), p. 62.

6. T. Barmby, A. Bryson, B. Eberth, "Human Capital, Matching and Job Satisfaction," *Economics Letters* (2012), 117(3), pp. 548–551.

7. J. Sprinks, J. Wardlaw, R. Houghton, S. Bamford, J. Morley, "Task Workflow Design and Its Impact on Performance and Volunteers' Subjective Preference in Virtual Citizen Science," *International Journal of Human-Computer Studies* (2017), 104, pp. 50–63.

8. H. C. W. Lau, G. T. S. Ho, K. F. Chu, W. Ho, C. K. M. Lee, "Development of an Intelligent Quality Management System Using Fuzzy Association Rules," *Expert Systems With Applications* (2009), 36(2), pp. 1801–1815.

9. G. Cravo, "Applications of Propositional Logic to Workflow Analysis," *Applied Mathematics Letters* (2010), 23(3), pp. 272–276.

10. Y. Gil, V. Ratnakar, J. Kim, P. A. González-Calero, P. Groth, J. Moody, E. Deelman, "Wings: Intelligent Workflow-Based Design of Computational Experiments," *IEEE Intelligent Systems* (2011), 26(1), pp. 62–72.

11. A. H. Memon, I. A. Rahman, A. A. Azis, "Assessing Causal Relationships Between Construction Resources and Cost Overrun Using PLS Path Modelling Focusing in Southern and Central Region of Malaysia," *Journal of Engineering and Technology (JET),* (2013), 4(1), pp. 67–78.

12. O. Henry, "Organisational Conflict and Its Effects on Organisational Performance," *Research Journal of Business Management* (2009), 2(1), pp. 16–24.

13. P. K. Thompson, "Help With Hiring," *Costco Connection* (December 2014), pp. 13–14.

14. F. P. Morgeson, M. Spitzmuller, A. S. Garza, M. A. Campion, "Pay Attention! The Liabilities of Respondent Experience and Carelessness When Making Job Analysis Judgments," *Journal of Management* (2016), 42(7), pp. 1904–1933.

15. J. I. Sanchez, E. L. Levine, "The Rise and Fall of Job Analysis and the Future of Work Analysis," *Annual Review of Psychology* (2012), 63, pp. 397–425.

16. "Overview," O*NET Resource Center, http://www.onetcenter.org/overview .html (retrieved June 19, 2018).

17. S. A. Woods, D. P. Hinton, "What Do People Really Do at Work? Job Analysis and Design" in *An Introduction to Work and Organizational Psychology: An International Perspective,* edited by N. Chmiel, F. Fraccaroli, M. Sverke (New York, NY: Wiley, 2017), pp. 7–11.

18. S. G. Gibson, "Generalized Work Dimension Analysis," in *The Handbook of Work Analysis: Methods, Systems, Applications and Science of Work Measurement in Organizations,* edited by M. A. Wilson, W. Bennett, S. G. Gibson, G. M. Alliger (New York, NY: Taylor & Francis, 2012), pp. 215–230.

19. W. J. Liccione, "Linking the Market and Internal Values of Jobs: Rethinking the

Market Line," *Compensation & Benefits Review* (2014), 46(2), pp. 80–88.

20. S. G. Gibson, "Generalized Work Dimension Analysis," in *The Handbook of Work Analysis: Methods, Systems, Applications and Science of Work Measurement in Organizations,*" edited by M. A. Wilson, W. Bennett, S. G. Gibson, G. M. Alliger (New York, NY: Taylor & Francis, 2012), pp. 215–230.

21. N. J. Gierlasinski, D. R. Nixon, "A Comparison of Interviewing Techniques: HR Versus Fraud Examination," *Oxford Journal: An International Journal of Business & Economics* (2014), 5(1).

22. M. Robinson, "Work Sampling: Methodological Advances and New Applications," *Human Factors and Ergonomics in Manufacturing & Service Industries* (2010), 20(1), pp. 42–60.

23. B. Beck, D. C. Billing, A. J. Carr, "Developing Physical and Physiological Employment Standards: Translation of Job Analysis Findings to Assessments and Performance Standards–A Systematic Review," *International Journal of Industrial Ergonomics* (2016), 56, pp. 9–16.

24. L. Weber, M. Korn, "Where Did All the Entry-Level Jobs Go?" *Wall Street Journal* (August 6, 2014), p. B6.

25. C. Hann, "Go Get 'Em," *Entrepreneur* (July 2014), p. 34.

26. L. Adler, "4 Common Leadership Fears and How to Avoid Them," *INC.* (April 2015), p. 10.

27. M. R. Barrick, G. R. Thurgood, T. A. Smith, S. H. Courtright, "Collective Organizational Engagement: Linking Motivational Antecedents, Strategic Implementation, and Firm Performance," *Academy of Management Journal* (2014), 58(1), pp. 111–135.

28. J. P. J. de Jong, S. K. Parker, S. Wennekers, C. H. Wu, "Entrepreneurial Behavior in Organizations: Does Job Design Matter?" *Entrepreneurship Theory and Practice* (2015), 39(4), pp. 981–995.

29. A. C. Keller, N. K. Semmer, "Changes in Situational and Dispositional Factors as Predictors of Job Satisfaction," *Journal of Vocational Behavior* (2013), 83(1), pp. 88–98.

30. J. Lahart, "Moment of Truth for Productivity Boom," *Wall Street Journal* (May 6, 2010), pp. A1, A16.

31. G. R. Oldham, J. R. Hackman, "Not What It Was and Not What It Will Be: The Future of Job Design Research," *Journal of Organizational Behavior* (2010), 31(2–3), pp. 463–479.

32. D. Shin, A. M. Konrad, "Causality Between High-Performance Work Systems and Organizational Performance," *Journal of Management* (2017), 43(4), pp. 973–997.

33. G. R. Oldham, Y. Fried, "Job Design Research and Theory: Past, Present and Future," *Organizational Behavior and Human Decision Processes* (2016), 136, pp. 20–35.

34. G. P. McClelland, D. J. Leach, C. W. Clegg, I. McGowan, "Collaborative Crafting in Call Centre Teams," *Journal of Occupational and Organizational Psychology* (2014), 87(3), pp. 464–486.

35. R. W. Proctor, K. P. L. Vu, "Cumulative Knowledge and Progress in Human Factors," *Annual Review of Psychology* (2010), 61, pp. 623–651.

36. R. Hackman, G. Oldham, *Work Redesign* (Reading, MA: Addison-Wesley, 1980).

37. A. M. Grant, "Giving Time, Time After Time: Work Design and Sustained Employee Participation in Corporate Volunteering," *Academy of Management Review* (2012), 37(4), pp. 589–615.

38. D. Liu, T. R. Mitchell, T. W. Lee, B. C. Holtom, T. R. Hinkin, "How Employees Are Out of Step With Coworkers: How Job Satisfaction Trajectory and Dispersion Influence Individual- and Unit-Level Voluntary Turnover," *Academy of Management Journal* (2012), 55(6), pp. 1360–1380.

39. S. K. Parker, "Beyond Motivation: Job and Work Design for Development, Health, Ambidexterity, and More," *Annual Review of Psychology* (2014), 65, pp. 661–691.

40. Generations website, www.generations .com (retrieved June 25, 2018).

41. C. Tate, "Work Simply," *BusinessWeek* (December 22–28, 2014), p. 71.

42. A. Jagoda, "Deskilling as the Dark Side of the Work Specialization," *International Journal of Academic Research* (2013), 5(3).

43. G. Colvin, "The Art of Doing the Unpopular," *Fortune* (June 15, 2016), p. 32.

44. K. Swisher, "A Question of Management," *Wall Street Journal* (June 2, 2009), p. R4.

45. J. P. J. de Jong, S. K. Parker, S. Wennekers, C. H. Wu, "Entrepreneurial Behavior in Organizations: Does Job Design Matter?" *Entrepreneurship Theory and Practice* (2015), 39(4), pp. 981–995.

46. J. Price, "If You Leave Me Now . . . ," *INC.* (January 2015), p. 20–21.

47. A. M. Grant, "Giving Time, Time After Time: Work Design and Sustained Employee Participation in Corporate Volunteering," *Academy of Management Review* (2012), 37(4), pp. 589–615.

48. M. R. Barrick, G. R. Thurgood, T. A. Smith, S. H. Courtirght, "Collective Organizational Engagement: Linking Motivational Antecedents, Strategic Implementation, and Firm Performance," *Academy of Management Journal* (2014), 58(1), pp. 111–135.

49. C. Tuna, "Micromanagers Miss Bull's-Eye," *Wall Street Journal* (November 3, 2008), p. B4.

50. M. R. Barrick, M. K. Mount, N. Li, "The Theory of Purposeful Work Behavior: The Role of Personality, Higher-Order Goals, and Job Characteristics," *Academy of Management Review* (2013), 38(1), pp. 132–153.

51. L. McNall, A. Masuda, J. Nicklin, "Flexible Work Arrangements, Job Satisfaction, and Turnover Intentions: The Mediating Role of Work-to-Family Enrichment," *Journal of Psychology: Interdisciplinary and Applied Issue* (2010), 144(1), pp. 61–81.

52. J. H. Wayne, W. J. Casper, "Why Having a Family-Supportive Culture, Not Just Policies, Matters to Male and Female Job Seekers: An Examination of Work-Family Conflict, Values, and Self-Interest," *Sex Roles* (2016), 75(9–10), pp. 459–475.

53. U.S. Office of Personnel Management, "Performance Management: Performance Management Cycle," http://www.opm .gov/perform/articles/2001/win01–1.asp (retrieved June 25, 2018).

54. Society for Human Resource Management, "Sample Policy: Flextime," http://www.shrm.org/templatestools/samples/policies/pages/cms_007473.aspx (retrieved June 25, 2018).

55. S. Kessler, "IBM, Remote-Work Pioneer, Is Calling Thousands of Employees Back to Office," *Quartz* (March 21, 2017), https://qz.com/924167/ibm-remote-work-pioneer-is-calling-thousands-of-employees-back-to-the-office/ (retrieved June 25, 2018).

56. T. Grant, "Marissa Meyer and Telecommuting: Yahoo CEO Got It Right," *Washington Post* (March 4, 2013), https://www.washingtonpost.com/lifestyle/on-parenting/marissa-mayer-and-telecommuting-yahoo-ceo-got-it-right/2013/03/04/3d377e66–8290–11e2-a350–49866afab584_story.html?utm_term=.834aeb4a5c5e (retrieved June 25, 2018).

57. M. R. Barrick, M. K. Mount, N. Li, "The Theory of Purposeful Work Behavior: The Role of Personality, Higher-Order Goals, and Job Characteristics," *Academy of Management Review* (2013), 38(1), pp. 132–153.

58. S. Rafiei, R. Mohebbifar, F. Hashemi, M. R. Ezzatabadi, F. Farzianpour, "Approaches in Health Human Resource Forecasting: A Roadmap for Improvement," *Electronic Physician,* (2016), 8(9), p. 2911.

59. L. S. Kleiman, "Human Resource Information Systems," *Reference for Business*, http://www.referenceforbusiness.com/management/Gr-Int/Human-Resource-Information-Systems.html(retrievedJune 25, 2018).

60. S. Strohmeier, F. Piazza, "Domain Driven Data Mining in Human Resource Management: A Review of Current Research," *Expert Systems With Applications* (2013), 40(7), pp. 2410–2420.

61. http://www.sandiegouniontribune.com/news/watchdog/sdut-age-discrimination-lawsuit-hp-2016ju112-story.html(retrieved June 2, 2018).

62. "How Layoffs Hurt Companies," Wharton School, University of Pennsylvania (April 12, 2016), http://knowledge.wharton.upenn.edu/article/how-layoffs-cost-companies/ (retrieved June 25, 2018).

63. Ibid.

64. A. Schenkel, R. Teigland, "Why Doesn't Downsizing Deliver? A Multi-Level Model Integrating Downsizing, Social Capital, Dynamic Capabilities, and Firm Performance," *International Journal of Human Resource Management* (2017), 28(7), pp. 1065–1107.

65. F. Gandolfi, "HR Strategies That Can Take the Sting out of Downsizing-Related Layoffs," *Ivey Business Journal* (July/August 2008), http://iveybusinessjournal.com/topics/strategy/hr-strategies-that-can-take-the-sting-out-of-downsizing-related-layoffs#.U40RwygKTv4/.

66. K. M. Day, A. A. Armenakis, H. S. Feild, D. R. Norris, "Other Organizations Are Doing It, Why Shouldn't We? A Look at Downsizing and Organizational Identity Through an Institutional Theory Lens," *Journal of Change Management* (2012), 12(2), pp. 165–188.

67. E. Krell, "Make It Easier to Say Goodbye," *HR Magazine* (2012), 57(10), pp. 40–44.

68. U.S. Department of Labor, Wage and Overtime Division, "Overtime Pay," http://www.dol.gov/whd/overtime_pay.htm (retrieved June 25, 2018).

69. H. S. Seo, H. Kim, S. M. Hwang, S. H. Hong, I. Y. Lee, "Predictors of Job Satisfaction and Burnout Among Tuberculosis Management Nurses and Physicians," *Epidemiology and Health* (2016), 38.

70. J. Manyika, S. Lund, J. Bughin, K. Robinson, J. Mischke, D. Mahajan, "Independent Work: Choice, Necessity, and the Gig Economy," McKinsey Global Institute (October 2016), http://www.mckinsey.com/global-themes/employment-and-growth/Independent-work-Choice-necessity-and-the-gig-economy (retrieved June 25, 2018).

71. Ibid.

72. M. E. Lapalme, G. Simard, M. Tremblay, "The Influence of Psychological Contract Breach on Temporary Workers' Commitment and Behaviors: A Multiple Agency Perspective," *Journal of Business and Psychology* (2011), 26(3), pp. 311–324.

73. M. J. Chambel, F. Sobral, "Training Is an Investment With Return in Temporary Workers: A Social Exchange Perspective," *Career Development International* (2011), 16(2), pp. 161–177.

74. U.S. Equal Employment Opportunity Commission, "Strategic Enforcement Plan, Fiscal Years 2017–2021," https://www.eeoc.gov//eeoc/plan/sep-2017.cfm (retrieved June 2, 2018).

75. K. Goodwin, "How Recent Changes in the Independent Contractors Law Can Impact Workers Comp in California," *Forbes* (May 30, 2018), https://www.forbes.com/sites/forbeslacouncil/2018/05/30/how-recent-changes-in-the-independent-contractors-law-can-impact-workers-comp-in-california/#149ed361494d (retrieved June 2, 2018).

76. B. Izzo, P Narancic, "*Vizcaino v. Microsoft* Raises the Stakes on Worker Classification; Other Major Changes Give Guidance to Employers," FindLaw, http://corporate.findlaw.com/human-resources/vizcaino-v-microsoft-raises-the-stakes-on-worker-classification.html (retrieved June 2, 2018).

77. "IRS Says Fedex Owed $319 mln in Back Taxes-Filing," Reuters (December 21, 2007), http://www.reuters.com/article/2007/12/24/idUSN2129616020071224 (retrieved June 2, 2018).

78. G. Jericho, "Alleviating Skills Shortages Takes Time (and Lots of It)," *The Drum* (June 6, 2012), http://www.abc.net.au/unleashed/4053438.html.

79. M. C. Davidson, Y. Wang, "Sustainable Labor Practices? Hotel Human Resource Managers' Views on Turnover and Skill Shortages," *Journal of Human Resources in Hospitality & Tourism* (2011), 10(3), pp. 235–253.

80. J. I. Hancock, D. G. Allen, F. A. Bosco, K. R. McDaniel, C. A. Pierce, "Meta-Analytic Review of Employee Turnover as a Predictor of Firm Performance," *Journal of Management* (2013), 39(3), pp. 573–603.

81. J. Manyika, S. Lund, J. Bughin, K. Robinson, J. Mischke, D. Mahajan, "Independent Work: Choice, Necessity, and the Gig Economy," McKinsey Global Institute (October 2016), http://www.mckinsey.com/global-themes/employment-and-growth/Independent-work-Choice-necessity-and-the-gig-economy (retrieved June 25, 2018).

82. "Venture: The Growth Guru." *Fortune* (December 15, 2015). p. 52.

83. HR News, "The Rise of the Agile Workforce," *HR Magazine* (June/July 2017) p. 27.

84. J. Manyika, S. Lund, J. Bughin, K. Robinson, J. Mischke, D. Mahajan, "Independent Work: Choice, Necessity, and the Gig Economy," McKinsey Global Institute (October 2016), http://www.mckinsey.com/global-themes/employment-and-growth/Independent-work-Choice-necessity-and-the-gig-economy (retrieved June 25, 2018).

85. E. Torpey, A. Hogan, "Working in a Gig Economy," *Career Outlook*, U.S. Bureau of Labor Statistics (May 2016), https://www.bls.gov/careeroutlook/2016/article/what-is-the-gig-economy.htm (retrieved June 25, 2018).

86. "Increased Use of AI and Robotics linked to Brighter Outlook for U.S. Business Growth," Randstad Sourceright Insights (May 17, 2017), http://insights.randstadsourceright.com/h/i/344301027-increased-use-of-ai-and-robotics-linked-to-brighter-outlook-for-u-s-business-growth (retrieved June 25, 2018).

87. D. Brin, "Dire or Rosy? Dueling Views on Automation's Impact on Employment," *SHRM Newsletter* (May 30, 2017), https://www.shrm.org/resourcesandtools/hr-topics/technology/pages/dire-or-dueling-views-on-automations-impact-on-employment.aspx (retrieved June 25, 2018).

88. C. B. Frey, M. A. Osborne, "The Future of Employment: How Susceptible Are Jobs to Computerisation?" *Technological Forecasting and Social Change* (2017), 114, pp. 254–280.

89. E. Rensi, "Thanks to 'Fight for $15' Minimum Wage, McDonald's Unveils Job-Replacing Self-Service Kiosks Nationwide," *Forbes* (November 29, 2016), https://www.forbes.com/sites/realspin/2016/11/29/thanks-to-fight-for-15-minimum-wage-mcdonalds-unveils-job-replacing-self-service-kiosks-nationwide/#3a681cfe4fbc (retrieved June 25, 2018).

90. D. Brin, "Dire or Rosy? Dueling Views on Automation's Impact on Employment," *SHRM Newsletter* (May 30, 2017), https://www.shrm.org/resourcesandtools/hr-topics/technology/pages/dire-or-dueling-views-on-automations-impact-on-employment.aspx (retrieved June 25, 2018).

91. "Corporate Human Resources," Walmart, https://careers.walmart.com/corporate/human-resources (retrieved March 29, 2017).

92. M. Gledhill, "WAL-MART STORES, INC." Hoovers, http://0-subscriber.hoovers.com.liucat.lib.liu.edu/H/company360/fulldescription.html?companyId=11600000000000 (retrieved March 29, 2017).

93. A. Thompson, "Walmart's HRM: HR Planning, Job Analysis & Design," Panmore Institute (January 28, 2017), http://panmore.com/walmart-human-resource-management-planning-job-analysis-design (retrieved March 29, 2017).

Chapter 5

1. H. J. Walker, T. N. Bauer, M. S. Cole, J. B. Bernerth, H. S. Feild, J. C. Short, "Is This How I Will Be Treated? Reducing Uncertainty Through Recruitment Interactions," *Academy of Management Journal* (2013), 56(5), pp. 1325–1347.

2. E. Chang, J. Green, J. Paskin, "Amazon Has Rare Change to Get More Diverse Fast," *Bloomberg Businessweek* (May 10, 2018), https://www.bloomberg.com/news/articles/2018–05–10/amazon-has-rare-chance-in-hq2-to-hire-more-women-and-minorities (retrieved June 10, 2018).

3. L. Frye, "The Cost of a Bad Hire Can Be Astronomical," SHRM (May 9, 2017), https://www.shrm.org/resourcesandtools/hr-topics/employee-relations/pages/cost-of-bad-hires.aspx (retrieved June 25, 2018).

4. J. Sundberg, "What Is the True Cost of Hiring a Bad Employee?" Under coverRecruiter, http://theundercoverrecruiter.com/infographic-what-cost-hiring-wrong-employee/ (retrieved June 25, 2018).

5. F. Fatemi, "The True Cost of a Bad Hire: It's More Than You Think," *Forbes* (September 28, 2016), https://www.forbes.com/sites/falonfatemi/2016/09/28/the-true-cost-of-a-bad-hire-its-more-than-you-think/#3530d2df4aa4 (retrieved June 25, 2018).

6. E. Fry, C. Zillman, "HR Is Not Your Friend," *Fortune* (March 1, 2018), pp. 99–108.

7. R. E. Ployhart, J. A. Weekley, J. Ramsey, "The Consequences of Human Resource Stocks and Flow: A Longitudinal Examination of Unit Service Orientation and Unit Effectiveness," *Academy of Management Journal* (2009), 52(5), pp. 996–1015.

8. A. Tumasjan, F. Kunze, H. Bruch, "Linking Employer Branding and Firm Performance: Testing an Integrative Mediation Model," *Academy of Management Proceedings* (January 2016), 2016(1), p. 14112.

9. "How Can Analytics Help Organizations Recruit Top Talent?" Cornerstone OnDemand, http://go.cornerstoneondemand.com/HowCanAnalyticsHelpOrganization_HCM.html (retrieved June 14, 2018).

10. A. B. Holm, "Institutional Context and e-Recruitment Practices of Danish Organizations," *Employee Relations* (2014), 36(4), pp. 432–455.

11. Y. Baruch, Y. Altman, "The Ecosystem of Labor Markets and Careers," *People & Strategy* (2016), 39(3), pp. 32–34.

12. J. Dodge, "The War for Tech Talent Escalates," *Boston Globe* (February 19, 2016), https://www.bostonglobe.com/business/2016/02/19/the-war-for-tech-talent-escalates/ejUSbuPCjPLCMRYlRZIKoJ/story.html (retrieved June 14, 2018).

13. C. E. Dawkins, D. Jamali, C. Karam, L. Lin, J. Zhao, "Corporate Social Responsibility and Job Choice Intentions: A Cross-Cultural Analysis," *Business & Society* (2016), 55(6), pp. 854–888.

14. D. Stillman, J. Stillman, "Move Over, Millennials; Generation Z Is Here," SHRM (April 11, 2017), https://www.shrm.org/resourcesandtools/hr-topics/behavioral-competencies/global-and-cultural-effectiveness/pages/move-over|-millennials-generation-z-is-here.aspx (retrieved June 14, 2018).

15. X. D. Lub, P. M. Bal, R. J. Blomme, R. Schalk, "One Job, One Deal . . . or Not: Do Generations Respond Differently to Psychological Contract Fulfillment?" *International Journal of Human Resource Management*, (2016), 27(6), pp. 653–680.

16. D. Stillman, J. Stillman, "Move Over, Millennials; Generation Z Is Here," SHRM (April 11, 2017), https://www.shrm.org/resourcesandtools/hr-topics/behavioral-competencies/global-and-cultural-effectiveness/pages/move-over-millennials-generation-z-is-here.aspx (retrieved June 14, 2018).

17. J. M. Henderson, "Job Stability vs. Job Satisfaction? Millennials May Have to Settle for Neither," *Forbes* blog (December 22, 2012), http://www.forbes.com/sites/jmaureenhenderson/2012/12/22/job-stability-vs-job-satisfaction-millennials-may-have-to-settle-for-neither/.

18. Department of Justice Antitrade Division, Federal Trade Commission, "Antitrust Guidance for Human Resource Professionals" (October 2016), https://www.justice.gov/atr/file/903511/download (retrieved June 14, 2018).

19. J. Passy, "Businesses Eliminated Hundreds of Thousands of Full-Time Jobs to Avoid Obamacare Mandate," MarketWatch (November 24, 2017), https://www.marketwatch.com/story/businesses-eliminated-hundreds-of-thousands-of-full-time-jobs-to-avoid-obamacare-mandate-2017-11-24 (retrieved June 14, 2018).

20. K. Lundby (Ed.), *Going Global: Practical Applications and Recommendations for HR and OD Professionals in the Global Workplace* (San Francisco, CA: Jossey-Bass, 2010), pp. 114–115.

21. A. Kurtz, "Tip Sheet Hiring Immigration Anxiety," *INC.* (Winter 2017/2018), pp. 50–51.

22. M. Lev-Ram, "Briefing," *Fortune* (December 2017), p. 22.

23. S. Raice, "Friend—and Possible Employee," *Wall Street Journal* (October 24, 2011), p. A-2.

24. S. Fiegerman, "Facebook Tops 1.9 Billion Monthly Users," CNN Business (May 3, 2017), money.cnn.com/2017/05/03/technology/facebook-earnings/index.html (retrieved June 14, 2018).

25. J. Hempel, "LinkedIn: How It's Changing Business," *Fortune* (July 1, 2013), p. 70.

26. J. Barrett-Poindexter, "How to Find Out What a Company's Culture Is Really Like," *Glassdoor* blog (July 22, 2013), http://www.glassdoor.com/blog/find-companys-culture/ (retrieved June 14, 2018).

27. T. Greenwald, "How AI Is Transforming the Workplace," *Wall Street Journal* (March 13, 2017), R1–R2.

28. L. Efron, "How AI Is About to Disrupt Corporate Recruiting," *Forbes* (July 12, 2016) https://www.forbes.com/sites/louisefron/2016/07/12/how-a-i-is-about-to-disrupt-corporate-recruiting/#6b2234743ba2 (retrieved June 25, 2018).

29. "Meet Olivia," Paradox, https://www.recruiting.ai/olivia/ (retrieved June 25, 2018).

30. R. Maurer, "Siri for Recruiting," SHRM (February 2, 2017), https://www.shrm.org/resourcesandtools/hr-topics/talent-acquisition/pages/siri-for-recruiting-debut-2017-hiringsolved.aspx (retrieved June 25, 2018).

31. E. N. Ruggs, S. S. Walker, A. Blanchard, S. Gur, "Online Exclusion: Biases That May Arise When Using Social Media in Talent Acquisition," in *Social Media in Employee Selection and Recruitment* (Springer International, 2016) pp. 289–305.

32. J. Valentino-Devries, "Social Media and Bias in Hiring," *Wall Street Journal*, (November 21, 2013), p. B-4.

33. S. Florentine, "How Artificial Intelligence Can Eliminate Bias in Hiring," *CIO*, (December 22, 2016), http://www.cio.com/article/3152798/artificial-intelligence/how-artificial-intelligence-can-eliminate-bias-in-hiring.html (retrieved June 10, 2018).

34. T. Greenwald, "How AI Is Transforming the Workplace," *Wall Street Journal* (March 13, 2017), R1–R2.

35. Staff, "How to Win at the Hiring Game," *INC.* (June 2018), p. 62.

36. Y. Liu, G. R. Ferris, J. Xu, B. A. Weitz, P. L. Perrewe, "When Ingratiation Backfires: The Role of Political Skill in the Ingratiation–Internship Performance Relationship," *Academy of Management Learning & Education* (2014), 13(4), pp. 569–586.

37. B. Farrow, "Wegmans," *Entrepreneur* (June 2018), p. 54.

38. Jobvite Index, http://www.jobvite.com/resources/jobvite-index/ (retrieved June 14, 2018).

39. J. I. Hancock, D. G. Allen, F. A. Bosco, K. R. McDaniel, C. A. Pierce, "Meta-Analytic Review of Employee Turnover as a Predictor of Firm Performance," *Journal of Management* (2013), 39(3), pp. 573–603.

40. R. Bonet, P. Cappelli, M. Hamori, "Labor Market Intermediaries and the New Paradigm for Human Resources," *Academy of Management Annals* (2013), 7(1), pp. 341–392.

41. Staff, "How to Win at the Hiring Game," *INC.* (June 2018), p. 62.

42. A. Ladkin, D. Buhalis, "Online and Social Media Recruitment: Hospitality Employer

and Prospective Employee Considerations," *International Journal of Contemporary Hospitality Management* (2016), 28(2), pp. 327–345.

43. Staff, "How to Win at the Hiring Game," *INC.* (June 2018), p. 62.

44. E. Fry, C. Zillman, "HR Is Not Your Friend," *Fortune* (March 1, 2018), pp. 99–108.

45. S. Choudhary, "A Study on Retention Management: How to Keep Your Top Talent," *International Journal of Advanced Research in Management and Social Sciences,* (2016), 5(3), pp. 17–31.

46. N. Leekha Chhabra, S. Sharma, "Employer Branding: Strategy for Improving Employer Attractiveness," *International Journal of Organizational Analysis* (2014), 22(1), pp. 48–60.

47. ADP Research reported in *Forbes* (November 23, 2015), pp. 102–103.

48. C. C. Chen, C. S. Hsu, P. S. Tsai, "The Process Mechanisms Linking Recruiter Positive Moods and Organizational Attraction," *International Journal of Selection and Assessment* (2013), 21(4), pp. 376–387.

49. S. Overman, "Help Recruiters Vault Ahead," *Staffing Management Magazine* (2006), 2(2), pp. 32–35.

50. C. B. Felsen, E. K. Shaw, J. M. Ferrante, L. J. Lacroix, B. F. Crabtree, "Strategies for In-Person Recruitment: Lessons Learned From a New Jersey Primary Care Research Network (NJPCRN) Study," *Journal of the American Board of Family Medicine* (2010), 23(4), pp. 523–533.

51. H. Weger Jr., G. Castle Bell, E. M. Minei, M. C. Robinson, "The Relative Effectiveness of Active Listening in Initial Interactions," *International Journal of Listening* (2014), 28(1), pp. 13–31.

52. C. C. Chen, C. S. Hsu, P. S. Tsai, "The Process Mechanisms Linking Recruiter Positive Moods and Organizational Attraction," *International Journal of Selection and Assessment* (2013), 21(4), pp. 376–387.

53. R. Maurer, "New Hires Skip Out When the Role Doesn't Meet Expectations," SHRM (March 31, 2017), https://www.shrm .org/resourcesandtools/hr-topics/talent -acquisition/pages/new-hires-retention -turnover.aspx (retrieved June 25, 2018).

54. D. R. Earnest, D. G. Allen, R. S. Landis, "Mechanisms Linking Realistic Job Previews With Turnover: A Meta-Analytic Path Analysis," *Personnel Psychology* (2011), 64(4), pp. 865–897.

55. A. Handley, "Get Outta Here!" *Entrepreneur* (January 2016), p. 26.

56. ADP Research reported in *Forbes* (November 23, 2015), pp. 102–103.

57. K. Rockwood, "Tip Sheet Corporate Culture: Beyond Fitting In," *INC.* (December 2015/January 2016), pp. 112–113.

58. R. Lussier, J. Hendon, *Human Resource Management,* 2nd ed. (Thousand Oaks, CA: Sage, 2016).

59. Society for Human Resource Management, "Cost per Hire," https://www .shrm.org/resourcesandtools/business -solutions/documents/shrm_ansi_cph_ standard.pdf (retrieved June 25, 2018).

60. D. G. Allen, P. C. Bryant, J. M. Vardaman, "Retaining Talent: Replacing Misconceptions With Evidence-Based Strategies," *Academy of Management Perspectives* (2010), 24(2), pp. 48–64.

61. C. Folz, "Why Millennials Are Who They Are—And What Employers Can Learn From Them," SHRM (July 20, 2016), https://www.shrm.org/resourcesand tools/hr-topics/global-hr/pages/millenni als-.aspx (retrieved June 25, 2018).

62. C. Groden, "Five Things You Can Do to Attract Millennial Talent," Fortune.com (March 15, 2016), pp. 15–16.

63. Ibid.

64. D. Stillman, J. Stillman, "Move Over, Millennials; Generation Z Is Here," SHRM (April 11, 2017), https://www.shrm .org/resourcesandtools/hr-topics/ behavioral-competencies/global-and -cultural-effectiveness/pages/move-over -millennials-generation-z-is-here.aspx (retrieved June 25, 2018).

65. Ibid.

66. L. Quast, "Why Grit Is More Important Than IQ," *Forbes* (March 6, 2017), https://www.forbes.com/sites/lisa quast/2017/03/06/why-grit-is-more -important-than-iq-when-youre-trying -to-become-successful/#44094ca67e45 (retrieved June 25, 2018).

67. A. Duckworth, *Grit: The Power of Passion and Perseverance* (New York, NY: Simon & Schuster, 2016).

68. "Residential Construction Contractors," Hoovers, http://0-subscriber.hoovers.com .liucat.lib.liu.edu/H/industry360/des cription.html?industryId=1154 (retrieved April 5, 2017).

69. "Residential Construction Contractors," Hoovers, http://0-subscriber.hoovers.com .liucat.lib.liu.edu/H/industry360/ callPrepQuestions.html?industryId=1154 (retrieved April 5, 2017).

70. "New Homes Spur Economic Growth," National Association of Home Builders, http://www.nahb.org/en/news-and -publications/press-releases/2017/04/ new-homes-strengthen-economy-spur -job-growth.aspx (retrieved April 5, 2017).

71. D. Olick, "Homebuilders Struggle to Fill Jobs 'Americans Don't Want,'" CNBC (March 29, 2017), http://www.cnbc .com/2017/03/29/homebuilders-struggle -to-fill-jobs-americans-dont-want.html (retrieved April 5, 2017).

72. "Construction Laborers and Helpers," U.S. Bureau of Labor Statistics (December 17, 2015), https://www.bls.gov/ooh/ construction-and-extraction/construc tion-laborers-and-helpers.htm (retrieved April 5, 2017).

73. C. Kimmel, "Recruit Construction Workers Now for 2020." *Constructor,* Associated General Contractors of America, http:// www.constructormagazine.com/recruit -construction-workers-now-for-2020/# .WOVHLYWcGUm (retrieved April 5, 2017).

74. D. Olick, "Homebuilders Struggle to Fill Jobs 'Americans Don't Want.'" CNBC (March 29, 2017), http://www.cnbc .com/2017/03/29/homebuilders-struggle -to-fill-jobs-americans-dont-want.html (retrieved April 5, 2017).

Chapter 6

1. B. Farrow, "Wegmans," *Entrepreneur* (June 2018), p. 54.

2. CareerBuilder, "Bad Hires Can Be Costly," *HR Magazine* (February 2013), p. 18.

3. Z. Syed, W. Jamal, "Universalistic Perspective of HRM and Organisational Performance: Meta-Analytical Study," *International Bulletin of Business Administration* (2012), 13, pp. 47–57.

4. P. Moen, J. Lam, S. Ammons, E. L. Kelly, "Time Work by Overworked Professionals: Strategies in Response to the Stress of Higher Status," *Work and Occupations* (2013), 40(2), pp. 79–114.

5. V. Elmer, "Hiring Without a Net: Groupon's Recruiter Speaks," *Fortune* (July 25, 2011), p. 34.

6. Staff, "How to Win at the Hiring Game," *INC.* (June 2018), p. 62.

7. J. Depeters, "Cultivating a Great Workplace Starts With Its People," *Fortune* (March 1, 2018), p. 40.

8. Staff, "How to Win at the Hiring Game," *INC.* (June 2018), p. 62.

9. M. A. C. Lee, "Do Criminal Background Checks in Hiring Punish?" *Washington University Jurisprudence Review* (2017), 9(2), pp. 327–352.

10. ADP Research reported in *Forbes* (November 23, 2015), pp. 102–103.

11. S. Y. Lee, M. Pitesa, S. Thau, M. M. Pillutla, "Discrimination in Selection Decisions: Integrating Stereotype Fit and Interdependence Theories," *Academy of Management Journal* (2015), 58(3), pp. 789–812.

12. T. Jefferson, *The Declaration of Independence,* http://www.archives.gov/exhibits/ charters/declaration_transcript.html (retrieved June 28, 2018).

13. T. A. Judge, C. P. Zapata, "The Person-Situation Debate Revisited: Effect of Situation Strength and Trait Activation on the

Validity of the Big Five Personality Traits in Predicting Job Performance," *Academy of Management Journal* (2015), 58(4), pp. 1149–1179.

14. L. Weber, E. Dwoskin, "As Personality Tests Multiply, Employers Are Split," *Wall Street Journal* (September 30, 2014), pp. A1, A12.

15. E. Grijalva, P. D. Harms, "Narcissism: An Integrative Synthesis and Dominance Complementarity Model," *Academy of Management Perspectives* (2014), 28(2), pp. 108–127.

16. T. Hahn, L. Preuss, J. Pinkse, F. Figge, "Cognitive Frames in Corporate Sustainability: Managerial Sensemaking With Paradoxical and Business Case Frames," *Academy of Management Review* (2014), 39(4), pp. 463–487.

17. Staff, "Special Report Job Market 2018," *Fortune* (February 1, 2018), pp. 50–52.

18. S. Woo, "In Search of a Perfect Team," *Wall Street Journal* (March 13, 2017), p. B1.

19. G. E. Leng, M. L. C. Chin, "Person-Job Fit, Personality, Organizational Commitment and Intention to Stay Among Employees in Marketing Departments," *Jurnal Psikologi Malaysia* (2016), 30(1).

20. Staff, "Special Report Job Market 2018," *Fortune* (February 1, 2018), pp. 50–52.

21. S. Woo, "In Search of a Perfect Team," *Wall Street Journal* (March 13, 2017), p. B1.

22. T. Greenwald, "How AI Is Transforming the Workplace," *Wall Street Journal* (March 13, 2017), pp. R1–R2.

23. J. L. Burnette, J. M. Pollack, "Implicit Theories of Work and Job Fit: Implications for Job and Life Satisfaction," *Basic and Applied Social Psychology* (2013), 35(4), pp. 360–372.

24. E. M. Nolan, M. J. Morley, "A Test of the Relationship Between Person-Environment Fit and Cross-Cultural Adjustment Among Self-Initiated Expatriates," *International Journal of Human Resource Management* (2014), 25(11), published online.

25. C. Beals, "From the Recruiter," *Fortune* (March 1, 2018), p. 70.

26. D. Meinert, "Cultural Similarities Influence Hiring Decisions," *HR Magazine* (February 2013), p. 18.

27. L. A. Rivera, "Hiring as Cultural Matching the Case of Elite Professional Service Firms," *American Sociological Review* (2012), 77(6), pp. 999–1022.

28. R. Karlgaard, "The Warp-Speed Entrepreneur," *Forbes* (November 14, 2017), p. 34.

29. Staff, "How to Win at the Hiring Game," *INC.* (June 2018), p. 62.

30. K. Rockwood, "Tip Sheet Corporate Culture: Beyond Fitting in." *INC.* (December 2015/January 2016), pp. 112–113.

31. Staff "Best New Jargon: 'Culture Add,'" *Fortune* (December 15, 2017), p. 22.

32. U.S. Equal Employment Opportunity Commission, "Employment Tests and Selection Procedures" (September 23, 2010), https://www.eeoc.gov/policy/docs/factemployment_procedures.html (retrieved June 28, 2018).

33. R. Hogan, "Find Out if Your Personality Fits Your Job," *Time* (June 22, 2015), p. 45.

34. U.S. Code of Federal Regulations, "Title 29: Labor, Part 1607: Uniform Guidelines on Employee Selection Procedures (1978)," https://www.eeoc.gov/policy/docs/qanda_clarify_procedures.html (retrieved June 28, 2018).

35. Ibid.

36. Ibid.

37. Ibid.

38. Uniform Guidelines on Employee Selection Procedures, "III. General Questions Concerning Validity and the Use of Selection Procedures" (2013), http://www.uniformguidelines.com/questionandanswers.html#3 (retrieved June 28, 2018).

39. Ibid.

40. U.S. Equal Employment Opportunity Commission, http://www.eeoc.gov (retrieved June 28, 2018).

41. D. G. Allen, P. C. Bryant, J. M. Vardaman, "Retaining Talent: Replacing Misconceptions With Evidence-Based Strategies," *Academy of Management Perspectives* (2010), 24(2), pp. 48–64.

42. V. Elmer, "Hiring Without a Net: Groupon's Recruiter Speaks," *Fortune* (July 25, 2011), p. 34.

43. T. Greenwald, "How AI Is Transforming the Workplace," *Wall Street Journal* (March 13, 2017), R1–R2.

44. S. Mintz, "More Than Half of Job Applicants Lie on Their Resumes," Workplace Ethics blog (August 2, 2012), http://www.workplaceethicsadvice.com/2012/08/more-than-half-of-job-applicants-lie-on-their-resumes-advice-for-employers-to-deal-with-manipulated-resume-information-a.html (retrieved June 28, 2018).

45. H. Williams, "A Resume You Can Trust," *Wall Street Journal* (March 12, 2018), p. R5.

46. A. Fisher, "Hiring Managers Are Seeing More Lies on Resumes," *Fortune* (Apr 20, 2016), http://fortune.com/2016/04/20/hiring-managers-are-seeing-more-lies-on-resumes (retrieved June 28, 2018).

47. Staff, "Special Report Job Market 2018," *Fortune* (February 1, 2018), pp. 50–52.

48. L. Weber, "To Get a Job, New Hires Are Put to the Test," *Wall Street Journal* (April 15, 2015), pp. A1, A10.

49. Uniform Guidelines on Employee Selection Procedures, "IV. A. Criterion-Related Validity" (2013), http://www.uniformguidelines.com/questionandanswers.html#5 (retrieved June 28, 2018).

50. U.S. EEOC, "Target Corporation to Pay $2.8 Million to Resolve EEOC Discrimination Finding" press release (August 24, 2015), https://www.eeoc.gov/eeoc/newsroom/release/8-24-15.cfm, retrieved June 28, 2018

51. Employee Polygraph Protection Act of 1988 (Pub. L. 100–347, June 27, 1988), http://www.dol.gov/whd/regs/statutes/poly01.pdf (retrieved June 28, 2018).

52. National Human Genome Research Institute, "Genetic Information Nondiscrimination Act of 2008," http://www.genome.gov/10002328/ (retrieved June 28, 2018).

53. Y. Kim, R. E. Ployhart, "The Strategic Value of Selection Practices: Antecedents and Consequences of Firm-Level Selection Practice Usage," *Academy of Management Journal* (2018), 61(1), pp. 46–66.

54. T. Gutner, "Should Businesses Hire Based on Personality?" Fox Business (March 4, 2011), http://smallbusiness.foxbusiness.com/biz-on-main/2011/03/04/businesses-hire-based-personality/ (retrieved June 28, 2018).

55. B. Leonard, "Study: U.S. Millennials' Skills Don't Match Education," SHRM (March 25, 2015), http://www.shrm.org/hrdisciplines/orgempdev/articles/pages/millennials-skills-study.aspx (retrieved June 28, 2018).

56. Organisation for Economic Co-operation and Development, "Skills," http://www.oecd.org/skills/ (retrieved June 13, 2017).

57. L. Weber, E. Dwoskin, "As Personality Tests Multiple, Employers Are Split," *Wall Street Journal* (September 30, 2014), pp. A1, A12.

58. J. M. McCarthy, C. H. Van Iddekinge, F. Lievens, M. C. Kung, E. F. Sinar, M. A. Campion, "Do Candidate Reactions Relate to Job Performance or Affect Criterion-Related Validity? A Multistudy Investigation of Relations Among Reactions, Selection Test Scores, and Job Performance," *Journal of Applied Psychology* (2013), 98(5), pp. 701–719.

59. *Watson v. Fort Worth Bank & Trust*, 487 U.S. 977 (1988), http://supreme.justia.com/cases/federal/us/487/977/case.html.

60. M. L. Cunningham, H. Douglas, S. Boag, "General Mental Ability Moderates the Link Between Confidence and Integrity Test Scores," *Personality and Individual Differences* (2018), 123, pp. 94–99.

61. P. R. Sackett, O. R. Shewach, H. N. Keiser, "Assessment Centers Versus Cognitive Ability Tests: Challenging the Conventional Wisdom on Criterion-Related Validity," *Journal of Applied Psychology* (2017), 102(10), pp. 1435–1447.

62. L. Weber, "To Get a Job, New Hires Are Put to the Test," *Wall Street Journal* (April 15, 2015), pp. A1, A10.

63. W. Talamonti, L. Tijerina, M. Blommer, R. Swaminathan, R. Curry, R. D. Ellis, "Mirage Events & Driver Haptic Steering Alerts in a Motion-Base Driving Simulator: A Method for Selecting an Optimal HMI," *Applied Ergonomics* (2017), 65, pp. 90–104.

64. Science Clarified, "Chapter 3: The Virtual Classroom: Virtual Reality in Training and Education," in *Virtual Reality,* http://www.scienceclarified.com/scitech/Virtual-Reality/The-Virtual-Classroom-Virtual-Reality-in-Training-and-Education.html (retrieved June 28, 2018).

65. J. Berke, S. Gould, "Map Shows Every US State Where Pot Is Legal," *Business Insider,* http://www.businessinsider.com/legal-marijuana-states-2018–1 (retrieved June 28, 2018).

66. Supreme Court of the State of Colorado, Case No. 13SC394, https://www.courts.state.co.us/userfiles/file/Court_Probation/Supreme_Court/Opinions/2013/13SC394.pdf (retrieved June 28, 2018).

67. J. E. Kenney, S. Hoffman, "Substance Abuse Program Administrators Association (SAPAA) Position Paper on Medical Marijuana" (September 4, 2013), http://www.sapaa.com/resource/resmgr/sapaa_med_marijuana_white_p.docx.

68. R. W. Bunch, "Fitness for Duty Testing and Safety Professionals," in *ASSE Professional Development Conference and Exposition* (January 2015), American Society of Safety Engineers.

69. U.S. Equal Opportunity Commission, "ADA: FMLA; Reasonable Accommodation—Leave; Medical Exams and Inquiries," http://www.eeoc.gov/eeoc/foia/letters/2008/ada_fmla_reasonableaccommodation_leave.html (retrieved June 28, 2018).

70. J. Meister, "Future of Work: How Using AI Creates an Enhanced Candidate and Employee Experience," *Forbes* (April 10, 2018), https://www.forbes.com/sites/jeannemeister/2018/04/10/future-of-work-how-using-artificial-intelligence-creates-a-best-in-class-employee-experience/#e3bfe8d620cb (retrieved June 28, 2018).

71. H. Ismail, S. Karkoulian, "Interviewers' Characteristics and Post-Hire Attitudes and Performance," *Contemporary Management Research* (2013), 9(4).

72. J. Alsever, "How to Get a Job: Show, Don't Tell," *Fortune* (March 19, 2012), pp. 29–31.

73. D. Meinert, "Cultural Similarities Influence Hiring Decisions," *HR Magazine* (February 2013), p. 18.

74. Staff, "Million-Dollar Questions," *Entrepreneur* (January-February 2018), p. 26.

75. J. Levashina, C. J. Hartwell, F. P., Morgeson, M. A. Campion, "The Structured Employment Interview: Narrative and Quantitative Review of the Research Literature," *Personnel Psychology* (2014), 67(1), pp. 241–293.

76. F. L. Schmidt, I. S. Oh, J. A. Shaffer, "The Validity and Utility of Selection Methods in Personnel Psychology: Practical and Theoretical Implications of 100 Years of Research Findings," Working Paper (2016), https://www.testingtalent.net/wp-content/uploads/2017/04/2016–100-Yrs-Working-Paper-on-Selection-Methods-Schmit-Mar-17.pdf.

77. J. Dana, R. Dawes, N. Peterson, "Belief in the Unstructured Interview: The Persistence of an Illusion," *Judgment and Decision Making* (2013), 8(5), p. 512.

78. T. Lytle, "Streamline Hiring," *HR Magazine* (April 2013), pp. 63–65.

79. E. Poucher, "From the Recruiter," *Fortune* (March 1, 2018), p. 60.

80. D. Lortscher, "Million-Dollar Questions," *Entrepreneur* (January-February 2018), p. 26.

81. A. Bryant, "In Head-Hunting, Big Data May Not Be Such a Big Deal," *New York Times* (June 19, 2013), http://www.nytimes.com/2013/06/20/business/in-head-hunting-big-data-may-not-be-such-a-big-deal.html (retrieved June 28, 2018).

82. H. Williams, "A Resume You Can Trust," *Wall Street Journal* (March 12, 2018), p. R5.

83. "Conducting Background Checks and Reference Checks," SHRM (September 20, 2018), https://www.shrm.org/resourcesandtools/tools-and-samples/toolkits/pages/conductingbackgroundinvestigations.aspx (retrieved March 4, 2019).

84. U.S. Equal Employment Opportunity Commission and Federal Trade Commission, "Background Checks: What Employers Need to Know," http://www.eeoc.gov/eeoc/publications/background_checks_employers.cfm (retrieved June 28, 2018).

85. L. Greene, "Are Credit Checks Essential to Hiring Good Employees? Yes—Here's Why," Glassdoor (February 16, 2018), https://www.glassdoor.com/employers/blog/are-credit-checks-essential-to-hiring-good-employees-yes-heres-why/ (retrieved June 28, 2018).

86. Federal Trade Commission, "Background Checks" (March 2018), https://www.consumer.ftc.gov/articles/0157-background-checks (retrieved June 28, 2018).

87. A. Preston, "Disney Sued for Misusing Background Checks" (November 20, 2013), https://www.shrm.org/resourcesandtools/hr-topics/risk-management/pages/disney-sued-background-checks.aspx (retrieved June 28, 2018).

88. 11 U.S. Code § 525: Protection Against Discriminatory Treatment, https://www.law.cornell.edu/uscode/text/11/525/ (retrieved June 28, 2018).

89. EEOC, "Consideration of Arrest and Conviction Records in Employment Decisions Under Title VII of the Civil Rights Act of 1964, https://www.eeoc.gov/laws/guidance/arrest_conviction.cfm#IIIB (retrieved June 28, 2018).

90. R. Maurer, "Indiana First State to Bar Local 'Ban the Box' Laws," SHRM (May 11, 2017) https://www.shrm.org/resourcesandtools/hr-topics/talent-acquisition/pages/indiana-first-state-bar-local-ban-box-laws.aspx (retrieved June 28, 2018).

91. R. Maurer, "HR Weeds Out Applicants Through Public Social Searches," SHRM (January 19, 2016), https://www.shrm.org/resourcesandtools/hr-topics/talent-acquisition/pages/hr-weeds-out-applicants-social-searches.aspx (retrieved June 28, 2018).

92. S. P. Joyce, "To Be Hired, You First Must Be Found," *Forbes* (May 17, 2017), https://www.forbes.com/sites/forbescoachescouncil/2017/05/17/to-be-hired-you-first-must-be-found/#1133d54e3394 (retrieved June 28, 2018).

93. D. Faulkner, "Why Googling Candidates Before You Decide to Interview Them Is Against the Law" *ADP* (March 1, 2017), https://www.adp.com/spark/articles/2017/03/why-googling-candidates-before-you-decide-to-interview-them-is-against-the-law.aspx (retrieved June 28, 2018).

94. G. M. Saylin, T. C. Horrocks, "The Risks of Pre-employment Social Media Screening" (July 18, 2013), http://www.shrm.org/hrdisciplines/staffingmanagement/articles/pages/preemployment-social-media-screening.aspx (retrieved June 28, 2018).

95. S. Barreiro, "Sexual Orientation Discrimination: Your Rights," NOLO, http://www.nolo.com/legal-encyclopedia/sexual-orientation-discrimination-rights-29541.html (retrieved June 28, 2018).

96. N. R. Kuncel, D. M. Klieger, B. S. Connelly, D. S. Ones, "Mechanical Versus Clinical Data Combination in Selection and Admissions Decisions: A Meta-Analysis," *Journal of Applied Psychology* (2013), 98(6), pp. 1060–1072.

97. Ibid.

98. S. Y. Lee, M. Pitesa, S. Thau, M. M. Pillutla, "Discrimination in Selection Decisions: Integrating Stereotype Fit and Interdependence Theories," *Academy of Management Journal* (2015), 58(3), pp. 789–812.

99. Links of London, "About Us," http://www.linksoflondon.com/us-en/about/about-us (retrieved April 13, 2017).

100. H. Sherman, T. Tae, "'Linking' Expectations and Culture at Links of London" *Journal of Business and Retail Management* (July 2016), 10(3), pp. 57–68.

101. Links of London, "Culture," http://www.linksoflondon.com/us-en/careers/culture (retrieved April 13, 2017).

102. Ibid.

Chapter 7

1. B. Farrow, "Wegmans," *Entrepreneur* (June 2018), p. 54.

2. T. Goetz, "You'd Better Get Write on It," *INC.* (June 2018), p. 52.

3. V. Kumar, A. Pansari, "Measuring the Benefits of Employee Engagement," *MIT Sloan Management Review* (2015), 56(4), pp. 67–72.

4. D. G. Allen, P. C. Bryant, J. M. Vardaman, "Retaining Talent: Replacing Misconceptions With Evidence-Based Strategies," *Academy of Management Perspectives* (2010), 24(2), pp. 48–64.

5. K. Pajo, A. Coetzer, N. Guenole, "Formal Development Opportunities and Withdrawal Behavior by Employees in Small and Medium-Sized Enterprises," *Journal of Small Business Management* (2010), 48(3), pp. 281–301.

6. T. Goetz, "You'd Better Get Write on It," *INC.* (June 2018), p. 52.

7. B. Shoot, "HR Made Easier," *Entrepreneur* (June 2015), p. 80.

8. V. Kumar, A. Pansari, A. "Measuring the Benefits of Employee Engagement," *MIT Sloan Management Review* (2015), 56(4), pp. 67–72.

9. M. Festing, "Strategic Human Resource Management in Germany," *Academy of Management Perspectives* (2012), 26(2), pp. 37–54.

10. A. Fox, "Help Managers Shine," *HR Magazine* (February 2013), pp. 43–46.

11. B. Schyns, T. Kiefer, R. Kerschreiter, A. Tymon, "Teaching Implicit Leadership Theories to Develop Leaders and Leadership: How and Why It Can Make a Difference," *Academy of Management Learning & Education* (2011), 10(3), pp. 397–408.

12. "100 Best Companies to Work For," *Fortune,* http://fortune.com/best-companies/ (retrieved June 29, 2018).

13. B. D. Blume, J. K. Ford, E. A. Surface, J. Olenick, "A Dynamic Model of Training Transfer," *Human Resource Management Review* (2019), 29(2), 270–283.

14. J. Daley, "Is an MBA Still Necessary?" *Entrepreneur* (October 2012), http://www.entrepreneur.com/article/224440/ (retrieved July 14, 2018).

15. T. Ungaretti, K. R. Thompson, A. Miller, T. O. Peterson, "Problem-Based Learning: Lessons From Medical Education and Challenges for Management Education," *Academy of Management Learning & Education* (2015), 14(2), pp. 173–186.

16. T. Sitzmann, K. Ely, K. G. Brown, K. N. Bauer, "Self-Assessment of Knowledge: A Cognitive Learning or Affective Measure?" *Academy of Management Learning & Education* (2010), 9(2), pp. 169–191.

17. Y. Dong, M. G. Seo, K. M. Bartol, "No Pain, No Gain: An Affect-Based Model of Developmental Job Experience and the Buffering Effects of Emotional Intelligence," *Academy of Management Journal* (2014), 57(4), pp. 1056–1077.

18. G. Colvin, "Ignore These Leadership Lessons at Your Peril," *Fortune* (October 28, 2013), p. 85.

19. R. Miller, "How Productive Is the U.S.?" *Businessweek* (March 2–8, 2015), pp. 16–17.

20. S. Ben-Hur, B. Jaworski, D. Gray, "Aligning Corporate Learning With Strategy," *MIT Sloan Management Review* (2015), 57(1), p. 53.

21. S. Liu, M. Wang, P. Barmberger, J. Shi, S. B. Bacharach, "The Dark Side of Socialization: A Longitudinal Investigation of Newcomer Alcohol Use," *Academy of Management Journal* (2015), 58(2), 334–355.

22. M. Voronov, K. Weber, "The Heart of Institutions: Emotional Competence and Institutional Actorhood," *Academy of Management Review* (2016), 41(3), 456–478.

23. L. Jia, J. D. Shaw, A. S. Tsue, T. Y. Park, "A Social-Structural Perspective on Employee-Organization Relationships and Team Creativity," *Academy of Management Journal* (2014), 57(3), pp. 869–891.

24. R. Lussier, J. Hendon, *Human Resource Management,* 2nd ed. (Thousand Oaks, CA: Sage, 2016).

25. G. O'Brien, "Putting Everyone at Ease," *Entrepreneur* (July 2015), p. 30.

26. D. G. Allen, P. C. Bryant, J. M. Vardaman, "Retaining Talent: Replacing Misconceptions With Evidence-Based Strategies," *Academy of Management Perspectives* (2010), 24(2), pp. 48–64.

27. R. E. Silverman, "First Day on Job: Not Just Paperwork," *Wall Street Journal* (May 28, 2013), p. D1.

28. D. G. Allen, L. R. Shanock, "Perceived Organizational Support and Embeddedness as Key Mechanisms Connecting Socialization Tactics to Commitment and Turnover Among New Employees," *Journal of Organizational Behavior* (2013), 34(3), pp. 350–369.

29. C. Tschopp, G. Grote, M. Gerber, "How Career Orientation Shapes the Job Satisfaction–Turnover Intention Link," *Journal of Organizational Behavior* (2014), 35(2), pp. 151–171.

30. S. Liu, M. Wang, P. Barmberger, J. Shi, S. B. Bacharach, "The Dark Side of Socialization: A Longitudinal Investigation of Newcomer Alcohol Use," *Academy of Management Journal* (2015), 58(2), pp. 334–355.

31. A. M. Meyer, L. K. Bartels, "The Impact of Onboarding Levels on Perceived Utility, Organizational Commitment, Organizational Support, and Job Satisfaction," *Journal of Organizational Psychology* (2017), 17(5), pp. 10–27.

32. C. Hann, "Go Get 'Em," *Entrepreneur* (July 2014), p. 34.

33. R. Lussier, J. Hendon, *Human Resource Management,* 2nd ed. (Thousand Oaks, CA: Sage, 2016).

34. D. G. Allen, P. C. Bryant, J. M. Vardaman, "Retaining Talent: Replacing Misconceptions With Evidence-Based Strategies," *Academy of Management Perspectives* (2010), 24(2), pp. 48–64.

35. R. Maurer, "Onboarding Key to Retaining, Engaging Talent," SHRM (April 16, 2017), https://www.shrm.org/resourcesand-tools/hr-topics/talent-acquisition/pages/onboarding-key-retaining-engaging-talent.aspx (retrieved July 14, 2018).

36. V. Fitoussi, "Top 10 Onboarding Programs," (March 1, 2019), https://www.saplinghr.com/blog/top-employee-onboarding-programs (retrieved March 6, 2019).

37. P. Gjerløv-Juel, C. Guenther, "Early Employment Expansion and Long-Run Survival Examining Employee Turnover as a Context Factor," *Journal of Business Venturing* (2019), 34(1), pp. 80–102.

38. R. Miller, "How Productive Is the U.S.?" *Businessweek* (March 2–8, 2015), pp. 16–17.

39. L. W. Chen, P. Thompson, "Skill Balance and Entrepreneurship Evidence From Online Career Histories," *Entrepreneurship Theory and Practice* (2016), 40(2), pp. 289–304.

40. A. M. Meyer, L. K. Bartels, "The Impact of Onboarding Levels on Perceived Utility, Organizational Commitment, Organizational Support, and Job Satisfaction," *Journal of Organizational Psychology* (2017), 17(5), pp. 10–27.

41. S. Ben-Hur, B. Jaworski, D. Gray, "Aligning Corporate Learning With Strategy," *MIT Sloan Management Review* (2015), 57(1), p. 53.

42. A. M. Dachner, B. Polin, "A Systematic Approach to Educating the Emerging Adult Learner in Undergraduate Management Courses," *Journal of Management Education* (2016), 40(2), pp. 121–151.

43. I. Nooyi, "CEO 101," *Fortune* (November 17, 2014), p. 129.

44. T. C. Bednall, K. Sanders, P. Runhaar, "Stimulating Informal Learning Activities Through Perceptions of Performance Appraisal Quality and Human Resource

Management System Strength: A Two-Wave Study," *Academy of Management Learning & Education* (2014), 13(1), pp. 45–61.

45. S. Robbins, M. Coulter, *Management* (Saddle River, NJ: Pearson Education, 2014), p. 466.

46. M. O'Callaghan, G. Thomas, "Pavlovian Principles and Behaviour Therapy," in *Applications of Conditioning Theory* (New York, NY: Routledge, 2017), pp. 129–148.

47. C. B. Sturdy, E. Nicoladis, "How Much of Language Acquisition Does Operant Conditioning Explain?" *Frontiers in Psychology* (2017), 8, p. 1918.

48. M. Muthukrishna, T. J. Morgan, J. Henrich, "The When and Who of Social Learning and Conformist Transmission," *Evolution and Human Behavior* (2016), 37(1), pp. 10–20.

49. I. P. Tussyadiah, "Technology and Behavioral Design in Tourism," in *Design Science in Tourism* (Cham, Switzerland: Springer, 2017), pp. 173–191.

50. Company Spotlight, "More Happiness, More Revenue: Ryan's Story," *Fortune* (March 15, 2015), p. 20.

51. B. M. Smith, G. S. Smith, T. A. Shahan, G. J. Madden, M. P. Twohig, "Effects of Differential Rates of Alternative Reinforcement on Resurgence of Human Behavior," *Journal of the Experimental Analysis of Behavior* (2017), 107(1), 191–202.

52. C. Borgmeier, S. L. Loman, M. Hara, B. J. Rodriguez, "Training School Personnel to Identify Interventions Based on Functional Behavioral Assessment," *Journal of Emotional and Behavioral Disorders* (2015), 23(2), pp. 78–89.

53. B. O. Martin, K. Kolomitro, T. C. Lam, "Training Methods: A Review and Analysis," *Human Resource Development Review* (2014), 13(1), pp. 11–35.

54. L. W. Chen, P. Thompson, "Skill Balance and Entrepreneurship Evidence From Online Career Histories," *Entrepreneurship Theory and Practice* (2016), 40(2), pp. 289–304.

55. B. L. Rau, "The Oxford Handbook of Evidence-Based Management," *Academy of Management Learning & Education* (2014), 13(3), pp. 485–487.

56. S. Ahadi, R. L. Jacobs, "A Review of the Literature on Structured On-the-Job Training and Directions for Future Research," *Human Resource Development Review* (2017), 16(4), pp. 323–349.

57. M. Kang, W. S. Shin, "An Empirical Investigation of Student Acceptance of Synchronous e-Learning in an Online University," *Journal of Educational Computing Research* (2015), 52(4), pp. 475–495.

58. L. Kolodny, "A New Way to Train Workers, One Small Bite at a Time," *Wall Street Journal* (March 14, 2016), p. R6.

59. M. Magni, C. Paolino, R. Cappetta, L. Proserpio, "Diving Too Deep: How Cognitive Absorption and Group Learning Behavior Affect Individual Learning," *Academy of Management Learning & Education* (2013), 12(1), pp. 51–69.

60. A. Ferracani, D. Pezzatini, L. Seidenari, A. Del Bimbo, "Natural and Virtual Environments for the Training of Emergency Medicine Personnel," *Universal Access in the Information Society* (2015), 14(3), pp. 351–362.

61. P. E. Kennedy, S. Y. Chyung, D. J. Winiecki, R. O. Brinkerhoff, "Training Professionals' Usage and Understanding of Kirkpatrick's Level 3 and Level 4 Evaluations," *International Journal of Training and Development* (2014), 18(1), pp. 1–21.

62. D. S. Chiaburu, J. L. Huang, H. M. Hutchins, R. G. Gardner, "Trainees' Perceived Knowledge Gain Unrelated to the Training Domain: The Joint Action of Impression Management and Motives," *International Journal of Training and Development* (2014), 18(1), pp. 37–52.

63. Ibid.

64. Information added based on reviewer David Biemer, Texas State University, suggestion May 9, 2017.

65. D. T. Hall, *Careers in and out of Organizations* (Thousand Oaks, CA: Sage, 2002).

66. R. A. Noe, A. D. Clarke, H. J. Klein, "Learning in The Twenty-First-Century Workplace," *Annual Review of Organizational Psychology and Organizational Behavior* (2014), 1(1), pp. 245–275.

67. ADP (Ed.), "Outsourcing and the Future of HR," ADP (2012), p. 3.

68. Jon Hay (Ed.), "HR Outsourcing Trends and Insights 2009," *Hewitt Associates* (2009), p. 10.

69. C. Hu, S. Wang, C. C. Yang, T. Y. Wu, "When Mentors Feel Supported: Relationships With Mentoring Functions and Protégés' Perceived Organizational Support," *Journal of Organizational Behavior* (2014), 35(1), pp. 22–37.

70. S. Humphrey, F. Morgeson, M. Mannor, "Developing a Theory of the Strategic Core of Teams: A Role Composition Model of Team Performance," *Journal of Applied Psychology* (2009), 94(1), pp. 48–61.

71. D. Super, D. Hall, "Career Development: Exploration and Planning," *Annual Review of Psychology* (1978), 29, pp. 333–372.

72. S. Parkin, "Was Gamification a Terrible Lie?" (November 18, 2017), https://how wegettonext.com/was-gamification-a-terrible-lie-3e845b97bb93 (retrieved June 20, 2017).

73. J. Meister, "The Future of Work: How to Use Gamification for Talent Management," *Forbes* (May 21, 2012), http://www.forbes .com/sites/jeannemeister/2012/05/21/ gamification-three-ways-to-use-gaming -for-recruiting-training-and-health-amp -wellness/ (retrieved June 13, 2014).

74. Gallup, "The Broken Link Between Higher Education and Workplace Readiness," (December 15, 2015), http://www .gallup.com/opinion/gallup/187685/ broken-link-higher-education-workplace -readiness.aspx?g_source=&g_medium= &g_campaign=tiles (retrieved June 20, 2017).

75. B. Carroll, E. Park, R. Singaraju, "Corporate Learning Factbook 2015: Benchmarks, Trends, and Analysis of the UK Training Market," Bersin by Deloitte (2016), http://www.bersin.com/Practice/ Detail.aspx?id=19469 (retrieved June 20, 2017).

76. Ibid.

77. J. Bersin, "The Disruption of Digital Learning: Ten Things We Have Learned," (March 17, 2017), http://joshbersin .com/2017/03/the-disruption-of-digital -learning-ten-things-we-have-learned/ (retrieved June 20, 2017).

78. Ibid.

79. "Lifelong Learning Is Becoming an Economic Imperative," *The Economist* (January 12, 2017), http://www.economist .com/news/special-report/21714169 -technological-change-demands-stronger -and-more-continuous-connections -between-education (retrieved June 20, 2017).

80. K. Gurchiek, "Digital Age Is Rewriting the Rules for Employee Learning," SHRM (May 15, 2017), https://www.shrm.org/resources andtools/hr-topics/organizational -and-employee-development/pages/ digital-age-is-rewriting-the-rules-for -employee-learning.aspx (retrieved June 20, 2017).

81. L. Oliver, "Nestlé S.A.," *Hoovers*, http://0-subscriber.hoovers.com.liucat.lib.liu .edu/H/company360/fulldescription .html?companyId=41815000000000 (retrieved April 26, 2017).

82. "Nestlé: At a Glance," http://www.nestle .com/aboutus/overview (retrieved April 26, 2017).

83. A. Francis, "Case Study of Nestlé: Training and Development," https://www .mbaknol.com/management-case-stud ies/case-study-of-nestle-training-and -development (retrieved April 26, 2017).

84. "Nestlé: Business Ownership of Skills," http://www.nestle.co.uk/ productivity/ owning-the-skills-pipeline (retrieved April 26, 2017).

85. A. Francis, "Case Study of Nestlé: Training and Development," https://www .mbaknol.com/management-case-studies/ case-study-of-nestle-training-and-devel opment (retrieved April 26, 2017).

Chapter 8

1. E. G. Barends, R. B. Briner, "Teaching Evidence-Based Practice: Lessons From the Pioneers: An Interview With Amanda Burls and Gordon Guyatt," *Academy of Management Learning & Education* (2014), 13(3), pp. 476–483.

2. D. G. Allen, P. C. Bryant, J. M. Vardaman, "Retaining Talent: Replacing Misconceptions With Evidence-Based Strategies," *Academy of Management Perspectives* (2010), 24(2), pp. 48–64.

3. E. Fry, C. Zillman, "HR Is Not Your Friend," *Fortune* (March 1, 2018), pp. 99–108.

4. E. Van Oosten, K. E. Kram, "Coaching for Change," *Academy of Management Learning & Education* (2014), 13(2), pp. 295–298.

5. J. Welch, S. Welch, "Dealing With the Morning-After Syndrome at Facebook," *Fortune* (March 19, 2012), p. 92.

6. M. K. Duffy, K. L. Scott, J. D. Shaw, B. J. Tepper, K. Aquino, "A Social Context Model of Envy and Social Undermining," *Academy of Management Journal* (2012), 55(3), pp. 643–666.

7. Ibid.

8. Mercer's 2017 Compensation Planning and Performance Management Webcast, Mercer (2016), https://www.mercer.com/content/dam/mercer/attachments/global/webcasts/gl-2016-talent-compensation-planning-performance-management-mercer.pdf (retrieved July 30, 2018).

9. A. S. DeNisi, "Managing Performance to Change Behavior," *Journal of Organizational Behavior Management* (2011), 31(4), pp. 262–276.

10. P. McCord, "How Netflix Reinvented HR," *Harvard Business Review* (2014), p. 1.

11. "The End of Annual Performance Reviews: Are the Alternatives Any Better?" Knowledge@Wharton, Wharton School of Business, University of Pennsylvania (September 19, 2016), http://knowledge.wharton.upenn.edu/article/the-end-of-annual-performance-reviews/ (retrieved July 30, 2018).

12. A. Wright, "Tech Company SAP Eliminates Annual Performance Reviews," SHRM (August 18, 2017), https://www.shrm.org/resourcesandtools/hr-topics/technology/pages/sap-eliminates-annual-performance-reviews.aspx (retrieved July 30, 2018).

13. E. Dunn, "Performance Anxiety," *Entrepreneur* (May 2018), pp. 18–19.

14. Ibid.

15. D. Wilkie, "If the Annual Performance Review Is on Its Way Out, What Can Replace It?" SHRM (December 7, 2015), https://www.shrm.org/resourcesandtools/hr-topics/employee-relations/pages/performance-reviews-dead.aspx (retrieved July 30, 2018).

16. A. Smith, "Without Performance Reviews, How to Handle Pay Equity, Firings," SHRM (May 9, 2017), https://www.shrm.org/resourcesandtools/legal-and-compliance/employment-law/pages/without-performance-reviews.aspx (retrieved July 30, 2018).

17. D. Meinert, "Is It Time to Put the Performance Review on a PIP?" SHRM, https://www.shrm.org/hr-today/news/hr-magazine/pages/0415-qualitative-performance-reviews.aspx (retrieved July 30, 2018).

18. "The End of Annual Performance Reviews: Are the Alternatives Any Better?" Knowledge@Wharton, Wharton School of Business, University of Pennsylvania (September 19, 2016), http://knowledge.wharton.upenn.edu/article/the-end-of-annual-performance-reviews/ (retrieved July 30, 2018).

19. ADP Research reported in *Forbes* (November 23, 2015), pp. 102–103.

20. P. Jacquart, J. Antonakis, "When Does Charisma Matter for Top-Level Leaders? Effect of Attributional Ambiguity," *Academy of Management Journal* (2015), 58(4), pp. 1051–1074.

21. L. Manganelli, A. Thibault-Landry, J. Forest, J. Carpentier, "Self-Determination Theory Can Help You Generate Performance and Well-Being in the Workplace: A Review of the Literature," *Advances in Developing Human Resources* (2018), 20(2), pp. 227–240.

22. "Master Class," *Businessweek* (May 6–12, 2013), p. 83.

23. E. Dunn, "Performance Anxiety," *Entrepreneur* (May 2018), pp. 18–19.

24. K. Gurchiek, "New HR Standard on Performance Management," *HR Magazine* (April 2013), p. 74.

25. L. Manganelli, A. Thibault-Landry, J. Forest, J. Carpentier, "Self-Determination Theory Can Help You Generate Performance and Well-Being in the Workplace: A Review of the Literature," *Advances in Developing Human Resources* (2018), 20(2), pp. 227–240.

26. C. Hann, "Looking Back," *Entrepreneur* (October 2014), p. 36.

27. E. Van Oosten, K. E. Kram, "Coaching for Change," *Academy of Management Learning & Education* (2014), 13(2), pp. 295–298.

28. S. Marikar, "Tools for Your Remote Team," *INC.* (December 2015/January 2016), pp. 88–89.

29. P. B. Whyman, A. I. Petrescu, "Workplace Flexibility Practices in SMEs Relationship with Performance via Redundancies, Absenteeism, and Financial Turnaround," *Journal of Small Business Management* (2015), 53(4), pp. 1097–1126.

30. S. A. Culbert, "Get Rid of the Performance Review," *Wall Street Journal* (October 20, 2008), p. R4.

31. D. G. Allen, P. C. Bryant, J. M. Vardaman, "Retaining Talent: Replacing Misconceptions With Evidence-Based Strategies," *Academy of Management Perspectives* (2010), 24(2), pp. 48–64.

32. E. Dunn, "Performance Anxiety," *Entrepreneur* (May 2018), pp. 18–19.

33. I. A. Scott, G. Phelps, C. Brand, "Assessing Individual Clinical Performance: A Primer for Physicians," *Internal Medicine Journal* (2011), 41(2), pp. 144–155.

34. Ibid.

35. "Managing Employee Performance," SHRM, http://www.shrm.org/templatestools/toolkits/pages/managingemployeeperformance.aspx (retrieved July 30, 2018).

36. Y. M. A. Amuna, M. J. Al Shobaki, S. S. A. Naser, "The Role of Knowledge-Based Computerized Management Information Systems in the Administrative Decision-Making Process," *International Journal of Information Technology and Electrical Engineering* (2017), 6(2), 1–9.

37. R. R. Hastings, "Performance Appraisals Used to Motivate, Weed Out," SHRM (July 20, 2009), http://www.shrm.org/hrdisciplines/employeerelations/articles/Pages/UsedtoMotivateWeedOut.aspx (retrieved July 30, 2018).

38. P. F. Buller, G. M. McEvoy, "Strategy, Human Resource Management and Performance: Sharpening Line of Sight," *Human Resource Management Review* (2012), 22(1), pp. 43–56.

39. A. L. Olsen, "Human Interest or Hard Numbers? Experiments on Citizens' Selection, Exposure, and Recall of Performance Information," *Public Administration Review* (2017), 77(3), pp. 408–420.

40. T. A. Judge, C. P. Zapata, "The Person–Situation Debate Revisited: Effect of Situation Strength and Trait Activation on the Validity of the Big Five Personality Traits in Predicting Job Performance," *Academy of Management Journal* (2015), 58(4), pp. 1149–1179.

41. P. Mussel, "Introducing the Construct Curiosity for Predicting Job Performance," *Journal of Organizational Behavior* (2013), 34(4), pp. 453–472.

42. K. Blanchard, D. Hudson, E. Wills, *The One Minute Entrepreneur* (New York, NY: Currency, 2008).

43. J. Goodale, "Behaviorally-Based Rating Scales: Toward an Integrated Approach to Performance Appraisal," *Contemporary Problems in Personnel* (Chicago, IL: St. Clair Press, 1977), p. 247.

44. K. Blanchard, D. Hutson, E. Wills, *The One Minute Entrepreneur* (New York, NY: Currency, 2008).

45. Company Spotlight, "More Happiness, More Revenue: Ryan's Story," *Fortune* (March 15, 2015), p. 20.

46. Ibid.

47. E. Fry, C. Zillman, "HR Is Not Your Friend," *Fortune* (March 1, 2018), pp. 99–108.

48. J. Mayne, "Accountability for Program Performance: A Key to Effective Performance Monitoring and Reporting," in *Monitoring Performance in the Public Sector* (New York, NY: Routledge, 2017), pp. 157–176.

49. A. Cohen, "When Do You Do Your Best Thinking?" M. Buckley response, *Businessweek* (May 14, 2015), p. 78.

50. E. Dunn, "Performance Anxiety," *Entrepreneur* (May 2018), pp. 18–19.

51. H. K. Fulk, R. L. Bell, N. Bodie, "Team Management by Objectives: Enhancing Developing Teams' Performance," *Journal of Management Policy and Practice* (2011), 12(3), pp. 17–26.

52. M. B. Bjerke, R. Renger, "Being Smart About Writing SMART Objectives," *Evaluation and Program Planning* (2017), 61, 125–127.

53. E. Dunn, "Performance Anxiety," *Entrepreneur* (May 2018), pp. 18–19.

54. H. K. Fulk, R. L. Bell, N. Bodie, "Team Management by Objectives: Enhancing Developing Teams' Performance," *Journal of Management Policy and Practice* (2011), 12(3), pp. 17–26.

55. S. McCartney, "How US Airways Vaulted to First Place," *Wall Street Journal* (July 22, 2009), p. D3.

56. R. E. Silverman, "GE Tries to Reinvent The Employee Review, Encouraging Risks," *Wall Street Journal* (June 8, 2016), p. B1.

57. R. Karlgaad, "Do Jerks Always Win?" *Forbes* (December 29, 2014), p. 44.

58. K. Blanchard, D. Hutson, E. Wills, *The One Minute Entrepreneur* (New York, NY: Currency, 2008).

59. E. Dunn, "Performance Anxiety," *Entrepreneur* (May 2018), pp. 18–19.

60. Ibid.

61. A. C. Loignon, D. J. Woehr, J. S. Thomas, M. L. Loughry, M. W. Ohland, D. M. Ferguson, "Facilitating Peer Evaluation in Team Contexts: The Impact of Frame-of-Reference Rater Training," *Academy of Management Learning & Education* (2017), 16(4), pp. 562–578.

62. R. E. Silverman, "Going Bossless Backfires at Zappos," *Wall Street Journal* (May 21, 2015), pp. A1, A10.

63. E. Dunn, "Performance Anxiety," *Entrepreneur* (May 2018), pp. 18–19.

64. A. Sudarsan, "Concurrent Validity of Peer Appraisal of Group Work for Administrative Purposes," *IUP Journal of Organizational Behavior* (2010), 9(1–2), pp. 73–86.

65. A. C. Loignon, D. J. Woehr, J. S. Thomas, M. L. Loughry, M. W. Ohland, D. M. Ferguson, "Facilitating Peer Evaluation in Team Contexts: The Impact of Frame-of-Reference Rater Training," *Academy of Management Learning & Education* (2017), 16(4), pp. 562–578.

66. R. R. Hastings, "Manager, Employee Perceptions of Performance Differ," SHRM (April 20, 2009), http://www.shrm.org/ hrdisciplines/employeerelations/articles/ Pages/ManagerEmployeePerceptions .aspx (retrieved July 30, 2018).

67. J. L. Brown, S. Farrington, G. B. Sprinkle, "Biased Self-Assessments, Feedback, and Employees' Compensation Plan Choices," *Accounting, Organizations and Society* (2016), 54, pp. 45–59.

68. M. Matthews, S. Beal, "Assessing Situation Awareness in Field Training Exercises," U.S. Army Research Institute for the Behavioral and Social Sciences Research Report 1795 (2002).

69. J. L. Brown, S. Farrington, G. B. Sprinkle, "Biased Self-Assessments, Feedback, and Employees' Compensation Plan Choices," *Accounting, Organizations and Society* (2016), 54, pp. 45–59.

70. M. Sonnenberg, V. van Zijderveld, M. Brinks, "The Role of Talent-Perception Incongruence in Effective Talent Management," *Journal of World Business* (2014), 49(2), pp. 272–280.

71. H. Han, S. S. Hyun, "Image Congruence and Relationship Quality in Predicting Switching Intention Conspicuousness of Product Use as a Moderator Variable," *Journal of Hospitality & Tourism Research* (2013), 37(3), pp. 303–329.

72. S. M. Nurudeen, G. Kwakye, W. R. Berry, E. L. Chaikof, K. D. Lillemoe, F. Millham, . . . L. Sato, "Can 360-Degree Reviews Help Surgeons? Evaluation of Multisource Feedback for Surgeons in a Multi-Institutional Quality Improvement Project," *Journal of the American College of Surgeons* (2015), 221(4), pp. 837–844.

73. E. Dunn, "Can the Annual Review Be Replaced By an App?" *Entrepreneur* (May 2018), pp. 18–19.

74. E. M. Mone, M. London, *Employee Engagement Through Effective Performance Management: A Practical Guide for Managers* (New York, NY: Routledge, 2011).

75. S. M. Nurudeen, G. Kwakye, W. R. Berry, E. L. Chaikof, K. D. Lillemoe, F. Millham, . . . L. Sato, "Can 360-Degree Reviews Help Surgeons? Evaluation of Multisource Feedback for Surgeons in a Multi-Institutional Quality Improvement Project," *Journal of the American College of Surgeons* (2015), 221(4), pp. 837–844.

76. J. P. Forgas, S. M. Laham, "Halo Effects," in *Cognitive Illusions: Intriguing Phenomena in Judgement, Thinking and Memory* (New York, NY: Taylor & Francis, 2016), p. 276.

77. A. N. Esfahani, M. Abzari, S. Dezianian, "Analyzing the Effect of Performance Appraisal Errors on Perceived Organizational Justice," *International Journal of Academic Research in Accounting, Finance and Management Sciences* (2014), 4(1), pp. 36–40.

78. E. Dunn, "Performance Anxiety," *Entrepreneur* (May 2018), pp. 18–19.

79. P. Jacquart, J. Antonakis, "When Does Charisma Matter for Top-Level Leaders? Effect of Attributional Ambiguity," *Academy of Management Journal* (2015), 58(4), pp. 1051–1074.

80. E. Bernstein, "The Smart Path to a Transparent Workplace," *Wall Street Journal* (February 23, 2015), p. R5.

81. C. Dusterhoff, J. B. Cunningham, J. N. MacGregor, "The Effects of Performance Rating, Leader-Member Exchange, Perceived Utility, and Organizational Justice on Performance Appraisal Satisfaction: Applying a Moral Judgment Perspective," *Journal of Business Ethics* (2014), 119(2), pp. 265–273.

82. R. Bommelje, "Managerial Coaching," *New Directions for Adult and Continuing Education* (2015), 2015(148), pp. 69–77.

83. D. G. Allen, P. C. Bryant, J. M. Vardaman, "Retaining Talent: Replacing Misconceptions With Evidence-Based Strategies," *Academy of Management Perspectives* (2010), 24(2), pp. 48–64.

84. E. Gibson, "The Stop-Managing Guide to Management," *Businessweek* (June 15, 2009), p. 73.

85. Ibid.

86. D. G. Allen, P. C. Bryant, J. M. Vardaman, "Retaining Talent: Replacing Misconceptions With Evidence-Based Strategies," *Academy of Management Perspectives* (2010), 24(2), pp. 48–64.

87. S. Soper, ""Inside Amazon's People's Court," *Businessweek* (July 2, 2018), pp. 22–23.

88. T. Gutner, "Ways to Make the Most of a Negative Job Review," *Wall Street Journal* (January 13, 2009), p. D4.

89. S. Shellenbarger, "It's Not My Fault! A Better Response to Criticism at Work," *Wall Street Journal* (June 18, 2014), pp. D1, D4.

90. S. L. Albrecht, A. B. Bakker, J. A. Gruman, W. H. Macey, A. M. Saks, "Employee Engagement, Human Resource Management Practices and Competitive Advantage: An Integrated Approach," *Journal of Organizational Effectiveness: People and Performance* (2015), 2(1), pp. 7–35.

91. K. Gurchiek, "Want to Build Engagement? Provide Latest Technology, Access to Leaders," SHRM (October 11, 2017), https://www.shrm.org/resourcesandtools/hr-topics/global-hr/pages/want-to-build-engagement-provide-latest-technology,-access-to-leaders-.aspx?_ga=2.256974091.1415210105.1498587577-39096977.1498587575 (retrieved July 30, 2018).

92. E. Mone, C. Eisinger, K. Guggenheim, B. Price, C. Stine, "Performance Management at the Wheel: Driving Employee Engagement in Organizations," *Journal of Business and Psychology* (2011), 26(2), pp. 205–212.

93. S. L. Albrecht, A. B. Bakker, J. A. Gruman, W. H. Macey, A. M. Saks, "Employee Engagement, Human Resource Management Practices and Competitive Advantage: An Integrated Approach," *Journal of Organizational Effectiveness: People and Performance* (2015), 2(1), pp. 7–35.

94. W. Carroll, "The Effects of Electronic Performance Monitoring on Performance Outcomes: A Review and Meta-Analysis," *Employment Rights & Employment Policy Journal* (2008), 29, pp. 29–47.

95. Ibid.

96. D. Perkins, "Electronic Performance Monitoring in Call Centers: An Ethical Decision Model," *EJBO: Electronic Journal of Business Ethics and Organization Studies* (2013), 18(1), pp. 4–14.

97. D. G. Allen, P. C. Bryant, J. M. Vardaman, "Retaining Talent: Replacing Misconceptions With Evidence-Based Strategies," *Academy of Management Perspectives* (2010), 24(2), pp. 48–64.

98. A. Biesada, "Jelly Belly Candy Company," *Hoovers,* http://0-subscriber.hoovers.com.liucat.lib.liu.edu/H/company360/fulldescription.html?companyId=57880000000000 (retrieved May 2, 2017).

99. "Jelly Belly Candy Company Mission Statement," Jelly Belly Candy Company, https://www.jellybelly.com/mission-statement (retrieved May 2, 2017).

100. "A Sweet Employee Performance Appraisal System for Jelly Belly," Halogen Software, http://www.halogensoftware.com/customers/stories/jelly-belly (retrieved May 2, 2017).

Chapter 9

1. E. Fry, C. Zillman, "HR Is Not Your Friend," *Fortune* (March 1, 2018), pp. 99–108.

2. N. Saif, N. Razzaq, S. U. Rehman, A. Javed, U. Ahmad, "The Role of Workplace Partnership Strategies in Employee Management Relations," *Information and Knowledge Management* (2013), 3(6), pp. 34–39.

3. M. W. Kramer, R. J. Meisenbach, G. J. Hansen, "Communication, Uncertainty, and Volunteer Membership," *Journal of Applied Communication Research* (2013), 41(1), pp. 18–39.

4. Dreamworks, http://www.dreamworksstudios.com (retrieved May 16, 2011).

5. J. Birkinshaw, "Why Good Management Is So Difficult," *Strategic HR Review* (2014), 13(2).

6. R. D. Costigan, K. E. Brink, "Another Perspective on MBA Program Alignment: An Investigation of Learning Goals," *Academy of Management Learning & Education* (2015), 14(2), pp. 260–276.

7. L. Tomkins, E. Ulus, "Is Narcissism Undermining Critical Reflection in Our Business Schools?" *Academy of Management Learning & Education* (2015), 14(4), pp. 595–606.

8. K. E. Brink, R. D. Costigan, "Oral Communication Skills: Are the Priorities of the Workplace and AACSB-Accredited Business Programs Aligned?" *Academy of Management Learning & Education* (2015), 14(2), pp. 205–221.

9. K. Davidson, "Hard to Find: Workers With Good 'Soft Skills'," *Wall Street Journal* (August 31, 2016), pp. B1, B6.

10. D. B. Arnett, C. M. Wittmann, "Improving Marketing Success: The Role of Tacit Knowledge Exchange Between Sales and Marketing," *Journal of Business Research* (2014), 67(3), pp. 324–331.

11. B. Jullien, I.-U. Park, "New, Like New, or Very Good? Reputation and Credibility," *Review of Economic Studies* (2014), 81(4), pp. 1543–1574.

12. E. C. Tomlinson, R. C. Mayer, "The Role of Causal Attribution Dimensions in Trust Repair," *Academy of Management Review* (2009), 34(1), pp. 85–104.

13. R. Hurley, "Trust Me," *Wall Street Journal* (October 24, 2011), p. R4.

14. A. C. Peng, J. M. Schaubroeck, Y. Li, "Social Exchange Implications of Own and Coworkers' Experience of Supervisory Abuse," *Academy of Management Journal* (2014), 57(5), pp. 1385–1405.

15. C. Hann, "Dedicated to You," *Entrepreneur* (September 2013), p. 24.

16. R. Karlgaad, "Do Jerks Always Win?" *Forbes* (December 29, 2014), p. 44.

17. P. J. Zak, "The Neuroscience of High-Trust Organizations," *Consulting Psychology Journal: Practice and Research* (2018), 70(1), p. 45.

18. "Declining Employee Loyalty: A Casualty of the New Workplace," Knowledge@Wharton, Wharton School of Business, University of Pennsylvania (May 9, 2012), https://knowledge.wharton.upenn.edu/article/declining-employee-loyalty-a-casualty-of-the-new-workplace/ (retrieved June 25, 2014).

19. D. Dowell, T. Heffernan, M. Morrison, "Trust Formation at the Growth Stage of a Business-to-Business Relationship: A Qualitative Investigation," *Qualitative Market Research: An International Journal* (2013), 16(4), pp. 436–451.

20. P. H. Kim, K. Dirks, C. D. Cooper, "The Repair of Trust: A Dynamic Bilateral Perspective and Multilevel Conceptualization," *Academy of Management Review* (2009), 34(3), pp. 401–422.

21. N. Brodsky, "Shut Up and Listen: Want a Good Deal? First Find Out What the Other Side Wants," *INC.* (March 2015) p. 58.

22. E. Bernstein, "How Well Are You Listening?" *Wall Street Journal* (January 13, 2015), pp. D1, D4.

23. Public Radio News Broadcast, WFCR 88.5 (May 28, 2010).

24. S. Diestel, J. Wegge, K. H. Schmidt, "The Impact of Social Context on the Relationship Between Individual Job Satisfaction and Absenteeism: The Roles of Different Foci of Job Satisfaction and Work-Unit Absenteeism," *Academy of Management Journal* (2014), 57(2). 353–382.

25. The Conference Board, Press release (September 1, 2017), https://www.conference-board.org/press/pressdetail.cfm?pressid=7184 (retrieved August 12, 2018).

26. K. Hannon, "It's Never Too Late to Love Your Job," *AARP Magazine* (May 2013), pp. 44–45.

27. A. Kirkman, "It's All About Attitude," *Fortune* (November 17, 2014), p. 34.

28. R. Dunham, J. Herman, "Development of a Female Faces Scale for Measuring Job Satisfaction," *Journal of Applied Psychology* (1975), 60(5), pp. 629–631.

29. C. Ai-Hong, J. S. Nafisah, M. N. A. Rahim, "Comparison of Job Satisfaction Among Eight Health Care Professions in Private (Non-government) Settings," *Malaysian Journal of Medical Sciences* (2012), 19(2), p. 19.

30. R. Silverman, "Are You Happy In Your Job? Bosses Push Weekly Surveys," *Wall Street Journal* (December 3, 2014), p. B1.

31. P. Spector, "Measurement of Human Service Staff Satisfaction: Development of the Job Satisfaction Survey," *American Journal of Community Psychology* (1985), 13(6), pp. 693–713.

32. D. C. Wyld, "Does More Money Buy More Happiness on the Job?" *Academy of Management Perspective* (2011), 25(1), pp. 101–102.

33. D. Wilkie, "Too Many Miserable Workers: Where Is HR Going Wrong?" SHRM (May 22, 2014), http://www.shrm.org/hrdisciplines/employeerelations/articles/pages/miserable-workers.aspx (retrieved August 5, 2018).

34. R. Reuteman, "Generation Gaps," *Entrepreneur* (March 2015), pp. 42–48.

35. R. McCammon, "I'm Sure You're Wondering Why I've Called You All Here," *Entrepreneur* (March 2015), pp. 28–29.

36. G. F. Cavanagh, D. J. Moberg, M. Velasquez, "The Ethics of Organizational Politics," *Academy of Management Review* (1981), 6(3), pp. 363–374.

37. J. Hughes, C. Babcock, F. Bass, "You're Fired, Now Get Back to Work," *Businessweek* (August 1–7, 2011), pp. 31–32.

38. United Nations, *Universal Declaration of Human Rights* (adopted by the General Assembly December 10, 1948), UN Doc. GA/RES/217 A (III).

39. H. L. Black, "The Bill of Rights," *New York University Law Review* (1960), 35, p. 865.

40. S. S. Wiltermuth, F. J. Flynn, "Power, Moral Clarity, and Punishment in the Workplace," *Academy of Management Journal* (2013), 56(4), pp. 1002–1023.

41. D. Ariely, "Why We Lie," *Wall Street Journal* (May 26–27, 2012), pp. C1–C2.

42. L. Guerin, "Employment At Will: What Does It Mean?" *NOLO* https://www.nolo.com/legal-encyclopedia/employment-at-will-definition-30022.html (retrieved August 10, 2018).

43. "Employment at-Will Exceptions by State," National Conference of State Legislatures, http://www.ncsl.org/research/labor-and-employment/at-will-employment-exceptions-by-state.aspx (retrieved August 10, 2018).

44. Y. Zhang, D. A. Waldman, Y. L. Han, X. Li, "Paradoxical Leader Behaviors in People Management: Antecedents and Consequences," *Academy of Management Journal* (2015), 58(2), pp. 538–566.

45. E. Van Oosten, K. E. Kram, "Coaching for Change," *Academy of Management Learning & Education* (2014), 13(2), pp. 295–298.

46. C. Hann, "Goofing Off Online," *Entrepreneur* (November 2014), p. 36.

47. R. C. Liden, S. J. Wayne, C. Liao, J. D. Meuser, "Servant Leadership and Serving Culture: Influence on Individual and Unit Performance," *Academy of Management Journal* (2014), 57(5), 1434–1452.

48. L. Jia, J. D. Shaw, A. S. Tsue, T. Y., Park, "A Social-Structural Perspective on Employee-Organization Relationships and Team Creativity," *Academy of Management Journal* (2014), 57(3), pp. 869–891.

49. M. R. Barrick, G. R. Thurgood, T. A. Smith, S. H. Courtright, "Collective Organizational Engagement: Linking Motivational Antecedents, Strategic Implementation, and Firm Performance," *Academy of Management Journal* (2015), 58(1), pp. 111–135.

50. D. Meinert, "7 Steps to Becoming a Better Coaching Leader," SHRM (September 29, 2016), https://www.shrm.org/hr-today/news/hr-news/pages/7-steps-to-becoming-a-better-coaching-leader.aspx (retrieved July 2, 2017).

51. A. Von Tobel, "Where Money Meets Morale," *INC.* (April 2014), pp. 48–49.

52. B. L. Rau, "The Oxford Handbook of Evidence-Based Management," *Academy of Management Learning & Education* (2014), 13(3), pp. 485–487.

53. S. K. Johnson, L. O. Garrison, G. H. Broome, J. W. Fleenor, J. L. Steed, "Go for the Goals: Relationships Between Goal Setting and Transfer of Training Following Leadership Development," *Academy of Management Learning & Education* (2012), 11(4), pp. 555–569.

54. M. Weber, "Culture Matters: 7 Ways of Great Leaders," *Forbes* (October 20, 2014), p. 113.

55. E. Van Oosten, K. E. Kram, "Coaching for Change," *Academy of Management Learning & Education* (2014), 13(2), pp. 290–292.

56. R. Shaich, "I Wish I'd Fired More People," *Entrepreneur* (March 2018), p. 26.

57. J. Segers, D. Vloeberghs, E. Henderickx, I. Inceoglu, "Structuring and Understanding the Coaching Industry: The Coaching Cube," *Academy of Management Learning & Education* (2011), 2(2), pp. 204–221.

58. E. De Haan, C. Bertie, A. Day, C. Sills, "Clients' Critical Moments of Coaching: Toward a 'Client Model' of Executive Coaching," *Academy of Management Learning & Education* (2010), 9(4), pp. 607–621.

59. Staff, margin note, *INC.* (March/April 2018), p. 44.

60. N. Tocher, M. W. Rutherford, "Perceived Acute Human Resource Management Problems in Small and Medium Firms: An Empirical Examination," *Entrepreneurship Theory and Practice* (2009), 33(2), pp. 455–479.

61. R. McCammon, "The Worst of Times," *Entrepreneur* (February 2016), pp. 15–16.

62. S. Shellenbarger, "Meet the Meeting Killers," *Wall Street Journal* (May 16, 2012), pp. D1, D3.

63. CareerBuilder, "Bad Hires Can Be Costly," *HR Magazine* (February 2013), p. 18.

64. J. R. Detert, A. C. Edmondson, "Implicit Voice Theories: Taken-for-Granted Rules of Self-Censorship at Work," *Academy of Management Journal* (2011), 54(3), pp. 461–488.

65. CareerBuilder, "Bad Hires Can Be Costly," *HR Magazine* (February 2013), p. 18.

66. E. Fry C. Zillman, "HR Is Not Your Friend," *Fortune* (March 1, 2018), pp. 99–108.

67. M. Voronov, R. Vince, "Integrating Emotions Into the Analysis of Institutional Work," *Academy of Management Review* (2012), 37(1), pp. 58–81.

68. P. Keegan, "The New Rules of Engagement," *INC.* (December 2014/January 2015), pp. 86–132.

69. CareerBuilder, "Bad Hires Can Be Costly," *HR Magazine* (February 2013), p. 18.

70. C. Hann, "Caught in the Cookie Jar," *Entrepreneur* (December 2014), p. 41.

71. J. A. Clair, "Procedural Injustice in the System of Peer Review and Scientific Misconduct," *Academy of Management Learning & Education* (2015), 14(2), pp. 159–172.

72. M. Goldsmith, "What Got You Here Won't Get You There: How Successful People Became Even More Successful," *Academy of Management Perspective* (2009), 23(3), pp. 103–105.

73. "Legal Standards of Proof," NOLO.com, http://www.nolo.com/legal-encyclopedia/legal-standards-proof.html (retrieved July 2, 2017).

74. L. A. Mainiero, K. J. Jones, "Sexual Harassment Versus Workplace Romance: Social Media Spillover and Textual Harassment in the Workplace," *Academy of Management Perspectives* (2013), 27(3), pp. 187–203.

75. S. Reddy, "Why Are You Always Late? It Could Be a Planning Fallacy," *Wall Street Journal* (February 3, 2015), pp. D1, D2.

76. C. Hann, "Caught in the Cookie Jar," *Entrepreneur* (December 2014), p. 41.

77. Ibid.

78. A. R. Gardner, "No Finding of Race Discrimination in Failure-to-Promote Case," *HR Magazine* (April 2013), p. 74.

79. R. Shaich, "I Wish I'd Fired More People," *Entrepreneur* (March 2018), p. 26.

80. C. Hann, "Caught in the Cookie Jar," *Entrepreneur* (December 2014), p. 41.

81. J. J. Miller, "Gross Negligence, Inherent Risks, Assumption of Risks: Using Waivers to Protect Fitness Clubs," Editor: Thomas H. Sawyer. *Journal of Physical Education, Recreation and Dance* (2015), 86(4), pp. 54–56.

82. L. McQuerrey, "The Definition of Gross Misconduct in the Workplace," *Houston Chronicle Online* (June 28, 2018), https://smallbusiness.chron.com/definition-gross-misconduct-workplace-20540.html (retrieved August 12, 2018).

83. National Mediation Board, The Railway Labor Act, http://www.nmb.gov/help-training/ (retrieved August 12, 2018).

84. National Labor Relations Board, National Labor Relations Act, http://www.nlrb.gov/national-labor-relations-act/ (retrieved August 12, 2018).

85. National Labor Relations Board, "What We Do," http://www.nlrb.gov/what-we-do/ (retrieved August 12, 2018).

86. National Labor Relations Board, National Labor Relations Act, http://www.nlrb.gov/resources/national-labor-relations-act/ (retrieved August 12, 2018).

87. http://law.justia.com/cases/california/ca12d/49/625.html (retrieved August 12, 2018).

88. California Public Relations Institute for Industrial Relations, University of California at Berkeley, "Glossary," http://www.perb.ca.gov/csmcs/glossary.pdf (retrieved August 12, 2018).

89. http://www.dol.gov/oasam/programs/history/glossary.htm (retrieved August 12, 2018).

90. Ibid.

91. Ibid.

92. B. Collins, *Right to Work Laws: Legislative Background and Empirical Research* (Washington, DC: Congressional Research Service, 2012), http://fas.org/sgp/crs/misc/R42575.pdf.

93. http://doleta.gov/programs/factsht/warn.htm (retrieved August 12, 2018).

94. Ibid.

95. Ibid.

96. J. Bravin, "Ruling on Public Unions Strikes at Labor Finance," *Wall Street Journal* (June 28, 2018), p. A1.

97. J. Eidelson, "Politics/Policy, *Business-Week* (February 20–March 5, 2017), pp. 25–26.

98. M. McGrath, with L. Gensler, S. Sharf, "Competition Is the New Union," *Forbes* (December 26, 2017), pp. 56–64.

99. National Labor Relations Board, National Labor Relations Act, http://www.nlrb.gov/resources/national-labor-relations-act/ (retrieved August 12, 2018).

100. National Labor Relations Board website, www.nlrb.gov (retrieved August 16, 2018).

101. "Interfering With Employee Rights (Section 7 & 8(a)(1))," https://www.nlrb.gov/rights-we-protect/whats-law/employers/interfering-employee-rights-section-7–8a1 (retrieved August 12, 2018).

102. J. Bravin, "Ruling on Public Unions Strikes at Labor Finance," *Wall Street Journal* (June 28, 2018), p. A1.

103. M. Valdez, "Boeing Machinists OK Contract Tied to 777X," Associated Press (January 4, 2014).

104. E. Fry, C. Zillman, "HR Is Not Your Friend," *Fortune* (March 1, 2018), pp. 99–108.

105. http://www.shrm.org/TemplatesTools/hrqa/Pages/decertifyaunion.aspx (retrieved August 12, 2018).

106. E. Bernstein, "Thou Shalt Not Send in Anger," *Wall Street Journal* (October 21, 2014), p. D1.

107. W. Deveney, "Employees' TV Interview Is Protected Speech," SHRM (November 3, 2016), https://www.shrm.org/resourcesandtools/legal-and-compliance/employment-law/pages/tv-interview-protected-speech.aspx (retrieved July 5, 2017).

108. Ibid.

Chapter 10

1. Staff, "How to Win at the Hiring Game," *INC.* (June 2018), p. 62.

2. P. White, D. White, "How Do I Make Employees Stay?" *Entrepreneur* (September 2018), p. 34.

3. S. Soper, "Inside Amazon's People's Court," *Businessweek* (July 2, 2018), pp. 22–23.

4. B. Farrow, "Wegmans," *Entrepreneur* (June 2018), p. 54.

5. P. White, D. White, "How Do I Make Employees Stay?" *Entrepreneur* (September 2018), p. 34.

6. J. DeVaro, "A Theoretical Analysis of Relational Job Design and Compensation," *Journal of Organizational Behavior* (2010), 31 (2–3), pp. 279–301.

7. "Comp ils Culture: 2017 Compensation Best Practices Report," *Payscale* (n.d.), http://www.payscale.com/content/report/2017-compensation-best-practices-report.pdf (retrieved November 3, 2018).

8. U.S. Bureau of Labor Statistics, "Economic News Release: Employment Cost Index Summary," https://www.bls.gov/news.release/eci.nr0.htm (retrieved November 3, 2018).

9. U.S. Bureau of Labor Statistics, "News Release: Employer Costs for Employee Compensation," https://www.bls.gov/news.release/pdf/ecec.pdf (retrieved November 3, 2018).

10. T. N. Martin, R. Ottemann, "Generational Workforce Demographic Trends and Total Organizational Rewards Which Might Attract and Retain Different Generational Employees," *Journal of Behavioral and Applied Management* (2016), 16(2), p. 1160.

11. "Employee Job Satisfaction and Engagement: The Doors of Opportunity Are Open," SHRM, https://www.shrm.org/hr-today/trends-and-forecasting/research-and-surveys/Documents/2017-Employee-Job-Satisfaction-and-Engagement-Executive-Summary.pdf (retrieved October 25, 2018).

12. S. Miller, "Bridge the 'Comp Chasm' With Trust, Transparency," SHRM (April 5, 2016), https://www.shrm.org/resourcesandtools/hr-topics/compensation/pages/bridge-comp-chasm.aspx (retrieved November 3, 2018).

13. R. Lloyd, D. Mertens, "Expecting More Out of Expectancy Theory: History Urges Inclusion of the Social Context," *International Management Review* (2018), 14(1).

14. V. Vroom, *Work and Motivation* (New York: John Wiley & Sons, 1964).

15. N. J. Fast, E. R. Burris, C. A. Bartel, "Managing to Stay in the Dark: Managerial Self-Efficacy, Ego Defensiveness, and

the Aversion to Employee Voice," *Academy of Management Journal* (2014), 57(4), pp. 1013–1034.

16. M. Renko, K. G. Kroeck, A. Bullough, "Expectancy Theory and Nascent Entrepreneurship," *Small Business Economics* (2012), 39(3), pp. 667–684.

17. R. L. Purvis, T. J. Zagenczyk, G. E. McCray, "What's in It for Me? Using Expectancy Theory and Climate to Explain Stakeholder Participation, Its Direction and Intensity," *International Journal of Project Management* (2015), 33(1), pp. 3–14.

18. "Balancing the Pay Scale: 'Fair' vs. 'Unfair,'" Wharton School of Business, University of Pennsylvania (May 22, 2013), http://knowledge.wharton.upenn.edu/article/balancing-the-pay-scale-fair-vs-unfair/ (retrieved November 3, 2018).

19. J. S. Adams, "Toward an Understanding of Inequity," *Journal of Abnormal and Social Psychology* (1963), 67, pp. 422–436.

20. C. P. Long, C. Bendersky, C. Morrill, "Fairness Monitoring: Linking Managerial Controls and Fairness Judgments in Organizations," *Academy of Management Journal* (2011), 54(5), pp. 1045–1068.

21. R. Lloyd, D. Mertens, "Expecting More Out of Expectancy Theory: History Urges Inclusion of the Social Context," *International Management Review* (2018), 14(1), pp. 28–43.

22. "Adams' Equity Theory: Balancing Employee Inputs and Outputs," Mind-Tools, http://www.mindtools.com/pages/article/newLDR_96.htm (retrieved October 27, 2018).

23. M. K. Duffy, K. L. Scott, J. D. Shaw, B. J. Tepper, K. Aquino, "A Social Context Model of Envy and Social Undermining," *Academy of Management Journal* (2012), 55(3), pp. 643–666.

24. C. Zárraga-Oberty, J. Bonache, "Compensating Global Careerists," in *The Management of Global Careers* (Cham, Switzerland: Palgrave Macmillan, 2018), pp. 319–340.

25. C. P. Long, C. Bendersky, C. Morrill, "Fairness Monitoring: Linking Managerial Controls and Fairness Judgments in Organizations," *Academy of Management Journal* (2011), 54(5), pp. 1045–1068.

26. J. S. Bourdage, A. Goupal, T. Neilson, E. R. Lukacik, N. Lee, "Personality, Equity Sensitivity, And Discretionary Workplace Behavior," *Personality and Individual Differences* (2018), 120, pp. 144–150.

27. K. Leavitt, S. J. Reynolds, C. M. Barnes, P. Schilpzan, S. T. Hannah, "Different Hats, Different Obligations: Plural Occupational Identities and Situated Moral Judgments," *Academy of Management Journal* (2012), 55(6), pp. 1316–1333.

28. "Adams' Equity Theory: Balancing Employee Inputs and Outputs,"

MindTools, http://www.mindtools.com/pages/article/newLDR_96.htm (retrieved October 27, 2018).

29. G. O'Brien, "It's All Your Fault!" *Entrepreneur* (February 2015), p. 30.

30. D. T. Kong, K. T. Dirks, D. L. Ferrin, "Interpersonal Trust Within Negotiations: Meta-Analytic Evidence, Critical Contingencies, and Directions for Further Research," *Academy of Management Journal* (2014), 57(5), pp. 1235–1255.

31. B. A. Scott, A. S. Garza, D. E. Conlong. Y. J. Kim, "Why Do Managers Act Fairly in the First Place? A Daily Investigation of Hot and Cold Motives and Discretion," *Academy of Management Journal* (2014), 57(6) pp. 1571–1591.

32. A. C. Peng, J. M. Schaubroeck, L. Li, "Social Exchange Implications of Own and Coworkers' Experiences of Supervisor Abuse," *Academy of Management Journal* (2014), 57(5), pp. 1385–1405.

33. D. T. Kong, K. T. Dirks, D. L. Ferrin, "Interpersonal Trust Within Negotiations: Mata-Analytic Evidence, Critical Contingencies, and Directions for Future Research," *Academy of Management Journal* (2014), 57(5), pp. 1235–1255.

34. C. O. Trevor, G. Reilly, B. Gerhart, "Reconsidering Pay Dispersion's Effect on the Performance of Interdependent Work: Reconciling Sorting and Pay Inequality," *Academy of Management Journal* (2012), 55(3), pp. 585–610.

35. S. Germano, "Nike Rethinks Pay, Bonus Practices," *Wall Street Journal* (July 24, 2018), pp. B1–B2.

36. H. Olen, "Mind the Gender Gap," *INC.* (June 2018), p. 56.

37. H. Yang, "Efficiency Wages and Subjective Performance Pay," *Economic Inquiry* (2008), 46(2), pp. 179–196.

38. Staff, "How to Ask for Your Next Big Raise," *Fortune* (February 1, 2018), p. 50.

39. R. A. Morris Morant, D. C. Jacobs, "Frontiers of Efficiency Wages: Unconventional Wisdom?" *Journal of Management History* (2018), 24(3), pp. 300–315.

40. Ibid.

41. C. N. Halaby, "Supervision, Pay, and Effort," *Social Forces* (2014), 92(3), pp. 1135–1158.

42. D. Harrison, E. Morath, "Boom Prods More to Job Hop," *Wall Street Journal* (July 5, 2017), pp. A1–A2.

43. K. Stock, "In Brief," *Businessweek* (October 8, 2018), p. 9.

44. B. B. Aguenza, A. P. M. Som, "Motivational Factors of Employee Retention and Engagement in Organizations," *International Journal of Advances in Management and Economics* (2012), 1(6), pp. 88–95. https://www.managementjournal.info/index.php/IJAME/article/viewFile/233/222 (retrieved October 27, 2018)

45. E. D. Campion, M. C. Campion, M. A. Campion, "Best Practices in Incentive Compensation Bonus Administration Based on Research and Professional Advice," *Compensation & Benefits Review* (2017), 49(3), pp. 123–134.

46. D. H. Bradley, *The Federal Minimum Wage: In Brief* (Washington, DC: Congressional Research Service, 2017), http://fas.org/sgp/crs/misc/R43089.pdf (retrieved November 3, 2018).

47. B. Bartling, F. A. von Siemens, "The Intensity of Incentives in Firms and Markets: Moral Hazard With Envious Agents," *Labour Economics* (2010), 17(3), pp. 598–607.

48. J. Kochanski, Y. Stiles, "Put a Lid on Salary Compression Before It Boils Over," SHRM (July 19, 2013), http://www.shrm.org/hrdisciplines/compensation/articles/pages/salary-compression-lid.aspx (retrieved October 27, 2018).

49. Fair Labor Standards Act of 1938, as Amended, https://www.dol.gov/whd/regs/statutes/FairLaborStandAct.pdf (retrieved November 3, 2018).

50. U.S. Department of Labor, "Employment Law Guide: Wages and Hours Worked: Minimum Wage and Overtime Pay," http://www.dol.gov/compliance/guide/minwage.htm (retrieved October 31, 2018).

51. National Conference of State Legislatures, "State Minimum Wages," http://www.ncsl.org/research/labor-and-employment/state-minimum-wage-chart.aspx (retrieved October 31, 2018).

52. M. Shoop, "DOL Announces 2019 Minimum Wage Increases for Federal Contractors," Littler (August 31, 2018), https://www.littler.com/publication-press/publication/dol-announces-2019-minimum-wage-increases-federal-contractors (retrieved March 25, 2019).

53. U.S. Department of Labor, "Employment Law Guide: Wages and Hours Worked: Minimum Wage and Overtime Pay," http://www.dol.gov/compliance/guide/minwage.htm (retrieved October 31, 2018).

54. Ibid.

55. http://www.dol.gov/whd/regs/compliance/fairpay/fs17g_salary.htm (retrieved October 31, 2018).

56. U.S. Department of Labor, Wage and Hour Division, "Fact Sheet #17H: Highly-Compensated Workers and the Part 541-Exemptions Under the Fair Labor Standards Act (FLSA)," https://www.dol.gov/whd/overtime/fs17h_highly_comp.htm (retrieved October 31, 2018).

57. U.S. Department of Labor, "Fair Labor Standards Act Advisor," http://www.dol.gov/elaws/faq/esa/flsa/016.htm (retrieved October 31, 2018).

58. U.S. Department of Labor, "Employment Law Guide: Wages and Hours Worked: Child Labor Protections," http://www.dol.gov/compliance/guide/childlbr.htm (retrieved October 31, 2018).

59. U.S. Census Bureau, "American Community Survey," https://www.census.gov/programs-surveys/acs/ (retrieved October 31, 2018).

60. J. Bell, "New Calif. Fair Pay Law Is Toughest in Nation," SHRM (October 7, 2015), https://www.shrm.org/resourcesandtools/legal-and-compliance/state-and-local-updates/pages/calif-fair-pay-act.aspx (retrieved November 3, 2018).

61. http://www.dol.gov/oasam/programs/history/flsa1938.htm (retrieved October 31, 2018).

62. "Comp Is Culture: 2017 Compensation Best Practices Report," *Payscale* (n.d.), http://www.payscale.com/content/report/2017-compensation-best-practices-report.pdf (retrieved November 3, 2018).

63. "How to Establish Salary Ranges," SHRM (May 23, 2018), https://www.shrm.org/resourcesandtools/tools-and-samples/how-to-guides/pages/howtoestablish-salaryranges.aspx (retrieved October 31, 2018).

64. https://www.shrm.org/resourcesandtools/tools-and-samples/toolkits/pages/performingjobevaluations.aspx (retrieved October 31, 2018).

65. AFL-CIO, "Executive Paywatch," https://aflcio.org/paywatch (retrieved March 30, 2019).

66. https://www.bloomberg.com/graphics/ceo-pay-ratio/ (retrieved October 31, 2018).

67. "Walmart CEO's Salary Is 1,188 Times the Median Employee's," MarketWatch (April 23, 2018), https://www.marketwatch.com/story/walmart-ceos-salary-is-1188-times-the-median-employees-2018-04-23 (retrieved October 31, 2018).

68. L. Burke, "Designing a Pay Structure," Student Workbook, SHRM, https://www.shrm.org/Membership/student-resources/Documents/Designing%20a%20Pay%20Structure_Student_9.08.pdf (retrieved October 31, 2018).

69. Ibid.

70. D. Aobdia, L. Cheng, "Unionization, Product Market Competition, and Strategic Disclosure," *Journal of Accounting and Economics* (2018), 65(2–3), 331–357.

71. G. O. Trevor, G. Reilly, B. Gerhart, "Reconsidering Pay Dispersion's Effect on the Performance of Interdependent Work: Reconciling Sorting and Pay Inequality," *Academy of Management Journal* (2012), 55(3), pp. 585–610.

72. "How to Establish Salary Ranges," SHRM (May 23, 2018), http://www.shrm.org/

TemplatesTools/HowtoGuides/Pages/HowtoEstablishSalaryRanges.aspx (retrieved November 3, 2018).

73. B. Kaye, L. Williams, L. Cowart, "Help Employees, Managers Recognize the Why of Lateral Moves," SHRM (October 2, 2017), https://www.shrm.org/resourcesandtools/hr-topics/organizational-and-employee-development/pages/help-employees-managers-recognize-the-why-of-lateral-moves.aspx (retrieved November 3, 2018).

74. https://www.shrm.org/resourcesandtools/tools-and-samples/toolkits/pages/buildingamarket-basedpaystructure fromscratch.aspx (retrieved November 3, 2018).

75. H. Olen, "Mind the Gender Gap," INC. (June 2018), p. 56.

76. S. Germano, "Nike Rethinks Pay, Bonus Practices," Wall Street Journal (July 24, 2018), pp. B1–B2.

77. Internal Revenue Service, "Independent Contractor Defined," http://www.irs.gov/Businesses/Small-Businesses-&-Self-Employed/Independent-Contractor-Defined (retrieved November 3, 2018).

78. https://www.dol.gov/whd/regs/compliance/whdfs13.htm (retrieved November 3, 2018).

79. J. Rosenblatt, E. Pettersson, "Uber Close to Settling Drivers' Suit With Billions at Stake," Bloomberg News (November 16, 2016), https://www.bloomberg.com/news/articles/2016-11-16/uber-close-to-settling-lawsuit-with-billions-at-stake (retrieved November 3, 2018).

80. "U.S. Judge Says Uber drivers Are Not Company's Employees," Reuters (April 12, 2018), https://www.reuters.com/article/us-uber-lawsuit/u-s-judge-says-uber-drivers-are-not-companys-employees-idUSKBN1HJ31I (retrieved November 3, 2018).

81. "The Gender Wage Gap," Fortune (September 15, 2015), p. 16.

82. A. Joshi, J. Son, H. Roh, "When Can Women Close the Gap? A Meta-Analytic Test of Sex Differences in Performance and Rewards," Academy of Management Journal (2015), 58(5), pp. 1516–1545.

83. A. Picchi, "What Could Finally Close the Gender Wage Gap?" CBS News (March 24, 2016), http://www.cbsnews.com/news/what-could-finally-close-the-gender-pay-gap/ (retrieved November 3, 2018).

84. A. Wright, "In Focus: DOL Accuses Google of 'Extreme' Gender Pay Disparity," SHRM (April 10, 2017), https://www.shrm.org/resourcesandtools/hr-topics/technology/pages/in-focus-dol-accuses-google-of-%E2%80%98extreme%E2%80%99-gender-pay-disparity.aspx (retrieved November 3, 2018).

85. L. Nagele-Piazza, "In Focus: Effort to Close the Gender Pay Gap Goes Global," SHRM (March 29, 2017), https://www.shrm.org/resourcesandtools/hr-topics/global-hr/pages/in-focus-effort-to-close-the-gender-pay-gap-goes-global.aspx (retrieved November 3, 2018).

86. "Google's Refusal to Give OFCCP Information Upheld," SHRM (April 6, 2017), https://www.shrm.org/resourcesandtools/legal-and-compliance/employment-law/pages/google-refusal-to-give-ofccp-information-upheld.aspx (retrieved November 3, 2018).

87. M. Gledhill, "Costco Wholesale Corporation," Hoovers, http://0-subscriber.hoovers.com.liucat.lib.liu.edu/H/company360/fulldescription.html?companyId=17060000000000 (retrieved May 3, 2017).

88. "Costco Careers," Costco Wholesale, https://www.costco.com/jobs.html (retrieved May 3, 2017).

89. "Costco Has Great Benefits," Costco Wholesale, https://www.costco.com/benefits.html (retrieved May 3, 2017).

90. T. Denman, "Costco Employees Rave About Compensation and Benefits," Retail Information Systems, https://risnews.com/costco-employees-rave-about-compensation-and-benefits (retrieved May 3, 2017).

91. Ibid.

Chapter 11

1. J. Gallus, "The Best Ways to Give Employees Performance Awards," Wall Street Journal (October 30, 2018), p. R9.

2. T. Greenwald, "How AI Is Transforming the Workplace," Wall Street Journal (March 13, 2017), pp. R1–R2.

3. P. White, D. White, "How Do I Make Employees Stay?" Entrepreneur (September 2018), p. 34.

4. Staff, "How to Win at the Hiring Game," INC. (June 2018), p. p. 62.

5. E. Schurenberg, "What Do You Owe Your Employees," INC. (November 2015), p. 12.

6. U.S. Bureau of Labor Statistics, "Economic News Release: Table 1. Civilian Workers, by Major Occupational and Industry Group" (September 2018), http://data.bls.gov/cgi-bin/print.pl/news.release/ecec.t01.htm (retrieved November 19, 2018).

7. Staff, "How to Win at the Hiring Game," INC. (June 2018), p. 62.

8. R. Feintzeig, "Who Gets Free Lunch and Other Tech Perks," Wall Street Journal (July 16, 2014), p. D2.

9. B. Farrow, "Wegmans," Entrepreneur (June 2018), p. 54.

10. Ibid.

11. D. Blanchard, D. Hutson, E. Wills, The One Minute Entrepreneur (New York, NY: Currency, 2008).

12. J. Gallus, "The Best Ways to Give Employees Performance Awards," Wall Street Journal (October 30, 2018). p. R9.

13. S. D. Levitt, S. J. Dubner, "SuperFreakonomics," Academy of Management Perspectives (2011), 25(2), pp. 86–87.

14. M. Pennington, "The 99% Movement Scorns American Creativity," Forbes (June 4, 2012), p. 30.

15. M. Houlihan, B. Harvey, "You Won't Learn This in Business School," Costco Connection (April 2014), p. 13.

16. P. White, D. White, "How Do I Make Employees Stay?" Entrepreneur (September 2018), p. 34.

17. R. E. Johnson, C. D. Chang, L. O. Yang, "Commitment and Motivation at Work: The Relevance of Employee Identity and Regulatory Focus," Academy of Management Review (2010), 35(2), pp. 226–245.

18. J. Gallus, "The Best Ways to Give Employees Performance Awards," Wall Street Journal (October 30, 2018), p. R9.

19. Ibid.

20. J. J. Martocchio, Strategic Compensation: A Human Resource Management Approach (Upper Saddle River, NJ: Prentice Hall, 2015), p. 86.

21. T. Greenwald, "How AI Is Transforming the Workplace," Wall Street Journal (March 13, 2017), R1–R2.

22. C. S. Jung, "Extending the Theory of Goal Ambiguity to Programs: Examining the Relationship Between Goal Ambiguity and Performance," Public Administration Review (2014), 74(2), pp. 205–219.

23. S. Germano, "Nike Rethinks Pay, Bonus Practices," Wall Street Journal (July 24, 2018), pp. B1–B2.

24. T. P. Chen, E. Morath, "Employers Choose Bonuses Over Raises," Wall Street Journal (September 19, 2018), pp. A1–A2.

25. K. Stock, "In Brief, Amazon.com," Businessweek (October 8, 2018), p. 9.

26. L.A. Myers Jr., "One Hundred Years Later: What Would Frederick W. Taylor Say?" International Journal of Business and Social Science (2011), 2(20), pp. 8–11.

27. H. Young Shin, W. Lee, "How Can We Introduce the Most Effective Incentive Plan for Non-exempt Employees?" (2013), http://digitalcommons.ilr.cornell.edu/student/18/.

28. J. Blasi, R. Freeman, D. Kruse, D. "Do Broad-Based Employee Ownership, Profit Sharing and Stock Options Help the Best Firms Do Even Better?" British Journal of Industrial Relations (2016), 54(1), 55–82.

29. J. Gallus, "The Best Ways to Give Employees Performance Awards," Wall Street Journal (October 30, 2018), p. R9.

30. S. Anand, P. R. Vidyarthi, R. C. Linden, D. M. Rousseau, "Good Citizens in Poor-Quality Relationships: Idiosyncratic Deals as a Substitute for Relationship Quality," *Academy of Management Journal* (2010), 53(5), pp. 970–988.

31. J. J. Martocchio, *Strategic Compensation: A Human Resource Management Approach* (Upper Saddle River, NJ: Prentice Hall, 2015), p. 92.

32. Ibid.

33. D. Kruse, R. B. Freeman, J. R. Blasi, *Shared Capitalism at Work: Employee Ownership, Profit and Gain Sharing, and Broad-Based Stock Options* (Chicago, IL: University of Chicago Press, 2010).

34. T. Greenwald, "How AI Is Transforming the Workplace," *Wall Street Journal* (March 13, 2017), pp. R1–R2.

35. J. Blasi, D. Kruse, D. Weltmann, "Firm Survival and Performance in Privately Held ESOP Companies," *Advances in the Economic Analysis of Participatory & Labor-Managed Firms* (2013), 14, pp. 109–124.

36. D. C. Wyld, "Do Employees View Stock Options the Same Way as Their Bosses Do?" *Academy of Management Perspectives* (2011), 25(4), pp. 91–92.

37. S. Gustin, "Two Years After Steve Jobs' Death, Is Apple a Different Company?" *TIME Magazine* (October 4, 2013).

38. http://ycharts.com/companies/AAPL/market_cap/ (retrieved July 13, 2014).

39. M. Krantz, B. Hansen, "CEO Pay Soars While Worker's Pay Stalls," *USA Today* (April 1, 2011), pp. B1–B2.

40. AFL-CIO Executive Paywatch, https://aflcio.org/paywatch (retrieved November 26, 2018).

41. "Executive Compensation Group Advisory," *Vedder Price P.C.* (July 2010).

42. J. McGregor, "As Companies Reveal Gigantic CEO-to-Worker Pay Ratios, Some Worry How Low-Paid Workers Might Take the News," *Washington Post* (February 21, 2018), https://www.washingtonpost.com/news/on-leadership/wp/2018/02/21/as-companies-reveal-gigantic-ceo-to-worker-pay-ratios-some-worry-how-low-paid-workers-might-take-the-news/?utm_term=.ad6395708620 (retrieved November 19, 2018).

43. AFL-CIO website, https://aflcio.org/paywatch/company-pay-ratios (retrieved November 26, 2018).

44. "Executive Compensation Group Advisory," *Vedder Price P.C.* (July 2010).

45. M. Tonello, "CEO and Executive Compensation Practices: 2017 Edition," Harvard Law School Forum on Corporate Governance and Financial Regulation, https://corpgov.law.harvard.edu/2017/10/04/ceo-and-executive-compensation-practices-2017-edition/ (retrieved November 19, 2018).

46. Ibid.

47. T. Greenwald, "How AI Is Transforming the Workplace," *Wall Street Journal* (March 13, 2017), R1–R2.

48. C. Austin, "The 10 Best Workplaces for Millennials," *Fortune* (July 1, 2018), p. 18.

49. https://www.fiscal.treasury.gov/fsreports/rpt/finrep/fr/17frusg/Executivesummary_2017.pdf (retrieved November 10, 2018).

50. https://www.ssa.gov/planners/retire/agereduction.html (retrieved November 10, 2018)

51. https://www.irs.gov/taxtopics/tc759 (retrieved March 30, 2019).

52. http://www.dol.gov/whd/fmla/index.htm (retrieved November 19, 2018).

53. http://www.dol.gov/whd/fmla/fmlaAmended.htm#SEC_101_DEFINITIONS (retrieved November 19, 2018).

54. http://www.littler.com/publication-press/publication/employer-mandate-delay-beware-ignoring-aca/ (retrieved November 19, 2018).

55. https://www.healthcare.com/blog/states-with-individual-mandate/ (retrieved November 27, 2018)

56. http://www.hhs.gov/ocr/privacy/ (retrieved November 19, 2018).

57. http://www.pbgc.gov/wr/benefits/guaranteed-benefits.html (retrieved November 19, 2018).

58. J. Gallus, "The Best Ways to Give Employees Performance Awards," *Wall Street Journal* (October 30, 2018). p. R9.

59. E. Fry, C. Zillman, "HR Is Not Your Friend," *Fortune* (March 1, 2018), pp. 99–108.

60. Staff, "How to Win at the Hiring Game," *INC.* (June 2018), p. 62.

61. Staff, "Headline," *Wall Street Journal* (October 4, 2018), p. A11.

62. U.S. Bureau of Statistics, "Employee Benefits in the United States—March 2018," News Release USDL-18–1182, https://www.bls.gov/news.release/pdf/ebs2.pdf (retrieved November 10, 2018).

63. T. P. Chen, E. Morath, "Employers Choose Bonuses Over Raises," *Wall Street Journal* (September 19, 2018), pp. A1–A2.

64. Internal Revenue Service, "Health Savings Accounts and Other Tax-Favored Health Plans," Publication 969, http://www.irs.gov/pub/irs-pdf/p969.pdf (retrieved November 19, 2018).

65. S. Miller, "Health Care Consumerism: HSAs and HRAs" SHRM (May 2, 2016), https://www.shrm.org/ResourcesAndTools/hr-topics/benefits/Pages/HRAsandHSAsAnOverview.aspx (retrieved July 29, 2017).

66. Ibid.

67. https://www.bls.gov/news.release/pdf/ebs2.pdf (retrieved November 19, 2018).

68. http://www.irs.gov/Retirement-Plans/Plan-Participant-Employee/Retirement-Topics-401k-and-Profit-Sharing-Plan-Contribution-Limits (retrieved November 19, 2018).

69. Ibid.

70. Society for Human Resources Management, *Examining Paid Leave in the Workplace* (Alexandria, VA: SHRM, 2008), http://www.shrm.org/research/surveyfindings/articles/documents/09–0228_paid_leave_sr_fnl.pdf.

71. Society for Human Resources Management, "2018 Employee Benefits" (Alexandria, VA: SHRM, 2018), p. 10, https://www.shrm.org/hr-today/trends-and-forecasting/research-and-surveys/Documents/2018%20Employee%20Benefits%20Report.pdf.

72. "Private Industry Workers Received Average of 15 Paid Vacation Days After 5 Years of Service in 2017," *Economics Daily,* U.S. Bureau of Statistics (June 28, 2018), https://www.bls.gov/opub/ted/2018/private-industry-workers-received-average-of-15-paid-vacation-days-after-5-years-of-service-in-2017.htm (retrieved November 19, 2018).

73. T. P. Chen E. Morath, "Employers Choose Bonuses Over Raises," *Wall Street Journal* (September 19, 2018), pp. A1–A2.

74. Society for Human Resources Management, "2018 Employee Benefits" (Alexandria, VA: SHRM, 2018, p. 10), https://www.shrm.org/hr-today/trends-and-forecasting/research-and-surveys/Documents/2018%20Employee%20Benefits%20Report.pdf.

75. Internal Revenue Service, "Group Term Life Insurance," https://www.irs.gov/government-entities/federal-state-local-governments/group-term-life-insurance (retrieved November 10, 2018).

76. P. Anand, D. Wittenburg, "An Analysis of Private Long-Term Disability Insurance Access, Cost, and Trends," *Monthly Labor Review,* U.S. Bureau of Labor Statistics (March 2017), https://www.bls.gov/opub/mlr/2017/article/an-analysis-of-long-term-disability-insurance-access-cost-and-trends.htm (retrieved November 10, 2018).

77. Society for Human Resources Management, "2018 Employee Benefits" (Alexandria, VA: SHRM, 2018, p. 30), https://www.shrm.org/hr-today/trends-and-forecasting/research-and-surveys/Documents/2018%20Employee%20Benefits%20Report.pdf.

78. B. Farrow, "Wegmans," *Entrepreneur* (June 2018), p. 54.

79. Staff, "Headline, Walmart Will Subsidize," *Wall Street Journal* (May 31, 2018), pp. A1, B6.

80. C. Austin, "The 10 Best Workplaces for Millennials," *Fortune* (July 1, 2018), p. 18.

81. J. Depeters, "Cultivating a Great Workplace Starts With Its People," *Fortune* (March 1, 2018), p. 40.

82. E. Dunn, "Making It Work Remotely," *Entrepreneur* (September 2018), pp. 20–21.

83. https://www.forbes.com/sites/adigaskell/2016/01/15/why-a-flexible-worker-is-a-happy-and-productive-worker/#241ce5bb14c4 (retrieved November 10, 2018).

84. D. Ladley, I. Wilkinson, L. Young, "The Impact of Individual Versus Group Rewards on Work Group Performance and Cooperation: A Computational Social Science Approach," *Journal of Business Research* (2015), 68(11), pp. 2412–2425.

85. R. Williams, "Why Financial Incentives Don't Improve Performance," https://raywilliams.ca/why-financial-incentives-dont-improve-performance/ (retrieved November 19, 2018).

86. Ibid.

87. Y. Garbers, U. Konradt, "The Effect of Financial Incentives on Performance: A Quantitative Review of Individual and Team-Based Financial Incentives," *Journal of Occupational and Organizational Psychology* (2014), 87(1), pp. 102–137.

88. "2016 Employee Benefits" SHRM (June 20, 2016), https://www.shrm.org/hr-today/trends-and-forecasting/research-and-surveys/Documents/2016%20SHRM%20Employee%20Benefits%20Full%20Report.pdf (retrieved November 19, 2018).

89. C. Huspeth, "Best Buy Co. Inc.," *Hoovers*, http://0-subscriber.hoovers.com.liucat.lib.liu.edu/H/company360/fulldescription.html?companyId=10209000000000 (retrieved May 10, 2017).

90. "Code of Business Ethics: Best Buy," (March, 2014, p. 8), http://s2.q4cdn.com/785564492/files/doc_downloads/Gov_docs/code_of_business_ethics.pdf (retrieved from May 10, 2017).

91. C. Heyne, "The Inside Story: A Prognosis of Best Buy from a Veteran Employee," *Audioholics* (March 4, 2016), http://www.audioholics.com/editorials/best-buy-prognosis-employee (retrieved from May 10, 2017).

92. Ibid.

93. "Employer: Best Buy Average Salary Range by Job," *Payscale*, http://www.payscale.com/research/US/Employer=Best_Buy/Salary (retrieved May 10, 2017).

94. C. Heyne, "The Inside Story: A Prognosis of Best Buy From a Veteran Employee," *Audioholics* (March 4, 2016), http://www.audioholics.com/editorials/best-buy-prognosis-employee (retrieved May 10, 2017).

95. "Confessions of a Former Best Buy Employee," *Geek in Heels*, http://www.geekinheels.com/confessions-of-a-former-best-buy-employee.html (retrieved May 10, 2017).

Chapter 12

1. R. King, "Companies Want to Know: How Do Workers Feel?" *Wall Street Journal* (November 14, 2015), p. R3.

2. E. Fry, C. Zillman, "HR Is Not Your Friend," *Fortune* (March 1, 2018), pp. 99–108.

3. OSHA, "42. Workplace Safety," *Businessweek* (December 8–14, 2014), p. 62.

4. A. Levin, "The Perils of Flying," *Businessweek* (May 18–24, 2015), pp. 26–27.

5. S. Grobart, "Daimler Veers Into Maximum Overdrive," *Businessweek* (May 18–24, 2015), pp. 34–35.

6. Occupational Safety and Health Administration website, http://www.osha.gov (retrieved November 23, 2018).

7. E. Fry, C. Zillman, "HR Is Not Your Friend," *Fortune* (March 1, 2018), pp. 99–108.

8. OSH Act of 1970 (Pub. L. 91–596, December 29, 1970), http://www.osha.gov/pls/oshaweb/owadisp.show_document?p_id=2743 &p_table=OSHACT (retrieved November 23, 2018).

9. https://www.osha.gov/osha40/timeline.html (retrieved November 23, 2018).

10. https://www.bls.gov/news.release/cfoi.nr0.htm (retrieved November 23, 2018).

11. http://www.bls.gov/news.release/osh.nr0.htm (retrieved November 23, 2018).

12. http://www.osha.gov/about.html (retrieved November 23, 2018).

13. http://www.osha.gov/Publications/3439at-a-glance.pdf (retrieved November 23, 2018).

14. E. Conn, "Know Your OSHA Inspection Rights," *SHRM* (October 11, 2013) https://www.shrm.org/resourcesand-tools/hr-topics/risk-management/pages/osha-employer-inspection-rights.aspx (retrieved November 23, 2018).

15. https://www.osha.gov/Publications/3439at-a-glance.pdf (retrieved November 23, 2018).

16. E. Conn, "Know Your OSHA Inspection Rights," *SHRM* (October 11, 2013) https://www.shrm.org/resourcesand-tools/hr-topics/risk-management/pages/osha-employer-inspection-rights.aspx (retrieved November 23, 2018).

17. https://www.osha.gov/FedReg_osha_pdf/FED20120326.pdf (retrieved November 23, 2018).

18. OSHA, "Hazard Communication: Appendix D to §1910.1200—Safety Data Sheets (Mandatory)," https://www.osha.gov/dsg/hazcom/hazcom-appendix-d.html (retrieved November 23, 2018).

19. http://www.osha.gov/Publications/osha3000.pdf (retrieved November 23, 2018).

20. http://cdc.gov/niosh/about/default.html (retrieved November 23, 2018).

21. Ibid.

22. E. Lehoczky, "Keeping Your Workers Well," *INC.* (March/April 2018), p. 42.

23. D. A. Sharar, J. Pompe, R. Lennox, "Evaluating the Workplace Effects of EAP Counseling," *Journal of Health & Productivity* (2012), 6(12), pp. 5–14.

24. Society for Human Resource Management, "2018 Employee Benefits" SHRM (June 2018) p. 21, https://www.shrm.org/hr-today/trends-and-forecasting/research-and-surveys/Documents/2018%20Employee%20Benefits%20Report.pdf (retrieved November 23, 2018).

25. M. K. Richmond, F. C. Pampel, R. C. Wood, A. P. Nunes, "Impact of Employee Assistance Services on Depression, Anxiety, and Risky Alcohol Use: A Quasi-Experimental Study," *Journal of Occupational and Environmental Medicine* (2016), 58(7), pp. 641–650.

26. http://www.cdc.gov/nchs/fastats/obesity-overweight.htm (retrieved November 23, 2018).

27. L. Berry, A. Mirabito, W. Baun, "What's the Hard Return on Employee Wellness Programs?" *Harvard Business Review* (2010), 88(12), pp. 104–112.

28. Ibid.

29. https://www.cdc.gov/workplacehealthpromotion/health-strategies/musculoskeletal-disorders/ (retrieved November 23, 2018).

30. Ibid.

31. https://www.osha.gov/SLTC/ergonomics/index.html (retrieved November 23, 2018).

32. https://www.osha.gov/SLTC/ergonomics/faqs.html (retrieved November 23, 2018).

33. http://www.ncbi.nlm.nih.gov/pmc/articles/PMC3736412/ (retrieved November 23, 2018).

34. M. Van Tulder, A. Malmivaara, B. Koes, "Repetitive Strain Injury," *Lancet* (2007), 369(9575), pp. 1815–1822.

35. A. Kirkman, "It's All About Attitude," *Fortune* (November 17, 2014), p. 34.

36. K. Dill, "Survey: 42% of Employees Have Changed Jobs Due To Stress," Forbes (April 18, 2014) http://www.forbes.com/sites/kathryndill/2014/04/18/survey-42-of-employees-have-changed-jobs-due-to-stress/ (retrieved July 27, 2014).

37. M. L. Marzec, A. F. Scibelli, D. W. Edington, "Examining Individual Factors According to Health Risk Appraisal Data as Determinants of Absenteeism Among U.S. Utility Employees," *Journal of Occupational and Environmental Medicine* (2013), 55(7), pp. 732–740.

38. The term *eustress* was added at the suggestion of reviewer Carl Blencke, University of Central Florida, added on May 23, 2017.

39. B. C. Deb, S. K. Biswas, "Stress Management: A Critical View," *European Journal of Business and Management* (2011), 3(4), pp. 205–212.

40. M. F. Marin, C. Lord, J. Andrews, R. P. Juster, S. Sindi, G. Arsenault-Lapierre, . . . S. J. Lupien, "Chronic Stress, Cognitive Functioning and Mental Health," *Neurobiology of Learning and Memory* (2011), 96(4), pp. 583–595.

41. Y. Zhang, J. A. Lepine, B. R. Buckman, F. Wei, "It's Not Fair . . . Or Is It? The Role of Justice and Leadership in Explaining Work Stressor-Job Performance Relationships," *Academy of Management Journal* (2014), 57(3), pp. 675–697.

42. C. R. Wanberg, J. Zhu, R. Kanfer, Z. Zhang, "After the Pink Slip: Applying Dynamic Motivation Frameworks to the Job Search Experience," *Academy of Management Journal* (2012), 55(2), pp. 261–284.

43. Ibid.

44. http://www.corporatewellnessmagazine .com/issue-24/worksite-wellness-issue-24/workplace-stress-strains-organizations-bottom-lines/ (retrieved November 23, 2018).

45. E. Agnvall, "Stress: Don't Let It Make You Sick," *AARP Bulletin* (November 2014), pp. 26–27.

46. "Preserve Your Health Like Your Wealth," *Wall Street Journal* (April 15, 2009), pp. D5–D6.

47. M. della Cava, "An Uber Engineer Killed Himself. His Widow Says the Workplace Is to Blame," *USA Today* (April 27, 2017), https://www.usatoday.com/story/tech/news/2017/04/27/is-uber-culture-to-blame-for-an-employees-suicide/100938330/ (retrieved July 31, 2017).

48. E. Monsen, R. W. Boss, "The Impact of Strategic Entrepreneurship Inside the Organization: Examining Job Stress and Employee Retention," *Entrepreneurship Theory and Practice* (2009), 33(1), pp. 71–104.

49. J. Schramm, "Manage Stress, Improve the Bottom Line," *HR Magazine* (February 2013), p. 80.

50. "Preserve Your Health Like Your Wealth," *Wall Street Journal* (April 15, 2009), pp. D5–D6.

51. H. Mitchell, "Does Being Stressed Out Make You Forget?" *Wall Street Journal* (March 17, 2015), p. D1.

52. S. S. Wang, "Never Procrastinate Again," *Wall Street Journal* (September 1, 2015), pp. D1, D2.

53. Ibid.

54. M. Gulati, "The Higher Your Stress, the Higher Your LDL," *Wall Street Journal* (February 9, 2016), pp. D1, D2.

55. http://www.cdc.gov/nchs/fastats/obesity-overweight.htm (retrieved November 23, 2018).

56. P. Biamond, "Exercise in Sound Management," *BusinessWest* (2011), 26(23), p. 22, https://0-search-proquest-com.library .ualr.edu/docview/868035112?accountid=14482.

57. S. Shellenbarger, "Are You Hard-Wired to Boil Over From Stress?" *Wall Street Journal* (February 13, 2013), p. D3.

58. M. Gulati, "The Higher Your Stress, the Higher Your LDL," *Wall Street Journal* (February 9, 2016), pp. D1, D2.

59. "Preserve Your Health Like Your Wealth," *Wall Street Journal* (April 15, 2009), pp. D5–D6.

60. M. Gulati, "The Higher Your Stress, the Higher Your LDL," *Wall Street Journal* (February 9, 2016), pp. D1, D2.

61. S. D. Sidle, "Workplace Stress Management Interventions: What Works Best?" *Academy of Management Perspective* (2008), 22(3), pp. 111–112.

62. J. Welch, S. Welch, "Finding Your Inner Courage," *Businessweek* (February 23, 2009), p. 84.

63. "Preserve Your Health Like Your Wealth," *Wall Street Journal* (April 15, 2009), pp. D5–D6.

64. S. Covey, "Time Management," *Fortune* (September 19, 2009), pp. 28–29.

65. A. J. Lombardi, "Tech Neck," *Strength & Conditioning* online (accessed May 23, 2017).

66. S. Shellenbarger, "When Stress Is Good for You," *Wall Street Journal* (January 24, 2012), pp. D1, D5.

67. Press Release: "Securitas USA Issues "Top Security Threats and Management Issues Facing Corporate America" Survey Report" Securitas USA (March 1, 2017), http://www.securitasinc.com/global assets/us/files/press-releases/top-security-threats-suvery-annoucement.pdf (retrieved November 23, 2018).

68. "Top Security Threats and Management Issues Facing Corporate America: 2012 Survey of Fortune 1000 Companies," *Securitas Security Services USA* (2013), p. 6.

69. http://www.cnn.com/2014/05/19/justice/china-hacking-charges/ (retrieved November 23, 2018).

70. J. Diamond, "Russian Hacking and the 2016 Election: What You Need to Know," CNN (December 16, 2016), http://www .cnn.com/2016/12/12/politics/russian-hack-donald-trump-2016-election/index .html (retrieved November 23, 2018).

71. A. M. Matwyshyn, "Before Companies Purchase that New Technology," *Wall Street Journal* (March 13, 2017), p. R10.

72. S. Madnick, "How Firms Can Create a Cybersafe Culture," *Wall Street Journal* (May 30, 2018), p. R4.

73. Ibid.

74. L. Nagele-Piazza, "How Can HR Professionals Respond to an Active-Shooter Situation in the Workplace?" SHRM (June 6, 2017), https://www.shrm.org/ resourcesandtools/legal-and-compliance/ employment-law/pages/disgruntled-former-employee-responsible-for-work

place-shooting-in-orlando.aspx (retrieved November 23, 2018).

75. K. Mollica, D. Danehower, "Domestic Violence and the Workplace: The Employer's Legal Responsibilities," *Journal of Management and Marketing Research* (2014), 17, 1.

76. R. Lussier, "Dealing With Anger and Preventing Workplace Violence," *Clinical Leadership & Management Review* (2004), 18(2), pp. 117–119.

77. Ibid.

78. H. Mitchell, "The Effect of Rudeness," *Wall Street Journal* (February 20, 2018), p. R4.

79. R. Lussier, "Dealing With Anger and Preventing Workplace Violence," *Clinical Leadership & Management Review* (2004), 18(2), pp. 117–119.

80. Ibid.

81. http://www.dol.gov/elaws/asp/drugfree/ drugs/screen92.asp (retrieved November 23, 2018).

82. P. Babcock, "Former Drug Czar: Drugs in Workplace Understated Crisis," SHRM (November 13, 2013) http://www.shrm. org/hrdisciplines/safetysecurity/arti cles/pages/drugs-workplace-crisis.aspx (retrieved November 23, 2018).

83. Society for Human Resource Management "Introduction to the Human Resource Discipline of Safety and Security," SHRM (November 13, 2017) https://www.shrm .org/resourcesandtools/tools-and-sam ples/toolkits/pages/introsafetyandsecu rity.aspx (retrieved November 23, 2018).

84. https://www.unodc.org/wdr2017/field/ Booklet_1_EXSUM.pdf (retrieved November 23, 2018).

85. Occupational Safety and Health Administration, "Standard Interpretations," (October 11, 2018), https://www.osha. gov/laws-regs/standardinterpretations/ 2018–10–11 (retrieved November 20, 2018).

86. G. W. Goodman, "OSHA Rule and Policy Changes Affecting Workers' Compensation," Paper presented at 2017 Workers' Compensation Midwinter Seminar and Conference (March 16, 2016), https:// www.americanbar.org/content/dam/aba/ events/labor_law/2017/03/work/papers/ osha_rule.pdf (retrieved November 20, 2018).

87. Occupational Safety and Health Administration, "Standard Interpretations," (October 11, 2018), https://www.osha .gov/laws-regs/standardinterpretations/ 2018–10–11 (retrieved November 20, 2018).

88. "About eDocAmerica," http://www.edo-camerica.com/about/ (retrieved November 23, 2018).

89. T. Green, "ActioNet Inc.," Hoovers, http://0-subscriber.hoovers.com.liucat.lib .liu.edu/H/company360/overview.html? companyId=130020000000000 (retrieved May 15, 2017).

90. "Who We Are," ActioNet, https://www .actionet.com/about-us/ (retrieved May 15, 2017).

91. J. DeSimone, "Workplace Violence Wrongful Termination Case," V. James DeSimone Law blog, (March 18, 2016), http://www.vjamesdesimonelaw.com/ Blog/2016/March/Workplace-Violence-Wrongful-Termination-Case.aspx (retrieved May 15, 2017).

92. K. Penton, "Tech Co. Must Pay $7.4M to Worker Choked at Office," Portfolio Media. Inc., http://www.vjamesdesi-monelaw.com/documents/law360.pdf (retrieved May 15, 2017).

93. J. DeSimone, "Workplace Violence Wrongful Termination Case," V. James DeSimone Law blog (March 18, 2016), http://www.vjamesdesimonelaw.com/ Blog/2016/March/Workplace-Violence-Wrongful-Termination-Case.aspx (retrieved May 15, 2017).

94. K. Penton, "Tech Co. Must Pay $7.4M to Worker Choked at Office," Portfo-lio Media Inc., http://www.vjamesdesi-monelaw.com/documents/law360.pdf (retrieved May 15, 2017).

95. J. DeSimone, "Workplace Violence Wrongful Termination Case," V. James DeSimone Law blog (March 18, 2016), http://www.vjamesdesimonelaw.com/ Blog/2016/March/Workplace-Violence-Wrongful-Termination-Case.aspx (retrieved May 15, 2017).

Chapter 13

1. R. L. Hughes, R. C. Ginnett, G. J. Curphy, *Leadership: Enhancing the Lessons of Experi-ence*, 7th ed. (Burr Ridge, IL: McGraw-Hill, 2011).

2. R. Murphree, "Visionary Leader: Gospel Is Key to Unlimited Success," *AFA Journal* (March 2013), p. 11.

3. C. Bonanos, "The Lies We Tell at Work," *Businessweek* (February 4–10, 2013), pp. 71–73.

4. P. Zak, *The Moral Molecule* (New York, NY: Penguin, 2012).

5. C. Downs, "Liar, Liar—Back's on Fire," *AARP Magazine* (October/November 2012), p. 22.

6. K. Leavitt, S. J. Reynolds, C. M. Barnes, P. Schilpzan, S. T. Hannah, "Different Hats, Different Obligations: Plural Occu-pational Identities and Situated Moral Judgments," *Academy of Management Jour-nal* (2012), 55(6), pp. 1316–1333.

7. B. C. Gunia, L. Wang, L. Huang, J. Wang, J. K. Murnighan, "Contemplation and Conversation: Subtle Influences on Moral Decision Making," *Academy of Manage-ment Journal* (2012), 55(1), pp. 13–33.

8. D. Lange, N. T. Washburn, "Understand-ing Attributions of Corporate Social Irre-sponsibility," *Academy of Management Journal* (2012), 37(2), pp. 300–326.

9. A. Rasche, K. U. Gilbert, I. Schedel, "Cross-Disciplinary Ethics Education in MBA Programs: Rhetoric or Reality?" *Academy of Management Learning & Educa-tion* (2013), 12(1), pp. 71–85.

10. C. Besio, A. Pronzini, "Morality, Ethics, and Values Outside and Inside Organiza-tions: An Example of the Discourse on Climate Change," *Journal of Business Eth-ics* (2014), 119(3), pp. 287–300.

11. S. Robbins, M. Coulter, *Management* (Upper Saddle River, NJ: Pearson, 2014), p. 136.

12. R. Chandra, *Business Ethics* (Self-published, 2013).

13. C. A. Rusnak, "Are You Confusing People With Your Leadership Style?" *Costco Con-nection* (March 2012), p. 11.

14. J. Geisler, "Forgive? Forget? Not Likely," *Costco Connection* (December 2012), p. 10.

15. C. Bonanos, "The Lies We Tell at Work," *Businessweek* (February 4–10, 2013), pp. 71–73.

16. D. Ariely, "Why We Lie," *Wall Street Jour-nal* (May 26–27, 2012), pp. C1–C2.

17. M. K. Duffy, K. L. Scott, J. D. Shaw, B. J. Tepper, K. Aquino, "A Social Context Model of Envy and Social Undermining," *Academy of Management Journal* (2012), 55(3), pp. 643–666.

18. D. M. Mayer, K. Aquino, R. L. Greenbaum, M. Kuenzi, "Who Displays Ethical Leader-ship, and Why Does It Matter? An Exami-nation of Antecedents and Consequences of Ethical Leadership," *Academy of Manage-ment Journal* (2011), 55(1), pp. 151–171.

19. M. K. Duffy, K. L. Scott, J. D. Shaw, B. J. Tepper, K. Aquino, "A Social Context Model of Envy and Social Undermining," *Academy of Management Journal* (2012), 55(3), pp. 643–666.

20. B. C. Gunia, L. Wang, L. Huang, J. Wang, J. K. Murnighan, "Contemplation and Conversation: Subtle Influences on Moral Decision Making," *Academy of Manage-ment Journal* (2012), 55(1), pp. 13–33.

21. C. Bonanos, "The Lies We Tell at Work," *Businessweek* (February 4–10, 2013), pp. 71–73.

22. D. Ariely, "Why We Lie," *Wall Street Jour-nal* (May 26–27, 2012), pp. C1–C2.

23. Ibid.

24. S. D. Levitt, S. J. Dubner, "SuperFreako-nomics: Global Cooling, Patriotic Prosti-tutes, and Why Suicide Bombers Should Buy Life Insurance," *Academy of Manage-ment Perspectives* (2011), 25(2), pp. 86–87.

25. D. Ariely, "Why We Lie," *Wall Street Jour-nal* (May 26–27, 2012), pp. C1–C2.

26. K. Leavitt, S. J. Reynolds, C. M. Barnes, P. Schilpzan, S. T. Hannah, "Different Hats, Different Obligations: Plural Occupational Identities and Situated Moral Judgments," *Academy of Management Journal* (2012), 55(6), pp. 1316–1333.

27. D. Ariely, "Why We Lie," *Wall Street Jour-nal* (May 26–27, 2012), pp. C1–C2.

28. Ibid.

29. Rotary International, "Our History," https://www.rotary.org/myrotary/en/ learning-reference/about-rotary/history-rotary-international/ (retrieved Nov. 23, 2018).

30. Berkshire Hathaway Inc., "Corporate Governance Guidelines," http://www .berkshirehathaway.com/govern/cor pgov.pdf (retrieved Nov. 23, 2018).

31. B. C. Gunia, L. Wang, L. Huang, J. Wang, J. K. Murnighan, "Contemplation and Conversation: Subtle Influences on Moral Decision Making," *Academy of Manage-ment Journal* (2012), 55(1), pp. 13–33.

32. D. Ariely, "Why We Lie," *Wall Street Jour-nal* (May 26–27, 2012), pp. C1–C2.

33. P. Zak, *The Moral Molecule* (New York, NY: Penguin, 2012).

34. K. Leonard, "What Are the Key Compo-nents of a Code of Ethics in Business?" *Houston Chronicle*, Chron.com, http:// smallbusiness.chron.com/key-compo nents-code-ethics-business-244.html (retrieved Nov. 23, 2018).

35. Ibid.

36. D. Meinert, "Creating an Ethical Culture," *HR Magazine* (April 2014), pp. 22–27.

37. J. R. Detert, M. C. Edmondson, "Implicit Voice Theories: Taken-for-Granted Rules of Self-Censorship at Work," *Academy of Management Journal* (2011), 54(3), pp. 461–488.

38. D. Ariely, "Why We Lie," *Wall Street Jour-nal* (May 26–27, 2012), pp. C1–C2.

39. P. Drucker, *Management* (New York, NY: Routledge, 2012).

40. P. Lattman, "Ralph Lauren Corp. Agrees to Pay Fine in Bribery Case," Deal-Book (April 22, 2013), http://dealbook .nytimes.com/2013/04/22/ralph-lauren-pays-1-6-million-to-resolve-bribery-case/ (retrieved Nov. 23, 2018).

41. C. A. Olson, R. b. Lapp, U. Chan-drasekaran, S. L. Slusher, "'Subjec-tive' Decision-Making After *Wal-Mart v. Dukes*," Seyfarth Shaw LLP (2012), https://www.americanbar.org/content/ dam/aba/events/labor_law/2012/03/ national_conference_on_equal_employ-ment_opportunity_law/mw2012eeo_ olson.authcheckdam.pdf (retrieved Nov . 23, 2018).

42. D. Lange, N. T. Washburn, "Understand-ing Attributions of Corporate Social Irre-sponsibility," *Academy of Management Journal* (2012), 37(2), pp. 300–326.

43. K. Freifeld, "BofA Could Still Put Coun-trywide Into Bankruptcy, Executive

Says," *Reuters* (June 10, 2013), http://www.reuters.com/article/2013/06/10/us-bofa-mbs-idUSBRE95916M20130610/ (retrieved Nov. 23, 2018).

44. N. Parish Flannery, "Monsanto's Pesticide Problems Raise Awareness About Corporate Environmental Responsibility," *Forbes* (September 3, 2011), http://www.forbes.com/sites/nathanielparishflannery/2011/09/03/monsantos-pesticide-problems-raise-awareness-for-corporate-environmental-responsibility/ (retrieved Nov. 23, 2018).

45. R. Albergotti, "Furor Erupts Over Facebook's Experiment on Users," *Wall Street Journal* (June 30, 2014), http://online.wsj.com/articles/furor-erupts-over-facebook-experiment-on-users-1404085840/ (retrieved Nov. 23, 2018).

46. PART 1608—Affirmative Action Appropriate Under Title VII of the Civil Rights Act of 1964, As Amended, https://www.govinfo.gov/content/pkg/CFR-2001-title29-v014/pdf/CFR-2001-title29-v014-part1608.pdf

47. L. M. Leslie, D. M. Mayer, D. A. Kravitz, "The Stigma of Affirmative Action: A Stereotyping-Based Theory and Meta-Analytic Test of the Consequences for Performance," *Academy of Management Journal* (2014), 57(4), pp. 964–989.

48. Call for papers, *Academy of Management Review* (2015), 40(4), pp. 669–670.

49. M. L. Besharov, "The Relational Ecology of Identification: How Organizational Identification Emerges When Individual Hold Divergent Values," *Academy of Management Journal* (2014), 57(5), pp. 1485–1512.

50. F. A. Miller, J. H. Katz, *The Inclusion Breakthrough: Unleashing the Real Power of Diversity* (San Francisco, CA: Berrett-Koehler, 2002).

51. http://www.shrm.org/templatestools/hrqa/pages/whenisanaapneeded.aspx (retrieved May 24, 2014).

52. 41 CFR 60–1.

53. Ibid.

54. http://www.supremecourt.gov/opinions/12pdf/11-345_15gm.pdf (retrieved May 25, 2014).

55. http://www.nytimes.com/2014/04/23/us/supreme-court-michigan-affirmative-action-ban.html?_r=0 (retrieved May 25, 2014).

56. E. Kearney, D. Gebert, S. C. Voelpel, "When and How Diversity Benefits Teams: The Importance of Team Members' Need for Cognition," *Academy of Management Journal* (2009), 52(3), pp. 581–598.

57. Z. T. Kalinoski, D. Steele-Johnson, E. J. Peyton, K. A. Leas, J. Steinke, N. A. Bowling, "A Meta-Analytic Evaluation of Diversity Training Outcomes," *Journal of Organizational Behavior* (2013), 34(8), pp. 1076–1104.

58. Call for papers, *Academy of Management Review* (2015), 40(4), pp. 669–670.

59. O. E. Varela, R. G. Watts, "The Development of the Global Manager: An Empirical Study on the Role of Academic International Sojourns," *Academy of Management Learning & Education* (2014), 13(2), pp.187–207.

60. U.S. Census Bureau website, www.census.gov (accessed June 7, 2018).

61. G. Bensinger, "Airbnb, Under Fire, Promotes Diversity," *Wall Street Journal* (September 9, 2016), p. B1.

62. O. E. Varela, R. G. Watts, "The Development of the Global Manager: An Empirical Study on the Role of Academic International Sojourns," *Academy of Management Learning & Education* (2014), 13(2), pp. 187–207.

63. S. Sandberg, "When Women Get Stuck, Corporate America Gets Stuck," *Wall Street Journal* (September 30, 2015), p. R3.

64. M. L. Besharov, "The Relational Ecology of Identification: How Organizational Identification Emerges When Individuals Hold Divergent Values," *Academy of Management Journal* (2014), 57(5), pp. 1485–1512.

65. M. E. M. Barak, *Managing Diversity: Toward a Globally Inclusive Workplace* (Thousand Oaks, CA: Sage, 2016), p. 8.

66. Ibid.

67. N. Vohra, V. Chari, P. Mathur, P. Sudarshan, N. Verma, N. Mathur, . . . V. Dasmahapatra, "Inclusive Workplaces: Lessons From Theory and Practice," *Vikalpa* (2015), 40(3), 324–362.

68. S. Sandberg, "When Women Get Stuck, Corporate America Gets Stuck," *Wall Street Journal* (September 30, 2015), p. R3.

69. M. Mayfield, J. Mayfield, "Developing a Scale to Measure the Creative Environment Perceptions: A Questionnaire for Investigating Garden Variety Creativity," *Creativity Research Journal* (2010), 22(2), pp. 162–169.

70. M. A. Runco, S. Acar, "Divergent Thinking as an Indicator of Creative Potential," *Creativity Research Journal* (2012), 24(1), pp. 66–75.

71. F. Stevens, V. Plaut, J. Sanchez-Burks, "Unlocking the Benefits of Diversity," *Journal of Applied Behavioral Science* (2008), 44(1), pp. 116–133.

72. S. Benard, L. Doan, "The Conflict-Cohesion Hypothesis: Past, Present, and Possible Futures," *Advances in Group Processes* (2011), 28, pp. 189–225.

73. Y. Chung, H. Liao, S. E. Jackson, M. Subramony, S. Colakglu, Y. Jiang, "Cracking but Not Breaking: Joint Effects of Faultline Strength and Diversity Climate on Loyal Behavior," *Academy of Management Journal* (2015), 58(5), pp. 1495–1515.

74. E. Fry, C. Zillman, "HR Is Not Your Friend," *Fortune* (March 1, 2018), pp. 99–108.

75. M. L. Stallard, "Building a Culture of Connections, *Costco Connection* (July 2015), p. 112.

76. Box item, "Three Diversity Strategies That Work," Fortune.com (accessed January 3, 2017).

77. Company Spotlight, Cadence, *Fortune* (December 1, 2015), p. 45.

78. R. Feintzerg, "More Firms Say Targets Are the Key to Diversity," *Wall Street Journal* (September 30, 2015), p. R3.

79. Box item, "Three Diversity Strategies That Work," Fortune.com (accessed January 3, 2017).

80. "Starbucks closed," *Wall Street Journal* (May 30, 2018), p. A1.

81. "The Best Advice," *Fortune* (October 1, 2015), p. 109.

82. N. Waller. J. Lublin, "What's Holding Women Back in the Workplace?" *Wall Street Journal* (September 30, 2015), pp. C1, C2.

83. B. Waber, "Gender Bias by the Numbers," *Businessweek* (February 3–9, 2014), pp. 8–9; M. L. McDonald, J. D. Westphal, "Access Denied: Low Mentoring of Women and Minority First-Time Directors and Its Negative Effects on Appointments to Additional Boards," *Academy of Management Journal* (2013), 56(4), pp. 1169–1198.

84. "Margin Note," *Entrepreneur* (June 2018), p. 52.

85. S. Y. Yousafzai, S. Saeed, M. Muffatto, "Institutional Theory and Contextual Embeddedness of Women's Entrepreneurial Leadership: Evidence from 92 Countries," *Journal of Small Business Management* (2015), 53(3), pp. 587–604.

86. Frito-Lay website, www.fritolay.com (accessed January 3, 2017).

87. S. Sandberg, "When Women Get Stuck, Corporate America Gets Stuck," *Wall Street Journal* (September 30, 2015), p. R3.

88. D. A. Waldman, R. M. Balven, "Responsible Leadership: Theoretical Issues and Research Directions," *Academy of Management Perspectives* (2014), 28(3), pp. 224–234.

89. I. Filatotchev. C. Nakajima, "Corporate Governance, Responsible Managerial Behavior, and Corporate Social Responsibility: Organizational Efficiency Versus Organizational Legitimacy," *Academy of Management Perspectives* (2014), 28(3), pp. 289–306.

90. E. Fry, C. Zillman, "HR Is Not Your Friend," *Fortune* (March 1, 2018), pp. 99–108.

91. A. B. Carroll, K. M. Shabana, "The Business Case for Corporate Social Responsibility: A Review of Concepts, Research and Practice," *International Journal of Management Reviews* (2010), 12(1), pp. 85–105.

92. C. Q. Trank, "Reading Evidence-Based Management: The Possibilities of Interpretation," *Academy of Management Learning & Education* (2014), 13(3), pp. 381–395.

93. "Master Class," *Businessweek* (May 6–12, 2013), p. 83.

94. D. Lange, N. T. Washburn, "Understanding Attributions of Corporate Social Irresponsibility," *Academy of Management Journal* (2012), 37(2), pp. 300–326.

95. R. Cohen, "Five Lessons From the Banana Man," *Wall Street Journal* (June 2–3, 2012), p. C2.

96. J. P. Doh. N. R. Quigley, "Responsible Leadership and Stakeholder Management: Influence Pathways and Organizational Outcomes," *Academy of Management Perspectives* (2014), 28(3), pp. 255–274.

97. S. Schaefer, "The Just 100: America's Best Corporate Citizens in 2016," *Forbes* (December 20, 2016), p. 82.

98. D. Bennet, D. Gambrell, "How CVS Quit Smoking," *Businessweek* (December 29, 2014–January 11, 2015), p. 58.

99. R. Karlgaard, "Society's Lottery Winners," *Forbes* (June 15, 2015), p. 30.

100. D. Seetharaman, A. Das, "Zuckerberg to Give Away Fortune," *Wall Street Journal* (December 2, 2015), pp. B1, B8.

101. J. Morelli, "Environmental Sustainability: A Definition for Environmental Professionals," *Journal of Environmental Sustainability* (2013), 1(1), p. 2.

102. A. Nadim, R. N. Lussier, "Sustainability as a Small Business Competitive Strategy," *Journal of Small Strategy* 21, no. 2 (2012), pp. 79–95.

103. D. S. Siegel, "Responsible Leadership," *Academy of Management Perspectives* (2014), 28(3), pp. 221–223.

104. D. Baden, "Look on the Bright Side: A Comparison of Positive and Negative Role Models in Business Ethics Education," *Academy of Management Learning & Education* (2014), 13(2), pp. 154–170.

105. C. L. Pearce, C. L. Wassenaar, C. C. Manz, "Is Shared Leadership the Key to Responsible Leadership?" *Academy of Management Perspectives* (2014), 28(3), pp. 275–288.

106. R. Karlgaard, "Riches From the Disruptive Dozen," *Forbes* (October 19, 2015), p. 38.

107. Ad "Green Building U.S.A." *Fortune* (November 1, 2015).

108. A. A. Marcus, A. R. Fremeth, "Green Management Matters Regardless," *Academy of Management Perspectives* (2009), 23(3), pp. 17–26.

109. D. Crilly, M. Hansen, M. Zollo, "The Grammar of Decoupling: A Cognitive-Linguistic Perspective on Firms' Sustainability Claims and Stakeholder' Interpretation," *Academy of Management Journal* (2016), 59(2), pp. 705–729.

110. L. Lorenzetti, "Southwest Airlines Is Flying High," *Fortune* (October 27, 2014), p. 38.

111. M. P. Johnson, S. Schaltegger, "Two Decades of Sustainability Management Tools for SMEs: How Far Have We Come?" *Journal of Small Business Management* (2016), 54(4), pp. 481–505.

112. A. Nadim, R. N. Lussier, "Sustainability as a Small Business Competitive Strategy," *Journal of Small Strategy* (2012), 21(2), pp. 79–95.

113. M. E. Porter, M. R. Kramer, "Profiting the Planet," *Fortune* (September 1, 2015), pp. 64–65.

114. "Walmart Marks Fulfillment of Key Global Responsibility Commitments," Walmart (November 17, 2105), https://news.walmart.com/news-archive/2015/11/17/walmart-marks-fulfillment-of-key-global-responsibility-commitments (retrieved June 24, 2018).

115. Briefs: Wal-Mart, *Businessweek* (February 13–19, 2012), p. 28.

116. K. Weise, "Sustainability: I'm With Wal-Mart," *Businessweek* (November 28–December 2, 2011), p. 60.

117. C. P. Withorn, "Thanks, Jeff Bezos!" *Forbes* (August 17, 2015), pp. 36–38.

118. Wikipedia, "Chief Sustainability Officer," http://en.wikipedia.org/wiki/Chief_sustainability_officer/ (retrieved May 22, 2013).

119. M. P. Johnson, S. Schaltegger, "Two Decades of Sustainability Management Tools for SMEs: How Far Have We Come?" *Journal of Small Business Management* (2016), 54(4), pp. 481–505.

120. D. Crilly, M. Hansen, M. Zollo, "The Grammar of Decoupling: A Cognitive-Linguistic Perspective on Firms' Sustainability Claims and Stakeholder' Interpretation," *Academy of Management Journal* (2016), 59(2), pp. 705–729.

121. World Economic Forum, "Action 2020: Can Business Help the World Become More Sustainable?" *Green Light* newsletter (January 2014), http://www3.weforum.org/docs/GAC/2014/WEF_GAC_GovernanceSustainability_GreenLight_January_Report_2014.pdf (retrieved March 25, 2019).

122. http://www.iso.org/iso/home/standards/management-standards/iso14000.htm (retrieved Nov. 23, 2018).

123. UN Global Compact, "The Ten Principles of the UN Global Compact," http://www.unglobalcompact.org/AboutTheGC/TheTenPrinciples/index.html (retrieved Nov. 23, 2018).

124. CSRwire, "About Us," http://www.csrwire.com/pages/about_us (retrieved Nov. 23, 2018).

125. N. Landrum, S. Edwards, *Sustainable Business: An Executive's Primer* (New York, NY: Business Expert Press, 2009), p. 32.

126. Clinton Presidential Center, "HEAL," https://www.clintonfoundation.org/clinton-presidential-center/about/heal (retrieved Nov. 23, 2018).

127. A. P. Brief (Ed.), *Diversity at Work* (Cambridge, UK: Cambridge University Press, 2008), pp. 265–267.

128. R. Anand, M. Winters, "A Retrospective View of Corporate Diversity Training From 1964 to the Present," *Academy of Management Learning & Education* (2008), 7(3), pp. 356–372.

129. Ibid.

130. C. Holladay, M. Quinones, "The Influence of Training Focus and Trainer Characteristics on Diversity Training Effectiveness," *Academy of Management Learning & Education* (2008), 7(3), pp. 343–354.

131. K. Leonard, "What Are the Key Components of a Code of Ethics in Business?" *Houston Chronicle*, Chron.com, http://smallbusiness.chron.com/key-components-code-ethics-business-244.html (retrieved Nov. 23, 2018).

132. R. Kerber, P. Szekely, "CEO Pay Still Dwarfing Pay of U.S. Workers: Union Report," *Reuters* (May 9, 2017), http://www.reuters.com/article/us-usa-compensation-ceos-idUSKBN1851SV (retrieved May 17, 2017).

133. D. Larcker, N. Donatiello, B. Tayan, "Americans and CEO Pay: 2016 Public Perception Survey on CEO Compensation," *Stanford Rock Center for Corporate Governance* (February 2016), https://www.gsb.stanford.edu/faculty-research/publications/americans-ceo-pay-2016-public-perception-survey-ceo-compensation (retrieved May 17, 2017).

134. C. Le Beau, "Is CEO Pay Too High?" *Crain's Custom Media* (August 20, 2013), http://www.chicagobusiness.com/article/20130820/NEWS01/130819903/is-ceo-pay-too-high (retrieved May 17, 2017).

135. Ibid.

136. A. Smith, "Executive Pay Controversy," *Business-know-how*, http://www.businessknowhow.com/growth/ceocompensation.htm (retrieved May 17, 2017).

Chapter 14

1. A. Murray, "The Hard Truths of Globalization," *Fortune* (August 1, 2016), p. 6.

2. M. L. Turner, "Remote Control," *Entrepreneur* (January 2016), pp. 75–79.

3. R. J. Reichard, S. A. Serrano, M. Condren, N. Wilder, M. Dollwet, W. Wang,

"Engaging in Cultural Trigger Events in the Development of Cultural Competence," *Academy of Management Learning & Education* (2015), 14(4), pp. 461–481.

4. J. R. Ramsey, M. P. Lorenz, "Exploring the Impact of Cross-Cultural Management Education on Cultural Intelligence, Student Satisfaction, and Commitment," *Academy of Management Learning & Education* (2016), 15(1), pp. 79–99.

5. "About FedEx," https://about.van.fedex .com/our-story/ (retrieved November 27, 2018).

6. M. Li, W. H. Mobley, A. Kelly, "When Do Global Leaders Learn Best to Develop Cultural Intelligence? An Investigation of the Moderating Role of Experiential Learning Styles," *Academy of Management Education & Learning* (2013), 12(1), pp. 32–50.

7. J. H. Marler, "Strategic Human Resource Management in Context," *Academy of Management Perspectives* (2012), 26(2), pp. 6–11.

8. U.S. Census Bureau, "U.S. and World Population Clock," http://www.census.gov/ popclock (retrieved March 25, 2019).

9. M. Schuman, "Emerging Markets Are Still the Future," *Businessweek* (September 7–13, 2015), pp. 8–9.

10. D. M. Ewalt, "The Modest Tycoon," *Forbes* (June 15, 2015), pp. 77–80.

11. J. Spiro, "The Great Leader Series: Jeff Bezos, Founder of Amazon.com," *INC.* (October 23, 2009), https://www.inc .com/30years/articles/jeff-bezos.html (retrieved November 27, 2018).

12. World Trade Organization "Overview," http://www.wto.org/english/thewto_e/ whatis_e/wto_dg_stat_e.htm (retrieved November 27, 2018).

13. Information taken from the World Trade Organization's website, http://www.wto .org (retrieved December 3, 2018).

14. B. Chappell, "USMCA: Trump Signs New Trade Agreement With Mexico and Canada to Replace NAFTA," NPR (November 30, 2018), https://www.npr .org/2018/11/30/672150010/usmca-trump -signs-new-trade-agreement-with-mexico -and-canada (retrieved December 1, 2018).

15. A. Molinsky, "The Psychological Processes of Cultural Retooling," *Academy of Management Journal* (2013), 56(3), pp. 683–710.

16. M. Mendenhall, A. Arnardottir, G. Oddou, L. Burke, "Developing Cross-Cultural Competencies in Management Education Via Cognitive-Behavior Therapy," *Academy of Management Learning & Education* (2013), 12(3), pp. 436–451.

17. Call for papers, *Academy of Management Review* (2015), 40(4), pp. 669–670.

18. S. Sandberg, "When Women Get Stuck, Corporate America Gets Stuck," *Wall Street Journal* (September 30, 2015), p. R3.

19. Equal Employment Opportunity Commission, "Employee Rights When Working for Multinational Employers," http:// www.eeoc.gov/facts/multi-employees .html (retrieved July 22, 2010).

20. Ibid.

21. J. Palazzolo, "Is It a Bribe . . . or Not?" *Wall Street Journal* (July 22, 2013), p. R3.

22. O. E. Varela, R. G. Watts, "The Development of the Global Manager: An Empirical Study on the Role of Academic International Sojourns," *Academy of Management Learning & Education* (2014), 13(2), pp. 187–207.

23. A. Chuang, R. S. Hsu, A. C. Wang, T. A. Judge, "Does West Fit with East? In Search of a Chinese Model of Person-Environment Fit," *Academy of Management Journal* (2015), 58(2), pp. 480–510.

24. C. Hardy, D. Tolhurst, "Epistemological Beliefs and Cultural Diversity Matters in Management Education and Learning," *Academy of Management Learning & Education* (2014), 13(2), pp. 265–289.

25. Call for papers, *Academy of Management Review* (2015), 40(4), pp. 669–670.

26. W. L. Bedwell, S. M. Fiore, E. Salas, "Developing the Future Workforce: An Approach for Integrating Interpersonal Skills Into the MBA Classroom," *Academy of Management Learning & Education* (2014), 13(2), pp. 171–186.

27. G. Colvin, "Humans Are Underrated," *Fortune* (August 1, 2015), pp. 100–113.

28. Ibid.

29. D. Baden, M. Higgs, "Challenging the Perceived Wisdom of Management Theories and Practice," *Academy of Management Learning & Education* (2015), 14(4), pp. 539–555.

30. H. G. Barkema, X. P. Chen, G. George, Y. Luo, A. S. Tsut, "West Meets East: New Concepts and Theories," *Academy of Management Journal* (2015), 58(2), pp. 460–479.

31. Hofstede Insights, "National Culture," https://www.hofstede-insights.com/mod els/national-culture (retrieved March 25, 2019).

32. "Hofstede's 5 Dimensions," home.sand iego.edu/~dimon/CulturalFrameworks .pdf

33. B. M. Cole, "Lessons From a Martial Arts Dojo: A Prolonged Process Model of High-Context Communication," *Academy of Management Journal* (2015), 58(2), pp. 567–591.

34. R. J. Reichard, S. A. Serrano, M. Condren, N. Wilder, M. Dollwet, W. Wang, "Engaging in Cultural Trigger Events in the Development of Cultural Competence," *Academy of Management Learning & Education* (2015), 14(4), pp. 461–481.

35. W. L. Bedwell, S. M. Fiore, E. Salas, "Developing the Future Workforce: An Approach for Integrating Interpersonal Skills Into the MBA Classroom," *Academy of Management Learning & Education* (2014), 13(2), pp. 171–186.

36. M. L. Besharov, "The Relational Ecology of Identification: How Organizational Identification Emerges When Individuals Hold Divergent Values," *Academy of Management Journal* (2014), 57(5), pp. 1485–1512.

37. W. L. Bedwell, S. M. Fiore, E. Salas, "Developing the Future Workforce: An Approach for Integrating Interpersonal Skills Into the MBA Classroom," *Academy of Management Learning & Education* (2014), 13(2), pp. 171–186.

38. O. E. Varela, R. G. Watts, "The Development of the Global Manager: An Empirical Study on the Role of Academic International Sojourns," *Academy of Management Learning & Education* (2014), 13(2), pp. 187–207.

39. R. J. Reichard, S. A. Serrano, M. Condren, N. Wilder, M. Dollwet, W. Wang, "Engaging in Cultural Trigger Events in the Development of Cultural Competence," *Academy of Management Learning & Education* (2015), 14(4), pp. 461–481.

40. P. C. Godart, W. W. Maddux, A. V. Shipilov, A. D. Galinsky, "Fashion With a Foreign Flair: Professional Experiences Abroad Facilitate the Creative Innovations of Organizations," *Academy of Management Journal* (2015), 58(1), pp. 195–220.

41. T. J. Huang, S. C. Chi, J. J. Lawler, "The Relationship Between Expatriates' Personality Traits and Their Adjustment to International Assignments," *International Journal of Human Resource Management* (2005), 16(9), pp. 1656–1670.

42. S. Mor, M. Morris, J. Joh, "Identifying and Training Adaptive Cross-Cultural Management Skills: The Crucial Role of Cultural Metacognition," *Academy of Management Learning & Education* (2013), 12(3), pp. 453–475.

43. C. Dörrenbächer, J. Gammelgaard, F. McDonald, A. Stephan, H. Tüselmann, "Staffing Foreign Subsidiaries With Parent Country Nationals or Host Country Nationals? Insights From European Subsidiaries," *Working Papers of the Institute of Management Berlin at the Berlin School of Economics and Law* (2013), 74.

44. P. J. Buckley, R. Strange, "The Governance of the Global Factory: Location and Control of World Economic Activity," *Academy of Management Perspectives* (2015), 29(2), pp. 237–249.

45. R. Ballhaus, M. Colias, "President Threatens to Cut GM Subsidies Over Layoffs," *Wall Street Journal* (November 28, 2018), pp. A1, A6.

46. R. Maurer, "Emerging Markets Drive Global Talent Strategy Shift," SHRM

(November 5, 2013), http://www.shrm .org/hrdisciplines/global/articles/pages/ emerging-markets-global-talent-strategy .aspx (retrieved August 21, 2014).

47. T. Chamorro-Premuzic, M. Sanger, "What Leadership Looks Like in Different Cultures," *SHRM* (May 6, 2016), https://hbr .org/2016/05/what-leadership-looks-like -in-different-cultures (retrieved December 1, 2018).

48. R. J. Reichard, S. A. Serrano, M. Condren, N. Wilder, M. Dollwet, W. Wang, "Engaging in Cultural Trigger Events in the Development of Cultural Competence," *Academy of Management Learning & Education* (2015), 14(4), pp. 461–481.

49. W. F. Smith, "Dynamic Decision Making: A Model of Senior Leaders Managing Strategic Paradoxes," *Academy of Management Journal* (2014), 57(6), pp. 1592–1623; I. Filatotchev, C. Nakajima, "Corporate Governance, Responsible Managerial Behavior, and Corporate Social Responsibility: Organizational Efficiency Versus Organizational Legitimacy," *Academy of Management Perspectives* (2014), 28(3), pp. 289–306.

50. G. K. Stahl, M. Y. Brannen, "Building Cross-Cultural Leadership Competence: An Interview With Carlos Ghosn," *Academy of Management Learning & Education* (2013), 12(3), pp. 494–502.

51. G. Colvin, "Humans Are Underrated," *Fortune* (August 1, 2015), pp. 100–113.

52. J. R. Ramsey, M. P. Lorenz, "Exploring the Impact of Cross-Cultural Management Education on Cultural Intelligence, Student Satisfaction, and Commitment," *Academy of Management Learning & Education* (2016), 15(1), pp. 79–99.

53. http://www.shrm.org/education/hredu cation/documents/international_hrm_ presentation.pptx (retrieved August 23, 2014).

54. R. L. Minter, "Preparation of Expatriates for Global Assignments: Revisited," *Journal of Diversity Management* (2011), 3(2), pp. 37–42.

55. N. Cole, K. Nesbeth, "Why Do International Assignments Fail? The Expatriate Families Speak," *International Studies of Management and Organization* (2014), 44(3).

56. K. van der Zee, J. P. van Oudenhoven, "Culture Shock or Challenge? The Role of Personality as a Determinant of Intercultural Competence," *Journal of Cross-Cultural Psychology* (2013), 44(6), pp. 928–940.

57. http://www.shrm.org/education/hredu cation/documents/international_hrm_ presentation.pptx (retrieved August 23, 2014).

58. B. M. Cole, "Lessons From a Martial Arts Dojo: A Prolonged Process Model of High-Context Communication," *Academy of Management Journal* (2015), 58(2), pp. 567–591.

59. "Repatriation: How Can My Company Best Retain Repatriated Employees?" SHRM, http://www.shrm.org/templates tools/hrqa/pages/howcanmycompanybe stretainrepatriatedemployees.aspx (retrieved August 23, 2014).

60. C. Bailey, L. Dragoni, "Repatriation After Global Assignments: Current HR Practices and Suggestions for Ensuring Successful Repatriation," *People & Strategy Journal* (2013), 36(1), pp. 48–57.

61. T. Shelton, "Global Compensation Strategies: Managing and Administering Split Pay for an Expatriate Workforce," *Compensation and Benefits Review* (January/February 2008), 40, pp. 56–60.

62. ORC Worldwide, *2006 Worldwide Survey of International Assignment Policies and Practices* (New York, NY: ORC, 2007).

63. "Global: Expatriate: How Should We Compensate an Employee on a Foreign Assignment?" SHRM (December 11, 2012), https://www.shrm.org/ resourcesandtools/tools-and-samples/ hr-qa/pages/howshouldwecompensate anemployeeonaforeignassignment.aspx (retrieved March 25, 2019).

64. K. Y. Ng, L. V. Dyne, S. Ang, "From Experience to Experiential Learning: Cultural Intelligence as a Learning Capability for Global Leader Development," *Academy of Management Learning & Education* (2009), 8(1), pp. 511–526.

65. C. Rose, "Charlie Rose Talks to Mike Duke," *Businessweek* (December 2–6, 2010), p. 30.

66. Hay Group, "Work on Your Winning Strategy," (July 2010).

67. M. Segalla, D. Rouzies, M. Besson, B. Weitz, "A Cross-National Investigation of Incentive Sales Compensation," *International Journal of Research in Marketing* (2006), 23(4), pp. 419–433.

68. Ibid.

69. L. Thomas, "The March of Globalization Is Grinding to a Halt," Reuters (September 21, 2016), https://www.blackrockblog .com/2015/11/12/how-the-world-retires/ (retrieved August 1, 2017).

70. R. Ottinger, "Disrupt or Be Disrupted," *Forbes* (April 3, 2013), http://www.forbes .com/sites/johnkotter/2013/04/03/how -to-lead-through-business-disruption/ (retrieved August 1, 2017).

71. L. Chandy, B. Seidel, "Is Globalization's Second Wave About to Break?" Brookings Institute (October 2016), p. 13.

72. http://www.bcg.com/media/pressrelease details.aspx?id=tcm:12–144944 (retrieved August 24, 2014).

73. "WTO Expects Global Trade to Grow at 2.4% in 2017," *Economic Times* (April 13, 2017), http://economictimes.indiatimes .com/news/international/business/wto -eyes-feeble-global-trade-recovery-in -2017/articleshow/58150346.cms (retrieved August 1, 2017).

74. "Brazil's Dilemma: How to Make Its Labor Market More Flexible" Wharton School of Business, University of Pennsylvania (May 16, 2007), http://www.wharton.universia .net/index.cfm?fa=viewArticle&id= 1349& language=english (retrieved May 11, 2011).

75. IBGE, "Union Membership Rate of Brazilian Workers Falls to 14.49%, the Lowest Since 2012," (November 8, 2018), https://agenciadenoticias.ibge.gov.br/en/ agencia-press-room/2185-news-agency/ releases-en/22957-ores-brasileiros-cai -para-14-4-a-menor-desde-2013

76. "Brazil: Labor Relations," *TozziniFriere Advogados* (2007), p. 1.

77. J. Almeida, *Brazil in Focus* (New York, NY: Nova Science, 2008), pp. 124–125.

78. "75% of Employers Expect Worse Labor Relations in 2011," *Korea Times* (December 19, 2010), http://www.koreatimes .co.kr/www/news/nation/nation_view .asp?newsIdx=78249 &categoryCode=113 Korea Times (retrieved May 11, 2011).

79. S. Hampton, "Robert Bosch Gesellschaft mit beschränkter Haftung," Hoovers, http://0-subscriber.hoovers.com.liucat .lib.liu.edu/H/company360/fulldescrip tion.html?companyId =41437000000000 (retrieved from May 22, 2017).

80. P. Sciacovelli, "Interview With Bosch Bari's HR Director: Francesco Basile," *Science for Work* (January 5, 2015), http:// scienceforwork.com/blog/interview -bosch-bari-hr-director-francesco-basile (retrieved May 22, 2017).

81. Marimari.com, *Singapore: General Information*. Retrieved August 4, 2014, from http://www.marimari.com/content/ singapore/general_info/main.html.

82. Marimari.com, *Singapore: Shopping*. Retrieved August 4, 2014, from http:// www.marimari.com/content/singapore/ shopping/main.html.

83. Jurong Point, *Jurong Point Shopping Centre: Singapore's Largest Suburban Life Style Paradise!* Retrieved August 4, 2014, from http://www.jurongpoint.com.sg/ corporate/.

84. S. V. Selvaretnam, *At Your Service*. Retrieved from http://www.hrmasia.com/ case-studies/at-your-service/185525/.

• Index •

Ability, 171
Ability-job fit, 140
Ability to pay, 257
Absenteeism, 9
ACA. *See* Affordable Care Act of 2010 (ACA)
Accenture, 194
Acceptability of performance measures, 197
Accountability, 342–343
Ackoff, Russell, 33
ActioNet, 331–332
Active listening, 123
ADA. *See* Americans with Disabilities Act of 1990 (ADA)
Addison Shoe Factory, 354
ADEA. *See* Age Discrimination in Employment Act of 1967 (ADEA)
Adobe Systems, 194
ADP, 182
Adverse employment action, 67
Advertising in recruiting, 120
Affirmative action, 345, 346 (exhibit)
Affordable Care Act of 2010 (ACA), 292
Age Discrimination in Employment Act of 1967 (ADEA), 58 (exhibit), 62
Agile workforce, 103
Ailes, Roger, 69
Airbnb, 6, 35, 72
    diversity at, 347
Alcoa, 325
AlertMedia, 326
Alibaba, 42
Allegiant, 37
Amazon, 18
    bonus pay at, 283
    compensation at, 257
    globalization of, 365
    recruiting at, 114
    sustainability at, 352
American Express, 350
Americans with Disabilities Act of 1990 (ADA), 58 (exhibit), 62–63
Anheuser-Busch InBev, 36
Annual leave, 297
Apple
    differentiation and, 37
    executive compensation at, 287
    external environment of, 32
    focus on profits versus being socially responsible at, 15
    as interactive company, 33
    inversion strategy and, 36
    objectives of, 36
    organizational culture at, 40
Applications, job, 144
Aqualon Company, 158

Artifacts of organizational culture, 40–41
Assertiveness vs. nurturing, 369 (exhibit)
Assessment, training program, 180
Assessment centers, 148
Association for Talent Development (ATD), 17
ATD. *See* Association for Talent Development (ATD)
Authority, 342
Automation at work, 103–104
Autonomy, 92

Background checks, 153–156
Bad hires, 138–139
Bakke v. California, 346
Balance sheet approach, 377
Bank of America, 344
BARS. *See* Behaviorally anchored rating scale (BARS) form
Base pay, 254
Behavioral appraisals, 199–200
Behaviorally anchored rating scale (BARS) form, 203–204, 203 (exhibit)
Behavior evaluations, 180
Behaviors, definition of, 199
Benefits, 254–255
    Affordable Care Act of 2010 (ACA), 292
    case, 305–306
    domestic partner, 301
    family and medical leave, 291
    flexible, 299–300
    in global firms, 378
    insurance, 297–298
    paid time off, 297
    retirement, 296–297
    Social Security and Medicare, 289–290
    statutory, 289–292
    statutory requirements when providing certain voluntary, 292–294
    trends and issues in HRM and, 300–301
    unemployment insurance, 290–291
    voluntary, 294–298, 298 (exhibit)
    workers' compensation, 290
    See also Incentives
Ben & Jerry's Ice Cream, 352
Berkshire Hathaway, 340
Bersin, Josh, 186
Best Buy, 305–306
BFOQ. *See* Bona fide occupational qualification (BFOQ)
Bias
    ethics of, 343–344
    in performance appraisals, 208 (exhibit), 209
Big data, 42
Biological job design, 90

Birchbox, 6
Birkman Method, 147
BlackBerry, 32
Blackboard, 178
Blanchard, Ken, 199–200
Bona fide occupational qualification (BFOQ), 61, 144
Bonus pay, 283
Boycotts, 240
Brazil, 379
Bribery, 343
Broadbanding, 270–271, 270 (exhibit)
Brodsky, Norm, 225
Buckley, Michael, 201
Budgetary constraints in recruiting, 121
Buffett, Warren, 40, 340
Burger King Worldwide, 36
Burnout, 320, 321
Business acumen, 7
Business necessity, 61
Business skills, 16
"Buy American" slogan, 366

Cadence, 348
Cafeteria plans, 299–300
Campbell Construction, 312
Career(s)
    career development consequences model and, 182–185, 183 (exhibit), 184 (exhibit)
    defined, 181
Cases
    compensation, 276–278
    employee engagement, 25–26
    employee incentives and benefits, 305–306
    ethics and executive compensation, 357–359
    globalization, 382–383
    labor relations, 247–248
    performance management and appraisal, 218–219
    recruiting, 130–133
    religious diversity, 76–77
    selection process, 161–163
    staffing strategy, 107–108
    strategy-driven HRM, 50–51
    training and development, 188–190
    workplace safety and security, 331–332
Catalya Hats, 50–51
Centralization, 39
Ceremonies in organizational culture, 41
Certifications, HRM, 17–18
Challenges, human resource management, 6–7
Chen, Ashley, 331

Child labor, 262
Citations, OSHA, 317
Civil Rights Act of 1964 (CRA), 58 (exhibit), 59–62, 61 (exhibit)
Civil Rights Act of 1991, 58 (exhibit), 63–64, 64 (exhibit)
Classical conditioning, 173
Classroom training, 178
Clinton Climate Initiative, 354
Closed-ended questions, 151
Closed shops, 240
Coaching, 233, 234 (exhibit)
COBRA. *See* Consolidated Omnibus Budget Reconciliation Act of 1985 (COBRA)
Coca-Cola, 322
    differentiation and, 37
    focus and niche of, 37
    globalization of, 364
Codes of conduct, 232
Codes of ethics, 341–344
Cognitive ability tests, 147–148
Cohesiveness, 348
Collective bargaining, 242
College of Business of the University of Arkansas at Little Rock, 35
Commissions, 283, 305–306
Communication
    defined, 224
    employee relations and, 224–225
    in performance appraisals, 198
    standards for hazard, 316, 316 (exhibit)
    training for global business, 375–376
Comparable worth, 263
Compensation
    ability to pay, 257
    about, 10
    at, above, or below market, 257
    case, 276–278
    defined, 254
    developing a pay system for, 266–271, 269 (exhibit), 270 (exhibit)
    executive, 265, 287–289
    global workforce, 376–378
    job evaluation and, 264–265
    legal and fairness issues in, 259–264, 259 (exhibit), 261–262 (exhibit)
    major HR responsibilities of HR staff and line management in, 14
    motivation and planning for, 255–257, 256 (exhibit)
    for performance or longevity, 258
    planning for, 255–257, 256 (exhibit)
    practitioner's perspective on, 253
    strategy in, 257–259
    trends and issues in HRM and, 272–273
    types of, 254–255, 257–258
    workers', 290
    See also Benefits; Incentives
Compensation planning, 255–257, 256 (exhibit)
    equity theory and, 256–257
    expectancy theory and, 255–256, 256 (exhibit)
Compensation strategy, 257–259
Compensatory damages, 63–64

Compensatory selection model, 156
Competency-based pay, 258
Competition, 31–32
    globalization of business and, 365
    recruiting and, 114
Complexity, 39
Compliance, 341
Conceptual and design skills, 16
Conflict, 348
Consistency in effect, in OUCH test, 57
Consolidated Omnibus Budget Reconciliation Act of 1985 (COBRA), 292
Constructive discharge, 67
Construct validity, 142–143
Content validity, 142
Contingency agencies, 119
Contract workers, 101–102
Contrast error in performance appraisals, 208 (exhibit), 210
Cook, Tim, 15
Core-plus plans, 299
Corporate learning imperative, 185–186
Corporate philanthropy, 336–337
Corporate social responsibility (CSR)
    business case for, 350
    defined, 349
    levels of, 350–351, 350 (exhibit)
Corrupt payments to government officials, 343
Cost centers, 5
Costco, 93
    compensation at, 257, 276–278
Cost leadership, 37
    human resource management and, 38
Cost per hire, 125
Counseling, management, 233–234
Countrywide Financial, 344
CRA. *See* Civil Rights Act of 1964 (CRA)
Creativity and innovation through diversity, 347–348
Credit checks, 154–155
Criminal background checks, 155
Criterion-related validity, 142
Critical evaluation, 7
Critical incidents method, 201
CSR. *See* Corporate social responsibility (CSR)
Cultural issues in business globalization, 367–370, 369–370 (exhibit)
Cultural training, 374–375, 375 (exhibit)
Culture, organizational.
    See Organizational culture
Culture shock, 374–375, 375 (exhibit)
Customers, 31
    globalization of business and finding new, 364
    performance appraisals by, 207
    privacy of, 344
CVS, 351
Cyber security, 324–325

Dakota Access oil pipeline, 32
Data analytics
    big data in, 42
    brief on, 42–43
    defined, 42

Debriefing after performance appraisals, 212–214
Decertification elections, 243
Decision making in performance appraisals, 198
Defined benefit plans, 296
Defined contribution plans, 296
Delayering, 270–271
Dell Computers, 204
    onshoring by, 373
Deloitte, 194
Delves, Donald, 358
Demographic diversity, 347
Demographics, labor, 7
Design, motivational jobs, 90, 93–95, 95 (exhibit)
Desired outcomes, 43
Development. *See* Talent management and development
Developmental performance appraisal interview, 213
Diaries, 88
Differentiation, 37
    human resource management and, 38
Digital learning, 186
Dillard's, 154
Direct compensation components, 254
Disability
    definition of, 62
    essential functions and, 63
    insurance against, 298
    marginal job functions and, 63
    reasonable accommodation for, 63
    and survivor benefits, 290
    undue hardship and, 63
Disability insurance, 298
Discernment and advice, 340
Discharge, 237
Discipline areas, HRM, 9–11
Disciplining, 234
    causes of immediate termination and, 238
    guidelines for effective, 235, 236 (exhibit)
    just cause and, 234–235
    model for, 237, 238 (exhibit)
    progressive, 236–237
Discrimination, 56
    illegal, 56
    organizational defenses against charges of, 61–62
    religious, 71
    reverse, 346
    sexual orientation and gender identity, 72
    systemic, 66–67
    types of, 59, 62, 62 (exhibit)
Disengagement stage in career development, 183–185
Disney, 154
Disparate impact, 61
Disparate treatment, 61
Distance learning, 178
Distributional errors in performance appraisals, 208 (exhibit), 209
Divergent thinking, 348
Diversity
    benefits of, 347
    creativity and innovation with, 347–348

defined, 346
demographic, 347
ethical organizations and, 345–349,
    346 (exhibit)
management of, 348–349
religious, 76–77
sexual orientation and gender identity, 72
training for, 349, 354–355
See also Legal environment and diversity
    management
Dodd-Frank Wall Street Reform and
    Consumer Protection Act of 2010,
    288–289
Domestic partner benefits, 301
Domino's Pizza, 154
Douglas, M. E., 202
Downsizing, 99, 101
Dr Pepper Snapple Group, 37
Drucker, Peter, 40, 342
Drug testing, 149
    post-incident, 328
Duckworth, Angela, 128
Dysfunctional stress, 320
    negative consequences of, 321

EAPs. *See* Employee assistance programs (EAPs)
Early retirement, 100–101
Ebony magazine, 37
Economic value added (EVA), 44
Economy, 32–33
EDocAmerica, 328–329
Educational institutions, recruiting at, 118
EEO. *See* Equal employment opportunity (EEO)
EEOC. *See* Equal Employment Opportunity
    Commission (EEOC)
Effectiveness, 6
Efficiency, 6
    technology's effect on, 8
E-learning, 178
Electronic performance monitoring (EPM),
    214–215
Employee assessment, 182
Employee assistance programs (EAPs), 318
Employee behavior
    organizational culture and, 41
    organizational structure and, 40
    shaping, 172 (exhibit), 173–175
Employee benefits. *See* Benefits
Employee complaints, 243–244, 243 (exhibit)
Employee development, definition of, 168
Employee engagement
    case, 25–26
    defined, 4
    importance of, 4
    improving productivity, 20
    performance management and, 214
    trends and issues in HRM and, 20–21
Employee health, 318–319
Employee misclassification under FLSA,
    262–263
Employee Polygraph Protection Act (EPPA),
    146, 147 (exhibit)
Employee privacy, 344
Employee readiness, 171–172

Employee relations, 10, 14
    See also Labor relations
Employee Retirement Income Security Act of
    1974 (ERISA), 292–294
Employee rights
    commonly accepted, 230–231, 231 (exhibit)
    under EEOC, 67
    and responsibilities under OSHA,
        314 (exhibit), 315
    right of free consent, 230, 231 (exhibit)
    right of freedom of conscience (limited),
        231, 231 (exhibit)
    right to due process, 230, 231 (exhibit)
    right to free speech (limited), 231,
        231 (exhibit)
    right to life and safety, 230, 231 (exhibit)
    right to privacy (limited), 231, 231 (exhibit)
    trends and issues in HRM and, 243–244,
        243 (exhibit)
    unions and, 241–243, 242 (exhibit)
    See also Labor relations
Employee selection. *See* Selection process
Employee stock plans, 286
Employee wellness programs (EWPs), 318
Employer rights
    codes of conduct, 232
    disciplining, 234–238, 236 (exhibit),
        238 (exhibit)
    employment-at-will, 232–233
    and prohibitions under EEOC, 67
    and responsibilities under OSHA, 313–315,
        314 (exhibit)
Employment agencies, recruiting by, 118–120
Employment-at-will, 232–233
Employment tests, 141–142, 144–150,
    147 (exhibit)
Engagement, employee.
    See Employee engagement
Enlargement, job, 94
Enrichment, job, 94
Enron, 335, 342
Environment
    external, 31–33, 32 (exhibit), 41 (exhibit)
    internal, 33, 33 (exhibit), 41 (exhibit)
    maintaining safe work, 86
    See also Legal environment and diversity
        management
EPPA. *See* Employee Polygraph Protection
    Act (EPPA)
Equal employment opportunity (EEO),
    9–10, 368
    affirmative action and, 345, 346 (exhibit)
    compensation and, 259–264, 259 (exhibit),
        261–262 (exhibit)
    laws related to, 58–59 (exhibit), 58–65
    technology creating new dangers in, 72–73
Equal Employment Opportunity Commission
    (EEOC), 66–68, 368
    employee rights, 67
    employer rights and prohibitions, 67
    employment testing and, 146
    enforcement actions by, 66–67
    HR leadership, 67–68
    responsibilities of, 66

Equal Pay Act of 1963, 58 (exhibit), 59
Equity theory, 256–257
Ergonomics and musculoskeletal disorders
    (MSDs), 318–319
Essential functions, 63
Establishment stage in career
    development, 183
Ethical dilemmas
    academic grades and incentives,
        286–287
    academic standards, 196
    bribery, 343
    "Buy American" slogan, 366
    discipline, 237
    downsizing, 101
    English language use, 64
    executive compensation, 265
    focus on profits versus being ethical and
        socially responsible, 15
    inversion strategy, 36
    obesity and smoking, 322
    recruiting, 122
    sexual orientation discrimination, 156
    virtual internships, 178
Ethics
    approaches to, 339–340
    business globalization and, 367–370,
        369–370 (exhibit)
    case, 357–359
    codes of, 341–344
    and contributing factors to unethical
        behavior, 338–339
    corporate social responsibility (CSR) and,
        349–351, 350 (exhibit)
    creating and maintaining ethical
        organizations and, 341–344
    defined, 11, 336–337
    diversity and inclusion, 345–349,
        346 (exhibit)
    major HR responsibilities of HR staff and
        line management in, 14
    practitioner's perspective on, 335
Eustress, 319
EVA. *See* Economic value added (EVA)
Evaluative performance appraisal interview,
    212–213
EWPs. *See* Employee wellness programs (EWPs)
Executive compensation, 265, 287–289
Executive Order 11246, 346
Executive recruiters, 119–120
Exercise, 323
Expansion, job, 94, 95 (exhibit)
Expatriate training and preparation, 374–376,
    375 (exhibit)
Expectancy theory, 255–256, 256 (exhibit)
Experience as development method, 182
Experience rating, 290
Expertise, HR, 7
Exploration stage in career development, 183
External environment, 31–33, 32 (exhibit),
    41 (exhibit)
External recruiting, 117–121, 118–120,
    119 (exhibit)
Extinction, 174–175

F5 Networks, 350
Fabricut Inc., 158
Facebook, 116, 120
    above average compensation at, 257
    corporate social responsibility (CSR) at, 351
    culture management at, 41
    data analytics and, 43
    employee and customer privacy at, 344
    labor force at, 32
    onboarding at, 169
    organizational culture at, 40
    performance appraisals at, 206
Faces scale of job satisfaction measurement, 227, 227 (exhibit)
Factor comparison method, 265
Fair Labor Standards Act of 1938, 259–264, 259 (exhibit), 261–262 (exhibit)
    on child labor, 262
    employee misclassification under, 262–263
Family and Medical Leave Act of 1993 (FMLA), 291
FCPA. *See* Foreign Corrupt Practices Act (FCPA)
Feasibility of measures, 197
Federal contractors, 346
FedEx, 102
    globalization of business and, 364
Feedback, 92
    good management and, 243–244
Fee-for-service plans, 294
Firstjob, 116
"Fit," looking for, 140–141
Fitness-for-duty testing, 149
Flexible benefit (cafeteria) plans, 299–300
Flexible job design, 94–95, 95 (exhibit)
Flextime, 94, 95 (exhibit)
FMLA. *See* Family and Medical Leave Act of 1993 (FMLA)
Focus or niche, 37
    human resource management and, 38
Ford, Henry, 171
Ford Motor Company, 36, 350
Forecasting, HR, 96–97
    methods of, 97, 98 (exhibit)
Foreign Corrupt Practices Act (FCPA), 368
Formal education, 182
Formalization, 39
Fortune 500, 42
4 Ms, 84–85, 85 (exhibit)
401(k) plans, 296
Four-Fifths Rule, 57–58, 57 (exhibit)
Four-way test, 340
Fowler, Susan, 72
Frito-Lay, 322, 349
Full-choice plans, 300
Functional stress, 319–320

Gainsharing plans, 286
Gamification, 185
Gap stores, 194
GE, 93
    performance appraisal process at, 194
    ranking method at, 204
Gender identity, 72
Gender wage gap, 272–273

General employment agencies, 119
Generation Z, 127–128
Generic strategies, 37
Genetic Information Nondiscrimination Act of 2008, 59 (exhibit), 65, 146
Gig work, 103
Glassdoor, 120
Globalization, business, 46
    benefit programs and, 378
    case, 382–383
    compensation of global workforce in, 376–378
    developing and managing global human resources for, 373–376, 375 (exhibit)
    differences in HRM with, 366–367
    global staffing for, 371–373, 373 (exhibit)
    human resource management and, 364–367
    national culture and, 368–370, 369–370 (exhibit)
    practitioner's perspective on, 363–364
    reasons for, 364–365
    trends and issues in HRM and, 378–379
Global managers, skills and traits for, 371–372
Global staffing, 371–373, 373 (exhibit)
Global village, 365
Global workforce, 158
GM, 36
Golden parachutes, 289
Golden Rule, 339
Good faith and fair dealing, 233
Google, 4, 72, 116
    above average compensation at, 257
    data analytics at, 42–43
    employee engagement, 4
    HR technology at, 43
    initial screening interviews at, 150
    People Operations at, 6
    recruiting using, 116, 120
Google for Jobs, 116, 120
Government officials, corrupt payments to, 343
Governments in external environment, 33
Graham, Robert, 201
Graphic rating scale form, 202
Green companies, 351–352
Grievances, 243
Grit: The Power of Passion and Performance, 128
Gross negligence, 238
Group health insurance, 294–295
Group incentives, 284–287, 285 (exhibit)

Halo error in performance appraisals, 208 (exhibit), 209
Harley Davidson, 37
Harvard Business Review, 43
Hazard communication standards, 316, 316 (exhibit)
HDHP. *See* High-deductible health plan (HDHP)
Health, employee, 318–319
Health insurance
    Consolidated Omnibus Budget Reconciliation Act of 1985 (COBRA) and, 292

Employee Retirement Income Security Act of 1974 (ERISA) and, 292–294
    group, 294–295
    Health Insurance Portability and Accountability Act of 1996 (HIPAA) and, 292
Health Insurance Portability and Accountability Act of 1996 (HIPAA), 292
Health maintenance organizations (HMOs), 294
Health reimbursement accounts (HRAs), 295
Health savings accounts (HSAs), 295
Heroes in organizational culture, 40
Hierarchy of needs, 183 (exhibit), 184
High-deductible health plan (HDHP), 295
High performance work practices (HPWPs), 38
HIPAA. *See* Health Insurance Portability and Accountability Act of 1996 (HIPAA)
Hiring, 157
    See also Selection process
Hiring freezes, 100
HiringSolved, 117
HMOs. *See* Health maintenance organizations (HMOs)
Hofstede, Geert, 369
Hofstede's model of national culture, 369–370, 369–370 (exhibit)
Holiday pay, 297
Holtz, Lou, 286
Honda, 169
Honesty tests, 148
Host-country nationals, 372, 373 (exhibit)
Hostile work environment, 68
HP (Hewlett Packard), 72
HPWPs. *See* High performance work practices (HPWPs)
HR. *See* Human resources (HR)
HRAs. *See* Health reimbursement accounts (HRAs)
HRCI. *See* Human Resource Certification Institute (HRCI)
HRM. *See* Human resource management (HRM)
HR Magazine, 273
HRMS. *See* Human resource management systems (HRMS)
HSAs. *See* Health savings accounts (HSAs)
Human Resource Certification Institute (HRCI), 17
Human resource management (HRM)
    certifications, 17–18
    challenges, 6–7
    disciplines within, 9–11
    effect of organizational structure on, 40
    effects of strategy on, 37–38
    globalization of business and, 364–367
    labor demographics and, 7
    measurement tools for strategic, 44–45
    organizational agility and, 20–21
    organizational revenue and, 5–6
    past and present, 5–9
    practitioner's model for, 18–20, 19 (exhibit)
    promoting strategy through high performance work practices, 38–39
    purpose for, 9

reasons for studying, 4–5, 5 (exhibit)
responsibilities, 14
skills, 15–16, 15 (exhibit)
technology and knowledge and, 7–8
trends and issues in (*See* Trends and issues
  in HRM)
Human resource management systems
  (HRMS), 43–44
Human resources (HR), 4
  EEOC on leadership in, 67–68
  expertise in, 7
  response to sexual harassment
    complaints, 69

IBM, 43
  performance appraisal process at, 194
  telecommuting at, 95
Illegal discrimination, 56
Immigration, 158
Implied contract, 233
Incentives
  case, 305–306
  executive, 289
  in global firms, 377–378
  group, 284–287, 285 (exhibit)
  individual, 282–284, 283 (exhibit)
  pay, 254, 282–284, 283 (exhibit), 300–301
  practitioner's perspective on, 282
  strategic value of, 282
  trends and issues in HRM and, 300–301
  See also Benefits
Inclusion and diversity, 345–349, 346 (exhibit)
Indeed.com, 116, 120
Independent contractors, 272
Individual incentives, 282–284, 283 (exhibit)
Individualism vs. collectivism, 369 (exhibit)
Individual retirement accounts (IRAs), 296–297
Informal coaching talk, 236
Information Age, 8
Insperity, 43
Instrumentality, 255–256
Insurance
  disability, 298
  life, 297–298
  unemployment, 290–291
Integrity tests, 148
Intel, 349
Interactive companies, 33
Interest tests, 147
Internal environment, 33, 33 (exhibit),
  41 (exhibit)
Internal recruiting, 117–118, 119 (exhibit)
International labor laws, 367
Internships, virtual, 178
Interpersonal skills, 15–16
Interviews, 87–88, 150–151
  preparing for and conducting,
    153, 153 (exhibit)
  types of, 151
  types of questions in, 151–153, 152 (exhibit)
IRA. *See* individual retirement accounts (IRAs)

JCM. *See* Job characteristics model (JCM)
Jelly Belly, 218–219

JetBlue, 37
Jet magazine, 37
Job analysis
  databases for, 86
  defined, 85
  job description and job specification
    outcomes of, 89
  methods of, 87–89
  observation, 88–89
  reasons for, 86
Job characteristics and recruiting, 122
Job characteristics model (JCM), 91–93,
  92 (exhibit)
Job design/redesign, 90
Job enlargement, 94
Job enrichment, 94
Job evaluation, 86
  compensation and, 264–265
Job expansion, 94, 95 (exhibit)
Job offers, 156–157
Job ranking, 264
Job relatedness, 62
  in OUCH test, 58
Job rotation, 94
Jobs, Steve, 15, 40, 287
Job satisfaction
  determinants of, 228
  measuring, 227–228, 227 (exhibit),
    228 (exhibit)
Job sharing, 94, 100
Job simplification, 93, 95 (exhibit)
Jobvite, 116, 117
Journal of Business Research, 300
Jumpstart:HR, 94
Junk foods, 322
Jurisdictional strikes, 240
Juron Point, 382–383
Just Cause, 234–235
  tests for, 243
Justification of unethical behavior, 339

Kelly Services, 118
Kmart, 154
Knowledge-based firms, 8
Knowledge workers, 8

L-3 National Security Solutions, 332
Labor demographics, 7
Labor force, 32
  children in, 262
Labor Management Relations Act of 1947
  (LMRA), 239 (exhibit), 240
Labor market, 114
  worldwide, 379
Labor relations
  about, 10
  case, 247–248
  coaching and, 233, 234 (exhibit)
  collective bargaining and, 242
  defined, 242
  disciplining in, 234–238, 236 (exhibit),
    238 (exhibit)
  job satisfaction and, 227–228, 227 (exhibit),
    228 (exhibit)

legal issues in, 239–241, 239 (exhibit)
  major HR responsibilities of HR staff and
    line management in, 14
  management counseling and, 233–234
  practitioner's perspective on, 224
  temporary or contract workers, 101–102
  trends and issues in HRM and, 243–244,
    243 (exhibit)
  trust and communication in, 224–225
  See also Employee rights; Employer rights
Labor shortage
  knowledge workforce, 8
  overtime and, 101
Labor surpluses, downsizing and layoffs for, 99
Laughter, 321
Laws. *See* Legal environment and diversity
  management
Layoffs, 99
Learning, 172–173
  corporate learning imperative, 185–186
  digital, 186
  distance, 178
  life-long, 186
  social, 173
  theories of, 173
  See also Training
Learning evaluations, 180
Learning management systems (LMS), 178
LEED (Leadership in Energy and
  Environmental Design), 352
Legal environment and diversity management
  about, 9–10
  Affordable Care Act of 2010 (ACA), 292
  business globalization and, 367–370,
    369–370 (exhibit)
  compensation and, 259–264, 259 (exhibit),
    261–262 (exhibit)
  Consolidated Omnibus Budget
    Reconciliation Act of 1985
    (COBRA), 292
  corporate social responsibility (CSR)
    and, 350
  Employee Retirement Income Security Act
    of 1974 (ERISA), 292–294
  employment laws, major, 58–59 (exhibit),
    58–65
  employment testing and, 144–150,
    147 (exhibit)
  Equal Employment Opportunity
    Commission (EEOC), 66–68
  executive compensation, 288–289
  Family and Medical Leave Act of 1993, 291
  Four-Fifths Rule, 57–58, 57 (exhibit)
  Health Insurance Portability and
    Accountability Act of 1996 (HIPAA), 292
  labor relations, 239–241, 239 (exhibit)
  limits on testing and, 157–158
  major HR responsibilities of HR staff and
    line management in, 14
  OUCH test guide for, 56–58, 56 (exhibit)
  practitioner's perspective on, 55
  religious discrimination, 71
  sexual harassment, 68–71, 70 (exhibit)
  trends and issues in HRM and, 71–73

Liability, 18
Life insurance, 297–298
Life-long learning, 186
Lilly Ledbetter Fair Pay Act of 2009 (LLFPA), 59 (exhibit), 65
Line managers, 14
LinkedIn, 41, 116, 120
   mentor programs at, 349
Listening skills, 225
LLFPA. *See* Lilly Ledbetter Fair Pay Act of 2009 (LLFPA)
LMRA. *See* Labor Management Relations Act of 1947 (LMRA)
Localization approach, 377
Lombardi, Vince, 321
Longevity, pay for, 258
Long-term disability insurance, 298
Long-term orientation vs. short-term orientation, 370 (exhibit)
Lyft, 72
   company culture at, 141

Ma, Jack, 42
Macy's, 41
Maintenance stage in career development, 183
Management by objectives (MBO) method, 201–202
Management counseling, 233–234
Management rights, 232–233
Management support, 341
Managers
   global, 371–372
   line vs. staff, 14
Margaritaville, 37
Marginal job functions, 63
Marijuana, 149
Mary Kay, 41
Masculinity vs. femininity, 369 (exhibit)
Maslow, Abraham, 183 (exhibit), 184
Maslow's hierarchy of needs, 183 (exhibit), 184
Matching contributions, 401(k) plans, 296
MBO. *See* Management by objectives (MBO) method
McDonald's, 322
   below average compensation at, 257
   formalization at, 39
   job simplification at, 93
   objectives of, 36
   organizational culture at, 41
   organizational structure of, 40
Measurement tools
   economic value added (EVA), 44
   return on investment (ROI), 45
Mechanistic job design, 90
Medical savings accounts (MSAs), 295
Medicare, 289–290
Mentor programs, 349
Merit pay, 284
Microlearning, 178
Microsoft
   complexity of, 39
   diversity at, 348
   mentor programs at, 349
   temporary workers at, 102, 119

Millennial generation, 127–128
Minimum wage, 260
Mission statement, 34–35
   performance management process based on, 197
   put together with vision, 35
Modular plans, 299
Monster.com, 89, 116, 120
Moodle, 178
Moral development, 338
Motivation
   compensation planning and, 255–257, 256 (exhibit)
   in performance appraisals, 198
Motivational job design, 90, 93–95, 95 (exhibit)
MSAs. *See* Medical savings accounts (MSAs)
MSDs. *See* Musculoskeletal disorders (MSDs)
Multiple-hurdle selection model, 156
Musculoskeletal disorders (MSDs), 318–319
Musk, Elon, 40
Myers-Briggs Type Indicator, 147

Nadella, Satya, 39
NAFTA. *See* North American Free Trade Agreement (NAFTA)
Narrative method or form, 202
Nassar, Larry, 69
National culture, 368–370, 369–370 (exhibit)
National Institute of Occupational Safety and Health (NIOSH), 317
National Labor Relations Act of 1935 (NLRA), 239–240, 239 (exhibit)
   on compensation, 263–264
National Labor Relations Board (NLRB), 240, 259
Natural attrition, 100
Needs assessment, 168–169, 171, 171 (exhibit)
Negative reinforcement, 174
Negligent hires, 138–139
Negotiation approach, 377
Nestlé, 188–190
Netflix, 84
   company culture at, 141
   performance appraisal process at, 194
   performance appraisals at, 206
Network diversity group, 349
New hires, 103
   onboarding of, 169
   performance of, 126
   turnover of, 126
Niche. *See* Focus or niche
Nike, 37, 150
   bonus pay at, 283
   gamification at, 185
   outsourcing by, 372
NIOSH. *See* National Institute of Occupational Safety and Health (NIOSH)
NLRA. *See* National Labor Relations Act of 1935 (NLRA)
NLRB. *See* National Labor Relations Board (NLRB)
Nonmonetary compensation components, 254
Nooyi, Indra, 172

North American Free Trade Agreement (NAFTA), 365
Norvig, Peter, 42
NO TIPS rules, 242
Noxious stimulus, 174
Nutrition and stress, 322

Obama, Barack, 41, 259
Obesity, 322
Objectives
   in OUCH test, 56
   performance management based on, 197
   setting of, 35–36
Observation, 88–89
Occupational Safety and Health Act (OSH Act), 312–313
Occupational Safety and Health Administration (OSHA), 313–317, 314 (exhibit), 316 (exhibit)
   employer and employee rights and responsibilities under, 313–315, 314 (exhibit)
   functions of, 313
   hazard communication standards under, 316, 316 (exhibit)
   on post-incident drug testing, 328
   violations, citations, and penalties under, 317
OJT. *See* On-the-job training (OJT)
Old-Age, Survivors, and Disability Insurance (OASDI), 289
Onboarding, 169
O'Neil, Cathy, 73
O*NET, 86–87, 89
Onshoring, 372–373
On-the-job training (OJT), 178
Open-ended questions, 151
Operant conditioning, 173
Oracle, 43, 72
Oral warnings, 236
O'Reilly, Bill, 69
Organizational agility and human resource management, 20–21
Organizational culture, 29, 141
   artifacts of, 40–41
   controlling employee behavior, 41
   defined, 40–41
   misalignment of structure, technology and, 46
   social media and, 41–42
Organizational image, 122
Organizational leadership and navigation, 7
Organizational output, 84
Organizational risk and sexual harassment lawsuits, 70–71, 70 (exhibit)
Organizational structure
   basics of, 39–40
   defined, 39
   employee behavior affected by, 40
   job design and, 90
   misalignment of culture, technology and, 46
OSHA. *See* Occupational Safety and Health Act (OSH Act); Occupational Safety and Health Administration (OSHA)

OUCH test, 56–58, 56 (exhibit), 144, 147, 210
  behaviors and, 199
  results appraisals and, 200
  traits and, 199
Outsourcing, 102, 182
  as alternative to international expansion, 372–373
Overtime, 260

Pace of technological change, 8
Paid personal leave, 297
Paid time off (PTO), 297
Palantir, 72
Pandora, 141
Parent- (home-) country nationals, 372, 373 (exhibit)
Parkin, Simon, 185
Parochialism, 369
Pattern or practice discrimination, 61
Pay equity, 263
Pay reductions, 100
Pay secrecy, 259
Pay structure, 269–271, 269 (exhibit), 270 (exhibit)
PDA. See Pregnancy Discrimination Act of 1978 (PDA)
Peers, performance appraisals by, 205–206
Penalties, OSHA, 317
PepsiCo, 37, 322
  corporate social responsibility (CSR) at, 350
  learning at, 172
Perceptual-motor job design, 90
Performance
  incentive pay effects on, 300–301
  measures of, 196–197
  new hire, 126
Performance appraisals
  avoiding problems with, 210–211
  calls to delete, 194–195
  case, 218–219
  conducting of, 198
  debriefing, 212–214
  defined, 195
  methods and forms in, 201–204, 201 (exhibit), 203 (exhibit)
  performance management versus, 195
  problems with, 208–211, 208 (exhibit)
  process in, 195, 196 (exhibit)
  reasons for conducting, 198
  trends and issues in HRM and, 214–215
  what is assessed in, 198–200
  who should conduct, 205–208
Performance management, 86
  case, 218–219
  compensation and, 258
  defined, 195
  performance appraisal versus, 195
  practitioner's perspective on, 193–194
  systems for, 194–197, 196 (exhibit)
  trends and issues in HRM and, 214–215
Performance measures, 196–197
Perquisites, 289
Personality-job fit, 140
Personality tests, 147

Personality traits and attitudes, 338
Personal responsibility, 341
Person-organization fit, 140–141
Philip Morris, 351
Physical exams, 148–149
Physical skill tests, 148
Physical testing
  decision to do, 149–150
  defined, 148
  drug testing, 149
  fitness-for-duty, 149
  physical exams, 148–149
  physical skills, 148
Piecework plans, 284
Point-factor method, 264
Policies, recruiting, 115, 121–122
Polygraphs, 146, 147 (exhibit)
Porter, Michael, 37
Position Analysis Questionnaire and the Management Position Description Questionnaire, 87
Positive reinforcement, 174
Positive thinking, 323
Post-incident drug testing, 328
Power-distance, 369 (exhibit)
PPOs. See Preferred provider organizations (PPOs)
Practitioner's model, human resources management, 18–20, 19 (exhibit)
Practitioner's perspective
  on company culture, 29
  compensation, 253
  on current state of the HR field, 3–4
  on ethics, 335
  on globalization, 363–364
  on hiring, 137–138
  on incentives and benefits, 282
  on labor relations, 224
  on legal environment, 55
  on performance evaluation, 193–194
  on recruiting, 113
  on training and development, 168
  on workforce planning, 84
  workplace safety, 311–312
Pratt Industries, 352
Predictive analytics, 44
Pre-employment inquiries, 144, 145 (exhibit)
Preferred provider organizations (PPOs), 294
Pregnancy Discrimination Act of 1978 (PDA), 58 (exhibit), 62
Preliminary screening, 144
Price, Joey, 94
PricewaterhouseCoopers, 150
  performance appraisal process at, 194
Principles, 341
Privacy, employee and customer, 344
Private employment agencies, 119–120
Probing questions, 152–153
Problem employees, 234
Productivity, 6
  bad hires and, 138
  employee engagement improving, 20
Productivity centers, 6
Professional responsibility and liability, 18

Profit sharing plans, 286
Progressive discipline, 236–237
"Project Oxygen," 4
Proximity error in performance appraisals, 208 (exhibit), 209
PTO. See Paid time off (PTO)
Public agencies for recruiting, 119
Public policy exceptions to employment-at-will, 233
Pulse surveys, 227
Punishment, 174
Punitive damages, 64

Qualcomm, 72
Qualitative forecasting, 97
Quantitative forecasting, 97, 98 (exhibit)
Questionnaires, 87
  job satisfaction measurement, 227, 228 (exhibit)
Quid pro quo harassment, 68

Race norming, 64
Railway Labor Act of 1926 (RLA), 239, 239 (exhibit)
Ralph Lauren, 343
Ranking method, 204
Ratio analysis, 97, 98 (exhibit)
Rave Guardian, 326
Reaction evaluations, 180
Realistic job preview (RJP), 122–123
Reasonable accommodation, 63
Reasonable person, 68
Recency error in performance appraisals, 208 (exhibit), 209–210
Recruiting
  alternatives to, 115–116
  budgetary constraints in, 121
  case, 130–133
  challenges and constraints in, 121–123
  cost per hire, 125
  defined, 114
  diversity, 348
  evaluation of, 124–126, 125 (exhibit)
  external, 118–120, 119 (exhibit)
  external forces acting on, 114–115
  global, 374
  internal, 117–118, 119 (exhibit)
  looking for grit in, 128
  millennial versus Generation Z, 127–128
  new hire performance, 126
  new hire turnover, 126
  organizational considerations in, 115–117
  policies on, 115
  policy constraints and organizational image in, 121–122
  practitioner's perspective on, 113
  process of, 114–115
  reach of, 116
  recruiter-candidate interaction and realistic job preview (RJP) and, 122–123
  technology in, 116–117
  time required to hire, 125
  timing of, 115
  trends and issues in HRM and, 126–128

yield ratio, 124
  See also Selection process
Recruiting.ai, 117
Reference checks, 155
Regression analysis, 97, 98 (exhibit)
Reinforcement, 174, 197
Relaxation, 321, 321–322 (exhibit)
Reliability, 197
  defined, 143
  HR forecasting, 96
  relationship between validity and, 143
Remediation, 170
Remington, 351
Repatriation after foreign assignments, 376
Responsibility
  in ethical organizations, 342
  human resources management, 14
  professional, 18
Results appraisals, 200
Results evaluations, 180
Résumés, 144
Retained search firms, 119–120
Retaliation, 67
Retirement
  benefit plans for, 296–297
  early, 100–101
  Employee Retirement Income Security Act
    of 1974 (ERISA) and, 292–294
  Social Security, 290
Retraining and transfers, 100, 102
Return on investment (ROI), 45
Revenue centers, 5–6
Reverse discrimination, 346
Right Guard deodorant, 37
Right of free consent, 230, 231 (exhibit)
Right of freedom of conscience (limited), 231,
  231 (exhibit)
Right to due process, 230, 231 (exhibit)
Right to free speech (limited), 231, 231 (exhibit)
Right to life and safety, 230, 231 (exhibit)
Right to privacy (limited), 231, 231 (exhibit)
Right-to-sue, 66
RLA. *See* Railway Labor Act of 1926 (RLA)
ROI. *See* Return on investment (ROI)
Rolex, 37
Rotation, job, 94
Roth IRA, 296–297

Safety. *See* Workplace safety
Safety and health management and
    training, 319
Sales commissions, 283, 305–306
Salesforce, 6
Samsung, 32, 84
SAP, 194
Sears, 18
Secondary boycotts, 240
Secrecy, pay, 259
Secret deodorant, 37
Securitas Security Services USA, 324
Security. *See* Workplace security
Selection, definition of, 138
Selection interviews, 150–153, 152 (exhibit),
  153 (exhibit)

Selection process
  applications and preliminary screening
    in, 144
  background checks in, 153–156
  case, 161–163
  global, 374
  importance of, 138–139
  interviews in, 150–153, 152 (exhibit),
    153 (exhibit)
  job offers and, 156–157
  looking for "fit," 140–141
  looking for "fit" in, 140–141
  practitioner's perspective on, 137–138
  steps in, 139–140, 139 (exhibit)
  testing and legal issues in, 144–150,
    147 (exhibit)
  trends and issues in HRM and, 157–158
  uniform guidelines for, 141–143
  uniform guidelines on employee selection
    procedures in, 141–143
  workplace security and, 326–327
  See also Recruiting
Self-assessment performance appraisals,
    206–207
Self-efficacy, 171
Serious misconduct, 238
Sexual harassment
  filing complaints and HR's response to, 69
  reducing organizational risk from lawsuits
    for, 70–71, 70 (exhibit)
  types of, 68
  what constitutes, 69
Sexual orientation, 72
Shaping behavior, 172 (exhibit), 173–175
Shareholders, 32
  Dodd-Frank Wall Street Reform and
    Consumer Protection Act of 2010
    and, 288–289
Sharing, job, 94, 100
SHI International, 364
Short-term disability insurance, 298
SHRM. *See* Society for Human Resource
    Management (SHRM)
Sick leave, 297
Similarity error in performance appraisals,
    208 (exhibit), 209
Simplification, job, 93, 95 (exhibit)
Simulations, 148, 178
Situational questions, 152
Skill-based pay, 258
Skills
  business, 16
  compensation based on, 258
  conceptual and design, 16
  for global managers, 371–372
  human resource management, 15–16,
    15 (exhibit)
  interpersonal, 15–16
  listening, 225
  technical, 15
  testing of, 147
Skill variety, 92
Skinner, B. F., 173
Slogans in organizational culture, 41

Smart phone checking, cutting back on, 323
Smith, Anthony, 358–359
Smoking, 322
Social learning, 173
Social media
  employee monitoring and, 244
  organizational culture and, 41–42
  and web searches in background checks,
    155–156
  for workplace safety and security, 326
Social Security, 258, 289–290
Society and determination of acceptable
    business practices, 32
Society for Human Resource Management
    (SHRM), 3, 17
South Korea, 379
Southwest Airlines
  corporate social responsibility (CSR), 350
  cost leadership of, 37
  People Operations at, 6
  sustainability at, 351
Specific measures, 197
Spirit, 37
Split-pay approach, 377
Staffing and workforce planning
  about, 10
  forecasting methods and, 97, 98 (exhibit)
  global, 371–373, 373 (exhibit)
  HR forecasting and, 96–97
  job analysis and, 85–89
  job characteristics model (JCM) and,
    91–93, 92 (exhibit)
  job design/redesign in, 90
  major HR responsibilities of HR staff and
    line management in, 14
  methods for reconciling labor shortage,
    101–103
  methods for reconciling labor surplus,
    99–101
  motivational job design and, 90, 93–95,
    95 (exhibit)
  practitioner's perspective on, 84
  workflow analysis and, 84–85, 85 (exhibit)
Staff managers, 14
Stakeholders
  approaches to ethics and, 340
  corporate social responsibility (CSR)
    and, 350
Standard hour plans, 284
Starbucks, 36
  above average compensation at, 257
  diversity at, 349
Statutory benefits
  Affordable Care Act of 2010 (ACA), 292
  family and medical leave, 291
  Social Security and Medicare, 289–290
  unemployment insurance, 290–291
  workers' compensation, 290
Stereotyping in performance appraisals,
    208 (exhibit), 209
Stock plans, employee, 286
Stories in organizational culture, 41
Strategic choice, 30 (exhibit)
Strategic planning, 30, 30 (exhibit)

external environment and, 31–33, 32 (exhibit)

HR management's role in, 31

Strategy, 33–34

defined, 34

generic, 37

human resource management effects of, 37–38

promoted through high performance work practices, 38–39

vision, mission, and objectives in, 34–36

Strategy-driven human resource management

case, 50–51

data analytics and HR technology in, 42–43

human resource management systems (HRMS) in, 43–44

introduction to, 30–33, 30 (exhibit), 32 (exhibit)

measurement tools for, 44–45

organizational culture and, 40–42, 41 (exhibit)

organizational structure and, 39–40

strategy in, 33–39

trends and issues in HRM and, 46

Stress

causes of, 320

cutting back on smart phone checking and, 323

defined, 319

exercise and, 323

functional and dysfunctional, 319–321

management of, 321

nutrition and, 322

positive thinking and, 323

relaxation for, 321, 321–322 (exhibit)

support network and, 323

time management and, 321

as tug-of-war, 323–324, 323 (exhibit)

Stressors, 320

Structure, organizational.

See Organizational structure

Student engagement, 5

Subordinates, performance appraisals by, 206

Sun Microsystems, 349

Sun Tzu, 34

Supervisors, performance appraisals by, 205

Suppliers, 32

Support network and stress, 323

Suspension, disciplinary, 236–237

Sustainability

corporate social responsibility (CSR) and, 349–351, 350 (exhibit)

culture of, 353

defined, 11, 351

HR and organizational, 351–352

internet resources for, 353–354, 353 (exhibit)

major HR responsibilities of HR staff and line management in, 14

management commitment to, 352

training in, 352

trends and issues in HRM and, 354–355

Symbols in organizational culture, 41

Synchronous distance learning, 178

Sysco, 8

Systemic discrimination, 66–67

Taft-Hartley Act, 239 (exhibit), 240

Talent management and development

careers and, 181

case, 188–190

common methods of, 181–182

global, 373–376, 375 (exhibit)

trends and issues in HRM and, 185–186

See also Training

Tan, Lip-Bu, 348

Target behaviors, 175

Target stores, 146

employment testing by, 158

Task identity, 92

Task significance, 92

Technical skills, 15

Technology

automation at work, 103–104

creating new dangers in equal opportunity and diversity management, 72–73

data analytics and HR, 42–43

efficiency effect of, 8

gamification, 185

growth of knowledge and, 7–8

HR, 43

for labor shortages, 102

misalignment of structure, culture, and, 46

as part of external environment, 32

recruiting, 116–117

Telecommuting, 94–95

Temporary agencies, 118–119

Temporary workers, 101–102

TEPCO, 39, 327

Termination, 237

causes of immediate, 238

options before, 237

Tesla

objectives at, 36

organizational culture at, 40

Testing, 144

cognitive ability, 147–148

EEOC and employment, 146

federal regulation limits on, 157–158

honesty or integrity, 148

personality and interest, 147

physical, 148–150

polygraph and genetic, 146, 147 (exhibit)

skills, 147

written, 146–148

Third-country nationals, 372, 373 (exhibit)

360-degree evaluations, 207–208

Time management, 321

Time required to hire, 125

Tim Hortons, 36

T-Mobile, 148

Trade barriers, declining, 365

Trade blocs, 365

Traditional health care plans, 294

Training, 86

about, 10

for advancement, 170

assessing, 180

case, 188–190

classroom, 178

defined, 168

design and delivery of, 175–179, 177 (exhibit), 178 (exhibit)

diversity, 349, 354–355

expatriate, 374–376, 375 (exhibit)

learning and shaping behavior in, 172–175, 172 (exhibit)

major HR responsibilities of HR staff and line management in, 14

need for, 168–170

needs assessment and process in, 170–172, 171 (exhibit)

new job requirements or processes in, 169

onboarding, 169

on-the-job (OJT), 178

practitioner's perspective on, 168

remediation, 170

safety and health management, 319

simulation, 178

steps in, 170

sustainability, 352

transfers and re-, 100, 102

trends and issues in HRM and, 185–186

See also Talent management and development

Trait appraisals, 199

Transfers and retraining, 100, 102

Travelers Insurance, 347

Trend analysis, 97, 98 (exhibit)

Trends and issues in HRM

compensation, 272–273

employee engagement, 20–21

employee incentives and benefits, 300–301

employee rights and labor relations, 243–244, 243 (exhibit)

globalization of business, 378–379

legal environment, 71–73

performance management and appraisal, 214–215

recruiting, 126–128

selection process, 157–158

staffing, 103–104

strategic planning, 46

sustainability, 354–355

training and development, 185–186

workplace safety and security, 328–329

Trust, 224–225

Tug-of-war, stress as, 323–324, 323 (exhibit)

Turnover, 9

new hire, 126

reduction of, 103

Twitter, 35

diversity at, 348

Uber, 72

temporary workers at, 102

UGESP. *See* Uniform Guidelines on Employee Selection Procedures (UGESP)

Uncertainty avoidance, 369 (exhibit)

Undue hardship, 63

Unemployment insurance, 290–291

Unethical behavior, contributing factors to, 338–339
See also Ethics
Uniformed Services Employment and Reemployment Rights Act (USERRA) of 1994, 58 (exhibit), 64–65
Uniform Guidelines on Employee Selection Procedures (UGESP), 141
Uniformity in application, in OUCH test, 56
Unilever, 185
Unions
  collective bargaining by, 242
  decertification elections, 243
  grievances and, 243
  NO TIPS rules, 242
  organizing of, 241–242, 242 (exhibit)
Union shops, 240
United Airlines, 42
United States–Mexico–Canada Trade Agreement (USMCA), 365
United Steel Workers Union, 325
Unstructured interviews, 151
U.S. Department of Defense, 185
U.S. Department of Health and Human Services, 38
U.S. Department of Labor, 86
USERRA. *See* Uniformed Services Employment and Reemployment Rights Act (USERRA) of 1994
USMCA. *See* United States–Mexico–Canada Trade Agreement (USMCA),

Vacation leave, 297
Valence, 255–256
Validity, 197
  construct, 142–143
  content, 142
  criterion-related, 142
  defined, 142
  HR forecasting, 96–97
  relationship between reliability and, 143
Values, 341
Variable pay, 282
VBIA. *See* Veterans Benefits Improvement Act of 2004 (VBIA)
Veterans Benefits Improvement Act of 2004 (VBIA), 59 (exhibit), 65
VEVRAA. *See* Vietnam Era Veterans Readjustment Assistance Act of 1974 (VEVRAA)

Vietnam Era Veterans Readjustment Assistance Act of 1974 (VEVRAA), 58 (exhibit), 62
Violations, OSHA, 317
Violence, workplace, 325–326
Virtual internships, 178
Vision, 34
  put together with mission, 35
Voluntary benefits, 292–294
  group health insurance, 294–295
Vroom, Victor, 255

WACC. *See* Weighted average cost of capital (WACC)
Wage and salary add-ons, 254
Wage compression, 258–259
Wage gap, gender, 272–273
Wage inversion, 258
Wagner Act, 239–240, 239 (exhibit)
Walk-ins, recruiting and, 118
Walmart
  below average compensation at, 257
  bias at, 343–344
  cost leadership of, 37
  organizational culture at, 41
  staffing strategy at, 107–108
  sustainability at, 352
WARN Act. *See* Worker Adjustment and Retraining Notification Act of 1988 (WARN Act)
Weapons of Math Destruction: How Big Data Increases Inequality and Threatens Democracy, 73
Weber, Max, 36
Wegmans, 117
Weighted average cost of capital (WACC), 44
Weight Watchers, 185
Weinstein, Harvey, 68, 71
Westinghouse, 325
Whistle-blowing, 11
Wildcat strikes, 240
Willingness, 172
Worker Adjustment and Retraining Notification Act of 1988 (WARN Act), 239 (exhibit), 241
Workers' compensation, 290
Workflow analysis
  defined, 84
  organizational output, 84
  tasks and inputs, 84–85

Workforce planning. *See* Staffing and workforce planning
Workplace safety, 86
  about, 10–11
  case, 331–332
  defined, 312
  employee health and, 318–319
  major HR responsibilities of HR staff and line management in, 14
  Occupational Safety and Health Act (OSH Act) and, 312–313
  Occupational Safety and Health Administration (OSHA) and, 313–317, 314 (exhibit), 316 (exhibit)
  practitioner's perspective on, 311–312
  social media for, 326
  stress and, 319–324, 321–322 (exhibit), 323 (exhibit)
  trends and issues in HRM and, 328–329
Workplace security
  case, 331–332
  cyber security, 324–325
  defined, 324
  employee selection and, 326–327
  general policies on, 327
  social media for, 326
  trends and issues in HRM and, 328–329
  workplace violence and, 325–326
Workplace violence, 325–326
Work samples, 148
WorldatWork, 18
World Economic Forum, 59, 353
World Trade Organization (WTO), 365
Written testing, 146–147
Written warnings, 236
WTO. *See* World Trade Organization (WTO)

Yahoo, 72
  telecommuting at, 95
Yang, Yowan, 332
Yap, Sally, 382–383
Yield ratio, recruiting, 124
Yowan Yang v. ActioNet, Inc., 332

Zappos, 40
  onboarding at, 169
  performance appraisals at, 205–206
Zuckerberg, Mark, 40, 351